Merl
BILINGUAL LAW DICTIONARY
DICCIONARIO JURÍDICO BILINGÜE

Cuauhtémoc Gallegos
Editor

Merl Publications
Chicago, IL

EDITOR
Cuauhtémoc Gallegos

EDITING CONTRIBUTORS
COLABORADORES EDITORIALES
Carolyn Hayes
Kiran Qureshi
Cyndia Pace

CONTRIBUTORS
COLABORADORES
Elizabeth Bricio Beauchamp
Patricia Dyess
Víctor Martínez Martínez
Cuauhtémoc Reséndiz Nuñez

COVER
PORTADA
Eric Gallegos

Library of Congress Catalog Number 2005920872

Library of Congress Cataloging-in-Publication Data
Merl bilingual law dictionary = diccionario jurídico bilingüe.
xvi. 416p. 23cm.
Includes bibliographic references
ISBN-10 1-886347-03-04
ISBN-13 978-1-886347-03-8
1.Law—Dictionaries—Spanish 2. Law—Dictionaries 3. Spanish language—Dictionaries—
English 4. English language—Dictionaries—Spanish 5. Español—Diccionarios—Inglés 6.
Inglés—Diccionarios—Español I. Title II. Gallegos, Cuauhtémoc

K52.S6
340/.03

Website: www.merlpublications.com

Dedication

To my parents, my sister Xochitl, and my brother-in-law Victor, for their example; and for Melissa and Eric, for their bright promise.

Contents
Indice

EXPLANATORY DIAGRAM

main entry ⟶ **by-laws**[1] CORP. n. *estatutos.*

entrada **by-laws**[2] LABOR n. *reglamento.*

legal notation **habeas corpus** [transpl.]*habeas corpus.*

disciplina jurídica **battery**[1] **(crime)** n. *lesiones, agresión* (PR).

• The unlawful application of force upon

transplant another person resulting in harm or offensive

término transplantado touching. – Syn. criminal battery.

Battery, being the actual use of force as op-

posed to assault or the threat of its use, always

legal comment includes an assault, and it is frequent to find the

comentario jurídico terms combined as the expression "assault and

battery."

aggravated battery *agresión física con agra-*

subentries *vantes, lesiones con agravantes.*

términos secundarios **assault and battery** *lesiones, agresión* (PR).◀

simple battery *agresión física simple, lesio-*

country notation *nes simples.*

identificación de país Rel: application of force, *uso de la fuerza;*

bodily injury or harm, *lesión o daño corporal;*

offensive touching, *tocar a alguien con ánimo*

background comment *de ofender;* physical contact, *contacto físico.*

comentario general Comment: Statutory law usually abandons the posi-

tion that any touching constitutes the offense. It is

frequently required that a bodily injury be caused

cross-reference or that the touching be "offensive".

remisión a otro término See: assault. *lesiones.*

Ref: (CA) Criminal Code R.S.C. 1985, c. C-46, s.

legal reference 265; (UK) 11(1) Halsbury's Laws para 488; (US)

referencias del derecho Newman v. Christensen, 31 N.W.2d 417, 418, 419,

149 Neb. 471.

equitable remedies [de]*remedios basados en el*

descriptive equivalent *régimen de derecho-equidad,* [de]*medios de*

equivalente descriptivo *defensa basados en el régimen de derecho-*

equidad.

fingerprints n. *huellas dactilares, huellas digita-*

part of speech *les, rostros papilares.*

parte de la oración Glossary: arch, *arco;* bifurcation, *bifurcación,*

fork; characteristics, *puntos característicos;*

cinta, *tape;* core, *punto central;* delta, *delta;*

development of latent fingerprints, *revelado*

glossary *de huellas latentes;* fingerprint card, *ficha*

glosario *dactiloscópica;* fingerprint powder, *polvo*

para huellas digitales; furrow, *surco;* island,

islote; latent fingerprints, *huellas latentes;*

loop, *presilla;* papillae, *papilas;* pores, *poros;*

ridge, *cresta;* ridge count, *conteo de crestas;*

silver nitrate, *nitrato de plata;* whorl, *verticilo.*

inflected form **insanity** n. [brder]*demencia, enajenación mental,*

palabra derivada *incapacidad mental* (PR), *trastorno mental per-*

manente. **insane** adj. *demente.*

definition • Presence of a mental disorder that relieves a

definición person from criminal or civil responsibility.

– Syn. legal insanity. lunacy. mental defect, *de-*

ficiencia o debilidad mental. mental derange-

EXPLANATORY DIAGRAM

ment, *enajenación mental.* mental disorder (CA),
trastorno mental. mental illness, *enfermedad
mental.* mental incompetence, *incapacidad mental.* unsound mind, *no tener juicio, estar demen-
te.* – Opp. sanity, *cordura, sensatez.*   — antonym / *antónimo*

Cf: **competency • credibility • insanity.**
Competency refers to the qualification of a   — comparison of similar or confusing terms / *comparación de términos afines o parecidos*
person or evidence to be accepted by the court.
Credibility refers to the veracity the person or
evidence brings to the court. Insanity denotes
lack of competency due to a condition of the
mind. <insanity defense> <competency hearing> ◄— example of usage / *ejemplo de su uso*
☛ Insanity is narrowly constructed as a mea-
sure of the mental disorder of a person to be
applied to the decision as to whether that person should be criminally responsible. *Demencia* is a similar term meaning mental disorder,
but mostly as a medical condition without   — comparison of target-language equivalents / *comparación de equivalentes del idioma de llegada*
direct legal implications. *Enajenación mental,
incapacidad mental* or *trastorno mental permanente* are the preferred terms used to designate
mental disorder as a reason to establish lack of
imputabilidad, together with unconsciousness,
uncontrollable fear, underage and sometimes
deaf muteness.

negotiable instrument [fe]*título de crédito,*   — functional equivalent / *equivalente funcional*
[le]*instrumento negociable* (PR). **acceptor** n.   — literal equivalent / *equivalente literal*
aceptante. **drawee** n. *girado,* **drawer or
maker** n. *girador.* **holder** n. *tenedor.*
• Negotiable instrument is an unconditional
promise or order to pay a fixed amount of mon-   — closely connected term / *términos vinculados*
ey, payable on demand or at a definite time,
and payable to bearer or to order. Examples
are a check, a note, a bill of lading, a bond or
a warehouse receipt.
Rel: acceptance, *aceptación;* dishonor, *falta de
pago o aceptación;* holder in due course, *tene-
dor legítimo, tenedor de buena fe;* indorsement,   — related terms / *términos relacionados*
endoso; pay to the order of, *páguese a la
orden de;* personal defenses, *defensas basadas
en la acción causal;* presentment, *presentación;*
protest, *protesto, protesta;* real defenses, *defen-
sas contra un tenedor legítimo.*   — lexical expansion / *expansión léxica*

prudent person test [lexical exp.]*figura jurídica
del hombre prudente.*
• In trust law, the rule that a trustee must make   — synonym / *sinónimo*
only those investments that a prudent man
would make to obtain a reasonable income and
preserve the principal. – Syn. prudent man rule,
regla del hombre prudente.

ultra vires CORP. [borr.] *ultra vires, doctrina de
actos fuera del objeto social (de una socie-
dad), actos sobre los que se carecen de facul-*   — borrowed term / *término prestado*
tades (según el objeto social).

vii

PREFACE

Merl Bilingual Law Dictionary is a descriptive dictionary that contains the most common legal terms and expressions used in English and in Spanish. Equivalents for the terms and expressions in one (source) language are given in the second (target) language. Entries and their definitions are based on terms and expressions found in various legal sources such as scholarly works, legal dictionaries, court proceedings, case law, and statutory law. Following legal tradition, emphasis is given to the writings of legal scholars and statutory law in Spanish-speaking countries and to case law holdings and selected statutory law in English-speaking countries.

Many entries are enhanced by a variety of relevant explanatory and contextual elements. These elements clarify and sharpen the meaning of the terms and are particularly useful when translating, interpreting, or understanding legal discourse. They consist of:

> Lexical comments
> Legal comments
> Comparisons of target-language equivalents
> Comparisons of similar or confusing terms
> Legal background notes
> Synonyms, antonyms, and abbreviations
> Related terms
> Specialized glossaries
> Cross references.

When an entry term or its target-language equivalent is used predominantly or solely in a specific country, the term or equivalent is labeled accordingly. Otherwise, that is when the entry term or equivalent is used or understood in most countries speaking the target-language, no country label is given.

Although many entries include detailed legal references, the references are for illustration purposes only, and no claim is made that such legal notation refers to current law or that it can be relied upon by users to provide legal advice.

EXPLANATORY NOTES

Main entries
Main entries are presented in alphabetical order. When two or more entries have the same spelling but different meanings or usage, they have numerical labels. Hyphenated words are considered as separate words and are alphabetized accordingly.

> **by-laws**[1] CORP. n. *estatutos.*
> **by-laws**[2] LABOR n. *reglamento.*
> **by mistake** *por error, equivocadamente.*

Main entries are usually followed by inflected forms (such as different parts of speech), which have their own target-language equivalents and identifying labels. In some instances, other closely connected terms, such as contractual party names, are added (for example "buyer" and "seller" in the sale contract entry term or "respondent" in the appeal entry below).

> **appeal** n. *apelación.* **appeal** v. *apelar.* **appellant** n. *apelante.* **appellee** n. *apelado, parte apelada.* **respondent** *apelado, parte apelada, recurrido* (PR). **appellate** adj. *de apelación.* **appealable** adj. *apelable.*

Synonyms, antonyms, and abbreviations

These terms appear immediately after the definition, or, if there is no definition, immediately after the main entry or its inflected forms. If the synonyms and antonyms appear without a target-language equivalent following them, the equivalent given for the main entry applies too.

> **insanity** n. [le]*demencia, enajenación mental, incapacidad mental* (PR), *trastorno mental.* **insane** adj. *demente.* – Syn. legal insanity. lunacy. mental defect, *deficiencia o debilidad mental.*

Definitions

Many entries include a definition providing meanings, and, when quoted from other sources, appropriate references. Every definition is preceded by a bullet (•).

> **guardian** adj. *tutor.* **guardianship** n. *tutoría.*
> • A legally appointed person who manages or cares for the person or estate of an incompetent.

Comments

Many entries contain one or more comments. Most comments refer to either a lexical notation or a legal explanation, which appears, without a label or flag, in one or two paragraphs following the paragraph containing the main entry or its definition. Relevant background comments, however, are labeled "Comment:" and they appear towards the end of an entry.

Comparison of similar terms

A paragraph labeled "Cf." includes a brief comparative discussion of the main entry and other similar or closely related terms.

> **damage** n. *daño.*
> Cf.: **damage•injury•harm.** All three of these terms are synonyms. Although not an established distinction, damage is generally used when applied to property, while injury is used when applied to persons. Harm, on the other hand, refers to a less severe or forceful loss or injury.

Comparison of target-language equivalents

Text identified by a ⤙ symbol presents a concise comparative discussion of the meaning of the target-language equivalents pertaining to that entry.

➻ *Amicus curiae* is unknown in civil law countries. In the civil law tradition judges are given broad powers to guide, control, and to act on their own in a lawsuit if necessary; as a consequence a judge can, in theory at least, request *dictámenes u opiniones* from third parties ...

Subentries

Subentries are listed in alphabetical order. They include expressions that contain the main entry or its inflected forms, their equivalents, and, in appropriate cases, applicable synonyms (which are preceded by the abbreviation – Syn.).

> **condition¹(contingent)** n. *condición.* **conditional** adj. *condicional.*
> **condition precedent** *condición suspensiva.*
> **constructive condition** *condición tácita por ministerio de ley.* – Syn. implied-in-law condition.

Related terms and cross-references

Terms closely associated with the main entry appear under the paragraph labeled "Rel:", while cross-references appear under the label "See:". The "Rel:" label lists terms closely related to the main entry, many not appearing elsewhere in the dictionary. The "See" label lists main entries in this dictionary where additional relevant information can be found.

> **false imprisonment (crime tort)** *privación ilegal de la libertad.*
> Rel.: false arrest, *detención o arresto ilegal.* wrongful imprisonment, *privación ilícita de la libertad.*
> See: kidnapping.

Glossaries

Several short glossaries are provided in selected entries to expand the number of terms and their degree of specialization. Most glossaries are so labeled, but those referring to a specific list, part of a generic term, are identified as "Specific Types:".

Target-language Equivalents

Equivalents in the target language appear as one or more words or expressions. When more than one equivalent is given, each is understood to be similar in meaning if they are separated by commas, but to be different when separated by the double line (‖) symbol.

> **fee (charge)** n. *honorarios* ‖ *cuota, tasa, derecho.*

In the case of Latin terms and certain terms in other languages, equivalents in both English and Spanish are given in the English-Spanish section as well as in Appendix C (Latin terms).

While most target-language equivalents denote their source language terms or expressions as having an exact equivalence (without any distinguishable different nature or features), many denote their equivalence as being of a particular nature or having specific characteristics. In these latter cases equivalents are labeled as falling in any of four basic designations:

> **[le] Literal equivalent,** one that is literally identical or similar to the source-language term or expression, but does not have its underlying legal meaning.

Miranda rights [le]*derechos Miranda.*

[fe] Functional equivalent, one that is functionally similar to the source-language legal term or expression, regardless of its lexical characteristics.

negotiable instrument [fe]*título de crédito.*

[de] Descriptive equivalent, one that describes the source-language term or expression in several words that constitute an atypical use or expression in the target language's legal terminology.

affirmative action program (US,CA) [de]*programa de participación de minorías.*

[borr.] Borrowed equivalent, one that has been adopted from a foreign source, usually because there is no similar legal term in the target language's legal system.

internet n. [borr.]*internet.*

Some borrowed equivalents have further distinctions:

[transpl.] Transplant, a borrowed equivalent that has taken permanent root in the legal system of the recipient.

habeas corpus [transpl.]*hábeas corpus.*

[lexical exp.] Lexical Expansion, a borrowed equivalent that is followed or preceded by additional qualifying words, from the target language's legal system, expanding the equivalent's meaning.

beneficial owner [lexical exp.] *propietario en "equidad."*

Quotations
In quotations, words appearing in italics in the original text are shown in compressed, sanserif type instead.

"synonym for one or more of the words title, ownership, and possession." instead of
"synonym for one or more of the words *title, ownership,* and *possession.*"

Examples of Usage
Examples are indicated with angle brackets (< >), unless stated otherwise.

<findings of fact> <conclusions of law>

PREÁMBULO

Diccionario Jurídico Bilingüe Merl es un diccionario descriptivo que contiene los términos y expresiones más comúnmente usados en inglés y en español. Los equivalentes de los términos y expresiones en uno de los idiomas (el de partida) son dados en el segundo (el de llegada). Las entradas y sus definiciones están basadas en diferentes fuentes legales tales como la doctrina, los diccionarios jurídicos, los procesos jurídicos, la ley y la jurisprudencia. Respetando la tradición jurídica se ha puesto mayor énfasis en las obras de los juristas y en la ley en los países de habla española, y en la jurisprudencia y en selectas leyes en los países de habla inglesa.

Muchas entradas incluyen además varios elementos contextuales y explicativos. Dichos elementos aclaran el significado de los términos, dándoles mayor precisión, y haciéndolos especialmente útiles para traducir, interpretar o, simplemente para entender su significado jurídico. Dichos elementos aparecen como:

> Comentarios lexicológicos
> Comentarios jurídicos
> Comparación de equivalentes del idioma al que se traduce o interpreta
> Comparación de términos similares o parecidos
> Notas jurídicas generales
> Sinónimos, antónimos y abreviaturas
> Términos relacionados
> Glosarios especializados
> Remisión a otra entrada.

Cuando el término de la entrada o sus equivalentes en el idioma al que se traduce o interpreta se usan predominante o exclusivamente en un solo país, los términos o los equivalentes son marcados con el rótulo correspondiente. Cuando no es así, esto es cuando el término de la entrada o sus equivalentes se usan y entienden en la mayoría de los países de habla del idioma al que se traduce o interpreta, no se hace indicación alguna.

Aunque muchas de las entradas contienen referencias legales detalladas, tal información aparece como ejemplo solamente y no se pretende que se refiera a derecho vigente, o que pueda ser usada por los usuarios para dar asesoría legal.

COMENTARIOS EXPLICATIVOS

Entradas
Las entradas aparecen en orden alfabético. Cuando la misma palabra tiene más de un uso o acepción se hace tal indicación enumerándolas. Las palabras compuestas que están divididas por un guión son consideradas como palabras separadas y aparecen en consecuencia listadas como tales.

> **ex post facto (lat.)** *ex post facto, after the fact, retroactively.*
> **ex-presidiario** n. *ex-convict.*
> **ex tempore (lat.)** *ex tempore, late in time.*

Las entradas principales son seguidas normalmente por sus palabras derivadas (tales como sus variaciones ortográficas), con sus equivalentes y rótulos correspondientes. En algunos casos se incluyen otros términos directamente relacionados, como la denominación dada a las partes contratantes (por ejemplo "comprador" y "vendedor" en la entrada de contrato de compraventa o "receptor" en la entrada de donación como aparece a continuación).

> **donación** n. *gift, donation,* [lat.]*donatio.* **donar** v. *to donate.* **donante** n. *donor.* **donatario** n. *donee.* **receptor** *recipient.*

Sinónimos, antónimos y abreviaturas
Estos términos se encuentran inmediatamente después de la definición, o, si no la hay, inmediatamente después de la entrada principal o sus derivados. En el caso de que a los sinónimos o antónimos no los sigan sus equivalentes del idioma al que se traduce o interpreta, se les aplicará también el equivalente de la entrada principal.

> **indemnización** n. *indemnity, compensation.*
> • El resarcimiento de un daño o un perjuicio. – Sin. compensación, *compensation.* reparación, *reparation, indemnity.* resarcimiento.

Definiciones
Muchas entradas incluyen una definición dando el significado, y, cuando se trata de una cita de otras fuentes, la referencia apropiada. Cada definición se encuentra precedida de un "botón" o círculo negro al inicio del renglón (•).

> **alimentos** FAMILIA n. *support payments.* **alimentante** n. *provider of support (payments).*
> • Es la prestación en dinero, hecha en forma periódica, que los obligados por la ley entregan a aquellos designados como recipientes para su sustento, habitación, vestido y asistencia médica.

Comentarios
Muchas entradas contienen uno o varios comentarios. La mayoría de los comentarios se refieren a anotaciones lexicológicas o jurídicas que aparecen, sin rótulo o identificación, en uno o dos párrafos a continuación del párrafo inicial de la entrada o del de su definición. Los comentarios relevantes de tipo general, sin embargo, aparecen identificados como "Comentario" en la parte final de la entrada.

Comparación de términos similares
El párrafo denomindado "Cf:" incluye una breve presentación comparativa del término de la entrada principal con otros términos similares o directamente relacionados.

> Cf. **condena** • **pena** • **sanción.** Estos tres términos se usan como sinónimos en ocasiones, significando castigo. Más frecuentemente condena se refiere a la declaración impositiva de un castigo con motivo de una sentencia de culpabilidad, mientras que pena y sanción definen el castigo específico y concreto que se le ha impuesto al condenado.

Comparación de los equivalentes del idioma al que se traduce o interpreta
Aquellas secciones que aparecen identificadas por el símbolo ⊶ ofrecen una presentación comparativa concisa del significado de los equivalentes del idioma al que se traduce o interpreta referentes a tal entrada.

> ⊶ Consideradas ampliamente, una asociación y una *association* son entidades similares, sin embargo cuando se les considera en forma más específica, estos términos tienen diferencias jurídicas importantes que inciden en su equiparación: la asociación es una

persona jurídica, y como tal releva de responsabilidad a sus miembros, lo que no sucede con la *association* que hace responsables a sus *associates* de las obligaciones sociales.

Términos secundarios

Los términos secundarios se listan alfabéticamente. Incluyen expresiones que contienen el término de la entrada principal o sus derivados, los equivalentes correspondientes, y, en casos especiales, los sinónimos apropiados (inmediatamente después de la abreviatura – Sin.).

> **línea de parentesco** *line of descent.*
> **línea ascendiente** *ascending line.*
> **línea descendiente** *descending line.*
> **línea transversal** *collateral line.* – Sin. línea colateral.

Términos relacionados y de remisión

Aquellos términos que se asocian directamente con la entrada principal aparecen en el párrafo denominado "Rel:", en tanto que las remisiones aparecen bajo la denominación "Ver:" El rótulo "Rel:" se refiere a un listado de términos directamente relacionados con el término de la entrada principal, muchos de los cuales no aparecen en ningúna otra parte del diccionario. El rótulo "Ver:" se refiere a un listado de términos que son parte de este diccionario y en donde se puede encontrar información adicional de relevancia.

> **huella** n. *print.*
> **huella de la mano** *handprint.*
> Rel: **impresión,** *print, impression;* **rastro,** *trace.*
> Ver: huellas digitales.

Glosarios

Varios glosarios especializados se encuentran incluídos en ciertas entradas selectas, incrementando el número de términos y su grado de especialización. A la mayoría de los glosarios se les denomina como tales, sin embargo aquellos que se refieren a una lista concreta del contenido de un término genérico, se les identifica como "Tipos:".

Equivalentes del idioma al que se traduce o interpreta

Los equivalentes en el idioma al que se traduce o interpreta aparecen como términos o expresiones únicos o múltiples. Cuando se trata de varios equivalents se considera que, si tienen el mismo o similar significado, aparecen separados por comas, pero que si son diferentes se encuentran separadas por el símbolo de doble barra (‖) .

> **partida de nacimiento** *record of birth ‖ birth certificate.*

En el caso de términos en latín y de ciertos términos en otros idiomas, sus equivalentes tanto en inglés como en español aparecen en la sección English-Spanish, así como en el Apéndice C (Latinismos).

Mientras la mayoría de los equivalentes del idioma al que se traduce o interpreta denotan a los términos o expresiones del idioma de partida como teniendo una correspondencia exacta (sin poseer características o naturaleza diferentes), muchos otros denotan su equivalencia como teniendo una naturaleza o características especiales. En éstos casos los equivalentes pueden caer bajo alguna de las siguientes cuatro designaciones:

[el] Equivalentes literales. Aquellos que son literalmente idénticos o similares a los términos del idioma de partida, pero sin tener la acepción jurídica sobre la que éstos se basan.

> **secretario del juzgado** [el]*court clerk.*

[ef] Equivalentes funcionales. Aquellos que son idénticos o similares a los términos del idioma de partida considerando la función legal que desempeñan, sin tomar en cuenta sus características lexicológicas.

> **comodato,** [ef]*gratuitous bailment.*

[ed] Equivalentes descriptivos. Aquellos que describen el término o expresión del idioma de partida respectivo mediante el uso de palabras que no se acostumbran normalmente dentro de la terminología legal del idioma al que se traduce o interpreta.

> **dación en pago** OBLIGACIONES n. [ed]*discharge of obligation by performance other than the one agreed upon.*

[prest.] Equivalente prestado. Aquellos que han sido adoptados de fuentes extranjeras, normalmente porque no hay un término jurídico similar en el sistema jurídico del idioma al que se traduce o interpreta.

> **usufructo** n. [prest.]*usufruct.*

Algunos equivalentes prestados pueden distinguirse en mayor detalle:

> [transpl.] Transplante. Aquellos términos prestados que han sentado raíces en el sistema jurídico del receptor.
>
> > **guerrilla** n. [transpl.]*guerrilla.* **guerrillero** n. *guerrilla fighter.*
>
> [exp.léxica] Expansión Léxica. Aquellos términos prestados que son calificados por palabras adicionales que los siguen o preceden, expandiendo su significado, y que pertenecen al sistema jurídico del idioma al que se traduce o interpreta.
>
> > **juicio de amparo,** [exp.léxica] *writ of amparo,* [exp.léxica]*amparo suit.*

Citas

En las citas, las palabras en letra itálica en el texto original han sido substituidas por el tipo de letra delgado san'serif.

> "Apelación posee dos acepciones procesales muy distintas..." en substitución de
> "*Apelación* posee dos acepciones procesales muy distintas..."

Ejemplos

Los ejemplos en este diccionario aparecen identificados por el símbolo (< >), a menos que se les indique como tales en alguna otra forma.

> <la voluntad del legislador> <la intención del legislador>

ENGLISH-SPANISH

Abbreviations
(English-Spanish)

A.	Atlantic Reporter (U.S.)
A.L.R.	American Law Reports
abbr.	abbreviation
adj.	adjective
admve.law	administrative law
adv.	adverb
All E.R.	All England Law Reports
Am. Jur.	American Jurisprudence
Ar	Argentina
AU	Australia
B.C.C.A.	British Colombia Court of Appeal
B.C.R.	British Columbia Reports
B.C.S.C.	Supreme Court of British Columbia
borr.	borrowed equivalent
Bo	Bolivia
brder	broader sense
C.B.N.S.	English Common Bench Reports, New Series
C.C.A.N.Y.	Circuit Court of Appeals (New York)
C.C.C	Canadian Criminal Cases
CA	Canada
C.A.	Court of Appeal (Canada)
Cal.App.	District Court of Appeal (California)
Cf.:	comparison of similar terms
Ch	Chile
civil proced.	civil procedure
Cl. & Finn.	Clark & Finnelly (England)
CLR	Commonwealth Law Reports (Australia)
Co	Colombia
const.	constitutional law
comm.law	commercial law
corp.	corporate law
CR	Costa Rica
criml.	criminal
criml.law	criminal law
criml.proced.	criminal Procedure
Cu	Cuba
D.L.R	Dominion Law Reports (Canada)
de	descriptive equivalent
DR	Dominican Republic
Ec	Ecuador
Engl.	England
euph.	euphemism
F & F	Foster & Finalson (England)
F.	Federal Reporter (U.S.)
fam.law	family law
fe	functional equivalent
Fed.R.Civil Proc.	Federal Rules of Civil Procedure (U.S.)
Fed.R.Crim Proc.	Federal Rules of Criminal Procedure (U.S.)
fmal	formal language
Gu	Guatemala
hist.	historical
Ho	Honduras
I.R.	Irish Reports
immgr.	immigration law
init.	initials
int.	International

interp.	interpretation usage
intl.law	international Law
K.B.	King's Bench (Engl.)
labor	labor law
L.Ed.	Lawyer's Edition. Supreme Court Reports (U.S.)
L.R.	Law Reports
L.R.A.	Lawyer's Reports Annotated (U.S.)
lat.	Latin
law fr.	Law French
law lat.	Law Latin
le	literal equivalent
lexical exp.	lexical expansion
M.P.C.	Model Penal Code (U.S.)
marit.law	maritime law
max.	maxim
mil.law	military law
Mx	Mexico
n.	noun
N.B.R	New Brunswick Reports
N.E.	North Eastern Reporter (U.S.)
Ni	Nicaragua
N.W.	Northwestern Reporter (U.S.)
N.Y.S.	New York Supplement
negot.instr.	negotiable instrument
new	Neologism
nrwer	narrower sense
NZ	New Zeland
O.L.R	Ontario Law Reports (Canada)
O.R	Ontario Reports (Canada)
obs.	archaism
Opp.	antonym
oral expr.	Oral expression
P.	Pacific Reporter (U.S.)
Pa	Panama
PACE	The Police and Criminal Evidence Act (England)
Pe	Peru
pop.	popular language
PR	Puerto Rico
prop.law	property law
Py	Paraguay
R.S.C.	Revised Statutes of Canada
R.S.M.	Revised Statutes of Manitoba
R.S.O.	Revised Statutes of Ontario (Canada)
Ref:	legal citations or legal reference
Rel:	related terms or crossreferences
S.C.	Statutes of Canada
S.C.A.D.	Supreme Court (Provincial), Appellate Division (Canada)
S.C.C.	Supreme Court of Canada
S.C.R.	Supreme Court Reports (Canada)
S.C.t	Supreme Court Reporter (U.S.)
S.E.	South Eastern Reporter (U.S.)
S.N.S.	Statutes of Nova Scotia
S.W.	South Western Reporter (U.S.)
Scot.	Scotland
sec.law	securities law
slg.	slang
So.	Southern Reporter (U.S.)
Sp	Spain
succession.	succession law
Spell.	spelling
Syn.	synonym

tax	tax law
traffic.	traffic law
transpl.	legal transplant
TRIPS	Agreement on Trade-Related Aspects of Intellectual Property Rights
U.C.C.	Uniform Commercial Code (U.S.)
UCC	Universal Copyright Convention
U.N.	United Nations
U.S.C.	United States Code
U.S.C.A.	United States Code Annotated
U.S.C.S.	United States Code Service
UK	United Kingdom
Ur	Uruguay
U.S. or US	United States of America
v.	verb
Ve	Venezuela
vul.	vulgar language
W.W.R.	Western Weekly Reports (Canada)
WIPO	World Intellectual Property Organization

AAAA

a contrario sensu (lat.) *a contrario sensu, en contrario*. On the other hand, in the opposite sense.
• A deduction made by being the opposite of something already proved or established as true.

a fortiori (lat.) *a fortiory, con mayor razón*. Even more so. Much more.
• Accepted as true because it is implicit in or part of something already proved or established as true.

a posteriori (lat.) *a posteriori, del efecto a la causa*. Inductively.
• Since a fact has been proved or established as true, a related second fact must also be true or proved.

a priori (lat.) *a priori, de la causa al efecto, lo que ocurrió antes*. Deductively.
• Once the cause has been proved or established as true, the corresponding effect must be considered proved or true.

ab intestato (lat.) *ab intestato, sin dejar testamento*. By intestacy.

abandonment of a proceeding *desistimiento de un proceso*.

abandonment of children *abandono de menores*.
• It occurs when there is an intention, express or implied, to terminate any relationship, neglecting any existent obligations, coupled with an actual desertion. – Syn. desertion of children.
Rel: child neglect, *descuido de menores, falta de atención a un menor*.

abandonment of copyright *abandono de derechos de autor*.

abandonment of patent *abandono de una patente*.

abandonment of permanent residence IMMGR. *abandono de la calidad de residente permanente*.

abandonment of property *abandono de bienes*.
• Intentional and absolute relinquishment of property. – Syn. dereliction, *derelicción*. res derelicta (lat.), *res derelicta*.

abandonment of spouse [le]*abandono de cónyuge*, [fe]*abandono de hogar o domicilio conyugal*.
• The unjustified separation of one spouse from the other with the deliberate intention of the offender to terminate the matrimonial relation. – Syn. desertion. spousal desertion.
Cf: **abandonment ● desertion.** These terms are interchangeable and synonymous. Abandon-

ment refers more to the fact of the relinquishment, while desertion usually emphasizes the breach of marital duty.
Ref: (US) Bennett v Bennett, 79 A.2d 513, 1197 Md. 408, 29 A.L.R.2d 467; Evan v. Evan, 90 A.2d 178, 179, 200 Md. 473.

abandonment of use ZONING [de]*abandono del uso expresamente permitido de un bien inmueble*.
• A voluntary, affirmative, completed act by which a property owner loses the right to resume a non-conforming use under the zoning law.

abatement[1] (decrease) n. *reducción o disminución*. **abate** v. *reducir o disminuir*. – Syn. reduction. decrease. lessening.
abatement of a debt *reducción de una deuda*.
abatement of a legacy *reducción de un legado*.
abatement of taxes *reducción de impuestos*.

abatement[2] (end) n. *terminación o eliminación*.
abatement of a nuisance *retiro de una molestia pública, eliminación de un perjuicio o molestia*.
abatement of action *extinción de la acción*.
abatement of debts *extinción de deuda*.

abbreviations n. *abreviaturas*.
Abbreviations in English are widely used in the courts and legal literature. Some are clearly regional and local in use, while others refer to scientific or legal judicial terminology handed down by longstanding tradition, still in use today.
See: Appendix A. Abbreviations.

abdication (obs.) n. *abdicación*. **abdicate** v. *abdicar*. **abdicable** adj. *abdicable*.
• The relinquishing by a sovereign of his or her throne or government. Also the renunciation of a person in office.

abduction (crime) n. *rapto*. **abduct** v. *raptar*. **abductor** n. *raptor*.
• Taking and carrying away a woman or child by fraud, persuasion or force.
"In England abduction is generally given a narrower sense: the offence of taking an unmarried girl under the age of 16 from the possession of her parents or guardian against her will or... taking away and detaining any woman with the intention that she shall marry or have unlawful sexual intercourse with a person by force or for the sake of her property or expectations of property." (Garner, 4)
Cf: **abduction ● kidnapping ● child stealing.** These terms have overlapping meanings.

Abduction is taking a woman or child away, while kidnapping refers to the abduction of a person, not only a woman or a child, often with a demand for ransom. Child stealing, on the other hand, is the technical statutory term for abduction of children.

abduction for marriage *matrimonio por rapto.*
child abduction *rapto o secuestro de menores, sustracción de menores* (Sp,Gu).
Rel: child stealing, *robo de infante;* interference with custody, *violación del derecho de custodia;* kidnapping, *secuestro.*

abet CRIML.LAW v. *instigar o provocar (la comisión de un delito).* **abettor/abetter** n. *instigador o provocador de un delito.* **abetment** n. *instigación o provocación.*
• To encourage or instigate in the commission of a crime.
aid and abet *asistir en la comisión de un delito.*
Rel: accessory, *cómplice;* accomplice, *coautor.*

abeyance n. *suspensión.* **abeyant** adj. *en suspenso.*
• In succession law, the lapse during which there is no person in whom title is vested. In property law, the condition of a freehold when there is no person in existence in whom it is vested.
inheritance in abeyance SUCCESSION *herencia yacente.*
lands in abeyance PROP.LAW *bienes vacantes.*

aboriginal peoples (CA,AU) *pobladores originales, aborígenes.*

abortion n. *aborto.* **abort** v. *abortar.*
abortionist n. *abortador, abortero.* **abortee** n. *mujer que aborta o abortó.*
• In strict terms abortion is the expulsion of the fetus from the womb, while the crime of abortion is the deliberate destruction of the life of an unborn child without legal justification.
– Syn. crime of abortion, *delito de aborto.*
criminal abortion, *aborto ilegal o penal.*
termination of pregnancy (euph), *terminación del embarazo.*
Cf: **abortion • miscarriage • criminal abortion.**
Abortion and miscarriage are neutral terms and do not connote illegality, although in general use abortion has come to have a criminal connotation. Both are used synonymously. Abortion is usually understood to be an artificially induced miscarriage, and miscarriage, in turn, is understood to be the expulsion of the fetus before it is capable of living outside the womb (sometimes referred to as spontaneous abortion). When referring to abortion as a criminal offense, the appropriate term is considered to

be criminal abortion or its equivalent term crime of abortion.
↦ Abortion and *aborto* are equivalents as are most of their related terminology. It is necessary to point out, however, that Hispanic countries seem to be reluctant to permit voluntary legal abortion during early pregnancy, thus rarely using such terms as parental notification, judicial bypass, and waiting period.
abortion clinic *clínica de abortos.*
conscientious objection to abortion (UK) *objeción de conciencia a efectuar un aborto.*
induced abortion *aborto provocado.*
procuring an abortion *conseguir u obtener un aborto, procurar un aborto.*
spontaneous abortion *aborto involuntario, malparto.*
therapeutic abortion *aborto terapéutico.*
Rel: feticide, *feticidio.*
Glossary: fetus, *feto;* gag rule, [de]*prohibición de sugerir y recomendar un aborto;* informed consent, *consentimiento debidamente informado, consentimiento informado;* judicial bypass, [de]*permiso judicial en substitución del consentimiento de los padres;* miscarriage, *aborto involuntario, malparto;* parental consent, *consentimiento de los padres;* parental notification, *notificación dada a los padres;* pregnancy, *embarazo, preñez;* pro-abortion, *pro aborto;* pro-choice, *pro aborto;* pro-life, *pro vida;* saline amniocentesis, *amniocentesis salina;* unborn child, *producto o niño no nacido, neonato;* unwanted pregnancy, *embarazo indeseado, no querer embarazarse;* waiting period, *período de espera;* viability, *viabilidad.*
Ref: (CA) Mortgentaler, Smoling & Scott v. The Queen[1988]1 S.C.R. 30; (UK) Abortion Act, 1967. Abortion Regulations, 1991; (US) Roe v. Wade, 410 U.S. 113, 163-64; Doe v. Bolton, 410 U.S. 179.

abroad n. *en el extranjero, fuera del país.*

abrogation n. [nrwer]*abrogación.* **abrogate** v. *abrogar.*
• The destruction or abolition of a former law or custom, either by an act of the legislature or by case law, custom or usage.
Rel: derogation, *derogación.*
See: repeal. *abrogación.*

abscond v. *evadir la justicia, substraerse a la acción de la justicia, eludir la acción de la justicia.* **absconder** n. *fugitivo.*
• To hide or be absent from domicile surreptitiously to avoid arrest or litigation.
Cf: **abscond • default.** These similar terms are usually distinguished. Abscond emphasizes

the hiding or absence while default underlines the avoidance of legal process.

abscond on bail *evadirse estando en libertad bajo fianza, fugarse estando bajo fianza.* Rel: in absentia, *in absentia;* in default, *en rebeldía.*

absence n. *absentismo.* **absent** adj. *absentista.* **absent** v. *absentarse.* – Syn. in absentia. nonattendance. nonpresence.

absent defendant *incomparecencia del acusado o demandado, ausencia del acusado.*

absentee landlord *casero o propietario absentista, casero o propietario que no habita en la propiedad.* – Syn. absentee management.

absolute conveyance *transmisión plena de la propiedad.*

absolute discretion *discrecionalidad total o absoluta.*

absolute gift *donación incondicional e irrevocable.*

absolute immunity *inmunidad absoluta.*

absolute liability *responsabilidad objetiva.* – Syn. strict liability.

absolute pardon *perdón absoluto.*

absolve v. *absolver.*

abstinence n. *abstinencia.* **abstinent** adj. *abstinente.* – Other spell.: abstinency (obs.).

abstract n. *extracto, resumen.*
• A summary of a legal document, text or proceedings. – Syn. abridgment, *compendio.* synopsis, *sinopsis.* summary, *resumen, sumario.*

abstract of judgment [de]*extracto o resumen del fallo o sentencia.* [fe]*puntos resolutivos de la sentencia.*

abstract of record [de]*resumen de lo actuado en un expediente judicial.*

abstract of title *resumen de los antecedentes de un título de propiedad, compendio de los antecedentes de la propiedad, estudio de título* (PR).

abuse of authority *abuso de autoridad.*

abuse of discretion *abuso de poder discrecional, abuso de discrecionalidad.*
• Any unreasonable determination inconsistent with the facts and law pertaining to the matter.

abuse of power AGENCY [de]*abuso de las facultades otorgadas en un poder.*

abuse of process *fraude procesal.*
• Improper use or perversion of legitimate process to obtain an unlawful or unwarranted result. – Syn. abuse of legal process. malicious

abuse of process. malicious abuse of legal process. malicious use of process, *uso ilícito de diligencias judiciales, uso ilícito de un proceso.* wrongful process.

Cf: **abuse of process ● malicious prosecution.** These terms are clearly distinguishable and are not interchangeable. While abuse of process is the use of a lawful process to obtain results considered wrongful or unjust, malicious prosecution is the commencement of a process considered malicious and without probable cause.

➤ Abuse of process is a broad concept including any improper and tortious use of process to obtain an improper result; in contrast, *fraude procesal* is in principle more limited, it refers to the same concept but includes an underlying element of fraud to achieve the unlawful result. In practice both terms are applied in very similar form and with similar results.

Rel: malicious prosecution, [de]*ejercicio de una acción penal improcedente con un propósito indebido o ilícito, persecución maliciosa* (PR). Ref: (CA) R v Heric [1975]4 W.W.R. 422 (B.C. Prov. Ct.); (UK) 45(2) Halsbury's Laws para 501; (US) McCartney v. Appalachian Hall, 51 S.E.2d 886, 230 N.C. 60.

abut v. *lindar, colindar.* **abutter** n. *colindante.*

acceptance[1] CONTRACTS n. *aceptación.* **accept** v. *aceptar.* **offeree** n. *aceptante.* **offeror** n. *proponente.*
• An agreeing either expressly or by conduct to the act or offer of another so that a contract is concluded.

acceptance by conduct *aceptación tácita, aceptación implícita.*

acceptance of an offer *aceptación de una oferta o propuesta.*

constructive acceptance *aceptación por determinación de la ley.*

Rel: assent, *asentimiento, asenso;* consent, *consentimiento;* sufferance, *aceptación por omisión.*

acceptance[2] COMMON LAW n. *aceptación.*
• The act of accepting a bill of exchange for payment when due.

absolute acceptance *aceptación absoluta o incondicional.*

acceptance for honor *aceptación por intervención.*

acceptance of a check *aceptación de un cheque.*

blank acceptance *aceptación en blanco.*

accession PROP.LAW n. *accesión.*

accessory CRIML.LAW n. *cómplice.* **accessory** adj. *cómplice.*

• Person who contributes to or aids in the commission of a crime. Participant in a crime who, without being present in the commission of a felony, acts not as a main perpetrator but as a person advising, instigating or concealing after the fact or commission. – Syn. abettor, *instigador o provocador de un delito.* confederate, *cómplice.* counsellor or procurer (UK), *consejero o asistente.*

Cf: **accessory • confederate • conspirator.** These terms are frequently considered synonyms, but they are not often used interchangeably. Accessory is the general term to designate a participant who aids or contributes in the commission of a crime. Confederate is a more specific and less often used term meaning an ally, a coconspirator or an accomplice, always in connection with a confederacy or association of persons. Conspirator means a participant in a conspiracy or agreement with others to commit an unlawful act; it is usually considered a crime by itself. Abettor, in contrast, refers to a participant in a crime who only encourages or assists in the commission of a crime.

accessory after the fact *encubridor.*
accessory before the fact *instigador.*
accessory to a crime *cómplice o implicado en un delito.*

Rel: accomplice, *coautor.*

Ref: (CA) Criminal Code, R.S.C. 1985, c. C-46, ss. 23(1), 21-22; (UK) Stacey v Whitehurst (1865)18 C.B.N.S. 344 at 355; (US) M.P.C. §2.06; Foster v. Com., 18 S.E.2d 314, 315, 179 Va. 96.

See: conspiracy.

accident n. *accidente.* **accidental** adj. *accidental.*

• An unforeseen and unplanned event or circumstance; a happening not by design. – Syn. casualty, *siniestro.* incident (euph.), *incidente.* mishap, *percance.*

Cf: **accident • casualty • mishap • incident.** These terms are synonyms that are distinguishable, but they are often used interchangeably. Accident is mostly used as a broad neutral term. Mishap also means an accident, but implies a negligible or slight consequence, while incident is a flexible term used as a euphemism to mean all these terms. Casualty is a very specific term, used mostly in the insurance world, meaning an accident, but it is also used as a noun to mean a fatality, property damage, or injuries resulting from an accident.

accident insurance *seguro contra accidentes.*

accident policy *póliza de seguro de accidente.*
accident-prone *con tendencia a accidentarse.*
accident report *reporte del accidente.*
accidental damage *daño accidental.*
accidental death *muerte accidental.*
accidental injury *lesión accidental.*
accidental killing *homicidio accidental.*
– Syn. homicide by misadventure. killing by misadventure.

hit and run accident *accidente en el que el conductor se da a la fuga.*
leaving the scene of an accident *abandonar el lugar de un accidente.*
unavoidable accident *accidente inevitable.*
– Syn. inevitable accident.

accomplice n. *coautor.*

• One who voluntarily engages with another in the commission or attempted commission of a crime. An accomplice is considered a principal. Rel: accessory, *cómplice;* principal, *autor principal (de un delito).*

accord n. *transacción, convenio.*

• An agreement; applies to both persons and nations.

accord and satisfaction *transacción, convenio transaccional, aceptación y finiquito* (PR).

• An agreement to substitute for a pending debt some alternative form of payment or discharge, coupled with the actual payment or performance promised. – Syn. compromise and settlement, *acuerdo compromisorio, compromiso.*

Cf: **accord and satisfaction • compromise and settlement.** These terms are similar but not usually used interchangeably. Accord and satisfaction usually appears in contractual contexts in the form of an agreement discharging a debt and executing the settlement agreed upon. Compromise and settlement, on the other hand, is considered a broader term associated with a dispute or litigation.

See: *transacción.*

account n. *cuenta.*
account in trust *cuenta fiduciaria.*
account payable *cuenta por pagar.*
account receivable *cuenta por cobrar.*
blocked account *cuenta bloqueada, cuenta congelada.* – Syn. frozen account.
checking account *cuenta de cheques.*
current account *cuenta corriente.*
deposit account *cuenta de depósito.*
savings account *cuenta de ahorros.*

Rel: accounting, *contabilidad.*

accounting¹ (accounts) n. *contabilidad.*

• The recording, classifying and summarizing of business transactions in terms of money. See: Appendix B. Accounting terms.

accounting² (**accountability**) *rendición de cuentas.*
• A rendition of an account.

accretion¹ PROP.LAW n. *aluvión, crecimiento natural.*
• Addition to a property by gradual accumulation caused by natural forces.

accretion² SUCCESSION *acrecimiento, derecho de acrecer.*
• The sharing among heirs or legatees of that part of an estate that a coheir or colegatee is unable to take or has rejected.

accusation (**generic**) CRIML.LAW n. *acusación.* **accuse** v. *acusar.* **accuser** n. *acusador.* **accusingly** adv. *acusadoramente.*
• A formal charge of the commission of a crime against a person, made before a court or magistrate having jurisdiction to inquire into the alleged crime. – Syn. indictment, *acusación formal (de un delito).* information, *acusación (por fiscal), acusación o denuncia* (PR). presentment, *acusación por iniciativa propia de un gran jurado.* impeachment, *acusación en un juicio político.*
Broadly understood, accusation includes indictment, presentment, information and any other form in which a charge of an offense can be made against a person.
Cf: **accusation • indictment • presentment • information•impeachment.** Accusation is the preferred generic term to connote a formal criminal charge. An indictment is a formal accusation originating with a prosecutor and issued by a grand jury in the United States and by committal proceedings in England. A presentment is an accusation initiated by the grand jury on its own initiative, using its own knowledge or observation. An information is a written accusation charging a person with a crime under the authority and signature of the prosecutor. Finally, impeachment refers to the accusation in impeachment proceedings as well as the proceedings themselves.
false accusation *acusación falsa.*
unfounded accusation *acusación infundada.*
Rel: arraignment, *presentación o lectura de la acusación;* charge, *cargo;* complaint, *denuncia.*

accusatory pleading *pliego de cargos.*

acquisition of property *adquisición de la propiedad.*

acquittal¹ CONTRACTS n. *liberación.*
• A discharge from an obligation or liability.

acquittal² CRIML.PROCED n. *declaración de inocencia, absolución.*
• Judicial discharge of a criminal accusation by jury verdict of not guilty.

act of God n. [de]*fuerza física irresistible.*
• An act occasioned exclusively by violence of nature beyond the intervention of man, such as a storm, tornado, flood, bolt of lightning or a tempest. – Syn. vis divina (lat.), *vis divina.* vis major (lat.), *vis major.*
Cf: **act of God • vis divina • vis major.** All three of these terms mean a superior natural force. Act of God is the term more often used, vis divina is used in civil law systems, though very infrequently, and vis major is the preferred Latin term.
Rel: force majeure (law fr.), *fuerza mayor.*

act of parliament (**UK**) *disposición parlamentaria, acto legislativo,* [nwrer]*ley.*

act of state doctrine *doctrina de la soberanía (estatal).*
• The legal principle that prevents domestic courts from questioning the validity of a foreign country's sovereign acts within its own territory.

action PROCEDURE n. *acción,* [lat.]*actio.* **actionable** adj. *que es una acción admisible o procedente, accionable.*
• A judicial or administrative proceeding in a court of justice in the nature of a litigation where one party sues or prosecutes and another defends or countersues. – Syn. lawsuit, *acción, juicio.* suit, *acción, juicio.*
Cf:**action • lawsuit • suit • claim • litigation • proceeding.** Action is the broadest and preferred term, as it includes any formal proceeding in a court of law. Lawsuit or suit used to be the equivalent term in equity. Both terms are now synonymous with and substituted by the term "action"; they are rarely used in criminal procedure. Claim is the making of an assertion of a right, and it more closely refers to the cause of action, rather than the action itself. Litigation is the term used to describe an adversarial action or lawsuit. Finally, proceeding refers to and emphasizes all steps and measures included in an action.
Action "has wide signification as including any method prescribed by those rules of invoking the court's jurisdiction for the adjudication or determination of a lis or legal right or claim or any justiciable issue, question or contest arising between two or more persons or affecting the

status of one of them." (Stroud's Words and Phrases, 31)

action for bodily injury *acción de responsabilidad civil por lesiones.*

action for damages *acción de daños y perjuicios.*

action for divorce *acción de divorcio.*

action for rescission and restitution *acción de rescisión y restitución.*

action in default *juicio en rebeldía.*

action in equity *acción basada en el régimen jurídico de la equidad, acción en derecho-equidad.*

action in personam *acción in personam, acción personal.* – Syn. *personal action.*

action in rem *acción in rem, acción real.* – Syn. *real action.*

action in tort *acción de responsabilidad civil.*

action of foreclosure *acción ejecutiva hipotecaria.*

cause of action *fundamento de la acción, hechos base de la acción.*

civil action *acción civil.*

class action *acción colectiva, acción o pleito de clase* (PR).

criminal action *acción penal.*

joint action *pluralidad de acciones.*

penal action *acción penal, acción criminal.*

third party action *tercería.*

uncontested action *acción sin respuesta de la contraria.*

Rel: claim, *pretensión jurídica.*

activism n. *activismo.*

actus reus (lat.) *actus reus, acto o conducta delictuosa.* The criminal act.

ad hoc (lat.) *ad hoc, para propósito específico.* For this special purpose.

addiction n. *adicción.* **addict** n. *adicto.* **addictive** adj. *adictivo.*

• Compulsive physiological need for a habit-forming drug.

alcohol addiction *adicción alcohólica.*

drug addiction *drogadicción.*

Rel: dependence, *dependencia.*

Ref: (CA) Mental Health Act, R.S.M. 1987, c. M 110, s. 1. 2. Lyman v Layman (1971), 20 D.L.R. (3d) 549; (US) 18 U.S.C.A. §4251.

adjacent land *terreno o tierra adyacente.*

adjective law *derecho adjetivo, derecho procesal.*

adjournment¹ (postponement) n. *suspensión, aplazamiento.* **adjourn** v. *suspender, aplazar.*

• A putting off or postponing of a session until another time.

Cf: **adjournment ● continuance.** Adjournment means generally a postponement of a session; continuance, on the other hand, is an adjournment motioned and granted in a court session.

adjournment sine die (lat.) *suspensión indefinida.*

Rel: continuance, *dársele una nueva fecha (a un caso), diferimiento;* recess, *receso.*

adjournment² (conclusion) n. *clausura, levantamiento.*

• The act of a court, assembly or meeting of dissolving a session, temporarily or finally. – Syn. close.

the court is adjourned *se levanta la sesión (de la corte o tribunal).*

the meeting is adjourned *se da por terminada la sesión, se levanta la sesión (de la reunión).*

Rel: to call to order, *abrir la sesión (de una asamblea).*

adjudication¹ (process) n. *dictar una sentencia, dictar una decisión judicial.* **adjudicate** v. *sentenciar, fallar.* **adjudicator** n. *juzgador.*

• Refers to the determination of a controversy and formal pronouncement of a judgment. – Syn. determination, *emitir una decisión judicial.*

Cf: **adjudication ● determination.** Both terms refer to the pronouncement of a decision by a court or similar body. Adjudication connotes the process of resolving a controversy, while determination usually emphasizes the finality of a court decision.

◦ *Adjudicación* is a false cognate. In Spanish-speaking countries *adjudicación* usually means the acknowledgment or recognition of a person's property rights by an authority qualified to do so.

adjudication of controversies *resolución de controversias.*

adjudication of insanity [le]*declaración de demencia.*

adjudicatory hearing ADMVE.LAW *audiencia en la que se dicta una decisión administrativa.*

administrative adjudication *decisión o resolución administrativa.*

adjudication² (decision) n. *decisión judicial.*

• The decision or final judgment issued by a court.

See: decision.

adjudication³ (Scot.) *adjudicación de bienes en garantía.*

administrative law [le]*derecho administrativo.*

• The law concerning the executive branch of

government and its relationship with the other branches of government and the public, especially emphasizing the operation of the government-controlled administrative agencies.

➥ Administrative law refers to the management, control and organization of the executive branch and related agencies and authorities. The most dynamic part of this body of law deals with agencies or authorities as regulatory entities and the control the courts exercise over them. *Derecho administrativo* refers to the organization and operation of the government, especially the organization and management of public services and government-controlled companies and institutions. While administrative law has a longstanding tradition as a body of law and is a major and modern part of the legal system in English-speaking countries, *derecho administrativo* is still considered a relatively new field in the legal tradition of Hispanic countries, lacking the history and sophistication of its civil doctrines and codifications. While it is evident that labels as broad as administrative law and *derecho administrativo* may not have a close functional correspondence, the more specific subjects and terms, like sovereign immunity (*inmunidad judicial del estado*), public interest (*interés público*), delegation (*delegación*), etc. are undoubtedly common and equivalent.

administrative agency *órgano administrativo de gobierno, organismo administrativo autónomo.*

administrative appeal *apelación en materia administrativa.*

administrative court *tribunal administrativo.*

administrative expense *gastos administrativos.*

administrative hearing *audiencia en materia administrativa.*

administrative law judge *juez de lo administrativo, juez de lo contencioso administrativo.* – Syn. hearing examiner. hearing officer.

administrative officer *funcionario administrativo.*

administrative procedure *procedimiento administrativo.*

administrative process *proceso administrativo* || *emplazamiento administrativo.*

administrative remedy *recurso administrativo.*

administrative review *revisión judicial de un acto o decisión administrativa.*

administrative rule-making *facultades legislativas de la administración.*

administrative tribunal (**Engl.**) *tribunal administrativo.*
Rel: delegation, *delegación;* discretion, *discreción;* public interest, *interés público;* sovereign immunity, *inmunidad judicial del estado.*

administrator[1] SUCCESSION n. *administrador judicial de una sucesión.* **administratrix** n. *administradora.*

Cf: **administrator ● executor.** An administrator is appointed by the court to manage the assets and liabilities of the deceased. An executor, on the other hand, is an administrator appointed by the testator to follow the testamentary provisions of a will, including the administration and disposition of property.

administrator ad litem *administrador ad litem.*

administrator de bonis non *administrador de bienes sucesorios excluidos de una administración anterior.*

administrator pendente lite *administrador pendente lite.*

ancillary administrator *administrador sucesorio ubicado en otra jurisdicción.*

special administrator *administrador especial.*
Rel: executor, *albacea.*

administrator[2] (**business**) n. *administrador.*
• A person in charge of managing a business, government office or agency; broadly, one who administers.

admiralty law *derecho marítimo, derecho de almirantazgo* (PR).
• The law governing marine commerce and navigation, transportation at sea of persons and merchandise and related matters. – Syn. maritime law.
"American English has two terms —admiralty and maritime law— to [refer to this body of law]. Although these terms are used synonymously today, etymologically they are quite distinct, and this tell us something about its history. Maritime means 'of or pertaining to the sea.' As such it has a broader scope than the word admiralty, which is derived from the connection between the American law and the jurisdiction exercised by a specialized English court that originated in the medieval period." (Schoenbaum, 2)

admiralty court *tribunal marítimo.*

admiralty jurisdiction *jurisdicción marítima.*
Rel: average, *avería;* charter, *fletamento ó fletamiento;* maritime liens, *privilegios maríti-*

mos; perils of the sea, *peligros del mar;* vessel, *embarcación, buque.*
See: law of the sea.

admission n. *admisión.*
• Voluntary acknowledgment that a fact or statement is true. It is also sometimes used in juvenile statutes to mean a guilty plea by a minor.
– Syn. acknowledgment, *aceptación, reconocimiento.* confession, *confesión.* statement, *declaración.*
Cf: **admission** ● **confession** ● **statement.** All three of these terms refer to voluntary acknowledgment of facts, statements or actions. An admission refers to the acknowledgment of factual allegations in view of their relevance to an adversarial proceeding and, in some instances, to a criminal case. A confession is an acknowledgment of the facts as well as of guilt made in a criminal case, usually in writing. A statement is an account given to the police or prosecutor about a crime during an investigation.
admission against interest *admisión contraria a los intereses de la persona (que la hace), admisión en contra.*
admission by demurrer *admisión de hechos de la demanda (hecha en la contestación).*
admission of guilt *admisión de culpabilidad.*
admission out of court *admisión extrajudicial.*
– Syn. extrajudicial admission.
by own admission *por admisión propia.*
implied admission *admisión implícita.*
incidental admission *admisión tácita.*
judicial admission *admisión judicial.*
admission of evidence *admisión de pruebas.*
admission to the bar *admisión a la Barra o Colegio de abogados.*

admonition n. *amonestación* || *apercibimiento*
• A reprimand directed to an attorney by the judge. It also refers to a warning.

adoption n. *adopción.* **adopt** v. *adoptar.*
adoptive adj. *adoptivo.*
• Legal process in which a child's legal rights and duties toward his or her natural parents are terminated and transferred to the child's adoptive parents.
adoption agency *agencia de adopción.*
adoption decree *declaración de adopción.*
adoption petition *solicitud judicial de adopción.*
adoptive child *hijo adoptivo.*
adoptive parents *padres adoptivos.*
black market adoption *adopción hecha a*

través del mercado negro o mercado ilegal.*
closed adoption *adopción con poca o ninguna información acerca de los padres.*
consent to adoption *otorgamiento de consentimiento para la adopción.*
de facto adoption *adopción de hecho, adopción de facto.*
emotional adoption *adopción informal no legalizada.*
foster adoption *adopciones hechas por los padres adoptivos temporales o de crianza.*
half adoption *adopciones de hijos de un cónyuge por el otro.*
independent adoption *adopciones hechas por los padres biológicos independientemente.*
international adoption *adopción internacional.*
kinship adoption *adopción hecha por un pariente o familiar.*
legal adoption *adopción legal.*
open adoption *adopciones manteniendo cierta relación con los padres.*
private adoption *adopción hecha por particulares.*
public adoption *adopciones hechas por instituciones públicas.*
transracial adoption *adopción interracial.*
Rel: foster parents, *padres adoptivos temporales o de crianza;* termination of parental rights (TPR), *terminación de los derechos y obligaciones de los padres (para con los hijos).*
Ref: (CA) Children and Family Services Act, S.N.S. 1990, c. 5 ss. 65-87 Amended; (UK) Adoption Act (1976) Amended; (US) Green v. Paul, 31 So2d 819, 821, 212 La. 337.

adulterate v. *adulterar.* **adulterated** adj. *adulterado.* **adulteration** n. *adulteración.* **adulterator** n. *adulterador.*

adultery n. *adulterio.* **adulterer** n. *adúltero.* **adulteress** n. *adúltera.* **adulterine** adj. *adulterino.* **adulterous** adj. *adúltero.*
• Voluntary sexual intercourse by a married person with someone other than his or her spouse.

adverse[1] **(hostile)** adj. *adverso.*
• Acting or serving to oppose. – Syn. antagonistic, *antagónico.* discordant, *discordante.*
adverse claim *derecho oponible.*
adverse enjoyment of property *disfrute de la propiedad sin derecho, posesión de mala fe.*

adverse[2] **(negative)** adj. *desfavorable, negativo.*
• Unfavorable or harmful. – Syn. injurious, *perjudicial.* unfavorable, *desfavorable.*
adverse verdict *veredicto desfavorable.*

adverse³ (opposite) adj. *contrario.*
• Moving in the opposite direction. – Syn. counter, *contra, opuesto.* counteractive, *contrario, opuesto.* inimical, *opuesto.*
adverse interest *interés opuesto o contrario.*
adverse party *la parte contraria.*
adverse possession *posesión prescriptiva.*
• A method of acquiring title to real property against all others, including record owner, by open, actual, continuous, exclusive, notorious and hostile occupation of land.
Rel: continuous, *continuo;* open and notorious, *público y notorio.*
adverse witness *testigo hostil, testigo desfavorable.*
• A witness giving adverse testimony to the party who called him or her to testify. Also, a hostile witness. – Syn. hostile witness.
advisory opinion ɪɴᴛʟ.ʟᴀᴡ *opinión consultiva.*
• A nonbinding statement by a court of its interpretation of the law, given to requesting government officials.
See: declaratory judgment.
advocate (Scot.) n. *abogado.*
affidavit n. *acta de declaración (hecha bajo juramento o protesta), declaración escrita,* [new][borr.]*afidávit.* **affiant** n. *declarante.*
• A written statement sworn to or affirmed under oath before an officer of the court or a person legally authorized to administer an oath.
affidavit of defense [de]*acta de declaración de las defensas promovidas (hecha bajo protesta o juramento).*
affidavit of good faith [de]*acta de declaración de buena fe de la parte apelante.*
affidavit of merits [de]*acta de declaración de las defensas sustanciales o de fondo promovidas (hechas bajo protesta o juramento).*
affidavit of service *acta de la diligencia de notificación.*
evidentiary affidavit *acta de declaración de pruebas (hecha bajo protesta o juramento).*
Rel: deposition, *testimonio extrajudicial.*
Comment: In most Spanish-speaking countries, in contrast with their English-speaking counterparts, notarization rather than oath is usually required for full legal effects in court proceedings.
affirm v. *declarar, aseverar.*
affirmance of judgment ᴀᴘᴘᴇᴀʟ *confirmación o ratificación de una sentencia.*
affirmation n. *bajo protesta, promesa solemne.*
affirmant n. *quien está bajo protesta.*

• "A solemn statement or declaration made as a substitute for a sworn statement by a person whose conscience will not permit him to swear." (39Am Jur.1st. Oath §13)
affirmative action program (US,CA) [de]*programa de participación de minorías,* [le]*acción afirmativa.*
• Programs designed to remedy the effects of past discrimination, to discurage its existing harmful practices and to prevent future manifestations. – Syn. equal opportunity (Engl.).
↪ *Acción afirmativa* is a literal equivalent frequently used by Hispanics in the United States and Puerto Rico, but rarely in any other Hispanic countries.
affirmative defense [de]*defensa o excepción basada en hechos o circunstancias no incluidos en la demanda o en la acusación,* [le]*defensa afirmativa.*
• A defense that asserts new matter not alleged by plaintiff or offers new evidence to defeat allegations against a defendant.
Specific types: accord, *transacción, convenio;* alibi, *coartada;* assumption of risk, *asunción de riesgo;* automatism, *automatismo;* coercion, *coerción;* contributory negligence, *culpa o negligencia inexcusable de la víctima;* duress, *coacción;* estoppel, *excepción basada en las consecuencias jurídicas de actos o declaraciones anteriores, impedimento;* insanity, *enajenación mental,* [le]*demencia;* intoxication, *intoxicación;* necessity, *estado de necesidad;* self-defense, *legítima defensa.*
Rel: defenses, *defensas.*
affirmative proof *prueba comprobatoria.*
affirmative relief *defensa basada en una acción que el demandado conserva contra el demandante.*
affirmative warranty ɪɴsᴜʀᴀɴᴄᴇ *representación o garantía (del asegurado), declaración.*
aforethought ᴄʀɪᴍʟ.ʟᴀᴡ adj. *pensado con anterioridad* ‖ *premeditación.*
• That which is designed in advance or premeditated. Thought of in advance. – Syn. premeditation. prepense.
Cf: **aforethought • premeditation • prepense.** All three of these terms have the same etymological meaning, aforethought being the old English term and prepense and premeditation the Latin synonyms.
malice aforethought *dolo específico de homicidio, intención homicida.*
age n. *edad.* **aged** v. *envejecido, añejado.*

age discrimination *discriminación basada en la edad.*

age of capacity *edad para tener capacidad (civil).*

age of consent *edad para contraer matrimonio.*

biological age *edad biológica.*

come of age *llegar a la mayoría de edad.*

legal age *edad legal, mayoría de edad.* – Syn. age of majority. lawful age.

mental age *edad mental.*

underage *menor de edad.*

agency[1] **(relationship)** n. *representación.* **agent** n. *representante, agente.* **principal** n. *principal.* **subagent** n. *representante substituto.*

• The fiduciary relation in which a person, called an agent, consents to act on behalf of another person and at that person's request. Cf: **agency ● master ● servant.** Agency creates a fiduciary relationship between principal and agent that is similar to the one created between master and servant. In the principal-agent relationship the agent has some discretion and acts before third parties on behalf of the principal, while in the master-servant relationship the servant is almost completely under the control of the master and does not act before third parties on the master's behalf.

agency agreement *contrato de representación.*

agency by estoppel *representación aparente.*

agency by operation of law *representación por disposición de la ley.*

agency by ratification *representación ratificada.*

agency coupled with an interest *representación en la que el representante tiene un interés jurídico propio.*

agency in fact *representación expresa.*

general agency *representación general.*

implied agency *representación tácita o implícita.*

special agency *poder especial.*

universal agency *representación amplísima.* Rel: authority, *facultades;* disclosed principal, *representante en nombre del representado;* fiduciary duty, *deber de confianza y buena fe;* independent contractor, *trabajador por su propia cuenta, trabajador independiente;* master-servant relationship, [fe]*relación individual laboral, relación individual de trabajo;* undisclosed principal, *representante en nombre propio.*

agency[2] ADMVE.LAW n. *órgano de gobierno, órgano de la administración, organismo autónomo,* [le]*agencia administrativa, agencia* (PR).

• Usually a government body with the authority to apply and enforce specific legislation. Also a private organization providing a public service. <relief agency> – Syn. administrative agency. government agency. regulatory agency.

agency proceeding *procedimiento administrativo de un órgano de gobierno, procedimiento de una agencia administrativa.*

federal agency *órgano de gobierno federal, agencia federal.*

aggravated v. *agravado.* **aggravate** v. *agravar.* – Syn. made worse. unmitigated.

aggravated arson *incendio con agravantes.*

aggravated assault *tentativa o amenazas de lesiones con agravantes.*

aggravated battery *lesiones con agravantes, agresión física con agravantes.*

aggravated burglary *robo de casa habitada con agravantes.*

aggravated kidnapping *secuestro con agravantes.*

aggravated rape *violación con agravantes, acceso carnal con agravación punitiva* (Co).

aggravated robbery *robo con agravantes.*

aggravating circumstances *circunstancias agravantes.*

aggression n. *agresión.* **aggressor** n. *agresor.*

aggrieved party *agraviado, parte agraviada, parte perjudicada.*

• A party whose rights have been infringed by the actions of another or who has suffered a legal grievance by a court judgment or decree. Rel: complaining witness, *denunciante.*

agreement n. *acuerdo, convenio, convención.*

• "An agreement is a manifestation of mutual assent on the part of two or more persons." (Restatement (Second) of Contracts §3) An agreement is made when one party accepts an offer made by the other. – Syn. meeting of minds, *acuerdo de voluntades.* mutual assent, *coincidencia de intención, consentimiento.* Cf: **agreement ● contract ● covenant ● accord.** Agreement and contract are often used synonymously. Agreement is a broader term that refers only to mutual assent and includes executed sales, gifts and other transfers of property, as well as promises without legal obligation. It is a broader term than bargain or promise. A contract requires as one of its essentials that an agreement be present, and implies in addition the creation of binding obligations, which an agreement does not. A covenant is an agreement entered into or a promise made in writing, often part of a contract. Accord, on the other hand, is an amicable arrangement, usually resolving a previous issue.

☛ Agreement in its broadest meaning corresponds to *acuerdo*, more specifically to *acuerdo de voluntades* in contractual matters. This meaning, however, is not the most commonly used in legal practice, where agreement is often used in its restricted meaning corresponding to *convenio, contrato* or even *pacto*.

agency agreement *mandato.*
ancillary agreement *convenio accesorio.*
binding agreement *convenio válido y obligatorio.*
by mutual agreement *de común acuerdo.*
conditional agreement *acuerdo condicional.*
enter into an agreement *celebrar un convenio.*
formal agreement *convenio que requiere de ciertas formalidades para su realización.*
implied agreement *convenio tácito || acuerdo implícito.*
international agreement *acuerdo internacional, tratado internacional.*
prenuptial agreement *contrato prenupcial.*
purchase agreement *compra, compraventa.*
sale agreement *venta, compraventa.*
separation agreement *convenio de separación.*
support agreement *convenio sobre pensión alimenticia, convenio de alimentos.*
to reach an agreement *llegar a un acuerdo.*
void agreement *convenio nulo.*
Rel: accord, *transacción, convenio;* compact, *convenio, pacto;* covenant, *acuerdo o estipulación obligatoria;* pact, *pacto;* understanding, *entendimiento.*
See: contract.

aid and abet *asistir en la comisión de un delito, complicidad.*
• To assist others in the commission of a crime. An aider and abettor may be also a principal, if present, or an accessory before or after the fact of crime.
Rel: accessory, *cómplice;* principal, *autor (del delito).*

aiding or allowing escape *ayudar o permitir una fuga.*

air piracy *piratería aérea.*

airspace law *derecho aéreo, derecho aeronáutico.*
• The rules governing the use of airspace, their application to aviation and to the benefits de-

rived by the general public and the nations of the world. – Syn. air law.
Rel: air rights, *derechos sobre el espacio aéreo;* aircraft, *aeronave;* airport, *aeropuerto;* navigable airspace, *espacio aéreo abierto a la navegación;* outer space law, *derecho espacial, derecho del espacio exterior.*

alcohol n. *alcohol.* **alcoholic** n. *alcohólico.* **alcoholic** adj. *alcohólico.* **alcoholism** n. *alcoholismo.*
• A colorless volatile flammable liquid that is the intoxicating agent in fermented and distilled liquors, also called ethyl alcohol. Also, a drink containing alcohol.

alcohol burn-off factor *coeficiente de catabolismo de alcohol.*
alcohol dependence *dependencia alcohólica.*
alcohol diversion program *programa de rehabilitación de alcohólicos.*
Alcoholics Anonymous *Alcohólicos Anónimos.* – Abbr. A.A.
blood-alcohol content *contenido de alcohol en la sangre.* – Abbr. BAC.
Rel: driving under the influence (DUI), *conducir en estado de ebriedad;* driving while intoxicated (DWI), *conducir en estado de intoxicación;* hangover, *cruda, goma, guayabo, resaca.*

alcoholic n. *alcohólico.* – Syn. boozer, *borracho,* ebrio. dipsomaniac, *dipsomaníaco, dipsómano.* drunk, *borracho.* drunkard, *borracho.* inebriate, *embriagado, ebrio.* wino, *briago, borracho.*

alias n. *alias.* – Syn. also known as (aka), *también conocido como.* nickname, *sobrenombre.*

alibi (lat.) n. *coartada.*
• A probable account of an individual's whereabouts at the time of a commission of a crime making it impracticable to place him or her at the scene of the crime. Negates physical possibility that suspect committed the crime.

alien IMMGR n. *extranjero.* **alienage** n. *condición de extranjero.*
• A foreign born person who is not a citizen of the country in which he or she is living. – Syn. foreigner, *extranjero.*
Cf: **alien ● foreigner.** These are synonymous terms that are used interchangeably. Both terms refer to a person being a citizen or owing allegiance to another country. Alien often implies a greater degree of exclusion or difference than foreigner does. <illegal alien> <foreign dignitaries>.
alien in transit *extranjero en tránsito.*

alienation

alien registration card *tarjeta o carta de registro de extranjero.*

enemy alien *ciudadanos del enemigo residentes en el país (en tiempo de guerra).*

harboring aliens *recibir y encubrir extranjeros ilegalmente en el país.*

illegal alien *extranjero ilegal.*

nonresident alien *extranjero no residente.*

reentry of deported alien *reentrada o readmisión de un extranjero deportado.*

resident alien *residente extranjero.*

smuggling aliens *introducir extranjeros ilegalmente (al país).*

undocumented alien *extranjero indocumentado, extranjero sin papeles.*

alienation n. *enajenación.* **alienable** adj. *enajenable.* **alienee** n. *adquirente.* **alienor** n. *enajenante.*

alimony n. *alimentos, pensión alimenticia (entre cónyuges).*
• An allowance for the support and maintenance of one spouse made by the other while separated, during the course of a marital lawsuit or after a divorce. – Syn. financial provision (UK.), [le]*provisión financiera.* maintenance (between spouses), *mantenimiento o manutención.* spousal support, *alimentos (entre esposos).*
Cf: **alimony • palimony • marital support.**
Alimony is an allowance granted to one spouse during separation, and during and after divorce proceedings. Palimony, in turn, is alimony granted during separation to one of the parties in a live-in relationship. Marital support is a duty of maintenance arising from marriage, lasting only as long as the marriage lasts.

alimony award *declaración de alimentos.*

alimony decree *sentencia de alimentos.*

alimony judgment *sentencia de alimentos.*

alimony pendente lite *alimentos pendente lite.*

permanent alimony *alimentos permanentes, pensión alimenticia permanente.*

temporary alimony *alimentos provisionales, pensión alimenticia provisional.*

Rel: ability to pay, *capacidad de pago;* divorce, *divorcio;* remarriage, *segundas nupcias.*

allegation¹ (assertion) n. *afirmar o asegurar la existencia de algo (un acto, delito o similar)* || *alegatos.*

allegation of corruption *afirmación de la existencia de corrupción, se asegura la existencia de corrupción.*

allegation² PLEADINGS n. [de]*afirmación o declaración de hechos (de una de las partes), pretensión (jurídica).*
• An assertion of fact that a party will attempt to prove in a proceeding.

alleged adj. *presunto.*

alleged crime *presunto delito.*

alleged victim *presunta víctima.*

altercation n. *altercado.*
• A heated dispute. – Syn. argument, *discusión acalorada, disputa.* dispute, *disputa.* fight, *pelea.* quarrel, *reyerta, riña.* wrangle, *reñir, disputar.*

altercation between employees *altercado entre empleados.*

alternative dispute resolution *resolución extrajudicial de conflictos.*
• The settling of disputes or controversies without court litigation, relying instead on other forms of conflict resolution such as mediation or arbitration. – Abbr. ADR.
Rel: arbitration, *arbitraje;* conciliation, *conciliación;* mediation, *mediación;* negotiation, *negociación;* summary jury trial, [de]*juicio simplificado ante jurados (que dictan un veredicto no obligatorio),* [le]*juicio abreviado ante jurados.*

ambassador INTL.LAW n. *embajador.*

ambassadorial adj. *referente a un embajador.*
• A diplomatic representative of the highest rank. – Syn. envoy, *enviado diplomático.* legate, *legado.* minister, *representante diplomático.* nuncio, *nuncio.* plenipotentiary, *plenipotenciario.*
Rel: consul, *cónsul;* diplomatic agent, *representante diplomático.*

amendment (change) n. *modificación, enmienda* (PR).
• An addition or modification to a statute or a legal instrument.

amendment of a will *modificación de un testamento.*

amendment to a pleading *subsanar la demanda o la contestación.*

constitutional amendment *reforma constitucional, enmienda constitucional.*
See: *reforma constitucional.*

amiable compositeur (fr.) INTL.LAW *amigable componedor.*
• An unbiased mediator in a controversy between international entities or nations.
– Syn. amiable compositor.

amicus curiae (lat.) [le]*amigo del tribunal,* [borr.] *amicus curiae,* [de]*persona interesada en un juicio que aporta una opinión (para que sea tomada en cuenta).*
• One who gives information to the court on

some matter of law that is in doubt and that might otherwise escape the court's attention, pointing to a particular result on behalf of the public or third parties who may be affected by the decision. – Syn. friend of the court.

➥ *Amicus curiae* is unknown in civil law countries. In the civil law tradition judges are given broad powers to guide, control, and to act on their own in a lawsuit if necessary; as a consequence a judge can, in theory at least, request *dictámenes u opiniones* from third parties, if deemed relevant. This practice, however, is usually neither common nor encouraged.

amnesty CRIML.LAW n. *amnistía.*
• A pardon that is extended to a group or class of persons usually, but not exclusively, to excuse political offenses.
Rel: pardon, *indulto, perdón.*

amortization *amortización.*
amortization of a mortgage *amortización de una hipoteca.*
amortization reserve (accounting) *fondo de amortización.*
See: *depreciación.*

amphetamines n. *anfetaminas.* – Syn. speed. uppers. whites.

ancient lights (Engl.) *derecho o servidumbre de vista.*
• Easement allowing a landowner to prevent an adjoining construction to block light passing through a window or similar opening.

annexation INTL.LAW n. *anexar (un territorio).*

annulment n. *anulación.*
• The act of voiding. – Syn. nullification, *nulificación.*
annulment decree *declaración de anulación.*
annulment of marriage *anulación de matrimonio.*
Rel: annul and set aside, *nulo y sin efecto;* void and null, *nulo y sin efecto, nulo absoluto.*

answer PLEADINGS n. *contestación (de la demanda).* || *contestación de la demanda de divorcio* (Ingl.). **answer** v.*contestar.*
• Answer is the formal written statement made by a defendant usually denying the allegations and setting forth the grounds of his or her defense. – Syn. plea.
Cf: **answer ● plea.** Both of these synonymous terms refer to a defendant's first pleading. Answer is the general term used in modern pleadings, while plea is the common law term.
frivolous answer *contestación infundada.*
irrelevant answer *contestación irrelevante.*

Rel: complaint, *demanda;* pleadings, *demanda-contestación y escritos complementarios.*

answer interrogatories CIVIL.PROC *absolver posiciones.*

antitrust laws (US) *leyes antimonopólicas, leyes de libre competencia,* [borr.]*leyes antitrust.*
• Statutes prohibiting restraints, monopolies, price-fixing, and price discrimination that interfere with trade and commerce. – Syn. competition law (Engl.), *leyes de libre competencia.*
Rel: cartel/cártel, *cartel;* discriminatory practices, *prácticas discriminatorias;* mergers and acquisitions, *fusiones y adquisiciones;* monopoly, *monopolio;* restraint of trade, *impedimento o restricción del libre comercio;* unfair practices, *prácticas comerciales ilegales, prácticas desleales de comercio.*

appeal n. *apelación.* **appeal** v. *apelar.* **appellant** n. *apelante.* **appellee** n. *apelado, parte apelada.* **respondent** *apelado, parte apelada, recurrido* (PR). **appellate** adj. *de apelación.* **appealable** adj. *apelable.*
• A request made to a superior court or tribunal to reverse or set aside the judgment or decision made by an inferior court or tribunal, on the grounds that an error was made or that justice requires it be corrected.
Cf: **appeal ● judicial review.** These terms are sometimes used synonymously. An appeal is usually achieved by way of a rehearing, using a transcript of the proceedings before the inferior court. Judicial review, besides referring to the court's power to review acts of the other branches of the government, also means reviewing an inferior court's decision by way of examining the record only, which is a more limited examination.
➥ While appeal refers to a rehearing of the case, (the main purpose being to determine the correctness of the appealed judgment) the rehearing is abbreviated when compared with the approach of the rehearing of *apelación* in the civil law system. *Apelación* in Spanish-speaking countries is considered a de novo proceeding; that is, the appellate court reviews the appealed judgment without deference to the decision issued by the trial court.
affirmed on appeal *firme en apelación.*
appeal allowed (UK) *se resuelve la apelación favorablemente.* – Syn. judgment reversed.
appeal bond *fianza o caución de apelación.*
appeal de novo *apelación de novo.*
appeal dismissed (UK) *se niega la apelación.* – Syn. judgment affirmed.

appealable judgment *sentencia apelable.*

appealable order *auto apelable.*

appellate brief *agravios (de apelación).*

appellate court *tribunal de apelación.*
– Syn. court of appeal.

appellate judge *juez de apelación.*

appellate jurisdiction *jurisdicción de alzada o apelación.*

appellate review *revisión en apelación.*

cross-appeal *contestación de la apelación.*

devolutive appeal *apelación con efecto devolutivo.*

direct appeal *apelación directa al tribunal de última instancia.*

grounds for appeal *causales de apelación.*

interlocutory appeal *apelación contra un resolución o auto interlocutorio.*

notice of appeal *notificación de la apelación.*

record on appeal *autos para apelación.*

suspensive appeal *apelación con efecto suspensivo.*

Rel: affirmed/dismissed, *se confirma, se ratifica (una sentencia);* new trial, *un nuevo juicio;* reversed/set aside/allowed, *se revoca, se invalida;* vacated and remanded, *se revoca y devuélvase (una sentencia).*

Ref: (CA) Supreme Court Act, R.S.C. 1985, c. S-26, s. 2. 4.; Clark v Orloff, [1955] 2 D.L.R. 472 (Man. CA); (US) US v District Court of Fourth Judicial Dist. In and for Utah County, Utah. 242 P.2d 774, 777.

appearance¹ (presence) n. *comparecencia.*
• The formal proceeding by which a defendant submits himself or herself to the jurisdiction of the court.

appearance by attorney *comparecencia siendo representado por un abogado, comparecencia en representación.*

appearance docket *registro de comparecencias en autos.*

appearance in court *comparecencia en juicio.*

compulsory appearance *comparecencia obligatoria.*

initial appearance *comparecencia inicial.*

voluntary appearance *comparecencia voluntaria.*

Rel: notice to appear, *notificación de la comparecencia del demandado (hecha al demandante);* summons, *emplazamiento.*

appearance² (look) n. *apariencia.* – Syn. aspect, *aspecto.* look, *parecido, apariencia.* semblance, *semblanza.*

personal appearance *presentación personal.*

physical appearance *apariencia física.*
Rel: demeanor, *comportamiento.*

application n. *solicitud.* **applicant** n. *solicitante.*

appointment¹ (designation) n. *nombramiento.*
• The act of designating someone for an office or position. – Syn. designation, *designación.* nomination, *nominación.*
Rel: name, *nombrar;* nominee, *persona nombrada o designada;* tap, *nombrar, designar.*

appointment² (position) n. *puesto, empleo.*
• The office or position to which a person has been appointed.

appointment³ (date) n. *cita, compromiso.*

appraisal n. *valuación.* **appraiser** n. *valuador.* **appraise** v. *valuar.*
• The estimation of the value of property made by an independent expert, usually an appraiser.
Cf: **appraisal • estimation • assessment • assay.** These terms are synonyms that are usually distinguished: appraisal implies an expert judgment while estimation means an approximated judgment. Assessment means an authoritative determination of value for tax purposes while assay refers to a careful examination, especially of chemical components.

appraisal at market value *valuación a precios de mercado.*

property appraisal *valuación de un bien o una propiedad.*
Rel: assessment, *tasación;* estimation, *estimación.*

appraisal rights CORP. *derecho de retiro de un accionista (en desacuerdo con importantes decisiones corporativas).*

apprehension¹ CRIML.PROCED n. *aprehensión.*
• The capture or seizure of a person charged with the commission of a crime. – Syn. arrest, *detención.*
See: arrest.

apprehension² n. *aprensión.*
• Fear or anxiety; perception or comprehension.

approach the bench (oral expr.) *acérquese o aproxímese al estrado (del juez).*

appropriation bill *ley de autorización de gastos y partidas presupuestarias.*

arbitration n. *arbitraje.* **arbitrator** n. *árbitro.* **arbitrate** v. *arbitrar.*
• Submission of a controversy to a third neutral party, often with an agreement to abide by the decision to be handed down.

arbitration agreement *contrato de arbitraje,*

contrato arbitral.
arbitration clause *cláusula de arbitraje, cláusula compromisoria.*
binding arbitration *arbitraje cuyo laudo es obligatorio (para las partes).*
compulsory arbitration *arbitraje forzoso u obligatorio.* – Syn. mandatory arbitration.
nonbinding arbitration *arbitraje cuyo laudo no es obligatorio (para las partes).*
voluntary arbitration *arbitraje voluntario.* – Syn. consented arbitration.
Rel: conciliation, *conciliación;* homologation, *homologación;* mediation, *mediación.*
See: alternative dispute resolution.

argument n. *alegatos (presentando argumentos).* **argue** v. *presentar alegatos.*
• An oral or written presentation before a court attempting to persuade a decision-maker.
– Syn. debate (Engl.).
closing argument *alegatos, alegatos finales.*
oral argument *alegatos orales.*

arm's length transaction *sin consideraciones especiales,* [de]*forma normal de realizar una operación entre empresas o partes no vinculadas entre sí.*
• Dealings between parties without a special relationship, that is, parties with an equal or similar bargaining position.

armistice *armisticio.*
• A temporary cessation of hostilities by mutual consent between warring parties.
– Syn. truce, *tregua.*

arraignment CRIML.LAW n. *presentación o lectura de la acusación.* [de]*comparecencia del acusado (ante el juez) para que le sea leída la acusación y declare su culpabilidad o inocencia.*
arraign v. *presentar al acusado para que le sea leída la acusación y declare su culpabilidad o inocencia.*
• The act of bringing a defendant before a court to answer the charge made against the defendant by asking him or her to plead "guilty" or "not guilty" or, where permitted, "nolo contendere."
Rel: indictment, *acusación formal (de un delito);* plea of guilty, *declaración de culpabilidad;* plea of nolo contendere, *declaración de nolo contendere, declaración de admisión penal sin admitir responsabilidad civil;* plea of not guilty, *declaración de no culpabilidad.*

arrears n. *pagos atrasados.*

arrest n. *detención, aprehensión, captura* (Co) *arresto* (PR,Cu). **arrest** v. *detener.* **arrestee** n.

detenido. **rearrest** *detener nuevamente, detener otra vez.*
• Taking a person into custody to answer for the commission of a crime or an offense.
– Syn. apprehension, *aprehensión.*
Cf: **arrest • apprehension • detention.** Arrest and apprehension are synonyms. Arrest is preferred and more commonly used in criminal cases, while apprehension is often used to simply mean seizure. Detention refers to the act or fact of restraining a person or exercising control over that person, without formal arrest. "An arrest represents the exercise of the power of the state to deprive a person of his or her liberty." (5 Am. Jur. 2d Arrest §2) Arrests can be made only pursuant certain legal guarantees, which provide the term arrest with the formality and importance that other similar terms lack.
arrest warrant *orden de detención, orden de aprehensión* (Mx), *orden de captura* (Co), *orden de arresto* (PR).
arrest without a warrant *detención sin una orden de detención.* – Syn. warrantless arrest.
arrestable offence (Engl.) [de]*delito cuya comisión permite la detención.*
arresting officer *policía que efectuó la detención.*
citizen's arrest *detención hecha por un particular.*
custodial arrest *confinamiento, detención preventiva.*
false arrest *detención ilegal.*
home arrest *arresto domiciliario.*
lawful arrest *detención legal, detención hecha con las formalidades legales.*
malicious arrest *detención ilegal hecha en forma intencional.*
parol arrest *detención decretada por el juez de su propia iniciativa.*
resisting arrest *resistirse a ser detenido, oponer resistencia a una detención.*
Rel: booking, *fichar (a un detenido);* detention, *detención;* in custody, *en detención, bajo custodia.*
Ref:(CA) R. v. Delong (1989), 47 C.C.C.(3d) 402 at 417 (Ont. C.A.); Criminal Code, R.S.C. 1985, c. C-46, ss. 494, 495 (S.C.C.); (US) Range v. State, 156 So.2d 534.

arson (crime) n. *incendio, incendio provocado o intencional, incendio malicioso* (PR). **arsonist** n. *incendiario.*
• In common law, "the willful and malicious burning of the dwelling house of another." (Ex parte Bramble, 187 P.2d 411, 414, 31 Cal. 2d 43) In

modern statutes, the intentional burning of another's or one's own property resulting in damages. – Syn. destruction of property by fire. malicious burning of property.

arson in the first degree *incendio de primer grado.*

arson of an occupied structure *incendio de una edificación habitada.*

arson with intent to defraud insurer *incendio en fraude de una compañía de seguros.*

suspected arson *sospecha de un incendio provocado o intencional.*

Rel: accelerator, *acelerador de combustión;* blaze, *en llamas, incendio;* charred, *carbonizado;* fire, *fuego, incendio;* incendiary device, *instrumento o artefacto incendiario;* reckless burning, *prender fuego en forma imprudente;* scorched, *chamuscado.*

articles of impeachment *acta de acusación de un juicio penal de altos funcionarios.*

articles of incorporation *escritura o acta constitutiva de una sociedad, acta constitutiva de una corporación.* – Syn: articles of association (Engl.). articles of organization.

articles of marriage *capitulaciones matrimoniales.*

artificial insemination *inseminación artificial.* Rel: embryo, *embrión;* in vitro fertilization, *fertilización in vitro;* surrogate mother, *madre sustituta, madre portadora, madre de alquiler.*

assassination n. *asesinato.* **assassin** n. *asesino.* **assassinate** v. *asesinar.* **assassinator** n. *asesino.*

• An intentional killing, usually one committed for hire, ransom or political reasons. See: homicide.

assault¹ (crime,tort) n. *tentativa o amenazas de lesiones, acometimiento* (pop)(mostly US).
assaultive adj. *referente a la tentativa o amenazas de lesiones.*

• "An attempt, with unlawful force, to inflict bodily injuries on another, accompanied with the apparent present ability to give effect to the attempt if not prevented." (Peasley v. Puget Sound Tug & Barge Co., 125 P.2d 681, 690) – Syn. simple assault.

"An assault is an attempt to commit a battery" (2 Wharton's Criminal Law, §179 at 418). Assault is both a crime and a tort. In popular usage assault refers to any attack; in strict legal terminology assault requires a show of force giving rise to apprehension in the mind of the victim as a main element, even if physical contact is not present.

Cf: **assault • battery.** "Assault should be distinguished from battery, in that assault is the threat of violence, whereas battery is actual violence. However because the two are so closely connected, the term 'assault' is frequently used as a general term for violence to a person." (Collin, Dictionary of Law 15)

↳ As a crime assault is a close equivalent to the civil law crime of *amenazas,* since both share the common elements of threat and raising fear in another. *Amenazas,* however, is considered a broader concept that includes as intended harm not only physical violence on a person, but also damage to property, attack on reputation, and coercion to force another to commit a crime.

aggravated assault *tentativa o amenazas de lesiones con agravantes.*

assault and battery *lesiones, agresión.*

assault causing bodily harm *lesiones.* – Syn. battery.

assault with a deadly weapon *tentativa o amenazas de lesiones con un arma que puede causar la muerte, acometimiento y agresión con una arma mortífera* (PR).

assault with intent to commit murder *tentativa o amenazas de lesiones con intención de cometer un homicidio calificado.*

assault with intent to commit rape *tentativa o amenazas de lesiones con la intención de cometer violación.* – Syn. assault to rape.

assault with intent to kill *tentativa o amenazas de lesiones con intención de causar la muerte.*

common assault (US) *tentativa o amenazas de lesiones simple.*

Rel: endangerment, *poner en peligro;* indecent assault, *abuso deshonesto;* intentional placing in fear, *provocar miedo o temor intencionalmente;* present ability to succeed, *posibilidad real de lograrlo;* threat to cause injury, *amenazas de lesiones.*

Comment: "There is no crime of battery in Canada per se. However, the statutory definition of **assault** in the Criminal Code recognizes, but obviates, the common-law distinction between assault and battery." (Yogis Canadian Law Dict., 30)

assault² (pop.) n. *ataque, asalto.*
• A violent physical or verbal attack.

assembly n. *asamblea.* **assemblyman** *miembro (hombre) de una asamblea.* **assemblywoman** *miembro (mujer) de una asamblea.* – Syn. gathering, *congregación, reunión.* meeting, *reunión, junta.*

general assembly *asamblea general.*

right of assembly *libertad de reunión.*
unlawful assembly *reunión ilícita o ilegal.*
Rel: session, *sesión;* take the floor, *hacer uso de la palabra.*
assessment n. *contribución* || *determinación.*
assess v. *tasar, valorar.* **assessor** n. *tasador, valuador.*
• Imposition of a tax based on the value of the property to be taxed. Also, determination of the amount of something.
assessment of damages *estimación de daños.*
assessment of deficiency *determinación de remanente.*
tax assessment *determinación de impuestos.*
assets¹ (thing) n. *bienes.*
• Anything owed which has value.
concealment of assets *ocultamiento de bienes.*
hidden assets *bienes ocultos.*
intangible assets *bienes intangibles.*
tangible assets *bienes tangibles.*
assets² (accounting) n. *activo.*
capital assets *bienes de capital.*
current assets *activo corriente, activo circulante.*
fixed assets *activo fijo.*
quick assets *activos líquidos.*
assignment n. *cesión.* **assign** v. *ceder,* **assignee** n. *cesionario.* **assignor** n. *cedente.*
• A transfer or setting over of property or rights from one party to another. – Syn. transfer, *transferencia.*
Cf: **assignment • negotiability • delegation.**
Assignment and negotiability both refer to the transfer of property. An assignment requires notification to the party or parties involved, and the assignor transfers his or her rights to the assignee, subject to all original defenses against the assignor. In the case of negotiability, transfer of a negotiable instrument requires no notification and if the transfer is made in good faith it passes a good title, free of any original defenses. While an assignment involves the transfer of rights, a delegation refers to the appointment of another to perform one's duties.
assignment for the benefit of creditors *cesión en beneficio de acreedores.*
assignment of accounts or accounts receivable *cesión de cuentas por cobrar.*
assignment of contract *cesión de un contrato.*
assignment of claim *cesión de un derecho.*
assignment of earnings *cesión de salario o sueldo.* – Syn. assignment of income. assignment of wages.

assignment of errors *expresión de agravios, agravios de apelación.*
assignment of mortgage *cesión de una hipoteca.*
assignment of lease *cesión de arrendamiento.*
collateral assignment *cesión de la garantía colateral.*
general assignment *cesión incondicional, cesión en favor de todos los acreedores.*
– Syn. voluntary assignment.
partial assignment *cesión parcial.*
Rel: delegation, *delegación;* novation, *novación.*
Comment: "Ordinarily parties to an assignment have one of two purposes in mind. They may intend an outright transfer of the right in question, or they may intend that the right be transferred as collateral security for an indebtedness ... An outright assignment may be defined as a manifestation of intent by the owner to the assignee to make a present transfer of the right to the assignee." (Calamari & Perillo, §18-3 at 724-25)
association n. *asociación.* **associate** n. *asociado.*
• A group of persons who have joined together for the pursuit of a particular common purpose, and usually meant to be a continuing organization. It can be a formal entity with by-laws, membership and other indications of an organization, or it can be a grouping of people without structure. – Syn. unincorporated association. voluntary association.
An association is an unincorporated society. It is not considered a legally established corporation or a partnership. Nevertheless, "an association that sometimes functions like a corporation may be treated as a corporation for some purposes by the law." (Ballentine's Legal Assistant, 37)
articles of association *acta o escritura constitutiva de asociación.*
homeowners' association *asociación vecinal, asociación de propietarios (de inmuebles).*
nonprofit association *organización sin afán de lucro, organización no lucrativa.*
professional association *asociación profesional.*
trade association *asociación comercial, cámara comercial o de comercio.*
See: *asociación.* partnership.
assumption¹ (undertaking) n. *asunción.* **assume** v. *asumir.*
• The undertaking or adoption of another's debt or obligation.
assumption clause *cláusula de asunción.*
assumption fee *cargo a pagar por asunción de una hipoteca.*

assumption of debt *asunción de deuda, cesión de deudas.*

assumption of mortgage *asunción de una hipoteca.*

assumption² **(supposition)** n. *suposición.*
• Something taken for granted.

assumption of risk TORTS *asunción de riesgo, aceptación de riesgo.*
• "A defense against liability for negligence which is based upon the principle that one who knows, appreciates, and deliberately exposes himself to a danger assumes the risk thereof." (Ballentine's Law Dict., 103) – Syn. assumption of the risk.
"Originally [assumption of the risk and contributory negligence] were separate doctrines, but *assumption of the risk* has been, in most jurisdictions, subsumed by the doctrine of *contributory* (or *comparative*) *negligence*." (Garner, 84)
Rel: contributory negligence (US), *culpa o negligencia inexcusable de la víctima.*

asylum INTL.LAW n. *asilo.* **asylee** n. *asilado.*
• A country to which a politically persecuted person flees to escape arrest in another country. Also the protection given from arrest by a foreign jurisdiction. – Syn. refuge, *refugio.* sanctuary, *santuario.*

political asylum *asilo político.*
Rel: exile, *exilio;* refugee, *refugiado;* right to return, *derecho de poder regresar (al país de origen), derecho de retorno;* well-founded fear of persecution, *miedo debidamente fundado de ser perseguido u oprimido.*

attachment n. [brder]*embargo.*
• A proceeding in law ordering the seizure of a person's property to secure payment of a judgment.
Cf: **attachment • sequestration • garnishment.**
Attachment is a seizure of property by a court to be used as security to satisfy a judgment. Sequestration refers to the removal of property by a court, usually to preserve it until the court has determined who has the right to it or to force compliance with an order or judgment. Garnishment is a judicial proceeding in which judgment notice is given to a third party in possession to hand property over to the judgment creditor.
↪ *Embargo* is broader than attachment. While *embargo* is a functional equivalent of attachment as provisional measure to secure judgment or to ensure execution, it is not its equivalent when *embargo* means seizure of property to levy execution of judgment, it is

then often called *embargo ejecutivo.*
attachable property *bienes embargables.*
attachment bond *fianza para garantizar un embargo.*
attachment of assets *embargo de bienes.*
attachment of earnings *embargo de ingresos.*
– Syn. attachment of wages.
attachment proceedings *diligencia de embargo.*
discharge of an attachment *liberación de un embargo.*
provisional attachment *embargo precautorio.*
Rel: garnishment, *embargo de bienes en manos de un tercero;* levy of execution, *embargo ejecutivo, embargo de ejecución, embargo en ejecución;* sequestration, *secuestro de bienes.*

attachment of persons *detención de personas.*

attachment of risk **(sale of goods)** *transmisión o traslado del riesgo (de pérdida de cosa o incumplimiento de contrato).*
• The moment risk of loss passes from seller to buyer. – Syn. passing of risk.

attempt CRIML.LAW n. *tentativa.*
• An overt act, beyond mere preparation, that moves directly towards the actual commission of a crime but that falls short of completion.
– Syn. criminal attempt.

attestation n. *testificación, certificación.* **attest** v. *atestar, testificar.* **attestant** n. *certificador.*
attested copy *copia atestada o certificada por un testigo.*
• To witness; to affirm that a document is truthful or authentic by signing as a witness.
See: certification.

attorney at law n. *abogado, representante legal.*
• A person authorized to practice law in a given jurisdiction. – Syn. attorney. counsel. lawyer. public attorney.
attorney-client privilege *secreto profesional, confidencialidad entre cliente y abogado.*
Attorney General (US) *Procurador Federal, Procurador General, Ministro de Justicia.*
Attorney General (Engl.) *Procurador o Fiscal de la Corona.*
attorney of record *abogado con personalidad acreditada en autos.*
attorney's fees *honorarios de un abogado.*
attorney's lien *derecho preferencial de garantía en favor de un abogado (para garantizar el pago de sus servicios).*
See: lawyer.

attorney-in-fact *apoderado.*
• The person authorized by a power of attorney

to represent or act as an agent of another in certain specified matters. – Syn. private attorney.
Rel: power of attorney, *poder.*

attorney's fees *honorarios de un abogado.*
– Syn. legal fees.
Rel: attorney's lien, *derecho preferencial de garantía en favor de un abogado (por sus servicios);* contingent fees, *honorarios basados en la cantidad recobrada, honorarios de cuota litis;* fee splitting or division of fees, compartir *honorarios (con otro abogado);* reimbursement of expenses, *reembolso de gastos;* retainer, *depósito a cuenta de honorarios, adelanto.*

auction n. *subasta.*
• Public sale where goods are sold to the highest bidder.
auction sale *venta en subasta.*
auction with reserve *subasta con precio de oferta mínimo.*
public auction *subasta pública.*

audit n. *auditoría.*
field audit *auditoría externa.*
independent audit *auditoría independiente.*
internal audit *auditoría interna.*
tax audit *auditoría fiscal.*

authentication n. *autentificación, autenticación.*
• The act or mode of giving authority or legal authenticity to a statute, record or other written instrument, or a certified copy, so as to render it legally admissible in evidence.
authentication of signature *autentificación o autenticación de firma.*
Rel: attestation, *atestación;* verification, *verificación.*

authority¹ (govmt.) n. *autoridad.*
• Governmental power or jurisdiction.
warning from the authorities *aviso de las autoridades.*

authority² (influence) n. *fuente de autoridad legal.*
• Legal writing, such as a precedent, statute, or scholarly work, considered conclusive, decisive or influential.
imperative authority *fuente con autoridad legal obligatoria.*

authority³ AGENCY n. *poderes o facultades de representación.*
• The power or authority delegated to another.
apparent authority *poder o facultades aparentes, autoridad aparente* (PR). – Syn. ostensible authority. authority by estoppel.
express authority *poderes o facultades expresas.*

general authority *poder general.*
implied authority *poder o facultades tácitas o implícitas.* – Syn. presumptive authority.
limited authority *poder especial en cuanto a las facultades otorgadas.*
special authority *poder especial en cuanto a su objeto.*
Rel: agency, *representación;* power, *poder.*

authorization n. *autorización.*
auto stripping *desmantelamiento de vehículo.*
auto theft *hurto o robo de vehículo.*
automatism n. *estados de inconsciencia, automatismo (fisiología).* **automaton** n. *autómata.*
• Action uncontrolled by thought or will.
Rel: hypnosis, *hipnosis;* sleepwalking, *sonambulismo.*

automobile n. *automóvil.*
automobile accident *accidente automovilístico.*
automobile insurance *seguro automovilístico.*

autopsy n. *autopsia.*
• An examination of a body after death, especially to determine the cause of death.
– Syn. post mortem examination. necropsy.
Rel: cause of death, *causa de la muerte;* coroner, *investigador de fallecimientos;* external examination, *examen externo;* internal examination, *examen interno.*
See: *autopsia.*

average¹ MARIT.LAW n. *avería.*
• Loss or damage accidentally resulting to a vessel or to its cargo at sea.
"The term 'average' means loss in maritime insurance and shipping law. In most cases when a loss occurs in a voyage either to the vessel or cargo, it is borne by the party that suffers it.... In contrast, general average refers to certain extraordinary sacrifices made or expenses incurred to avert a peril that threatens the entire voyage. In such case the party sustaining the loss confers a common benefit on all the parties to the maritime venture." (Schoenbaum, 522)
average agreement *garantía de avería.*
average bond *fianza o caución de avería.*
general average *avería general.*
gross average *avería gruesa.*

average² INSURANCE n. *distribución de la pérdida.*
• A reduction in the amount payable under an insurance policy in respect of a partial loss of property.

particular average *avería particular.*
– Syn. simple average. partial average.

avulsion n. *avulsión.*
• An abrupt addition or loss of land caused by a change in the course of a river or stream.

award n. *laudo.*
• "The decision of arbitrators determining the disputed matters submitted to them." (4 Am. Jur. 2d Alternative Dispute Resolution, §193 at 95) Also the amount of a judgment or verdict.
– Syn. arbitrament, *laudo arbitral.*
award of damages *sentencia de daños y perjuicios.*

award v. *otorgar, adjudicar.*
award a contract *adjudicar un contrato.*
award custody *otorgar la custodia.*

BBBB

bad debts (accounting) *cuentas incobrables, malas cuentas.*

bad check *cheque incobrable.*
• A check that is dishonored on presentation for payment because of insufficient funds or a closed bank account.

bad faith *mala fe.*
• An act made with dishonest intent.
Rel: good faith, *buena fe.*

bail n. *fianza penal, caución.* **bailable** adj. *que alcanza fianza.*
• Money or security given to ensure the appearance of a defendant in court.
bail bond *certificado de fianza penal, fianza penal.*
bail bond forfeiture *pérdida de la garantía dada en fianza, caducidad de la fianza.*
free on bail *libertad bajo fianza, libertad bajo caución.* – Syn. free on bond.
jump bail *falta de comparecencia (garantizada mediante fianza), saltar una fianza* (PR).
violation of bail bond *violación de las condiciones de la fianza.*
Rel: bond, *fianza, certificado de caución o garantía.*

bailiff n. *alguacil, oficial judicial.*
• The court officer in charge of maintaining order in the courtroom. Also, sometimes a sheriff executing writs and serving processes.
– Syn. marshal (US-federal), *márshal* (PR). sheriff, *sheriff.*

bailment n. [nrwer]*depósito,* [borr.]*bailment.* **bailor** n. *depositante.* **bailee** n. *depositario.*

• A delivery of personal property by the bailor to the bailee for a specific purpose, with the understanding that the property will be returned or delivered over when that special purpose is accomplished.
Cf: **bailment** • **custody** • **pledge** • **sale.** A bailment involves intent to control and possession of chattels. Custody refers instead to mere dominion over personalty (for example, the handing over of goods to a customer in a store to examine in the presence of the clerk). In a pledge, the debtor deposits with the creditor, as bailee, the goods to hold as security for a debt until performance. A sale involves a transfer or passage of title to the goods from the seller to the buyer for a price; in contrast, a bailment does not involve a transfer of title from the bailor to the bailee.
⌐ Bailment developed in the common law tradition as a noncontractual generic concept granting possession of movables while *depósito* and *comodato,* performing a similar legal function, became specific contracts in the civil law tradition. *Depósito* is more closely identified with bailment and is often used as its equivalent, but bailment is broader in that it is present whenever there is rightful possession of goods by someone who is not the owner, while *depósito* is always a consensual agreement, a contract. Similarly, *comodato,* or a gratuitous loan of non-fungible goods, is also a narrower concept, since it refers to a specific type of goods and is again, unlike bailment, always a contract.
bailment for hire *depósito oneroso.*
bailment for mutual benefit *depósito en beneficio mutuo.*
constructive bailment *depósito por ministerio de ley.*
gratuitous bailment *depósito gratuito,* [fe]*comodato.*
involuntary bailment *depósito involuntario.*
– Syn. involuntary deposit.
Rel: chattel, *bien mueble;* custody, *custodia de bienes.*
Comment: "Courts and text writers have been prone to consider bailment as a peculiar transaction or relationship from which as from a matrix certain rights, powers, duties and liabilities arise. If there is a bailment, then it is said that bailee is under a duty to exercise a certain degree of care over the bailed chattel, and to return it to the bailor on demand. It is frequently assumed that if there is no bailment then such rights and obligations do not exist." (Brown, The Law of Personal Property §73 at 253)

Ref: (CA) Lessor v. Jones (1920), 47 N.B.R. (S.C.A. D.); (UK) 2 Halsbury's Laws para 1801; (US) Lash v. Knapp, 143 N.Y.S.2d 516, 518.

balance (account) n. *saldo.*
balance due *saldo a pagar.*
balance outstanding *saldo por pagar.*
balance sheet *balance general.*
ballistics n. *balística.*
• The science that deals with the motion of projectiles such as bullets, shells, rockets and aerial bombs.
Ballistics has three branches: interior ballistics deals with the behavior of a projectile within a gun barrel; exterior ballistics refers to the motion of a projectile in flight; and terminal ballistics deals with the effect of the projectile on its target.
exterior ballistics *balística exterior.*
forensic ballistics *balística forense.*
interior ballistics *balística interior.*
terminal ballistics *balística de arribada o efecto.*
See: *balística.* gun.

ban[1] **(prohibit)** n. *prohibición.*
ban[2] **(expel)** n. *expulsión.*

bank n. *banco.* **banker** n. *banquero.*
• An institution formed for the purposes of receiving and maintaining deposits of money, issuing loans and credit, and discounting commercial paper.
bank acceptance *aceptación bancaria.*
bank account *cuenta bancaria.*
bank assets *activos bancarios.*
bank branch *sucursal bancaria.*
bank charges *cargos bancarios.*
bank deposit *depósito bancario.*
bank draft *letra bancaria.*
bank loan *préstamo bancario.*
bank money order *orden de pago bancario.*
bank note *billete de banco.*
bank overdraft *sobregiro bancario.*
bank rate *tasa bancaria.*
bank receiver *interventor bancario.*
bank statement *estado de cuenta bancario.*
bank syndicate *consorcio bancario. operación bancaria sindicada.*
commercial bank *banco comercial.*
savings and loan bank (US) *banco o sociedad de préstamos y ahorros.* – Syn. savings and bank association.
savings bank *banco de ahorros.*
Rel: credit, *crédito;* money, *dinero.*

bankruptcy n. *quiebra, bancarrota.*
• A legal process aimed at rearranging rights

and liabilities between a debtor and his or her creditors allowing the former to start anew, exempt from liabilities arising from preexisting debts.
bankruptcy act *ley de quiebras.*
bankruptcy code *código de quiebras.*
bankruptcy court *tribunal de quiebras.*
bankruptcy estate *masa de la quiebra.*
bankruptcy procedure *procedimiento de quiebra.*
bankruptcy proceeding *juicio de quiebra, juicio concursal.*
bankruptcy trustee *síndico de la quiebra.*
– Syn. trustee in bankruptcy.
chapter VII bankruptcy (US) *quiebra bajo el capítulo VII.* – Syn. liquidation or straight bankruptcy.
chapter XI bankruptcy (US) *quiebra bajo el capítulo XI.* – Syn. reorganization.
chapter XIII bankruptcy (US) *quiebra bajo el capítulo XIII.* – Syn. adjustment of debts of individuals.
discharge in bankruptcy *rehabilitación del quebrado.* – Syn. discharge of the bankruptcy.
involuntary bankruptcy *quiebra fortuita.*
petition in bankruptcy *demanda de la declaración de quiebra.* – Syn. bankruptcy petition.
receiver in bankruptcy *administrador de la quiebra.*
trustee in bankruptcy *síndico de la quiebra.*
voluntary bankruptcy *quiebra voluntaria.*
Rel: creditors' meeting, *asamblea de acreedores.*
Glossary: automatic stay, *suspensión de pagos;* debtor rehabilitation, *rehabilitación del deudor;* dischargeable debts, *deudas extinguibles, deudas relevables* (PR); disputed debts, *créditos sujetos a objeción;* exempt property, *bienes exentos;* non-dischargeable debts, *deudas no extinguibles, deudas no relegables* (PR); plan of reorganization, *plan de reorganización;* priority claims, *créditos privilegiados;* proof of claims, *prueba de los créditos;* public examination (UK.), *interrogatorio judicial;* reaffirmation of a debt, *acuerdo de pago de un crédito extinguible;* redemption of property, *recuperación de bienes;* statement of affairs (UK.), *estado de cuentas.*
Comment: "Bankruptcy provides a collective forum for sorting out the rights of 'owners' (creditors and others with rights against a debtor's assets) and can be justified because it provides protection against the destructive effects of an individual remedies system when there are not enough assets to go around. This makes the basic process one of determining who

gets what, in what order. Who is fundamentally a question of claims, or what shall often be referred to as liabilities. What is fundamentally a question of property of the estate, or what shall often be referred to as assets." (Jackson, 20)

See: *quiebra.* receivership.

Ref: (CA) Bankruptcy and Insolvency Act, 1985, R.S.C.; (UK) Insolvency Act (1986); (US) US Constitution Art I §8, cl 3,4; Art VI, cl 2; Amend 5,10; 7 U.S.C.S. §24(a); 11 U.S.C.S. §§101ss.

bar¹ (obstruction) *impedimento, excepción.*

bar² (lawyer's assoc.) *abogados (en oposición a los jueces), foro.*

bar association *barra de abogados, colegio de abogados.*

admission to the bar *admisión a la barra de abogados* || *admisión al ejercicio de la abogacía.*

bargain CONTRACTS n. *policitación, negociación contractual.* **bargain** v. *negociar.*

• Agreement of two or more persons to exchange promises, performances or both. "The term bargain is both narrower than the term agreement in that it is not applicable to all agreements, and yet broader than the term contract, since it includes a number of promises that in themselves are not properly definable as contracts. For example, a promise given in exchange for an insufficient consideration is clearly within the definition of bargain, although it is outside the definition of contract." (1 Williston, §1:4 at 16-17)

Rel: contract, *contrato;* promise, *declaración unilateral de voluntad.*

barrister (UK,AU) n. *abogado litigante.*

barter n. *permuta, trueque* (pop.). **barter** v. *permutar, intercambiar, trocar.* **barterer** n. *permutante, trocador.*

• The exchange of goods or services for other goods or services. – Syn. exchange, *permuta, intercambio.* swap, *trueque.* trade, *permuta, intercambio.*

See: exchange.

bastard adj.n. *bastardo.* – Syn. adulterine, *adulterino.* illegitimate child, *hijo ilegítimo.*

Rel: illegitimacy, *ilegitimidad.*

battered-spouse *esposa golpeada.*

battered -spouse syndrome *síndrome de la esposa golpeada.* – Syn. battered-woman syndrome.

battery¹ (crime) n. *lesiones, agresión* (PR).

• The unlawful application of force upon another person resulting in harm or offensive

touching. – Syn. criminal battery.

Battery, being the actual use of force as opposed to assault or the threat of its use, always includes an assault, and it is frequent to find the terms combined as the expression "assault and battery."

aggravated battery *agresión física con agravantes, lesiones con agravantes.*

assault and battery *lesiones, agresión* (PR).

simple battery *agresión física simple, lesiones simples.*

Rel: application of force, *uso de la fuerza;* bodily injury or harm, *lesión o daño corporal;* offensive touching, *tocar a alguien con ánimo de ofender;* physical contact, *contacto físico.*

Comment: Statutory law usually abandons the position that any touching constitutes the offense. It is frequently required that a bodily injury be caused or that the touching be "offensive."

See: assault. *lesiones.*

Ref: (CA) Criminal Code R.S.C. 1985, c. C-46, s. 265; (UK) 11(1) Halsbury's Laws para 488; (US) Newman v. Christensen, 31 N.W.2d 417, 418, 419, 149 Neb. 471.

battery² (tort) n. *lesiones.*

• Intentional and wrongful physical contact with another without his or her consent, resulting in injury or offensive touching. – Syn. tortious battery.

bearer n. *al portador.*

bearer bond *bono al portador.*

bearer check *cheque al portador.*

bearer stock *acciones al portador.*

before me *ante mí.*

behavior n. *conducta, comportamiento.* – Syn. conduct, *conducta.*

behavior modification *modificación de conducta.*

criminal behavior *conducta criminal.*

Rel: demeanor, *comportamiento;* deportment, *porte;* manners, *modales.*

belligerency INTL.LAW n. *beligerancia.* **belligerence** n. *beligerancia.* **belligerent** adj. *beligerante.*

• The status given to a nation waging war against another nation; likewise, the designation of a de facto statehood given to a group of rebels legalizing its hostilities.

Rel: combatant, *combatiente.*

bench¹ (court) *tribunal, estrado judicial.*

bench warrant *orden judicial.*

bench² (judge) *juez, magistratura.*

before the bench *ante el juez, comparecer.*

bench trial *juicio ante un juez.*

beneficial interest [de]*derecho de beneficiario*

(en derecho-equidad), [borr.]*beneficial interest.*
• The right to the use and benefit of property as contrasted with legal title to property.

beneficial owner [de]*propietario conforme al sistema de derecho-equidad o "equity",* [lexical exp.]*propietario en "equidad",* [borr.] *beneficial owner.*
• A person enjoying the benefit of property (who has equitable title) of which another is the legal owner (who has legal title).
– Syn. equitable owner.
↝ The Anglo-Saxon legal tradition has created the possibility of dual ownership over the same property by allowing the right to hold legal title *(titularidad del derecho de propiedad)* to rest in one person, while the right to use and benefit *(derecho de uso y disfrute)* from the same property rests in another person. This distinction of property rights does not exist in civil law countries, where the terms legal and beneficial ownership are unknown.
Rel: legal owner, [le]*propietario legal,* [de]*propietario conforme al sistema de derecho estricto o "common law."*

beneficial use PROP.LAW *uso y aprovechamiento de un bien como beneficiario (bajo el derecho-equidad),* [de]*derecho de uso y aprovechamiento efectivo de la propiedad,* [fe]*ejercicio del derecho de usufructo.*
• "The right to use property and all that makes that property desirable or habitable, such as light, air, and access, even if someone else owns the legal title to the property." (Black's Law Dict., 8th. ed., 1577)
See: beneficial owner.

beneficiary n. *beneficiario.*
bequest beneficiary *legatario.*
incidental beneficiary *beneficiario indirecto.*
third-party beneficiary *tercero beneficiado.*

benefit of discussion *beneficio de orden y excusión.*
See: *beneficio de orden y excusión.*

benefit of inventory *beneficio de inventario.*
See: beneficio de inventario.

benefit of the doubt *(dar el) beneficio de la duda.*

bequest n. *legado de bienes muebles.* **to bequeath** v. *legar.*
• A gift of personal property by will.
conditional bequest *legado condicional de bienes muebles.*
general bequest *legado proveniente del fondo*

general del patrimonio sucesorio.
Rel: devise, *legado de bienes inmuebles;* to bequeath, *legar.*
See: legacy.

best evidence *originales, pruebas primarias.*
best evidence rule *regla de que son admisibles sólo originales o pruebas primarias, regla de la mejor evidencia* (PR).

best of my knowledge and belief (to the) *a mi leal saber y entender.*

betting *apuestas.* **bet** n. *apuesta.* **bet** v. *apostar.*
illegal betting operation *operación ilegal de apuestas.*
Rel: bookie, *corredor de apuestas;* bookmaking, *apuestas;* gamble, *juego.*

beyond a reasonable doubt *fuera de toda duda razonable, más allá de duda razonable* (PR).

bias n. *parcialidad, predilección.*

bid n. *propuesta, oferta.* **bidder** n. *postor.*
• An offer by an intending purchaser to pay a designated price for property that is about to be sold at auction. Also an offer made to be considered in awarding a contract, especially a construction contract. – Syn. offer, *oferta.*
bid for a contract *concursar por un contrato, hacer una oferta para ganar un contrato.*
competitive bidding *licitación, abierto a concurso.*
legal bid *postura legal.*
open bid *oferta pública, oferta abierta.*
sealed bid *propuesta cerrada, oferta cerrada.*
Rel: tender, *licitación.*

bigamy n. *bigamia.* **bigamist** n. *bígamo.*

bigotry n. *fanatismo.*
Rel: bias, *parcialidad;* intolerance, *intolerancia;* narrow-mindedness, *de mente estrecha, intolerancia;* prejudice, *prejuicio.*

bill[1] **(obs.)** PLEADINGS n. *demanda (bajo el régimen de derecho-equidad).*

bill[2] **(legislation)** n. *iniciativa de ley, proyecto de ley.*
• The draft of a proposed statute to be discussed and approved by the legislature. – Syn. bill for an act.
bill draft *proyecto de ley.*
engrossed bill *iniciativa o proyecto de ley aprobado por una cámara.*
enrolled bill *iniciativa o proyecto de ley aprobado por ambas cámaras.*
omnibus bill *iniciativa o proyecto de ley de materias varias, iniciativa o proyecto de ley de miscelánea legislativa.*

bill³ (invoice) n. *factura, cuenta.*

bill⁴ (document) n. *documento, certificado.*

bill⁵ (money) n. *billete.*

bill of exchange *letra de cambio.* – Syn. draft, giro, *letra de cambio.* letter of exchange.

bill of lading *conocimiento de embarque, guía de embarque, póliza de cargamento.*
• "A written acknowledgment signed by the master of a vessel, that he or she has received the goods therein described, from the shipper, to be transported on the terms therein expressed, to the described place of destination, and there to be delivered to the consignee or parties therein designated." (Ballentine's Law Dict., 136) – Abbr. B/L. – Syn. waybill, *carta de porte, conocimiento de embarque.*

clean bill of lading *conocimiento de embarque libre a bordo.*

negotiable bill of lading *conocimiento de embarque a la orden.*

ocean bill of lading *conocimiento de embarque marítimo.*

straight bill of lading *conocimiento de embarque nominativo.* – Syn. nonnegotiable bill of lading.

bill of particulars *relación pormenorizada de cargos, pliego de particulares* (PR).
• A more specific and detailed statement of the claims or charges set forth in the pleadings, indictment or information, provided at the request of the defendant. – Syn. statement of particulars. Rel: motion for more definite statement, *promoción pidiendo se enmiende y clarifique la demanda o su contestación.*

Bill of Rights (US) *Declaración de Derechos Constitucionales, garantías individuales o constitucionales.*
• The enumeration of the rights of individuals legally protected against violation by government.

> Comment: "The American Bill of Rights is found in the federal Constitution and its amendments, especially the first ten. The Bill of Rights is broader than the first ten amendments with which it has been traditionally identified." (Chandler, Endler & Renstrom, 7)

bill of sale *título translativo de propiedad de bienes muebles, factura de venta.*

binder INSURANCE *nota de cobertura, póliza provisional.*
• A memorandum providing temporary coverage to the insured, spelling out the most important terms of an insurance contract, later to be issued in detail and in full text.

binding adj. *obligatorio.* – Syn. compulsory. mandatory.

binding arbitration *arbitraje obligatorio.*

binding contract *contrato obligatorio.*

birth n. *nacimiento.* – Syn. childbirth, nacimiento, *alumbramiento.*

birth certificate *certificado de nacimiento, acta de nacimiento.*

birth date *fecha de nacimiento.*

birth record *partida de nacimiento.*

birth defect *defecto de nacimiento.*

birthday *cumpleaños.*

birthmark *marca de nacimiento.*

birthright *derechos de nacimiento, derechos de primogenitura.*

by birth *de nacimiento.*

to give birth *dar a luz, alumbrar.*

black market *mercado negro.*

blackmail n. *chantaje.* **blackmailer** n. *chantajista.* – Syn. criminal coercion, *coerción criminal.* extortion, *extorsión.*

blood relations *parentesco por consanguinidad.* – Syn. kin, *parentesco.* consanguinity, *consanguinidad.*

blood-alcohol content *contenido de alcohol en la sangre.*

blue sky laws SEC.LAW *leyes sobre emisión y venta de valores.*

board of appeals *Junta de apelación.*

board of directors *consejo de administración* (Gu,Ho,Mx,Sp), *junta de directores* (PR), *junta directiva* (Co,CR,Ve), *directorio* (Ar,Bo,Ch,Pa, Pe,Ur).
• The governing body of a corporation elected to set company policy and appoint chief executives and operating officers.

chairman of the board *presidente del consejo de administración, presidente del directorio.* Rel: directors' and officers' insurance (D & O insurance), *seguro de consejeros y directores;* self-dealing, *actos realizados en interés propio.*

board of review ADM.LAW *Junta de revisión (en materia administrativa).*

board of trustees *Junta de síndicos.*

bodily injury or harm *lesión corporal.*

bogus adj. *falso.* – Syn. false. phony. sham. counterfeit, *falsificación.*

bogus check *cheque sin fondos.*

bogus documents *documentos falsos.*

bogus money *dinero falso.*

bona fide (lat.) *de buena fe.*

bond[1] **(guarantee)** n. *fianza, certificado de caución o garantía.*
• "… [A] written instrument with sureties, guaranteeing faithful performance of acts or duties contemplated." (Fidelity & Casualty Co. of New York v. Niles Bank Co., 71 N.E.2d 742,749)
appeal bond *fianza de apelación.*
bail bond *certificado de la fianza penal, fianza penal.*
bid bond *caución de licitación, fianza de participación (en una licitación).*
bond forfeiture *pérdida de la fianza por violación de sus condiciones, caducidad de la fianza, confiscación de la fianza* (PR).
bond forfeiture warrant (BFW) *orden de detención por violación de las condiciones de la fianza.*
bond forfeiture warrant vacated *se revoca la orden de detención por violación de las condiciones de la fianza.*
bond reduction *reducción de la fianza.*
fiduciary bond *garantía dada por un administrador o representante.*
judicial bond *fianza judicial.*
original bond stands *se confirma la fianza fijada originalmente.*
payment bond *fianza garantizando pago.*
performance bond *fianza de ejecución o cumplimiento.*

bond[2] **(debt)** n. *bono.*
• A document giving evidence of a corporate or government interest-bearing debt issued to take care of a specific financial need and secured by a lien on property. – Syn. debenture, *obligación quirografaria.*
Cf: **bond • debenture • note.** A bond is an instrument secured by a lien or mortgage on corporate property. A debenture is an unsecured corporate obligation. While a bond is usually a long term debt, a note is a shorter term obligation.
bond discount *bono con pago inferior a su valor nominal.*
bond redemption *rescate de bonos.*
bond yield *rendimiento de un bono.*
bearer bond *bono al portador.*
callable bond *bono redimible.*
consolidated bond *bono consolidado.*
convertible bond *bono convertible.*
government bond *bono emitido por el gobierno.*
junk bond *bono basura.*
mortgage bond *bono hipotecario.*

municipal bond *bono municipal.*
savings bond *bono de ahorros.*
treasury bond *bono de la tesorería.*

bookkeeping *teneduría de libros, llevar los libros.* **bookkeeper** n. *tenedor de libros, contable.*

border n. *frontera, límite.*
border country *zona fronteriza.*
border patrol *patrulla fronteriza.*
border search *registro fronterizo.*
border warrant *orden de detención en el puerto de entrada.*
Rel: customs, *aduana.*

boundary n. *lindero, límite.*
boundary mark *mojonera, demarcación.*

boycott n. *boicot.*

brand n. *marca.*
• A name identifying a product or service, usually from a known source or organization. While brands are usually differentiated from the name of the source or tradename, it is not uncommon for a tradename to be also used as a brand.
Rel: tradename, *nombre comercial;* trademark, *marca comercial.*

breach n. *violación, incumplimiento.* **breach** v. *violar, incumplir.*
• Violation of a duty imposed by law owed to another or to society. – Syn. nonperformance, *falta de cumplimiento, falta de ejecución.* infringement, *infracción.* violation, *violación.*
breach of covenant *incumplimiento de un acuerdo o convenio.*
breach of duty *incumplimiento de un deber.*
breach of fiduciary duties *violación de deberes basados en una relación de confianza o fiduciaria.*
breach of law *violación de la ley.*
breach of warranty *incumplimiento de la garantía.*
Rel: performance, *cumplimiento.*

breach of contract *incumplimiento de contrato.*
• Failure to perform obligations under a contract.
↪ "Unlike the Continental systems the Common law in principle treats every contract as containing a guarantee. If the debtor fails to do what he promised, he is liable in damages for 'breach of contract', regardless of whether or not he himself or any of his assistants or subcontractors has been at fault." (Zweigert & Kotz, 503)

anticipatory breach *incumplimiento anticipado.*

constructive breach *incumplimiento implícito.*

material breach *incumplimiento sustancial.*
Ref: (UK) Jarvis v Moy, Davies, Smith, Vandervell & Co[1936]1 KB 399 at 404, 405; (US) Friedman v. Katzner, 114 A. 884, 886, 139 Md. 195.

breach of the peace (crime) *alteración o perturbación del orden público, escándalo en la vía pública.*
• A generic criminal offense including the commission of a public disturbance or a disruption of public order. – Syn. disturbance of the peace.

breaking and entering *penetración, escalamiento.*
Rel: breaking, *fractura o escalamiento.*
Comment: Breaking and entering are necessary elements of the offense of burglary. They refer to a breakage, either actual or constructive, that involves the application of physical force, followed by unlawful entry; that is, entry for the purpose of committing an offense.
See: burglary.

breaking the law *transgresión de la ley, violación de la ley.*

bribery n. *soborno, cohecho* (Mx,Sp). **bribe** n. *soborno, cohecho, mordida* (slg.)(Mx), *picada* (slg.)(Cu). **bribe** v. *sobornar.* **bribee/bribe-taker** *sobornado.* **briber/bribe-giver** *sobornador.*
• Voluntary giving of something of value to influence performance of official duty. The giving or receiving of a reward to influence any official act.
bribing a public official *soborno o cohecho de funcionarios públicos.*
Rel: conflict of interest, *conflicto de intereses;* kickback, *comisión secreta e indebida;* on the take, *que acepta o toma sobornos;* pay-off, *soborno;* payola (slg.), *cohecho, soborno;* slush /hush money, *dinero para sobornar;* unlawful gratuity, *dádiva o gratificación indebida.*
See: corruption.
Ref: (CA) Criminal Code R.S.C. 1985, c. C-46 119-125, 139, 426; (UK) 11(1) Halsbury's Laws Para 281 at 284; (US) People v. Siciliano, 123 N.E.2d 725, 728, 4 Ill.2d 581.

brief¹ (writing) n. [de]*escrito de conclusiones de hecho y de derecho.*
• A written statement submitted to a court, prepared by the counsel arguing a case, for the purpose of stating the essential facts and the legal arguments upon which a favorable judgment or ruling is requested. – Syn. legal brief.

appellate brief *escrito de apelación (ya sea del apelante o del apelado).*

appellant's brief *escrito de agravios de una apelación, demanda de apelación.*

legal brief *conclusiones, resumen de un caso.*

respondent's brief *contestación de la apelación.*
Rel: memorandum, *escrito de alegatos.*
Comment: "It contains a summary of the facts of the case, the pertinent laws, and an argument of how the law applies to the facts supporting counsel's position." (Black's Law Dict., 5th. ed., 100)

brief² (advocacy)(UK) n. *instrucciones y resumen del caso (dadas a un abogado litigante para que tome el caso).*
• A document by which a solicitor instructs a barrister to appear as an advocate in court.

bringing a cause to trial *proceder judicialmente, entablar un juicio.* – Syn. bring an action. bring suit.

broker n. *agente, comisionista, corredor.*

exchange broker *comisionista de cambio, cambista.*

insurance broker *agente de seguros, corredor de seguros.*

merchandise broker *comisionista de ventas.*

note broker *agente de descuento de documentos.*

pawn broker *prestamista, usurero.*

real estate broker *agente inmobiliario, agente de bienes raíces.*

ship broker *agente marítimo.*

stock broker *agente de bolsa, comisionista de valores.*

budget n. *presupuesto.* **budget** v. *presupuestar.*
• Estimate of revenue and expenditure for a specified period.
balanced budget *presupuesto equilibrado.*
capital budget *presupuesto de capital.*
cash budget *presupuesto de caja.*

buggery n. *sodomía.*

bugging *intercepción de conversaciones.* **bug** v. *interceptar conversaciones.* – Syn. eavesdropping, *interceptar conversaciones privadas en forma ilegal y subrepticia.* wiretapping, *intercepción de una comunicación telefónica.*
bugging device *interceptor de conversaciones.*

builder n. *constructor.*
builder's lien *derecho preferencial de garantía en favor de un constructor.*
builder's risk insurance *seguro sobre el riesgo de construcción.*

building¹ (edifice) n. *edificio.* – Syn. edifice,

edificio. premises, *propiedad (inmobiliaria).* structure, *estructura.*
apartment building *edificio de departamentos o apartamentos.*
office building *edificio de oficinas, edificio comercial.*
rental building *edificio de rentas, edificio rentado.*
building² (construction) n. *construcción.*
building code *reglamento de construcción.*
building permit *permiso de construcción.*
building restrictions *limitaciones a la construcción.*
bullet n. *bala.* – Syn. pellet, *balín, munición.* projectile, *proyectil.*
astray bullet *bala perdida.*
bulletproof *a prueba de balas.*
expanding bullet *bala de expansión.*
explosive bullet *bala explosiva.*
rubber bullet *bala de goma.*
Rel: ballistics, *balística;* caliber, *calibre.* cartridge, *cartucho;* jacket, *blindaje (camisa).* See: *cartucho.*
burden of proof *carga de la prueba, peso de la prueba* (PR).
• The obligation by a party in a proceeding to show convincing evidence proving an allegation or issue.
burglary (crime) n. *robo de casa habitada, robo con fuerza en las cosas, escalamiento* (PR).
burglarize v. *robar (una habitación, oficina o comercio).* **burglarious** adj. *relativo a un robo (de habitación, oficina o comercio).* **burglar** n. *ladrón, robacasas.*
• Burglary in common law means the breaking and entering of a dwelling house of another in the night time with the intent to commit a felony. In modern statutes, breaking and entering is neither restricted to a house nor limited to night time. – Syn. statutory burglary. housebreaking.
Cf: **burglary • breaking and entering.**
Burglary and breaking and entering are often considered and used as synonyms. In common law, however, breaking and entering is but one of the elements of the crime of burglary, the act of entering a building without permission.
↬ In most Hispanic countries both *penetración* and *escalamiento* are widely used and understood as equivalents of breaking and entering. While *penetración* means an unusual form of entry, usually implying the overcoming of some type of resistance, *escalamiento* usually means entry by climbing or trespassing in all

jurisdictions but Puerto Rico, where it is often used as the equivalent of burglary.
breaking and entering *penetración, escalamiento.*
burglary in the first degree *robo de casa habitada de primer grado.*
possession of burglar's tools *posesión de implementos o herramientas para robar.*
residential burglary *robo de casa habitada.*
Rel: criminal trespass, *entrar o permanecer ilícita e intencionalmente en una propiedad,* unauthorized entry of a dwelling, *entrada sin autorización en una propiedad habitada.* See: theft.
business¹ (commerce) n. *negocios, administración.* – Syn. commerce, *comercio.* trade, *negocio, comercio.*
business administration *administración de negocios.*
business deal *trato comercial, acuerdo de negocios.*
business guest *visitante de un negocio o establecimiento comercial o industrial.*
business hours *horas hábiles.*
business losses *pérdidas de negocios.*
business plan *propuesta de un negocio.*
business records *libros y registros de un negocio o establecimiento.*
business school *escuela de administración.*
Rel: accounting, *contabilidad;* finances, *finanzas;* marketing, *mercadotecnia, mercadeo.*
business² (occupation) n. *ocupación, profesión.*
business forms *sociedades comerciales o mercantiles.* – Syn. business enterprises, *empresas comerciales o mercantiles.* business entities, *entidades comerciales o mercantiles.* business organizations, *organizaciones comerciales o mercantiles.*
Specific types: cooperative, *cooperativa;* corporation, *corporación, sociedad anónima;* joint-stock company, *compañía por acciones;* limited liability company, *compañía o sociedad de responsabilidad limitada;* limited partnership, *sociedad en comandita;* nonprofit organization, *organización no lucrativa;* partnership, *sociedad colectiva;* sole proprietorship, *comerciante individual.*
businessman n. *hombre de negocios, comerciante, negociante.* **businesswoman** n. *mujer de negocios.*
Rel: entrepreneur, *empresario;* manager, *gerente.*
by-laws¹ CORP. n. *estatutos.*
• Rules of government adopted by an association or corporation.

by-laws[2] LABOR n. *reglamento.*

by mistake *por error, equivocadamente.*

by mutual agreement *de común acuerdo.*

by operation of law *por determinación de la ley, por ministerio de ley.*

by own admission *por admisión propia.*

by proxy *por poder, por poderes.*

bystander n. *circunstante, espectador.*

CCCC

cabinet n. *gabinete.*
• A body of ministers and high officials who advise the President or Prime Minister on formulating government policy and carrying it out. See: Parliament.

cadaver n. *cadáver.* – Syn. body, *cuerpo.* corpse, *cadáver.* remains, *restos.*

calendar n. *calendario.*
   calendar days *días naturales.*
   calendar year *año calendario.*
   court calendar *lista de casos para acuerdo.*
   settlement calendar *lista de asuntos en conciliación.*
   trial calendar *calendario de juicios, lista de juicios.*
   Rel: date, *fecha.*

call[1] SEC.LAW n. *opción de compra (de acciones).*
• An option or contract granting the holder the right to buy or sell designated securities or commodities at a specified price within a stipulated period.

call[2] PROCEDURE n. *llamada a participar (en una actuación judicial), lista de casos a ser llamados (ante un juez).*
• A request to be present or to assemble.
   bond call *llamada a participar en las audiencias de fijación de fianza, lista de casos para señalar fianza a ser llamados (ante el juez).*
   domestic violence call *llamada a participar en las actuaciones (judiciales) de casos de violencia doméstica, lista de casos de violencia doméstica a ser llamados (ante el juez).*
   preliminary hearing call *llamada a participar en las audiencias preliminares, lista de casos de audiencias preliminares a ser llamados (ante el juez).*

call[3] **(pago)** n. *pago exigible.* **call** v. *exigir pago.*
• A demand for payment.
   call loan *préstamo exigible en cualquier momento.*

cancellation n. *cancelación.* **cancel** v. *cancelar.*

• The termination of a contract or instruments evidencing a contract or arising under it. Also the mark or marks showing that a document or instrument is cancelled. – Syn. annulment, *anulación.* termination, *terminación.*
Cf: **cancellation • termination • rescission.** Cancellation and termination are synonyms that are used interchangeably with few exceptions. <the employee received notice of termination> They are usually used to express ending, sometimes as duplets. <the agreement is cancelled and terminated> Rescission is distinguished from cancellation and termination since it connotes unmaking or discharging rather than ending.
   cancellation clause *cláusula de cancelación.*
   cancellation of a contract *cancelación de un contrato.*
   cancellation of a lease *cancelación de un arrendamiento.*
   cancellation of a mortgage *cancelación de una hipoteca.*
   cancellation of a will *revocación de un testamento.*
   cancellation of an insurance policy *cancelación de una póliza de seguro.*
   cancelled check *cheque cancelado.*
   Rel: expunge, *borrar retroactivamente;* revocation, *revocación;* vacate, *revocar, invalidar.*
   See: rescission.

cannabis n. *canabis.* – Syn. hashish, *hashish.* marihuana/marijuana, *mariguana.*

canon law *derecho canónico.* **canonical** adj. *canónico.*
   See: *derecho canónico.*

capacity n. *capacidad.*
• Ability to understand the nature and effects of one's acts. A legal qualification. – Opp. disability, *incapacidad.* incapacity, *incapacidad.*
   capacity defense *defensa de falta de capacidad.*
   criminal capacity *capacidad criminal o penal.*
   diminished capacity *capacidad reducida.*
   disposing capacity *capacidad para disponer de bienes.*
   fiduciary capacity *capacidad fiduciaria.*
   legal capacity *capacidad legal.*
   mental capacity *capacidad mental.*
   testamentary capacity *capacidad testamentaria.*
   Rel: legal age, *edad legal.*
   See: competency.

capital n. *capital.* – Syn. resources, *recursos.* means, *medios.*

capital assets *activo fijo.*
capital expenditures *gastos de capital.*
capital gains *ganancias de capital.*
capital investment *inversión de capital.*
capital losses *pérdidas de capital.*
capital market *mercado de capital.*
capital stock *capital social.*
capital tax *impuesto sobre capitales.*
flight capital *fuga de capital.*
paid-in-capital *capital pagado, capital desembolsado* (Sp), *capital exhibido (*Mx).

capital punishment *pena capital.* – Syn. death punishment. death penalty.

caption of a petition *rubro de la demanda o petición.*

capture[1] (detención) n. *arresto* || *detención.*

capture[2] INTL.LAW n. *captura.*
In technical terms capture is a taking by military personnel, while a taking by civil authorities is considered a seizure.

care[1](attention) n. *cuidado, atención.*
• To provide close attention and to watch over; to heed.
care provider *encargado de proveer cuidados y atención.*
due care *atenciones y cuidados necesarios.*
health care *atención médica, cuidados médicos.*

care[2] TORTS n. *diligencia, prudencia.*
• The conduct demanded from a person taking into account the circumstances of the situation.
great care *diligencia o prudencia extraordinaria.*
highest degree of care *el más alto grado de diligencia o prudencia.*
ordinary care *diligencia o prudencia ordinaria o común.*
reasonable care *diligencia o prudencia razonable.*
slight care *diligencia o prudencia mínima.*
standard of care *criterio usado para determinar la diligencia o prudencia necesaria.*
Rel: negligence, *negligencia.*

carjacking [de]*robo de un automóvil tomado de su ocupante (generalmente mediante el uso de la fuerza), robo de automóvil (en circulación),* [le]*secuestro de automóvil.*

carrier n. *transportista, compañía de transportación.*
• Individual or organization dedicated to the transportation of goods or persons for a price.
– Syn. shipper, *compañía de carga.* transport

company, *compañía de transportación, compañía de transporte.*
carrier's lien [de]*derecho preferencial de garantía en favor de un transportista (creado por ministerio de ley).*
common carrier *transportista público.*
freight carrier *transporte de carga.*
private carrier *transportista particular.*

case[1] (action) n. *caso.* **caseload** n. *carga de trabajo (de casos).*
• "A contested question in a court of justice." (Ballentine's Law Dict., 177) When used in a loose form, case may refer to an action, cause or suit. <civil case> <criminal case>
case at common law *caso al que se aplica el régimen jurídico de derecho estricto o "common law."*
case continued *cítese a las partes nuevamente, se continúa el caso a una nueva fecha, caso prorrogado.*
case dismissed *caso sobreseído, caso desestimado* (PR).
case in equity *caso al que se aplica el régimen jurídico de derecho-equidad.*
case on appeal *caso en apelación, apelación.*
case reserved [de]*escrito en el que las partes acuerdan describir los hechos del caso para que el tribunal de apelación decida sobre el derecho de ciertas cuestiones.*
disposition of a case *resolución o acuerdo en un proceso,* [le]*disposición en un caso.*
pass the case *déjese el caso pendiente para ser llamado después (durante la misma sesión).*
pending case *caso o proceso pendiente.*
reinstate a case *reposición de un proceso.*
reopening a case *reabrir un caso.*
write-in case *caso agregado (a la lista de casos).*
Rel: action, *acción;* cause, *causa;* suit, *juicio.*

case[2] EVIDENCE n. *pruebas.*
case in chief *pruebas de la parte con la carga probatoria.*
prima facie case *elementos probatorios prima facie de la acción.*
rebuttal case *pruebas de la parte que contradice las presentadas por la contraria.*

case[3] (decision) n. *precedente, ejecutoria.*
leading case *precedente judicial, precedente jurisprudencial, caso que sienta precedente.*

case law *jurisprudencia, precedentes judiciales.*
• The law as expressed in the decisions of the courts; that which is created by judicial decision rather than by statute. – Syn. adjudicative law.

jurisprudence.

cash n. *dinero en efectivo, dinero al contado.*
  cashier n. *cajero.*
  cash bail *fianza en efectivo.*
  cash basis accounting *contabilidad con base en lo percibido, método contable de lo percibido.*
  cash bond *certificado de caución en efectivo.*
  cash discount *descuento por pago en efectivo.*
  cash dividend *dividendos pagados en efectivo.*
  cash flow *flujo de efectivo, flujo de fondos.*
  cash market value *valor de mercado al contado.*
  cash on hand *efectivo disponible.*
  cash price *precio en efectivo, precio al contado.*
  cash register *caja registradora.*
  cash sale *venta en efectivo, venta al contado.*
  cash surrender value *valor de rescate (de una póliza de seguro).*
  Rel: money, *dinero.*

casual criminals *delincuentes por necesidad.*

casualty[1] (accident) n. *accidente, accidente serio.*
  casualty insurance *seguro contra accidentes.*
  casualty loss *monto de la pérdida por el accidente.*
  See: accident.

casualty[2] (fatality) n. *baja, pérdida.*
  human casualty *fatalidad, baja.*
  casualties of war *bajas, víctimas de la guerra.*

cause n. *causa.*
  • An action or a lawsuit; a case.
  cause célèbre *causa célebre.*
  cause pending *causa pendiente, proceso pendiente.*

cause n. *causa.*
  • That which produces an effect.
  intervening cause *causa independiente del acto o conducta.*
  probable cause *causa probable.*

cause of action *fundamento de la acción, hechos base de la acción.*
  • A right to sue based on the existence of a factual situation entitling one person to redress a grievance before a court.
  Cf: **cause of action ▪ action.** Both terms are sometimes used as synonyms when cause of action is used broadly and loosely. Most times, however, they are clearly differentiated: cause of action refers to a set of facts justifying a suit or action, while action refers to the resulting civil or criminal proceeding.

  failure to state a cause of action *omisión del fundamento de la acción, falta de los hechos base de la acción.*

cause of death *causa de la muerte.*
  immediate cause of death *causa inmediata de la muerte.*
  proximate cause of death *causa legal de la muerte.*
  Rel: deadly gunshot, *disparo mortal de un arma;* drowning, *ahogado;* hanging, *ahorcamien to;* natural causes, *causas naturales;* poisoning, *envenenamiento;* smother, *asfixia, sofocación;* stabbing, *apuñalamiento;* strangulation, *estrangulación;* suffocation, *sofocación.*
  See: death.

caveat emptor (max.)(lat.) [le]*que el comprador sepa.* [fe]*a riesgo de comprador.*
  "Let the buyer beware, a maxim of the common law expressing the rule that the buyer purchases at his peril. Implied warranties in the sale of personal property are an exception to the rule thus expressed." (Ballentine's Law Dict., 183)

cease-and-desist order *orden judicial o administrativa prohibiendo una conducta ilegal.*

certificate n. *certificado.* **certify** v. *certificar.*
  certification n. *certificación.*
  • A document in which an attestation of a fact or facts is made.
  birth certificate *acta de nacimiento, partida de nacimiento, certificado de nacimiento.*
  certificate of citizenship *certificado de ciudadanía.*
  certificate of deposit *certificado de depósito.*
  certificate of good conduct *certificado de buena conducta.*
  certificate of membership *certificado de membresía.*
  certificate of occupancy *certificado de satisfacer los requisitos necesarios para la ocupación o habitabilidad (de un inmueble).*
  certificate of origin *certificado de origen.*
  certificate of title *título.*
  death certificate *acta de defunción, certificado de defunción.*
  marriage certificate *certificado de matrimonio.*
  Rel: document, *documento.*

certification n. *certificación.* **certificate/certify** v. *certificar.* – Syn. verification.
  • A written representation that something has occurred, or has not been done, or is valid, authentic or true. – Syn. jurat, *certificación (de*

una declaración o testimonio).
Rel: acknowledgment, *reconocimiento;* attestation, *testificación;* authentication, *autenticación;* ratification, *ratificación.*
certified check *cheque certificado.*
certified mail *correo certificado.*
certiorari (law lat.) [borr.]*certiorari.*
• An order issued by a superior court directed to a court of inferior jurisdiction requiring the certification and delivery of the record of the proceedings for review. – Syn. writ of certiorari, *mandamiento de certiorari,* [borr.]*writ de certiorari.*
"The writ of certiorari and certiorari are terms of art, used especially in U.S. Supreme Court practice; in some other courts, writ of review serves the same function. When procedural rules call for a petition for a writ of certiorari, no other words will do." (Mellinkoff's Dict., 69)
chain of custody *control ininterrumpido de la prueba, posesión ininterrumpida de la prueba.* – Syn. chain of possession.
chain of title *antecedentes de un título de propiedad.*
challenge[1] (jury) n. *descalificación, recusación.*
challenge v. *desafiar, oponerse.*
• A party's objection taken against a potential juror.
challenge for cause *descalificación con causa de un jurado, recusación motivada* (PR). – Syn. causal challenge. general challenge.
peremptory challenge *descalificación sin causa de un jurado.*
challenge[2] (objection) n. *impugnación.*
• Objecting the validity or authority of a person, an action or a thing.
challenge of a decision *impugnación de una decisión.*
challenge of a will *impugnación de un testamento.*
constitutional challenge *pedir se declare inconstitucional (una ley o un acto de autoridad).*
Rel: objection, *objeción.*
change of name *cambio de nombre.*
change of venue *cambio de competencia territorial.*
charge[1] (accusation) n. *cargo, acusación.*
charged v. *acusado de un delito.*
• An accusation; also more specifically, the underlying substantive offense contained in an accusation.
criminal charge *acusación penal o criminal.*

Rel: accusation, *acusación.*
charge[2] (cost) *cargo, obligación.*
inspection charge *derechos o cargos de inspección.*
delinquent charge *cargo por falta de pago.*
without charge *sin cargo.*
charge[3] (encumbrance) *gravamen.*
charge account *cuenta de crédito,* [le]*cuenta de cargo.*
charge to the jury *instrucciones sobre el caso y la ley aplicable dadas al jurado (por el juez).*
charitable adj. *caritativo, benéfico.* **charity** n. *caridad.* – Syn. altruistic, *altruista.* generous, *generoso.* philanthropic, *filantrópico.*
charitable deduction *deducción de impuestos por donaciones a instituciones de beneficencia, deducciones por obras caritativas.*
charitable foundation *fundación de caridad o beneficencia.*
charitable gift *donación con fines de caridad o beneficencia.* – Syn. charitable contribution.
charitable institution *institución de caridad o beneficencia.*
charitable trust *fideicomiso con fines de caridad o beneficencia.*
charter[1] MARITIME n. *fletamiento/fletamento.*
charterer n. *fletante, fletador, naviero.*
shipowner n. *propietario de un buque, fletador.*
• "The leasing or hiring of an airplane, ship, or other vessel." (Black's Law Dict., 8th. ed., 250)
bareboat charter *fletamiento a casco limpio, desnudo o descubierto.*
charter agreement *contrato de fletamiento.* – Syn. charter-party.
charter company *armador u operador de buques.*
demise charter *contrato de fletamiento de la totalidad de un buque (sin tripulación por el propietario del buque), contrato de fletamiento de un buque armado y equipado.*
time charter *fletamiento por tiempo,* [borr.] *time-charter.*
voyage charter *fletamiento por viaje.* – Syn. trip charter.
Rel: demurrage, *sobreestadía;* laytime, *período de carga y descarga, tiempo de estadía;* vessel, *embarcación, buque.*
charter[2] (document) n. *escritura constitutiva, carta constitutiva.*
• A special act of the government by or under which a corporation or business is created.
bank charter *escritura constitutiva de un banco.*

corporate charter *escritura constitutiva de una sociedad (por acciones).*

Charter of Rights and Freedoms (CA) [le]*Carta de Derechos y Garantías, Carta Constitucional de Canadá.*

Charter of the United Nations *Carta de las Naciones Unidas.*

chattel n. [nrwer]*bien mueble,* [lexical exp.] [de]*todo bien que no es un inmueble en "freehold".*

• A thing personal, as opposed to real. Visible, tangible, moveable, personal property. Chattels are a class of things defined by exclusion.

↪ Chattels and *bienes muebles* are equivalent for most practical purposes. While chattels include leasehold interests in land, which are considered as having characteristics of both real and personal property (and labeled chattel real), *bienes muebles* are foreign to leasehold interests in land but usually include leases on real estate that are considered contracts.

chattel lien [de]*derecho preferencial de garantía sobre bienes muebles.*

chattel mortgage [de]*gravamen sobre un bien mueble registrable dado en garantía, hipoteca mobiliaria.*

chattel paper [de]*documentación de una obligación de pago garantizada con bienes muebles.*

chattel real [lexical exp.][de]*derechos sobre inmuebles que no constituyen una "freehold" ó "fee",* [fe]*derecho de posesión de un inmueble en arrendamiento.*

Rel: choses in action, *derechos intangibles que pueden ejercitarse judicialmente;* choses in possession, *bienes muebles tangibles;* goods, *bienes muebles, mercaderías.*

Ref: (UK) 35 Halsbury's Laws para 1204,1105; (US) Curington v. State, 86 So. 344, 345, 80 Fla. 494.

check n. *cheque.* **drawee** n. *librado.* **maker /drawer** n. *librador.* **payee** n. *beneficiario, tomador.*

• A draft drawn upon a bank and payable on demand, signed by the maker or drawer, containing an unconditional promise to pay a specified amount of money to the order of the payee.

acceptance of a check *aceptación de un cheque.*

bad check *cheque incobrable.*
– Syn. rubber check. bogus check. false check.

bearer check *cheque al portador.*

blank check *cheque en blanco.*

bounced check *cheque devuelto (por incobrable).*

cashier's check *cheque de caja.*

certified check *cheque certificado.*

check stub *talón de cheque.*

endorsed check *cheque endosado.*

forged check *cheque falsificado.*

personal check *cheque personal.*

postdated check *cheque postdatado.*

registered check *cheque registrado.*

traveler's check *cheque de viajero.*

Ref: (CA) The Bills of Exchange Act R.S.C. 1985, c. B-4; (UK) Bills of Exchange Act (1882) s. 73; (US) U.C.C. §3-104(2)b.

checks and balances *sistema de pesas y contrapesos (gubernamentales).*

chicanery n. *chicaneria, trampa.*

chief executive *director ejecutivo.*

chief executive officer (CEO) *Presidente ejecutivo.*

chief judge *juez en jefe, presidente del tribunal.*

child n. *niño, menor.*

Cf: **child ● infant ● minor.** These are synonymous and interchangeable terms that mean underage, and more specifically that a person is not an adult. Child is the only term to express family relationship, usually a son or daughter. Infant refers mostly to the fact of being very young. Minor is used when referring to the period of being underage, and often in cases and legislation relating to abuse, neglect and delinquency.

abandoned child *niño abandonado.*

adopted child *niño adoptado.*

battered-child syndrome *síndrome del niño golpeado.*

best interest of the child *en el mayor beneficio del niño, en beneficio del menor.*

child abduction *rapto o secuestro de menores, sustracción de menores (Gu,Sp).*

child care *cuidado de menores.*

child custody *custodia de un menor.*

child desertion *abandono de menores.*

child endangerment *poner en peligro a un menor.*

child labor *trabajo de menores.*

child pornography *pornografia de menores.*

dependent child *niño o menor dependiente.*

disobedient child *niño o menor desobediente.*
– Syn. incorrigible child.

illegitimate child *hijo ilegítimo.*

natural child *hijo natural.* – Syn. biological child.

unborn child, *niño aún no nacido.*

neglected child *niño descuidado.*

Rel: foundling, *infante abandonado de padres desconocidos;* kid, *chamaco;* teenager, *joven entre los trece y diecinueve años, adolescente;* youngster, *joven.*

child abuse *abuso de menores.* – Syn. cruelty to children, *crueldad a menores.*

child molestation *abuso sexual de un menor.* – Syn. child sexual abuse, *abuso sexual de menores.*

child neglect *descuido de menores, falta de atención a un menor.*

choses in action *derechos intangibles que pueden ejercitarse judicialmente.* – Syn. things in action.

choses in possession *bienes muebles tangibles.*

circuit court *corte de circuito.*

circuit court of appeals *corte de circuito de apelaciones.*

circumstantial evidence *pruebas circunstanciales.*

citation[1] **(request)** n. *citatorio.*

citation[2] **(reference)** n. *referencia legal.*

citizen's arrest *detención hecha por un particular.*

citizenship n. *ciudadanía, nacionalidad.* **citizen** n. *ciudadano, nacional.*

• The status of being a member in a political society or nation, implying a duty of allegiance on the part of the member, and a duty of protection on the part of the society or nation. Cf: **citizenship • nationality.** These synonymous terms are used ambiguously. While both refer to that existing link between a person and a nation or a state, there is a tendency to use citizenship in contexts where the term is applicable mostly to individuals and nationality when referring primarily to entities.

British citizenship *ciudadanía británica.*

British Overseas citizenship *ciudadanía británica de ultramar.*

native-born citizen *ciudadano por nacimiento.*

naturalized citizen *ciudadano por naturalización o naturalizado.*

sale of naturalization or citizenship papers *venta de documentos de naturalización o ciudadanía.*

Rel: nationality, *nacionalidad;* naturalization, *naturalización.*

city n. *ciudad.*

city attorney *abogado representante de la ciudad.*

city clerk *secretario de actas y del registro civil (de una población o ciudad).*

city council *Consejo de la ciudad.*

city hall *ayuntamiento, palacio municipal.*

Rel: megalopolis, *megalópolis, zona conurbada;* metropolis, *metrópolis;* metropolitan area, *área metropolitana;* slum, *barrio miserable, ciudad perdida;* suburb, *suburbio;* town, *pueblo, población;* village, *villa, colonia.*

civil adj. *civil.* – Syn. civic, *cívico.* laic, *laico.* secular, *secular.*

civil action *acción civil.*

civil code *código civil.*

civil court *corte civil, juzgado civil.*

civil damages *daños y perjuicios civiles.*

civil defense *defensa civil.*

civil disobedience *desobediencia civil.*

civil jurisdiction *jurisdicción civil.*

civil liability *responsabilidad civil.*

civil marriage *matrimonio civil.*

civil rights *derechos civiles,* [fe]*libertades individuales.*

civil service *servicio civil.*

civil status *estado civil.*

civil suit *demanda civil, juicio civil.*

civil law[1] **(legal tradition)** *sistema legal romano-germánico, sistema legal continental.*

• Systems of law based in the Justinian and Napoleonic codes as distinguished from the common law of England and the canon law. – Syn. civil law tradition, *tradición jurídica continental.* ius civile (lat.), *ius civile.*

➥ Some of the relevant characteristics of civil law systems are: a reliance on the principles derived from the Roman law (*derecho romano*); the use of codes setting up in an abstract, general and systematized way the rights and duties of persons (*códigos*); the strong influence of academic lawyers through their writings (*doctrina*); and the lesser importance of case law and other procedural institutions like examinations, juries and adversarial litigation (*jurisprudencia y procedimiento*).

Comment: "It is today the dominant legal tradition in most of Western Europe, all of Central and South America, many parts of Asia and Africa, and even a few enclaves in the common law world (Louisiana, Quebec, and Puerto Rico)." (Merryman, Civil Law Tradition. Legal Systems of Western Europe and Latin America 3)

civil law[2] **(non-criminal law)** *derecho civil.*

• The non-criminal part of the law as opposed to criminal law. <civil liability> <civil procedure>

civil law[3] **(state law)** *derecho civil, derecho positivo.*
• The law enacted by the state as opposed to natural law.
Rel: canon law, *derecho canónico;* natural law, *derecho natural.*

civil procedure *procedimiento civil.*
• Civil procedure refers to the methods, procedures and practices by which civil litigation functions.
rules of civil procedure *reglas del procedimiento civil.*
⌐ "The development of English civil procedure, particularly since the 16th century, has constituted a process of continual refinement, reflected in the periodic alterations to correct immediate deficiencies which distract a court from reaching a just result. This development contrasts significantly with the more methodical, external development of civil procedure in most civil law nations, where procedure is guided by legislative enactments and by the writings of legal scholars, detached of any particular, current dispute." (Glendon, Gordon & Carozza, 235)
Rel: appeal, *apelación;* discovery, *requerimiento y producción de pruebas;* execution, *ejecución;* judgment, *sentencia;* jurisdiction, *jurisdicción;* pleadings, *demanda-contestación y escritos complementarios;* trial, *juicio.*
See: civil trial. *procedimiento civil.*

civil trial *enjuiciamiento civil, juicio civil.*
• That part of a lawsuit by which a civil action is decided, usually after an examination of the issues, whether of fact or of law, raised by the parties.
The trial phase of civil procedure involves two main developments: hearing of evidence and the court determination of the matter at issue. Trials are conducted orally and usually in a continuous session or in a series of sessions constituting a single event. While most civil trials are rarely before a jury, some kinds of civil litigation are customarily tried before jurors (tort liability in the United States, for example).

claim[1] **(legal subject matter)** n. *pretensión jurídica.* **claimant** n. *persona que ejerce una pretensión.*
• "The demand or the subject matter for which any action, suit or proceeding is brought." (Dukelow and Nuse, 189)

claim[2] **(demand)** n. *acción, demanda, reclamación.*
• A demand made as a matter of right, usually for money due, property, damages or enforcement of a right.
claim adjustment *ajuste o liquidación de una reclamación de seguros.*
claim for damages *acción por daños y perjuicios.*
claims adjuster *ajustador o liquidador de seguros.*
counterclaim *contrademanda.*
frivolous claim *demanda o reclamación infundada.* – Syn. vexatious litigation.
insurance claim *reclamación de seguro.*

claim[3] **(right)** n. *derecho, ejercicio de un derecho.*
• An interest or remedy recognized at law.
mining claim *derecho minero, pertenencia minera, reclamación de derechos mineros.*
priority claim *derecho de prioridad, derecho prioritario.*

class action *acción colectiva,* [de]*acción en beneficio de un grupo de personas,* [le]*acción o pleito de clase* (PR).
• An action brought by one or several plaintiffs on behalf of a class of persons. – Syn. class suit. A class action is indicated when a group is so large that individual suits are impractical.
⌐ This is an institution which has no equivalent in civil law systems, at least not to the extent, complexity, and widespread use class action suits have in common law countries, especially in the United States. A multiparty suit in a civil law country typically has only a few litigants, and the applicable rules are those contemplating a small number of parties. In contrast, a class action suit in a common law country involves hundreds, if not thousands, of plaintiffs and benefits from rules and procedures specifically designed to handle the complexities of such multiparty litigation. Modern doctrinal tendencies in Spanish-speaking countries have often used the term *acción colectiva* to refer to class action suits.

clause n. *cláusula.*
• A paragraph or an identifiable section or provision of a legal document. – Syn. stipulation, *estipulación, cláusula.*
acceleration clause *cláusula de vencimiento anticipado.*
escalation clause *cláusula con escala ajustable.*
grandfather clause *cláusula que excluye casos o personas regidos por el régimen aplicable anteriormente.*
penalty clause *cláusula penal.*

clear and convincing evidence [le]*prueba clara*

y convincente, prueba concluyente.

clear and present danger doctrine [le]*peligro claro e inmediato,* [de]*doctrina de la necesidad de la existencia de un peligro claro e inmediato para considerar procedentes restricciones a la libertad de expresión.*

clerk¹ n. *secretario, administrador.*
court clerk *secretario del juzgado, secretario de la corte.*
See: city clerk.

clerk² (**Engl.**) *asistente de un abogado.* – Syn. law clerk (US), *pasante.*
clerk to the justices *asistente de un juez o un ministro.*

closing arguments *alegatos, alegatos finales.*

cloud on title *defecto o irregularidad del título de propiedad (de un inmueble), título turbio* (PR).

cocaine n. *cocaína.* – Syn. candy, *azúcar.* coke, coca. crack, [borr.]*crack.* snow, *nieve.*

code n. *recopilación,* [le]*código.* – Syn. consolidated laws.
☛ Codes in common law countries are unlike those in the civil law tradition. In common law countries Codes are usually either a compilation of laws (United States Code) or a consolidation of statutory laws and precedent on a specific subject (Criminal Code). In contrast, in civil law countries Codes are a systematic body of principles laid down mostly in a general and abstract form on a given subject. While common law Codes are said to be a "terminated product" in the sense that they are based on precedent, civil law Codes are labelled as "unfinished product" in the sense that they are based on abstract rules.

codeine n. *codeína.*

coercion n. *coerción, coacción.* **coercive** adj. *coercitivo, coercible.*
• Compelling someone to do something by threat of force or persuasion.
coerced confession *confesión forzada.*
criminal coercion *coerción penal, delito de coerción.*
Rel: compulsion, *compulsión;* duress, *coacción, miedo grave;* pressure, *presión;* undue influence, *coerción, presión o influencia.*

coinsurance n. *coseguro.*

collateral adj. *accesorio.*
collateral attack on a judgment [de]*recurso contra una sentencia basado en una causal indirecta,* [le]*ataque colateral a una sentencia* (PR).

collateral consanguinity *consanguinidad colateral.*
collateral contract *contrato accesorio.*
collateral estoppel [de]*preclusión de cuestiones o determinaciones de hecho litigadas anteriormente,* [le]*impedimento colateral* (PR).
collateral issues *cuestiones incidentales.*
collateral proof *prueba indirecta.*

collateral n. *garantía.*
collateral security *garantía colateral.*

collect on delivery (**C.O.D.**) *pago contra entrega.*

collection n. *cobranza.* **collection agent** *cobrador.*
collection agency *agencia de cobranzas.*
collection fee *comisión de cobro.*

collective bargaining LABOR *negociación colectiva.*

collective security system INTL.LAW *sistema colectivo de seguridad.*

collision n. *colisión.*
collision insurance *seguro de colisión.*
head-on collision *choque de frente.*
rear-end collision *choque por atrás.*
Rel: crash, *choque;* traffic accident, *accidente de tráfico.*

collusion n. *colusión.*

color of law *apariencia de legalidad.*
color of title *apariencia de legitimidad, apariencia de titularidad, título colorado* (PR).

comity INTL.LAW n. *cortesía internacional.*
• A principle by which a country may allow another country's law to operate in its territory not as a matter of obligation but as a matter of deference and mutual respect.
Rel: full faith and credit (US), *cláusula constitucional que otorga reconocimiento de los actos jurídicos celebrados en un estado en todos los demás, reconocimiento de actos jurídicos (en los otros estados de la federación).*

commander-in-chief *comandante en jefe, jefe supremo de las fuerzas armadas.*

commercial law *derecho mercantil.*
• The body of law dealing with matters concerning merchants, such as the sale and distribution of goods, the financing of credit transactions, shipping, insurance, and negotiable instruments. – Syn. mercantile law. [hist.]law merchant. Commercial law as a separate branch of private civil law was well established before the time of the great codifications in the civil law

countries. "In Napoleon's code system, and in most of the later codifications, the dichotomy between 'civil' and commercial law was preserved by the enactment of separate commercial codes, and by provisions (either in the code of commerce or in the procedural codes) perpetuating the separate commercial courts. … In England, the law merchant was absorbed into the common law during the 17th and 18th centuries…. In the process, many of the merchants' substantive rules and customs, especially those dealing with negotiable instruments, were transformed into common law rules." (Schlesinger, 185-86) Most American commercial law is governed by the Uniform Commercial Code.

Rel: negotiable instruments, *títulos de crédito;* sale of goods, *compraventa de mercancías,* [fe]*compraventa mercantil;* secured transactions, *operaciones comerciales de garantía.*

commercial paper *papel comercial, títulos de crédito comerciales.*

• A general designation given to negotiable instruments, which includes bills of exchange, checks, notes and certificates of deposit.

– Syn. negotiable instruments, *títulos de crédito.*
See: negotiable instruments.

commission n. *comisión.*

  commission agent *comisionista.*
  commission broker *corredor bursátil.*
  commission merchant *comerciante a comisión, factor.*
  commission of a crime *comisión de un delito.*

commissioner n. *comisionado.*

  common carrier *transportista o transportador público.*

common land *tierra comunal, copropiedad.*

common law¹ (legal tradition) [borr.]*common law, derecho angloamericano.*

• The system of judge-made law that originated in England as compared with the system of law based on the Roman law, which is mostly statutory and usually referred to as civil law.

↪ Some relevant characteristics of the common law system are: the judicial opinion is the major form in which the law is stated (*jurisprudencia);* a major distinction between the principles developed by the courts of law and the courts of equity is still observed (*equidad);* procedure in common law has developed its own institutions like juries, discovery and accusatory litigation (*procedimiento);* and precedent is considered more important than

academic work when seeking to advance the development of law (*precedente).*

Rel: equity, *derecho-equidad;* jury, *jurado;* precedent, *precedente judicial;* procedure, *procedimiento.*

  Comment: "As a result of the remarkable expansion and development of the British Empire during the age of colonialism and empire, however, the common law was very widely distributed. It is today the legal tradition in Great Britain, Ireland, United States, Canada, Australia and New Zealand, and [it] has had substantial influence on the law of many nations in Asia and Africa," especially India and South Africa. (Merryman, The Civil Law Tradition. Legal Systems of Western Europe and Latin America, 4)

See: English law.

common law² (body of law) [borr.]*common law,* [le]*derecho común, derecho jurisprudencial.*

• Body of law found in the decisions of the courts, rather than in the statutes or enacted legislation.

Cf: **common law ● statutory law.** These terms are often used to contrast each other. Common law is the designation for that body of law derived from or contained in judicial decisions, while statutory law is that body of law which similarly derives from or is contained in statutes.

common-law action *acción basada en derecho común.*

common-law crime *delitos basados en el derecho común.*

common-law marriage *matrimonio por comportamiento, matrimonio consensual.*

Rel: case law, *jurisprudencia;* statute, *ley escrita.*

common law³ (hist.) *derecho estricto,* [borr.] *common law.*

• Body of laws derived from law court decisions as opposed to laws derived from decisions of courts sitting in equity.

Cf: **common law ● equity.** The "classification between the common law in the narrow sense and equity, [is] due solely to the historical circumstance that in English history two types of courts developed, those of the common law, and those of chancery or equity, in which not only different remedies but even different substantive rights were recognized." (Brown, The Law of Personal Property §73 at 253)

See: equity¹.

common market *mercado común.*

community law (European Union) *derecho de las Comunidades Europeas, derecho comunitario.*
See: European law.

community property *comunidad de bienes, sociedad conyugal* (Mx).
• Property acquired during marriage and owned in common by husband and wife, each one holding one-half interest in the property.
Cf: **community property • marital property • family assets.** All three of these terms refer to property acquired by the spouses from the beginning of the marriage until its dissolution. Community property considers common property as divided in half and each spouse as holding one half each. In the United States, marital property is the expression used in equitable-distribution states (those not under a community property system) to refer to property acquired during marriage. In England the term "family assets" is often used to mean not only property acquired during marriage but refers also to the right to share those assets upon dissolution of marriage.

community-property state (US) *estado (parte de la federación) en el que rige la comunidad de bienes.*
Rel: apportionment, *reparto, división;* commingled property, *incorporación (mezcla, confusión), bienes mezclados que no pueden ser identificados;* equitable distribution, *distribución de bienes bajo el régimen de derecho-equidad;* gifts between spouses, *donaciones entre esposos;* premarital property, *propiedad adquirida antes del matrimonio;* separate property, *separación de bienes;* transmutation, *cambio de régimen de propiedad.*

> Comment: The nine community property states in the United States are Arizona, California, Idaho, Nevada, Louisiana, New Mexico, Washington, Texas and Wisconsin. All other common law states have treated community property as a form of tenure, a method of holding title to assets, without regard to corresponding liabilities. Community property goes beyond the typical spousal protection provisions that are found in common law states because it establishes a lifetime division of the property as well as a method for dividing an estate upon the death of a spouse.

community service (punishment) *servicio a la comunidad, servicio en la comunidad.*

commutation n. *conmutación de pena.*
See: pardon.

company (generic) n. *compañía.*
• A generic and loosely used term that indiscriminately designates corporations, partnerships and less formal associations.
Company is a statutory term widely used in England. – Abbr. co.

"At common law , the technical legal term for an entity having a legal personality was corporation. The word company could refer to a partnership or other unincorporated association of persons. In current usage, however, company almost always refers to an incorporated company –i.e., a corporation." (Garner, 182)
company store *tienda de raya, tienda de la compañía.*
company union *sindicato de la compañía.*
charter company (UK) *compañía constituida mediante carta de autorización.*
holding company *compañía controladora.*
investment company *compañía de inversiones.*
joint-stock company *compañía por acciones.*
limited company (UK) [de]*compañía de responsabilidad limitada.*
limited liability company *compañía o sociedad de responsabilidad limitada.*
parent company *compañía afiliada.*
private company (UK) *sociedad anónima (cuyas acciones no se ofrecen al público).*
public company (UK) *sociedad anónima (cuyas acciones se ofrecen al público).*
public limited company (UK) *sociedad anónima (cuyas acciones pueden ser ofrecidas al público).* – Syn. registered company limited by shares.
registered company (UK) *compañía constituida mediante su registro.*
surety company *compañía afianzadora, compañía de fianzas.*
trust company *compañía fiduciaria.*
Rel: firm, *firma;* head office, *oficina matriz;* headquarters, *casa matriz, centro de operaciones;* subsidiary, *subsidiaria.*
See: business forms.

comparative law *derecho comparado.*
• The discipline studying the similarities, differences and the relationship between legal systems of the world.
Rel: functional analysis, *análisis funcional;* in context, *en contexto;* legal system, *sistema legal;* legal tradition, *tradición legal;* legal transplant, *transplante legal.*

compensation[1] **(indemnity)** n. *compensación.*
amount of compensation *cantidad de la compensación.*
compensatory damages *daños compensatorios.*
worker's compensation *seguro de accidentes de trabajo.*
Rel: indemnity, *indemnización;* reparation, *repa-*

ración; restitution, *restitución.*

compensation² (remuneration) *remuneración.*
– Syn. emolument, *emolumento.* fees, *honorarios.* remuneration, *remuneración.* salary, *salario.* wages, *sueldo.*

compensation of attorney *pago a un abogado, compensación de un abogado.*

competence¹ (person's ability) n. *competencia, capacidad.* **competent** adj. *competente.*

competence of a witness *capacidad de un testigo.*

competence of an expert witness *competencia de un perito.*

competence² (entity's capacity) n. *competencia.*

competent authority *autoridad competente.*

competent court *corte o juzgado competente.*

competent jurisdiction *órgano o jurisdicción competente.*

Rel: jurisdiction, *jurisdicción;* venue, *competencia territorial.*

competency n. *capacidad.* **competent** adj. *capaz.*
• The ability to understand problems and make decisions; also the ability to understand proceedings and to stand trial. – Syn. capacity.
Cf: **competency • capacity • competence.** These terms are very similar in meaning, and they are used loosely within convention. Capacity refers to legal ability or qualification, as in the capacity to contract, commit crimes or file a lawsuit; competency is a similar word usually used in connection with evidence or evidentiary proceedings <competency to testify >, it may also mean basic general ability to do something as it applies to the ability to understand problems and stand trial; incompetency is the usual word used in legal writing <incompetency to stand trial>. Finally, competence has the same meaning of general basic ability to do something but it is often associated with a popular rather than legal context.

competency to stand trial *capacidad procesal.*

competency to testify *capacidad para ser testigo, capacidad para testificar.*

Rel: credibility, *credibilidad;* insanity, [le]*demencia, enajenación mental.*

complaining witness *denunciante, querellante.*

complaint¹ PLEADINGS n. *demanda.* **plaintiff** n. *demandante.* **complainant** n. *demandante.* **defendant** n. *demandado.*
• The first pleading of the plaintiff stating the facts on which relief is sought. – Syn. bill. count. libel. declaration. petition. statement of

claim (UK).
Cf: **complaint • declaration • libel • bill • petition • count.** All of these terms are synonymous. The declaration is the common law equivalent of the complaint in code and rule pleading, libel is the corresponding term in ecclesiastical and admiralty law, bill is the term used in equity, petition is the term used in civil law, and count the term used in real actions.

amended complaint *demanda enmendada, subsanar la demanda.*

service of the complaint *notificación y traslado de la demanda.*

third party complaint *solicitud del demandado hecha a un tercero en una tercería necesaria.*

Rel: action, *acción;* counterclaim, *contrademanda;* pleadings, *demanda-contestación y escritos complementarios.*

Ref: (UK) 36(1) Halsbury's Laws para 6, 47; (US) Fed.R.Civ.Proc. 3; Willison v. Norhtern Pac. R. Co., 127 N.W. 4, 111 Minn. 370.

complaint² CRIML.PROCED n. *denuncia, querella.*

complainant n. *denunciante, querellante.*
• The preliminary charge or accusation before a court or officer that a person has committed a certain crime.
Cf: **complaint • accusation.** Complaint refers to the specific formal charge, made by a complaining witness in a sworn affidavit before a prosecutor or other authority, that a crime has been committed. Accusation, in turn, means presentation of charges before a court or magistrate, usually after the prosecution decides to initiate criminal proceedings once a complaint has been investigated and reviewed.

verified complaint *denuncia ratificada.*

Rel: charge, *cargo;* grievance, *queja.*

Ref: (US) Fed.R.Crim.Proc. 3; Hebebrand v. State, 196 N.E. 412, 414, 129 Ohio St. 574.

complaint³ (protest) n. *queja, reclamación.*
• A protest, objection or criticism; a grievance.

complexion n. *color de la piel, color del cutis.*

Rel: identification, *identificación;* portrait a parle, *retrato hablado.*

compliance n. *cumplimiento.* **comply** v. *cumplir.* **compliant** adj. *que cumple.*

failure to comply *falta de cumplimiento.*

Rel: performance, *cumplimiento.*

composition with creditors *compromiso o concordato extrajudicial con los acreedores.*

compounding a crime *colusión para no presentar una denuncia penal, [de]desistirse de una acusación por retribución hecha a la víctima (por el acusado).*

compromise n. *avenencia, compromiso.*
• An agreement to settle a matter by means of mutual concessions.
compromise agreement *avenencia, compromiso.*
compromise and settlement *acuerdo compromisorio, compromiso.*
See: accord and satisfaction.
compulsory adj. *obligatorio.* – Syn. mandatory, *obligatorio.*
compulsory arbitration *arbitraje obligatorio.*
compulsory insurance *seguro obligatorio.*
compulsory payment *pago forzado.*
computer n. *computadora, ordenador* (Sp).
computer crime *delitos mediante el uso de computadoras u ordenadores.*
computer fraud *estafa mediante el uso de una computadora u ordenador.*
computer tampering *acceso o alteración ilícita de una computadora u ordenador.*
Rel: hardware, [borr;]*hardware;* internet, [borr;]*internet;* software, [borr.]*software.*
See: online law.
concealment n. *ocultación.* **conceal** v. *ocultar.*
concealed weapon *arma oculta.*
concealment of assets *ocultación de bienes.*
concealment of birth *ocultamiento de parto.*
conciliation n. *conciliación.* **conciliate** v. *conciliar.* **conciliator** n. *conciliador.* **conciliatory** adj. *conciliatorio.*
• The resolution of a dispute in an amicable manner. – Syn. mediation, *mediación.*
Cf: **conciliation ● mediation.** Conciliation and mediation are usually differentiated by practitioners, but there is no clear consensus about their differentiation. Both terms are often used synonymously and interchangeably. Conciliation is mostly considered a nonbinding arbitration, while mediation is often considered an assisted negotiation.
Rel: arbitration, *arbitraje.*
conclusion n. *conclusión.*
conclusion of fact *conclusión de hecho.*
conclusion of law *conclusión de derecho.*
conclusive adjudication *adjudicación definitiva.*
conclusive evidence *pruebas concluyentes.*
conclusive presumption *presunción concluyente.*
concurrent adj. *concurrente.*
concurrent jurisdiction *jurisdicción concurrente.*
concurrent sentences *condenas concurrentes.*

condition concurrent *condición concurrente.*
condemnation n. *expropiación.* **condemnee** n. *expropiado.*
• The taking of private property for public use by authority of eminent domain. – Syn. expropriation.
condemnation proceedings *procedimiento de expropiación.*
excess condemnation *expropiación excesiva.*
inverse condemnation *indemnización compensatoria (por la devaluación de propiedad contigua a una propiedad expropiada).*
See: eminent domain.
condition[1] **(contingent)** n. *condición.* **conditional** adj. *condicional.*
• An uncertain future act or event whose occurrence or nonoccurrence limits or modifies the rights or obligations of a party in a contract, deed, will or similar instrument.
condition concurrent *condición concurrente.*
condition precedent *condición suspensiva.*
condition subsequent *condición resolutoria.*
conditional judgment *sentencia condicional.*
conditional release *liberación condicional de una obligación.*
constructive condition *condición tácita por ministerio de ley.* – Syn. implied-in-law condition.
implied conditions *condiciones implícitas, términos supletorios.*
implied-in-fact condition *condición implícita en el contrato o la naturaleza de la transacción.*
Rel: contingency, *contingente.*
condition[2] **(state)** *condición.*
• "A particular mode of being of a person or thing." (Webster Encyclopedic Unabridged Dict., 306)
conditions of employment *términos de empleo.*
conditions of sale *términos de venta.*
conditional discharge CRIML.LAW *remisión condicional* || *liberar o dejar en libertad condicional (a un detenido o convicto).* – Syn. conditional release.
condominium n. *régimen de propiedad en condominio, condominio.* **condónimo** *condominium owner.*
• A form of ownership of real property in which owners separately own portions of the property (as separate units of a building) and undivided common areas (like lobbies and hallways). Term refers to the system of ownership as well as the real estate so organized. – Syn. horizontal property, *propiedad horizontal.*

condominium association *asociación de condóminos.*

condominium ownership *propiedad en condominio, régimen de condominio.*

Rel: common areas, *áreas comunes;* condominium by-laws, *estatutos del régimen de condominio, estatutos del condominio;* master deed, *escritura constitutiva del régimen de condominio.*

condonation n. *condonación.* **condoner** n. *condonante.* **condone** v. *condonar.* – Syn. pardon.

conduct n. *conducta.* **conduct** v. *conducirse.* – Syn. behavior.

disorderly conduct *escándalo en la vía pública, alteración del orden público.*

unprofessional conduct *falta de profesionalismo, conducirse en forma poco profesional.*

Rel: action, *acción;* omission, *omisión.*

conference n. *junta,* [le]*conferencia.*

• A meeting of several persons to deliberate, to resolve a dispute or an objection, or simply to exchange opinions to try to reach a common view. – Syn. discussion group.

international conference *conferencia internacional.*

predisposition conference *junta previa a una resolución judicial.*

presentence conference *junta previa al dictamen de una condena.*

pretrial conference *junta previa al inicio del juicio.*

confession CRIML.LAW n. *confesión.* **to confess** v. *confesar.*

• An admission of guilt by the accused, usually an acknowledgment in written form specifying in detail his or her alleged criminal behavior.

Cf: **confession ● admission.** In a confession all the necessary elements for a conviction are acknowledged by the accused, while in an admission there is an acknowledgment of facts, which may or may not establish guilt.

coerced confession *confesión forzada.*

extrajudicial confession *confesión extrajudicial.*

involuntary confession *confesión no voluntaria.*

naked confession *confesión sin corroboración alguna.*

oral confession *confesión oral.*

plenary confession *confesión plena.*

written confession *confesión por escrito.*

Rel: admission, *admisión;* incrimination, *incriminación;* interrogation, *interrogatorio.*

confidential adj. *confidencial.*

confidential communication *confidencialidad.*

confidential relationship *relación fiduciaria, relación basada en la confianza otorgada a una persona.* – Syn. fiduciary relationship.

confinement n. *confinamiento, reclusión.*

house confinement *confinamiento domiciliario, restricción domiciliaria* (PR).

solitary confinement *en solitario, confinamiento solitario.*

Rel: commitment, *internación, reclusión;* imprisonment, *poner en prisión;* incarceration, *encarcelación.*

conflict of interest *conflicto de intereses.*

• A variance, real or apparent, between one's private interests and one's public or fiduciary duties.

conflict of jurisdictions *conflicto de jurisdicciones.*

Rel: in rem jurisdiction, *jurisdicción in rem;* long arm jurisdiction, *jurisdicción extraterritorial;* quasi in rem jurisdiction, *jurisdicción quasi in rem.*

conflict of laws *conflicto de leyes.*

• That body of law by which the court in which the action is maintained determines or chooses which law to apply where a diversity exists between the applicable law of that court's state and the applicable law of another jurisdiction interested in the controversy.

Cf: **conflict of laws ● choice of law.** Conflict of laws in a broad sense refers to three related areas of law: choice of law, conflict of jurisdictions, and recognition and enforcement of judgments. Choice of law is then only one of the three parts in which conflict of laws is traditionally divided; however, tradition has kept these two terms closely identified and often used interchangeably.

Rel: characterization, *calificación;* choice of law, *ley aplicable;* comity, *cortesía internacional;* connecting factor, *punto de conexión;* domicile, *domicilio;* enforcement of foreign judgments, *aplicación de sentencias extranjeras;* lex domicilii, *lex domicilii;* lex fori, *lex fori;* lex loci, *lex loci;* renvoi, *reenvío.*

Comment: "It is customary to divide conflict of laws into three topics – jurisdiction, choice of law, and foreign judgments. Jurisdiction raises the question of whether the local court can hear the case. This is always determined in accordance with local law (the *lex fori*). The inquiry concerns the competence of the forum court to adjudicate, in view of the existence of a non-local element, and the further question whether, given it has competence, it ought to do so. If jurisdiction exists, and it is appropiate that it be exercised, the court will then proceed to determine the substantive controversy between the parties. But the court will have to decide in accordance with local law on whether the local nature of the transaction renders it appropriate to defer to a foreign rule of decision. In some areas, mostly pertaining to family law, the *lex fori* is generally applied. But in other fields – contracts, torts and property – there may well be reference to foreign law." (Sykes & Pryles, 3)

conflicting evidence *pruebas contradictorias.*

confrontation[1] **(face to face)** *careo, confrontación.*
• In the United States, the constitutional right of a criminal defendant to have his or her accusers present during trial and to hear and cross-examine them.
confronting a witness *confrontación de un testigo.*
See: *careo.*

confrontation[2] **(altercation)** *enfrentamiento.*
• The act of confronting, especially a face to face meeting. – Syn. encounter, *encuentro.*

confusion of goods *confusión de bienes.*

conjugal adj. *conyugal.* – Syn. marital, *marital.*
conjugal rights *derechos conyugales.*
conjugal visit *visita conyugal.*

conscientious objector *opositor de conciencia* [de]*que se rehusa a servir en las fuerzas armadas basado en principios de conciencia o espirituales.*

consensual interrogation *interrogatorio consensual.*

consent n. *consentimiento, conformidad.*
• Approval or compliance of what is done or proposed by another.
consent decree *sentencia u orden convenida (por las partes).*
consent judgment *sentencia convenida (por las partes), sentencia por mutuo acuerdo, sentencia consensual.*
consent jurisdiction *jurisdicción consensual.*
consent search *registro consensual, dar consentimiento para un registro.*
consent to adoption *otorgamiento de consentimiento para la adopción.*
express consent *consentimiento expreso.*
implied consent *consentimiento tácito.*
informed consent *consentimiento debidamente informado, consentimiento informado.*
without consent *sin consentimiento.*
Rel: sufferance, *consentimiento por omisión.*

consequential damages *indemnización por daños indirectos.*

consequential loss *pérdidas indirectas.*

consideration CONTRACTS n. [de]*contraprestación* [brder][fe]*causa,* [borr.]*consideration.*
• "Inducement to a contract, something of value given in return for a performance or a promise of performance by another." (Gifis, 98) "Consideration requires that a contractual promise be the product of a bargain. However, in this usage, 'bargain' does not mean an exchange of things of equivalent, or any, value. It means a negotiation resulting in the voluntary assumption of an obligation by one party upon condition of an act or forbearance by the other.... It is noteworthy that the civil law has a corresponding doctrine of 'causa' which, to the eye of a common-law lawyer, is not much different than consideration." (Baher v. Penn-O-Tex Oil Corp., 104 N.W.2d 661 258 Minn 533)
↦ Although different in style and technique, consideration and *causa* pursue the same functional end: to declare a contract invalid if it is legally or morally offensive. In spite of this common functionality, important differences remain, such as the many different answers to what is legally or morally offensive, which varies from country to country, or the existence of various competing definitions of *causa.*
bargained-for consideration *contraprestación efectivamente negociada, causa efectivamente considerada.*
for valuable consideration *por una causa válida, con motivo de una contraprestación válida.*
moral consideration *deber moral.*
nominal consideration *contraprestación nominal, causa simbólica.*
Rel: assent, *asentimiento, asenso, manifestación de voluntad;* bargain, *policitación, negociación contractual;* mutual assent, *consentimiento;* promise, *declaración unilateral de voluntad.*
See: contract.
Ref: (UK) Currie v Misa (1875) LR 10 Exch 153 at 162; (US) Restatement (2nd) Contracts, §71; Wheeler v. Williams, 81 N.E.2d 175, 176, 400 Ill. 438.

consignment n.*consignación.* **consignee** n. *consignatario.* **consignor** n. *consignador.*
Cf: **consignment • conditional sale.** These are two different legal concepts: consignment is a bailment for sale, while a conditional sale is a sale contract. Consignment implies no transfer

of title or ownership of property while the property is on consignment, while a conditional sale means an actual transfer of ownership of property subject to the contingency specified on the contract.

consignment contract *contrato de consignación.*

consignment sale *venta por consignación.*

Rel: conditional sale, *venta sujeta a condición, venta condicional.*

conspiracy (crime) n. *acuerdo para cometer un delito, confabulación delictiva, conspiración* (PR,Gu,Sp), *concierto para delinquir* (Co), **conspirator** n. *parte o participante de un acuerdo para cometer un delito, conspirador* (PR).

• "Conspiracy is the result of an agreement between two or more persons to commit an unlawful act or to commit a lawful act by unlawful means." (4 Wharton's Criminal Law §678 at 532) – Syn. confederacy, *acuerdo para cometer un delito.*

Cf: **conspiracy • confederacy.** Both of these terms are synonymous in criminal matters. Confederate is used sometimes with a neutral meaning, implying participation for mutual support or joint action rather than criminal or malicious purpose.

↝ The crime of conspiracy in common law countries is defined and treated as a separate crime than the crime that the conspirators are accused of committing or attempting. In contrast, civil law Hispanic countries usually consider the equivalent crime of *acuerdo para cometer un delito* as either an element of the crime being committed or an aggravating circumstance.

conspiracy or combination in restraint of trade *instigación o acuerdo para restringir el libre comercio.*

conspiracy to defraud *acuerdo para defraudar, acuerdo para cometer un fraude.*

constitution n. *constitución.* **constitutionalism** n. *constitucionalismo.* **constitutionalist** n. *constitucionalista.* **constitutional** adj. *constitucional.* **constitutionality** n. *constitucionalidad.* **constitutionalize** v. *constitucionalizar.* **constitutionally** adv. *constitucionalmente.*

• A system of fundamental laws or principles for the government of a nation, state, society, corporation or other similar aggregation of individuals.

constitutional amendments *enmiendas o*

reformas constitucionales.

constitutional convention *congreso o convención constituyente.*

constitutional rights *derechos constitucionales.* Rel: Bill of Rights (US), *Declaración de Derechos Constitucionales, Garantías individuales o constitucionales;* Canadian Charter of Rights and Freedoms, *Carta Canadiense de Derechos y Garantías.*

Comment: "No single written constitutional document exists in England as in many other civil and common law nations. English constitutional law is thus frequently noted as being based on an 'unwritten constitution.' That contains more myth than truth. It is true only in the sense that constitutional law is not contained in a single document; the complex and abstract nature of the English Constitution results from it being an aggregation of numerous sources, mostly written but all identifiable." (Glendon, Gordon & Carozza, 276-77)

constitutional law *derecho constitucional.*

• The body of law establishing the fundamental elements of the legal structure of government of a political entity, as well as its powers and form of operation.

Rel: civil rights, *derechos civiles,* [fe]*libertades individuales;* due process of law, *debido proceso legal;* executive power, *poder ejecutivo;* federalism, *federalismo;* individual rights, *garantías individuales;* judicial review, *control constitucional de actos del gobierno;* legislative power, *poder legislativo.*

construction n. *interpretación.* **construe** v. *interpretar.*

• The process of interpreting a legal writing such as a statute, deed or will and determining its meaning as it applies to the controversy being considered. – Syn. interpretation.

Cf: **construction • interpretation.** There is no general agreement as to the distinction between interpretation and construction. They are considered synonymous and interchangeable for the most part. For some, interpretation is used when referring to statutory words or language within a writing, and construction when referring to finding the intention of the legislator or the legal meaning of an entire writing.

constructive adj. *tácito, implícito.*

constructive acceptance *aceptación tácita.*

constructive breach of contract *incumplimiento por disposición o ministerio de la ley.*

constructive conversion *apropiación por disposición o ministerio de la ley.*

constructive delivery *entrega jurídica o*

virtual.

constructive fraud *fraude por disposición o ministerio de la ley.*

constructive mortgage *hipoteca tácita.*

constructive possession *posesión jurídica o virtual.*

constructive trespass *violación de derechos por determinación de la ley.*

constructive trust *fideicomiso creado por disposición o ministerio de la ley.*

consumer n. *consumidor.*

consumer advocate *defensor del consumidor.*

consumer boycott *boicot del consumidor.*

consumer credit *crédito al consumidor.*

consumer debt *deuda incurrida por el consumidor.*

consumer price index (CPI) *índice de precios al consumidor.* – Abbr. CPI.

consumer protection law *ley de protección al consumidor.*

contemplation of death *causa mortis, en contemplación de la muerte.*

Rel: anticipation of death, *anticipándose a la muerte, en prevención de la muerte.*

contempt of court *en desacato de la corte o juzgado.* **contemnor/contemner** *persona que desacata, persona en desacato.*

• Conduct that tends "to bring the authority and administration of the law into disrespect or disregard, interferes with or prejudices parties to their witnesses during a litigation or otherwise tends to impede, embarrass, or obstruct the court in the discharge of its duties." (17 Am. Jur. 2d Contempt §2).

Cf: **contempt ● contumacy ● contemptuous.** Contempt is the generic term that includes disobedience and disrespect to the court. Contumacy is restricted to deliberate disobedience <contumacious defendant>. Contemptuous means expressing scorn or contempt.

⊷ Contempt of court is an important instrument of punishment by the court in the common law system, embodying "the respect and authority courts are perceived to possess" (David & Brieley, 332). An extreme example is the survival of prison for debts in cases where the defaulting debtor acts in bad faith and rejects the judge's order to pay. The equivalent *desacato* is a term similar in formal description but clearly short in authority and measures to implement it, since failure to comply a *desacato* order is typically sanctioned only by fine or admonition. Prison for debts, on the other hand, has not survived in the civil law systems

where the courts have neither the authority nor the legal basis to order it.

civil contempt *desacato civil.*

constructive contempt *desacato de la autoridad judicial (fuera de la sala o juzgado).* – Syn. consequential contempt.

contempt in the face of the court *desacato en el tribunal, desacato ante el tribunal.*

criminal contempt *desacato penal.*

direct contempt *desacato del tribunal (en la sala o juzgado).*

Rel: contempt of Congress, *en desacato del Congreso.*

Ref: (UK) 9 Halsbury's Laws para 2; (US) Rust v. Pratt, 72, P.2d 533, 535, 157 Or. 505.

contest v. *disputar, combatir.*

contest a will *oponerse a un testamento.*

contest an action *contestar una acción, litigar.*

contest an election *disputar una elección, no estar de acuerdo con una elección.*

contingency n. *contingencia, eventualidad.*

contingent adj. *condicional, sujeto a condición.*

contingent claim *acción o reclamación sujeta a una condicion.*

contingent damages *indemnización por daños eventuales.*

contingent estate *propiedad o patrimonio cuya adquisición, modificación o extinción están sujetas a condición.*

contingent fee *honorarios de cuota litis.*

contingent legacy *legado condicional.*

contingent liability *responsabilidad condicional.*

continuance PROCEDURE n. *dársele una nueva fecha (para promover o proceder en una causa), diferimiento, [le]continuación (PR).*

• The adjournment of a cause to a future date.

Cf: **continuance ● postponement ● adjournment ● stay.** An adjournment means to suspend a session to another time or place, or to suspend a session indefinitely. Continuance, a term often used in court proceedings, "may sometimes mean an adjournment or recess of a trial already in progress, but its more common meaning is the postponement to a later date of the commencement of trial." (State v Rourick, 60, N.W.2d 529, 532, 245 Iowa 319) Postponement means to hold back to a later time and is generally limited to delays within the same term. Finally, a stay of an action is a postponement of all future proceedings until the happening of a specified event, regardless of any term of court.

⊷ Continuance is the common term used in

U.S. courts to express the postponement of proceedings to a later date. "Pass the case" is the expression used to mean a delayed presentation of the case by the parties before the judge on the day's court call. In Spanish-speaking countries a formal request for a continuance is usually phrased as *petición de una nueva fecha*, that is a request for a new date to be granted. Delaying the presentation of the case, on the other hand, is usually handled in an informal way, reflecting the non-oral nature of the proceedings.

Rel: postponement, *aplazamiento;* stay, *suspensión.*

contraband[1] **(crime)** n. *contrabando.* **smuggler** n. *contrabandista.*

• Contraband is the possession or transportation of anything prohibited or excluded by law. – Syn. carrying contraband, *contrabando.* Contraband refers most often to the property being transported, but it is also considered synonymous with illegal trade, as such, it is frequently used in cases of international transportation of illegal property.

contraband[2] **(property)** n. *bienes prohibidos, matute* (slg.)(PR), *fayuca* (slg.)(Mx).

• Goods not allowed to be imported, exported or possessed. <the automobile was searched for contraband>

contraband per se *bienes prohibidos por sí mismos, bienes prohibidos por su naturaleza.*

contract n. *contrato.* **contracting party** *parte contratante.* **contract** v. *contratar.* **contractual** adj. *contractual.*

• An agreement between two or more persons resulting in obligations that the law will enforce or recognize. Also the document in which such agreement is written.

Cf: **contract • memorandum of understanding.** A contract refers to an agreement that is considered binding by the parties and that the law will recognize by enforcing its resulting obligations. Memorandum of understanding, on the other hand, is a preliminary understanding of the parties regarding an intended contract or agreement, in which the parties do not consider themselves to be bound.

↪ While in the common law contract is distinguishable from gift, trust or bailment (because in the past they were not sanctioned by the action of assumpsit), in the civil law systems *contrato* applies to any agreement falling under the statutory definition of contract, and as a consequence *donación, fideicomiso,* and *depó-*

sito are traditionally considered and regulated as contracts.

accessory contract *contrato accesorio.*

adhesion contract *contrato de adhesión.*

adoption of contract *ratificación de un contrato.*

bilateral contract *contrato bilateral.* – Syn. mutual contract. reciprocal contract.

breach of contract *incumplimiento de un contrato.*

collateral contract *contrato accesorio.*

conditional contract *contrato sujeto a condición.*

contract not to compete *acuerdo estableciendo la obligación de no competir (con la otra parte).*

contract obligation *obligación contractual.*

contract of agency *contrato otorgando representación.*

contract of employment *contrato de trabajo.*

contract of insurance *contrato de seguro.*

contract of marriage *contrato de matrimonio.*

contract of sale *contrato de compraventa.* – Syn. contract for sale.

contract of suretyship *contrato de fianza.*

contract to lease *contrato de arrendamiento.*

executory contract *contrato sin ser aún ejecutado.*

gambling contract *contrato de juego.* – Syn. gaming contract.

government contract *contrato de suministro del gobierno.* – Syn. procurement contract.

implied contract *contrato implícito, o tácito.*

implied-in-law contract [de]*contrato implícito por disposición de la ley.* – Syn. constructive contract.

marriage contract *contrato de matrimonio.*

parol contract *convenio modificatorio hecho en forma oral, contrato oral.*

principal contract *contrato principal.*

rescission of a contract *rescisión de un contrato.*

retail installment contract *contrato de venta al menudeo a plazos, contrato al menudeo en abonos.* – Syn. conditional sales contract.

unenforceable contract *contrato que no puede ser ejecutado judicialmente.*

valid contract *contrato válido.*

variation of a contract *modificación de un contrato.*

void contract *contrato nulo.*

voidable contract *contrato anulable, contrato sujeto a nulidad.*

written contract *contrato escrito.*

Rel: acceptance, *aceptación;* agreement, *convenio;* bargain, *policitación, negociación;* consideration, *contraprestación;* performance, *cumplimiento;* privity, *relación contractual entre las partes;* promise, *declaración unilateral de voluntad;* remedies, *recursos.*

Comment: The law of contracts is confined to promises, and to promises that the law will enforce. The Restatement (Second) "defines a promise to be 'a manifestation of intention to act or refrain from acting in a specified way', made in such a way 'as to justify a promisee in understanding that a committ ment has been made.'" (1 Williston, §1:2 at 10) The law enforces promises on the following basis: "1) because the promise was made for valid consideration; 2) because the promisee has detrimentally relied upon the promise, or 3) because the promise comes within a statute which makes it enforceable despite the absence of consideration." (Schaber & Rohwer, §46 at 75)

contractor n. *contratista.*

contractor's lien *derecho preferencial de garantía en favor de un contratista.*

independent contractor *contratista independiente.*

Rel: subcontractor, *subcontratista.*

contributing cause TORTS *causa contribuyente.*

contributory negligence[1] TORTS **(US)** *culpa o negligencia inexcusable de la víctima, negligencia contribuyente* (PR).

Rel: comparative negligence (US), *culpa o negligencia parcial de la víctima, negligencia comparada* (PR).

contributory negligence[2] TORTS **(UK)** *culpa o negligencia parcial de la víctima, negligencia comparada* (PR).

controlled purchase [de]*venta ficticia hecha por la policía (de una sustancia o artículo ilegal),* [de]*compra hecha a un agente policíaco en cubierto (de una sustancia o artículo prohibido).*

controlled substance *sustancia bajo regulación especial, sustancia ilegal o prohibida.*

– Syn. controlled drugs (RU).

delivery of controlled substances *entrega de sustancias ilegales o de uso prohibido.*

possession of controlled substances *estar en posesión de sustancias ilegales o de uso prohibido.*

Rel: drugs, *drogas.*

controversy[1] **(lawsuit)** n. *controversia.*

• A concrete dispute that is adversarial in nature and that can be resolved by the judicial system.

controversy[2] **(dispute)** n. *controversia, conflicto.* – Syn. altercation, *altercado.* argument, *discusión, alegato.* bickering, *pleito.* debate, *debate.* discord, *discordia.* dispute, *disputa.* dissension, *disensión.* friction, *fricción.*

convention[1] **(meeting)** n. *convención.* – Syn. assembly, *asamblea.*

convention[2] **(treaty)** n. *convención, tratado general.*

Rel: compact, *pacto, acuerdo;* treaty, *tratado.*

convention[3] **(practice)** *convencionalismo, convencionalismos sociales.*

conversion[1] **(tort crime)** *apropiación ilícita, conversión* (PR).

• The tortious or wrongful deprivation of the personal property of another as if it were one's own.

Conversion includes "acts such as taking possession, refusing to give up the goods on demand, giving them to a third person, or destroying them." (Garner, 221)

constructive conversion *apropiación ilícita por disposición o ministerio de la ley.*

direct conversion *apropiación ilícita de hecho.*

fraudulent conversion *apropiación fraudulenta, apropiación indebida.*

conversion[2] **(change)** *conversión, modificación.*

• A transformation; an alteration.

conversion of insurance policy *conversión de la póliza de seguro.*

equitable conversion [de]*el considerar bienes reales como personales y viceversa.*

conveyance[1] n. *transmisión de la propiedad inmueble, acto translativo de dominio de un inmueble.* **conveyancing** *trámites y documentación referentes a la transmisión de inmuebles.* **convey** v. *transmitir, trasladar (el dominio).*

• The voluntary transfer of property or title to property from one person to another.

In its broad sense conveyance refers to a voluntary transfer of an interest in land; in a more narrow sense it is used to mean the activity related to the creation and transfer of interests and estates in land.

absolute conveyance *transmisión de propiedad inmueble libre de gravámenes.*

fraudulent conveyance *transmisión de propiedad inmueble en fraude de acreedores.*

Rel: transfer, *transmisión.*

conveyance[2] n. *título de propiedad.*

• An instrument conveying an interest in real property from one person to another.

Cf: **conveyance • deed.** These terms are synonymous but are not usually interchangeable. Conveyance refers to the document, usually a deed, by which a transfer of an interest in land is made. Deed, being broader in definition, refers to any written instrument that was signed, sealed and delivered (although in the United States, deed has the narrower meaning of a writing by which land is conveyed).

conviction CRIML.LAW n. *sentencia condenatoria, encontrar culpable (a una persona), convicción* (PR). **convict** n. *condenado.*

• A finding by a judge or a jury that a person accused of a crime is guilty.

convicted of a crime *haber sido encontrado culpable de un delito.*

to have prior convictions *tener antecedentes penales.*

Rel: judgment, *sentencia;* sentence, *condena.*

cooperative n. *cooperativa.*

• Corporation or association organized for the sole purpose of providing economic services to its shareholders without pursuing profits of itself. – Syn. co-op, *cooperativa, convertirse en miembro de una cooperativa.*

agricultural cooperative *cooperativa agrícola.*

consumer's cooperative *cooperativa de consumidores.*

cooperative apartment *propiedad de un inmueble en cooperativa.*

• "A dwelling (as an apartment building) owned by its residents, to whom the apartments are leased." (Black's Law Dict., 8th. ed., 359)

Rel: cooperative corporation, *cooperativa constituida como persona jurídica.*

co-ownership *copropiedad.*

copyright n. *derechos de autor, propiedad literaria,* [borr.]*copyright.* **copyright** v. *registrar como derecho de autor (una obra, etc.).* **copyrighted** adj. *protegido por los derechos de autor (un libro, etc).*

• The exclusive right given to an author, composer, artist or photographer to publish and sell exclusively a work for specified period of time. ↦ "The copyright system grew from the British Act of 1710 and spread throughout the British dominions and to the United States. The copyright system grants rights of an economic nature, covering exploitation of works by copying, public performance, broadcasting and other uses… each of the rights covered by copyright can be separately assigned or licensed, as can the copyright as a whole. [In contrast] The

[*sistema de derechos de autor*] is generally regarded as stemming from the French Laws of 1791 and 1793. In the nineteenth century, the concept evolved in the French jurisprudence that the right of the author in his works stemmed from his personality and that there were two aspects to this right, the economic and the moral." (Sterling, 15-16) This "dual" system influenced the development in the Continent (and thus in countries outside Europe having laws derived from the Continental model).

copyright notice *aviso de los derechos de autor (en una obra, libro, etc.).*

copyright protection *protección que otorgan los derechos de autor.*

Glossary: architectural works, *trabajos arquitectónicos;* artistic works, *trabajos artísticos;* author, *autor;* Berne Convention, *Convención de Berna;* coauthor, *coautor;* collective work, *obra colectiva;* derivative work, *obra derivada;* employee's works, *obras de empleados;* exclusive rights, *derechos exclusivos;* fair use, *uso razonable;* literary works, *obra literaria;* original expression, *expresión original;* piracy, *piratería;* public domain, *de dominio público;* recording, *grabación;* registration, *registro;* related rights, *derechos relacionados;* reproduction right, *derecho de reproducción;* royalty, *regalía;* term of protection, *plazo o duración de la protección;* work for hire, *trabajo u obra encomendada (a su autor), obra a pedido.*

See: intellectual property.

Ref: (CA) Copyright Act, R.S.C. 1985, Amended; (Int) Berne Convention; UCC; TRIPS; WIPO; (UK) 9(2) Halsbury's Laws para 1; (US) Copyright Act (1976) 17 USCA §101-1332.

cornering the market *acaparar el mercado, acaparamiento del mercado.*

coroner n. [de]*investigador de fallecimientos.*

Cf: **coroner • medical examiner • forensic pathologist.** These terms are often used as synonyms, but sometimes they must be distinguished: forensic pathologists are physicians specialized in the field of forensic pathology; medical examiners are also physicians, not necessarily pathologists, whose appointment underlines their function as political officers of a government entity. Finally, coroners are also political officers like medical examiners, but they don't necessarily need to be physicians to be appointed.

Rel: forensic pathologist, *patólogo forense;* medical examiner, *médico forense o legista.*

corporal punishment *castigo corporal.*

corporate crime [le]*criminalidad corporativa,* [fe]*responsabilidad penal de una sociedad,* [de]*delitos imputables a una sociedad (a través de actos de sus funcionarios).*
corporate law *ley de sociedades mercantiles.* – Syn. company law (RU).
corporation¹ (entity) n. *persona jurídica o moral.* **corporate** adj. *corporativo.* **incorporated** adj. *entidad con personalidad jurídica.* **unincorporated** adj.*entidad sin personalidad jurídica.*
• A group of individuals or office-holders who are considered by law to be a legal entity.
– Syn. aggregate corporation. body corporate. Corporation "in the U.S. refers to 'an entity (usu. a business) with authority under law to act as a single person, with rights to issue stock and act indefinitely.' In England, corporation (or body corporate, q.v.) is defined more broadly as 'an entity that has legal personality, i.e., that is capable of enjoying and being subject to legal rights and duties.' Often, in G.B., where company is the more usual term, corporation is used elliptically to mean a municipal corporation." (Garner, 225)
dormant corporation *sociedad inactiva.*
municipal corporation *entidad u organismo municipal.*
nonprofit corporation *sociedad o compañía sin afán de lucro.*
professional corporation (P.C.) *sociedad profesional, sociedad civil.*
public corporation *entidad u organismo público.* – Syn. publicly held corporation.
public corporation (UK) *empresa nacionalizada.*
corporation² (business) n. [fe][nrwer]*sociedad anónima,* [borr.]*corporación.* [de]*sociedad por acciones.* **corporate** adj. *corporativo.*
• "An entity (usu. a business) having authority under law to act as a single person distinct from the shareholders who own it and having rights to issue stock and exist indefinitely." (Black's Law Dict., 8th. ed., 365)
Cf: **corporation • association • company.** Besides being an incorporated entity, a corporation is also capable of issuing stock and existing indefinitely. An association is an unincorporated, looser organization pursuing a common purpose and having no legal personality separate from that of its members. Company, on the other hand, usually refers to an incorporated entity, although in common law it appears as an imprecise term used mostly in England

to refer to corporations, partnerships and other less formal entities. Company is now the preferred statutory term in England.
⌐ Corporation refers mostly to the legal entity that issues stock and operates as a business, best described in Spanish as *sociedad anónima.* This equivalence is by no means exact. The term *sociedad anónima* is narrower in scope and underlines the pooling of capital as a main distinguishing feature, while corporation is a broader concept and emphasizes the separateness of the entity from its members.
Corporación, used as equivalent of corporation, is a borrowed literal equivalent without an underlying similar legal concept in Spanish-speaking countries, with the exception of Puerto Rico. As a term used in administrative law *corporación* usually means a government-related entity not part of the central government. Finally, *sociedad por acciones* is a loose description of a corporation accurately defining its main features, but the term, being generic, falls short in precision.
chartered corporation (UK) *sociedad constituida mediante registro (por la autoridad), sociedad registrada.* – Syn. common law corporation.
closed corporation *sociedad cerrada, sociedad anónima cerrada.* – Syn. close corporation. closely held corporation.
corporate charter *escritura constitutiva.*
corporate domicile *domicilio social.*
corporate name *denominación.*
corporate officers *directores.*
corporate veil [borr.]*velo corporativo.*
corporation de facto *sociedad irregular.*
domestic corporation *sociedad constituida en el estado o país del lugar de que se trate.*
foreign corporation *sociedad constituida en otro estado o país.*
multinational corporation *corporación multinacional.*
private corporation *sociedad de derecho privado, sociedad que no es gubernamental o de participación estatal.*
public corporation *sociedad cuyas acciones se encuentran en poder del público, sociedad registrada en la bolsa de valores.*
statutory corporation (UK) *sociedad constituida de conformidad con los lineamientos de la ley.*
Rel: articles of incorporation, *escritura constitutiva;* board of directors, *consejo de administración;* by-laws, *estatutos;* officers, *directores;*

corpse

shareholder's meetings, *asambleas generales de accionistas.*

Comment: "Conducting a business in this way often has advantages over conducting business in the name of one or more individuals. The most obvious advantage is that the corporation is unlimitedly liable for the debts and obligations of the business but the shareholders are not, since in theory all debts are the artificial entity's obligations, not the shareholder's. In effect, the shareholders risk what they have invested but no more; in legal language the shareholders enjoy *limited liability.*" (Hamilton, 1-2)

Ref: (CA) Business Corporations Act, R.S.O. 1990, c. B16, s. 1; (UK) 9 Halsbury's Laws para 1001; (US) In re Clarke's Will, 284 N.W. 876, 878, 204 Minn. 574.

See: business forms. company.

corpse n. *cuerpo, cadáver.* – Syn. body, *cuerpo.* cadaver, *cadáver.* remains, *restos.*

corpus delicti (lat.) *corpus delicti, cuerpo del delito.* Body or substance of the crime.

corroborating evidence *pruebas confirmatorias o corroborativas.*

corruption n. *corrupción,* **corrupt** adj. *corrupto.*
• In general, the lack of integrity, virtue or moral rectitude; in particular, conduct that tends to unduly favor or discriminate against some persons in the discharge of official duties or in the implementation or enforcement of rights.
Rel: blackmail, *chantaje;* bribery, *cohecho, soborno;* extortion, *extorsión;* graft, *corrupción oficial, concusión.*

cost-of-living adjustment *compensación por el costo de vida, ajuste del costo de vida, indexación del costo de la vida.*

counterclaim n. *contrademanda.* – Syn. recon-vention, *reconvención.* cross-demand. cross-complaint. cross-claim.
compulsory counterclaim *contrademanda restringiéndose a los puntos originales.*
permissive counterclaim *contrademanda introduciendo nuevos puntos.*
Rel: cross-claim, *demanda entre codemandantes o codemandados.*

counterfeit n. *falsificación.* **counterfeiter** n. *falsificador.* – Syn. falsification. forgery, *falsificación.*
counterfeit of money and securities *falsificación de moneda y valores o títulos-valor.*

county n. *condado.*
county board *consejo del condado.*
county court *juzgado o tribunal del condado.*

court n. *juzgado, tribunal, corte.*
• A place where justice is administered, but also a body, formed by one or several judges, with specific powers to hear and decide cases brought before it. – Syn. bench. tribunal, *tribunal.*
↪ Court and *juzgado* are similar concepts, but court is considered a wider term. *Juzgado* usually refers to courts having only one judge, while court is used in either collegiate or single judgeship bodies. *Tribunal* is preferred when several judges preside in a court, and *corte* is preferred when referring to the Supreme Court (but this is not the only use by any means). *Corte,* instead of *juzgado,* is used as an equivalent of court in Puerto Rico.

civil court *juzgado o tribunal civil.*
court call *orden del día, lista de casos del día.*
court costs *costas judiciales.*
court date *fecha en que se debe comparecer ante un juzgado o tribunal.*
court en banc or in bank *tribunal en pleno.*
court of appeals *juzgado o tribunal de apelación o de segunda instancia, tribunal de última instancia* (US-New York, Maryland).
– Syn. appellate court. court of review. appeal court.
court of bankruptcy *juzgado o tribunal de quiebras.*
court of domestic relations *juzgado o tribunal de relaciones familiares, juzgado de lo familiar.* – Syn. family court. domestic court.
court of original jurisdiction *juzgado o tribunal de primera instancia.* – Syn. court of first instance.
court of probate *juzgado o tribunal sucesorio o testamentario.* – Syn. probate court.
courthouse *edificio del juzgado o tribunal, juzgado.*
criminal court *juzgado o tribunal penal.*
federal court *tribunal federal.*
housing court *juzgado o tribunal en materia de arrendamiento de inmuebles.*
in open court *en audiencia pública.*
juvenile court *tribunal para menores.*
kangaroo court *parodia de tribunal, burla de tribunal.*
moot court *tribunal de práctica.*
municipal court *juzgado o tribunal municipal.*
rule of court [lat.]*usus fori, práctica forense.*
small-claims court *juzgado menor, juzgado de reclamaciones de menor cuantía.*
state court *juzgado o tribunal estatal.*

54

trial court *juzgado o tribunal de primera instancia.* – Syn. court of first instance.

Comment: While court and *juzgado* are very similar institutions from a functional point of view, the powers and political role played by Anglo-American judges are substantially different than those given to their Hispanic counterparts. Courts have been given extraordinary powers to execute their decisions, to remedy unjust situations and to force actions or redress omissions even from public officials. In addition, courts hold the power to control and influence most administrative and legislative acts by means of judicial review, powers unequalled in Hispanic countries.

court interpretation *interpretación judicial.*
court interpreter *intérprete judicial.*
• Language interpretation performed in court proceedings or matters related to court functions.

Cf: **court interpretation** ● **judicial interpretation** ● **legal interpretation.** Court interpretation and judicial interpretation are synonymous and interchangeable; both mean language interpretation in a court setting or in a forum connected to court proceedings. Legal interpretation is a wider term meaning any interpretation pertaining to the application, enforcement or practice of law or in a legal setting.

court interpreter confidentiality *secreto profesional del intérprete judicial.*
team court interpreting *interpretación judicial en equipo.*
See: interpretation.

court reporter *taquígrafo judicial, transcriptor o taquimecanógrafo judicial.*

court-martial *corte marcial, consejo de guerra.* Rel: enlisted panel, *jurado de reclutas;* investigating officer (IO), *investigador policíaco o policial, investigador militar;* military judge, *juez militar;* officer panel, *jurado de oficiales;* prefer charges, *acusar.*

covenant[1] (agreement) n. *acuerdo, estipulación, cláusula.*
• Agreement or promise in writing, appearing usually as a contractual provision.
↪ Covenant as a broad term may appear as an equivalent of several legal concepts in Spanish, including most often *estipulación*, but also *acuerdo, convenio, contrato* and the narrower concept of *cláusula.*
absolute covenant *estipulación incondicional.*
concurrent covenant *estipulaciones concurrentes.*
conditional covenant *estipulación condicional.*

covenant not to compete *cláusula de no concurrencia o no competencia, acuerdo de no competencia o concurrencia.*
covenants under seal *convenios celebrados bajo la solemnidad del sello.*
dependent covenant *estipulación cuya exigibilidad depende de la realización de un acto o condición, estipulación sujeta a condición.*
express covenant *estipulación expresa.*
implied covenant *cláusula tácita o implícita en un contrato.*
independent covenant *estipulaciones cuya exigibilidad no dependen de ninguna condición u obligación de la otra parte.*
negative covenant *estipulación de no hacer.*
restrictive covenant *estipulaciones que establecen limitaciones.*
See: agreement.

covenant[2] (obligation) n. *estipulación obligatoria en una escritura referente a un inmueble.*
• An obligation in a deed burdening or favoring a landowner.
Covenant in a restricted sense is currently used mostly with respect to promises in conveyances pertaining to real estate.
Cf: **covenant** ● **easement.** "In concept, the main difference between easements and covenants is that, whereas an easement allows its holder to go upon and to do something upon the servient tenement, the beneficiary of a covenant may not enter the burdened land, but may require the owner of the land to do, or more likely not to do, something on that land." (Cunningham, Stoebuck & Whitman, 8.3 at 467)
affirmative covenant *estipulación obligatoria de dar o hacer.*
covenant for quiet enjoyment *saneamiento para el caso de evicción.*
covenant of warranty *cláusula de garantía.*
covenant running with the land *obligación propter rem.* – Syn. real covenant.

cover up n. *encubrimiento.*

coverage INSURANCE n. *cobertura.*
full coverage *cobertura completa.*

credible witness *testigo veraz o testigo capaz.*

credit[1] (business) n. *crédito.* **creditor** n. *acreedor.* **debtor** n. *deudor.*
• "The right granted by a creditor to a debtor to defer payment of debt or to incur debt and defer its payment." (U.C.C. §1.301(7))
credit agreement *convenio de crédito.*
credit bureau *oficina de información crediticia o de crédito.*

credit rating *evaluación crediticia de una persona o empresa.*
credit sale *venta a crédito.*
credit terms *condiciones de crédito.*
credit union *cooperativa de crédito, unión de crédito.*
credit-card fraud *fraude mediante el uso de tarjetas de crédito.*
letter of credit *carta de crédito.*
line of credit *línea de crédito.*
Rel: borrowing power, *capacidad crediticia o de crédito;* loan, *préstamo.*
See: accounting.
credit² tax n. *crédito fiscal.* – Syn. tax credit.
credit for child care expenses *crédito para gastos de cuidado de menores.*
credit for the elderly or the disabled *crédito para ancianos o para personas incapacitadas.*
crime (offense) n. *delito.*
• A wrong against society made punishable by the law. – Syn. criminal wrong. criminal offense.
accessory to crime *cómplice de un delito.*
commission of a crime *comisión de un delito.*
computer crime *delitos que requieren el uso de sistemas de computación.*
continuous crime *delito continuo.*
crime against humanity *crimen contra la humanidad.*
crime against nature *crimen contra natura.*
crime lab *laboratorio criminológico.*
crime of passion *crimen pasional.*
crime prevention *prevención de la delincuencia, prevención del delito.*
crime scene *escena del crimen.*
elements of a crime *elementos del delito.*
hate crime *delito motivado por odio contra un cierto grupo de personas.*
infamous crime *delito infamante.*
organized crime *crimen organizado.*
political crime *delito político.*
violent crime *delito con violencia.*
white collar crime *delito de guante blanco.*
See: criminals. offense.
crimes *delitos.*
crimes against persons *delitos contra la persona.*
crimes against property *delitos contra la propiedad.*
crimes mala in se (lat.) *delitos mala in se, delitos por su propia naturaleza.* Wrongs in themselves.
crimes mala prohibita (lat.) *delitos mala prohibita, delitos por disposición de la ley.* Prohibited wrongs.

Rel: felony, *delito mayor;* misdemeanor, *delito menor.*
criminal adj. *criminal, penal.*
criminal act (actus reus) *acto o hecho delictivo.*
criminal action *acción penal.*
criminal background *antecedentes penales.*
criminal charge *acusación de un delito.*
criminal conviction *habérsele encontrado culpable (de un delito).*
criminal court *juzgado o corte penal.*
criminal damage to property *daño en propiedad ajena.*
criminal facilitation *ayudar a la comisión de un delito.*
criminal intent *intención delictiva, dolo.*
criminal lawyer *abogado penalista, abogado criminalista.*
criminal negligence *negligencia culposa, negligencia criminal* (PR).
criminal proceeding *proceso penal.*
criminal rate *índice de criminalidad.*
criminal record *antecedentes penales, récord criminal.*
criminal law *derecho penal, derecho criminal.*
• The area of the law concerned with specifying which conduct constitutes a crime and stipulating what punishment should be imposed.
criminal procedure *procedimiento penal, enjuiciamiento penal.*
• The rules governing the way crimes are investigated, prosecuted and punished.
↳ Criminal procedure follows the so called accusatorial or common law system, while *procedimiento penal* follows the so called inquisitorial or civil law system. In the latter, a neutral judicial officer conducts the criminal investigation and a judge (or a panel of judges) having access to the investigation file (*expediente*) determines guilt or innocence. In the former, investigation is made by the police who focus on a suspect and collect evidence to prove that suspect guilty in an adversarial procedure before a neutral judge who has no prior knowledge of the case.
rules of criminal procedure *reglas de procedimiento penal.*
Rel: accusation, *acusación;* bail, *fianza;* discovery, *requerimiento y producción de pruebas;* hearing, *audiencia;* plea, *declaración formal de culpabilidad o no culpabilidad hecha ante el juez;* trial, *juicio.*
See: *procedimiento penal.*
criminal trial *juicio penal.*
A criminal trial is the final phase of criminal

procedure. Like a civil trial, it includes the examination of evidence and the final determination of the case; unlike a civil trial, a criminal trial is usually, but not always, presented before a jury.

criminals n. *criminales, delincuentes.*
– Syn. crooks, *pillos, truhanes.* delinquents, *delincuentes.* offenders.
Rel: defendant, *inculpado, acusado.*

criminology n. *criminología.* **criminologist** n. *criminólogo.* **criminological** adj. *criminológico.*
• The study of crime, criminals and criminal punishment.

cross-appeal *contestación de la apelación.*

cross-complaint *contradenuncia, contrademanda.*

cross-examination *repreguntar, contrainterrogatorio.*

Crown n. *la Corona.*
• The King or Queen as representing the State. In legal reports the Crown is referred to as Rex or Regina. – Abbr. R.
Rel: Royal prerogative, *derechos, facultades o privilegios reales,* [le]*prerrogativa real.*

cruel and unusual punishment *castigo cruel e inusitado* (PR), [fe]*pena inhumana y extraordinaria.*
Rel: Eighth Amendment (US), *Octava Enmienda (constitucional).*

cruelty to animals *crueldad a los animales.*

curfew n. *hora de regresar o llegar a casa, toque de queda (militar).*

current adj. *corriente, actual.*
   current assets *activo corriente, activo circulante.*
   current events *sucesos de actualidad.*
   current income *ingreso actual.*
   current liabilities *pasivo corriente, pasivo circulante.*

custodial account (bank) *cuenta en administración.*

custodial arrest *detención precautoria, detención preventiva.*

custodial interference FAM.LAW *violación del derecho de custodia o de la patria potestad.*

custodial interrogation *interrogatorio bajo custodia, interrogatorio del detenido.*

custodial search *registro hecho durante una detención o arresto.*

custody[1] FAM.LAW n. *custodia.*
• The physical control, care and maintenance of a child by a parent in a divorce or separation proceeding.
Cf: **custody • parental authority • parental rights.** These are similar terms that are usually differentiated. Custody refers to actual control or to a mere right to control; it normally means the right to keep a child and to control his or her upbringing. Parental authority is a similar but broader term referring to the authority parents have to control, but also to act on behalf of a minor. Finally, parental rights is a general term to refer to the rights arising from the child-parent relationship as a whole.
↦ *Custodia,* when used as equivalent of controlling a child, is usually understood broadly as the parents' rights and duties of care of a minor, and often referred to as *custodia de "un menor"* or *custodia "de menores."* In most cases the term *patria potestad* is preferred. In contrast, custody which is more specific, means the care, control and maintenance of a minor as ordered by a judge as a result of court proceedings.

actual custody *custodia efectiva.*
child custody *custodia de menores.*
divided custody *custodia dividida.*
joint custody *custodia en común.* – Syn. shared custody.
protective custody (juvenile) *custodia protectora, custodia de protección (de un menor).*
split custody *custodia alternada.*
temporary custody *custodia temporal.*
to have custody *tener la custodia.* – Syn. to have legal custody, *tener la custodia legal.*
Rel: divorce, *divorcio.*

custody[2] CRIML.LAW n. *bajo custodia.* **custodial** adj. *estando bajo custodia.*
• Restraint and physical control over a person. Equivalent of "detention" in civil law and synonymous with "imprisonment".
in custody *bajo custodia.*
released from custody *ser puesto en libertad.*
Rel: arrest, *detención;* detention, *detención.*

custody[3] PROP.LAW n. *custodia de bienes.*
• Control of a chattel.
↦ *Custodia* is mostly used in contractual terminology, meaning a duty of care and custody over property; as such, *custodia* is the essential element of the *contrato de depósito.*
Rel: possession, *posesión.*
See: bailment.

custom[1] (usage) n. *costumbre.* **customary** adj. *referente a la costumbre.*
   custom and usage *usos y costumbres.*
   legal custom *costumbre sancionada*

legalmente (o a la que la ley da aplicación).
local custom *costumbre local.*
custom²(duty) n. *aduana, derechos aduanales.*
custom broker *agente aduanal o aduanero.*
custom duties *derechos aduanales o aduaneros.*

DDDD

dactylography n. *dactilografía.*
dactyloscopy n. *dactiloscopia.*
damage n. *daño.*
• Loss, injury or deterioration.
Cf: **damage • injury • harm.** All three of these terms are synonyms. Although not an established distinction, damage is generally used when applied to property, while injury is used when applied to persons. Harm, on the other hand, refers to a less severe or forceful loss or injury.
criminal damage to property *daño en propiedad ajena (en forma intencional).*
property damage *daño en propiedad ajena.*
Rel: damnify, *damnificar, perjudicar;* harm, *daño;* injury, *lesión;* loss, *pérdida.*

damages n. *indemnización por daños y perjuicios.*
• "It is the pecuniary compensation or indemnity that may be recovered in the courts by any person who has suffered loss, detriment or injury, whether to his person, property, or rights, through the unlawful act or omission or negligence of another." (Stein, 1-2) – Syn. compensation, *compensación.* indemnity, *indemnización.*
Cf: **damages • compensation • indemnity.**
These terms are often used synonymously to mean payment by a person who caused injury to another. In insurance they refer to the restoration of the victim of a loss, in whole or in part, by payment or in kind. While damages and compensation are used interchangeably, indemnity or indemnify applies only to an obligation to make good a loss.
actual damages *daños y perjuicios compensatorios.* – Syn. compensatory damages.
assessment of damages *estimación de daños y perjuicios.*
award of damages *adjudicación de indemnización por daños y perjuicios.*
consequential damages *indemnización por daños indirectos.*
contingent damages *indemnización por daños eventuales o condicionales.*
damages actually sustained *indemnización por daños efectivamente sufridos, daños.*

discretionary damages *daños discrecionales.*
excess damages *indemnización en exceso de la cobertura de la póliza.*
exemplary damages *indemnización por daños a título punitivo o ejemplar.*
general damages *daños normales que resultan del acto ilícito.*
incidental damages *daños resultantes (que se derivan de los daños compensables).*
irreparable damages *daños irreparables.*
liquidated damages *cantidad líquida y determinada como indemnización por daños y perjuicios.*
loss-expectation damages *indemnización de la ganancia no adquirida,* [brder]*lucro cesante.*
– Syn. expectation damages. loss-of-bargained damages. damages for lost expectations.
nominal damages *indemnización nominal por daños y perjuicios.*
pecuniary damages *indemnización en dinero.*
punitive damages *indemnización por daños y perjuicios a título de pena.*
restitution damages *indemnización restitutoria.*
statutory damages *daños y perjuicios sancionados por una ley.*
Ref: (CA) Leistikow v Liggett Co. Ltd.[1925] 1 D.L. R. 210 Man.KBD; (UK) 12 Halsbury's Laws para 802; (US) Thomas v. Ware, 204 So.2d 501, 505, 44 Ala. App. 157.

dangerous adj. *peligroso.* **danger** n. *peligro.*
– Syn. fraught with danger, *lleno de peligro.* hazardous, *peligroso, aventurado.* perilous, *peligroso, arriesgado.* threatening, *amenazante.*
Cf: **danger • peril • hazard.** Danger is the general term used to denote liability for injury or evil to any degree or likelihood of occurrence. Peril suggests great and imminent danger. Hazard emphasizes the element of chance in a foreseeable but uncontrollable possibility of danger.
dangerous criminal *criminal peligroso.*
dangerous weapon *arma peligrosa.*

date n. *fecha.*
admission date *fecha de admisión.*
court date *fecha en que se debe comparecer en la corte.*
date certain *fecha cierta.*
date certain for trial *fecha en definitiva para llevar a cabo el juicio.*
date of birth *fecha de nacimiento.*
date of death *fecha de fallecimiento.*
date of execution *fecha de ejecución.*
date of issue *fecha de emisión.*
date of maturity *fecha de vencimiento.*

delivery date *fecha de entrega.*
due date *fecha de vencimiento.*
expiration date *fecha de expiración.*
filing date *fecha de presentación.*
trial date [de]*fecha del juicio (oral).*
day in court *derecho de comparecer en juicio, derecho de ejercer un derecho ante un tribunal, día en corte* (PR).
de facto (lat.) adv.adj. *de facto, de hecho.* In fact, in deed.
 de facto corporation *sociedad anónima irregular.*
 de facto government *gobierno de facto.*
 de facto marriage *matrimonio de facto.*
de jure (lat.) *de jure, de derecho.* Of right, lawful.
dead n. *muerto.* **dead** adj. *muerto.*
 – Syn. decedent, *fallecido, de cujus/cuius.* the deceased, *el fallecido.* the defunct, *el difunto.* the departed (euph), *el desaparecido.* the late, *el finado.*
 dead on arrival (DOA) *fue pronunciado muerto a su llegada.* – Abbr. DOA.
 presumed dead *se presume muerto.*
dead time *tiempo en prisión no elegible para la pena.*
deadbeat (pop.) *deudor moroso.*
deadly adj. *mortal.* – Syn. fatal, *fatal.* mortal, *mortal.* lethal, *letal.*
 deadly force *fuerza que puede causar la muerte, fuerza que pone en peligro la vida.*
 deadly gun-shot *disparo mortal de un arma.*
 deadly weapon *arma mortífera.*
deaf adj.n. *sordo.* **deafness** n. *sordera.*
 Rel: hard of hearing, *con dificultad para oír;* hearing impaired, *con impedimento auditivo;* telephone communication for the deaf (TDD), *comunicación telefónica para sordos.*
dealer¹ (trader) n. *comerciante.*
 art dealer *comerciante de arte.*
dealer² (intermediary) n. *distribuidor, intermediario.*
 car dealer *distribuidor de automóviles.*
 drug dealer *traficante de drogas, narcotraficante.*
dealer³ SEC.LAW n. *corredor.*
 stock dealer *corredor de acciones.*
death n. *muerte.* **die** v. *morir.*
 • The cessation of life. – Syn. deceased, *deceso.* casualty, *fatalidad.* passing.
 accidental death *muerte accidental.*
 brain death *muerte cerebral.* – Syn. legal death.

cause of death *causa de la muerte.*
civil death *muerte civil.*
death benefits *cantidad pagadera al beneficiario de un seguro de vida.*
death by natural causes *muerte por causas naturales.*
death certificate *acta o certificado de defunción.*
death penalty *pena de muerte, pena capital.*
death row *los condenados a muerte.*
death sentence *condena de pena de muerte.*
death squad *escuadrón de la muerte.*
death warrant *orden de ejecución de la pena de muerte.*
estimation of the time of death *estimación de la hora de la muerte.*
immediate death *muerte repentina, muerte inmediata.*
manner of death *causa legal de la muerte.*
mechanism of death *mecanismo de la muerte.*
natural death *muerte natural.*
presumption of death *presunción de muerte.*
wrongful death *muerte resultante de actos ilícitos de otro, muerte por negligencia de otro.*
Rel: homicide, *homicidio;* suicide, *suicidio.*
debenture¹ (US) n. *obligación quirografaria, bono,* [borr.]*debenture.*
 • An unsecured long-term debt instrument.
 – Syn. naked debenture. plain bond. unsecured bond.
debenture² (UK) *obligación en garantía (de una sociedad).*
debt n. *deuda.*
 acknowledgment of debt *reconocimiento de deuda.*
 bad debt *cuentas malas, cuentas incobrables, créditos incobrables.*
 debt cancellation *cancelación de deuda.*
 debt consolidation *consolidación de deudas.*
 debt financing *financiamiento de pasivo (de una empresa).*
 debt service *servicio de la deuda.*
 fraudulent debt *fraude financiero.*
 junior debt *deuda subordinada.*
 preexisting debt *deuda preexistente o anterior.*
debtor n. *deudor.*
 debtor rehabilitation *rehabilitación del deudor.*
 debtor relief *ayuda a deudores, protección de deudores.*
deceit¹ (false impression) n. *engaño.*
 • The act of deceiving; concealment of the

truth for the purpose of misleading.

deceit² (tort) n. *falsedad de declaraciones (en materia civil).*
• False representation knowingly made that causes harm to another.
Rel: fraud, *defraudación.*

deceptive practices *engaño con intención fraudulenta, engaño con intención de defraudar.*
Rel: fraud, *defraudación.*

decision (generic) n. *decisión, dictamen.*
• A judicial determination based on consideration of the facts and law involved, which usually includes a final judgment or ruling.
Cf: **decision • award • judgment • verdict.** Decision is regarded as a broad and generic term, while award, judgment and verdict are each considered a specific kind of determination of a controversy in an arbitral case, a trial and a jury trial, respectively.
appealable decision *decisión apelable.*
landmark decision *precedente importante, decisión judicial que establece nueva jurisprudencia.*
Rel: decree, *sentencia, decreto;* disposition, *disposición,* finding, *determinación;* judgment, *sentencia, fallo;* pronouncement, *pronunciamiento;* ruling, *fallo, orden;* sentence, *condena, sentencia condenatoria;* verdict, *veredicto.*

declaration¹ (statement) n. *declaración.*
• A usually formal statement, either sworn or unsworn, written or oral, made by a person for a specific purpose.
customs declaration *declaración aduanal.*
declaration of dividends *declaración de dividendos.*
self-serving declaration *declaración que beneficia al declarante.*

declaration² PLEADINGS (obs.) n. *demanda.*
• In common law pleading, the first pleading by the plaintiff in an action at law.
The term complaint or petition is used today in the United States, while statement of claim is its English equivalent.
See: complaint¹.

declaration³ INT'L.LAW n. *declaración.*
• Formal statement or pronouncement issued by a country or an international body affecting the rights or duties of any other member of the international community.
Declaration of Independence (US) *declaración de independencia.*
declaration of war *declaración de guerra.*

declaration⁴ (judgment) n. *declaración, declaratoria.* – Syn. declaratory judgment, *sentencia declaratoria.*
declaration of legitimacy *declaración o declaratoria de la legitimidad de un hijo.*
declaration of paternity *declaración o declaratoria de paternidad.*

declaratory judgment *sentencia declaratoria.*
• A judgment that establishes the rights of the parties or the opinion of the court regarding a question of law without ordering enforcement.
Cf: **declaratory judgment • advisory opinion.** An advisory opinion is issued by a judge in response to a question made by a governmental official who is not a party in an adversarial proceeding. It has no binding force as law. A declaratory judgment does not seek execution or performance from the opposing party, but it is binding as to the future and present rights of the parties to the action.

declaratory suit *jurisdicción voluntaria.*

decree (judgment) n. *sentencia.*
• The judicial decision given by a court of equity in ruling on a cause. Similarly, this term is also used by the courts of admiralty, divorce and probate when deciding a litigated case.
The term judgment has generally replaced decree.
☞ Decree is also broadly used in some cases to mean a court order. When used with such connotation, the most appropriate Spanish language equivalent is *orden* or *orden judicial.*
alimony decree *sentencia de pensión alimenticia.*
annulment decree *declaración de nulidad.*
consent decree *sentencia u orden convenida (por las partes).* – Syn. consent order.
decree of distribution *sentencia de distribución del haber hereditario.*
decree of divorce *sentencia de divorcio.*
decree of insolvency *declaración de insolvencia.*
decree of support *sentencia de alimentos.*
default decree *sentencia en rebeldía, juicio en rebeldía.*
deficiency decree *sentencia de pago de sumas no cubiertas por la ejecución de una hipoteca.* – Syn. deficiency judgment.
foreclosure decree *sentencia de ejecución forzosa.*
interlocutory decree *sentencia interlocutoria.*

deduction TAX n. *deducción.* **deductible** adj.

deducible.
• Amount taken off from gross income in calculating net income. – Syn. tax deduction.
business deduction *deducción del costo de hacer negocios.*
deductible expenses *gastos deducibles.*
itemized deduction *deducción desglosada, deducción detallada.*
marital deduction *deducción marital.*
standard deduction *deducción estándar, deducción fija.*
deed[1] **(US)** n. *escritura o instrumento traslativo de derechos sobre inmuebles.*
• In the United States, as opposed to in the United Kingdom, a deed is more narrowly defined as a writing that conveys an interest in land. – Syn. conveyance, *título de propiedad (de un inmueble).*
Cf: **deed ● covenant.** A covenant is an obligation favoring or burdening a landowner or sometimes a promise made in an agreement. A deed is the document or writing in which a covenant is conveyed or created. Deeds are of two types: warranty deeds or quitclaim deeds.
absolute deed *escritura de propiedad libre de cargas o gravámenes.*
bargain and sale deed *escritura de propiedad sin garantía de la legitimidad del título.*
– Syn. full covenant and warranty deed.
deed of conveyance *título de propiedad, escritura de transmisión de un bien inmueble.*
deed of land recorded *escritura de propiedad inscrita en el registro de la propiedad o catastral.*
deed of trust *escritura constitutiva de fideicomiso sobre bienes inmuebles dados en garantía.*
– Syn. trust deed.
estoppel by deed *excepción o impedimento basados en una escritura.*
execution of deed *celebración o perfeccionamiento de la escritura o instrumento.*
general warranty deed *escritura que transmite los derechos sobre un inmueble garantizando su legitimidad.*
quitclaim deed *escritura de propiedad que transmite los derechos que se tengan sobre un inmueble sin garantizar su legitimidad, escritura traslativa de propiedad sin garantía de legitimidad.* – Syn. deed without covenants or fiduciary deed.
special warranty **deed** [de]*escritura de propiedad que incluye solamente la garantía de la legitimidad del título en el caso de acciones procedentes contra el otorgante.*

Ref: (US) McMee v. Henry, 174 S.W. 746, 747.
deed[2] **(UK)** n. [de]*documento o instrumento escrito que cumple con las formalidades legales (específicamente la firma, el sello y la entrega),* [de]*documento formalizado por escrito.*
grantor n. *otorgante.* **grantee** n. *a quien se otorga (el documento), beneficiario.*
• In common law, a written document that is signed, sealed and delivered.
deed of arrangement *convenio de quita y espera.*
deed of assignment *cesión de bienes (del deudor al acreedor).*
deed of covenant *convenio que crea una obligación.*
deed of partnership *escritura constitutiva de una sociedad colectiva, escritura constitutiva de un "partnership".*
deed poll *escritura o instrumento hecho en forma unilateral.*
title deed *escritura de propiedad (de un bien).*
Rel: delivery, *entrega;* seal, *sello.*
Ref: 13 Halsbury's Laws para 1.
See: conveyance[2].
defacing property *estropear o deteriorar una propiedad ajena, dañar una propiedad ajena.*
defalcation n. *desfalco.*
See: embezzlement.
defamation (generic) n. *difamación.* **defame** v. *difamar.* **defamatory** adj. *difamatorio.*
• Defamation is a generic term that appears as a legal concept as either slander (oral defamation) or libel (written defamation).
Rel: fair comment, *comentario apropiado;* libel, *difamación escrita;* public figure, *figura pública;* slander, *difamación oral.*
default[1] **(failure)** n. *incumplimiento.*
• A failure to discharge a duty – Syn. breach.
default in payment *falta de pago.*
default interest *interés moratorio.*
default on a debt *incumplimiento de una obligación (monetaria), falta de pago de una deuda.*
in default *(estar) en incumplimiento, haber incumplido.*
default[2] **(absence)** *rebeldía.*
• The failure to appear in court or the omission to plead when under duty to do it.
– Syn. contumacy, *contumacia.*
default decree *declaratoria de rebeldía.*
default hearing *audiencia de acuse de rebeldía.*
judgment by default *sentencia en rebeldía.*

motion for default *acuse de rebeldía.*

motion to vacate default *promoción pidiendo la revocación de la declaratoria o declaración de rebeldía.*

defect n. *vicio, defecto.* defective adj. *defectuoso.*

• Deficiency, insufficiency, absence of something essential for the purpose intended.

defect in the pleading *vicio o defecto de la demanda o la contestación.*

defect of form *vicio o defecto de forma.*

defect of title *vicio o defecto de un título de propiedad.*

fatal defect *vicio de los elementos de validez (de un acto o contrato).*

hidden defect *vicios ocultos.* – Syn. latent defect.

product defect *producto defectuoso.*

defection MIL.LAW n. *deserción.*

defendant[1] CRIML.PROCED n. *acusado, indiciado.* – Syn. accused, *acusado.*

defendant demands trial (oral expr.) *el acusado pide se proceda en juicio.*

defendant is ready (proceeding) *el acusado pide se proceda (en un procedimiento).*

defendant rests (proceeding) *la defensa ha terminado (una actuación judicial).*

third party defendant *tercero acusado.*

Rel: codefendant, *coacusado;* parties, *partes.*

defendant[2] CIVIL PROCED *demandado.* – Syn. respondent.

defense n. *defensa, excepción.*

• The reasons or allegations given by the defendant in a cause supporting the defendant's assertion that there is no case against him or her. – Other spell.: defence (RU,CA).

affirmative defense [de]*defensa o excepción basada en hechos o circunstancias no incluidos en la demanda o en la acusación,* [le] *defensa afirmativa.*

alibi defense *coartada.*

capacity defense *defensa de falta de capacidad.*

dilatory defense *defensa dilatoria.*

equitable defense *defensa basada en el régimen de derecho-equidad.*

frivolous defense *defensa infundada.*

legal defense *defensa legal.*

meritorious defense *defensas de fondo.*

motion to strike defense *promoción o petición de la improcedencia de una defensa.*

self-defense *legítima defensa.*

sham defense *defensa sin fundamento.*

Rel: immunity, *inmunidad;* privilege, *privilegio.*

See: affirmative defense.

defense attorney *abogado defensor.*

defense rests (trial) *la defensa ha terminado su presentación de pruebas.*

deficiency judgment or decree *sentencia de pago de sumas no cubiertas por la ejecución de una hipoteca.*

defraud v. *defraudar.*

delegation n. *delegación.* delegate v. *delegar.*

delegation of powers *delegación de poderes.*

deliberate adj. *deliberado, intencional.* – Syn. calculated, *calculado.* cogitative, *reflexión, meditación.* done on purpose, *hecho a propósito.* intentional, *intencional.* premeditated, *premeditado.* willful, *intencional, voluntario.*

deliberation n. *deliberación.*

delinquency n. *delincuencia.* delinquent n. *delincuente.*

juvenile delinquency (JD) *delincuencia juvenil.*

delinquent (late) adj. *en mora.*

delinquent debt *deuda vencida, deuda en mora.*

delinquent taxpayer *contribuyente moroso.*

delivery[1] (transfer) n. *entrega.*

• Giving or surrendering possession or control of something to another. Also, the formal act of transfer or conveyance.

actual delivery *entrega real.*

conditional delivery *entrega condicional.*

constructive delivery *entrega jurídica.*

delivery in escrow *entrega en depósito condicional en favor de un tercero.*

delivery of goods *entrega de mercancía.*

delivery of property *tradición, entrega.*

symbolic delivery *entrega simbólica.*

delivery[2] (of a child) n. *parto.*

• Giving birth. – Syn. childbirth, *parto, alumbramiento.*

breech delivery *presentación de nalgas.*

premature delivery *parto prematuro.*

Rel: birth, *nacimiento;* brau or face presentation, *presentación de brau o de cara;* labor, *trabajo de parto, dolores de parto;* midwife, *partera, comadrona;* miscarriage, *malparto;* stillborn, *niño nacido muerto, nonato.*

demeanor n. *comportamiento, proceder, porte.*

Rel: character, *carácter.*

dementia (lat.) n. *dementia, demencia.*

demise¹ (conveyance) n. *transmisión de la tenencia sobre inmuebles (mediante testamento o arrendamiento).*

demise² SUCCESSION n. *transmisión sucesoria de la propiedad.*

demise³ (death) n. *fallecimiento.*

demurrer (obs.)(law fr.) *pedir la improcedencia de la demanda por carecer de fundamento.*

• "A demurrer, in reality, does not admit anything, but merely asserts that, even if everything stated in complaint were true, it does not state facts sufficient to constitute a cause of action." (State v. California Packing Corp., 145 P.2d 784,105 Utah 191)
In modern procedure demurrer is termed a motion to dismiss in most U.S. jurisdictions, and it has been replaced by provision for hearing objections on points of law in England.

general demurrer *pedir la improcedencia basada en aspectos sustantivos.*

special demurrer *pedir la improcedencia basada en las formalidades del procedimiento.*

denial n. *negación, denegación* (PR).
– Syn. traverse (plea), *negación.*

denial of motion *negar o denegar una promoción o petición.*

denial of paternity *negación de la paternidad.*

denial of relief *negar o denegar un recurso o la tutela jurídica de derechos o defensas.*

denial of responsibility *sin responsabilidad, negar la responsabilidad, negar el ser responsable.*

general denial *negación de la demanda en todos sus puntos.*

Department of Corrections (DOC)
Departamento de correcciones, correccional.

dependent TAX n. *dependiente.*

depletion n. *reducción, agotamiento de un recurso.*

deportation IMMGR n. *deportación.* **deport** v. *deportar.* **deportee** n. *deportado.*
• The expulsion of an alien, who has entered the country, to another country.
Cf: **exclusion • extradition • expulsion.**
Exclusion is the denial of entry to a country. Extradition is the surrender to another country (or state) of one accused of an offense against its laws. Expulsion is the ejection or banishment from a country, resulting in deprivation of the rights and privileges normally granted to its citizens.

appeal from a deportation hearing *apelación de la resolución de una audiencia de deportación.*

deportation appeal *apelación de la orden definitiva de deportación.*

deportation bond *fianza otorgada en un caso de deportación, fianza de deportación.*

deportation defenses *defensas en contra de una orden de deportación.*

deportation grounds *causales de deportación.*

deportation hearing *audiencia de deportación.*

deportation proceedings *procedimiento de deportación.*

deportation relief *impugnación de una orden o procedimiento de deportación.* – Syn. relief from deportation.

deportation suspension *suspensión de la orden de deportación.*

extended voluntary departure *extensión del plazo para salir voluntariamente (del país).*

judicial recommendation against deportation (JRAD) *recomendación judicial contra la deportación.*

stay of deportation *aplazamiento de la deportación.*

withholding of deportation *retención o detención de la orden de deportación.*
Rel: exclusion, *exclusión;* expulsion, *expulsión;* extradition, *extradición;* motion to reopen or reconsider, *petición para que se dicte o reconsidere nuevamente una resolución, moción de reconsideración* (PR); voluntary departure, *salida voluntaria.*

deposit¹ n. *depósito.* **deposit** v. *depositar.*
• Money or property given to another for safekeeping, preservation or use to be returned in kind.

bank deposit *depósito bancario.*

demand deposit (bank) *depósito a la vista.*

deposit in court *depósito judicial.*

insured deposit *depósito garantizado (por entidad pública).*

security deposit (lease) *depósito en garantía, depósito de garantía.*

time deposit (bank) *depósito a plazo fijo.*
Rel: bailment, *depósito.*

deposit² n. *depósito en dinero como garantía de cumplimiento.*
• Money deposited with a person as earnest money or security for the execution of an obligation.

deposition n. *testimonio extrajudicial, deposición* (PR). **deponent** n. *declarante.* **depose** v. *declarar, dar testimonio (extrajudicialmente).*
• The procedural means by which one party asks oral questions of the other party or one of

that party's witnesses under oath, out of court and on record.

☞ Deposition is a common and popular discovery device in English-speaking countries, particularly in the United States, without an equivalent in Hispanic countries. Although *testimonio extrajudicial* is an acceptable description of deposition, its role, implementation and purpose are clearly different. Depositions are conceived and executed as evidence in preparation for trial, carried on by the parties themselves out of court and under strictly applied evidence rules; *testimonio extrajudicial*, on the other hand, is considered a neutral event, in most cases carried out by a public notary or other nonjudicial authority out of court, without being primarily considered evidence to be produced for trial. Also, *testimonio extrajudicial* is often simply understood as any statement made out of court.

Comment: In England depositions are made before a magistrate or court official. In criminal cases depositions are taken during commital proceedings before the magistrate's court. In civil proceedings the court may order an examiner of the court to take depositions from any witnesses who are ill or likely to be unavailable during the hearing. Unlike in the United States, pretrial depositions out of court are uncommon.

See: discovery.

depreciation (accounting) n. *depreciación.*
  accelerated depreciation *depreciación acelerada.*
  accumulated depreciation *depreciación acumulada.*
  declining balance depreciation method *método de depreciación del saldo decreciente.*
  replacement cost depreciation method *método de depreciación de costo de reposición.*
  sinking fund depreciation method *método de depreciación de fondo de amortización.*
  straight method of depreciation *método de depreciación directa.*
  See: *depreciación.*

depredation n. *depredación.*

dereliction¹ (abandonment) *derrelicción.*

dereliction² (accession) *adquisición de tierra por accesión debido al retiro de aguas.*

derogation n. *derogación.* **derogatory** adj. *derogatorio.*

derogatory clause (will) *cláusula secreta de validación testamentaria.*

descent¹ (relation) *descendencia.* **descendant** n. *descendiente.*

• Ancestry; lineage.
  collateral descent *descendencia colateral.*
  immediate descent *descendencia inmediata.*
  lineal descent *descendencia lineal.*
  mediate descent *descendencia mediata.*
  Rel: direct line, *línea directa;* maternal line, *línea materna;* paternal line, *línea paterna.*

descent² SUCCESSION n. *transmisión de bienes por sucesión intestada.*
• "It is the passing of title in realty from a person dying intestate to someone related to him by consanguinity."(Sodhi, 116)
Cf: **descent • distribution • inheritance.** "At common law, intestate real property passes by descent and intestate personal property passes by distribution. Both heirs (who take by descent) and distributees (who take by distribution) may properly be said to inherit or take by inheritance. In the U.S., the Uniform Probate Code has simplified the historical terminology, supplanting all these specific terms for the general phrase intestate succession." (Garner, 269)

description CRIML.LAW n. *descripción.*
– Syn. portrayal, *retrato, representación.*
Rel: accessories, *accesorios de vestir;* clothing, *prendas de vestir;* colors, *colores;* ethnicity, *etnia;* height, *estatura;* marks, *marcas;* measurements, *medidas;* piercing, *perforaciones;* scar, *cicatriz;* tattoo, *tatuaje;* weight, *peso.*

desertion¹ n. *abandono.* **desert** v. *abandonar.*
  deserter n. *quien abandona.*
• "Abandoning a duty (e.g., marital or child support) without legal cause and with an intent to make the abandonment permanent." (Mellinkoff's Dict., 167)
  constructive desertion *abandono causado por la conducta del otro cónyuge.*
  desertion and nonsupport *abandono y falta de pago de sustento o alimentos.*
  malicious desertion *abandono intencional, abandono sin causa justificada*[Sa].
  Rel: abandonment, *abandono.*

desertion² MIL.LAW n. *deserción.* **deserter** n. *desertor.*
Rel: absent without leave (AWOL), *ausente sin permiso.*

detainer¹ (possession) n. *retención (de bienes).*
• The act of withholding or keeping from someone, with legal right, the possession of land or goods.
  forcible detainer *retención ilegal y hostil de la posesión de bienes || procedimiento judicial de desalojo*
  unlawful detainer *retención ilegal de la posesión de un inmueble.*

detainer²(restraint) *detención ilegal.*
• The restraint of a person's personal liberty against his or her will. A detention.
detention n. *detención.* **detainee** n. *detenido.*
• Restraining a person for some official purpose by establishing control over that person.
investigative detention *detención con motivo de una investigación.*
pretrial detention *detención previa al juicio.*
preventive detention *detención preventiva.*
See: arrest.

deterrence *disuasión.*

detriment n. *perjuicio.*
detriment to promisee *perjuicios causados a aquél que se hace una oferta (contractual).*
detrimental reliance *perjuicios causados con motivo de la aceptación de una promesa o declaración unilateral.*

devise n. *legado de bienes inmuebles.* **devise** v. *legar.* **devisee** n. *legatario.* **devisor** n. *otorgante.*
• A gift of real estate property by will. However, devise is often used loosely as the act of giving either real or personal property by will.
general devise *legado general de bienes inmuebles.*
lapsed devise *legado imposible de bienes inmuebles (por haber fallecido el legatario antes que el otorgante).*
specific devise *legado de inmuebles específicamente identificados.*
Rel: legacy, *legado de bienes personales.*

dictum (lat.) n. *obiter dictum, comentarios (hechos por el juez en la sentencia) que no constituyen parte del precedente, señalamiento incidental en una resolución, opinión no vinculante.* A remark by the way.
• A statement, remark or observation. Remarks contained in a court's opinion that are nonbinding and incidental to the disposition of the case. – Syn. dicta. obiter dicta.
Rel: holding, *principio legal.*

digest n. *índice de casos judiciales ordenados sistemáticamente, digestos o prontuarios de jurisprudencia.* – Abbr. D.
Digest as a translation of Digesto or Digesta refers to the Civil law monumental compilation and systematic discussion of the law embodied in the Pandects of Justinian.

dilatory adj. *dilatorio.* – Syn. delaying.
dilatory defense *defensa dilatoria.*
dilatory exceptions *objeciones dilatorias.*

dilatory pleas *excepciones dilatorias.*

diplomacy n. *diplomacia.* **diplomat** n. *diplomático.* **diplomatic** adj. *diplomático.*
diplomatic agent *agente diplomático.*
diplomatic relations *relaciones diplomáticas.*
Rel: good offices, *buenos oficios;* letters of credence, *cartas credenciales;* persona non grata, *persona non grata;* ultimatum, *ultimátum.*

dipsomania n. *dipsomanía.* **dipsomaniac** n.adj. *dipsomaniaco.*
• An insatiable craving for alcoholic beberages.
Rel: addiction, *adicción;* alcohol, *alcohol.*

direct adj. *directo.*
direct examination *examen testimonial inicial, interrogatorio directo* (PR).
direct finding *sentencia sumaria sobre el fondo del asunto.*
directed verdict *veredicto dictado por el juez (en un juicio ante jurados).*

disability¹ (legal disqualification) n. *incapacidad.*
disable n. *incapaz.* **disabled** n. *incapacitado*
• Incapacity in the eyes of the law. – Syn. incapacity, *incapacidad.*
civil disability *incapacidad civil.*
disability to enter into a contract *incapacidad contractual.*

disability² (physical inability) n. *invalidez.*
disabled n. *inválido, impedido.* **disablement** n. *invalidez.*
• The lack of ability to perform some function. – Syn. defect, *defecto.* handicap. impairment, *deterioro, daño, impedimento.* inability, *inhabilidad.* infirmity, *enfermedad deshabilitante.*
Cf: **disability • incapacity • disablement.**
Disability and incapacity are synonyms connoting the idea of disablement. Disablement, in turn, refers to the action of crippling or incapacitating.
disability benefits *prestaciones por invalidez.*
disability compensation *indemnización por invalidez.*
disability insurance *seguro de invalidez.*
disability plan *plan de invalidez.*
disability retirement *jubilación por invalidez.*
general disability *incapacidad total.*
personal disability *incapacidad personal.*
preexisting disability *invalidez preexistente.*
special disability *incapacidad parcial.*
temporary disability *invalidez temporal, incapacidad temporal.*

disabled adj. *incapacitado, inválido, discapaci-*

tado, minusválido. – Syn. crippled, *lisiado.* handicapped, *incapacitado.* impaired, *inhabilitado, deteriorado físicamente, disminuido, impedido.* invalid, *inválido.*

disagreement n. *desacuerdo.* **disagree** v. *disentir.*

disbarment n. *revocación de la autorización para ejercer como abogado || expulsión de la Barra (de abogados).* **to disbar** *desaforar* (PR).

discharge¹ (extinguish) n. *resolución, extinción.*
• Form of satisfying or extinguishing a legal duty or obligation.
discharge a duty *resolución de una obligación.*
discharge of contract *resolución de obligaciones contractuales.*

discharge² (release) n. *liberación.*
• A release from an obligation.
discharge of an attachment *levantamiento de un embargo.*
discharge of lien *liberación de un gravamen.*

discharge³ (dismissal) n. *despido.*
• The termination of employment of an employee.
discharge from military service *dar de baja del servicio militar, ser dado de baja.*
discharge from work *ser despedido del trabajo.*
dishonorable discharge MIL.LAW *baja deshonrosa.*
honorable discharge MIL.LAW *dar de baja honorablemente, ser dado de baja honorablemente.*
wrongful discharge *despido injustificado.*

discharge⁴ CRIML.LAW n. *remisión || liberación, dejar en libertad.*
• Conditional dismissal of a case. Also, conditional release of a defendant from custody.
conditional discharge *remisión condicional || liberar o dejar en libertad condicional (a un detenido o convicto).*

discharge in bankruptcy *rehabilitación del quebrado.*

discharge of a firearm *disparo de un arma de fuego, abuso de arma* (Ar).

disclaimer¹ (renunciation) n. *repudio o renuncia.*

disclaimer² (denial) n. *negación.*

disclosure of assets *declaración de bienes.*

discount n. *descuento.* – Syn. markdown, *rebaja.* rebate, *descuento en devolución.*
Rel: refund, *reembolso;* surcharge, *recargo.*

discovery n. *requerimiento y producción de pruebas, descubrimiento de pruebas* (PR).
• Procedure by which a party in litigation ob-

tains disclosure of information or documents relevant to the matters in question. – Syn. discovery proceedings, *procedimiento de requerimiento y producción de pruebas.*
Discovery usually includes depositions, interrogatories, production of documents or things, permission to enter upon land or other property, physical and mental examinations and requests for admission.
Cf: **discovery • disclosure • investigation.** While discovery and disclosure are sometimes used interchangeably, investigation is always considered to have a different meaning. All three terms are clearly distinguishable. Discovery refers specifically to legal proceedings that force a party to reveal facts or documents relevant to the litigated matter at the opposing party's request; disclosure refers only to the revelation of something previously unknown; and investigation means to inquire carefully and systematically into an event or matter.
↦ Discovery is practically nonexistent in civil law countries. While production of pretrial probatory material is part and parcel of the common law (being an adversarial system), it is unnecessary in civil law (being an inquisitorial system) where the parties have, in principle, unlimited access to *pruebas*, and the judge presides over the production of evidence with powers to have it disclosed if he or she so chooses. Discovery, as a tool in the hands of the parties, is closest to the term *requerimiento y producción de pruebas*, meaning a compelled form of obtaining information and knowledge about the issues in dispute, provided the different legal context in which discovery and *requerimiento y producción* operate is taken into account.

abuse of discovery *uso abusivo del requerimiento y producción de pruebas.*

discovery of facts *requerimiento y producción de pruebas sobre los hechos.*

discovery proceeding *procedimiento de requerimiento y producción de pruebas.*

motion for discovery *petición o promoción del requerimiento y producción de pruebas.*

pretrial discovery *requerimiento y producción de pruebas previos al juicio.*

tender discovery *exhibición u ofrecimiento de pruebas obtenidas mediante su requerimiento y producción.*

Specific Types: deposition, *testimonio extrajudicial;* interrogatories, *pliego de posiciones;* permission to enter on land, *permisos para entrar en una propiedad;* physical and mental examinations, *exámenes físicos y mentales;* production of documents and things, *presentación de documentos y objetos;* request for admission, *petición de que se niegue o acepte una admisión hecha por una de las partes.*

discretion n. *discreción.*
• The freedom to act following one's own judgment or conscience. Also a reasonable exercise of power to act in an official capacity.
judicial discretion *discreción judicial.*
legal discretion *discreción legal.*

discretionary account *cuenta discrecional.*

discrimination n. *discriminación.*
age discrimination *discriminación por edad.*
employment discrimination *discriminación laboral, discriminación en el trabajo.*
gender discrimination *discriminación basada en el sexo (de la persona), discriminación por razón del sexo.*
price discrimination *prácticas discriminatorias con los precios.*
racial discrimination *discriminación racial.*
religious discrimination *discriminación religiosa.*
reverse discrimination [de]*discriminación perpetrada por aquellos que son normalmente discriminados,* [de]*discriminación por los discriminados.*
Rel: discriminatory practices, *prácticas discriminatorias;* equal protection, *principio de igualdad jurídica.*

disease n. *enfermedad.* – Syn. ailment, *padecimiento, achaque.* disorder, *desorden físico.* illness, *enfermedad.* malady, *mal.* sickness, *enfermedad.*
infectious disease *enfermedad infecciosa.*
mental disease *enfermedad mental.*
occupational disease *enfermedad profesional.*
sexually transmitted disease *enfermedad transmitida sexualmente.*

disinherit v. *desheredar.*

dismissal[1] **(termination)** n. *sobreseimiento* || *desistimiento.*
• Termination of an action, claim, motion or appeal, usually without a resolution of the issues involved.
dismissal agreed *desistimiento por acuerdo entre las partes.*
dismissal for want of prosecution *suspensión del procedimiento penal.* – Abbr. DWP.
dismissal of an appeal *sobreseimiento de una apelación.*

dismissal on the merits *sobreseimiento por motivos de fondo.*
dismissal with prejudice *sobreseimiento precluyendo el ejercicio de cualquier acción, desistimiento con perjuicio* (PR).
dismissal without prejudice *sobreseimiento sin precluír el ejercicio de acciones procedentes, desistimiento sin perjuicio* (PR).
involuntary dismissal *sobreseimiento, caducidad.*
motion to dismiss *promoción o petición de sobreseimiento.*
voluntary dismissal *desistimiento.*

dismissal[2] **(discharge)** *despido.*
• The discharge of an employee from his or her employment.

dismissal and nonsuit *sobreseimiento o desistimiento de una de las partes, desistimiento y nonsuit* (PR).

disobedience n. *desobediencia.*
civil disobedience *desobediencia civil.*
disobedience of traffic signs *no respetar las señales de tráfico.*

disorderly conduct *escándalo en la vía pública, alteración del orden público.*
• A broad concept usually defined in vague terms embracing a variety of violations of public decency and order.
"The term 'disorderly conduct' is one of general or indefinite meaning, but generally signifies any conduct which tends to breach the peace or to disturb those who see or hear it; to endanger morals, safety or health of community; or to shock public sense or morality." (State v. Cherry, 173 N.W.2d 887, 888)
Rel: breach of the peace, *alteración o perturbación del orden público;* drunkenness, *alcoholismo, embriaguez;* loitering, *vagancia.*

disposition[1] **(transfer property)** *transferencia.*
disposition of property *transferencia de propiedad.*

disposition[2] **(determination)** *resolución.*
• A court determination or ruling, especially one settling or deciding a case.
disposition of a case *resolución de un caso, disposición* (PR).

dissenting or minority opinion *opinión en contrario o en discrepancia, opinión de la minoría.*

dissolution of a corporation *disolución de una persona jurídica o moral, disolución de una sociedad.*

• The end of the legal existence of a corporation.

articles of dissolution *acta de liquidación, acta de disolución.*

de facto dissolution *disolución de facto.*

involuntary dissolution *disolución por determinación legal o judicial.*

voluntary dissolution *disolución voluntaria.*

dissolution of marriage *disolución de matrimonio.* – Syn. divorce, *divorcio.* marital dissolution.

Rel: prove-up, [de]*diligencia probatoria (que establece un derecho).*

See: divorce.

district attorney (US) *fiscal de Distrito, fiscal estatal.* – Abbr. DA.

diversion program *programa de rehabilitación.*

diversity of citizenship *partes de jurisdicciones diferentes.*

divestiture (antitrust) n. *desprendimiento o renuncia de bienes por mandato judicial.*

dividend n. *dividendo.*

cash dividend *dividendo en efectivo.*

cumulative dividend *dividendo acumulativo.*

dividend income *ingreso proveniente de dividendos.*

dividend yield *rendimiento de los dividendos.*

preferred dividend *dividendo preferente.*

share dividend *dividendo en acciones.*

Rel: distributions, *distribuciones de utilidades o capital;* earnings, *ganancias, utilidades.*

divorce n. *divorcio.* **to divorce** v. *divorciar.* **divorcé** *divorciado.* **divorcée** *divorciada.*

– Syn. marital dissolution. dissolution of marriage *disolución de matrimonio.*

Cf: **divorce • dissolution of marriage.** Both of these terms are synonymous and mean the ending of the marital relationship. Dissolution of marriage is a term brought back by the introduction of the no-fault divorce. It is considered broader than divorce since it includes both divorce proper and annulment of marriage. From another perspective, divorce is said to focus on the parties to the marriage while dissolution underlines the marriage bond itself.

divorce by consent *divorcio por mutuo consentimiento.*

divorce decree *sentencia de divorcio.*

foreign divorce *divorcio de otra jurisdicción, divorcio extranjero.*

grounds for divorce *causales de divorcio, causa legal (aducida en un procedimiento de divorcio).*

no-fault divorce *divorcio sin determinación de culpa, divorcio sin causa.*

Rel: alimony, *alimentos (entre cónyuges);* separation, *separación.*

Glossary: child support, *alimentos, pensión alimenticia para un menor;* desertion, *abandono;* irreconcilable differences, *diferencias irreconciliables;* irretrievable breakdown, *rompimiento irreparable, rompimiento matrimonial definitivo;* legal separation, *separación legal;* living apart, *vivir separadamente;* marital assets, *bienes del matrimonio;* mental cruelty, *crueldad mental;* reconciliation, *reconciliación;* separate property, *separación de bienes;* visitation, *derecho de visita.*

See: separation.

Ref: (UK) Deacock v Deacock [1958]2 All E.R. 633 at 635; (US) Johnson v. Davis, 198 S.W.2d 129, 130.

DNA (deoxyribonucleic acid)(init.) *ADN (ácido desoxirribonucleico).*

DNA profiling *identificación de sospechosos mediante el uso de ADN.*

DNA fingerprint *identificación genética, dactilografía genética.* – Syn. genetic fingerprint.

DNA pattern *configuración del ADN.*

Glossary: acid phosphatase, *fosfatasa ácida;* adenine, *adenina;* adenosine deaminase, *adenosina deaminasa;* adenylate kinase, *adenilatokinasa;* agar, *agar;* agarose, *con agar, agarosa;* allele, *alelo;* allelomorph, *alelomorfo;* antigen, *antígeno;* bands, *cintas;* base pair, *par de base;* bases, *bases;* cell fusion, *fusión de células;* chromosome, *cromosoma;* cluster, *agrupación repetitiva;* cytosine, *citosina;* electrophoresis, *electroforesis;* endonuclease, *endonucleasa;* enzyme, *enzima;* eukaryote, *célula eucariota;* exonuclease, *exonucleasa;* extraction, *extracción;* gel, *solución coloidal, gel;* gene, *gene;* gene frequency, *frecuencia genética;* genetic code, *código genético;* guanosine, *guanosina;* interpolation, *interpolación;* karyotype, *cariotipo;* ligase, *ligasa;* loci, *lugares;* locus, *lugar o punto;* marker, *marcador;* nucleotides, *nucleótidos;* polymorphic, *polimórficos;* probes, *tientas, sondas;* ribosomes, *ribosomas;* smear, *frotis;* thymidylic acid, *ácido timidílico.*

docket[1] (record) n. *registro (resumido) de las actuaciones en autos.*

• A summary of all the proceedings in a case, usually recorded by the judge or the court clerk. – Syn. judicial record.

docket number *número del registro de anotaciones,* [fe]*número de expediente.*

docket[2](calendar) n. [fe]*lista de casos para*

acuerdo, lista de casos.
• A list of cases set for disposition or review by a court.
trial docket *lista de casos listos para proceder en juicio.*

document n. *documento.* **document** v. *documentar.* **documentary** adj. *documental.*
document of title *título translativo de dominio.*
documentary draft *letra de cambio documentada.*
documentary evidence *prueba documental.*
export documents *documentos de exportación.*
original document *documento original.*
public document *documento público.*
Rel: certificate, *certificado;* instrument, *instrumento.*
document under seal *documento sellado.*
A promise without consideration "must be in a particular documentary form. Originally the document had to be given 'under seal', but the need for actual wax was dropped long ago: it was enough if the document bore the letters 'LS' (*loco sigilli*), the word 'seal', or even a red sticker put there by the promisor or his attorney. Sealing has now been abolished in England and replaced by the 'deed', a document in writing which is signed by the promisor with a declaration that it is intended as a 'deed', his signature being witnessed and the witnesses signing as such. Most of the states of the United States have abolished the formality of documents under seal by legislation." (Zweigert & Kotz, 373)
Rel: deed, *documento o instrumento que cumple con las formalidades legales.*

doing business as *operando mercantilmente como, en negocios bajo el nombre de ,* [le]*haciendo negocios como.* – Abbr. d.b.a.

domestic[1] (indigenous) adj. *nacional.*
domestic corporation *sociedad local, sociedad del estado correspondiente* (US).
domestic jurisdiction *jurisdicción local.*

domestic[2] (household) adj. *doméstico.*
domestic worker *trabajador doméstico.*
live-in domestic worker *trabajador doméstico que vive en el lugar de trabajo.*

domestic relations law *derecho de relaciones familiares.*
• The body of law dealing with marriage, divorce, adoption, child custody and support, paternity and other family matters. – Syn. family law.
Rel: adoption, *adopción;* custody, *custodia;* paternity, *paternidad;* support, *alimentos.*

domestic violence *violencia doméstica, violencia familiar, violencia intrafamiliar.*
• Violence between members of the same household.
Rel: abusive husband, *esposo abusivo o abusador;* abusive relationship, *relación en la que hay abuso;* battered child syndrome, *síndrome del niño golpeado;* battered woman, *mujer golpeada;* child abuse, *maltrato de menores, abuso de menores;* domestic battery, *lesiones en contra de un miembro de la familia;* order of protection, *orden de protección;* physical abuse, *abuso físico.*

domicile n. *domicilio.*
• The place where an individual has a permanent home or a principal establishment, to where, whenever that person is absent, he or she has the intention of returning. – Syn. permanent abode.
"Despite rigorous efforts to keep domicile separate from **residence** ..., domicile and residence are frequently equated. **Legal residence** and permanent residence are synonymous of domicile." (Mellinkoff's Dict., 180)
commercial domicile *domicilio comercial.*
corporate domicile *domicilio social.*
elected domicile *domicilio convencional, domicilio estipulado en una cláusula jurisdiccional.*
matrimonial domicile *domicilio matrimonial o conyugal.*
Rel: address, *dirección;* habitancy, *habitación;* home, *hogar.*
See: residence.

donatio (lat.) n. *donatio, donación.* **donator** n. *donador.* **donatarius** *donatario.* – Syn. gift, *donación.*
donatio inter vivos *donación inter vivos.*
donatio mortis causa *donación mortis causa.*
Rel: animus donandi (lat.), *animus donandi, intención de donar.*

donation n. *donación.* **donor** *donante.* **donee** n. *donatario, recipiente, beneficiario.*
Cf: **gift • donation • gratuitous promise.** Gift and donation are sometimes used synonymously, but donation, derived from Latin, is usually considered a charitable gift rather than a plain gift. While gift and donation refer to a transfer of property without consideration, a gratuitous promise refers to a promise, that is

double jeopardy

a manifestation of intention to act or not to act creating a commitment with another, also without consideration.

double jeopardy [de]*estar sujeto doblemente al riesgo de una misma decisión judicial, doble exposición* (PR).
• A second prosecution or punishment for the same offense.
Rel: Fifth Amendment (US), *Quinta Enmienda (constitucional).*

double taxation *doble imposición tributaria.*

doubt n. *duda.* **doubt** v. *dudar.*

finding of guilt beyond a reasonable doubt *encontrar al acusado culpable fuera de toda duda razonable.*

dowry n. *dote.* **dower** n. *bienes dotales.*
Rel: curtesy, *derecho hereditario del marido sobre los bienes de su esposa.*

draft[1] MIL.LAW n. *conscripción militar obligatoria.*
• Mandatory military enlistment in the armed forces.

draft[2] NEG. INSTR n. *giro, letra de cambio.* **maker or drawer** n. *girador.* **drawee** n. *girado.* **payee** n. *tenedor, portador, beneficiario.* **bearer** n. *portador.*
• An unconditional order in writing issued by the drawer directing the drawee to pay a specified sum of money to a third person or payee or to bearer. – Syn. bill of exchange, *letra de cambio.*

bank draft *giro bancario.*

sight draft *giro a la vista.* – Syn. demand draft.

time draft *giro a día fijo.*

draft[3] (preliminary) n. *borrador, anteproyecto.*
• A preliminary version of a writing, document or idea.

final draft *último borrador, borrador final.*

first draft *primer borrador, primer antepro-yeto.*

drinking in the public way *beber alcohol en la vía pública.*
Rel: alcohol, *alcohol.*

drive-by-shooting (pop.)(crime) *disparar desde un vehículo en marcha.*

driver's license TRAFFIC *licencia de conductor, cartera dactilar* (Cu), *pase* (Co), *permiso de conducción* (Sp). **driver** n. *conductor, chofer.*

driving without a license *conducir sin licencia.*

duplicate driver's license *duplicado de la licencia.*

out-of-state driver's license *licencia de conductor expedida fuera del estado.*

probationary driver's license *licencia condicional.*

renewed driver's license *licencia renovada.*

revoked driver's license *licencia revocada.*

suspended driver's license *licencia suspendida.*
Rel: driving permit, *permiso para conducir.*

driving under the influence (DUI) *manejar o conducir bajo los efectos del alcohol u otras drogas, manejar o conducir en estado de ebrie-dad, manejar o conducir* bajo *la influencia del alcohol u otras drogas.* – Syn. driving while in-toxicated (DWI), *manejar o conducir en estado de intoxicación.* driving while ability-impaired (DWAI), *manejar o conducir con capacidad reducida.* drunken driving (RU). operating a motor vehicle while intoxicated (OMVI), *ope-rar un vehículo motorizado estando intoxicado.* operating under the influence (OUI), *manejar o conducir bajo la influencia de drogas o alcohol.*
Rel: breathalyzer test, *prueba del analizador de aliento;* erratic driving, *conducir erráticamente;* impaired driving, *inhabilitado para conducir, no estar en condición de conducir;* sobriety tests, *pruebas de sobriedad;* statutory summary suspension, *suspensión summaria por ministe-rio de ley (del derecho de conducir), suspen-sión automática por disposición o ministerio de ley.*

drug n. *droga.*

drug abuse *uso excesivo de drogas, uso abusivo de drogas.*

drug addict *drogadicto, toxicómano, vicioso.*

drug overdose *sobredosis.* – Abbr. OD.

drug withdrawal *crisis de abstinencia o privación del consumo de drogas, síntomas de abstinencia de drogas, síndrome de abstinencia de drogas.*

Glossary: aerosols, *aerosoles;* alcohol, *alcohol;* amphetamines, *anfetaminas;* analgesics, *ana-lgésicos;* barbiturates, *barbitúricos;* benzedrine, *bencedrina;* chloroform, *cloroformo;* cocaine, *cocaina;* codeine, *codeina;* depressants, *depre-sivos;* DMT, *DMT;* DOM, *DOM;* dope, *droga;* downers, *depresivos;* gasoline, *gasolina;* glue, *cemento, pegamento;* hallucinogens, *halicinó-genos;* hashish, *hashish;* heroin, *heroina;* inha-lants, *inhalantes;* lacquer, *lacas;* LSD, *LSD;* marijuana, *mariguana;* MDA, *MDA;* mescaline, *mescalina;* methadone, *metadona;* morphine, *morfina;* nail polish remover, *acetona;* narcotics, *narcóticos;* opiates, *opiato;* PCP, *PCP;* peyote, *peyote;* psilocybin, *psilocibina, psilocybina;*

psychotropics, *psicotrópicos;* sedatives, *sedativos;* sleeping pills, *píldoras para dormir;* stimulants, *estimulantes;* thinner, [borr;]*thiner;* tranquilizer, *tranquilizante;* valium, *valium;* varnish, *barniz.*

drug addiction *drogadicción.*

Rel: acid freak, *adicto a LSD;* cokehead, *cocacolo, coco;* cube head, *adicto a LSD;* doper, *mariguano, vicioso;* glass eyes, *adicto;* hophead, *adicto, vicioso;* hype, *adicto;* junkie, *adicto, vicioso;* pill freak, *píldoro;* pothead, *mariguano;* sleep walker, *adicto a la heroína;* speed freak, *adicto a anfetaminas;* stoned, *tronado, en onda;* user, *adicto;* weed head, *mariguano.*

drug dealer *traficante de drogas.*

Rel: courier, *mula, camello, cruzador;* drug pusher, *que induce al consumo de las drogas;* mule, *mula;* peddler, *vendedor;* runner, *caballo;* smuggler, *contrabandista.*

drug paraphernalia *aditamentos o implementos para el uso de drogas.*

Rel: balance, *balanza, báscula;* blades, *navajas;* eyedropper, *gotero;* hype kit, *equipo hipodérmico, estuche;* layout or outfit, *equipo para inyectarse, estuche;* nail, *punta;* needle, *aguja;* pipe, *pipa;* spike, *hierro;* syringe, *jeringa;* triple beam scale, *báscula de astil triple.*

drug taking *forma de tomar la droga.*

Rel: blow a stick, *fumar mariguana;* blow snow, *aspirar cocaína;* joy pop, *inyección;* skinning, *inyectarse;* smoke, *fumar;* sniff, *inhalar;* snort, *aspirar por la nariz;* to bang, *picarse;* to fix, *picarse, pincharse;* to get high, *ponerse pacheco, (estar) moto, (estar) encandilado;* to inject, *inyectarse;* to jab, *picarse, clavarse;* to shoot, *picarse.*

drug tests *análisis de drogas.*

Rel: chemical color test, *análisis químico de color;* gas test, *análisis de gas;* infrared spectroscopy test, *análisis de espectroscopia infrarroja.*

drunk adj,n. *borracho.* – Syn. alcoholic, *alcohólico.* loaded (slg.), *borracho, pedo, marrano.* wasted (slg.), *borracho, marrano, mamado.*

drunkard n. *borracho.* **drunkenness** n. *embriaguez.* – Syn. alcoholic, *alcohólico.*

Rel: hangover, *resaca, cruda* (Mx), *ratón* (Ve), *guayabo* (Co).

due care *atención y cuidado necesario.*

due process of law *debido proceso legal, procedimiento legal debidamente establecido, debido procedimiento de ley* (PR), *garantía de audiencia.*

• Legal concept representing the normal and regular administration of law.

"Due process of law is founded on the principle that government may not act arbitrarily or capriciously. It means that government may only act in ways established by law and under such limitations as the law imposes to protect individual rights." (Renstrom, 15)

☛ Due process of law is a principle which has been adopted by practically all constitutions of Hispanic countries, it is also often referred to as *principio de legalidad* or *garantía o derecho de audiencia.*

Rel: Fifth Amendment (US), *Quinta Enmienda (constitucional).*

duel n. *duelo.* **duelist** n. *duelista.*

dumping [transpl.]*dumping, saturación ilegal* (PR).

duress n. *coacción, miedo grave* (Mx). **duressor** n. *persona que ejerce la coacción.*

• Threat or harm used to compel a person to do or refrain from doing something.

Cf: **duress • coercion • undue influence • compulsion.** All of these terms are loosely synonymous and overlapping. Written in the order of their level of intensity, duress appears as being the more forceful application of power, coercion is understood as less of a threat, but not as low as undue influence (usually considered not illegal). Compulsion, on the other hand, is considered extremely forceful threats made in the commission of a crime and it is used as a defense, especially in Canada.

duress of goods *coacción mediante la apropiación ilegal de bienes.*

duress of the person *coacción hecha contra la persona directamente.*

economic duress *coacción económica.*

moral duress *coacción moral.*

under duress *bajo coacción.*

Rel: coercion, *coerción;* undue influence, *coerción, presión o influencia.*

duty¹ (obligation) n. *deber.*

• An obligation or responsibility. A legal obligation.

contractual duty *obligación contractual.*

delegable duty *deber delegable.*

duty of due care *deber de prestar la atención y cuidados necesarios.*

duty to mitigate damages *deber de reducir los daños al mínimo.*

fiduciary duty *obligación fiduciaria.*

legal duty *deber legal, obligación.*

moral duty *deber moral, obligación moral.*

neglect of duty *abandono del deber.*
preexisting duty *deber preexistente.*
duty[2] TAX n. *impuesto, tasa de impuestos.*
• A tax imposed on things, usually upon the importation or exportation of goods.
customs duty *impuesto aduanal.*
import duty *impuesto de importación.*

EEEE

earnest money *depósito en garantía de la celebración de un contrato, adelanto* (pop.)*, arras.*
• A sum of money or other valuable item given as a formal sign of commitment by a contracting party, usually forfeited if that party defaults.
Cf: **earnest money • escrow • option.** Earnest money is given to one of the parties to a transaction, usually to the seller as a binding action by the buyer. In an escrow, a third party holds the goods or money to effect transfer; the goods or money are not given directly by buyer to seller. By owning an option to buy, on the other hand, the buyer only acquires the right to purchase, not an obligation to buy.
Rel: escrow, *depósito condicional en favor de un tercero;* option, *opción de compra.*
earnings (accounting) n. *ingresos, ganancias, utilidades.*
earnings per share *utilidades por acción.*
gross earnings *ingresos brutos.*
net earnings *ingresos netos.*
easement n. *servidumbre.*
• A grant of an interest in land that entitles a person to use land possessed by another.
– Syn. servitude, *carga.*
Cf: **easement • servitude • license.** Servitude is usually considered a generic term that includes easements, licenses and profits. Broadly defined, easement and servitude are synonymous. Easement is the common law name, while servitude is the civil law designation. Easement emphasizes the enjoyment of a benefit, while servitude emphasizes the burdening of land for the sake of that benefit. License, on the other hand, is a revocable permission to commit some act that would otherwise be unlawful.
affirmative easement *servidumbre positiva.*
apparent easement *servidumbre aparente.*
discontinuing or discontinuous easement *servidumbre discontinua.*
easement appurtenant *servidumbre de disfrute. servidumbre real* (der.Rom.).

easement by estoppel *servidumbre voluntaria y aparente.*
easement by necessity *servidumbre forzosa.*
– Syn. easement of necessity. necessary easement.
easement by prescription *servidumbre adquirida por prescripción.*
easement in gross (US) *servidumbre de uso, servidumbre personal* (der.Rom.).
easement of access *servidumbre de paso.*
equitable easement *servidumbre resultante en la división de una propiedad.*
implied easement *servidumbre legal.*
negative easement *servidumbre negativa.*
Rel: dominant estate or tenement, *predio dominante;* equitable servitude, *carga sobre un inmueble bajo el régimen de derecho-equidad;* real covenant, *obligación propter rem;* right of way, *derecho de paso;* servient estate or tenement, *predio sirviente.*
eavesdropping *interceptar conversaciones privadas ilegal y subrepticiamente.*
ejectment[1] **(ejection)** n. *desalojo de la propiedad inmueble.*
• An expulsion or ejection of a person in possession of land.
Rel: ouster, *expulsión de ocupantes legítimos.*
ejectment[2] **(action)** n. *acción reivindicatoria (de inmuebles).*
• The common law action for the recovery of possession of property and damages.
– Syn. action for the recovery of land.
Rel: eviction, *desahucio;* forcible detainer, *procedimiento judicial de desalojo,* [fe]*interdicto posesorio.*
election n. *elección.* **elected** adj. *elegido.*
electorate n. *electorado.*
elected official *funcionario público electo, funcionario electo.*
elected to office *ser electo, resultar electo.*
election board *junta electoral.*
election returns *actas de las casillas electorales.*
general election *elección general.*
primary election *elección primaria.*
electronic monitoring *custodia mediante medios electrónicos,* [borr.] *monitoreo electrónico.*
electronic surveillance *vigilancia subrepticia por medios electrónicos.*
elopement n. *fugarse (con un amante).*
emancipation n. *emancipación.*
Rel: age of majority, *mayoría de edad.*

embezzlement (crime) n. *abuso de confianza, apropiación indebida.* **embezzler** n. *desfalcador.*
• The fraudulent conversion or appropriation of property of another by a person who is in lawful possession of it. – Syn. criminal breach of trust (CA).
Cf: **embezzlement • peculation • defalcation.** Broadly synonymous, all three of these terms mean to misappropriate money or other property in one's charge. Embezzlement is the term most often used and is considered a broad enough term to include most other crimes involving a fraudulent conversion of property. Peculation refers to the embezzlement of public funds by a public official, while defalcation is mostly used to mean either the act of embezzling, the property embezzled, or the amount embezzled.
embezzlement by trustee *abuso de confianza de un administrador o fiduciario.*
Rel: being in lawful possession, *estando legalmente en posesión de, tener la tenencia;* fraudulent conversion, *apropiación fraudulenta de bienes.*
embracery (crime) n. *intento de influir o sobornar al jurado.* **embraceor** n. *sobornador.*
• An attempt to influence a jury in a form that is corrupting or illegal.
eminent domain *derecho de expropiación (que tiene el estado).*
• The right of the state or sovereign to take private property for public use. – Syn. dominium eminens (lat.).
Cf:**eminent domain • condemnation • expropriation.** Eminent domain refers to the power of the federal and local governments in the United States to convert property to public use. Exercising the power of eminent domain is referred to as condemnation or expropriation. In the United Kingdom, eminent domain is primarily a term used in international law, and expropriation is the taking by the state of private property for public purposes, normally without compensation, while compulsory purchase is the term used when compensation must be paid.
Rel: compulsory purchase (UK), *expropiación, venta forzosa;* condemnation (US), *expropiación mediante compensación;* expropriation (UK), *expropiación.*
employee stock purchase plan *plan de compra de acciones para los trabajadores o empleados.*
employment n. *empleo, trabajo.* **employ** v. *emplear.* **employer** n. *patrón.* **employee** n. *emple-*

ado.
• State of being employed. – Syn. work, *trabajo.* occupation, *ocupación.*
Cf: **employment • employment at will.** Employment is the general term used to refer to an employer-employee relationship, while employment at will is employment performed without a contract and which can be terminated at will by either party without cause.
abandonment of employment *abandono de trabajo.*
conditions of employment *condiciones de trabajo.*
contract of employment *contrato de trabajo.*
duration of employment *duración del trabajo.*
employment at will *contrato de trabajo por tiempo indeterminado, relación de trabajo por tiempo indeterminado.*
employment discrimination *discriminación en el empleo.*
full-time employment *trabajo de tiempo completo.*
gainful employment *ocupación remunerada, trabajo retribuido o lucrativo.*
seasonal employment *ocupación temporal, trabajo por temporada.*
Rel: equal opportunity, *oportunidades de empleo sin discriminación alguna;* unemployment, *desempleo.*
employment agency *agencia de empleos, agencia de contrataciones o colocaciones.*
empower v. *facultar, dar poder.*
enactment n. *promulgación.*
enacting clause *cláusula de promulgación, decreto de promulgación.*
encroachment n. *intrusión o usurpación ilegal.*
encumbrance n. *carga o gravamen.*
encumbrancer n. *titular de una carga o gravamen.*
• "A claim or liability that is attached to property or some other right, and that may lessen its value, such as a lien or mortgage." (Black's Law Dict., 8th. ed., 568) – Other spell.: incumbrance. Encumbrance is a term often construed broadly to include any right in real property other than an ownership interest, such as liens, attachments, leases, easements and other restrictions on use.
encumbrance of property *cargas o gravámenes de la propiedad.*
endorsement n. *endoso.*
See: indorsement.
enemy n. *enemigo.*

enemy alien *extranjero de un país enemigo.*

enemy belligerent *enemigo beligerante.*

public enemy *enemigo público.*

enforcement n. *ejecución, hacer cumplir.*
• To compel compliance.

enforcement of a contract *ejecución de un contrato, hacer cumplir un contrato.*

enforcement of a judgment *ejecución de una sentencia, hacer cumplir una sentencia.*
See: law enforcement.

enforcement proceeding *procedimiento de ejecución.* – Syn. execution, *ejecución.*

English law *derecho inglés.*
• That law which applies in England and Wales. The United Kingdom (UK) has three separate distinct legal systems: one operating in England and Wales, a second in Scotland, and a third in Northern Ireland.
"It is inappropriate, nonetheless, to suggest that it is English law which exists in the United States or Australia or India or South Africa, or that there is a Commonwealth law applied in the Commonwealth, or a British law of Great Britain. English law applies only in England and Wales. Great Britain, the political geographic term for England, Wales and Scotland, has no common legal system. Many English statutes are applicable in Scotland, but the Scottish private law is based primarily on the civil law derived from Roman law.... Northern Ireland and Great Britain comprise the United Kingdom, the principal geographic area to which most parliamentary expressions apply, the latter referred to as UK law. As in the case of Great Britain, the United Kingdom is a larger area than one associates with English law." (Glendon, Gordon & Carozza, 168-69)

enjoin v. *ordenar judicialmente una acción o abstención.*
See: injunction.

enter an appearance *comparecer.*

enter into an agreement *celebrar un convenio o contrato.*

entitled v. *tener derecho.*

entitlement n. *derecho, legitimación.*

entrapment n. *incitación a la comisión de un delito por personal policíaco, entrampamiento* (PR). **entrap** v. *incitar a la comisión de un delito, entrampar* (PR).
• The instigation or inducement of a person to commit a crime by a law-enforcement officer.

entry[1] (record) *registro, asiento.*

• A setting down in writing, making or entering a record.

entry in the regular course of business *asiento contable en el curso normal de los negocios.*

entry of judgment *registro de una sentencia.*

entry[2] (entrance) *entrada, entrar.*
• The act of entering real property.

forcible entry and detainer *procedimiento judicial de desalojo,* [ef]*interdicto posesorio.*

right of entry *derecho de paso.*

surreptitious entry *entrar subrepticiamente.*

unlawful entry *entrar ilegalmente a un inmueble.* – Syn. illegal entry.

environmental law *derecho ambiental.*
"What we call environmental law is a complex combination of common law, legislation, and international agreements. After centuries of wrestling with environmental conflicts, the common law has now been eclipsed by an explosion of environmental statutes." (Percival & Alevizatos, 205)
Rel: hazardous waste, *deshechos peligrosos;* motor vehicle emission standards, *reglas de la emisión de gases de combustión de los vehículos de motor;* pollution, *contaminación;* riparian rights, *derechos de los propietarios ribereños, derechos de los propietarios de las márgenes de un río;* toxic substances, *sustancias tóxicas.*
See: *medio ambiente.*

equal protection of the laws *principio de igualdad jurídica, igual protección de la ley* (PR). – Syn. equality before the law (CA).

equitable action [de]*acción basada en el régimen de derecho-equidad.*

equitable estoppel *excepción o impedimento basado en declaraciones o acciones anteriores (que contradicen lo alegado).*

equitable interest in land [de]*derecho de propiedad sobre un inmueble basado en el régimen de derecho-equidad.*

equitable remedies [de]*remedios basados en el régimen de derecho-equidad,* [de]*medios de defensa basados en el régimen de derecho-equidad.*
Specific types: accounting, *rendición de cuentas;* discovery, *requerimiento y producción de pruebas;* injunction, *interdicto;* interpleader, *tercería;* partition, *partición, división;* removing cloud on title, *subsanar el defecto o irregularidad de un título de propiedad de inmuebles;* rescission, *rescisión;* specific performance, *cumplimiento forzado de la obligación con-*

tractual (o convencional).

Rel: equitable relief, *tutela jurídica o protección otorgada a través del régimen de derecho-equidad.*

equitable right [de]*derecho bajo el régimen de derecho-equidad.*

equitable servitude [de]*carga de un inmueble basada en el régimen de derecho-equidad.*

• Right enforceable in equity regarding the use or restriction of the use of land.

Cf: **equitable servitude • equitable easement.** Equitable servitude is considered a contractual right, while an easement is an interest in land. As such, it follows that unlike prescriptive easement, "there is no prescriptive equitable servitude; prescription involves no promise." (Mellinkoff's Dict., 188)

equity[1] **(body of law)** n. *derecho-equidad,* [de]*régimen de la equidad,* [borr.]*equity.* **equitable** adj. *basado en el régimen de derecho-equidad.*

• Separate body of law developed in England to ameliorate the strictness of the common law rules and practices.

Even though equity and common law were merged during the last century in most jurisdictions, equity jurisprudence and equitable doctrines are still being applied today.

↪ Although both equity and *equidad* refer broadly to the idea of fairness and consequently the application of standards of fairness (see next entry), each term has also developed an important legal concrete meaning that is as different in description as it is in legal function. Equity describes a legal system differentiated from the common law. *Equidad,* in contrast, is the application by the judge of the principle of fairness to an individual case pursuant to the judge's discretionary power as a decision-maker. Equity provides legal avenues to achieve results that are impractical or not available through the common law principles; *equidad,* in turn, gives a judge an element of flexibility when reaching a decision, when there is no law applicable to the case (legal gap), to direct it towards a just result.

equity action *acción basada en el régimen de derecho-equidad.*

equity acts in personam not in rem (max.) *la equidad actúa en personam.*

equity aids the vigilant not one who sleeps on his rights (max.) *la equidad asiste al diligente no a aquél que desatiende sus derechos.*

equity follows the law (max.) *la equidad está subordinada a la ley.*

equity jurisdiction *jurisdicción en equidad.*

equity regards substance rather than form (max.) *la equidad considera más el fondo que la forma.*

equity will not suffer a wrong without a remedy (max.) *la equidad no tolera un agravio sin su reparación.*

he who comes into equity must come with clean hands (max.) *aquél que aprovecha el derecho de equidad lo debe hacer con las manos limpias, doctrina de la conciencia pura o tranquila.*

he who seeks equity must do equity (max.) *aquél que demanda equidad debe actuar en equidad.*

suit in equity *juicio bajo el régimen de derecho-equidad.*

Comment: "To counter the severity of the writ system and provide relief other than money damages, the king and later his Chancellor, the 'keeper of the king's conscience,' accepted petitions for equitable relief. Heard in an inquisitorial fashion modeled in canon and Roman law, these equitable proceedings focused on avoiding the strictures of common law. It was successful, and a formal Court of Chancery soon assumed jurisdiction of pleas in equity. If the addition of such equitable concepts as injunctive relief and specific performance to supplement the common law was equity's paramount general contribution, the origin of the trust was its most important conceptual addition." (Glendon, Gordon & Carozza, 158-59)

equity[2] **(justice)** n. *equidad.*

• The application of standards of fairness and justice to particular circumstances, as contrasted with the direct application of a rule of law that may not provide for such application. "In the general juristic sense, equity means the power to meet the moral standards of justice in a particular case by a tribunal having discretion to mitigate the rigidity of the application of strict rules of law so as to adapt the relief to the circumstances of the particular case." (McClintock, 1)

equity[3] **(share of ownership)** *capital* ‖ *plusvalía.*

• A share or part in the stock capital of a publicly traded company; an interest in property defined as the value found after any amounts owed have been deducted from its fair market price.

equity financing *financiamiento mediante la emisión de acciones o capital.*

equity of partners *partes sociales de los socios.*

equity shares *acciones del capital social, partes sociales del capital.*

property equity *plusvalía de una propiedad.*

equity of redemption *rescate de un bien hipotecado, extinción de una hipoteca por pago durante el procedimiento de remate.*

error¹ (wrong perception) n. *error.*

• A departure from objective reality.

error in corpore *error en el objeto.*

error in negotio *error en el tipo de contrato.*

error² PROCEDURE n. *error del procedimiento, error en materia procesal.*

• A mistake made by a court in a judgment, opinion or order.

clerical error *error tipográfico o secretarial, error clerical* (PR).

error in fact *error de hecho.*

error in law *error de derecho.*

fundamental error *error grave.* – Syn. plain error.

harmless error *error enmendable, error excusable.* – Syn. technical error.

manifest error *error grave e indiscutible.*

reversible error *error apelable.* – Syn. harmful error. fatal error. prejudicial error.

Rel: writ of error, *auto de admisión de la apelación basada en error.*

See: mistake.

escape n. *fuga, evasión de presos* (Mx), *escape* (pop.). **escapee** n. *fugitivo.* – Syn. evasion, *evasión.* flight, *escape, fuga.* getaway, *huída, escape.*

Rel: abscond, *evadirse de la justicia;* flee, *huir;* manhunt, *persecución de un delincuente o reo.*

escape clause *cláusula de excepción, cláusula de escape.*

escrow n. *depósito condicional en favor de un tercero.*

• A deposit or delivery of the necessary writings, property or money with a third party until the occurrence of a condition or a deadline in accordance with the instructions set forth.

close of escrow (C.O.E.) *ejecución o cierre del depósito condicional.*

escrow instructions *condiciones del depósito condicional.*

escrow officer *depositario.* – Syn. escrowee.

in escrow or in an escrow account *en depósito sujeto a condición resolutoria.*

See: earnest money.

espionage n. *espionaje.*

estate¹ (ownership) n. *patrimonio.*

• All that a person or entity owns, including both real and personal property.

bankruptcy estate *patrimonio del quebrado.*

deceased's estate *patrimonio del decujus.*

marital estate *patrimonio marital.*

estate² SUCCESSION n. *patrimonio hereditario, patrimonio sucesorio.*

• The aggregate of all property a person leaves after death. – Syn. inheritance, *herencia.* patrimony, *patrimonio.*

administration of an estate *administración de una sucesión.*

estate planning *planeación sucesoria.*

estate tax *impuesto sucesorio o hereditario, impuesto sobre herencias.*

settling an estate *administración, distribución y liquidación de una sucesión.*

Rel: administrator, *administrador judicial de una sucesión;* distribution, *reparto de bienes;* executor, *albacea.*

Comment: "Broadly speaking, such an estate [of a deceased person] is deemed to exist only from the death of the decedent until it is finally wound up by an order of the court having jurisdiction of it. After the property of the decedent's estate has been paid out or otherwise distributed to those entitled thereto in accordance with the court's orders, and thereupon the estate has been declared closed, it can no longer be said to exist." (Ballentine's Law Dict., 419)

See: succession¹.

estate³ PROP.LAW n. *derecho de propiedad (que se tiene) sobre un bien inmueble,* [borr.]*estate.*

• "The degree, quantity, nature and extent of interest which a person has in real property." (28 Am. Jur. 2d Estate §1)

"Under common law, a physical person or an entity with legal personality is not the owner of a piece of land, but rather is the owner of an estate. The estate is a purely conceptual notion, an abstraction introduced between a person and the land; the person possesses the estate, which is an interest in land." (Clark, 311) Especially in conveyances, estate is used sometimes in an imprecise form to mean property, right, title or interest.

Cf: **estate • tenancy.** The clear differentiation between the terms estate and tenancy amounts to the distinction between "the property and holding it." (Mellinkoff's Dict., 209) When estate is referred to as an interest in real property, however, this differentiation blurs and both estate and tenancy are synonymous and often used interchangeably. In some instances, however, estate is preferred to tenancy and vice versa.

estate by the entirety [fe]*sociedad conyugal, comunidad de los bienes conyugales (con derecho de acrecer).* – Syn. tenancy by the entirety.

estate for life *propiedad perpetua.* [fe]*usufructo vitalicio.* – Syn. life estate. life tenancy.

estate in fee simple [de]*derecho de dominio pleno en forma absoluta sobre un inmueble, derecho absoluto (de propiedad),* [fe]*nuda propiedad,* [borr.]*fee simple.*

estate in severalty *derechos sobre un inmueble que tiene una persona individualmente (a diferencia de varias en copropiedad).*

estate in remainder [le]*derechos residuales (de propiedad),* [de]*derechos de propiedad que se adquieren al terminar los derechos de otro (sobre la misma propiedad).* – Syn. remainder.

estate tail [de]*derecho de dominio pleno sobre un inmueble heredable solamente a ciertos descendientes (señalados por el otorgante).* – Syn. fee tail. entailed estate.

freehold estate [de]*dominio pleno sobre un inmueble —ya en forma absoluta, ya limitando la transmisión a ciertos herederos, ya determinando que su duración sea igual a la de la vida del recipiente.* || *clase de derechos de propiedad de dominio pleno sobre inmuebles.* – Syn. freehold.

future estate [de]*derecho futuro sobre un bien inmueble.* – Syn. future interest.

leasehold estate [de]*derecho de tenencia u ocupación de un inmueble (bajo arrendamiento)* || [de]*clase de derechos posesorios sobre un inmueble.* – Syn. leasehold.

vested estate *derecho adquirido sobre un inmueble.*

Rel: ownership, *propiedad;* tenancy, *tenencia.*
Ref: (CA) Thompson v Jockney (1912) 8 D.L.R. 776 (Man, KBD); (UK) 39(2) Halsbury's Laws para 2; (US) Boyd v. Sibold, 109 P.2d 535, 539, 7 Wash.2d 279.

estate[4] (land) n. *una porción o lote de tierra o terreno.*

estoppel n. [de]*excepción o impedimento basado en las consecuencias jurídicas de actos o declaraciones anteriores,* [interp.]*defensa, excepción.*
• The principle that precludes a party from alleging or proving a fact in contradiction to what has been established by the party's own deeds or representations or by that of judicial or legislative officers.

equitable estoppel [de]*excepción o impedimento basado en declaraciones o acciones anteriores (que contradicen lo alegado).*

estoppel by deed [de]*excepción o impedimento basado en una escritura (que contradice lo alegado).*

estoppel by judgment [de]*excepción o impedimento basado en una sentencia (que contradice lo alegado).*

estoppel by record [de]*excepción o impedimento basado en un registro (que contradice lo alegado).*

promissory estoppel [de]*excepción o impedimento basado en una declaración unilateral (que contradice lo alegado).*

estrangement n. *separación, alejamiento.*

et al.(lat.) *et al., y otros.* And others.

ethnic cleansing *eliminación de minorías étnicas.*

ethnocentrism n. *etnocentrismo.*

European Union (EU) *Unión Europea.*
• Organization pursuing the process of economic and eventual political integration among European nations. – Syn. European Common Market, *Mercado Común Europeo.* European Communities (EC), *Comunidades Europeas.* Rel: Commission, *Comisión;* Council of Ministers, *Consejo de Ministros;* Court of First Instance, *Corte de primera instancia;* European Atomic Energy Community (Euratom), *Comunidad Europea de Energía Atómica* (Euratom); European Coal and Steel Community (ECSC), *Comunidad Europea del Carbón y del Acero;* European Court of Justice, *Corte Europea de Justicia;* European Economic Community (EEC), *Comunidad Económica Europea;* European Parliament, *Parlamento Europeo.* See: *derecho comunitario.*

euthanasia n. *eutanasia.*
• Painlessly terminating life of a person or animal. – Syn. mercy killing.

evasion n. *evasión.*
tax evasion *evasión de impuestos.*

eviction n. *desahucio, desalojo.*
• Depriving a person of possession of land or rental property.
Cf: **eviction ● ejectment at common law.**
Eviction is the act of depriving a person of the possession of real property either by reentry or by legal process. Ejectment at common law, on the other hand, was the legal term used for the court action seeking to dispossess tenants at common law.

constructive eviction *desalojo de hecho, desalojo mediante actos que impiden el uso*

evidence

habitable de una vivienda.
eviction notice *notificación de desahucio.*
eviction proceedings *juicio de desahucio.*
retaliatory eviction *desalojo a título de venganza.*
unlawful eviction *desalojo ilegal.* – Syn. forcible entry and detainer. summary process. summary ejectment. unlawful detainer.
Rel: lease, *arrendamiento.*

evidence¹ (proof) n. *prueba, medios de prueba, evidencia* (PR). **evidence** v. *probar.*
• "The means whereby a fact in controversy may be proved or disproved." (2 Wharton's Criminal Evidence, §1 at 2) – Syn. demonstration, *demostración.* proof, *prueba.*
Cf: **evidence • proof.** Evidence includes any means by which an alleged fact can be established or disproved. To offer proof is to persuade the fact finder to accept the fact as true. Proof is an ambiguous term usually referring to both evidence and the resulting belief.
↳ Evidence is regarded as an important part of the law in the common law tradition, while *pruebas* is a less important subject in the civil law system. Historically, evidence developed as a set of rules designed to allow illiterate jurors to make fair and reasonable decisions; for that reason, evidence became a more detailed and technical subject. *Pruebas*, in contrast, were seldom used in oral suits before a jury and, as a result, remained a set of rules broad in scope and relatively undeveloped. While hearsay rules, objections, exclusionary rules and examination are weighty legal concepts in both theory and practice in common law countries. These same terms are concepts hardly identifiable as relevant issues, often falling under the judge's discretionary powers, in civil law countries.
admissible evidence *pruebas admisibles.*
best evidence *prueba plena.*
character evidence *prueba de carácter moral, evidencia de carácter* (PR).
circumstantial evidence *pruebas circunstanciales.* – Syn. indirect evidence.
clear and convincing evidence *prueba clara y convincente.*
conclusive evidence *prueba conclusiva.*
conflicting evidence *pruebas contradictorias.*
corroborating evidence *pruebas corroborativas.*
demonstrative evidence *pruebas tangibles.* – Syn. real evidence.

direct evidence *prueba directa.* – Syn. positive evidence.
documentary evidence *prueba documental.*
evidence contamination *contaminación de la prueba.*
evidence rules *reglas en materia probatoria.*
evidence sufficient to support a finding *pruebas suficientes para fincar o fundamentar una conclusión.*
exclusion of evidence *exclusión de pruebas.*
exculpatory evidence *pruebas exculpatorias.*
expert evidence *pruebas periciales.* – Syn. expert testimony.
hearsay evidence *testimonio de lo dicho por un tercero, prueba de referencia* (PR). – Syn. hearsay.
illegally obtained evidence *pruebas obtenidas ilegalmente.*
in evidence *como consta en autos.*
incompetent evidence *pruebas inadmisibles.* – Syn. inadmissible evidence.
incriminating evidence *pruebas incriminatorias o incriminantes.*
inculpatory evidence *pruebas que establecen culpabilidad.*
insufficient evidence *pruebas insuficientes.*
irrelevant evidence *pruebas irrelevantes.*
newly discovered evidence *pruebas sobrevinientes.*
offer in evidence *presentar como prueba, ofrecer como prueba.*
preponderance of the evidence *por mayoría de pruebas, preponderancia de la prueba* (PR).
presumptive evidence *presunciones.*
rebuttal evidence *pruebas que contradicen lo asentado o probado.*
suppression of evidence *deshechamiento de las pruebas, supresión de evidencia* (PR).
tainted evidence *prueba contaminada.*
weight of the evidence *carga de la prueba, peso de la prueba* (PR).
withholding of evidence *supresión de pruebas.*
Rel: physical evidence, *pruebas materiales;* presumption, *presunción;* testimony, *prueba testimonial.*
Ref: (CA) R. v. Schwartz (1988), 55 D.L.R. (4th) 1 at 26; Rex v Whittake [1924] 3 D.L.R. 63 (Alta. SC); (UK) 17 Halsbury's Laws para 1; (US) Bednarik v. Bednarik, 16 A.2d 80, 89, 18 N.J.Misc. 633.

evidence² (body of law) *derecho probatorio* (PR).
• Body of law which refers to the rules controlling what evidence is admissible and what value is to be attached to it. – Syn. law of evidence.

evidentiary facts *hechos probatorios que son admisibles* || *hechos secundarios necesarios para probar los hechos principales.*
• Evidentiary facts are facts necessary to prove the essential or ultimate fact.

ex aequo et bono INTL.LAW **(lat.)** *ex aequo et bono, conforme a la equidad.* According to what is equitable and good.

ex officio (lat.) *ex oficio, de oficio.* From office, by virtue of the office.

ex parte (lat.) *ex parte, de una parte.* From the part.
• At the instance of one side only.

ex parte motion *pedimento o promoción ex parte, pedimento de una de las partes.*

ex post facto (lat.) *ex post facto, después del hecho.* After the fact.

examination[1] **(interrogation)** n. *interrogatorio (bajo juramento o protesta). [fe]examen testimonial, examen oral, desahogo de la prueba testimonial.*
• Questioning of a person under oath or affirmation. – Syn. interrogation, *interrogatorio.*
cross-examination *repreguntar, interrogatorio del testigo por la parte contraria, contrainterrogatorio* (PR).
direct examination *interrogatorio inicial del testigo (por la parte que lo propuso), interrogatorio directo* (PR). – Syn. examination-in-chief.
redirect examination *interrogatorio de seguimiento al interrogatorio inicial, interrogatorio re-directo* (PR).
Rel: deposition, *testimonio extrajudicial*; impeachment of a witness, *tacha de testigo*; refreshing recollection, *ayudar a recordar, refrescar memoria* (PR); testimony, *testimonio.*

examination[2] **(inspection)** *investigación, examen.*
examination of books *exámen de los libros.*
Rel: inspection, *inspección.*

exception n. *excepción.*
exception to a ruling *inconformarse o impugnar una resolución.*
statutory exception *exclusión o excepción introducida en una ley.*

excessive bail *fianza excesiva.*

excessive punishment *castigo excesivo.*

exchange n. *permuta, intercambio o cambio (de bienes).*
• To give goods or services and, in return, to get goods or services of equal value. – Syn. barter, *trueque.* permutation, *permuta.*

Cf: **exchange • sale • barter.** Exchange and barter are synonymous, the former meaning to give goods or services in return for goods or services of equal value, the latter usually stressing the absence of money. Sale, in contrast, involves a transfer of goods or services in return for money.
like-kind exchange *permuta o trueque de bienes similares.*
owelty of an exchange *cantidad de dinero pagada para completar la equivalencia de una permuta o trueque, pago de la diferencia de un trueque.*

exchange controls *control de cambios.*

exchange rate *tipo de cambio.*

excise tax *impuestos interiores, impuestos indirectos.*
• A tax payable on certain goods or on an occupation or activity. It has been extended to include most internal revenue tax, excluding income and property taxes.

excited utterance *declaración hecha durante la emoción del evento, declaraciones espontáneas por excitación* (PR).
• A statement about an event made under the excitement and emotion of such an occurrence. It is an exception of the hearsay rule.

exclusionary rule *inadmisibilidad o improcedencia de pruebas obtenidas en forma ilegal.*
• The rule that evidence illegally obtained cannot be used at trial.
The exclusion of evidence illegally obtained is a rule well established in the United States because of its constitutional origins, but applied with variance or replaced in other common law countries. England, for example, allows illegally obtained evidence to be used if relevant to the case, and Australia takes into consideration questions of "public policy," while Canada has developed the so called "Canadian duty" rule.

↤ Civil law systems have not developed well defined rules regarding admission of illegally obtained evidence. In most cases admission is granted, since both evidence and any alleged surrounding circumstances are to be reviewed and evaluated by a professional judge, who is likely to exclude illegal or inappropriate proof in reaching a decision. This position is opposite from the detailed rules relating to exclusion of illegally obtained evidence in common law systems, where a lay jury is presented with carefully selected and weighed evidence in an excuse

attempt to simplify its task of reaching a verdict.
Rel: exclusion hearing, *audiencia del incidente de la inadmisibilidad o improcedencia de pruebas,* [le]*audiencia de exclusión de pruebas;* exclusion of evidence, *declaración de la improcedencia de pruebas,* [le]*exclusión de pruebas;* fruit of the poisonous tree, *inadmisibilidad de pruebas obtenidas en registros, detenciones o confesiones ilegales.*
Ref: (AU) Bunning v. Cross (1978), 141 C.L.R. 54; (CA) R. v. Collins (1987), 1 S.C.R. 265; (UK) PACE, Sec 78; (US) Mapp v. Ohio, 367 U.S. 643, 81 SCt 1684, 6 L.Ed.2d 1081.

excuse n. *excluyente de responsabilidad (penal), eximentes.*
Traditional excuses are: duress, entrapment, infancy, insanity and involuntary intoxication. – Syn. legal excuse.

execution¹ (carry on) n. *ejecución.*
• The carrying into effect of a court's resolution. – Syn. implementation, *ejecución.*
execution of a judgment *ejecución de una sentencia.*
execution of a sentence *ejecución de una condena.*
execution of a warrant *ejecución de una orden de detención.*
execution sale *venta judicial.* – Syn. forced sale. judgment sale. sheriff's sale.
writ of execution *auto de ejecución.*

execution² (completion) n. *perfeccionamiento.*
• The completion of a written instrument by signing or otherwise. – Syn. closing, *cierre, celebración (de un instrumento).* signing, *firma (de un instrumento).*
execution of a contract *celebración o perfeccionamiento de un contrato.*
execution of a trust *constitución de un fideicomiso.*
execution of an instrument *celebración o perfeccionamiento de un instrumento.*

execution³ (killing) n. *ejecución (de la pena capital).* **to execute** v. *ejecutar.* **executioner** n. *verdugo.*
• The carrying out of the death penalty.
Rel: death penalty, *pena de muerte.*

executive¹ (govmt.) n. *ejecutivo, poder ejecutivo.* – Syn. executive power, *poder ejecutivo.*
chief executive *jefe del ejecutivo.*
executive clemency *indulto del poder ejecutivo, indulto otorgado por el ejecutivo.* – Syn. executive pardon.
executive privilege *inmunidad presidencial.*

executive² (management) n. *ejecutivo.* **executive** adj. *ejecutivo.*

executor SUCCESSION n. *albacea testamentario.*
executrix n. *albacea (mujer).* **coexecutor** n. *coalbacea.*
Rel: administrator, *administrador judicial de una sucesión.*

exemption¹ (privilege) n. *exención, excepción.*
• Freedom from duty or obligation.

exemption² TAX n. *exención.*
• An allowance in the nature of a deduction used to calculate taxable income. – Syn. tax exemption, *exención fiscal.*
personal exemptions *exenciones personales.*

exhibit¹ (document) n. *documento anexo, anexo.*
• A document attached to a pleading, contract or other instrument.

exhibit² EVIDENCE n. *medio de prueba material,* [borr.]*exhíbit* (PR), [interp.] *prueba.*
• Any tangible item tendered as evidence.
people's exhibit *prueba material del fiscal.*

exigent circumstances *circunstancias urgentes, circunstancias apremiantes.*

exile n. *exilio.*

existing laws *leyes en vigor.*

exonerate v. *exonerar.* **exoneration** n. *exoneración.* – Syn. exculpate, *exculpar.*

expatriation n. *expatriación.* **expatriate** n. *expatriado.* – Syn. banishment, *destierro.* deportation, *deportación.* exile, *exilio.*

expel v. *expulsar.*

expenditure n. *erogación, gasto.*

expense (accounting) n. *gasto.* – Syn. cost, *costo.*
account expense *cuenta de gasto.*
accrued expense *gastos devengados.*
business expense *gasto del negocio, gasto de representación.*
capital expense *gasto de capital.*
deductible expense TAX *gasto deducible.*
entertainment expense TAX *gastos de agasajo, gasto de representación.*
medical expense *gastos médicos.*
moving expense *gastos de mudanza.*
operating expense *gasto de operación.*
organization expense *gastos de organización de un negocio, gastos iniciales.*
personal expense *gastos personales.*
travel expenses *gastos de viaje, viáticos, gastos de desplazamiento.*

expert adj. *experto, perito.*
• Having a high degree of skill or knowledge in a specific field.

expert evidence *pruebas periciales.*
expert opinion *dictamen o informe pericial.*
expert testimony *peritaje.*
expert witness *perito.*
expert n. *perito.* **expert** adj. *experto.*
• Person with special skill or knowledge in a particular subject. – Syn. authority, *autoridad.* specialist, *especialista.*
consulting expert *perito consultor.*
handwriting expert *perito grafólogo o calígrafo.*
expiration n. *expiración, vencimiento.* **expire** v. *expirar, vencer.*
expiration date *fecha de expiración.*
expired insurance policy *póliza de seguro expirada.*
export n. *exportación, exportaciones.* **export** v. *exportar.* **exporter** n. *exportador.*
export financing program *programa de financiamiento de exportaciones.*
export letter *carta de crédito.*
export license *permiso de exportación.*
export trade *comercio de exportación.*
exposure of sexual organs (crime) [fe]*exhibiciones obscenas,* [le]*exposición de los órganos sexuales.*
See: indecent exposure.
expropriation n. *expropiación.*
expunge v. *cancelar, borrar retroactivamente.*
expungement n. *cancelación.*
• To erase or physically delete the official record of something.
expungement of record *borrar retroactivamente un registro (al cumplirse un término), destrucción de un registro, cancelación de un registro* || *destrucción de antecedentes penales, cancelación de antecedentes penales.*
Rel: erasure of record, *borrar un registro (al cumplirse una condición);* sealing of records, *cerrar registros al público.*
extension of stay *extensión del aplazamiento.*
extenuating circumstances *atenuantes, circunstancias atenuantes.* – Syn. mitigating circumstances.
extortion (crime) n. [brder]*extorsión.*
• The offense of extortion consists of the corrupt collection, under color of office, of an illegal fee by a public official. – Syn. common-law extorsion.
In modern statutory law, the offense of extortion has been broadened to include the illegal taking of property by anyone using actual or threatened force, violence or fear in addition to color of office (being often considered synonymous with blackmail in this form).
Cf: **extortion • bribery.** Often used as synonyms, both extortion and bribery are considered similar enough to find their distinction difficult in many cases. An often mentioned distinction involves looking at who takes the initiative when a public official illegally receives property: if the briber takes the initiative, it is bribery; if the recipient takes the initiative, it is extortion.
extradition n. *extradición.* **extradite** v. *extraditar.* **extraditable** adj. *extraditable.*
• The surrender of a person accused of committing a crime to another state that claims jurisdiction.
de facto extradition *extradición de facto.*
extradition crimes *delitos extraditables.*
extradition hearing *audiencia de extradición.*
extradition of nationals *extradición de nacionales.*
extradition of war criminals *extradición de criminales de guerra.*
extradition treaty *tratado de extradición.*
interstate extradition *extradición interestatal.*
Rel: asylum state, *país de asilo;* double criminality, *delito perseguible en ambos países;* political crime exception, *defensa de tratarse de un delito político, la no extradición de delitos políticos;* requesting state, *país que pide la extradición.*
Ref: (UK) 17(2) Halsbury's Laws para 1101; (US) 18 U.S.C.A. §3181; Waller v. Jordan, 118 P.2d 450, 451, 58 Ariz. 169.
extrajudicial confession *confesión extrajudicial.*
extraterritoriality n. *extraterritorialidad.*
extreme cruelty *crueldad extrema.*
extreme hardship *circunstancias extremadamente duras o difíciles.*
eyewitness n. *testigo presencial u ocular.*

FFFF

fabrication of evidence *falsificación de pruebas.*
fabrication of facts *invención de hechos, hechos falsos.*
facias (law lat.) *que se haga.* That you cause.
facio ut facias *que yo haga lo que usted pueda hacer.*
scire facias *que usted haga para que se sepa.* That you cause to know.
ut facias *para que se haga.* So that you do.

fact n. *hecho.* **fact finder** n. *juzgador, [de]persona u órgano a cargo de la averiguación y determinación de los hechos.*

• "An event that has occurred or circumstances that exist, events whose actual occurrence or existence is to be determined by the evidence." (Gifis, 190)

fact-finding *comprobación de hechos.*

facts in evidence *hechos probados.* – Syn. established facts.

facts in issue *hechos controvertidos.*

facts not in evidence *hechos no probados.*

material fact *hecho sustantivo.*

question of fact *cuestión de hecho.*

stipulated facts *hechos sobre los que hay acuerdo, hechos en los que se está de acuerdo.*

undisputed facts *hechos incontrovertidos, hechos no controvertidos.*

factoring COMM.LAW [transpl.]*factoring.* **factor** n. [borr.]*factor.*

• The operation of buying accounts receivable at a discount by a broker.

factual basis *hechos sobre los que se basa (un acto, una decisión), base de hecho.*

factual basis for the plea *hechos sobre los que se basa la declaración de culpabilidad o no culpabilidad.*

failure of proof *sin haber probado (una pretensión, un hecho).*

failure to act *dejar de hacer, dejar de realizar un acto esperado.*

failure to comply *incumplimiento.*

failure to prosecute *dejar de proceder penalmente, no proceder penalmente.*

failure to state a cause of action *omisión del fundamento de la acción, falta de los hechos base de la acción.*

fair competition *competencia leal.*

fair play *actuar de buena fe, actuar con justicia y equidad.*

fair trial *juicio justo e imparcial, juicio legal y equitativo.*

fait accompli *fait acompli. Hecho consumado.* Fact or deed accomplished.

false adj. *falso.* – Syn. contrary to fact, *contrario a los hechos.*

false accusation *acusación falsa.*

false arrest *detención ilegal, arresto ilegal* (PR).

false personation *suplantación de persona, impostura* (PR), *personificación.* – Syn. false impersonation.

false representation *actuación o declaración falsa.*

false statement *declaración falsa.*

false witness *testigo falso.*

false imprisonment (crime tort) *privación ilegal de la libertad.*

• "False imprisonment is the unlawful violation of the personal liberty of another." (Penal Code of the State of California §236)

Cf: **false arrest ● false imprisonment ● wrongful imprisonment.** False imprisonment is a common law misdemeanor and a tort; it is an unlawful restraint applying to both private and governmental detention. False arrest is a false imprisonment imposed only by a real or apparent legal authority. Wrongful imprisonment, on the other hand, is the preferred term in tort.

Rel: false arrest, *detención o arresto ilegal;* wrongful imprisonment, *privación ilícita de la libertad.*

See: kidnapping.

false pretenses (crime) [brder]*estafa, fraude* (Mx). – Other spell.: false pretences (UK,CA,AU).

• A statutory offense emphasizing the appropriation of title to property through fraudulent representation. – Syn. fraudulent pretenses.

Cf: **false pretenses ● deceptive practices.** These terms are often used as synonyms. False pretenses is the traditional broad common law term used to designate appropriation of title through fraudulent representation, while deceptive practices is a more limited term used in consumer protection statutes emphasizing improper conduct that is likely to deceive a consumer.

↳ *Estafa* is the equivalent crime in civil law systems; however, in contrast with false pretenses, most definitions of *estafa* are broader, usually referring to the appropriation as arising from deceit or from taking advantage of a false perception, and resulting in unlawful gain. In some instances false pretenses is simply too narrowly defined to correspond to *estafa,* like when instead of title to property, possession of property is appropriated, in such case larceny by trick is likely to be a closer equivalent.

Rel: deception, *engaño;* embezzlement, *abuso de confianza;* intent to defraud, *intención fraudulenta o de defraudar;* larceny by trick, *hurto mediante engaño;* misrepresentation, *afirmación o declaración falsa;* swindle, *estafa, timo;* trickery, *trampa, embuste.*

falsify v. *falsificar.* – Syn. counterfeit. forge.

family n. *familia.*

family law *derecho familiar.*

family leave *permiso o licencia para ausentarse del trabajo para atender a familiares.*
family man *hombre de familia.*
family ties *lazos familiares.*
Rel: relatives, *parientes.*

family automobile doctrine INSURANCE *responsabilidad del propietario de un automóvil (por daños causados con el vehículo por miembros de su familia).* – Syn. family group. family purpose doctrine.

father n. *padre.* – Syn. dad, *pa, papá.* dada, *pa.* daddy, *papi, papá.* old man, *viejo.* pa, *pa.*
adoptive father *padre adoptivo.*
father-in-law *suegro.*
natural father *padre natural.*
putative father *padre putativo.*
Rel: grandfather, *abuelo;* paternity, *paternidad;* stepfather, *padrastro.*

federalism n. *federalismo.* **federal** adj. *federal.*
federation n. *federación.*
"The term *federalism* is usually reserved for federations at the national political level. Strictly speaking 'federal government' refers to an overall system containing both central and state governments. Common usage, however, equates 'federal government' with 'central government.'" (Chandler, Enslen & Renstrom, 30)
Cf: **federation • confederation • league • common wealth.** These terms all refer to the political structure of nations, indicating the degree of control and sovereignty among those entities that make up a country or group of countries. A federation consists of a strong central authority and autonomous but limited state entities. A confederation is a looser arrangement in which each state retains sovereignty and the central government retains only limited authority. A league of nations is an alliance of countries pursuing common protection or common interests. Finally, a commonwealth is a loose association of countries recognizing one sovereign. <British Commonwealth>
↪ Currently there are only three Spanish-speaking countries with a *sistema federal*: Argentina, Mexico and Venezuela.
federal courts *tribunales federales, cortes federales.*
federal government *gobierno federal.*
federal law *leyes federales.*
Ref: (US) C,10Amend.; Erie Railroad v. Tompkins 304 US 64(1938).
fee (charge) n. *honorarios* || *cuota, tasa, derecho.*

• A charge or compensation paid for acts or services provided by either a public officer or a private person. – Syn. dues. honorarium.
attorney's fees *honorarios del abogado.* – Syn. legal fees.
contingent fee *honorarios basados en la cantidad recobrada, honorarios de cuota litis.*
fee splitting/division of fees *compartir honorarios (con otro abogado).*
license fee *cuota o derecho de licencia.*
origination fee (loan) *pago de gestoría, comisión de apertura.*

fee simple [de]*derecho de dominio pleno sobre un inmueble, derecho absoluto (de propiedad),* [fe]*nuda propiedad,* [borr.]*fee simple.*
• A fee simple is the most complete estate in land. It is an estate that has the potential of enduring forever. It resembles absolute ownership, and its holder is commonly called the owner of the land. – Syn. fee simple absolute. estate in fee simple.
"In modern times the fee simple absolute has become the most common form of estate. Therefore, a conveyance of 'Blackacre to A' is presumed to be a conveyance to A in fee simple absolute. This was not always the case ... the phrase 'to A and his heirs' had to be used if A was to get a fee simple." (Rabin, 169)
fee simple conditional [de]*derecho de dominio pleno sobre un inmueble sujeto a condición.*
fee simple defeasible [de]*derecho de dominio pleno sobre un inmueble sujeto a condición resolutoria.*
fee simple determinable [de]*derecho de dominio pleno sobre un inmueble sujeto a plazo o condición resolutoria.*
Rel: estate, [de]*derecho que una persona tiene sobre un inmueble;* to A and his heirs, *para A y sus herederos.*
See: estate[3].

fee tail [de]*derecho de dominio pleno sobre un inmueble heredable solamente a ciertos descendientes (señalados por el otorgante).* [borr.]*fee tail.*
• A freehold estate in which the inheritable succession is limited to the grantee's specified lineal descendants only. – Syn. entail. estate tail. tenancy in tail.
Rel: and the heirs of his body, *y a los descendientes en línea directa.*

felony n. *delito grave, delito mayor, felonía* (PR).
felon n. [de]*delincuente que ha cometido un delito grave,* [fe]*criminal peligroso.* **felonious** adj. *criminal.*

feticide

• A crime or offense more serious than a misdemeanor. – Syn. major crime, *delito mayor.* indictable offense (UK,CA). serious crime. Term used to distinguish high crimes from lesser crimes. Statutes usually define felonies as those punishable by death or imprisonment for more than one year. In the United Kingdom, this term has been abandoned with few remaining exceptions.
capital felony *delito capital.*
felonious intent *intención criminal.*
felony conviction *haber sido encontrado culpable de un delito grave o mayor.*
felony murder *homicidio calificado por haberse cometido durante la comisión de otro delito grave.*
forcible felony *delito grave o mayor violento, delito grave o mayor cometido con violencia.*
Rel: misdemeanor, *delito menor.*

feticide n. *feticidio.* **feticide** adj. *feticida.*
• Causing the death of a fetus. – Syn. child destruction (UK).

fiction of law *ficción de la ley.*

fictitious adj. *ficticio.* – Syn. fictional. invented, *inventado.*
fictitious action *acción ficticia.*
fictitious name *nombre ficticio.*

fidelity insurance *seguro contra abuso de confianza y deshonestidad de empleados.*

fiduciary n. *fiduciario, persona depositario de la confianza de otro.* **fiduciary** adj. *fiduciario.*
• A person entrusted to act with the utmost good faith in handling money or property for another person.
fiduciary bequest *legado fiduciario.*
fiduciary capacity *actuando en capacidad de fiduciario, actuando en virtud de la confianza que otro le ha depositado.*
fiduciary relationship *relación de confianza, relación fiduciaria.* – Syn. confidential relationship.
Rel: trust, *fideicomiso.*

fight (pop.) n. *pelea, riña.*
to pick a fight *empezar una pelea, armar camorra.*
to put up a fight *ofrecer resistencia, defenderse.*
Rel: altercation, *altercado;* attack, *ataque;* bout, *pelea, encuentro;* brawl, *refriega;* come to blows, *pelearse a puñetazos o golpes, liarse a golpes;* fray, *riña;* quarrel, *pelea, reyerta;* scrimmage, *golpeo, forcejeo;* scuffle, *forcejeo;* struggle, *lucha;* wrestle with, *luchar contra.*
See: battery, *lesiones.*

file n. *expediente, autos.* – Syn. records, *autos.* Rel: docket, *registro de las actuaciones en autos.*
file¹ (hand in) v. *presentar, promover* (Mx), *radicar* (PR).
• To deliver and enter a legal document with a clerk court or an official in charge of records.
file a claim *demandar.*
file a complaint *denunciar un delito, promover una demanda.*
file a motion *presentar una promoción, hacer una petición, presentar una moción* (PR).
file a petition *presentación de una petición.*
file a suit *demandar, promover una demanda.*
file an appeal *apelar, promover una apelación.*
file an appearance *comparecer en juicio.*
file² (arrange) v. *archivar.*
• To place records in an organized system designed to preserve and retrieve them.

filiation n. *filiación.*

filing date *fecha de presentación.*

filing status TAX *categoría para efectos de la declaración de impuestos, tipo de causante.*

final decision *decisión o sentencia definitiva.*

final disposition *decisión final.*

final judgment *sentencia definitiva.*

final order *orden definitiva, orden final.*

finance n. *finanzas.* **financing** *financiamiento, financiación.*
• From the corporate viewpoint, the planning and acquisition of funds and the management of these funds for various operations.
refinancing *refinanciamiento.*
See: stock exchange.

finding¹ (determination) n. [fe]*determinación judicial.*
• Decision of a court, either by a judge or a jury, on issues of fact. Applied by extension to other adjudicative bodies such as administrative entities and the like.
Cf: **finding • holding • conclusion.** These terms are synonymous, but they are used in distinguishable form in legal context. The term finding is commonly used to refer to decisions of fact, that is, determinations of fact supported by evidence made by a fact finder. Conclusions and holdings refer to determinations of law; that is, decisions or inferences made on a matter of law based on facts already in evidence. <findings of fact> <conclusions of law>.
direct finding *resolución sumaria sobre el*

fondo del asunto.

finding of fact *determinación de una cuestión de hecho.*

finding of guilt *encontrar culpable, se le encuentra culpable, declaración de culpabilidad.*

finding of law *determinación de una cuestión de derecho.*

finding[2] **(discovery)** *resultado.*
• Result of a judicial examination or investigation by a court, jury, referee, arbitrator or other authority.

findings of an investigation *resultados de una investigación.*

fine n. *multa.*
• An amount of money imposed as a punishment for the commission of a crime or offense. – Syn. penalty.
Rel: penalty, *castigo, pena.*

fingerprints n. *huellas dactilares, huellas digitales, rostros papilares.*
Glossary: arch, *arco;* bifurcation, *bifurcación, fork;* characteristics, *puntos característicos;* cinta, *tape;* core, *punto central;* delta, *delta;* development of latent fingerprints, *revelado de huellas latentes;* fingerprint card, *ficha dactiloscópica;* fingerprint powder, *polvo para huellas digitales;* furrow, *surco;* island, *islote;* latent fingerprints, *huellas latentes;* loop, *presilla;* papillae, *papilas;* pores, *poros;* ridge, *cresta;* ridge count, *conteo de crestas;* silver nitrate, *nitrato de plata,* whorl, *verticilo.*
See: huellas digitales.

fire[1] **(flame)** n. *fuego.* – Syn. blaze, *en llamas.*
Rel: pyromania, *piromanía;* pyrophobia, *pirofobia;* smolder, *quemar sin llama, arder.*

fire[2] **(conflagration)** n. *incendio.*
• Destructive burning.

fire insurance *seguro contra incendio.*

fire regulations *reglamentación preventiva de incendios, reglamentación contra incendios.*
Rel: arson, *incendio intencional;* conflagration, *conflagración;* firebomb, *bomba incendiaria;* wildfire, *incendio violento e indiscriminado, incendio destructor.*

firearm n. *arma de fuego.*
• A small arms weapon that fires a projectile by using an explosive charge.
Rel: weapon, *arma.*
See: ballistics. gun.

firing[1] **(shooting)** *disparo, descarga.*

close range firing *disparo a poca o corta distancia.*

firing squad *pelotón de fusilamiento.*

firing[2] **(dismissing)** *despedir de un empleo.*

first n. *primero.*

at first sight *a primera vista.*

first cousin *primo, primo de primer grado.*

first degree murder *homicidio calificado de primer grado.*

first name *nombre de pila.*

first offender *acusado por primera vez, (persona) sin antecedentes penales.*

first-born *primogénito.*

firsthand *de primera mano, directamente.*

fishing expedition (interrogation)
[de]*interrogatorio sin un propósito definido (para que el testigo mencione información relevante que no es conocida).* – Syn. fishing trip.

fitness[1] **(relevancy)** n. *idoneidad.*

fitness for a particular purpose *propiedad o idoneidad para un propósito determinado.*

fitness[2] **(ability)** n. *capacidad, aptitud.*

fitness hearing *audiencia para determinar la capacidad de una persona.*

fitness to stand trial *capacidad para ser procesado, capacidad procesal.*

fixture n. *inmueble por accesión o adhesión.*
• An article of personal property so annexed to real property that it is considered part of the land.

trade fixtures *accesorios (considerados parte del inmueble).*

flagrante delicto (lat.) *delito flagrante, delito in fraganti.*
• In the act of committing an offense. – Syn. in flagrante delicto.

flotsam MARIT.LAW n. *pecio, bienes echados al mar que flotan a la deriva.*
• Abandoned goods floating in the sea.
Rel: jetsam, *echazón, bienes echados al mar que se han hundido al fondo del mar;* lagan, *bienes echados al mar y marcados con una boya.*

food stamps *cupones para alimentos.*

footprints n. *huellas de los pies.*

forbearance[1] **(abstention)** n. *abstención, omisión.*
• Refraining from doing something which one has a right to do.
Cf: **forbearance ● omission.** Forbearance and omission are usually distinguished in that forbearance is understood as a holding back which is voluntary, while omission is considered a holding back which is involuntary.

forbearance[2] **(term)** n. *período de gracia para el*

force majeure

cumplimiento de obligaciones.

force majeure (law fr.) *fuerza mayor.*
- An event or effect that can be neither foreseen, prevented or resisted. Includes both acts of nature and of people.
Rel: act of god, *fuerza física irresistible.*

forced labor *trabajos forzados.*

forcible detainer¹ (legal proceeding) *procedimiento judicial de desalojo,* [fe]*interdicto posesorio.*
- A remedy to recover possession of land and damages from one wrongfully taking or refusing to surrender it. – Syn. forcible entry and detainer.

forcible detainer² (unlawful possession) *retención ilegal y hostil de la posesión de bienes.*

forcible detention *detención mediante el uso de la fuerza.*

forcible entry *toma de un inmueble mediante el uso de la fuerza, invasión de tierras o inmuebles.*
- At common law, the taking possession of lands violently and without legal authority.

forcible rape *violación con violencia, violación mediante el uso de la fuerza, violencia carnal* (Co).

forcible trespass *apoderamiento sin derecho y por la fuerza de un bien mueble.*

foreclosure¹ (loss of property) n. *pérdida legal del derecho de propiedad (por parte del deudor hipotecario).*
- Termination of a right to property by legal process.

foreclosure² (court proceeding) n. *procedimiento ejecutivo hipotecario o de ejecución de una garantía.*
- "An equitable action to compel payment of a mortgage or other debt secured by a lien." (Gifis, 206)

foreclosure decree *sentencia de ejecución forzosa de una garantía hipotecaria o de otra garantía similar.*

foreclosure of a mortgage *ejecución de una garantía hipotecaria.*

judicial foreclosure *ejecución judicial hipotecaria o de otras garantías similares.*

foreign adj. *extranjero.* – Syn. alien. nonindigenous, *que no es nativo.*

foreign corporation *corporación constituida en otro país o en otro estado (en el caso de un sistema federal).*

foreign currency *moneda extranjera.*

foreign judgment *sentencia expedida por otro país o estado (dentro de un sistema federal), sentencia de otra jurisdicción.*

foreign jurisdiction *jurisdicción correspondiente a otro país o a otro estado (dentro de un sistema federal).*

foreign law *ley de diferente jurisdicción, ley extranjera.*
See: alien.

foreign divorce *divorcio obtenido en el extranjero o en otro estado (dentro de un sistema federal), divorcio de otra jurisdicción.*

recognition of foreign divorce *reconocimiento de un divorcio obtenido en el extranjero.*

foreign investment *inversión extranjera.*

forensic medicine *medicina forense, medicina legal.*

forfeiture n. *pérdida de un derecho o un bien (a título de pena o sanción), pérdida de un derecho o un bien (por violación o incumplimiento) || confiscación.*
- "The loss of a right, a privilege or property because of a crime, breach of obligation or neglect of duty." (Black's Law Dict., 8th. ed., 677)

bond forfeiture *pérdida de la fianza por violación de sus condiciones, caducidad de la fianza, confiscación de la fianza* (PR).

bond forfeiture warrant *orden de detención por violación de las condiciones de la fianza.*

forfeiture clause *cláusula penal para el caso de incumplimiento.*

forfeiture of deposit *pérdida del depósito, caducidad del depósito.*

forfeiture of lease [fe]*rescisión de un arrendamiento por incumplimiento (de las obligaciones del arrendatario).*

relief from forfeiture *impugnación de la pérdida por incumplimiento.*
Rel: default, *incumplimiento, rebeldía.*

forgery n. *falsificación.* **forge** v. *falsificar.* – Syn. falsification. counterfeit.

forged check *cheque falsificado.*

forged I.D. *documento o papel de identificación falso.*

formalities n. *formalidades, trámites.*

fortuitous adj. *fortuito.*

forum n. *foro, tribunal.*

forum conveniens (lat.) *forum conveniens, foro o tribunal de conveniencia (para las partes).*

forum non conveniens (lat.) *forum non*

conveniens, foro o tribunal que se inhibe o excusa del conocimiento de una causa (para la conveniencia de las partes). – Syn. forum inconveniens.

forum-shopping *tribunal elegido por una o ambas partes para su conveniencia.*

law of the forum *ley del foro.*

foster child *hijo adoptivo temporal, provisional o de crianza.*

foster home *hogar adoptivo temporal o provisional, hogar de crianza.*

foundation¹ (organization) n. *fundación.*

• An organization established for charitable, educational, religious or other benevolent purposes.

charitable foundation *fundación caritativa o de beneficencia.*

private foundation *fundación privada.*

foundation² (basis) n. *fundamento.*

• Basis upon which something, especially evidence, is to be admitted.

laying the foundation *planteando o estableciendo el fundamento (de un alegato o una presentación).*

objection of lack of foundation *objeción de falta de fundamento (en un interrogatorio).*

franchise¹ (license) n. *permiso, autorización.*

franchiser/ franchisor n. *permisionario.*

• "The right conferred by the government to engage in a specific business or to exercise corporate powers." (Black's Law Dict., 8th. ed., 683)

Cf: **franchise ● license.** Franchise and license are often used synonymously. Some authors differentiate attributing more substantial rights to franchise, while attributing lesser rights to license. In practice, however, the differentiation issue does not seem to have been clearly settled.

franchise² (commercial rights) n. *franquicia, concesión,* [borr.]*franchise.* **franchisor/ franchiser** n. *concesionario.* **franchisee** *otorgante de la franquicia o concesión.*

• The exclusive right granted to a manufacturer, distributor or person to manufacture or sell a product or service in a limited area for a specified period of time, usually with the provision to permit use of an identifiable trademark or trade name and to supply financial and technical know-how.

"More broadly stated a 'franchise' has evolved into an elaborate agreement under which the franchisee undertakes to conduct a business or sell a product or service in accordance with methods and procedures prescribed by the franchisor,

and the franchisor undertakes to assist the franchisee through advertising, promotion and other advisory services." (Black's Law Dict., 5th. ed., 336)

franchise agreement *contrato de concesión o franquicia.*

franchise clause INSURANCE *cláusula de estipulación de una pérdida máxima como condición para pago total del siniestro.*

franchise tax *impuesto sobre concesiones o franquicias.*

franchise³ (vote) n. *derecho de voto.*

• The right to vote. – Syn. elective franchise, *derecho de voto.*

fratricide n. *fratricidio.* **fratricide** n. *fratricida.*

• The killing of a brother or a sister.

fraud¹ (injury) *defraudaciones, fraude* (Mx).

fraudulent *fraudulento.*

• A false representation of fact by one person that causes a second person to act in reliance on it, resulting in damage suffered by the second person.

constructive fraud *defraudación o fraude por disposición o ministerio de la ley.*

fraud in law *presunción de fraude.*

– Syn. constructive fraud.

fraud on creditors *fraude en perjuicio de acreedores.*

fraudulent conversion *apropiación fraudulenta, apropiación indebida.*

fraudulent conveyance *transmisión de propiedad fraudulenta o con intención de defraudar.*

fraudulent debt *simulación fraudulenta de deuda o crédito.*

fraudulent insolvencies by a corporation *insolvencia fraudulenta de una sociedad.*

fraudulent intent *intención fraudulenta, intención de defraudar.*

fraudulent representation *declaraciones hechas con intención fraudulenta o intención de defraudar.*

mail fraud *defraudación o fraude mediante el uso de los servicios del correo.*

tax fraud *defraudación o fraude fiscal.*

Rel: false pretenses, *estafa.*

fraud² (deceit) *engaño.*

• Gaining an advantage by deceiving someone. – Syn. deceit.

Rel: artifice, *artificio;* cheating, *engañar;* deception, *engaño;* pretense, *simulación;* swindling, *estafa, trampa;* trickery, *trampa, embuste.*

free adj. *libre.*

free and clear *libre de gravámenes.*

free competition *libre competencia.*
free of duty *libre de derechos.*
free on bail *libre bajo fianza.*
free on board (FOB) *Libre a bordo* (LAB).
free port *puerto libre.*
free trade *libre comercio.*
own free will *en forma voluntaria.*
freedom n. *libertad.*
  freedom of assembly *libertad de reunión.*
  freedom of press *libertad de prensa.*
  freedom of religion *libertad de creencias.*
  freedom of speech *libertad de expresión.*
  See: liberty.
freehold n. [de]*derecho de dominio sobre un inmueble—ya en forma absoluta, ya limitando la transmisión a ciertos herederos, ya determinando que su duración sea igual a la de la vida del recipiente—* [borr.]*freehold.*
  • An estate in fee simple, fee tail or a life estate. – Syn. estate of freehold. freehold estate. Freehold was the highest form of holding under feudal tenure. It designates a group of estates to be differentiated from other possessory estates labeled leasehold estates having a less important form of holding. Like leasehold, freehold includes possession, but in addition, unlike leasehold, also includes the right to such possession (seisin).
  See: estate³.
freelancer n. *trabajador independiente, trabajar por cuenta propia* [borr.]*freelancer.*
  freelance translator or interpreter *traductor o intérprete independiente.*
  Rel: per diem, *trabajador contratado diariamente.*
freight *flete, carga.*
  freight booking *contratación de carga.*
  freight charges *gastos de transporte o transportación.*
  freight forwarder *agente de carga, comisionista de transporte.*
  freight insurance *seguro de carga.*
  freight rate *tarifa de transporte o transportación de carga.*
fresh pursuit *persecusión continua.*
  See: hot pursuit.
friend of the court [lat.]amicus curiae, [de]*persona que aporta una opinión en un juicio (sin ser parte pero teniendo algún tipo de interés en la materia).*
  See: amicus curiae.
friendly suit *juicio consentido,* [de]*juicio sustanciado formalmente en el que las partes han*

acordado aceptar la decisión judicial (que normalmente corresponde a sus actuaciones).
fringe benefits *prestaciones sociales, beneficios marginales* (PR), *beneficios extrasalariales.*
  • Benefits given to employees other than wages or salary.
  employee fringe benefits *prestaciones para los trabajadores o empleados, beneficios extrasalariales (para los trabajadores).*
  Specific types: accident insurance, *seguro contra accidentes;* dental plan, *plan dental;* disability plan, *plan de incapacidad o invalidez;* employee stock purchase plan, *plan de compra de acciones para los empleados;* leave of absence, *licencia sin goce de sueldo;* life insurance, *seguro de vida;* medical coverage, *cobertura médica;* paid holidays, *días de fiesta o feriados pagados;* pension plan, *plan de jubilación;* profit sharing plan, *plan de reparto de utilidades;* sabbatical, *sabático;* savings incentive plan, *plan de incentivos para el ahorro;* paid sick days, *días de enfermedad pagados;* vacation, *vacaciones.*
frisk v. *registrar, cachear.*
  Rel: pat down, *cachear palpando;* search, *registro.*
frivolous adj. *carente de fundamento o justificación.*
  frivolous answer *contestación infundada.*
  frivolous appeal *apelación infundada, apelación frívola* (PR).
  frivolous cause of action, *los hechos base de la acción no tienen fundamento, acción infundada.*
  frivolous claim *demanda o reclamación infundada.*
  frivolous complaint *denuncia infundada* || *demanda infundada, demanda temeraria.*
  frivolous defense *defensa infundada.*
  frivolous demurrer *petición infundada de la improcedencia de la demanda.*
  frivolous objection *objeción infundada.*
fruit of the poisonous tree doctrine *inadmisibilidad de pruebas obtenidas en registros, detenciones o confesiones ilegales; frutos del árbol ponzoñoso* (PR).
  • The doctrine that evidence fom illegal arrests, searches or interrogations is inadmissible against the defendant. – Syn. the fruits doctrine. the tainted fruit doctrine.
fugitive adj. *fugitivo, prófugo.*
  fugitive warrant *orden de detención de un fugitivo o prófugo.*

full faith and credit (US) *reconocimiento o validez de actos públicos celebrados en un estado diferente (dentro de un estado federal).*
• Constitutional principle under which every state within the United States must recognize the legislative acts, public records and judicial decisions of the other states.
Rel: comity, *cortesía internacional.*

full force and effect *válido y vigente.*

full proof *prueba plena.*

furlough n. *licencia, permiso.*

furnish bail *otorgar fianza.*

furnish proof *exhibir o presentar pruebas.*

future advance clause *cláusula de cobertura de garantía de cantidades adicionales futuras de un préstamo.*

future interest [de]*derecho sobre un inmueble que permite su posesión o disfrute a futuro,* [le]*interés futuro,* [borr.]*future interest.*
• A property interest that is to come into existence at a future time. – Syn. future estate.
"The essence of a future interest is that (1) it involves the privilege of possession or enjoyment in the future, and (2) it is looked upon as a portion of the total ownership of the land or other thing which is its subject matter (Simes, 2). A future interest should be carefully distinguished from a mere possibility, such as the expectancy of a person who is the heir apparent of a living person.
↪ There is no equivalency for future interests in the civil law system. *Derechos sobre inmuebles que otorgan su posesión a futuro* is a loose description at best, which cannot accurately define the various proprietary combinations of interests created by the common law. Civil law systems have regulated mostly actual possessory rights, seldom referring to future interests.
Glossary: executory interest, [de]*un "future interest" en favor de un tercero que no es una reversión o un derecho residual;* remainder, [le]*derecho residual (de propiedad),* [borr;]*remainder;* reversion, [borr;]*reversión (de un inmueble);* rule against perpetuities, [borr.]*regla contra la perpetuidad (en materia de derechos de inmuebles), regla de prohibición de la transmisión de derechos sobre inmuebles (si ésta no es ejecutada dentro de los 21 años siguientes a la fecha de su creación);* possessory interest, *derecho a ejercer la posesión (de un inmueble);* waste, *deterioro del valor de un "future interest."*

futures n. *futuros.*
futures contract *contrato de futuros.* – Syn. futures.
futures market *mercado de futuros.*

GGGG

gag order[1] (immobilization) *orden de amordazamiento e inmovilización de un acusado hostil (en caso necesario).*

gag order[2] (secrecy) *orden de confidencialidad de la publicidad de un proceso.*

gambling (crime) *juegos y apuestas, juegos prohibidos* (Mx), *juegos ilícitos* (Sp). **gambler** n. *jugador.*
compulsive gambler *jugador compulsivo.*
Rel: bet, *apuesta;* wager, *apuesta.*

gang n. *pandilla, ganga* (US). – Syn. band, *banda.*
gang banger *pandillero.*
gang colors *colores de la pandilla.*
gang leader *jefe de la pandilla.*
gang member *pandillero.*
gang signs *señales usadas por los pandilleros.*
Rel: graffiti, [borr.]*grafiti,* [borr.]*graffiti;* hand signals, *señales manuales, señas;* tattoo, *tatuaje.*

gangster n. *gángster.* – Syn. Mafioso, *mafioso.* mobster.
Rel: underworld, *bajo mundo.*

garnishment n. *embargo de bienes en manos de un tercero.* **garnishee** n. *embargado.* **garnisher** n. *embargante.*
• Attachment of money or property that is due to be paid to a party pursuant to a judicial proceeding and that is in the hands of a third party. Cf: **garnishment • trustee process.** These terms are considered synonyms. Trustee process is also known as factorizing process or process by foreign attachment.
garnishment of income *embargo de salario, retención o deducción de salario (por orden judicial).* – Syn. garnishment of wages.
garnishment proceeding *procedimiento de embargo de bienes en manos de un tercero.*
See: attachment. *embargo.*

general adj. *general.*
general agency *mandato general.*
general average *avería común o gruesa.*
general election *elección general.*
general intent *dolo genérico.*
general strike *huelga general.*
general welfare *beneficencia pública.*

genocide n. *genocidio* || *genocida.*

germane adj. *relacionado, pertinente.*

gerrymander v. *reconfiguración partidaria de distritos electorales.*

gift n. *donación.* **grantor** n. *donador, donante, otorgante.*
• A voluntary transfer of property to another made without consideration.
Cf: **gifts inter vivos • gifts causa mortis.** Gifts inter vivos are those ordinary present unconditional gifts given by the grantor to take effect during his or her lifetime; by contrast, gifts causa mortis are those made in contemplation of immediate approaching death.
absolute gift *donación incondicional e irrevocable.*
charitable gift *donación caritativa, donación con fines benéficos.*
gift causa mortis *donación causa mortis.*
gift inter vivos *donación inter vivos.*
gift tax *impuesto sobre transmisión gratuita de bienes.*
revocable gift *donación revocable.*
testamentary gift *donación testamentaria.*
See: donation.

good behavior *buena conducta.*

good faith *buena fe.*
• Honesty, fair play. The belief that one's actions are proper. – Syn. bona fide (lat.).
good faith purchaser *comprador de buena fe.*

good moral character *buenos principios morales, solvencia moral, alta calidad moral.*

good will COMMON LAW n. *plusvalía, llave* (Ar), *fondo de comercio* (Sp).

goods *mercaderías, bienes muebles tangibles.*
• In the legal sense, tangible or movable personal property (excluding money), especially merchandise; in the economic sense, things that have value, whether tangible or not.
Cf: **chattels • personal property • goods.** These terms often overlap. Chattels and personal property are usually considered synonyms; however, in the strict sense, chattels is a broader term that includes all property that is not freehold property, thus including leasehold land in its scope; personal property can be similarly defined as property that is not real property, excluding leasehold land. Goods, on the other hand, is a term describing a group of moveable property that is tangible and closely identified with commercial operations.
capital goods *bienes de capital.*
conforming goods *bienes o mercancía de conformidad con los términos pactados.*

consumer goods *bienes de consumo.*
delivery or tender of goods *entrega de bienes o mercancía.*
durable goods *bienes duraderos.*
fungible goods *bienes fungibles.*
identified goods *bienes identificables (individualmente).*
inspection of goods *inspección de bienes o mercancía.*
Rel: contract for sale, *contrato de compraventa mercantil;* sale of goods, *venta de mercaderías.*

government n. *gobierno.* – Syn. administration, *administración.* authorities, *autoridades.* regime, *régimen.* rule, *gobierno, autoridad.*
de facto government *gobierno de facto.*
federal government *gobierno federal.*
government-in-exile *gobierno en el exilio.*
head of government *jefe de gobierno.*
provisional government *gobierno provisional.*
recognition of government *reconocimiento de gobierno.*
Rel: anarchy, *anarquía;* aristocracy, *aristocracia;* democracy, *democracia;* despotism, *despotismo;* dictatorship, *dictadura;* monarchy, *monarquía;* oligarchy, *oligarquía;* republic, *república;* tyranny, *tiranía.*

grace period *período de gracia.*

graffiti n. [borr.]*grafiti,* [borr.]*graffiti, pintarrajear propiedades ajenas, pintas* (slg.) (Mx).

graft n. *corrupción oficial.*
• The obtaining of an undue gain by taking advantage of one's position, especially one in public office.

grand jury (US) [fe]*jurado de acusación.* [le]*gran jurado* (PR).
• A group of lay people summoned to enquire into alleged crimes and to decide whether to issue presentments or indictments. The grand jury was abolished in England in 1933. – Syn. accusing jury. jury of indictment.
↦ Grand jury is a practically unknown institution in Spanish-speaking countries. In Mexico, *Gran Jurado* refers to impeachment proceedings before members of the legislature against public officials for the commission of certain crimes.
investigative grand jury *jurado de acusación con facultades de investigación.*

grand larceny *hurto de mayor cuantía.*

grand theft *hurto mayor, hurto de mayor cuantía.*

grant[1] **(creation of a right)** n. *concesión, otorga-*

miento de un derecho en exclusividad. **grant** v. *conceder, otorgar.*

grant of patent *concesión de una patente.*

grant²(transfer) n. *transmisión de un inmueble.* **grant** v. *transmitir (un inmueble).*

grant (permit) v. *conceder, acordar judicialmente.*
grant a motion *acordar favorablemente una petición o promoción.*
grant an injunction *conceder un interdicto.*

grievance¹ LABOR n. *demanda de violación del contrato colectivo || queja laboral, inconformidad laboral.*
• Formal complaint filed by a worker or a labor representative alleging violation of the worker's rights or of the collective bargaining agreement.
grievance procedure *procedimiento de queja o inconformidad laboral.*

grievance²(complaint) n. *queja o inconformidad, reclamación.*

grievance³(injury) n. *agravio.*

gross earnings *ganancias brutas.*

gross income *ingreso bruto.*

gross misconduct *falta grave.*

gross national product (GNP) *producto nacional bruto* (PNB).

gross negligence *negligencia grave.*

gross profit *ganancias brutas.*

grounds n. *causales o fundamento.*
grounds for an objection *fundamento de una objeción o excepción.*
grounds for appeal *causales de apelación.*
grounds for dismissal LABOR *causales de terminación.*
grounds for divorce *causales de divorcio.*
grounds of excludability IMMGR. *causales de exclusión.*

guaranty n. *garantía* n. **guarantee** n. *titular de una garantía.* **guarantor** n. *garante.*
• A collateral agreement in which a party promises to answer for the debt, default or lack of performance of another party. – Other spell.: guarantee.
Cf: **guaranty • warranty • suretyship.**
Guaranty and warranty are often considered synonymous. They are both collateral promises by third parties to ensure against default or nonperformance, but while guaranty is designed to be exercised in response to the failure or default of the principal obligation, a warranty is created as an independent obligation that will be exercised regardless of the compliance or default of the principal obligation, provided the terms of the warranty have been violated. In the case of suretyship, the collateral undertaking is created as a joint promise, that is, a surety is a party to the principal obligation, being equally liable with the principal debtor.
collateral guaranty *garantía colateral.*
guaranty clause *cláusula de garantía.*
guaranty fund *fondo de garantía.*
guaranty insurance *seguro de personal de confianza, seguro contra fraudes de empleados o funcionarios.*
limited guaranty *garantía limitada.*

guardian adj. *tutor.* **guardianship** *tutela.*
• A legally appointed person who manages or cares for the person or estate of an incompetent. – Syn. conservator.
guardian ad litem *curador ad litem.*
legal guardian *tutor legal.*
testamentary guardian *tutor testamentario.*
Rel: custody, *custodia;* incompetent, *incapaz.*

guilty n. *culpable.* **guilty** adj. *culpable.* **guilt** n. *culpa.* – Syn. culpable, *culpable.* – Opp. not-guilty, *no culpable.*
finding of guilt *encontrar culpable, declaración de culpabilidad.*
guilty as charged *culpable del delito que se le imputa, culpable del delito que se le acusa.*
guilty plea *[de]declararse culpable formalmente (a la acusación hecha), declaración de culpabilidad.*
guilty verdict *veredicto de culpabilidad.*
Rel: conviction, *sentencia condenatoria;* plea, *[de]declaración formal de culpabilidad o no culpabilidad (hecha ante el juez por parte del acusado al iniciarse el proceso), alegación* (PR).

gun n. *rifle || pistola || cañón.*
• A weapon made of a heavy, usually metallic tube from which a projectile is discharged by means of an explosive detonation. Also, similar weapons in either shape or mode of operation. In popular parlance gun refers mostly to a pistol or revolver.
Glossary: automatic revolver, *revólver automático o de repetición, escuadra;* automatic rifle, *rifle automático, fusil automático;* assault rifle, *rifle de asalto, fusil automático ligero;* barrel, *cañón;* blank, *bala de salva;* bolt, *cerrojo;* bolt action rifle, *fusil de cerrojo;* bolt assembly, *mecanismo de cerrojo;* bore, *alma, ánima;* breech, *recámara;* buckshot, *perdigón;* butt, *cacha, cu-*

lata; caliber, *calibre;* carbine, *carabina;* cartridge, *cartucho;* cartridge case or casing, *casquillo;* chamber, *cámara;* clip, *cargador, peine;* cylinder, *cilindro, tambor;* dud, *cartucho fallido;* ejector, *expulsor;* extractor, *eyector;* groove, *estría, ranura;* gun powder, *pólvora;* hammer, *martillo, percutor;* handgun, *pistola;* lands, *campos;* live ammunition, *cartucho con bala;* machine gun, *ametralladora;* magazine, *cargador, peine;* magnum, *magnum;* muzzle, *boca (del cañón de una arma);* pellet gun, *pistola de perdigón o postas;* pistol, *pistola;* powder, *pólvora;* recoil, *patada (de un arma);* revolver, *revólver;* repeating rifle, *rifle de repetición;* rifle, *rifle, fusil;* sawed -off rifle, *rifle recortado;* shotgun, *escopeta;* shotgun shell, *cartucho de perdigones;* semi-automatic, *semiautomática, escuadra;* service revolver, *revólver reglamentario;* sight, *mira;* silencer, *silenciador;* slide lock, *seguro corredizo;* sub-machine gun, *metralleta;* telescopic sight, *mira telescópica;* thumb latch, *guarda-monte;* trigger, *gatillo, disparador.* See: ballistics. bullet.

gun runner n. *traficante de armas, contrabandista de armas.*

gunfight *balacera, tiroteo, agarrarse a balazos.*

gunman n. *pistolero, aquél que tiene una pistola.* – Syn. gunslinger, *pistolero.* hit man, *sicario, asesino a sueldo.*

gunshot n. *disparo.*
   gunshot wound *herida infligida por arma de fuego, herida de arma de fuego.*
   point blank gunshot *disparo de arma de fuego a quemarropa.*

HHHH

habeas corpus [transpl.]*hábeas corpus.*
   • "Meaning literally: 'That you may have the body.' It is a writ directing a jailer, a warden, or someone else who has a person in custody to bring the person before a court to inquire into the legality of the restraint." (Mellinkoff's Dict., 279) – Abbr. H.C. – Syn. Great Writ. habeas.
   ☞ Habeas corpus, as a writ bringing a person before a judge to determine the legality of his or her detention, has been transplanted and has taken root in most Hispanic countries. No attempt has been made to introduce an equivalent term in Spanish, and the English usage has been adopted by both scholars and legislation. In spite of this acceptance, habeas corpus' other meanings in English countries, like extradition review, review and verification of proper jurisdiction or review of bail or bail amount, have not been adopted.
   habeas corpus ad prosequendum [de]*orden judicial de traslado de un detenido a la jurisdicción de la acusación.*
   habeas corpus ad respondendum [de]*orden judicial de traslado del detenido a la jurisdicción del proceso civil en su contra.*
   habeas corpus ad subjiciendum [de]*orden judicial de presentación del detenido con expresión del fundamento de su detención.*
   habeas corpus ad testificandum [de]*orden judicial de comparecencia del detenido para que testifique.*
   habeas corpus proceeding *procedimiento de habeas corpus.*
   Ref: (CA) In re John Henderson [1930] S.C.R. 45 at 55; (UK) 31Car.II, c.2; St.56 Geo.III, c.100; (US) C Art 1 §9; 28 U.S.C.A. §2241ss.

habit n. *hábito.*

habitual *habitual, usual.*

habitual criminal (US) *reincidente.* – Syn. habitual offender.

habitual residence (UK) *residencia habitual.*

hallucinogens n. *alucinógenos.*
   Rel: DMT, *DMT;* DOM, *DOM;* LSD, *LSD;* MDA, *MDA;* mescaline, *mezcalina;* PCP, *PCP;* peyote, *peyote;* psilocybin, *psilocibin, psilocybina.*
   See: drugs.

handicap n. *invalidez, desventaja.*
   See: disability.

hangover *cruda, goma, guayabo, mona, pea* (Ve), *ratón, resaca* (Ar, Ur), *perseguidora* (Pe).

harassment n. *hostigamiento, hostilidad, vejación, acoso.*
   • Behavior that annoys, threatens or abuses, usually causing distress to another.
   – Syn. annoyance, *molestia.* bother, *molestia.*
   debt collection harassment *hostigamiento de deudores, prácticas hostiles de cobro.*
   harassing a witness *hostigar a un testigo.*
   sexual harassment *acoso u hostigamiento sexual, insinuación sexual.*

harboring aliens *recibir y encubrir extranjeros ilegalmente en el país.*

hardship n. *privación.*
   extreme hardship *circunstancias excepcionalmente difíciles.*

harm n. *daño, perjuicio.* **harmful** adj. *dañino, perjudicial.*
   • Loss or detriment of any kind to a person or group or to property.

bodily harm *daño corporal.*

physical harm *daños físicos (a una cosa o persona).*

harmful error PROCEDURE *error apelable.* – Syn. reversible error. prejudicial error.

harmful product *producto defectuoso (que causa un daño).*

hate crime *delito motivado por odio contra un cierto grupo de personas.*
• A crime committed against a victim because he or she belongs to a certain race, religion, ethnicity, sexual orientation or a group similarly defined.

hazard[1] n. *peligro.* **hazardous** adj. *peligroso.*

hazard pay *bonificación por trabajo peligroso.*

hazardous contract *contrato aleatorio.*

hazardous employment *trabajo peligroso.*

hazard[2] INSURANCE n. *riesgo.*

hazardous insurance *seguro con agravación de riesgo.*

head of state *jefe de estado.*

head of the household *jefe de familia.* – Syn. head of the family.

headquarters n. *casa matriz, centro de operaciónes, cuartel general* (mil.).

health insurance *seguro médico.*
• Insurance covering insureds for medical expenses as a result of injury or illness.
Glossary: deductible, *deducible;* health care, *cuidado o atención médica;* inpatient, *paciente interno;* major coverage, *cobertura mayor;* mental health, *salud mental;* out of pocket expenses, *gastos efectivamente incurridos;* outpatient, *paciente externo;* waiting period, *período de espera.*

Hear ye, hear ye, hear ye (oral expr.) *(Oyez, Oyez, Oyez)* ¡Oíd, Oíd, Oíd!

hearing *audiencia, vista, debate oral.*
• Proceeding to reach a decision about an issue of fact or of law in which witnesses are heard and/or evidence is presented.
↦ Broadly, hearing and *audiencia* in civil and criminal procedure are very similar terms when both refer to a court proceeding that is oral and usually involves a complete procedural step. In a more restricted sense, however, hearing and *audiencia* are different in that hearing is mostly a preliminary procedural step in a lawsuit or case, while *audiencia* is often used to carry on matters traditionally considered part of trial in common law countries, like a case-in-chief examination of a witness per example. In adminis-

trative matters, hearing and *audiencia* are usually equivalent; they describe a simplified procedure consisting mostly of direct oral allegations before an examiner or judge. In legislative practice *audiencia*, used as a noun, usually designates an assembly formed by political representatives, especially in Spain; hearing, on the other hand, refers only to testimony given to legislators regarding a piece of legislation or an inquiry under consideration.

adjudicative hearing *audiencia de adjudicación.*

default hearing *audiencia de acusación de rebeldía.*

evidentiary hearing *audiencia de pruebas.*

exclusionary hearing *audiencia de admisibilidad de pruebas, audiencia de exclusión de pruebas.*

final hearing *audiencia sobre materias de fondo.*

full hearing *audiencia que permite la presentación completa de las posiciones de las partes respecto a la cuestión debatida.*

hearing de novo *repetición de una audiencia.*

hearing on damages *audiencia de daños y perjuicios.*

hearing on the merits *audiencia sobre materias de fondo, audiencia sobre el fondo del asunto.*

interlocutory hearing *audiencia interlocutoria.*

omnibus hearing *audiencia que incluye cuestiones varias.*

preliminary hearing *audiencia preliminar, vista preliminar* (PR).

public hearing *audiencia pública.*

revocation hearing *audiencia de revocación.*

suppression hearing *audiencia que resuelve la improcedencia de ciertas pruebas.*

Rel: examination, *examen, interrogatorio;* statement (UK), *declaración de un testigo (por escrito);* testimony, *testimonio;* witness, *testigo.*

hearing officer *funcionario a cargo de una audiencia administrativa.* – Syn. administrative-law judge. hearing examiner.

hearsay n. *lo dicho por un tercero, de oídas, testimonio por referencia, prueba de referencia* (PR).
• "Evidence that consists in something that has been told to a witness rather than something he has himself observed or of which he has personal knowledge." (Radin, 149) – Syn. secondhand evidence.

↪ Hearsay refers to a well established fact in evidence practice: that testimony given by witnesses who testify about another's statements or observations, as a rule, has reduced or no evidentiary value. Hearsay is usually excluded from jury trials since an unsophisticated juror (one illiterate in the early stages of common law) was considered unlikely to grasp such distinction. *Lo dicho por un tercero*, in contrast, is usually included as part of evidence in civil law systems. This can be attributed to the absence of juries and the presence, instead, of professional judges who do not need guidance about admissibility and proper evaluation of evidence.

hearsay evidence *testimonio de lo dicho por un tercero, prueba de referencia* (PR).

hearsay rule *regla sobre la inadmisibilidad de lo dicho por un tercero, regla de prueba de referencia* (PR).

heat of passion *crimen pasional, estado de emoción violenta* (Gu), *arrebato de cólera* (PR).

• An emotional state of rage or hatred suddenly aroused by provocation and lasting enough time to impede reason to prevail.

heir n. *heredero.* **heiress** n. *heredera.* **heirs** n. *herederos.* **coheir** n. *coheredero.*

• A person who, on intestacy, inherits realty or personalty from a decedent. – Syn. inheritor. distributee. next of kin.

The term heirs applies today indiscriminately to those who inherit by will as well as by law. Cf: **heir • inheritor • distributee • next of kin • successor.** Heir, used broadly, is synonymous with all these terms; strictly defined, however, heir is equivalent to inheritor, meaning a person entitled by the laws of intestacy to succeed an intestate decedent's real property. A distributee or next of kin is the person entitled to an intestate's personal property (although heir is often used). Finally, successor means a person who acquires property upon the death of another by descent or will.

forced heir *heredero forzoso.*

heir apparent *heredero aparente.*

heir at law *heredero legal.* – Syn. legal heir.

heir beneficiary *herencia a beneficio de inventario.*

heir by adoption *heredero por adopción.*

heirless state *herencia vacante.*

heirs and assigns *sucesores.*

heirs of the body *heredero que es descendiente directo del decujus, heredero en línea recta.*

heir presumptive *heredero presunto.*

illegitimate heirs *herederos ilegítimos.*

legitimate heirs *herederos legítimos.*

sole heir *heredero único.*

testamentary heir *heredero testamentario.*

Rel: inheritance, *herencia;* next of kin, *familiar más cercano.*

hereby adv. *de conformidad con la presente.*

hereditary succession *sucesión hereditaria.*

herein adv. *en la presente, en el presente (documento, etc.).*

hereinabove adv. *más arriba, arriba.*

hereinafter adv. *en adelante, en lo sucesivo.*

hereto adv. *al presente, del presente.*

heretofore adv. *hasta ahora, anteriormente.*

hereunder adv. *en el presente (documento, etc.), más abajo.*

herewith adv. *adjunto al presente, con el presente.*

heroin n. *heroína.* – Syn. blow. "H", *"H".* horse, *caballo.* scag. smack.

hidden assets *bienes ocultos.*

hidden defect *vicio oculto.*

high seas INTL.LAW *alta mar.*

high treason *alta traición.*

highway n. *carretera, autopista.*

highway robbery *asalto en carretera, asalto en caminos.*

interstate highway *carretera interestatal.*

Rel: expressway, *vía rápida;* freeway, *carretera libre;* overpass, *paso a desnivel (superior o arriba);* road, *camino;* roadway, *camino;* toll road, *camino de cuota;* underpass, *paso a desnivel (inferior o abajo).*

hijack n. *secuestro (de bienes o personas en tránsito).* **hijack** v. *secuestrar.* **hijacker** n. *secuestrador.*

• Taking control of a vehicle by force or threat. Also to rob cargo from a carrier while in transit. – Other spell.: highjack. – Syn. hijacking.

Rel: aircraft piracy, *piratería aérea;* carjacking, *secuestro de automóvil (en circulación);* hostage taking, *toma de rehenes;* skyjacking, *secuestro aéreo, secuestro de un avión.*

hired killer *sicario, asesino a sueldo.* – Syn. hired assassin.

hit and run accident *accidente de tráfico en el que se huye del lugar.*

hitchhiking *auto-stop, aventón* (Mx), [borr.]*raite.*

holder in due course *tenedor de buena fe.*

holding[1] **(principle)** n. *principio de derecho, ratio decidendi.*

• The determining principle adopted on a point of law in a court's decision. – Syn. legal rule.

holding[2] **(decision)** n. *fallo, decisión.*
• A ruling at trial.

holding[3] PROPERTY n. *propiedad.*
• Land or securities held by a person.

holding company *compañía controladora.*

holdup n. *asalto a mano armada, atraco.*

holiday n. *día feriado.*
  legal holiday *día de descanso obligatorio o legal.*
  public holiday *día feriado.*

holocaust n. *holocausto.*

holographic will *testamento ológrafo.*

home n. *hogar, casa.* – Syn. household. house, *casa.* residence, *residencia.*
  home arrest *arresto domiciliario.* – Syn. home confinement. home detention.
  home invasion *allanamiento y agresión en morada habitada.*
  home intrusion *penetración indebida en una morada.*
  home owner *propietario de una casa, dueño de un hogar.*
  Rel: domicile, *domicilio;* dwelling, *morada;* habitation, *habitación;* lodging, *alojamiento.*

homeland n. *tierra natal o de origen.*

homeless n. *persona que vive en la calle, persona de la calle.* – Syn. street people, *gente de la calle.* vagabond (old), *vagabundo.*

homestead n. *patrimonio de familia, bien de familia* (Ar).

homicide n. *homicidio.*
• "The killing of a human being under any circumstances, by the act, agency, or omission of another." (Ballentine's Law Dict., 565)
Homicide is a generic term that includes both murder and manslaughter.
Cf: **homicide • murder • assassination.** These terms are synonyms. From the broadest to the most specific: Homicide refers simply to the killing of a person regardless of circumstance or intent; murder refers to the killing of a person with malice aforethought; assassination refers to the killing of a person usually for payment or for political reasons.
  felonious homicide *homicidio sin justificantes.*
  homicide by misadventure *homicidio accidental.* – Syn. accidental killing.
  justifiable homicide *homicidio con justificantes.* – Syn. excusable homicide.

premeditated homicide *homicidio premeditado.*
Rel: assassination, *asesinato;* elimination (euph), *eliminación;* feticide, *feticidio;* fratricide, *fratricidio;* genocide, *genocidio;* infanticide, *infanticidio;* killing, *matar, dar muerte;* liquidation (euph), *liquidar;* manslaughter, *homicidio no intencional;* massacre, *masacre;* murder, *homicidio con agravantes;* parricide, *parricidio.*

homosexual n. *homosexual.* – Syn. fag, *loca, marica* (Mx), *pájaro* (Cu), *pato* (Cu). fairy (slg.), *marica, maricón.* gay, *homosexual.* lesbian, *lesbiana, tortillera* (Cu). queer (slg.), *afeminado.*
Rel: bisexual, *bisexual;* pederast, *pederasta;* transsexual, *transexual;* transvestite, *transvestista, transvestido.*

honor n. *honor.* **honorable** adj. *honorable.*
Rel: dignity, *dignidad;* prestige, *prestigio.*

honor v. *aceptación (de una título de crédito).*
  honor a debt *pagar una deuda.*

hooligan n. *rufián, malhechor.* – Syn. hoodlum. ruffian.
Rel: criminal, *delincuente;* gang banger, *pandillero;* thug, *gángster.*

hostage n. *rehén.*

hostile adj. *hostil.* – Syn. actively opposed, *activamente en contra.* antagonistic, *antagonista.* combative, *combativo.* ill-disposed, *adverso, en contra.*
  hostile fire *fuego enemigo.*
  hostile possession *posesión hostil.*
  hostile witness *testigo hostil, testigo renuente.*

hostilities (war) n. *hostilidades.*

hot pursuit INTL.LAW *persecución en caliente, persecución ininterrumpida.*
• The legal pursuit of a vessel in the high seas after it has allegedly committed a flagrant violation in the jurisdiction of the pursuing country.
Cf: **hot pursuit • fresh pursuit.** Hot pursuit and fresh pursuit are sometimes synonymous but usually not interchangeable. Hot pursuit is the legitimate persecution of a vessel outside the national jurisdiction of a country, whereas fresh pursuit is also a persecution outside the jurisdiction of the persecuting authorities, but often not restricted to a vessel and usually without international implications.
Rel: fresh pursuit, *persecución continua.*

house[1] **(dwelling)** n. *casa.*
  dwelling house *casa habitada.*
  house arrest *arresto domiciliario.*

house of corrections *correccional, reformatorio.*
Rel: home, *hogar;* homemaker, *ama de casa (persona a cargo);* househusband, *hombre a cargo de la casa;* housewife, *ama de casa;* residence, *residencia.*

house² (assembly) n. *cámara, asamblea.*
House of Commons *Cámara de los Comunes.*
House of Lords *Cámara de los Lores.*
House of Representatives *Cámara de Representantes.*
house of worship *iglesia, casa de Dios.*

housebreaking (burglary) *robo con fuerza en las cosas.* – Syn. burglary.
Today housebreaking refers not only to the breaking into a dwelling, but also breaking into any building. Housebreaking, instead burglary, is still used in Scotland.
See: burglary.

household n. *hogar, hogar familiar.*
head of the household *jefe de familia.*

household adj. *familiar, doméstico.*
household help *empleado doméstico, ayuda doméstica.*
household income *ingreso familiar.*

housing code *código de construcciones, reglamento de construcción.*

human rights *derechos humanos.*
• Human rights are widely considered to be those fundamental moral rights of the person that are necessary for a life with human dignity. – Syn. international human rights. international protection of human rights.
American Convention on Human Rights *Convención Americana de Derechos Humanos.*
European Convention on Human Rights *Convención Europea de los Derechos Humanos.*
European Court of Human Rights *Corte Europea de Derechos Humanos.*
Inter-American Court of Human Rights *Corte Interamericana de Derechos Humanos.*
Universal Declaration of Human Rights *Declaración Universal de los Derechos del Hombre.*
Rel: discrimination, *discriminación;* genocide, *genocidio;* humanitarian intervention, *intervención humanitaria;* torture, *tortura.*
Ref: (CA) Canadian Human Rights Act, R.S.C. 1985, c.H-6; (Int) UN Charter A1(3), 55, 56; (UK) 8(2) Halsbury's Laws para 101.

hung jury *jurado en desacuerdo (en cuanto al veredicto).*

husband n. *esposo.*
husband-wife privilege *confidencialidad entre esposos.*

I I I I

identification CRIML.LAW n. *identificación.* – Syn. recognition, *reconocimiento.*
Rel: biological fingerprints, *huellas biológicas;* build, *complexión;* complexion, *color de la piel;* handprint, *huella de la mano;* portrait parle, *retrato hablado;* speech, *habla.*

identity n. *identidad.*
identity papers *papeles de identidad.*

idiocy n. *idiotez.* **idiot** n. *idiota.* – Syn. imbecility, *imbecilidad.* feeblemindeness, *debilidad mental.*
Rel: mental disease, *enfermedad mental.*

idiom¹ (expression) *expresión idiomática, modismo.*
• An expression meaning something different than what is conveyed by the words forming it.

idiom² (language) *lengua, dialecto.*
• A language or dialect spoken by a people.

ignorance of the law *ignorancia de la ley.*

ill fame *mala reputación.*

ill will *mala voluntad, hostilidad.*

illegal adj. *ilegal.* – Syn. illicit, *ilícito.* unlawful.
Cf: **illegal • illicit • unlawful.** These words are synonyms that mean a general sense of what is contrary to law. Illicit, in addition, carries moral implications. Illegal and unlawful, being from Latin and French origins respectively, are often interchangeable. Attempts at a generalized distinction of these terms have not succeeded in reaching widespread acceptance.
illegal acts *actos ilegales.*
illegal alien *extranjero indocumentado, ilegal.*
illegal contract *contrato ilegal.*
illegal detention *detención ilegal.*
illegal discrimination *discriminación ilegal.*
illegal entry IMMGR. *entrada (al país) ilegal.*
illegal possession *posesión ilegal.*
illegal search *registro ilegal.*
illegal search and seizure *registro y secuestro ilegal.*
illegal transaction *transacción ilegal.*
Rel: lawless, *sin ley;* unlawful, *ilegal;* wrongful, *ilícito.*

illegitimacy n. *ilegitimidad.* **illegitimate** adj. *ilegítimo.* – Syn. bastardy, *bastardía.*
Rel: bastard, *bastardo;* out of wedlock, *extramarital.*

illicit adj. *ilícito.*

illicit trade *tráfico ilegal.*
Rel: wrongful, *ilícito, ilegal.*
illness n. *enfermedad.*
imbecility n. *imbecilidad.* **imbecile** n. *imbécil.*
– Syn. feeblemindedness, *debilidad mental.*
deficiencia o disminución mental, *deficiencia mental, debilidad mental.* idiocy, *idiotez.*
moronity, *debilidad mental.* retardation, *retardo mental.*
immaterial n. *insustancial, sin consecuencias, sin efectos.*
immigration n. *inmigración.* **immigrant** n. *inmigrante.* **immigrate** v. *inmigrar.*
• Entering a foreign country with the intention to reside there permanently.
adjustment of immigrant status *regularización de calidad migratoria.*
Board of Immigration Appeals (US) *Junta de Apelaciones de Inmigración.* – Abbr. BIA.
change of immigrant status *cambio de calidad migratoria.*
Executive Office for Immigration Review (US) *Oficina Ejecutiva de Revisión de Inmigración.* – Abbr. EOIR.
immigrant status *calidad migratoria.*
immigrant visa *visa de inmigrante.*
Immigration and Naturalization Service (US) *Servicio de Inmigración y Naturalización, la migra* (pop.) – Abbr. INS.
immigration hold *continuación o extensión de una detención por petición de las autoridades migratorias.*
Rel: alien, *extranjero;* asylee, *asilado;* citizenship, *nacionalidad;* deportation, *deportación;* migrant, *migrant;* refugee, *refugiado.*
Glossary: arrival category, *calidad migratoria de entrada;* continuous residence, *residencia continua;* date of entry, *fecha de entrada;* denaturalization, *desnaturalización;* employment permit, *permiso de trabajo;* exclusion hearing, *audiencia para determinar la exclusión;* expatriation, *expatriación, destierro;* extension of status, *extensión de la duración de la calidad migratoria;* green card, *tarjeta o carta de residente permanente;* grounds for exclusion, *causales de exclusión;* grounds for deportation, *causales de deportación;* employment authorization, *autorización de* trabajo; labor certification, *certificación del Departamento de Trabajo;* naturalization, *naturalización;* nonimmigrant visa, *visa de no inmigrante;* notice to appear, *notificación para que (la persona) justifique su permanencia en el país;* offer of employment, *ofrecimiento de trabajo;*

parole, *admisión condicional (en el país);* permanent resident, *residente permanente;* removal proceeding, *procedimiento de expulsión;* suspension of deportation, *suspensión de la deportación;* voluntary departure, *salida voluntaria (del país);* withholding of removal or deportation, *suspensión de la deportación o expulsión.*
immorality n. *inmoralidad.*
immunity n. *inmunidad.*
• An exception from duty, liability or service of process granted by law. – Syn. privilege, *privilegio.*
Cf: **immunity • privilege.** These terms are frequently synonymous. Both of these words refer to a right or exception not enjoyed by others. Immunity underlines an exception from what others must bear, while privilege connotes the freedom not to do what others are obliged to comply with.
diplomatic immunity *inmunidad diplomática.*
immunity from prosecution *inmunidad penal.*
legislative immunity *inmunidad legislativa.*
sovereign immunity *inmunidad judicial del estado.* – Syn. government immunity.
testimonial immunity *inmunidad testimonial.*
impaired v. *inhabilitado, deteriorado físicamente, disminuido, impedido.* – Syn. disabled, *incapacitado, inválido.*
hearing impaired *persona con un defecto auditivo.*
impaired driving *inhabilitado para conducir.*
Rel: handicapped, *en desventaja, inhabilitado.*
impaneling a jury *seleccionar a un jurado.*
impeachment[1] (accusation) *acusación de altos funcionarios o magistrados.*
• Formal accusation charging a public official with wrongdoing while in office.
articles of impeachment *acta de acusación y desafuero de altos funcionarios o magistrados.*
impeachment proceeding *juicio de altos funcionarios o magistrados.*
Rel: accusation, *acusación.*
impeachment[2] (discrediting) *tachas.*
• The contradiction of testimony given by a witness by either providing conflicting evidence or discrediting the witness's veracity.
impeachment of a witness *tacha de testigo.*
impeachment of testimony *impugnación de un testimonio, desvirtuar o tachar un testimonio.*
impeachment of verdict *impugnación de un veredicto, petición de la anulación de un veredicto.*

impersonation n. *suplantación, impostura* (PR), *personificación* (Mx). **impersonate** v. *suplantar, sustituir a una persona.* **impersonator** n. *suplantador.*
• The act of assuming another person's appearance, character or identity, especially with a fraudulent intent. – Syn. personation.
false impersonation *usurpación de funciones públicas o profesionales* || *suplantación de persona.*

implementation n. *implementación, aplicación.*

implicate v. *implicar.*

implied adj. *implícito, tácito.* – Opp. express, expreso.
implied acceptance *aceptación tácita.*
implied agreement *convenio tácito.*
implied confession *confesión implícita.*
implied consent *consentimiento tácito.*
implied malice *presunción de intención ilícita.*
implied warranties *garantías implícitas.*
implied-in-fact contract *cuasicontrato.*

import n. *importación.* **importer** n. *importador.* **importable** adj. *importable.* **import** v. *importar.* – Syn. importation.

importation, manufacture, distribution, and storage of explosive materials *importación, manufactura, distribución y almacenamiento de materiales explosivos.*

impound v. *confiscar.* – Syn. confiscate. seize, *secuestrar.*

imprints n. *impresiones.*
See: physical evidence.

imprisonment n. *ser puesto en prisión, encarcelamiento, reclusión.* – Syn. confinement, *confinamiento.* incarceration, *encarcelamiento.*
false imprisonment *privación ilegal de la libertad.*
term of imprisonment *plazo de la pena de prisión.*

impunity n. *impunidad.*

in camera (law lat.) *en privado, en la oficina del juez o magistrado.* In chambers.

in loco parentis (lat.) *in loco parentis, en lugar de uno de los padres, tutor temporal (de un menor).* In the place of a parent.

in open court *en audiencia pública.*

in pari delicto (lat.) *in pari delicto, igualmente responsable.* In equal fault.

in personam (lat.) *in personam.* Against the person.
• "An action is in personam when its purpose is to determine the rights and interests of the parties themselves in the subject matter of the action." (Garner, 451)
action in personam *acción in personam.*
in personam jurisdiction *jurisdicción in personam.*

in rem (lat.) *in rem.* Against the thing.
• "An action is in rem when the court's judgment determines the title to property and the rights of the parties, not merely among themselves, but also against all persons at any time claiming an interest in the property at issue." (Garner, 451)
action in rem *acción in rem.*
in rem jurisdiction *jurisdicción in rem.*

in toto *totalmente, en total.*

inadmissible adj. *inadmisible.*
inadmissible evidence *pruebas inadmisibles.*
inadmissible testimony *testimonio inadmisible.*

incapacity n. *incapacidad.* – Opp. capacity, *capacidad.*
legal incapacity *incapacidad legal.*
total incapacity *incapacidad total.*

incarceration n. *encarcelación.* – Syn. imprisonment, *ser puesto en prisión, encarcelamiento.* confinement, *confinamiento.*

incest (crime) n. *incesto.*
• Sexual relations between very closely related persons.

inchoate crimes *delitos preparatorios, delitos incoados.*
Specific types: attempt, *tentativa;* conspiracy, *acuerdo para cometer un delito;* solicitation, *invitación a la comisión de un delito.*

incident[1] **(event)** n. *incidente, acontecimiento. accidente* (euph.).
• An event, occurrence or happening.

incident[2] **(accompanying)** n. *incidente, relacionado, concomitante.*
• A dependant, related or connected event.
incident to employment *relacionado con el trabajo, en el trabajo.*

incidental adj. *incidental.*

inciting a riot *incitación a un motín.*

income (accounting) n. *ingreso.*
actual income *ingreso real.*
current income *ingreso actual.*
earned income *ingreso por concepto de trabajo.*
estimated income *ingreso estimado.*
gross income *ingreso bruto.*

net income *ingreso neto.*

retirement income *ingreso de jubilación.*
Rel: earnings, *ingresos, ganancias, utilidades;* proceeds, *ingresos, productos;* profit, *ganancia;* revenue, *ingreso, ganancia;* wage, *sueldo.*

income tax[1] **(individuals)** *impuesto sobre ingresos de las personas, contribución sobre ingresos* (PR).
alternative minimum tax (US) [le]*impuesto mínimo alternativo (al ingreso).*
earned income *ingreso del trabajo.*
deferred income *ingreso diferido.*
income tax return *declaración del impuesto sobre ingresos.*
reportable income *ingreso que debe declararse, ingreso declarable.*
taxable income *ingreso gravable.*
unearned income *ingresos no derivados del trabajo.*
See: tax.

income tax[2] **(corporations)** *impuesto sobre ingresos de las empresas.*
Rel: corporate tax rate, *tasa de impuesto a las empresas;* corporate taxable income, *ingreso gravable de las empresas;* corporation double tax, *doble imposición tributaria a las empresas;* distributions, *distribuciones;* worldwide income, *ingreso mundial.*

incommunicado adj. *incomunicado.*

incompetency n. *incapacidad.* **incompetent** adj. *que es incapaz o no tiene habilidad.*
incompetent to stand trial *con incapacidad para ser procesado, falta de capacidad procesal.*
See: competency.

incorporeal rights *derechos inmateriales.*

incorrigible adj. *incorregible.*

incoterms (int.) *incoterms.*
See: *incoterms (Spanish-English section).*

incredible testimony *testimonio inverosímil.*

incriminate v. *incriminar.* **incrimination** n. *incriminación.* **incriminatory** adj. *incriminatorio, incriminante.*
incriminating circumstances *circunstancias incriminatorias.*
incriminating evidence *pruebas incriminatorias.*
self-incrimination *autoincriminación.*

indecent assault (crime) *abuso deshonesto.*

indecent exposure (crime) *exhibiciones obscenas, exposiciones deshonestas* (PR).
• To expose the genitals in a way and place as to outrage public decency. – Syn. indecent exhibition.

indemnity[1] **(repayment)** n. *indemnización.* **indemnitee** n. *indemnizado.* **indemnitor** n. *indemnizador.* **to indemnify** v. *indemnizar.*
• "An obligation or duty resting on one person to make good on any loss or damage another has incurred or may incur by acting at his request or for his benefit." (Bohannon v. Southern Ry. Co., 104 S.E.2d 603, 605, 97 Ga.App. 849) Also, the right a person suffering the loss or damage is entitled to claim.
Cf: **indemnity • suretyship • contribution.**
"[Indemnity] differs from suretyship or guaranty with which it is often confused in the fact that it is made with a debtor and not the creditor. Indemnity is implied in suretyship or guaranty between the surety and the principal." (Radin, 160) Contribution, on the other hand, means the demand made to a person, who is jointly responsible for injury to another, to contribute his or her share to another jointly responsible person who was already required to compensate the injured party.
indemnity bond *garantía de indemnización, certificado de la garantía de indemnización.*
indemnity contract *contrato de indemnización.*
indemnity insurance *seguro de indemnización.*
Rel: contribution, *derecho de repetición;* suretyship, *fianza o garantía.*

indemnity[2] **(compensation)** n. *compensación.* – Syn. compensation, *compensación.*

indemnity[3] **(free of damage)** n. *indemnidad.*

indictment CRIML.LAW n. *acusación formal (de un delito), acusación por gran jurado* (PR). || *escrito de acusación.*
• A formal accusation, and the document in which it is written, against one or several persons for the commission of an indictable crime or offense. – Syn. committal for trial.
An indictment is issued by a grand jury in the United States and by committal proceedings in the United Kingdom, Canada and Australia.
reindictment [de]*reposición de la acusación formal (de un delito).*
Rel: arraignment, *presentación o lectura de la acusación.*
See: accusation.

indigent adj. *indigente.*

individual retirement account (US) *cuenta personal de jubilación.* – Abbr. IRA.

indorsement n. *endoso.* **indorser** n. *endosante.* **indorsee** n. *endosatario.*

• Signature placed upon the back of an instrument, with or without other words, to transfer or assign the property of the same to another. – Other spell.: endorsement.

blank indorsement *endoso en blanco.*

conditional indorsement *endoso limitado.*

indorsee in due course *tenedor de buena fe.*

qualified indorsement *endoso sin mi responsabilidad.* – Syn. indorsement without recourse.

restrictive indorsement *endoso restrictivo.*

special indorsement *endoso nominal o nominativo.* – Syn. full endorsement.

inducement to commit suicide *inducción a cometer suicidio, instigación al suicidio.*

ineligibility n. *ineligibilidad.* – Syn. exclusion, *exclusión.*

infamy n. *infamia.*

infamous crime *delito infamante.*

infancy n. *minoría de edad.* **infant** n. *infante.* Rel: child, *niño;* minor, *menor.*

infanticide n. *infanticidio, infanticida.*

• The killing of a newborn child. Also the offender.

information *acusación (por fiscal), procesamiento, acusación o denuncia* (PR), *consignación* (Mx.).

• An accusation of a crime made by a prosecutor, of his or her own authority, charging a person with the commission of a crime. – Syn. laying an information.

Information is an alternative to grand jury indictment as a means of starting a criminal prosecution. Rel: arraignment, *presentación o lectura de la acusación;* indictment, *acusación formal.* See: accusation.

informed consent *consentimiento debidamente informado, consentimiento informado.*

informer n. *informante, informador, confidente policíaco.*

• A person who informs or accuses another of a criminal violation before the appropriate authorities. – Syn. informant, *informante.* fink, *soplón.* weasel, *soplón.* stool pigeon, *soplón.* police tipper, *delator (ante la policía), chivato.* squealer, *soplón.*

In most cases the informer remains undisclosed and the information provided is of a voluntary and confidential nature.

informer's privilege *confidencialidad sobre la divulgación de la identidad del informante.* – Syn. informant's privilege.

paid informer *informante pagado.*

reliable informer *informante confiable.*

infraction n. *infracción.*

• Broadly an infringement, more specifically a minor violation of the law. Rel: crime, *delito.*

infringement n. *violación de una disposición.* **infringe** v. *infringir.* **infringer** n. *infractor.*

• An encroachment; a violation of a right or privilege of another.

infringement of copyright *violación de derechos de autor.*

infringement of patent *violación de patente.*

infringement of trademark *violación de marca comercial.*

inhalants n. *inhalantes.* Rel: chloroform, *cloroformo;* ether, *éter;* glue, *pegamento.* See: drugs.

inheritance n. *herencia.* **inherit** v. *heredar.* **inheritor** n. *heredero.* **inheritable** adj. *heredable.*

• That which is inherited or to be inherited by intestacy. It refers to property acquired by descent, as an heir of another.

inheritance tax *impuesto hereditario.* Rel: intestate, *intestado;* succession, *sucesión.*

injunction n. [fe][nwrer]*interdicto.* [de]*mandamiento judicial prohibitorio,* [borr.]*injunction.*

• A judicial remedy awarded for the purpose of requiring a party to refrain from doing or continuing to do a particular act or activity. – Syn. writ of injunction.

Cf: **injunction • preliminary injunction • temporary restraining order.** A preliminary or temporary injunction is a court order issued after the party ordered to refrain has been given notice and opportunity to participate in a hearing regarding the request for the injunction. A temporary restraining order is also a preliminary or temporary injunction, but one that has been issued by the court without notifying the other party.

↪ Injunction, when compared to *interdicto,* is of far wider range and more everyday use in the courts. *Interdicto* is usually restricted only to providing legal relief in cases involving possessory rights. Injunctions without a statutory equivalent *interdictos* have no legal Spanish equivalent in most cases, and the word injunction or its descriptive equivalents are often used to render an accurate translation.

interlocutory injunction [nwrer]*interdicto interlocutorio,* [de]*mandamiento judicial prohibitorio interlocutorio o pendente lite.* – Syn. temporary injunction.

mandatory injunction *mandamiento judicial ordenando una acción o un comportamiento dado,* [le]*interdicto o mandamiento judicial mandatorio.*

preliminary or temporary injunction *interdicto o mandamiento judicial prohibitorio provisional.*

prohibitory injunction *interdicto o mandamiento judicial imponiendo una prohibición,* [de]*interdicto o mandamiento judicial prohibitorio.* – Syn. restraining order.

Rel: temporary restraining order, *medida inhibitoria provisional,* [nwrer]*interdicto prohibitorio,* [de]*mandamiento judicial temporal de prohibición.*

Comment: An injunction is a preventive measure developed by the courts of equity to protect against future injuries that cannot be redressed by an action at law. "An injunction operates in personam; it does not of itself, affect legal rights even within the state; and it may order a party to do, or refrain from doing, acts outside of the jurisdiction or which affect property located outside of the jurisdiction." (McClintock , 88)

Ref: (US) Ladner v. Siegel, 148 A. 699, 701, 298 Pa. 487, 68 A.L.R. 1172; (UK) 24 Halsbury's Laws para 801

injury[1] **(wrong)** n. *lesión, agravio.* **injure** v. *lesionar, agraviar.* **injurious** adj. *lesivo, agraviante.*

• An actionable wrong or damage done to another in person, reputation or property.
– Syn. wrong, *violación de un derecho.*
Unlike physical injury, legal injury is any damage from the violation of a legal right.

cause of injury *causa de la lesión.*

injury to property *daño a la propiedad.*

intentional injury *lesión causada en forma intencional.*

irreparable injury *lesión sin recurso legal.*

permanent injury *lesión consumada.*

Rel: damages, *daños;* personal injury, *responsabilidad civil (por lesiones físicas o morales)*

injury[2] **(bodily harm)** n. *lesión física.*
• Harm or damage made to the body of an individual.

accidental injury *lesión accidental.*

aggravation of injuries *empeoramiento de las lesiones.*

bodily injury *lesión corporal.* – Syn. physical injury.

injuries after regular working hours *lesiones sufridas fuera de la jornada normal de trabajo.*

on the job injuries *lesiones sufridas en el trabajo.*

permanent injury *daño permanente, lesión permanente.*

personal injury *lesiones físicas causadas a una persona.*

Inland Revenue (UK,NZ) *Hacienda pública, fisco.*

inmate n. *preso, recluso, reo.*

innocent adj. *inocente.* **innocence** n. *inocencia.*

innocent passage *paso inocente.*

innocent purchaser *comprador de buena fe.*

insane impulse to act *impulso irracional.*

insanity n. [brder]*demencia, enajenación mental, incapacidad mental* (PR), *trastorno mental permanente.* **insane** adj. *demente.*
• Presence of a mental disorder that relieves a person from criminal or civil responsibility.
– Syn. legal insanity. lunacy. mental defect, *deficiencia o debilidad mental.* mental derangement, *enajenación mental.* mental disorder (CA), *trastorno mental.* mental illness, *enfermedad mental.* mental incompetence, *incapacidad mental.* unsound mind, *no tener juicio, estar demente.* – Opp. sanity, *cordura, sensatez.*
Insanity is a legal term with no definite medical equivalent. While mental disease, defect or disorder describes a mental condition that may exempt a person from punishment for a criminal act, the assertion of insanity can only be established after the application of the standards that may be appropriate for the type of case under consideration.

Cf: **competency** • **credibility** • **insanity.**
Competency refers to the qualification of a person or evidence to be accepted by the court. Credibility refers to the veracity the person or evidence brings to the court. Insanity denotes lack of competency due to a condition of the mind.

☞ Insanity is narrowly constructed as a measure of the mental disorder of a person to be applied to the decision as to whether that person should be criminally responsible. *Demencia* is a similar term meaning mental disorder, but mostly as a medical condition without direct legal implications. *Enajenación mental, incapacidad mental* or *trastorno mental permanente* are the preferred terms used to designate mental disorder as a reason to establish lack of *imputabilidad,* together with unconsciousness, uncontrollable fear, underage and sometimes deaf muteness.

adjudication of insanity [brder][de] *declaración o declaratoria de demencia, declaración o declaratoria de la enajenación mental (del acusado).*

insane delusion *alucinaciones demenciales.*

insanity defense [brder][de]*defensa de demencia,* [fe]*defensa o alegatos de inimputabilidad por la enajenación mental del acusado.* – Syn. plea of insanity.

insanity hearing [brder][de]*audiencia para determinar la validez del alegato de demencia (del acusado).*

Rel: competency, *capacidad;* derangement, *trastorno mental;* diminished capacity, *capacidad mental reducida;* Durham rule, *regla Durham;* guilty but mentally ill, *culpable pero afectado de enfermedad mental;* madness, *locura;* mental disorder, *enfermedad mental;* McNaghten rule, *regla McNaghten;* psychiatric evaluation, *evaluación psiquiátrica.*

> Comment: "In 1843, the House of Lords answered a series of questions about what a criminal defendant must show to succeed on the defense of insanity. These answers are generally known as the *McNaghten rules*." (Garner, 540)
> Ref: (US) Sollars v. State, 316 P.2d 917, 919, 73 Nev. 248; (UK) McNaghten case (1843)10 Cl & Fin 200 at 210

insolvency n. *insolvencia.*
• A person is insolvent when he or she has ceased to pay his or her debts in the ordinary course of business or cannot pay his or her debts as they fall due.

insolvency proceedings *procedimiento de insolvencia.*
Rel: bankruptcy, *quiebra.*

inspection n. *inspección.*
inspection of documents *inspección de documentos.*
inspection warrant *orden judicial de inspección.*
Rel: search, *registro.*

installment n. *pago parcial, abono.* – Other spell.: instalment (UK).
installment contract *contrato de prestaciones periódicas o a plazos.*
installment sale *venta en abonos.*
Rel: sale, *compraventa.*

instanter (oral expr.) adv. *inmediatamente.* Instantly.

instigation n. *instigación.* **instigator** n. *instigador.*
instigation of a crime *instigación de un delito.*

instrument n. *instrumento.*

instrument under seal *instrumento sellado.*
negotiable instrument *título negociable, título de crédito.*

insult n. *insulto, ofensa, injuria.* – Syn. affront, insulto.

insurance n. *seguro.* **insured** n. *asegurado.* **beneficiary** n. *beneficiario.* **insurer** n. *compañía de seguros.*
• "A contract whereby one party, the insurer, undertakes, in return for a consideration, the premium, to pay the other, the insured or assured, a sum of money in the event of the happening of a, or one of various, specified uncertain events." (Walker, 627)
"The concept of sharing risks has long been generally understood and employed in societies throughout the world, and agreements to share risk continue to be among the most important types of consensual arrangements. Insurance is generally understood to be an arrangement for transferring and distributing risks. Unfortunately, this characterization is neither very precise nor universally applicable as a definition of insurance because it describes many other arrangements and relationships which almost uniformly are not regarded or treated as insurance transactions." (Keeton & Widiss, 3)
Cf: **insurance ● suretyship.** In a suretyship, one party simply assumes the liability of another for some consideration. In an insurance, the risk is distributed among a substantial number of members.

accident insurance *seguro de accidente.*
– Syn. casualty insurance.
automobile insurance *seguro de automóvil, seguro automovilístico.*
casualty insurance *seguro de daños por accidente.*
collision insurance *seguro de colisión (de vehículos).*
comprehensive insurance *seguro total.*
fidelity insurance *seguro contra abuso de confianza y deshonestidad de empleados, seguro de fidelidad.*
fire insurance *seguro de incendio.*
group insurance *seguro de grupo, seguro colectivo.*
health insurance *seguro de salud.*
homeowners insurance *seguro de vivienda, seguro de habitación.*
insurance adjuster *ajustador de seguros,*
– Syn. insurance assessor (UK).
insurance agent *agente de seguros.*

insurance carrier *compañía aseguradora.*
insurance company *compañía de seguros.*
insurance law *ley de seguros.*
insurance premium *prima de seguro.*
insurance rate *tasa de seguros.*
liability insurance *seguro de responsabilidad civil.*
life insurance *seguro de vida.*
loss marine insurance *seguro de pérdida marina.*
marine insurance *seguro marítimo.*
no-fault auto insurance *seguro de automóvil sin determinación de culpabilidad, seguro de automóvil de responsabilidad objetiva.*
renters insurance *seguro de arrendatario, seguro de habitación rentada o arrendada.*
term life insurance *seguro de vida a plazo fijo o a término.*
title insurance [de]*seguro de título de propiedad.*
unemployment insurance *seguro de desempleo.*
Rel: loss, *pérdida;* surety, *fianza, garantía.*
See: suretyship.
Ref: (CA) The Insurance Act, R.S.O. 1990; (US) Commissioner of Banking and Insurance v. Community Health Service, 30 A.2d 44, 46, 129 N.J.L. 427; (UK) 25 Halsbury's Laws para 1 at 6.
insurrection *insurrección.* **insurrectionist** *insurgente.*
• Insurrection is "a raising against civil or political authority, but something more than a mob or riot." (45 Am Jur §1) – Syn. rebellion, *rebelión.* revolt, *revuelta.* uprising, *levantamiento.*
intangible property *bienes intangibles.*
integration n. *integración.*
economic integration *integración económica.*
horizontal integration *integración horizontal.*
vertical integration *integración vertical.*
integrity n. *integridad.*
intellectual property *propiedad intelectual.*
• Rights protecting the creation of valuable original thought. It normally includes patents, trademarks, copyrights and design rights.
Rel: copyright, *derechos de autor;* patent, *patente;* service mark, *marcas de servicios;* trade name, *nombre comercial;* trademark, *marca comercial.*
intent¹ (intention) n. *intención.*
• The design or mental determination to do or not to do something. The state of mind behind an act.

Cf: **intent ● motive.** Terms traditionally distinguished: motive refers to the reasons or inducement to carry on an act, while intent describes the resolve or determination to commit the same.
constructive intent *intención implícita o tácita.*
legislative intent *intención legislativa, intención del legislador.*
testamentary intent *intención testamentaria.*
Rel: aforethought, *pensado con anterioridad;* manifestation of intention, *expresión de intención;* motive, *motivo.*
intent² CRIML.LAW n. *intención, intencionalidad,* [fe] *dolo.*
• A state of mind in which the person knows and desires the consequences of his or her act.
– Syn. criminal intent *intención delictiva, dolo.*
felonious intent *intencionalidad en la comisión de delitos mayores.*
fraudulent intent *intención fraudulenta, intención de defraudar.*
general intent *dolo genérico.*
intent to kill *intención de matar.*
specific intent *dolo específico.*
Rel: motive, *móvil;* negligence, *negligencia, culpa, imprudencia;* premeditation, *premeditación;* recklessness, *imprudencia grave.*
intent³ TORTS n. *intención (como elemento de la responsabilidad civil).*
• A purpose to accomplish certain result or the knowledge, with substantial certainty, that the defendant's actions will bring about such result.
– Syn. purpose.
"The intent with which tort liability is concerned is not necessarily a hostile intent, or a desire to do any harm. Rather it is an intent to bring about a result which will invade the interest of another in a way that the law forbids." (Prosser & Keeton on The Law of Torts, 36)
immediate intent *intención de cometer un ilícito.*
inter vivos (lat.) *inter vivos, de una persona viva a otra, entre vivos.* Between the living.
interest¹ (profit) n. *interés.*
• "A sum paid or charged for the use of money or for borrowing money." (Webster Encyclopedic Unabridged Dict., 741)
accrued interest *interés devengado.*
compound interest *interés compuesto.*
conventional interest *interés convencional.*
gross interest *interés bruto.*
interest rate *tasa de interés.*
legal interest *interés legal.*
nominal interest *interés nominal.*
simple interest *interés simple.*

Rel: Truth-in-Lending Act (US), *Ley de trans-parencia en el otorgamiento de préstamos;* usury, *usura.*

interest² (share) n. *interés jurídico.*
• A legal share in something.
adverse interest *interés jurídico de la contraparte.*
controlling interest *parte del capital social que permite controlar la sociedad.*
security interest *derecho sobre un bien dado en garantía.*
vested interest *derecho adquirido pleno y simple sobre un bien,* [le]*derecho presente sobre un bien.*

interest³ PROP.LAW n. *derecho inmobiliario, derecho relativo a bienes inmuebles.*
• A claim, right or title to which a holder of property rights is or may be entitled.
absolute interest *derecho inmobiliario pleno.*
interest for years *derecho inmobiliario limitado a cierto número de años.*
interest in remainder *derecho inmobiliario de tipo residual.*
merger of property interests [de]*consolidación de los derechos inmobiliarios (sobre un bien).* [le]*fusión de los intereses de la propiedad.*
possessory interest *derechos posesorios.*

interference with custody *violación del derecho de custodia o de la patria potestad, privación ilegal de custodia* (PR).

interlocutory adj. *interlocutorio.*
• provisional, temporary, not final. – Syn. intermediate.
interlocutory decree *sentencia interlocutoria.*
interlocutory hearing *audiencia interlocutoria.*
interlocutory judgment *sentencia interlocutoria.*
interlocutory order *decreto interlocutorio, orden interlocutoria.*

interloper n. *comerciante sin autorización, intruso.*

Internal Revenue Service (US) *Hacienda pública, fisco,* [le]*Servicio de Impuestos Internos, Servicio de Rentas Internas* (PR). – Syn. Inland Revenue (UK,NZ). Canada Customs and Revenue Agency (CA). Australian Taxation Office (AU). – Abbr. IRS.

International Bank for Reconstruction and Development (IBRF) *Banco Internacional de Reconstrucción y Fomento* (BIRF), *Banco Inter-*

nacional para la Reconstrucción y Desarrollo (BIRD). – Syn. World Bank.

international business transactions *operaciones internacionales de comercio o de negocios.*

International Court of Justice (ICJ) *Corte Internacional de Justicia.*

International Criminal Police Organization *Organización Internacional de Policía Criminal.* – Abbr. Interpol.

international dispute resolution *resolución extrajudicial internacional de conflictos.*
Rel: good offices, *buenos oficios;* negotiation, *negociación.*
See: alternative dispute resolution (ADR).

International Labor Organization (ILO) *Organización International del Trabajo* (OIT).
See: *Organización Internacional del Trabajo.*

international law *derecho internacional.*
• The law of the international community.
– Syn. ius gentium, *ius gentium.* law of nations, *derecho de gentes.* public international law, *derecho internacional público.*
"International law consists of rules and principles of general application dealing with the conduct of states and of international organizations and with their relations inter se, as well as with some of their relations with persons, whether natural or juridical." Restatement (Revised) Foreign Relations Law §101
Rel: airspace law, *derecho aéreo;* asylum, *asilo;* human rights, *derechos humanos;* law of the sea, *derecho del mar;* state, *estado;* treaty, *tratado;* war, *guerra.*

international licensing *otorgamiento internacional de licencias.* **licensee** *licenciatario, licenciador.* **licensor** *licenciante.*
international licensing agreement *contrato internacional de otorgamiento de licencia.*
Rel: applicable law, *ley aplicable;* know-how, *conocimientos técnicos,* [borr.]*know-how;* royalties, *regalías.*

International Monetary Fund (IMF) *Fondo Monetario Internacional.*

international organizations *organizaciones internacionales.*

international private law *derecho internacional privado.*
Rel: conflict of laws, *conflicto de leyes.*

international relations *relaciones internacionales.*

international taxation *derecho fiscal internacional, tributación internacional.*
Glossary: advance pricing agreement (APA), *acuerdo anticipado con la autoridad fiscal del método de transferencia de precios;* arm's length price, *precio de mercado;* back-to-back loan, *préstamo compensatorio;* cross-border transactions, *transacciones fronterizas;* direct investment, *inversión directa;* double taxation, *doble imposición tributaria;* dual-resident taxpayer, *causante con doble residencia;* effectively connected income, *ingreso vinculado efectivamente;* engaged in a trade or business, *estar dedicado a una ocupación o negocio;* exemption method, *método de exención de ingresos de fuente extranjera;* foreign currency, *divisa extranjera;* foreign income exclusion, *exclusión de ingresos generados en el extranjero;* foreign tax credit, *acreditación de impuestos pagados en el extranjero;* in-bound transactions, *transacciones de extranjeros realizadas en el país;* income tax treaty, *tratado o convenio fiscal sobre la renta;* intercompany pricing, *precios de transferencia entre empresas asociadas;* inter-nation equity, *distribución fiscal equitativa del ingreso entre países;* outbound transactions, *transacciones realizadas en el extranjero;* permanent establishment (PE), *establecimiento o negocio permanente;* place of incorporation, *lugar de su constitución;* place of management, *lugar de su administración;* source country, *país de origen, país de tributación original;* tax haven, *paraíso fiscal;* treaty shopping, *elección del tratado más ventajoso para el causante.*
See: off shore companies. tax.

international trade *comercio internacional.*
Rel: import, *importación;* export, *exportación.*

interpleader n. [nrwer]*tercería,* [de]*petición de que se resuelva una controversia entre terceros (respecto del objeto de la demanda).*
• An action exercised by a disinterested party to force rival claimants to assert who, if any, has a legitimate claim against such disinterested party.

interpretation¹ (language) n. *interpretación de idiomas.* **interpreter** n. *intérprete.*
• The rendering of discourse from a source language to a target language without change of register or meaning.
conference interpretation *interpretación de conferencia.*
consecutive interpretation *interpretación consecutiva.*

court interpretation *interpretación judicial.*
disqualification of an interpreter *remoción de un intérprete (de una sesión o caso), descalificación de un intérprete.*
sight interpretation *interpretación oral de un texto.*
simultaneous interpretation *interpretación simultánea.*
verbatim interpretation *interpretación palabra por palabra.*
Glossary: accreditation examinations, *exámenes de acreditación;* clarification, *clarificación;* editing speech, *editar lo dicho;* false start, *comienzo sin seguimiento;* fragmentary statements, *fragmentos de oraciones o frases;* level or register, *nivel o registro;* lengthening testimony, *alargar lo dicho en testimonio;* nonverbal communication, *comunicación no verbal;* repetition, *repetición;* self-correction, *corregirse a sí mismo, autocorrección;* source language, *idioma original, idioma de partida;* tape transcription, *transcripción de cintas (gravadas);* target language, *idioma al que se interpreta, idioma de llegada.*
See: court interpretation.

interpretation² (legal text) n *interpretación jurídica.* **interpret** v. *interpretar.* **interpretative** adj. *interpretativo.* **interpretive** adj. *interpretativo.*
• The ascertaining of the meaning of legal text.
– Syn. construction.
constitutional interpretation *interpretación constitucional, interpretación de preceptos constitucionales.*
contract interpretation *interpretación de un contrato, interpretación contractual.*
legal interpretation *interpretación legal.*
restrictive interpretation *interpretación restrictiva.*
strict interpretation *interpretación estricta.*
See: construction.

interrogation n. *interrogatorio, interrogación.*
interrogate v. *interrogar.* **interrogator** n. *interrogador.*
custodial interrogation *interrogación del detenido.*
third degree interrogation *interrogatorio agresivo y extenuante, interrogatorio exhaustivo.*
Rel: inquiry, *averiguación;* confession, *confesión.*

interrogatories n. *pliego de posiciones.*
• Written questions put to one party by the other in a lawsuit as a form of discovery.

intervening cause TORTS *causa independiente del*

acto o conducta, causa interviniente (PR).

intervening damages APPEAL *daños causados durante el procedimiento de apelación.*

intervention[1] CIVIL PROCED n. *tercería.* **intervenor** n. *tercero.*

intervention by right *tercería por disposición legal, tercería por ministerio de ley.*

intervention by the leave of the court *tercería por determinación del juez, tercería por discreción del juez.*
Rel: interpleader, *tercería.*

intervention[2] INTL.LAW n. *intervención.* **intervene** v. *intervenir.*
• Interference in the internal affairs of another country.
foreign intervention *intervención extranjera.*
humanitarian intervention *intervención humanitaria.*

interview n. *entrevista.*

intestacy n. *intestado.* **intestate** adj. *intestado.*
• To die without making a will.
intestate succession *sucesión intestada.*
– Syn. [obs.]descent and distribution.
Rel: next of kin, *heredero* || *pariente más cercano;* will, *testamento.*
See: succession[1].

intimidation n. *intimidación.*

intoxication n. *intoxicación.*

intrusion n. *intrusión.* **intruder** n. *intruso.*
• Entry in a place without permission.
home intrusion *penetración indebida en una casa habitada.*
intrusion of rights *violación de derechos.*

invalid[1] **(disabled)** adj.n. *inválido.*
• A weak or sickly person, especially one disabled.

invalid[2] **(null)** adj. *sin validez, inválido.*
• Having no legal force or effect. – Syn. nugatory, *nugatorio.* null, *nulo.* void, *nulo.* voidable, *anulable.*
invalid contract *contrato sin validez.*
invalid gift *donación sin validez.*
invalid transfer *transferencia sin validez.*
invalid will *testamento sin validez.*

invasion of privacy *violación del derecho de privacía o privacidad, atentados a la vida privada.*

invention n. *invención.*
• A new devise, composition of matter, process or a new use of these that is described or claimed in a patent.
Rel: patent, *patente.*

inventory[1] **(accounting)** n. *inventario.*
inventory turnover *rotación del inventario.*

inventory[2] CRIML.LAW *inventario.*
• An itemized list of property, especially of evidence pieces.
inventory of seized property *inventario de bienes decomisados o confiscados.*
inventory search *registro para efectos de inventario.*

investigation n. *investigación.* **investigate** v. *investigar.* **investigator** n. *investigador.*
police investigation *investigación de la policía, investigación policíaca.*
presentence investigation *investigación preparatoria de la condena.*
pretrial investigation *investigación preparatoria del juicio, investigación preliminar del acusado.*

investment n. *inversión.* **investor** n. *inversionista.*
investment broker *corredor de valores.*
investment company *compañía de inversiones.*
investment security *valores de inversión.*
investment trust *fideicomiso de inversión.*

invoice n. *factura.* **invoice** v. *facturar.*

involuntary confession *confesión no voluntaria.*

involuntary manslaughter *homicidio no intencional inconsciente,* [fe]*homicidio culposo con previsión o representación, homicidio accidental involuntario.*

ipso facto (lat.) *ipso facto, como resultado del acto mismo.* By the fact or act itself.

ipso jure (lat.) *ipso jure, por ministerio de ley.* By the operation of the law itself.

irrelevant adj. *irrelevante.* – Syn. beside the point, *que no viene al caso.* not applicable, *no es aplicable.* not pertinent, *no es pertinente.* unrelated, *no está relacionado.*
irrelevant evidence *pruebas irrelevantes.*
irrelevant question *pregunta irrelevante.*
irrelevant testimony *testimonio irrelevante.*
See: material.

irreparable damages *daños irreparables.*

irreparable injury *lesión sin recurso legal.*

irresistible force *fuerza mayor.*

irresistible impulse *impulso irresistible, impulso incontrolable* (PR). – Syn. uncontrollable impulse.

irretrievable breakdown of marriage [de]*quebrantamiento irreversible de un matrimonio,* [de]*rompimiento irreparable de un matrimonio.*

irrevocable adj. *irrevocable.* – Syn. indefeasible. unalterable, *inalterable.* unchangeable, *incambiable.*

irrevocable letter of credit *carta de crédito irrevocable.*

irrevocable trust *fideicomiso irrevocable.*

issuance of a bad check *expedir o emitir un cheque incobrable.*

issuance of a check without provision of funds *expedición o emisión de un cheque sin provisión de fondos.*

Rel: bounce a check, *rebotar un cheque, recibir de regreso un cheque (por incobrable);* rubber check, *cheque de hule, cheque incobrable.*

issue in pleading *cuestión en litigio, cuestión controvertida.*

issue of fact *cuestión de hecho.*

issue of law *cuestión de derecho.*

issue of stock CORP. *emisión de acciones.*

itinerant adj. *ambulante.* – Syn. ambulant.

Rel: migratory, *migratorio;* wandering, *vagabundo, errante.*

JJJJ

jail n. *cárcel.* **jailer** n. *carcelero.*

• A place of confinement for defendants awaiting trial and for those convicted of misdemeanors. – Syn. gaol (Engl.). detention center, *centro de detenciones.* cooler or slammer (slg.), *cárcel, bote* (Mx), *reja* (Cu), *cafúa* (Ar). the can (slg.), *bote, reja, cafúa.*

jail bird *ex-convicto.*

jail search *búsqueda de un detenido en la cárcel.*

Rel: house of corrections, *correccional, reformatorio;* lockup, *celda de detenidos;* reformatory, *reformatorio.*

jailbreak n. *fugarse de la cárcel, fuga (de una prisión o cárcel).*

jailhouse lawyer [de]*reo que da consejos legales (dentro de la prisión),* [de]*reo que aconseja a otros (acerca de cuestiones legales).*

jargon n. *jerga, jerigonza.*

• Specialized language used by members of any social, occupational, or professional group to communicate among themselves.

Cf: **jargon ● terms of art.** In the legal field, jargon is the broad range of specialized words used by lawyers; term of art is an even more specific and precise group of terms. <Reasonable care is a jargonistic word; promissory estoppel is a term of art.>

jeopardy n. [de]*(el encontrarse) sujeto al riesgo de una decisión judicial.*

• The danger of conviction or punishment in which a person is placed when put on trial for a criminal offense. – Syn. legal jeopardy.

double jeopardy [de]*doble riesgo de una misma decisión judicial, doble exposición* (PR).

jetsam MARIT.LAW n. *bienes en echazón.*

• Goods thrown overboard which sank and remained underwater.

See: flotsam.

jettison MARIT.LAW n. *echazón.*

• Throwing cargo overboard to save a ship floundering or in danger of sinking.

job¹ (task) n. *trabajo, tarea.*

to do a job *hacer una tarea, hacer un trabajo.*

job² (occupation) n. *trabajo, ocupación.*

to be on the job *estar en el trabajo.*

to have a job *tener un empleo, tener un trabajo.*

joinder¹ (bring together) n. *acumulación (de partes o acciones).*

• Uniting either several causes of action or several parties in a single lawsuit.

Cf: **joinder ● consolidation.** "Whereas joinder has come to be used usually in the sense of uniting parties in a suit, consolidation has become in [American English] the more usual word for uniting two or more lawsuits into a single suit." (Garner, 478)

compulsory joinder *litisconsorcio necesario.* – Syn. needed joiner.

joinder of defendants *acumulación de partes (en acciones penales).*

joinder of offenses *concurso de delitos.*

joinder of parties *acumulación de partes, litisconsorcio.*

permissive joinder *litisconsorcio voluntario.*

Rel: class action, *acción colectiva;* consolidation, *acumulación de acciones;* misjoinder, *acumulación o litisconsorcio improcedente.*

joinder² (adding to) *adhesión.*

• Acceptance of acting jointly.

joinder in pleading [de]*admisión de la acción y la litis planteadas (por la contraria).*

joinder of plaintiffs *adhesión a la demanda.*

joint adj. *conjunto, unido, común.* **jointly** adv. *solidariamente, conjuntamente.*

joint account *cuenta mancomunada y solidaria.* – Syn. joint and survivorship account.

joint and several liability *responsabilidad solidaria y mancomunada.*

joint custody *custodia en común.*

joint ownership *copropiedad.*

joint trial *acumulación de procesos.*

joint tenancy *copropiedad (con derecho de acrecer).*

Cf: **joint tenancy • tenancy in common.** Both terms refer to co-ownership. In a joint tenancy each coowner has a right of survivorship in the other's share, while in a tenancy in common each person has an equal right to possess the property but not the right of survivorship.

joint venture *asociación en participación, empresa común* (PR).

• A relationship between two or more persons combining their labor or property and sharing profits or losses for a single business undertaking. – Syn. syndicate, *sindicación, asociación o consorcio.*

Cf: **partnership • joint venture.** A partnership is an association of persons who jointly own and carry on a business for profit. A joint venture is an undertaking carried on by two or more persons in a single project, but it does not rise to the level of being a permanent entity like partnership does.

joint-venture corporation *asociación en participación en la que participan una o varias sociedades, coinversión.*

See: partnership.

joy ride *robo de uso (de un vehículo),* [de]*tomar un vehículo sin permiso (para viajar en él sin intención de apropiárselo), vehículo robado sólo para "dar la vuelta".*

judge n. *juez.*

• One who presides over a court with power to adjudicate controversies and decide matters brought before him or her. – Syn. adjudicator, *juzgador.* arbiter, *árbitro.* justice, *juez.*

Cf: **judge • arbiter • justice • arbitrator.** Judge and justice are not synonyms, but in some restricted cases these terms are interchangeable. The generic is judge and includes justice. In general contexts justice does not include judge. Arbiter, on the other hand, refers to the power a person has to decide conflicts or disputes and is a broader term than both judge and justice. In contrast, arbitrator is strictly defined as a neutral person called to resolve a dispute, usually following a formal arbitration proceeding.

⤝ Judges in common law countries are not case managers like the *jueces* in the civil law countries. An English judge acts more like an impartial decision-maker in a contest, a "silent umpire" between two adversaries burdened with providing their own evidence and allega-tions in a mostly oral process. In contrast, a *juez* in civil law countries is considered a main participant, more outspoken and inquisitorial, in charge of finding and providing evidence in addition to handing down a ruling in a mostly written process.

appellate judge *magistrado.*

associate judge *juez asociado.*

chief judge *juez en jefe, juez que preside otros jueces (en toda la jurisdicción).*

Justice of the Supreme Court *Magistrado de la Suprema Corte, Ministro de la Suprema Corte.*

lay judge *juez lego.*

presiding judge *juez presidiendo un tribunal.*

removal of a judge *remoción de un juez.*

substitution of judge [fe]*recusación de un juez,* [le]*substitución de juez.* – Abbr. SOJ.

trial judge *juez de la causa, juez del proceso.*

Rel: magistrate, *magistrado;* trier of fact, *juzgador de hecho (en contraste con "de derecho").*

judgment n. *sentencia, fallo.*

• The final determination in a cause, based on the verdict of a jury, on the plea of a defendant, or on findings following a bench trial of the matters submitted for decision. – Syn. adjudication, *adjudicación.* decision, *decisión.* decree, *decreto.* finding, *determinación.* ruling, *fallo, decisión.*

A distinction is usually made between opinion as the reasons for the disposition and the judgment proper as the disposition itself. This distinction is usually not observed in England where opinion and judgment are used as synonyms.

Cf: **judgment • decision • decree • ruling.**

Although decree is the final disposition in equity, judgment is often used to refer to the final decision in both equitable and legal proceedings. Decision is a more general, non-technical term, while a ruling is the outcome of a court's decision on a point of law or on the adjudication of the case itself.

⤝ Some differences between judgment and *sentencia* are: the former is usually given orally while the latter is handed down in writing; judgments are usually pronounced immediately after the conclusion of the corresponding trial, while *sentencias* are usually delayed for several days and even weeks, when the sentencing judge is to review and become familiar with the record or *autos.*

arrest of judgment *suspensión temporal de los efectos de una sentencia.*

cognovit judgment *sentencia basada en la admisión (de una obligación) hecha por parte del demandado.*

collateral attack on a judgment *impugnación de una sentencia hecha en forma indirecta.*

conditional judgment *sentencia condicional.*

consent judgment *sentencia por mutuo acuerdo o consensual, proceso simulado o juicio consentido, sentencia por confesión* (PR). – Syn. agreed judgment. stipulated judgment.

declaratory judgment *sentencia declaratoria.*

default judgment *sentencia dictada en rebeldía.*

deficiency judgment *sentencia de pago de sumas no cubiertas por la ejecución judicial.*

domestic judgment *sentencia estatal o nacional.*

dormant judgment *sentencia incumplida.*

enforcement of a judgment *ejecución de una sentencia.*

entry of judgment *inscripción y fecha en que surte efectos una sentencia.*

execution of a judgment *ejecución de una sentencia.*

final judgment *sentencia definitiva.*

foreign judgment *sentencia de otra jurisdicción.*

interlocutory judgment *sentencia interlocutoria.*

judgment call *vista de los casos para sentencia.*

judgment in rem *sentencia determinando la situación jurídica de una cosa o derecho cuyo efecto recae sobre las personas.*

judgment in personam *sentencia dirigida a una persona que afecta sus derechos u obligaciones.*

judgment non obstante verdicto or notwithstanding verdict (N.O.V.) *sentencia no obstante veredicto en contrario.*

judgment of acquittal *sentencia absolutoria, fallo absolutorio* (PR).

judgment of conviction *sentencia condenatoria, sentencia de condena.* – Syn. judgment of guilt.

judgment of dismissal *sentencia absolutoria.*

judgment on the merits *sentencia sobre el fondo del asunto.*

money judgment *sentencia de pago de dinero.*

personal judgment *sentencia que resulta en responsabilidad personal de la parte culpable.*

relief from judgment *impugnación de una sentencia.*

reversal of judgment *revocación de una sentencia.*

summary judgment *dictar sentencia sumariamente, sentencia sumaria* (PR).

vacating a judgment *revocación de una sentencia.*

See: *fallo.* sentence².

judicial adj. *judicial.* **judicially** adv. *judicialmente.*

judicial activism *actuación política de la judicatura.*

judicial decision *decisión judicial.*

judicial driving permit *permiso judicial para conducir.*

judicial circuit *circuito judicial.*

judicial discretion *discreción judicial.*

judicial district *distrito judicial.*

judicial officer *funcionario judicial.*

judicial recommendation against deportation (JRAD)(US) *recomendación judicial contra la deportación.*

judicial sale *venta judicial.*

Rel: juristic, *jurídico.*

judicial notice *conocimiento judicial, hecho notorio.*

• "The power of a court to accept as proved certain notorious facts." (Radin, 176) – Syn. judicial cognizance.

judicial notice of foreign law *conocimiento judicial de leyes extranjeras.*

to take judicial notice *dar por admitido en autos un conocimiento judicial o un hecho notorio.*

judicial review¹ (control) [de]*facultad del poder judicial para determinar la constitucionalidad de los actos del gobierno, control constitucional de los actos de gobierno.*

• "The power of courts to examine governmental actions to determine whether they are within constitutional limits." (Renstrom, 20)

↦ Judicial review is a major development arising from tradition, history and political institutions in English-speaking countries. In Hispanic countries, where traditions conducive to the creation of this institution are absent, judicial review or *control constitucional de los actos de gobierno*, is not a vigorous living legal institution, but rather a constitutional formality obscured by the preeminence of a strong presidential power in most cases.

Ref: (US) Madbury v. Madison 5 U.S. 87

judicial review² APPEAL *revisión judicial.*

judiciary n. *poder judicial.*

jump bail *fugarse estando bajo fianza.*

jurat *certificación (de una declaración o testimonio).*
• An authentication made by an officer certifying that an affidavit was sworn and signed by the person subscribing it.
Rel: sworn and subscribed before me, *jurado y suscrito ante mi.*

juris et de jure (lat.) *jure et de jure, por ley y por derecho.* Of law and from law.

juris tantum (lat.) *juris tantum, presunción que admite prueba en contrario.*

jurisdiction¹ (power) n. *jurisdicción.*
• The power to hear and determine a case. Jurisdiction is also used to refer to particular legal systems. – Syn. authority to hear and decide a case, *autoridad legal para juzgar y decidir un caso.* capacity to decide the matter in issue, *capacidad para decidir la materia en cuestión.* legal power to decide a case, *facultad legal para decidir un caso.*

ancillary jurisdiction *jurisdicción prorrogada sobre cuestiones accesorias o incidentales.*
civil jurisdiction *jurisdicción civil.*
concurrent jurisdiction *jurisdicción concurrente.*
equity jurisdiction *jurisdicción en derecho-equidad.*
exclusive jurisdiction *jurisdicción exclusiva.*
limited jurisdiction *jurisdicción limitada.*
original jurisdiction *jurisdicción original.*
pendent jurisdiction *jurisdicción prorrogada sobre la materia.* – Syn. supplemental jurisdiction.
personal jurisdiction *jurisdicción sobre la persona.*
submission to a jurisdiction *sometimiento a una jurisdicción.*
Ref: (UK) 10 Halsbury's Laws para 314; (US) Jacubenta v. Dunbar, 198 N.E.2d 674, 675, 120 Ohio App. 249.

jurisdiction² (place) n. *competencia territorial.*
• A geographical area to which a court's power to adjudicate is circumscribed.
See: venue.

jurisdictional plea *excepción de incompetencia.*

jurisprudence n. *jurisprudencia.*
• The science of law. – Syn. legal philosophy, *filosofía del derecho.*
↦ In the common law tradition, jurisprudence refers to the science of law, the study of the structure of the legal system, and to the case law as a system; it is also a synonym for "law." In the civil law tradition, *jurisprudencia* means mostly the collectivity of decisions of a particular court or a particular jurisdiction; it has also been used, like in the common law tradition, to mean the science of law and "law" but these connotations are rare today.

jurist n. *jurista.*

jury n. *jurado, jurados.* **juror** n. *jurado.*
• A group of persons selected from a given community to assist a court by indicting a person or deciding a question of fact after hearing evidence to that effect.
Cf: **jury • triers of fact • array.** All three terms are used synonymously, but they are not interchangeable in most cases. Jury is the more precise term, meaning a group of jurors for the purpose of hearing a case and rendering a verdict. Triers of fact refers to the jury's obligation to make findings of fact in deliberating and reaching a verdict, or the judge's obligation to do so in a bench trial. Array, on the other hand, means a panel of potential jurors or a list of impaneled jurors; it is equivalent to venire.
↦ *Jurados* is not an institution often used in civil law countries, even though from time to time attempts to use them in the courts are introduced, usually without success. In contrast, common law countries have traditionally used the jury successfully, although its presence has been steadily reduced, and it is used today mostly in criminal trials and some limited civil matters.

advisory jury *jurado de consulta únicamente.*
alternate juror *jurado suplente.*
challenge for cause *descalificación con causa de un jurado.*
charge to the jury *instrucciones sobre la ley aplicable.*
foreman of a jury *presidente del jurado.*
– Syn. **foreperson of a jury.**
grand jury *jurado de acusación,* [le]*Gran jurado* (PR).
hung jury *jurado en desacuerdo (en cuanto al veredicto).* – Syn. deadlocked jury.
impaneling a jury *seleccionar un jurado.*
– Syn. empaneling a jury.
jury box *estrado del jurado.*
jury deliberation *deliberación del jurado.*
jury duty *servicio de jurado obligatorio.*
jury misconduct *actuación ilegal del jurado, actos ilegales del jurado.*
jury instructions *instrucciones del juez dadas al jurado.* – Syn. jury directions (GB).
jury selection *selección de jurados.*
jury tampering *intento de influir o sobornar al jurado.* – Syn. embracery.
jury trial *juicio de jurados, juicio ante*

jurados, juicio ante un jurado popular.
peremptory challenge *descalificación sin causa de un jurado.*
petit jury [borr.]*jurado petit, jurado menor.*
polling the jury *encuesta del jurado (acerca de su voto).*
sequestering the jury *aislamiento o confinamiento de un jurado.*
Rel: motion for directed verdict, *petición para que el juez dicte el veredicto (en vez del jurado);* right to trial by jury, *derecho de tener un juicio de jurados;* venire selection, *selección de un grupo de posibles jurados;* verdict, *veredicto;* voir dire, *voir dire, proceso de selección de jurados.*
See: trial.
Ref: (CA) Jury Act, R.S.M. 1987, c. J30, s. 1.; R. v Meunier (1942) 80 C.C.C. 125 (Que. SC); (US) Freeman v. U.S., C.C.A.N.Y., 227 F. 732, 74; State v. Dalton, 174 S.E. 422, 424, 206 N.C. 5073; (UK) 26 Halsbury's Laws para 401.

justice¹ (fairness) n. *justicia.* – Syn. equity, *justicia, equidad.* fairness, *justicia, imparcialidad.* righteousness, *justicia, rectitud.*
obstruction of justice *obstrucción de justicia.*
speedy justice *justicia expedita.*

justice² (judge) n. *magistrado, juez.*
justice of the peace *juez de paz.*
Justice of the Supreme Court *Magistrado de la Suprema Corte, Ministro de la Suprema Corte.*

justifiable homicide *homicidio con justificantes.*

justification CRIML.LAW n. *justificantes, causas de justificación.* – Syn. justification defense.
Cf: **justification ● excuse.** "A justification challenges the wrongfulness of an action which technically constitutes a crime. In contrast excuse concedes the wrongfulness of the action but asserts that the circumstances under which it was done are such that it ought not to be attributed to the actor." (International Encyclopaedia of Laws. Criminal Law, vol. I at 111) In modern law, justification and excuse have become synonymous for all practical purposes, although there is still a moral connotation in distinguishing criminal behavior considered lawful and justified, rather than wrongful but excused. Justifications traditionally include the following: consent, self-defense, necessity, and use of force by public authority.
Rel: consent, *consentimiento por el agraviado;* necessity, *estado de necesidad;* self-defense,

defensa propia; use of force by public authority, *uso de la fuerza pública.*
See: excuse.

juvenile adj. *juvenil.*
juvenile delinquency (JD), *delincuencia juvenil.*
juvenile detention center *centro de detención para menores.*
juvenile record *antecedentes penales como menor.*

juvenile n. *menor, joven.*
• A person who is not an adult.
juvenile delinquent *menor encontrado culpable (en un proceso judicial).* – Syn. juvenile offender. youthful offender.
Rel: minor, *menor de edad;* teenager, *adolescente (entre los 13 y 19 años),* [nwrer] *quinceañero;* truant, *remiso escolar, que no asiste a la escuela, que hace novillos, que se va de pinta* (Mx)(pop).

juvenile court *tribunal para menores.*
Rel: Department of Children and Family Services (DCFS) (US), *Departamento de Menores y Servicios Familiares;* secure custody (CA), *detención para menores.*

juvenile proceedings *procedimiento judicial en materia de menores.*
Glossary: adjudicatory hearing, *audiencia de adjudicación;* caseworker, *trabajador social asignado al caso;* commitment to the Department of Corrections, *ser enviado al Departamento de Correcciones;* child in need of services (CHINS), *menor que requiere de servicios de ayuda;* disposition hearing, [le]*audiencia de disposición, audiencia para resolver la situación jurídica del menor;* guardian at litem, *tutor judicial provisional, tutor at litem;* minor in need of supervision (MINS), *menor que requiere de supervisión;* minor respondent, *menor responsable, menor acusado;* temporary custody hearing, *audiencia de custodia temporal;* to be adjudged a ward of the court, *quedar bajo la tutela o custodia del tribunal.*

KKKK

kickback n. *pago de comisión secreta e ilegal, comisión ilegal, mochada* (slg.)(Mx).

kidnapping (crime) n. *secuestro.* **kidnapper** n. *secuestrador.*
• Unlawful taking and carrying away of a person against that person's will by force or fraud, usually for ransom. – Syn. abduction,

rapto. child stealing, *secuestro o rapto de menores.* hijacking, *secuestro.*

Cf: **kidnapping • false imprisonment.** These terms are close but clearly differentiated: false imprisonment does not require taking and carrying away, while kidnapping is a false imprisonment with the added removal of the victim to another location.

aggravated kidnapping *secuestro con agravantes.*

kidnapping in the first degree *secuestro de primer grado.*

kidnapping for ransom *secuestro para pedir recompensa, secuestro extorsivo* (Co).

simple kidnapping *secuestro simple, secuestro sin agravantes.*

Rel: false arrest, *detención ilegal;* false imprisonment, *privación ilegal de la libertad;* interference with custody, *violación del derecho de custodia.*

See: abduction.

Ref: (UK) People (AG) v Edge[1943] I.R. 115 at 146; (US) State v. Bruce, 150 S.E.2d 216, 223, 268 N.C. 174.

killing *dar muerte, matar.* **killer** n. *asesino.* – Syn. annihilation, *aniquilación.* elimination, *eliminación.* extermination, *exterminación.* slaying, *matar.*

indiscriminate killing *matanza indiscriminada.*

killing by destructive device or explosive *homicidio mediante el uso de un artefacto destructivo o explosivos.*

killing by torture *homicidio por tortura.*
See: homicide. manslaughter.

kinship n. *parentesco.* **kinsman** n. *pariente.*
Rel: relatives, *parientes.*

kleptomania n. *cleptomanía.* **kleptomaniac** n. *cleptomaníaco.*
• An obsessive impulse to steal.

know all men by these presents (legalese) *hágase saber a todos por la presente.*

know-how n. *conocimientos técnicos, conocimientos técnicos especiales,* [borr.]*know-how.*
•"The information, practical knowledge, techniques and skill required to achieve some practical end, particularly in industry or technology." (Garner, 495)

knowingly and willfully *a sabiendas e intencionalmente.*

LLLL

labor¹ (work) *trabajo, labor.*

hard labor *trabajos forzados.*

labor agreement *contrato colectivo de trabajo.* – Syn. union contract.

labor code *código de trabajo, código laboral.*

labor crew *cuadrilla de trabajo.*

labor dispute *conflicto laboral.*

labor² (social group) *clase obrera, trabajadores.*

labor law *derecho laboral, derecho del trabajo.* – Syn. industrial relations. – Other spell.: labour law (RU).

In England labor law is traditionally divided into contractual rights, statutory employment protection and collective labor law.

Rel: collective bargaining agreement; *convenio colectivo de trabajo;* contract of employment, *contrato de trabajo;* union, *sindicato.*

Labor Relations Board (US) *Junta de Relaciones Laborales.*

labor union *sindicato.*

labor organization *organización laboral.*
See: union.

laches (law fr.) n. [fe]*caducidad de la instancia,* [de]*pérdida de derechos por inactividad procesal, incuria* (PR).
• Equitable defense against the enforcement of long-neglected rights.

Cf: **laches • statute of limitations.** "[Statute of limitations] refers to a fixed statutory period of time within which an action may be brought to preserve a claim, and which if not brought within the statutory period is barred. 'Laches' signifies such inexcusable and prejudicial delay, independent of statute, as in equity would operate to bar a claim." (Kaplan, 6)

estoppel by laches [de]*preclusión de un derecho por inactividad procesal, excepción o impedimento de caducidad de la instancia.*
Rel: dereliction of duty, *abandono de un deber;* inexcusable delay, *retrazo injustificado;* lapse, *caducidad.*
See: *caducidad de la instancia.*

lack of evidence *falta de pruebas.*

lack of jurisdiction *falta de jurisdicción.*

land n. *tierra, terreno, suelo* || *derecho sobre un inmueble.* **landholder** n. *terrateniente.* **landowner** n. *propietario, hacendado.*
• Any soil, ground or earth whatsoever. Also, an estate or interest in real property. – Syn. earth, *tierra.* ground, *tierra, suelo.* soil, *suelo.* tract, *tracto, extensión.*

Cf: **land • real property • realty • real estate.**
All these terms are often used interchangeably. Land is usually the term giving a general de-

scription of the soil, ground or earth. Real property underlines the legal description of land including, in addition to the soil, the ground below and the space above. Realty and real estate underline the physical components of land, such as any additions, deposits, constructions, etc. and they are usually used as generic terms that include all others.

abutting land *terreno colindante.*

adjacent land *terreno contiguo, terreno cercano.*

appurtenance to land *anexo a un terreno o un inmueble.*

common land *tierra comunal, copropiedad.*

convey an interest in land *transmitir un derecho de propiedad sobre un inmueble.*

equitable interest in land *derechos de propiedad sobre inmuebles basados en el derecho-equidad.*

land certificate *certificado de inscripción de un inmueble.*

land contract *contrato de compraventa de bienes inmuebles.*

land grant *concesión de tierras.*

land tax *impuesto sobre inmuebles.*

lease of land *arrendamiento de un predio o terreno.*

lien on land [de]*derecho preferencial de garantía sobre un predio o terreno, gravamen sobre un inmueble.*

subdivision of land *subdivisión de terrenos.*

title in land *título de propiedad de un inmueble.*

trespass on land *entrar u ocupar un inmueble sin derecho.*

vacant land *propiedad vacante.*

Rel: real estate, *bienes raíces;* real property, *bienes inmuebles.*

See: real estate.

Ref: (UK) 26 Halsbury's Laws para 507; Land Charges Act 1972; (US) Reynard v. City of Caldwell, 42 P.2d 292, 296, 55 Idaho, 342.

landlord and tenant *arrendamiento de inmuebles* || *relación jurídica entre arrendador y arrendatario.*

See: lease.

language¹ (speech) n. *habla, palabras, expresión.*
• The communication of human thought and emotion by speech or by signing.

abusive language *insultos, palabras insultantes.*

ambiguous language *expresiones ambiguas.*

foreign language *idioma extranjero.*

foul language *malas palabras, groserías.*

obscene language *expresiones obscenas.*

precatory language *palabras de súplica o ruego.*

Rel: expression, *expresión;* speech, *habla.*

language² (dialect) n. *lenguaje, idioma.*
• The sounds, words and symbols constituting a system of communication used by a particular group of people. – Syn. dialect, *dialecto.* idiom, *idioma.* tongue, *lengua.*

Rel: communication, *comunicación;* idiom, *modismo;* jargon, *jerga;* lingo, *dialecto, jerga;* linguistics, *lingüística;* parlance, *dicción, idioma;* rhetoric, *retórica;* slang, *modismo, habla informal;* terminology, *terminología;* vernacular, *vulgar.*

lapse n. *caducidad.*
• "The termination of a right or privilege because of a failure to exercise it within some time limit or because a contingency has occurred or not occurred." (Black's Law Dict., 8th. ed., 896)

lapsed devise *legado (de bienes reales) caduco o caducado.*

lapsed legacy *legado (de bienes personales) caduco o caducado.*

lapsed license *licencia caducada o expirada.*

lapsed policy INSURANCE *póliza caducada o expirada.*

Rel: laches, *caducidad de la instancia.*

larceny (crime) n. *hurto, robo* (Mx).
• Trespassory taking of another's personal property with intent to deprive the possessor of it permanently.

Cf: **larceny • theft.** Larceny and other related common-law crimes have been combined and substituted by the modern statutory crime of theft in most jurisdictions. Larceny is recognized as being more limited than theft and as requiring the asportation or carrying away of the property.

↪ *Hurto* is the Spanish equivalent of larceny and theft, which can be used broadly as theft, and narrowly as larceny; although sometimes other terms like *latrocinio, substracción* and *ratería,* for example, are sparingly used.

constructive larceny *considerado hurto por ministerio de ley.*

grand larceny *hurto de mayor cuantía.*

larceny by deception *hurto mediante engaño.*

larceny by extortion *hurto mediante extorsión.*

larceny by false pretenses *hurto mediante estafa.*

larceny by fraud *hurto mediante defraudación.*

larceny by trick *hurto mediante engaño.*
Rel: burglary, *robo de casa habitada;* robbery, *robo con violencia, asalto;* shoplifting, *hurto de mercancía en una tienda o almacén;* theft, *hurto.*

lascivious adj. *lascivo.* – Syn. lewd, *obsceno, lujurioso.* licentious, *licencioso.*

latch the warrant *ejecutar una orden judicial.*

latent defect *vicio oculto.*

latent fingerprints *huellas latentes, impresión de huellas digitales.*

Latin n. *latín.*
See: Appendix C. Latin terms.

laundered money *lavado o blanqueado de dinero.*

law¹ (body of rules) n. *derecho, sistema jurídico.*
lawful adj. *legal.*
• The body of rules created and enforced by the government of a given society. – Syn. law of the land, *leyes en vigor, orden jurídico vigente.*
The word law is used with several different meanings: as a body of legal principles that includes all those principles and rules issued, within their authority, by the executive, legislative or judicial branches of government; in other words, the law is what it is usually refer to as the legal order. As a science, law refers to a systematic structure of principles or rules of human conduct. Law has also been used in the English language as a substitute for the lost meaning of the word right, equivalent to an all-inclusive body of rules used as a source of rights, duties and powers, corresponding to the Spanish *Derecho* and the German *Recht.*
Cf: **law • morality.** Moral and legal rules have been clearly distinguished. In contrast with the enforceable nature of the law, rules of morality are not enforced by the courts and depend for their effect solely on the force of public opinion or their voluntary adoption by individuals and communities.

as a matter of law *de pleno derecho.*
attorney at law *abogado, representante legal.*
authorized by law *autorizado legalmente.*
bankruptcy law *ley de quiebras.*
blue sky laws *ley sobre emisión y venta de valores.*
breach of the law *violación de la ley, trangresión de la ley, incumplimiento de la ley.*
choice of law *derecho aplicable.*
color of law *apariencia de legalidad.*
existing laws *derecho vigente.*

federal law *leyes federales.*
foreign laws *leyes de diferente jurisdicción, leyes extranjeras.*
issue of law *cuestión de derecho.*
law and order *orden público.*
law firm *bufete o despacho jurídico.*
law library *biblioteca de derecho.*
law of the case *la aplicación de la norma al caso concreto es firme en apelación.*
law of the land *derecho vigente.*
private law *derecho privado.*
public law *derecho público.*
question of law *cuestión de derecho.*
remedy at law *recursos legales (bajo el derecho estricto —en contraste con recursos bajo el derecho-equidad), remedio legal* (PR).
– Syn. legal remedy.
state law *derecho estatal.*
to the full extent of the law *como mejor proceda en derecho.*
Rel: legal order, *orden jurídico y su aplicación;* natural law, *derecho natural;* positive law, *derecho positivo;* Roman law, *derecho romano.*
Comment: While the civil law world developed a dogmatic conception of what is law recognizing only statutes, regulations and customs as law in principle, the common law world, "less compelled by the peculiar history and the rationalist dogmas of the French Revolution, developed a different attitude. The common law of England, an unsystematic accretion of statutes, judicial decisions, and customary practices, is thought of as the major source of law…. [L]egislation, of course, is law, but so are other things, including judicial decisions. In formal terms the relative authority of statutes, regulations, and judicial decisions may run in roughly that order, but in practice such formulations tend to lose their neatness and their importance. Common lawyers tend to be less rigorous about such matters than civil lawyers." (Merryman, The Civil Law Tradition. Legal Systems of Western Europe and Latin America 24-5)

law² (statute) *ley, leyes.*
• The aggregate of rules promulgated by a legislative body. – Syn. statute, *ley.*
antitrust laws *leyes antimonopólicas.*
statutory law *ley escrita.*
written law *derecho escrito, leyes.*
Rel: canon, *canon;* custom and usage, *costumbre y convencionalismos sociales;* legislation, *legislación;* ordinance, *ordenanza;* provision, *disposición;* regulation, *reglamentación;* rule, *regla.*

law³ (discipline) *derecho, disciplina jurídica.*
• "The set of rules and principles dealing with a specific area of a legal system." (Black's Law Dict., 8th. ed., 900)

administrative law *derecho administrativo.*

civil law *derecho civil.*

commercial law *derecho mercantil.*
– Syn. business law.

constitutional law *derecho constitucional.*

corporate law *derecho corporativo.*

criminal law *derecho penal.*

domestic relations law *derecho de relaciones familiares.*

family law *derecho familiar, derecho de familia.*

insurance law *ley de seguros.*

international law *derecho internacional.*
– Syn. law of nations. public international law.

labor law *derecho laboral, derecho del trabajo.*

maritime law *derecho marítimo.*
– Syn. admiralty law.

military law *derecho marcial o militar.*

municipal law *derecho municipal.*

patent and trademark law *ley de patentes y marcas.*

procedural law *derecho procesal.*

real estate law *ley de bienes inmobiliarios, ley de bienes raíces.*

tax law *derecho fiscal, derecho tributario.*

law[4] (case law) *derecho estricto, jurisprudencia.*
• The law as expressed in the decisions of the courts. – Syn. common law.

at law (as opposed to equity) *de derecho, de derecho estricto.*

case law *jurisprudencia, precedentes judiciales.*

law enforcement *administración de justicia || aplicación o cumplimiento de la ley.*
• The duty of investigating and punishing the violation of the law.

law enforcement officer *agente de la ley, agente de la policía.* – Syn. enforcement officer.

Law French *francesismos anglo-normandos.*

Law Latin *latinismos usados antiguamente.*

law of the sea *derecho del mar.*
• "The body of international law governing how nations use and control the sea and its resources." (Black's Law Dict., 8th. ed., 904)

Cf: law of the sea • admiralty • maritime law. Law of the sea refers to the international rules regulating the use and control of the sea; in contrast, admiralty and maritime law, which are synonyms, refer to domestic laws as they apply to commerce and navigation and transportation over water of persons and goods and related matters.

Glossary: archipelago, *archipiélago;* bay, *bahía;* contiguous zone, *zona contigua;* continental shelf, *plataforma continental;* exclusive economic zone (EEZ), *zona económica exclusiva;* fisheries, *zonas pesqueras;* flag of convenience, *bandera de conveniencia;* high seas, *alta mar;* hot pursuit, *persecución ininterrumpida, persecución en caliente;* innocent passage, *derecho de paso inocente;* internal waters, *aguas interiores;* island, *isla;* piracy, *piratería;* strait, *estrecho;* territorial sea, *mar territorial.*
See: admiralty.

law practice *ejercicio de la abogacía.*
↳ Law practice and *ejercicio de la abogacía* are most fundamentally distinguished by the all-important participation of a professional association or organization (namely, bar association) in the admission and regulation of law practice, while professional organizations are not nearly as relevant in most aspects of *ejercicio de la abogacía.*
Rel: admission to law practice, *admisión al ejercicio de la abogacía;* client-lawyer relationship (privilege), *confidencialidad entre cliente y abogado;* discharge of attorney by client, *retirar a un abogado de un caso (a petición de su representado);* effectiveness of counsel, *eficacia o competencia profesional de un abogado;* representation adverse to client, *representación en perjuicio del representado.*
See: compensation of attorney. lawyer.

law reports *publicación de jurisprudencia, publicación de fallos judiciales, repertorio de jurisprudencia.*

lawbreaker *transgresor de la ley.*

lawful adj. *de acuerdo a derecho, legal.* – Syn. in accordance with the law, *de acuerdo con la ley, de conformidad con la ley.* within the law, *dentro de la ley.* – Opp. unlawful, *ilegal.*
Cf: lawful • legal • licit. Lawful and legal are not interchangeable even though they often overlap and are used as synonyms. Lawful, licit and legal share the meaning "according or not contrary to law, permitted by law" <lawful or legal activity> <legal fees> <licit use of force>.

lawful arrest *detención legal.*

lawful discharge *despido justificado.*

lawful money *dinero de curso legal.*

lawfully wedded husband *esposo legítimo.*

lawfully wedded wife *esposa legítima.*

lawsuit[1] (court proceedings) n. *juicio, pleito, procedimiento judicial.*
• An adversarial proceeding in a court of law.
– Syn. suit.

lawsuit

Lawsuit is the preferred popular use of the word suit. It is almost exclusively used in civil cases.
Rel: action, *acción;* case, *caso.*
See: suit.

lawsuit[2] (equity) n. *acción (en derecho-equidad), procedimiento judicial (en derecho-equidad).*
• An equitable action.
See: suit.

lawyer n. *abogado.*
• Person licensed or professionally qualified to practice law. – Syn. advocate *abogado.* barrister (UK,AU) *abogado litigante.* counsel *asesor jurídico.* counselor *abogado.* jurist *jurista.* jurisconsultus *jurisconsulto.* legal advisor *consejero jurídico.* legal practitioner *abogado en ejercicio (del derecho).* legist *legista.* litigator *litigante.* solicitor (UK,AU) *abogado asesor.*
"The two most common terms [in American English], lawyer and attorney, are not generally distinguished even by members of the profession. In the U.S., attorney, attorney at law, and lawyer are generally viewed as synonymous.
Today there seems to be a notion afoot, however, that attorney is a more formal (and less disparaging) term than lawyer. Technically, lawyer is the more general term, referring to one who practices law. Attorney, literally means 'one who is designated to transact business for another'. An attorney, technically and archaically (except in the phrase attorney in fact) may or may not be a lawyer." (Garner, 90)
Cf: **lawyer ● attorney at law ● counsel.** All three terms, used synonymously and interchangeably, refer to the professional legal practitioner. Lawyer stresses professional qualifications and legal admission to licensing bodies. Attorney at law, of old English ancestry, is a synonym used in the United States to imply broad legal practice, as opposed to specialization among barristers, solicitors and proctors or advocates. Counsel infers legal advice and service to a client. In England counsel refers to a barrister or barristers acting for one of the parties in a legal action.
☞ Lawyer and *abogado* are usually considered very close equivalents, but some qualifications are in order: lawyers are always licensed law practitioners, while *abogados* may or may not be licensed. In this sense, *abogado* may be closer to attorney. A licensed *abogado* is specifically designated as *licenciado en Derecho.* *Abogado* also refers to an active supporter of a social cause, which, of course, the term lawyer

does not include.
ambulance chaser [brder]*abogado inescrupuloso, abogado aprovechado.*
barrister (UK,AU) *abogado litigante.*
corporate lawyer *abogado corporativo, abogado de empresas.*
corporation lawyer *abogado representante de una entidad pública, abogado representante del gobierno.*
criminal lawyer *penalista, criminalista.*
house counsel *abogado de una empresa, abogado de empresa.*
retain a lawyer *contratar a un abogado.*
– Syn. retain counsel.
sole practitioner *en práctica por sí solo, ser un abogado particular.*
shyster lawyer *abogado leguleyo, abogado chicanero*
trial lawyer *abogado litigante.*
Rel: advocate, *consejero, defensor de una causa.*
See: compensation of attorney. law practice.

lay judge *juez lego.*

leading case *precedente judicial, precedente jurisprudencial, caso que sienta precedente.*

leading question (testimony) *pregunta tendenciosa o sugestiva.*

lease n. *arrendamiento, alquiler* (pop.). **lease,** v. *arrendar.* **lessor** n. *arrendador.* **landlord** n. *propietario.* **lessee** n. *arrendatario.* **tenant** n. *inquilino.*
• An agreement by which a party, in rightful possession of real property, conveys its use and occupation to another for a definite period in exchange for a consideration called rent, retaining legal ownership.
"A tenancy is created when an owner of an estate in land grants to another the right to exclusive possession of the land. Without such an agreement, there can be no landlord and tenant relationship. The agreement is called a lease, and the relationship may be referred to as lessor-lesee or landlord-tenant. Similarly, the parties may be referred to as lessor and lesee, or as landlord and tenant. The possession of the tenant must be in subordination to the interest of the landlord, as the owner of the supporting estate, and with the landlord's consent." (Hill, 4)
Cf: **lease ● license ● rent ● demise.** A lease conveys an interest in land and transfers possession of land. A license conveys no property right or interest to the land but merely allows the licensee to do certain acts without consti-

tuting trespass. As a verb, rent is a synonym of lease, which is its main meaning (rather than the payment made by the lessee). Demise, on the other hand, means the conveyance of an estate by will or lease.

➥ "The lease, even when it pertains to commercial premises in an urban area, is considered to be an instrument of conveyance of an estate in the land, like the deed. It is not a contract. Promises may be contained in the lease, but they are not treated in the same way as promises in contracts. Instead they retain the characteristics of an earlier age, aptly conveyed by the name 'covenants.'" (Merryman, The Loneliness of the Comparative Lawyer, 359) In contrast, in civil law countries *arrendamiento* is always a contract and as such follows strictly contractual rules. It is not a conveyance of an estate in the land, since there are no estates in civil law ownership, and its clauses are, therefore, interpreted and applied as regular contractual promises.

assignment of lease *cesión de arrendamiento.*
cancellation of a lease *cancelación de un arrendamiento.*
forfeiture of lease *violación de los términos de un arrendamiento.*
lease of land *arrendamiento de un terreno.*
lease-back *cesión-arrendamiento, operación de compraventa y subsecuente arrendamiento entre las mismas partes.*
lease-sale *arrendamiento con opción de compra.*
long-term lease *arrendamiento a largo plazo.* – Syn. long lease.
month-to-month lease *arrendamiento mensual.*
renewal of lease *renovación de arrendamiento.*
short-term lease *arrendamiento a corto plazo.* – Syn. short lease.
term of lease *plazo del arrendamiento, término del arrendamiento.*
termination of lease *terminación del arrendamiento.*
voidable lease *contrato anulable o sujeto a nulidad.*
Rel: demise, *transmisión de un estate;* eviction, *desalojo;* fitness for use, *apropiado para el uso al que se le destina;* illegal use, *uso ilegal;* indenture, *escritura, instrumento;* latent defects, *vicios ocultos;* quiet enjoyment, *garantía para el caso de evicción;* rent, *renta;* security deposit, *depósito de seguridad;* sublease, *subarriendo, subarrendamiento;* warrant of habitability, *garantía de habitabilidad.*

Ref: (CA) Johnston v. British Canadian Insurance Co. [1932] 4 D.L.R. 281 at 284, [1932] S.C.R. 680, Lamont J. 2.; Garland Mfg. Co. v Northumberland Paper etc Co. (1899) 31 OR 40 at 52 (Div. Ct.); (UK) 27(1) Halsbury's Laws para 77; (US) Willys of Marin Co. v. Pierce, 296 P.2d 25, 28, 140 Cal. App.2d 826.
See: . rent[1].

leasehold estate [de]*derecho de tenencia u ocupación de un inmueble (bajo arrendamiento),* [borr.]*leasehold.* **landlord** n. *propietario.* **tenant** n. *inquilino.*
• Tenancy under a lease. "A tenant's possessory estate in land or premises." (Black's Law Dict., 8th. ed., 909) – Syn. leasehold.
"While a leasehold was an estate in real property, it was not real property for purposes of determining a leaseholder's property rights. The leasehold became a hybrid known as a chattel real." (Hill, 2)
Cf: **leasehold • non-freehold estate • chattel real.** All three terms are used as synonyms. All refer to leasehold estates, underlying different features: leasehold is the generally preferred term, usually implying its mixed property and contractual features; a non-freehold estate, in contrast with a freehold estate, alludes to historical concepts like seisin, while chattel real emphasizes the personal property nature of this legal concept.
➥ Leasehold estate as a hybrid concept between *contrato de arrendamiento* and *derecho real de propiedad* has no equivalent in Spanish-speaking countries, where *contrato de arrendamiento* regulates most aspects of this legal institution in a strictly contractual basis.
Rel: tenancy at sufferance, *tácita reconducción de un arrendamiento.*
See: personal property. tenancy.

leasing *arrendamiento financiero,* [transpl.]*leasing.*
• Contract granting use of real estate, equipment or other fixed assets for a specified period in exchange of payment, usually in the form of rent.

leave n. *permiso, autorización.*
leave of absence *licencia, licencia sin goce de sueldo (de un trabajo), excedencia* (Sp).
leave of the court *permiso o autorización del juez.*
maternity leave *permiso o licencia por maternidad.*
sick leave *permiso o licencia por enfermedad.*
leaving the scene of an accident *abandonar el lugar de un accidente.*

legacy n. *legado.* **legatee** n. *legatario.*
• A gift or bequest by will of personal property, often including money. – Syn. bequest. *legado de bienes muebles.* devise, *legado de bienes inmuebles.*
Cf: **legacy** • **bequest** • **devise.** At common law, bequest is synonymous with legacy and both mean personalty left by will. In modern usage, however, a bequest may include both real and personal property. Devise is the term used to refer to realty left by will.
alternate legacy *legado alternativo.*
conditional legacy *legado condicional.*
contingent legacy *legado sujeto a condición suspensiva.*
cumulative legacy *legados acumulables.*
demonstrative legacy *legado pagado de una fuente de origen específica.*
general legacy *legado pagado de los bienes generales.*
specific legacy *legado específico.*
void legacy *legado nulo.*
Rel: will, *testamento.*
Ref: (CA) Re Tyhurst [1932] S.C.R. 713; (UK) 17 Halsbury's Laws para 1228 at 1230; (US) Blakeslee v. Pardee, 56 A. 503, 505, 76 Conn. 263; Festorazzi v. First National Bank of Mobile, 264 So.2d 496,505.

legal adj. *legal.*
legal advice *asesoramiento jurídico, asesoría jurídica.*
legal age *mayoría de edad.*
legal aid *asesoría legal gratuita.*
legal capacity *capacidad legal.*
legal custody *custodia legal.*
legal duty *deber jurídico.*
legal forms *formulario legal.*
legal fiction *ficción legal.*
legal interest *interés legal.*
legal matter *cuestión jurídica.*
legal remedy *medios legales, recursos legales.*
legal separation *separación legal.*
legal subtleties *argucias legales.*
legal tender *postura legal (tender)* || *curso legal (moneda).*
legal test *figura jurídica, doctrina* (PR).
legal title *título legal.*
legal weapon *arma reglamentaria.*
See: lawful, *legal.*
legal culture *cultura legal.* – Syn. legal tradition.
Rel: common law family, *familia de derecho común, familia de la "common law";* Romano-Germanic family, *familia romano-germánica;* Scandinavian family, *familia escandinava.*

legal language *legalismos.* – Syn. legal parlance. legalese.
Rel: oral formalisms, *formalismos orales;* written formalisms, *formalismos escritos.*
legal rule [le]*regla de derecho,* [lat.]*ratio decidendi,* [fe]*norma individualizada,* [brder]*principio de derecho.*
• A principle of law expressed in the grounds or reasons of a court decision. – Syn. ratio decidendi. rule of law. holding.
"The English concept of legal rule, much narrower than the corresponding continental notion, is historically explained by the fact that the Common law was formed by the judges and that their technique was one of making distinctions, rather than one of interpretation, and this remains the basic approach of English law today." (David & Brierley, 335-36)
↳ Legal rule and *norma jurídica* are similar fundamental concepts in their respective legal systems. Both refer to a legal statement regarding an issue of fact, but while *norma jurídica* is typically a hypothetical and abstract rule described in general terms, a rule of law is a principle expressed in concrete terms in the grounds or reasoning of a court decision. Also, in spite of their similar functional role as rules upon which decisions are based, they are also concepts with different purposes, since legal rule seeks to provide a solution to an actual dispute or trial while *norma jurídica* formulates a general rule of conduct for hypothetical cases. While *norma jurídica* may be used sometimes as an appropriate equivalent of legal rule, often a closer term in Spanish may be "*norma individualizada.*" Similarly, an often closer English term to convey the meaning of *norma jurídica* may be "legal principle".

legislation[1] **(enactments)** n. *legislación.*
enact legislation *promulgar legislación.*
Rel: statute, *ley escrita.*
legislation[2] **(law making)** n. *acto de legislar.*
legislature n. *legislatura, cuerpo legislativo.*
legislator n. *legislador.* **legislative** adj. *legislativo.*
legislative branch *poder legislativo.*
legislative hearing *comparecencia ante la legislatura.*
legislative power *facultades del poder legislativo.*
legislative resolution *resolución legislativa.*
Rel: appropriations, *asignaciones presupuestarias;* bill, *iniciativa de ley, proyecto de ley;* committee hearing, *sesión del comité, audiencia*

del comité (parlamentario o camaral); reading, *lectura (de una iniciativa o proyecto).*

legitimate child *hijo legítimo.*

leniency n. *clemencia.*

lesion n. *lesión física.*

letter of credit *carta de crédito.* – Abb. L/C

• "An engagement by a bank or other person made at the request of a customer that the issuer will honor the drafts or other demands for payment upon compliance with the conditions specified in the credit." (2 West's Law & Commercial Dictionary in Five Languages, 43) – Syn. bill of credit.

confirmed letter *carta de crédito confirmada.*

documentary letter of credit *crédito documentario.*

export letter *carta de crédito de exportación.*

import letter *carta de crédito de importación.*

irrevocable letter *carta de crédito irrevocable.*

open letter of credit *carta de crédito abierta.*

revocable letter *carta de crédito revocable.*

letter of intent *declaración de intención, acuerdo preliminar.*

letters of administration *auto de nombramiento de administrador testamentario, nombramiento de administrador testamentario.*

letters of guardianship *auto de nombramiento de tutor, nombramiento de tutor.*

letters patent *patente, carta patente, cédula de patente.*

letters rogatory *carta rogatoria.*

• A request made by a local court to a foreign court to obtain evidence by answering interrogatories or to serve process on a person domiciled abroad. – Syn. letter of request. requisitory letter.

letters testamentary *auto de nombramiento de albacea, nombramiento de albacea.*

leveraged buy out *adquisición forzada mediante apalancamiento, compra de una compañía mediante apalancamiento.*

levy¹ (exactment) n. *gravamen, impuesto.* – Syn. tax levy.

levy² (execution) n. *embargo ejecutivo, incautación* (PR). – Syn. levy of execution.

lewdness (crime) n. *faltas a la moral, actos lascivos o impúdicos* (PR). **lewd** adj. *obsceno, lujurioso.*

• "The common law offense of 'lewdness' means open and public indecency, and in order to amount to an indictable crime it must al-

ways amount to a common nuisance, committed in a public place, and seen by persons lawfully in that place." (Ballentine's Law Dict., 729)

lex domicilii (lat.) *lex domicilii, la ley del domicilio.* The law of the domicile.

lex fori (lat.) *lex fori, la ley del foro o tribunal.* The law of the forum.

lex loci actus (lat.) *lex loci actus, la ley del lugar en que se realiza un acto.* The law of the place where a legal act takes place.

lex loci contractus (lat.) *lex loci contractus, la ley del lugar en que se ha celebrado el contrato.* The law of the place where a contract was made.

lex loci delicti (lat.) *lex loci delicti, la ley del lugar de la comisión del acto ilícito.* The law of the place of the wrong.

lex loci situs (lat.) *lex loci situs, la ley del lugar en que se encuentra la cosa.* The law of the place where an object is situated.

liability¹ (obligation) n. *responsabilidad.* **liable** adj. *responsable.*

• A broad legal term that means an obligation or accountability; a duty as correlative to a right; responsibility to another, such as criminal or tort liability; an obligation to pay a debt.

civil liability *responsabilidad civil.*

contingent liability *responsabilidad condicional.*

criminal liability *responsabilidad penal.*

joint and several liability *responsabilidad solidaria y mancomunada.*

liability for bodily injury or death *responsabilidad por lesiones corporales o muerte.*

liability insurance *seguro de responsabilidad civil.*

product liability *responsabilidad civil del fabricante, responsabilidad del producto.*

release from liability *liberación de la responsabilidad.*

several liability *responsabilidad solidaria.*

strict liability *responsabilidad objetiva.*

third party liability *responsabilidad de tercero.*

vicarious liability *responsabilidad por terceros.*

liability² (debt) n. *pasivo, deuda.*

libel n. *difamación escrita, libelo* (PR). **libelee/libellee** n. *difamador, demandado por difamación.* **libelant/libellant** n. *difamado, demandante por difamación.* – Syn. defamation, *difamación.* slander, *difamación oral.*

group libel *difamación contra un grupo de personas.*

seditious libel *comunicación escrita de carácter sedicioso.*

Rel: First Amendment (US), *Primera Enmienda (constitucional).*

See: defamation.

liberty n. *libertad.*

Cf: **liberty ● freedom.** These are synonymous but usually not used interchangeably. "Freedom is the broader, all encompassing term, that carries strong positive connotations," while liberty, being more specific, is slightly less emotive and usually evokes the removal of past restraints (Garner, 528).

liberty of contract *libertad contractual.*

liberty of speech *libertad de expresión.*

liberty of the press *libertad de prensa.*

personal liberty *libertad personal.*

religious liberty *libertad religiosa.* – Syn. religious freedom.

license n. *licencia, autorización, permiso.* **licensee** *licenciatario.* **licenser/licensor** *licenciante.*

• "A grant of permission to do a particular thing, to exercise a certain privilege, or to carry on a particular business or to pursue a certain occupation." (Blatz Brewing Co. v. Collins, 160 P.2d 37, 39, 69 Cal.App.2d 639) – Other spell.: licence (RU,CA). – Syn. permit, *permiso.* patent, *patente.*

Cf: **license ● permit ● patent.** License and permit are usually used as synonyms, but they are some times distinguished, considering that license refers to a revocable permission while permit refers to the certificate granting permission. Patent, on the other hand, is a grant given to an inventor that lasts a specified number of years to exclusively control the manufacture and sale of his or her invention.

↪ License is usually a broader term than *licencia.* When referring to entry onto real property, *autorización* and *permiso* are mostly used, but when indicating a grant of permission by the government or other authority *licencia* is usually preferred.

driver's license *licencia de conductor.*

gaming license *licencia de juego.*

hunting license *licencia de caza.*

liquor license *licencia para vender alcohol.*

patent license *licencia de patente.*

renewal of a license *renovación de una licencia.*

revocation of a license *revocación de una licencia.*

Rel: international licensing, *otorgamiento internacional de licencias.*

See: *franquicia.*

Ref: (AU) Federal Comr. of Taxation v. United Aircraft Corpn. (1943) 68 C.L.R. 525 at 533; (CA) Jenny Lind Co. v. Bradley-Nicholson (1883) 1 B.C.R.(pt II) 185 (B.C.S.C.); (US) 160 P.2d 37, 39.

lie detector *detector de mentiras.*

– Syn. polygraph.

lien n. [de]*derecho preferencial o preferente de garantía sobre bienes, derecho de retención,* [brder]*gravamen,* [nrwer]*privilegio.* **lienee** n. *propietario de bienes sujetos a un derecho preferencial.* **lien creditor** [de]*deudor cuya garantía está constituida por un derecho preferencial.* **lienor/lienholder** [de]*titular o acreedor de un derecho preferencial.*

• A right of any nature in the property of another as security for the duration of an outstanding obligation or debt of the owner of the property.

– Syn. encumbrance, *carga o gravamen.*

"In G.B., it is customary for the lienholder to retain possession of the property on which the lien has been obtained, whereas in the U.S. it is more usual that a lien does not involve retention by the lienholder. In the U.S. when the creditor possesses the collateral, *pledge* is the most usual term." (Garner, 528)

Cf: **lien ● encumbrance ● charge.** Lien is synonym of encumbrance, which is a generic term referring to most security devices, including liens. Charge is a loosely used term that also means lien or encumbrance.

↪ Lien is a widely used institution created by law, arising automatically when the operating facts give rise to such security. There is no exact equivalent in the Roman-Germanic tradition, specifically one where the automatic perfection is given by law. Sometimes *derecho de retención* and *embargo preventivo* are used to best describe a lien in Spanish, but in most cases a looser description such as a *derecho preferencial o preferente de garantía* or even *gravamen* may be preferred.

agricultural lien [de]*derecho preferencial de garantía sobre bienes agrícolas.*

artisan's lien [de]*derecho preferencial de garantía en favor de un artesano.*

attorney's lien [de]*derecho preferencial de garantía en favor de un abogado.*

builder's lien [de]*derecho preferencial de garantía en favor de un constructor.*

carrier's lien [de]*derecho preferencial de garantía en favor de un transportista.*

contractor's lien [de]*derecho preferencial de garantía en favor de un contratista.*

discharge of lien [de]*extinción de un derecho preferencial de garantía sobre bienes.*

equitable lien [de]*derecho preferencial de garantía bajo el régimen jurídico de derecho-equidad.*

factor's lien [de]*derecho preferencial de garantía en favor de un comisionista o agente comercial.*

floating or shifting lien [de]*gravamen negociable (circulante).*

landlord's lien [de]*derecho preferencial de garantía en favor de un arrendador.*

lien on land [de]*derecho preferencial de garantía sobre un predio o terreno.*

liens on cargo *privilegios sobre la carga.*

maritime liens *privilegios marítimos.*

mechanic's lien [de]*derecho preferencial de garantía en favor de constructores.*

tax lien *gravamen fiscal,* [de]*derecho preferencial de garantía fiscal.*
See: encumbrance.
Ref: (UK) 28 Halsbury's Laws para 701 at 708; (US) Page v. Francis, 120 S.W.2d 161, 164, 196 Ark. 822.

life annuity *anualidad.*

life estate [de]*derecho de tenencia vitalicia sobre un bien, derecho de propiedad vitalicio.*
• An estate lasting as long as a person's life, usually the life of the person in possession. See: estate[3].

life expectancy *esperanza de vida, expectativa de vida.*

life insurance *seguro de vida.* **beneficiary** n. *beneficiario.* **cestui que vie** *beneficiario vitalicio.* **owner** n. *titular (del seguro de vida).*
• Insurance issued on the life of an individual to pay a certain amount of money to the beneficiary upon the death of the insured.
endowment life insurance *seguro de vida del valor de efectivo, seguro dotal* (PR).
group life insurance *seguro de vida de grupo, seguro colectivo de vida.*
industrial life insurance *seguro de vida industrial.*
term life insurance *seguro de vida de término.*
universal life insurance *seguro de vida universal.*
whole life insurance *seguro de vida entera.*
Rel: cancellation, *cancelación;* lapse, *caducidad;* surrender value, *valor de rescate.*

life interest *derecho vitalicio sobre un inmueble.*

life sentence *condena de por vida, condena de cadena perpetua.*

limited jurisdiction *jurisdicción limitada.*

limited liability *responsabilidad limitada.*

limited liability company *compañía o sociedad de responsabilidad limitada.* – Abbr. L.L.C. – Syn. limited liability corporation.

limited partnership [fe]*sociedad en comandita,* [borr.]*limited partnership.*
• A limited partnership is a partnership consisting of one or more general partners and one or more limited partners. – Abbr. L.P.
"A limited partnership allows a person, by becoming a limited partner, to be a co-owner of a partnership, sharing in profits and enjoying the benefits of partnership taxation, without liability for the debts of the partnership." (Hynes, 31)
↬ "The antecedents of the limited partnership form of enterprise can be traced back to the European continent during the Middle Ages where it was known as a *'commenda'* or *'societé en commandité.'* It was unknown, however, to the English common law or to the common law of the United States." (Kaplan, 674)
limited liability partnership *sociedad profesional, sociedad profesional organizada como comandita.*
See: partnership.

line of credit *línea de crédito.*

line of succession *línea de sucesión.*

line up n. *identificación en rueda de presos, confrontación en fila, reconocimiento en fila.*
• Police identification procedure of an offender, by a victim or witness, out of a line of people standing next to each other.
Rel: identification, *identificación.*

lineal consanguinity *consanguinidad en línea directa.*

lineal descendant *descendiente en línea directa.*

linguistics n. *lingüística.*

liquidation[1] **(paying)** n. *liquidación.* **liquidator** n. *síndico.*
• The adjustment or settlement of debts; the paying of debts. The conversion of assets into cash; the selling of assets.
liquidated amount *cantidad cierta y determinada, cantidad pagada.*
liquidated damages *daños y perjuicios estimados, indemnización convencional por daños y perjuicios.*

liquidated damages clause *cláusula de daños y perjuicios estimados, cláusula de indemnización convencional por daños y perjuicios.*
liquidation of assets *liquidación de activo o existencias.*
liquidation price *precio de liquidación.*
liquidation proceeding *procedimiento de liquidación.*
Rel: distribution (succession), *partición de herencia.*
liquidation[2] **(winding up)** n. *liquidación, disolución.*
• The winding up of a business entity upon dissolution.
compulsory liquidation *liquidación forzosa o forzada.*
liquidation of a company *liquidación de una compañía.*
voluntary liquidation *liquidación voluntaria.*
Rel: dissolution, *disolución;* merger, *fusión.*
liquidity *liquidez.*
lis pendens (lat.) *lis pendens, litispendencia.* A pending suit.
listed securities *valores listados (en la bolsa de valores).*
literal adj. *literal, al pie de la letra, textual.* – Syn. verbatim, *palabra por palabra.*
literary property *propiedad literaria.*
litigation n. *litigio.* **litigant** n. *litigante.* **litigate** v. *litigar.* **litigious** adj. *litigioso.*
• The process of engaging in a lawsuit; a lawsuit. – Syn. contest, *litigar, impugnar.*
Rel: advocacy, *litigio;* trial lawyer, *abogado litigante.*
loan n. *préstamo.* **lender** n. *otorgante de crédito, prestamista (derogatorio).*
• Property or money given temporarily to another under contract for its use under an obligation to return it and to pay interest if so agreed.
amortized loan *préstamo amortizado.*
call a loan *exigir el pago anticipado de un préstamo.*
collateral loan *préstamo en garantía.*
consumer loan *préstamo al consumidor.*
installment loan *préstamo en abonos, préstamo a plazos.*
loan shark *prestamista usurero o leonino.*
nonperforming loan *préstamo delincuente, préstamo en mora.*
personal loan *préstamo personal.*
secured loan *préstamo garantizado.*
short term loan *préstamo a corto plazo.*

soft loan *préstamo subsidiado, préstamo subvencionado.*
unpaid loan *préstamo pendiente de pago.*
location n. *ubicación.* – Syn. place, *lugar.* site, *sitio.* spot, *lugar.*
prime location *la mejor ubicación, ubicación de primera.*
lockdown *cierre temporal de una prisión (por una emergencia).*
lockout *paro patronal.*
lockup n. *celda de detenidos.* **lock up** v. *encerrar.*
loitering *vagancia (en un lugar), estar de vago, permanecer en un lugar sin hacer nada.* **loiter** v. *vagar, holgazanear.*
Rel: hobo, *vagabundo;* vagrancy, *vagancia (permanente), vivir en la calle, deambular sin tener domicilio.*
looting *saqueo.* **loot** n. *botín.*
loss n. *pérdida.*
"Loss is a generic and relative term. It signifies the act of losing or the thing lost. It is not a word of limited, hard and fast meaning and has been held synonymous with or equivalent to 'damage', 'damages', 'deprivation', 'detriment', 'injury', and 'privation'." (Black's Law Dict., 5th. ed., 486) In insurance it is the basis for a claim for indemnity or damages. It refers to any diminution of quantity, quality or value of property.
actual loss *pérdida realmente sufrida.*
business loss (business) *pérdidas económicas.*
business loss TAX *pérdidas del negocio, pérdidas.*
carryover loss TAX *pérdida trasladada al año siguiente.*
casualty loss *pérdidas con motivo de un accidente, pérdida por siniestro.*
consequential loss *pérdidas indirectas.*
general average loss *pérdida por avería común.*
marine insurance loss *seguro de pérdida marítima.*
net loss *pérdidas netas.*
operating losses *pérdidas de operaciones.*
profit and loss statement *estado de pérdidas y ganancias.*
salvage loss *pérdida de salvamento.*
total loss *pérdida total, siniestro total.*
lost property *bienes mostrencos, bienes perdidos (pop.).*
• Property that is not in possession of the owner and that cannot be located by diligent search.
Cf: **lost property** • **mislaid property** • **aban-**

doned property. Lost property refers to property accidentally or inadvertently dispossessed and which may not be recovered by diligent search. Property is mislaid when its owner has placed it in a location and then inadvertently has lost track of it, but knows where it was left and can recover it by diligent search. Abandoned property is that which its owner has willingly given up.
Rel: abandoned property, *bienes abandonados;* mislaid property, *bienes extraviados, bienes olvidados;* treasure trove, *tesoro.*

lottery n. *lotería.*
Rel: numbers game, *lotería ilegal;* raffle, *rifa;* wager, *apuesta.*

LSD *LSD.* – Syn. acid, *ácido.* tabs.

lump sum distribution *reparto o distribución de bienes o dinero en una sola remesa o en un pago único.*

lump sum payment *pago global, pago único, pago a precio alzado.*

lunacy n. *locura, demencia.* **lunatic** n.adj. *lunático.* – Syn. insanity, [brder]*demencia, enajenación mental.*

lynching *linchamiento.*
lynching mob *multitud que lincha.*

MMMM

Mafia n. *mafia.* **Mafioso** n. *mafioso.* – Syn. Cosa Nostra, *Cosa Nostra.* mob, *la mafia.*
Rel: capo, *jefe;* drug trafficking, *tráfico de drogas;* extortion, *extorsión;* gambling, *juego y apuesta;* godfather, *padrino;* money laundering, *lavado de dinero;* organized crime, *crimen organizado;* racketeering, *extorsión e intimidación organizada;* soldier, *soldado, miembro menor (de la mafia);* underworld, *bajo mundo.*

magistrate[1] (official) n. *magistrado.*
• A local civil official with specifically assigned powers.

magistrate[2] (judicial official) n. *magistrado judicial menor, magistrado* (PR).
• A judicial officer usually with reduced local jurisdiction.
examining magistrate (UK) *juez de instrucción.*
lay magistrate (UK) *juez de paz.*
stipendiary magistrate (UK) *juez letrado.*
See: *magistrado[2].*

Magna Carta *Carta Magna.*

mail n. *correo, correspondencia.*
acknowledgment of mail receipt *acuse de recibo de correo.*

certified mail *correo certificado.*
mail fraud *defraudación o fraude usando el correo.*
mail order bride *matrimonio por procuración (de una mujer extranjera).*
mail order divorce *divorcio fuera de la jurisdicción de la residencia de las partes, divorcio en el extranjero.* – Syn. foreign divorce.
mailing obscene or crime-inciting matter *enviar por correo material obsceno o que incita a la criminalidad.*
notification by mail *notificación por correo.*

mala fides (lat.) *mala fides, mala fe.* – Syn. bad faith.

malfeasance n. *realización de un acto ilícito o ilegal.* **malfeasor** n. *quien comete un acto ilícito o ilegal.* **malfeasant** adj. *ilícito o ilegal.*
• Commission of a wrongful or unlawful act, especially one affecting an official duty.
Cf: **malfeasance • misfeasance • nonfeasance.** Terms often used imprecisely. Malfeasance denotes the unmitigated commission of a wrongful or unlawful act; misfeasance refers to behavior otherwise considered lawful, but done in an actively unlawful manner; while nonfeasance, in contrast, describes neglect of duty or passive misconduct.

malice[1] (intent) n. *intención ilícita, mala intención, malicia* (PR).
• Wrongful intention, intent to commit a wrongful act without justification or excuse.
constructive malice *intención ilícita tácita.*
malice in fact *intención ilícita expresa.*
malice in law *intención ilícita por determinación de la ley.*
Ref: (UK) Melia v Neate (1863) 3F & F 757 at 763, 764; (US) Chisley v. State, Md., 95 A.2d 577, 585.
malice[2] (evilness) n. *malicia, maldad.*
Rel: evil intent, *intención diabólica o malévola;* ill will, *mala voluntad;* malevolence, *malevolencia.*

malice aforethought *dolo específico de homicidio, intención homicida, malicia premeditada* (PR).

malicious arrest *detención intencionalmente ilegal, detención ilegal hecha en forma intencional.*

malicious injury *daño intencional o doloso.*

malicious mischief (crime) *delito menor de daño en propiedad ajena, daños maliciosos* (PR,Ve).
• The common-law misdemeanor of intentionally destroying or damaging the property of

another. – Syn. criminal mischief. malicious damage. malicious mischief and trespass. Rel: criminal damage to property, *daño en propiedad ajena.*

malicious prosecution [le]*persecución maliciosa* (PR). [de]*ejercicio de una acción penal improcedente con un propósito indebido o ilícito.*
See: abuse of process.

malinger v. *fingirse enfermo o deshabilitado.*

malpractice n. *negligencia profesional, mala praxis* (Ar).
• Incompetence or negligence in the practice of a professional activity. – Syn. professional negligence, *negligencia profesional.*
healing art malpractice *negligencia en la práctica de las artes curativas.*
legal malpractice *negligencia legal profesional.*
medical malpractice *negligencia médica profesional, impericia profesional médica* (PR).

malum in se (lat.) *malum in se, un acto intrínsecamente malo.*
• An evil in itself. An act intrinsically wrong.

malum prohibitum (lat.) *malum prohibitum, un acto que es malo por estar prohibido.*
• A prohibited evil. An act wrong only because prohibited.

malversation (obs.) n. *malversación.* – Syn. official corruption, *corrupción de funcionarios públicos.*

mandamus (lat.) n. [de]*orden o mandamiento judicial extraordinario,* [borr.] *mandamus,* [de]*mandamiento judicial exigiendo el cumplimiento de un acto o el resarcimiento de derechos (dirigida normalmente a una autoridad o juez inferior).*
• An extraordinary writ, issued by a superior court, to compel a lower court or government officer to perform a ministerial act that is recognized as an absolute duty by the law.
– Syn. writ of mandamus. writ of mandate.
↪ Mandamus is an unknown institution in civil law countries. While courts in common law countries can order an administrative body to refrain from carrying on or executing an act deemed illegal, courts in civil law countries are usually restricted from doing so by the constitutional division of powers, so the underlying problem, being the lack of enforcement of a specific legal provision or an illegal action of government, must be resolved through other

avenues, such as constitutional redress or direct political action.
Comment: "It is considered quite normal in England for the court to issue orders to the various branches of the government administration in order that the law be respected. English courts do not limit themselves to quashing an illegal administrative act; they will direct by a mandamus order that the legally required administrative step be taken; they will also order the police, or any person, through the writ of habeas corpus, to put at liberty a person who has been illegally detained or confined." (David & Brierley, 331)

mandate[1] (court order) n. *orden o mandato judicial.* **mandate** v. *ordenar.* **mandatory** adj. *obligatorio.*
• A command or a request directed to an officer of the court to have an order enforced.

mandate[2] APPEAL n. *mandamiento devolviendo los autos y ordenando que se cumpla lo resuelto (en apelación).*
• A request from an appellate court directing a lower court to follow its findings and conclusions.

mandate[3] INTL.LAW n. *mandato.*
• Power given by the United Nations to certain governments to control specified territories.

mandatory adj. *obligatorio.*
mandatory relief *recursos obligatorios.*
mandatory sentence *condena mínima obligatoria.*
mandatory statutory provisions *estipulaciones o disposiciones escritas legales obligatorias.*

mania n. *manía.*
• A form of mental disease characterized by exaltation and excitement that manifests itself in delusions, an obsession or a craze.
– Syn. craze. obsession, *obsesión.*
dipsomania *dipsomanía,* craving for alcoholic beverages.
kleptomania *cleptomanía,* obsessive impulse to steal.
megalomania *megalomanía,* obsession with grandiose or extravagant things.
necromania *necromanía,* obsession with the souls of the dead.
nymphomania *ninfomanía,* obsession with sexual desire (in a female).
pyromania *piromanía,* uncontrollable impulse to start fires.

manic depressive *maniaco depresivo.*

manslaughter n. *homicidio no intencional o culposo.*

• The unlawful killing of a person without malice aforethought.

Cf: **manslaughter • murder.** Manslaughter is a homicide without malice aforethought, while murder is a homicide with it.

involuntary manslaughter *homicidio no intencional inconsciente,* [fe]*homicidio culposo sin previsión o representación, homicidio accidental involuntario.*

killing in the heat of passion *homicidio pasional, matar estando bajo estado pasional.*

manslaughter by accountability *homicidio no intencional por responsabilidad indirecta.*

voluntary manslaughter *homicidio intencional bajo estado pasional o emoción violenta (arrebato u obcecación).*

Rel: homicide, *homicidio;* murder, *homicidio con agravantes.*

manufacture or delivery of a controlled substance *producción o tráfico de una sustancia regulada.*

manufacture or delivery of cannabis *producción o tráfico de canabis.*

marijuana n. *mariguana/marihuana.* – Syn. cannabis, *canabis.* dope. grass, *la verde.* hashish, *hashish.* Mary Jane. pot. weed, *yerba.* – Other spell.: marihuana.

marijuana user *mariguano.*

marijuana wrappings *envolturas de la marihuana.*

See: drugs.

marine insurance *seguro marítimo.*

• An insurance covering the risk of loss of a vessel or its cargo either during a certain voyage or during a fixed period of time.

Glossary: barratry, *baratería de capitán o patrón;* cargo insurance, *seguro de mercancías;* doctrine uberrimae fidei (utmost good faith), *de máxima buena fe, de confianza plena;* free of captures and seizures clause (F.C.& S.), *exento de responsabilidad por piratería;* hull insurance, *seguro de casco;* insurable interest, *riesgo asegurable;* perils of the sea, *peligros del mar;* protection and indemnity insurance (P&I), *clubes P&I (protección e indemnización);* warranty of seaworthiness, *garantía de poderse hacer a la mar, garantía de navegabilidad.*

marital adj. *marital.*

marital communications privilege *confidencialidad entre esposos.* – Syn. husband-wife privilege.

marital deduction *deducción fiscal marital, deducción matrimonial.*

marital home *hogar marital, domicilio conyugal.*

marital partnership *sociedad conyugal.*

marital rape *violación entre esposos.*

marital rights *derechos maritales, matrimoniales o conyugales.*

marital status *estado civil.*

Rel: divorced, *divorciado;* married, *casado;* separated, *separado;* significant other, *pareja;* single, *soltero;* widow, *viudo.*

maritime law *derecho marítimo.*

See: admiralty law.

markdown n. *rebaja.* – Syn. discount.

market price *precio de mercado.*

market value *valor de mercado.*

marketing *mercadotecnia, mercadeo.*

Rel: advertising, *publicidad;* consumer, *consumidor;* distribution, *distribución;* product, *producto;* promotion, *promoción;* transportation, *transportación.*

marriage n. *matrimonio.*

• The legal union of a man and a woman to form a relationship as husband and wife. – Syn. wedlock.

Tentative adoption of gay marriages, mostly in Canada and the U.S., is changing the traditional definition of marriage by introducing, not without controversy, same-sex marriages. The term civil union, meaning a less formal and solemn union, is often used in the U.S. to connote homosexual legal unions.

Cf: **marriage • matrimony.** Both terms are synonymous. While marriage is used indistinctly in legal or common language expressions, matrimony is a rather formal term rarely used outside a legal context.

annulment of marriage *anulación del matrimonio.*

articles of marriage *capitulaciones matrimoniales.*

bond of marriage *vínculo matrimonial.*

civil marriage *matrimonio civil.*

common law marriage *matrimonio consensual, matrimonio por comportamiento.*

gay marriage *matrimonio de homosexuales.*

marriage broker *proxeneta, alcahuete.*

marriage ceremony *ceremonia de matrimonio.*

marriage certificate *certificado de matrimonio.*

marriage license *solicitud de matrimonio, licencia matrimonial* (PR).

marriage of convenience *matrimonio de*

conveniencia.

proxy marriage *matrimonio por poder, matrimonio por representante.*

putative marriage *matrimonio putativo.*

sham marriage *matrimonio en fraude de la ley.*

void marriage *matrimonio nulo.*

voidable marriage *matrimonio anulable, matrimonio sujeto a nulidad relativa.*

Rel: civil union, [de]*unión civil;* domestic partner, [de]*pareja doméstica;* remarriage, *contraer nuevas nupcias;* unmarried cohabitation, *cohabitación sin estar casados, unión libre;* wedding; *boda.*

marshal (US)(federal govmt.) n. *alguacil (federal).* – Syn. bailiff. [nrwer]constable (UK). sheriff, *sheriff.*

martial law *ley marcial.*
• Emergency set of strict rules to be applied when civil government is endangered and actual unrest is prevalent or likely to spread.

massacre n. *masacre.*

master and servant [fe]*relación individual laboral,* [fe]*relación individual de trabajo, patrono y empleado* (PR).
• An employer-employee relationship. The legal relation between two persons, one of whom has authority over the other, regarding the time, form and place of the services rendered.
Cf: **master and servant ● principal and agent.** Each phrase represents a similar, but distinguishable, relationship. A master has more control over a servant than a principal over an agent. An agent usually acts for the principal before third parties while the servant does not.
↳ Master and servant and *relación individual laboral* are equivalent terms, and both are used to describe the employee-employer relationship. Master and servant was the initial common law term used, and it is still in use today. Master and servant and *relación individual* refer to the content and nature of the rights and duties between employee and employer, which has changed over time, depending on the theories used. Today, while some consider these rights and duties to arise only from conractual arrangements (contract of employment), others consider them as arising from statute, regardless of any contractual agreements. In contrast to individual labor rights and duties, modern collective labor relations are referred to as industrial law or *derechos colectivos laborales* or *derecho colectivo de trabajo.*

Rel: contract of employment, *contrato de trabajo.*

Master of the Rolls (UK) *presidente del Tribunal de Apelación.*

material adj. *sustancial, importante.*
• Essential, important, relating to a given matter. – Syn. consequential, *importante.* crucial, *crucial.* decisive, *decisivo.* essential, *esencial.* key, *clave.* pertinent, *pertinente.* significant, *significante.* substantial, *sustancial.* vital, *vital.*
Cf: **material ● relevant.** Material means "having some logical connection with the consequential facts." Relevant means a "tender to prove or disprove a matter in issue." (Garner, p550)

material allegation *afirmación sustancial, afirmación esencial.*

material breach *incumplimiento sustancial.*

material defect *vicio o defecto determinante.*

material evidence *prueba material o relevante.*

material fact *hecho fundamental o esencial.*

material representation *declaración determinante o esencial.*

material witness *testigo esencial.*

matricide n. *matricidio.* **matricidal** adj. *matricida.*

maturity n. *vencimiento.*

mayhem (crime) n. *mutilación que causa incapacitación o lesiones que dejan una marca permanente, mutilación* (PR).
• A malicious injury that disables or disfigures the person of another. – Syn. grievous bodily harm.
Rel: maim, *desfigurar, mutilar, desmembrar.*

mayor n. *alcalde.* **mayoral** adj. *de alcalde, del alcalde.*

mediation *mediación.* **mediate** v. *mediar.* **mediator** n. *mediador.*
• A method of settling disputes through the intervention of a disinterested third party who helps to reach a mutually acceptable solution.
Rel: arbitration, *arbitraje.*
See: conciliation.

medical adj. *médico.*

medical care *cuidados médicos.*

medical coverage *cobertura médica.*

medical doctor *médico.*

medical evidence *pruebas periciales médicas.*

medical examination *examen médico.*

medical examiner *médico forense.*

medical expenses *gastos médicos.*

medical history *historia médica.*

medical malpractice *negligencia profesional médica.*

medical records *historial médico, reportes médicos.*

meeting *reunión, asamblea, junta.* **meet** v. *reunirse.* – Syn. gathering.
  call a meeting *convocar a una asamblea.*
  call a meeting to order *abrir la sesión.*
  meeting of creditors ʙᴀɴᴋʀᴜᴘᴛᴄʏ *junta de acreedores.*
  meeting of shareholders ᴄᴏʀᴘ. *asamblea de accionistas.*

memorandum of understanding *memorandum de entendimiento.*

mens rea (law lat.) *dolo o intención delictuosa o delictiva.* A guilty mind.
• Criminal intent or recklessness. – Syn. criminal intent. criminal purpose. criminal state of mind. guilty mind.
  general mens rea *dolo general.*
  specific mens rea *dolo específico.*

mental adj. *mental, intelectual.*
  mental anguish *angustia mental.*
  mental cruelty *crueldad mental.*
  mental deficiency *deficiencia mental.*
  mental incompetence *incapacidad mental.*
  mental retardation *retrazo mental.*
  mental state *estado mental.*
  mental suffering *sufrimiento mental.*

mental disease *enfermedad mental.*
Rel: mania, *manía;* insanity, [ʙʀᴅᴇʀ]*demencia, enajenación mental.*
Glossary: amnesia, *amnesia;* anxiety, *ansiedad;* compulsion, *compulsión;* delirium, *delirio;* depression, *depresión;* idiocy, *idiotez;* madness, *locura;* manic-depressive, *maniacodepresivo, maniaco-depresivo;* multiple personality, *personalidad múltiple;* nervous breakdown, *crisis nerviosa;* neurosis, *neurosis;* obsession, *obsesión;* psychosis, *psicosis;* schizophrenia, *esquizofrenia;* sleepwalking, *sonambulismo.*

merchandise n. *mercancía o mercadería.*
  merchant n. *comerciante o mercader* (obs.).
  merchantable adj. *comerciable, sujeto a comercio.*
  See: goods.

mercy killing *homicidio piadoso.* – Syn. euthanasia, *eutanasia.*

merger[1] ᴄᴏɴᴛʀᴀᴄᴛꜱ n. *inclusión de un contrato o un acuerdo en otro posterior.*

merger[2] ᴄʀɪᴍʟ.ʟᴀᴡ n. *acumulación y simplificación de cargos, concurso o acumulación ideal o formal* – Syn. merger of offenses.

merger[3] ᴄᴏʀᴘ. n. *fusión.*
• "A combination whereby one of the constituent companies remains in being –absorbing or merging in itself all the other constituent corporations." (19 Am. Jur. 2d Corporation §2510)
Cf: **merger • consolidation • amalgamation.** In a merger one company is absorbed by another. In a consolidation the corporations that are absorbed into a new entity lose their previous identities to form a new corporation. Amalgamation, on the other hand, is the term used in England and Canada to refer to the different forms of corporate union.
  conglomerate merger *fusión de empresas sin relación alguna.*
  horizontal merger *fusión horizontal.*
  mergers and acquisitions *fusiones y adquisiciones,* [borr.] *mergers and acquisitions.*
  mergers and consolidations *fusiones y consolidaciones.*
  short form merger *fusión simplificada.*
  vertical merger *fusión vertical.*
Rel: amalgamation, *unión de sociedades;* buy out, *compra de una porción controladora de acciones de una sociedad o de su activo;* [borr.]*buy out;* consolidation, *consolidación;* pooling of interests, *método de la fusión de intereses.*

middleman n. *intermediario.* – Syn. intermediary.
Rel: broker, *corredor, comisionista;* factor, *comisionista;* finder, *gestor.*

migrant worker *trabajador migratorio.*

militancy n. *militancia.*

military adj. *militar, castrense, marcial.*
  military court *tribunal militar.*
  military jurisdiction *jurisdicción militar.*
  military law *derecho marcial, derecho militar.*
  military officer *oficial de las fuerzas armadas.*
  military operation *operación militar.*
  military police *policía militar.*
  military service *servicio militar.*
  military testament *testamento militar.*

military law *derecho marcial, derecho militar.*
• Statutory provisions governing the service of the personnel in the armed forces. – Syn. military justice.
Glossary: absence without leave, *ausentarse sin licencia o permiso;* aiding the enemy, *ayudar al enemigo;* conduct unbecoming an officer, *conducta impropia de un oficial;* conscientious objection, *oposición de conciencia;* conscription, *conscripción;* court martial, *corte marcial;* deferment, *diferimiento;* dereliction of duty, *abandono de los deberes militares;* desertion, *deserción;* enlistment, *alistamiento, recluta-*

miento; failure to obey order or regulation, *desobedecer órdenes o reglamentos;* mutiny, *motín;* reservists, *reservistas;* veteran's benefits, *prestaciones a los veteranos de guerra.*

militia n. *milicia.*

mineral right *derecho minero.* – Syn. mineral interest.

minimum sentence *pena mínima.*

minimum wage *salario mínimo.*

mining law *ley minera.*
• "The special body of law that covers the acquiring and dealing with all manner of natural resources that are usually in the ground." (Mellinkoff's Dict., 409)
Rel: minerals ferae naturae, *hallazgo de minerales (en forma natural),* [le]*minerales ferae naturae;* mining claim, *derecho minero,* [de]*pertenencia minera, reclamación de derechos mineros;* mining lease, *concesión minera.*

minor n. *menor de edad.*
• A person who has not yet reached legal age. Also insignificant, small, petty.
emancipated minor *menor emancipado.*
minor dependent *menor dependiente.*
minor respondent *menor acusado.*
Rel: adolescent, *adolescente;* child, *niño;* juvenile, *menor, joven;* teenager, *adolescente (entre los 13 y 19 años);* youth, *joven.*

minority member *miembro de una minoría.*

minority opinion *opinión de la minoría.*

minutes n. *minutas.*
• A record of a business or proceeding.
minutes book *libro de minutas.*
Rel: transcripts, *actas.*

Miranda rights [le]*derechos Miranda.*
Mirandize v. *expresar o explicar los derechos Miranda.*
• The right of a suspect in police custody to be informed of his or her right to remain silent, to have an attorney present and to exercise other constitutional protections before an interrogation can take place.
Miranda rules [le]*reglas Miranda.*
Miranda warnings [le]*prevenciones Miranda.*
Rel: Fifth Amendment (US), *Quinta Enmienda (constitucional).*
Text: "You have the right to remain silent. Anything you say can and will be used against you in a court of law. You have the right to talk to a lawyer and have him present with you while you are being questioned. If you cannot afford to hire a lawyer one will be appointed to represent you before any questioning if you

wish one." (Miranda v. Arizona 384 U.S. 436, 444-45)
"Usted tiene derecho a no decir nada. Cualquier cosa que usted diga podrá y será usada en su contra en una corte judicial. Usted tiene el derecho de hablar con un abogado y de que él esté presente con usted cuando se le esté interrogando. Si usted no puede pagar para contratar a un abogado uno le será nombrado, si usted desea tenerlo, para que lo represente antes de cualquier interrogatorio." (translation by editor)

misapplication n. *uso ilegal o indebido de fondos.*

misappropriation n. *malversación, defraudación.*
misappropriate v. *malversar, defraudar.*
• The dishonest application of another's property in favor of the person doing it.
Rel: embezzlement, *abuso de confianza.*

misconduct n. *falta.*
• Disobedience of a legal duty; improper conduct.
gross misconduct *falta grave.*

misconduct in office *faltas en el ejercicio de funciones públicas, ejercicio indebido de funciones públicas.*

misdeed n. *fechoría.*

misdemeanor n. *delito menor, delito menos grave* (PR).
• At common law, a lesser crime that was neither a treason nor a felony. In the United States, any offense other than a felony. – Syn. minor crime, *delito menor.* summary offence (CA,UK,NZ).
Cf: **misdemeanor • felony.** The distinction between felonies and misdemeanors, based on the greater seriousness of the former as contrasted with the later, has been replaced by the classification of crimes by degrees in some jurisdictions in the United States, and abolished and replaced by indictable, summary and mixed (referred to as "either way") offences in England and, in a modified form, in New Zealand, as well as by indictable and summary offences in Canada and Australia.
misdemeanor complaint *denuncia de un delito menor.*
Rel: felony, *delito grave.*

misleading *engañoso.*

misnomer n. *error en el nombre, nombre equivocado o erróneo.*

misprision n. [de]*dejar de reportar la ocurrencia de un delito grave (por alguien que no*

participó en el ilícito), ocultamiento de delito.
• Concealment of the commission of a crime by a person who did not participate in it.

misrepresentation n. *declaración falsa.* **misrepresent** v. *declarar falsamente.*
• A misstatement about a material fact in a contract or other transaction designed to deceive. – Syn. false misrepresentation, *declaración falsa.*

fraudulent misrepresentation *declaración falsa hecha en forma dolosa.*

material misrepresentation *declaración falsa de hechos o elementos esenciales o fundamentales.*
Rel: false pretenses, *estafa;* deceit, *engaño.*

missing in action MIL.LAW *desaparecido en acción, desaparecido en combate.* – Abbr. MIA

missing person *persona desaparecida.*

mistake n. *error.*
• An act or omission arising from ignorance, misconception or the like.
Cf: **mistake ● error.** Mistake differs from error in that mistake focuses on the act or omission caused by the error or erroneous perception or belief, while error refers mostly to the faulty judgment or incorrect belief about matters of fact or the application of the law.
☞ In the Spanish language, *error* stands for both mistake and error. *<cometió un error> <error en el golpe>*

mistake as to the subject matter *error en cuanto al objeto.*

mistake of fact *error de hecho.*

mistake of law *error de derecho.*

mistaken identity *identidad equivocada, error en la persona.* – Syn. mistake as to the person.

mutual mistake *error mutuo, error de ambas partes.*

unilateral mistake *error unilateral.*
Rel: error, *error.*

mistreat n. *maltratar.*

mistress n. *amante.* – Syn. concubine, *concubina.* lover, *amante.* paramour, *querida, manceba.*

mistrial *nulidad de actuaciones, nulidad de lo actuado.*
• A trial aborted because of incurable error.
Rel: hung jury, *jurado dividido (al deliberar).*

misunderstanding *malentendido.*

mitigating circumstances *circunstancias atenuantes.*

mitigation n. *atenuación, reducción (de un pena o castigo), mitigación* (PR).

mitigation of damages *medidas tendientes a mitigar o reducir los daños.*
• Doctrine requiring plaintiff to use ordinary care after an injury or breach to alleviate the resulting damages. – Syn. avoidable consequences, *consecuencias que pueden evitarse.*

duty to mitigate damages *deber legal de mitigar o reducir los daños.*

mob[1] n. *turba, tumulto.*
• A riotous assemblage. A disorganized assemblage of many persons intent on unlawful violence either to persons or property. – Syn. horde, *horda.* multitude. throng, *tumulto.*

mob control *control de multitudes.*
Rel: active crowd, *muchedumbre enardecida;* demonstration, *manifestación;* multitude, *multitud;* press, *muchedumbre, multitud.*

mob[2] n. *mafia, banda.* **mobster** n. *mafioso.*
– Syn. criminal syndicate, *agrupación criminal.*

modify v. *modificar.*

modify a contract *modificar un contrato.*

modify a court order *modificar un mandato o mandamiento judicial.*

modus operandi (lat.) *modus operandi, forma de operación.* Method of operating or doing things.

modus vivendi (lat.) *modus vivendi, forma de vivir, arreglos para vivir (juntos).* Means of living (together).

money[1] **(currency)** n. *dinero.*
• Coins and paper currency used as a means of exchange. A medium of exchange enforced by a government to facilitate economic transactions. – Syn. currency, *divisa, moneda.* funds, *fondos.*

bogus money *dinero falso.*

counterfeit money *dinero falsificado.*

earnest money *depósito en garantía de la celebración de un contrato.*

money demand *pedir el pago de una suma de dinero.*

money had and received *dinero pagado por error o sin la correspondiente contraprestación.*

money judgment *sentencia de pago de dinero.*

money laundering *lavado de dinero.*

money market *mercado de valores a corto plazo.*

money order *orden de pago, giro.*

paper money *papel moneda.*

phony money *imitación de dinero, dinero simulado.*

Rel: cash, *efectivo;* legal tender, *de curso legal.*

money² (wealth) n. *riqueza.*
moneyed corporation *sociedad de gran capital.* – Syn. deep pockets company.
moneylender *prestamista.*
monopoly n. *monopolio.*
• The capture of the control of an article of trade in a given market by a single individual or a small group of persons.
monopoly power *poder monopólico.*
natural monopoly *monopolio natural.*
Rel: combination in restraint of trade, *asociación o acuerdo en contra del libre comercio;* divestiture, *despojarse de operaciones o bienes (por orden judicial);* price fixing, *establecimiento de precios en común, colusión de precios.*
month n. *mes.* **monthly** adj. *mensual.*
monthly payments *mensualidades.*
monthly premium *prima mensual.*
moot adj. *cuestión meramente académica, hipotético.*
moot case *caso hipotético, caso académico* (PR).
moot court *práctica procesal* || *[de]tribunal de práctica.*
moral adj. *moral.*
moral character *calidad moral, solvencia moral.*
moral consideration *consideración moral.*
moral damages *daños morales.*
moral duty *deber moral.*
moral obligation *obligación moral.*
Rel: ethical, *ético;* high-minded, *de una alta calidad moral;* principled, *de buenos principios morales, tener principios;* righteous, *justo, honrado.*
moratorium n. *moratoria.*
• A period during which a debtor or obligor has the right to postpone payment or performance of an obligation.
morgue n. *depósito de cadáveres, anfiteatro.*
morphine n. *morfina.*
mortgage n. [fe]*hipoteca.* **mortgagee** n. *acreedor hipotecario.* **mortgagor** n. *deudor hipotecario.*
• "An interest in property created as a form of security for a loan or payment of a debt and terminated on payment of the loan or the debt." (Oxford Dictionary of Law, 298)
"A mortgage is the transfer of an interest in land as security for the performance of an obligation. The typical mortgage transaction is relatively uncomplicated. A landowner borrows

money from an institutional lender and enters a written agreement with the lender that the landowner's land is collateral for repayment of the loan. In legal terminology the landowner-borrower is a mortgagor, the lender is a mortgagee, and the agreement is a mortgage. If the mortgagor fails to pay the mortgage loan, the mortgagee may enforce his security interest by using appropriate foreclosure procedures to have the mortgaged land sold to satisfy the debt." (Bruce, 1)
adjustable-rate mortgage (ARM) *hipoteca con tasa de interés variable.*
amortization of a mortgage *amortización de una hipoteca.*
assignment of a mortgage *cesión de una hipoteca.*
assumption of a mortgage *asunción de una hipoteca.*
balloon mortgage *hipoteca con un pago final global.*
blanket mortgage *hipoteca general.*
chattel mortgage *gravamen sobre un bien mueble.*
constructive mortgage *hipoteca tácita.*
conventional mortgage *hipoteca convencional.* – Syn. conventional loan.
first mortgage *primera hipoteca.*
foreclosure of a mortgage *ejecución de la garantía hipotecaria.*
junior mortgage *segunda o posterior hipoteca.*
mortgage bond *bono hipotecario.*
mortgage certificate *cédula hipotecaria.*
mortgage discharge *liberación de la hipoteca.*
mortgage note *cédula hipotecaria.*
mortgaged property *propiedad hipotecada.*
recording of a mortgage *inscripción de una hipoteca.*
redemption of a mortgage *pago o extinción de una hipoteca en ejecución.*
second mortgage *segunda hipoteca.*
Rel: acceleration clause, *cláusula de aceleración;* defeasance clause, *cláusula resolutoria de una hipoteca (al cumplirse con las condiciones estipuladas);* deficiency judgment, *sentencia del pago de sumas no cubiertas por la ejecución de una hipoteca;* equity of redemption, *recuperación de un bien hipotecado sujeto a remate;* pledge, *prenda;* power of sale clause, *cláusula otorgando poder para vender;* right of redemption, *derecho de rescate o recuperación.*
Comment: In the United States, the nature of the interest in land in a mortgage has been defined in three basic different ways: as a conveyance of legal title

to the mortgagee; as giving the mortgagee a lien on the mortgaged property, but not legal title; and a hybrid system considering the transaction a conveyance but limiting the mortgagee's right to possession, creating merely a security interest.

mortis causa *mortis causa, por causa de muerte.*

mortmain statutes *leyes de manos muertas.*

most-favored-nation clause ɪɴᴛʟ.ʟᴀᴡ *cláusula de nación más favorecida.*

motion[1] (in court) n. *pedimento, petición,* [brder]*promoción,* [nrwer]*incidente,* [borr.] *moción* (PR). **move** v. *promover, pedir, solicitar.*

• An application made to a court for the purpose of obtaining a ruling or order directing something be done in favor of the applicant.

Cf: **motion • petition • application.** Motion is a broad term that is sometimes interchangeable with concepts like petition and application. In most cases motion is the better term, but in some selected instances petition and application have become the appropriate terms. <petition for a writ of certiorari> <application for an injunction>

↦ Motion, as part and parcel of an adversarial system, does not have an exact equivalent in the civil law systems where the judge, presiding over an inquisitorial system, has enhanced powers of direction and control over the parties. Unlike motion in the common law systems — where the parties are expected to participate in a legal contest and the judge is expected to play the role of an impartial arbiter— civil law equivalents refer to requests made to the judge as case manager (and as an active participant), asking from him or her to follow the proper procedural steps and to accept the legal conclusions of their arguments. Due to the above considerations Spanish language legal discourse is usually not inclined to use noun equivalents of the term motion, often using instead the verbs *pedir, promover* or similar and, in some instances, only the name of the underlying substantive matter being requested. <*promover la nulidad*> <*pedir el saneamiento para el caso de evicción*> <*pido la recusación*> <*desistimiento de la acción*> *Pedimento* and *petición* refer to the action of requesting something specific from the authorities (either judicial or administrative) and they are perhaps closest to the broadness of motion; *pedimento* is sometimes favored as equivalent, if the adversarial and inquisitorial distinction is put

aside, but for that very same reason it is used sparingly in legal discourse. *Petición* is a term more imbedded and pervasive in legal language and text but it is generally recognized as having too strong an administrative leaning. An *incidente* is a request made before the court asking that an incidental issue to a lawsuit be resolved, thus being equivalent to motion in a reduced number of cases. *Promoción* means an appearance before a judge that involves pleading, petitioning or filing a motion. It appears to be a broader but less precise term than motion, since *promoción* is customarily used in any kind of court filings, regardless of the content of the request being made. *Promoción* and *promover* are the preferred terms in Mexican forensic terminology.

ex parte motion *pedimento de una de las partes, pedimento ex-parte.*

motion for a directed verdict [de]*petición para que el veredicto sea dictado por el juez (en vez del jurado).*

motion for a nonsuit *petición de sobreseimiento, promover el sobreseimiento.*

motion for acquittal [de]*petición de la declaración de absolución.*

motion for discovery [de]*petición del requerimiento y producción de pruebas.*

motion for judgment [de]*petición para que se dicte sentencia,* [fe]*dése vista para sentencia.*

motion for judgment notwithstanding verdict [le]*petición para que se dicte sentencia no obstante veredicto en contrario.*

motion for new trial [le]*petición de un nuevo,* [fe]*recurso de revisión, juicio,* [borr.]*moción de juicio nuevo* (PR).

motion for nonsuit *petición de sobreseimiento, petición de caducidad.*

motion for substitution of judge (SOJ) *petición de la substitución del juez,* [fe]*inhibitoria del juez.*

motion for summary judgment *petición para que se dicte sentencia sumariamente.*

motion in arrest of judgment [de]*petición de la nulidad de la sentencia,* [fe]*promover la nulidad de la sentencia.*

motion to continue [de]*petición de que se dé una nueva fecha, petición de prórroga, petición de continuación* (PR).

motion to dismiss *petición de sobreseimiento, promover el sobreseimiento,* [borr.]*moción para desestimar* (PR).

motion to dissolve an injunction [de]*petición de que se extinga un interdicto (o un manda-*

motion

miento judicial prohibitorio).

motion to produce [de]*petición de que se exhiban pruebas,* [fe]*pido se proceda a la presentación o exhibición de pruebas.*

motion to quash [de]*petición de que se deje sin efectos,* [fe]*pido se deje sin efectos.*

motion to quash summons *pedir la nulidad del emplazamiento.*

motion to reopen *petición para reabrir un caso,* [fe]*reposición de un proceso.*

motion to set aside information or indictment *petición de que se declarare improcedente la acusación o denuncia.*

motion to stay *pedimento de suspensión.*

motion to strike *petición de que se deseche,* [fe]*improcedencia.*

motion to strike defense [de]*petición de la improcedencia de una defensa,* [fe]*téngase por improcedente la defensa (de la contraria).*

motion to suppress *petición de que no se admita la prueba,* [borr.]*moción de supresión de evidencia* (PR).

motion to transfer venue [de]*petición de cambio de competencia,* [borr.]*moción de traslado* (PR).

motion to vacate *petición de la declaración de revocación.*

motion to vacate a judgment *petición de la revocación de una sentencia.*

pretrial motion *providencias preparatorias a juicio.*

withdrawal of a motion *desistimiento de una petición.*

Rel: order, *orden judicial;* petition, *petición, demanda, promoción.*

See: *procedimiento civil.*

motion² **(in parliament)** n. *moción.*

• A proposal formally made in parliamentary proceedings.

motive¹ **(impulse)** n. *móvil.*

• That desire which induces action. – Syn. ulterior intent.

Rel: intent, *intención, intencionalidad.*

motive² **(reason)** n. *motivo.*

• Evidential circumstance which presumes the presence of certain desire.

movable¹ n. *bien mueble.*

See: movable property.

movable² **(Scot.)** n. *bienes no sujetos a sucesión.*

movable property *bienes muebles.*

• Property which can be moved or transported, as opposed to property which cannot be moved, called immovable. – Syn. personal property.

Cf: **movable property ● personal property.**

Movables and personal property are usually synonyms. Sometimes movable property is understood as only including tangible personal property. At other times it is considered to refer only to personal property that is movable now, excluding personal property that will be movable in the future, such as growing crops.

See: *bienes muebles.*

moving traffic violation *infracción de tráfico (al conducir o manejar), infracción de circulación (de tráfico).*

municipal adj. *municipal.*

municipal bonds *bonos municipales.*

municipal code *reglamento municipal, código municipal.*

municipal court *corte municipal.*

municipal ordinance *ley municipal, ordenanza municipal.*

murder **(crime)** n. *homicidio calificado, homicidio con agravantes, asesinato* . **murderer** n. *homicida, asesino.*

• "Murder is the unlawful killing of another human being, or a fetus, with malice aforethought." (Penal Code of the State of California §187)

attempted murder *intento de homicidio calificado.*

capital murder *homicidio de pena capital.*

first degree murder *homicidio calificado de primer grado.*

murder for hire *mandar matar a otro, mandar cometer un homicidio.*

premeditated murder *homicidio con premeditación.*

second degree murder *homicidio calificado de segundo grado.*

serial killing *asesinatos en serie.*

Rel: intent to kill, *intención de causar la muerte, intencionalidad homicida;* manslaughter, *homicidio no intencional.*

See: *asesinato.* homicide.

mute adj. *mudo.*

mutilation¹ **(damage)** n. *mutilación (de un documento o récord), daño.*

mutilation² **(maim)** n. *mutilación.*

• Cutting off or damaging an essential body part. – Syn. maim, mutilación.

mutiny n. *motín.*

• An insurrection or insubordination of sailors or soldiers against the authority of their commanders.

mutual agreement *mutuo consentimiento, de*

común acuerdo.

mutual assent *coincidencia de intención, consentimiento.*

mutual fund *fondo de inversiones bursátiles (de renta variable), fondo mutual de inversiones* (Ve), *fondo común de inversiones* (Ar), *fondo mutuo de inversión* (Co).

mutual insurance company *compañía mutualista de seguros.*

NNNN

name n. *nombre.*

   birth name *nombre de nacimiento.*

   corporate name *razón social,* [le]*nombre corporativo.*

   fictitious name *nombre ficticio.*

   full name *nombre completo.*

   generic name *nombre genérico.*

   given name *nombre de pila.*

   last name *apellido paterno.*

   legal name *nombre legal.*

   maiden name *apellido de soltera.*

   nickname *sobrenombre, nombre de cariño.*

   second last name *apellido materno.*

   surname *apellido familiar, nombre de familia*
   – Syn. family name.

   Rel: alias, *alias;* also known as (aka), *también conocido como;* pseudonym, *seudónimo.*

narcotics n. *narcóticos.*

   Rel: analgesics, *analgésicos;* codeine, *codeína;* darvon, *darvon;* demeral, *demeral;* dilaudid, *dilaudid;* heroin, *heroína;* morphine, *morfina;* opiates, *opiatos.*
   See: drugs.

nation n. *nación.*

   • A large group of people who inhabit a territory and share common ancestry and traditions, and who usually have the same government. Cf: **nation ● state.** A nation usually refers to an identifiable group of people who share a common culture and live under the same government. A state usually refers to the system of rules or legal structures that make possible the participation of individuals in a societal group.

national government *gobierno nacional.*

national origin (int.trade) *origen nacional.*

nationalism n. *nacionalismo.*

nationality n. *nacionalidad.*

   • The relationship between a person, sometimes an entity, and a nation. The status of belonging to a particular nation.

   double nationality *doble nacionalidad.*

   See: citizenship.

native-born citizen *ciudadano por nacimiento.*
   – Syn. natural-born citizen.

natural cause *causa natural.*

natural child *hijo natural.*

natural death *muerte natural.*

natural law *derecho natural.*

   • The law considered as a set of immutable principles beyond human control reflecting the essence of human nature or a divine order. – Syn. ius naturale (lat.), ius naturale, derecho natural.

natural person *persona natural.*

   • An individual or human being as distinguished from an artificial person such as a corporation.
   Rel: artificial or fictitious person, *persona moral o jurídica.*

naturalized citizen *ciudadano por naturalización.*

naval law *derecho naval, derecho de la marina.*

   naval officers *oficiales navales.*

   Rel: Code of Military Justice, *Código de Justicia Militar;* Navy, *Marina.*

necessaries n. *necesidades, cosas de primera necesidad.*

   • Things indispensable to life.

necessity CRIML.LAW n. *estado de necesidad.*

   • An irresistible compulsion of natural forces or the forces of humankind, barring other choices of conduct. Acting in a way that is necessary to prevent a greater evil. – Syn. choice of evils defense, necessity defense.
   Rel: irresistible impulse, *impulso irresistible;* justification, *justificantes, causas de justificación.*

necropsy n. *necropsia.*
   See: autopsy, *autopsia.*

negative adj. *negativo.*

   negative covenant *acuerdo o declaración prohibitiva.*

   negative easement *servidumbre negativa.*

   negative evidence *prueba de hechos negativos.*

   negative pregnant *negación que implica una admisión, negativa que implica afirmativa* (PR).

   negative testimony *testimonio negativo.*

neglect n. *descuido, falta de cuidado.* **neglect** v. *descuidar.* **neglectful** adj. *descuidado.*

   • The disregard of a duty owed to a person or thing, whether inadvertent, careless or willful.

   excusable neglect *descuido u omisión justifi-*

cado.
neglect of duty *incumplimiento de un deber.*
willful neglect *abandono intencional.*
neglected child *niño descuidado.*
Rel: child abuse, *abuso o maltrato de menores.*
negligence n. *negligencia, culpa, imprudencia.*
negligent adj. *negligente.* **negligently** adv.
negligentemente.
• The failure to exercise the standards of care
that a reasonable and prudent person would
apply in a similar situation or the doing of
what a reasonable and prudent person would
not do. – Syn. actionable negligence. ordinary
negligence.
Cf: **negligence • neglect.** These are distinguishable terms. Neglect refers to the fact that the
person has not done what it was his or her duty to do; negligence refers to the reason why
the person has failed to exercise the standard
of care he or she ought to have exercised.
Neglect is an objective fact, while negligence
is a subjective state of mind.
comparative negligence *culpa o negligencia
parcial de la víctima, negligencia comparada*
(PR). – Syn. comparative fault.
contributory negligence *culpa o negligencia
inexcusable de la víctima, negligencia
contribuyente* (PR), *imprudencia temeraria* (Sp).
criminal negligence *imprudencia criminal,
negligencia criminal, culpa.* – Syn. culpable
negligence.
gross negligence *culpa o negligencia grave,
imprudencia temeraria.* – Syn. wanton
negligence.
imputed negligence *negligencia o culpa por
actos de terceros.*
negligence per se *culpa o negligencia por
ministerio de ley.*
slight negligence *culpa o negligencia leve.*
Rel: assumption of risk, *asunción de riesgo;* duty of care, *deber de diligencia;* recklessness,
imprudencia grave.
> Comment: The basis of liability in negligence is
> the creation of an unreasonable risk to harm
> another. The general standard applicable in most
> negligence cases is one of reasonable care under
> the circumstances.
See: *culpa*[1].
negligent crime *delito imprudencial o culposo.*
negligent homicide *homicidio imprudencial o
culposo por negligencia.*
negligent manslaughter [fe]*homicidio culposo con previsión o representación, homicidio
imprudencial involuntario.*

– Syn. involuntary manslaughter.
involuntary manslaughter *homicidio no intencional inconsciente,* [fe]*homicidio culposo con
previsión o representación, homicidio
accidental involuntario.*
negotiable instrument [fe]*título de crédito,*
[le]*instrumento negociable* (PR). **acceptor** n.
aceptante. **drawee** n. *girado,* **drawer or
maker** n. *girador.* **holder** n. *tenedor.*
• Negotiable instrument is an unconditional
promise or order to pay a fixed amount of money, payable on demand or at a definite time,
and payable to bearer or to order. Examples
are a check, a note, a bill of lading, a bond or
a warehouse receipt.
Cf: **negotiable instrument • commercial paper.** These terms are synonymous but not
interchangeable. Commercial paper is the
broader term, and in a strict sense it includes
negotiable as well as nonnegotiable paper.
Negotiable instruments are by definition those
which are issued to be negotiable in the ordinary course of business.
Rel: acceptance, *aceptación;* dishonor, *falta de
pago o aceptación;* holder in due course, *tenedor legítimo, tenedor de buena fe;* indorsement,
endoso; pay to the order of, *páguese a la orden
de;* personal defenses, *defensas basadas en la
acción causal;* presentment, *presentación;*
protest, *protesto, protesta;* real defenses, *defensas contra un tenedor legítimo.*
See: note.
Ref: (CA) Martin v National Union Fire Insurance
Co. of Pittsburgh [1923] 3 D.L.R. 574 (Alta S.C.A.
D.); (US) U.C.C. §3-104; (UK) 4(1) Halsbury's
Laws para 303.
negotiation n. *negociación.*
nepotism n. *nepotismo.*
• Favoring the appointment of one's relatives
to public office or their preference in business
or promotions.
net adj. *neto.* – Opp. gross, *bruto.*
net assets *activo neto.*
net cost *costo neto.*
net income *ingreso neto.*
net loss *pérdidas netas.*
net operating income *ingreso neto de
operaciones.*
net pay *sueldo o salario neto.*
net price *precio neto.*
net profits *utilidades netas, ganancias netas.*
net revenues *ingreso neto, percepción neta.*
net sales *ventas netas.*
net value *valor neto.*

net weight *peso neto.*

net yield *rendimiento neto.*

net worth *capital líquido, capital neto, patrimonio neto* (Ar), *pasivo no exigible* (Ch), *activo líquido, capital contable* (Mx), *neto patrimonial* (Sp).

neutrality INTL.LAW n. *neutralidad.*

next of kin *pariente más cercano* || *heredero (de bienes personales).*

no-fault auto insurance *seguro de automóvil sin determinación de culpabilidad, seguro de automóvil de responsabilidad objetiva.*
"Insurance policies typically provide for the payment of benefits upon the occurrence of described events and without regard to whether those events were caused by the fault of either the insured or another person." (Keeton & Widiss, 411-12)

no-fault divorce *divorcio sin causa o causal, divorcio basado en responsabilidad objetiva.*

nolle prosequi (lat.) *nolle prosequi, desistimiento de la acción penal.*
• Formal entry in the record by a prosecutor indicating that a charge will not be prosecuted any further. – Abbr. nol-pros. nolle pros.
Cf: **nolle prosequi • non prosequitur (non pros).** Nolle prosequi (not to wish to prosecute) indicates the legal notice of abandonment of suit or a docket entry showing that the plaintiff or the prosecution has relinquished the action. Non prosequitur (he does not prosecute) is the judgment against a plaintiff who has not pursued the case.

nolo contendere (lat.) *nolo contendere.* [le]*no quiero litigar,* [le]*no lo disputaré,* [de]*admisión de culpabilidad penal sin aceptar responsabilidad civil.* I will not contest it.
Cf: **plea of guilty • nolo contendere • no contest.** A plea of guilty is an unconditional admission of guilt before the court; nolo contendere on the other hand, is an admission of guilt as to the criminal charges brought against the defendant but without acknowledgment of any wrongdoing regarding any civil claims that may arise from the facts of the case. Nolo contendere is also termed a "no contest" plea in some jurisdictions.

nominal adj. *nominal.*

nominal damages *indemnización por daños y perjuicios nominales.*

nominal interest rate *tasa nominal de interés.*

nominal salary *sueldo o salario nominal.*

nominal value *valor nominal.*

non sequitur (lat.) *non sequitur.* It does not follow.

nonappearance n. *incomparecencia.*

non-bailable offense *delito sin derecho a fianza.*

nonfeasance n. *omisión, no hacer.*

nonimmigrant n. *no inmigrante.*

nonprofit corporation *sociedad o compañía sin afán de lucro.*
• A corporation organized for purposes other than turning a profit, usually for charitable, educational or other humanitarian activities.
– Syn. charitable institution, *institución de beneficencia.*

nonprofit association *organización sin afán de lucro, organización no lucrativa, asociación.*

nonresident *extranjero no residente.*

nonsuit[1] (voluntary dismissal) n. *desistimiento.*
• A voluntary dismissal of a lawsuit or criminal action without a decision on the merits.
– Syn. voluntary discontinuance. voluntary dismissal.
motion for nonsuit, *desistimiento de la actora o del órgano de acusación.*
Rel: mistrial, *nulidad de actuaciones, sobreseimiento.*

nonsuit[2] (involuntary dismissal) n. *sobreseimiento, desestimación.*
• Dismissal of a case or of a defendant because plaintiff failed to prosecute or prove his or her case. – Syn. judgment of nonsuit.
involuntary nonsuit *sobreseimiento por causas ajenas a la actora.* – Syn. compulsory nonsuit.
motion for nonsuit *petición de la declaración de sobreseimiento, promover el sobreseimiento.*
peremptory nonsuit *sobreseimiento por falta de pruebas.*
voluntary nonsuit *abandono de la acción.*

non-tariffs barriers (intl.trade) *barreras no arancelarias.*

North American Free Trade Agreement (NAFTA) *Tratado Norteamericano de Libre Comercio* (TNLC).

no-strike clause *cláusula de prohibición de huelga.*

not guilty *no culpable.*

not guilty by reason of insanity
[brder][de]*(encontrar al acusado) no culpable por demencia* || [brder][de]*defensa de no culpabilidad por demencia,* [fe]*defensa o alegato de inimputabilidad por la enajenación mental del acusado.*

plea of not guilty *declaración de no culpabilidad.*

verdict of not guilty *veredicto de no culpabilidad.*

Rel: innocent, *inocente.*

notary public [brder]*notario público.* **notarize** v. *notarizar.* **notarial** adj. *notarial.*

• A public officer whose function is to administer oaths, to attest to the authenticity of certain types of documents, and to formalize some commercial acts, such as protesting commercial paper.

↦ Any similarities between the civil law notary and the notary public in the common law countries is only superficial. The notary public in civil law countries is a person of greater importance when compared to the common law notary. In the civil law countries the notary public normally serves three main functions: drafts important legal instruments (such as wills, corporate charters, conveyances and contracts), authenticates documents, and acts as a kind of a public record regarding instruments drafted or authenticated by his or her office. The public notary in common law systems, in contrast, attests to the validity and correctness of deeds and documents, administers oaths and take affidavits. In some jurisdictions, lay persons as well as lawyers are admitted as public notaries.

note n. *pagaré.* **maker** n. *suscriptor, otorgante.* **noteholder** n. *tenedor, portador.* **payee** n. *beneficiario.*

• A written promise by the maker to pay money to the payee or to bearer. – Syn. promissory note. Cf: note • **promissory note** • draft. Note and promissory note are synonymous. A note is a promise to pay money to another or to bearer; it is a two-party instrument. A draft is an order by the drawer to another, the drawee, demanding that the drawee pay money to the payee or to bearer; it is, in contrast, a three-party instrument.

demand note *pagaré a la vista.*

installment note *pagaré en serie, pagaré seriado, pagarés continuados.*

mortgage note *pagaré hipotecario.*

negotiable note *pagaré negociable.*

secured note *pagaré con garantía colateral, pagaré garantizado.* – Syn. collateral note.

unsecured note *pagaré sin garantía colateral.*

notes payable *efectos, documentos o pagarés por pagar.*

notes receivable *efectos, documentos o pagarés*

por cobrar.

notice[1] (communication) n. *notificación.* **notify** v. *notificar.*

• Communication of information of a legal nature following a specified formal procedure. – Syn. notification.

actual notice *notificación efectivamente hecha.*

constructive notice *notificación considerada hecha por determinación de la ley, notificación por ministerio de ley.*

express notice *notificación expresa.*

implied notice *notificación tácita.*

notice by publication *notificación por publicación.*

notice of appeal *presentación de la apelación.*

notice of appearance *notificación de la comparecencia del demandado.*

notice of claim *notificación de la demanda.*

notice of dishonor *notificación o aviso de falta de pago o aceptación.*

notice of entry of a default order *notificación del auto de la declaración de rebeldía.*

notice of motion *notificación de un pedimento o petición, notificación de una promoción.*

notice to creditors *notificación a los acreedores.*

notice to terminate tenancy *notificación de la terminación de una tenencia o un arrendamiento.*

personal notice *notificación personal.*

to serve notice on *notificar legalmente.*

Rel: judicial notice, *conocimiento judicial, hecho notorio;* subpoena, *citatorio, citación.*

notice[2] (announcement) n. *aviso.*

• An intimation; a warning.

public notice *aviso público.*

to give notice *dar aviso.*

until further notice *hasta nuevo aviso.*

notorious possession *posesión pública y notoria.*

novation n. *novación.* **novate** v. *novar.* **novatory** adj. *novatorio.*

• Substitution of an old obligation with a new one that either extinguishes the existing obligation or replaces an original party with a new party.

Rel: assignment, *cesión.*

nuisance[1] (public interference) n. *molestia pública,* [brder]*perjuicio,* [borr.]*estorbo público* (PR).

• An unreasonable interference with the rights of the public. – Syn. public nuisance.

"Nuisance is a word derived from the French word for harm. A public nuisance can be defined as an unreasonable interference with a right common to the general public. A private nuisance is a substantial and unreasonable interference with the use and enjoyment of land." (Rodgers, 102)

abatement of a nuisance *retiro de una molestia pública, eliminación de una molestia o perjuicio.*

nuisance in fact *que constituye una molestia o perjuicio en forma circunstancial.*

nuisance per se *que constituye una molestia o perjuicio por sí misma.* – Syn. nuisance at law.

nuisance² (private interference) n. [de]*interferencia en el uso y aprovechamiento del derecho de propiedad,* [borr.]*estorbo privado* (PR).

• A considerable and unreasonable interference with the use, possession and enjoyment of another person's land. – Syn. private nuisance.

null and void *nulo y sin efecto.* – Syn. void, *nulidad.*

nulla poena sine lege (max.) *no hay pena sin que la ley lo autorice.*
Rel: nullum crimen sine lege (max.), *no hay delito sin que la ley lo autorice.*

nunc pro tunc (lat.) *nunc pro tunc,* [le]*ahora por entonces, con efectos retroactivos.* Now for then.

• Act allowed to be done after it should have been done.

nuncupative will *testamento oral o verbal.* – Syn. oral will. unwritten will.

OOOO

oath n. *juramento.* – Syn. affirmation, *protesta.* pledge. promise, *promesa.* swearing. word of honor, *palabra de honor.*

• A declaration that a statement or testimony is the truth, usually invoking God or another venerated being or thing as a witness.

oath of a witness *juramento de un testigo.*
oath of allegiance *juramento de lealtad.*
oath of office *juramento de cumplir un cargo.*
Cf: **oath ● affirmation.** These are equivalent terms used synonymously. An affirmation is a similar declaration to an oath, without the religious connotation.

obiter dictum (lat.) *comentarios (hechos por el juez en la sentencia) que no constituyen parte del precedente, opinión no vinculante, señalamiento incidental (en una sentencia).*
See: dictum.

objection n. *objeción, excepción.*

• Reason for opposing a contention or argument. "The act of a party who objects to some matter or proceeding in the course of a trial, or an argument or reason urged by him in support of his contention that the matter or proceeding objected to is improper or illegal." (Black's Dictionary 5th ed., 556)

Cf: **objection ● challenge ● exception.** An objection is sometimes called a challenge, in particular when the objection protests the admissibility of expert testimony of a lay witness or the qualification of prospective jurors. On the other hand, an "exception [is] a form of objection in some jurisdictions. E.g., to preserve a point for appeal, especially when the court has overruled an objection." (Mellinkoff's Dict., 437)

↳ While an objection is traditionally an oral rebuke by one of the parties in a proceeding, and especially in the phrasing of a question or statement in the examination of a witness, *excepción* refers to the content of a written plea introducing a specific defense to the affirmations of the plaintiff or the accusation of the accusing party. In this light, *excepción* is an appropriate equivalent only in those cases where objection amounts to a full defense, usually in the pleading stage of trial.

frivolous objection *objeción o excepción infundada.*

grounds for an objection *fundamento de una objeción o excepción.*

overrule an objection *la objeción es improcedente, no procede la objeción.*

sustain an objection *ha lugar la objeción, procede la objeción.*

Specific types: argumentative, *controvertida;* calling for a conclusion, *insinuando una conclusión;* hearsay, *declaración o mención hecha por un tercero, de oídas;* immaterial, *insustancial;* irrelevant, *irrelevante;* leading, *tendenciosa;* not being pleaded, *no parte de la litis;* privileged, *inmunidad;* self-serving declaration, *manifestación que le favorece a sí mismo;* untimely, *no ha lugar;* violates privilege against self-incrimination, *infringe el derecho contra autoincriminación;* violates the best evidence rule, *infringe la regla de que son admisibles sólo originales o pruebas primarias;* violates the oral evidence rule, *infringe la regla de la prueba oral;* without sufficient foundation, *no lo suficientemente fundada, falta de fundamento.*

Rel: examination, *examen testimonial, examen oral de un testigo.*

obligation

obligation¹ (duty) n. *obligación.* **obligee** n. *acreedor.* **obligor** n. *deudor, obligado.*
• "A legal or moral duty to do or not to do something." (Black's Law Dict., 8th. ed., 1104)
Cf: **obligation • duty.** Obligation is a word of broad meaning that is usually interpreted in context. Derived from the Latin word *obligatio,* it may mean legal or moral duty, contractual duty or simply what a person is bound to do or forbear. Obligation, broadly considered, is often used as synonym of duty.
↦ Obligation in English-speaking countries includes both legal and moral connotations and is often equated with duty; in Spanish-speaking countries, *obligación* has a similar loose meaning, but in addition has a very important specific definition, meaning an acknowledgment of liability to pay or to do or abstain from doing certain things for another. It includes both rights and duties deriving from this acknowledgment of liability.
conditional obligation *obligación condicional.*
contractual obligation *obligación contractual.*
fiduciary obligation *obligación fiduciaria.*
joint obligation *obligación mancomunada.*
moral obligation *obligación moral.*
parental obligation *obligación paterna.*
personal obligation *obligación personal.*
statutory obligation *obligación legal.*
Rel: contract, *contrato;* duty, *deber.*
See: *obligación.*

obligation² (liability) *obligación.* **obligee** n. *acreedor.* **obligor** n. *deudor.*
• A bond by deed. – Syn. legal obligation.

obscene adj. *obsceno.* **obscenity** n. *obscenidad .*
• Content offensive to accepted standards of decency or to what is considered appropriate.
Cf: **obscene • indecent.** Both terms "are sometimes considered interchangeable, although indecency is arguably broader because it may encompass anything which is outrageously disgusting ... As a matter of degree, however, obscene is the term to which stronger disapproval attaches." (Garner, 610)
obscene material *material obsceno, materia obscena* (PR). – Syn. obscene matter.
obscene publications (UK) *publicaciones obscenas.*
Rel: corrupting morals, *obscenidad, ultrajes a la moral pública;* pornography, *pornografía.*

obsolescence n. *obsolescencia.* **obsolete** adj. *obsoleto.*

obstructing a police officer *obstruir el cumplimiento del deber de un policía.*

obstructing justice *obstrucción de justicia.*
Rel: withholding of evidence, *ocultación o retención de pruebas.*

occupation¹ (possession) *ocupación.*
occupation² (livelihood) n. *ocupación.* – Syn. career, *carrera.* job, *empleo, trabajo.* profession, *profesión.* trade, *oficio, ocupación.* work, *trabajo.*
occupational adj. *ocupacional.*
occupational accident *accidente de trabajo.*
occupational disease *enfermedad profesional.*
occupational hazard *riesgo profesional.*

odometer fraud (crime) *modificar ilegalmente el contador de kilometraje.*

of age *mayor de edad.*
of record *registrado, inscrito.*
attorney of record *abogado acreditado en autos.*
matter of record *en autos, conforme a los autos.*

off the record *sin que se transcriba, sin que conste en autos, sin que se anote en el acta.*

offense n. *delito.* **offender** n. *delincuente.* – Other spell.: offence (AU,CA,UK,NZ)
• A violation of the law; a crime. – Syn. crime.
Cf: **crime • offense.** Both are synonyms. Crime is mostly used to refer to specific criminal wrongs, especially to the more serious infractions. Offense is used to refer to felonies and misdemeanors generically, and often to the less serious wrongs. In England, Canada and Australia the modern tendency is to refer to crimes as offences.
arrestable offence (UK) [de]*delito con pena de prisión de más de cinco años.*
bailable offense *delito que alcanza fianza.*
continuing offense *delito continuo.*
indictable offence (CA,UK) *delito mayor,* [de]*delito perseguible mediante acusación de gran jurado.*
lesser included offense [de]*delito menor incluido en otro mayor, acumulación de delitos (uno de ellos de menor penalidad).*
lesser offense *delito menos grave.*
notifiable offence (CA,UK) *delito reportable.*
offense against property *delitos contra la propiedad.*
summary offence (CA,UK) *delito menor.*
See: criminals.

offensive language *lenguaje ofensivo o insultante.*

offer¹ SEC.LAW n. *precio de oferta (de acciones).*
offeror n. *ofertante, vendedor (de acciones).*

• The price at which someone owning shares offers to sell them. – Syn. asked price.

offer² CONTRACTS n. *oferta, propuesta.* **offeree** *destinatario.* **offeror** *oferente, proponente.*
• A proposal made with the purpose of inviting an acceptance that will create a contract.
irrevocable offer *oferta irrevocable.*
offer and acceptance *oferta y aceptación.*
revocable offer *oferta revocable.*
unilateral offer *oferta unilateral.*
Rel: acceptance, *aceptación;* bargain, *policitación, negociación contractual;* consideration, *contraprestación;* promise, *declaración unilateral de voluntad.*

offer of proof *petición sobre la admisibilidad de pruebas (generalmente para efectos de apelación).*

officer n. *funcionario.*
civil officer *funcionario civil.*
military officer *oficial militar.*
officer in court (oral expr.) *el oficial (de policía) se encuentra presente (en el juzgado o tribunal).*
officer of the court *funcionario judicial auxiliar.*
police officer *oficial de policía, agente de la policía, policía.*
public officer *funcionario público.*

official languages (CA) *idiomas oficiales.*

official misconduct *responsabilidad oficial.*
Rel: graft, *corrupción oficial.*

offshore *fuera de la jurisdicción nacional,* [borr.] *offshore.*
• An international term meaning not only out of one's country (jurisdiction) but out of the tax reach of one's country of residence or citizenship.
offshore bank *banco con sucursales o matrices establecidas en el extranjero,* [borr.]*offshore bank.*
offshore investments [borr.]*inversiones offshore, inversiones hechas en paraísos fiscales.*
Rel: asset protection trust (APT), [le]*fideicomiso para la protección de activos;* badges of fraud, *indicios de probable abuso o fraude;* international business company (IBC), [le]*compañía internacional de negocios;* tax haven, *paraíso fiscal, refugio fiscal.*

oligopoly n. *oligopolio.*

on all fours (jargon) [de]*aplicación exacta (de un precedente al nuevo caso bajo consideración).*

• Exactly applicable to a case with regard to both facts and law when considering a precedent's authority in support of a new case.

on demand *a la vista.* – Syn. on call, *a la vista.*

on duty *en activo, en servicio.*

on record *en actas.*

onerous adj. *oneroso.*

online law *derecho de computación en línea.*
– Syn. cyberlaw, *ciber-ley.* internet law, *ley aplicable al internet, derecho del internet.*
online contracts *contratos en línea.*
online sales *ventas en línea.*
Rel: computer fraud, *fraude cometido mediante el uso de una computadora;* digital signatures, *firmas electrónicas;* domain name, *nombre de dominio;* e-mail, *correo electrónico;* encryption, *cifrado;* hacker, *ciber-pirata* [borr.]*hacker;* software, [borr.]*software;* web site, *sitio de la red, sitio en el internet, página web.*

open adj. *abierto.*
in open court *en audiencia pública.*
open account *cuenta abierta.*
open letter of credit *carta abierta de crédito.*
open port *puerto libre, puerto franco.*
open-end credit *crédito revolvente.*

opening statement *discurso de apertura, presentación oral en la apertura de un juicio.*

operating expenses (accounting) *gastos de operación o explotación, gastos de explotación* (Sp), *gastos operativos* (Ar). – Syn. operating cost, *costo o coste de operación o explotación.*

operating losses (accounting) *pérdida de operaciones, pérdida operativa, pérdida de explotación.*

operating margin (accounting) *margen de operación, margen operativo, margen de explotación.*

operation of law *por disposición de la ley, por ministerio de ley, operación de ley* (PR).

opinion¹ (belief) n. *opinión.*
• A statement or conclusion of belief; a formal judgment of an expert or knowledgeable person.
expert opinion *opinión de un perito.*
witness opinion *opinión de un testigo.*

opinion² (judicial decision) n. *ponencia, opinión.*
• Written reasons given by the court explaining a decision in a case. – Syn. judicial opinion. An opinion in the United States includes points of law, statements of fact, the grounds or reasons for the court's decision and dicta. The equivalent word in the United Kingdom is judg-

ment, but the word opinion is also used. In the United Kingdom, opinion more often refers to legal advice given by counsel in writing.

concurring opinion *ponencia coincidente (en cuanto a la sentencia pero no en cuanto a los motivos o fundamento), opinión individual (coincidente).*

dissenting or minority opinion *ponencia disidente, opinión disidente.*

majority opinion *ponencia mayoritaria, opinión mayoritaria.*

per curiam opinion *ponencia del tribunal (sin identificar a sus autores).*

opium n. *opio.*

option[1] CONTRACTS n. *opción.* **optionee** n. *beneficiario (de una opción).* **optionor** n. *obligado (de una opción).*

• A contractual obligation to keep an offer open for a specified time in exchange for consideration.

option to purchase *opción de compra.*

option[2] SEC.LAW n. *opciones financieras.*

• The right to buy or sell stock, commodities or other assets at a fixed price within a specified period of time.

commodity futures option *opciones financieras de productos cotizados en bolsa,* [lexical exp.]*opciones de commodities.*

stock option *opciones financieras de valores, opciones de valores, opción sobre acciones.*

oral argument *alegato oral.*

oral confession *confesión oral.*

oral contract *contrato oral.* – Syn. parol contract.

oral formalisms (legalese) *formalismos orales (legales).* – Syn. oral expressions (law).
Rel: by the authority vested in me, *en uso de mis facultades;* Hear ye, hear ye, hear ye;, *(Oyez,Oyez,Oyez)* ¡*Oíd, Oíd, Oíd;!* honorable, *honorable;* may it please the court, *con el permiso de la corte, con la venia de la corte;* my Lord (UK), *su Señoría* (Sp), *vuestra señoría* (Ar), C; *(ciudadano) juez* (Mx); the truth, the whole truth, and nothing but the truth, *la verdad, toda la verdad y nada más que la verdad;* your Honor, *su señoría* (Sp), *vuestra señoría* (Ar), C; *(ciudadano) juez* (Mx).
See: written formalisms.

order[1] **(judicial directive)** n. *orden judicial, mandamiento.*

• A direction or mandate of the court on some subsidiary or incidental matter to the main proceeding. – Syn. court order. judicial order. decree.

final order *orden definitiva.* – Syn. final judgment.

interlocutory order *decreto interlocutorio.*

order for assignment of wages *orden de cesión de salario.*

order of commitment *orden de reclusión (de un demente o incompetente)* || *orden de participación en un programa de rehabilitación (de un delincuente).*

order of dismissal *auto declarando el sobreseimiento.*

order of protection *orden de protección* (RD, PR).

order of restitution *orden de restitución.*

order of separation *orden de separación.*

order of withholding *orden de retención.*

order to show cause *auto pidiendo se fundamente lo actuado, auto pidiendo que se demuestre que el incumplimiento o lo actuado tiene justificación legal.*

restraining order *interdicto o mandamiento judicial prohibitivo provisional.*

support order *orden de pensión alimenticia.*

suspension order *orden de suspensión.*
Rel: motion, [de]*petición;* warrant, *orden judicial (de detención o requisición).*

order[2] **(purchase)** n. *orden, pedido.*

order[3] SEC.LAW n. *orden.*

• Instruction given to a broker to buy or sell securities.

day order *orden abierta por un día.*

limit order *orden límite.*

market order *orden de mercado.*

stop order *orden tope.*

ordinance n. *ordenanza, ley local.*

ordinary course of business *en el curso normal de los negocios, durante el ejercicio habitual de su actividad.*

ordinary income *ingresos ordinarios.*

organized crime *crimen organizado.*

original jurisdiction *jurisdicción original.*

out of commission *fuera de servicio.*

out of wedlock *fuera de matrimonio.*

out-of-court settlement *convenio extrajudicial.*

out-of-pocket expenses *gastos efectivamente incurridos.*

outcry *desahogo, desahogarse (de haber sido víctima de un delito, especialmente sexual), exclamación expontánea* (PR).

outer space law *derecho espacial, derecho del espacio exterior.* – Syn. airspace law, *derecho espacial.*

outer space treaty *tratado sobre el espacio exterior.*
Rel: air law, *derecho aéreo.*

outlaw n. *bandido, forajido.* **outlaw** v. *declarar la ilegalidad (de algo o alguien).*

outrageous conduct *conducta ultrajante o indignante.*

outstanding debt *deuda por pagar, deuda pendiente de pago.*

overcome a presumption *refutar una presunción.*

overdue n. *vencido.*

overrule a decision *invalidar o revocar una decisión.*

overrule an objection *declarar una objeción improcedente, que no ha lugar (la objeción), denegar la objeción.*

overturn a judgment *revocar una sentencia.*

ownership n. *derecho de propiedad, titularidad.*
owner n. *propietario, titular, dueño.*
• The status or rights of an owner, including the right to possess and control property.
– Syn. proprietorship, *propiedad.* seisin, *posesión efectiva de un inmueble (basada en un derecho).*
Cf: **ownership** • **property** • **title.** Ownership, property and title are used synonymously. Ownership is the recognition of lawful possession, use, enjoyment and right of conveyance over property. When contrasted with property, ownership means or implies the right of control over an object, as opposed to any actual or constructive control. While usually considered interchangeable, title and ownership are sometimes distinguished by the emphasis placed by ownership on the right of possession and control, as opposed to the relevance title gives to all the elements of the rights to property.
"In England, ownership resided in the king, and the distribution and retention of lands throughout the kingdom was carried out according to the theory of tenure. Those who actually occupied and used the great mass of English land were not owners of it but holders of derivative rights from the king or from the king's tenants, and hence English land law was concerned not with ownership and the rights and duties of owners but with tenure and the rights and duties of tenants. The concept of ownership simply did not come into play." (Merryman, Clark & Haley, 1193) Ownership, as a consequence, means that what one owns is

not the land, but an estate in the land, that is the rights of possession, use, enjoyment and conveyance over property.
absolute ownership *propiedad absoluta.*
joint ownership *propiedad mancomunada.*
legal ownership [le]*propiedad legal,* [de]*propiedad conforme al sistema de derecho-estricto o "common law" (en contraste con el sistema de derecho-equidad o "equity").*
owner of record *propietario registrado.*
sole ownership *propietario o dueño único.*
Rel: possession, *posesión;* title, *título, titularidad.*
See: property. seisin. title.

PPPP

pact n. *pacto, acuerdo.*
• An agreement, especially one between countries or government entities. – Syn. compact. treaty, *tratado.*

pacta sunt servanda (max.)(lat.) *pacta sunt servanda, los acuerdos deben cumplirse conforme se pactaron.* Agreements are to be kept.
Rel: rebus sic stantibus (lat.), *rebus sic stantibus.*

pain and suffering *daños físicos o morales sufridos por una persona.*

palimony n. [de]*pensión alimenticia otorgada en disolución de uniones no legalizadas.*

pandering[1] **(solicitation)** n. *proxenetismo, lenocinio* (Mx). **panderer** n. *proxeneta, lenón.*
• Soliciting customers for a prostitute; recruiting a prostitute.

pandering[2] **(distribution)** n. *ofrecimiento de material pornográfico.*
• Distributing material to appeal to someone's sexual interest.
pandering of obscenity *ofrecimiento de publicaciones pornográficas.*
Rel: white slave trade, *trata de blancas;* prostitution, *prostitución.*

paralegal n. *asistente de abogado, asistente legal.*

paranoia n. *paranoia.*

pardon n. *indulto, perdón.*
• "An act of grace proceeding from the power entrusted with the execution of laws, which exempts the individual on whom it is bestowed from the punishment the law inflicts for a crime he has committed." (Ballentine's Law Dict., 911) – Syn. executive pardon.
conditional pardon *indulto condicional.*

executive pardon *perdón del Ejecutivo, perdón presidencial.* – Syn. presidential pardon.
general pardon *amnistía.* – Syn. amnesty.
unconditional pardon *indulto incondicional.*
Rel: amnesty, *amnistía;* clemency, *clemencia;* commutation, *conmutación de pena;* reprieve, *aplazamiento (de la ejecución de una condena);* suspended sentence, *condena suspendida.*
parents n. *padres.* **parent** n. *el padre o la madre.*
biological parents *padres biológicos.*
foster parents *padres adoptivos temporales, padres de crianza.*
natural parents *padres naturales.*
Rel: paternity, *paternidad;* in loco parentis (lat.), *in loco parentis, tutor temporal (de un menor).*
parental authority *autoridad de los padres.*
parental care *cuidado de los padres.*
parental consent *consentimiento de los padres.*
parental rights *derechos de los padres.*
parliament n. *parlamento.* **parliamentary** adj. *parlamentario.*
parliamentary elections *elecciones parlamentarias.*
parliamentary law *derecho parlamentario.*
parliamentary privilege *inmunidad parlamentaria.*
parliamentary session *sesión parlamentaria.*
parliamentary vote *voto parlamentario.*
Rel: Prime Minister, *Primer Ministro.*
parol evidence rule [de]*el acuerdo escrito final entre las partes no admite prueba que lo modifique o contradiga,* [fe]*regla de que el acuerdo escrito final hace prueba plena.*
• The rule that a written agreement between parties intended as final cannot be changed by prior or contemporaneous oral understanding.
parole n. *libertad condicional, libertad preparatoria* (Mx), **parolee** *persona bajo libertad condicional.*
• A conditional release of an inmate, after the inmate has served part of his or her sentence, under the supervision of a parole officer.
parole board *comité de libertad condicional.*
parole officer *funcionario a cargo de la libertad condicional.*
Rel: probation, [nrwer]*condena condicional;* suspended sentence, *sentencia suspendida.*
parricide n. *parricidio.* **parricide** n. *parricida.*
parricidal adj. *parricida.*
• The killing of a parent.
Rel: patricide, *patricidio.*
parties n. *partes.*

• Persons opposing each other as litigants in a lawsuit, or those participating in a transaction or agreement.
Cf: **parties** • **plaintiff** • **defendant** • **prosecution** • **complainant** • **respondent** • **libelant** • **libelee** • **appellant** • **appellee.** Parties in legal proceedings have different names depending on the nature of the legal relief pursued. In common law, parties in a civil suit are called plaintiff and defendant, in a criminal case defendant and prosecution; in equity, parties are called complainant and defendant; in maritime law, the parties are the libelant and the respondent or libelee; in appellate proceedings, the parties are the appellant and the respondent or appellee. Parties in contractual or other relationships are increasingly identified functionally rather than simply as parties, like buyer and seller, lender and borrower, etc.
joinder of parties *acumulación de partes, litisconsorcio.*
necessary parties *litisconsorcio necesario.*
parties to crime *partícipes de un delito.*
Rel: appellant, *apelante, parte apelante;* complainant (equity), *demandante;* defendant, *demandado;* defendant (criml.), *acusado;* defendant (equity), *demandado;* libelant (marit.), *demandante;* plaintiff, *demandante;* prosecution, *fiscal;* respondent/appellee, *la contraria/el apelante;* respondent/libelee (marit.), *demandado.*

partition n. *partición, división.*
• Division into severalty of lands held by joint tenants, copartners, or tenants in common.
defintive partition *partición definitiva.*
partition wall *muro medianero.*

partnership n. [borr.]*partnership.*
[nrwer]*sociedad colectiva o en nombre colectivo.* **partner** n. *socio.*
• "Association of two or more persons to carry on as co-owners a business for profit." (U.S. Uniform Partnership Act (1996) §101(6))
Cf: **partnership** • **association.** These terms describe different types of unincorporated organizations. An association is a broad concept that means a gathering of people pursuing a common purpose; partnership, being a more limited term, is the joining together of a group pursuing a business purpose for profit.
↪ Partnership and *sociedad mercantil* are terms following different criteria and having imprecise lines of equivalence. Both partnership and *sociedad mercantil* refer to the pursuit by a group of a business purpose for profit, but while

a partnership is usually considered an unincorporated entity, *sociedad mercantil* is always an incorporated business enterprise. Partnership is a general denomination that includes an undistinguished variety of informal business situations as well as systematically organized entities; *sociedad mercantil,* on the other hand, being also a general label, is divided into several specific categories, making reference to any one type more precise. Partnership and *sociedad mercantil* are equivalents if they are considered a generic label only; when more specific considerations are taken into account, partnership must be qualified to match an appropriate Spanish equivalent. *Sociedad en nombre colectivo o sociedad colectiva,* for example, emphasizes the unlimited responsibility of the partners, which is often the case in a general partnership, while *sociedad en comandita simple* or *sociedad de responsabilidad limitada* underscore the limited nature of the partner's personal liability in the business, a defining characteristic of the limited partnership.

articles of partnership *estatutos de una sociedad colectiva,* [lexical exp.]*estatutos de un partnership.*

dissolution of partnership *disolución de una sociedad colectiva,* [lexical exp.]*disolución de un partnership.*

general partnership *sociedad colectiva.*

limited partnership *sociedad en comandita simple.*

limited liability partnership (LLP) *sociedad profesional, sociedad profesional organizada como comandita.*

partnership agreement *contrato de una sociedad colectiva,* [lexical exp.]*contrato de partnership.*

Rel: full or general partner, *socio comanditado;* junior partner, *socio asociado;* senior partner, *socio principal;* silent partner, *socio capitalista.*

Comment: "Although civil law jurisdictions, such as Louisiana, have invariably treated a partnership as a separate legal entity or person, this has not been true either under the common law or under the English or American codification of the law of partnership. The tradition of the common law was to treat as legal persons only incorporated groups. The mercantile view of the nature of a partnership, influenced as it was by the civil law, was to treat a commercial partnership as a legal person. Modern partnership law has taken an ambivalent view, treating a partnership as a legal person or entity for some purposes, and not for other purposes." (Kaplan, 630)

See: corporation.

Ref: (CA) Ottawa Lumbermen's Credit Bureau v. Swam, [1923] 4 D.L.R. 1157 at 1163, 53 O.L.R. 135 (C.A.), Orde J.A.; Sproulev Mc Connell [1925] 1 W.W.R. 609 (Sask. CA); UK) 35 Halsbury's Laws para 1 at 5; (US) Eggleston v. Eggleston, 47 S.E.2d 243, 247, 249, 228 N.C. 668; Winslow v. Boyd, Tex. Civ.App., 195 S.W.2d 384, 386.

party[1] **(transaction)** n. *parte.*
• The person taking part in an act or transaction.
contractual party *parte contractual.*
third party *tercero.*

party[2] **(lawsuit)** n. *parte.*
• The person prosecuting or defending in a lawsuit.
adverse party *parte con un interés jurídico opuesto.*
aggrieved party *parte agraviada, parte perjudicada.*
party opponent *la contraria, la parte contraria.*
prevailing party *parte ganadora (de un juicio), parte en cuyo favor se dicta la sentencia.*
real party in interest *titular del derecho sustantivo que se hace valer procesalmente.*
third party *tercero, tercería.*
See: parties.

pass judgment *sentenciar, dictar una sentencia.*

pass the case (oral expr.) *posponer la presentación de un caso (ante el juez), el caso se llamará posteriormente (durante la misma sesión).*

pat down *registro superficial, registro palpando a la persona.* – Syn. frisk, *cachear.*
protective pat down *palpación de armas.*

patent[1] **(invention)** n. *patente.* **patentee** n. *titular (de una patente).* **patentable** adj. *patentable.*
• A governmental grant made to an inventor, giving the inventor the exclusive right to make, use and sell his or her invention for a certain number of years.
design patent *patente de diseño.*
letters patent *carta patente.*
patent and trademark law *ley de patentes y marcas.*
patent attorney *abogado de patentes.*
patent infringement *violación de una patente.*
patent license *licencia de patentes.*
patent rights *derechos de patente.*
patent royalty *regalías de una patente.*
patented drug *medicina de patente.*
process patent *patente de proceso.*
Rel: invention, *invención;* nonobviousness, *que no es obvio (que la invención es un resultado*

normal del desarrollo actual), que no es evidente; novelty, *novedad;* utility, *utilidad.* See: intellectual property.

patent² (grant) n. *concesión.*
• The grant of a right, privilege, or authority given by the government. – Syn. public grant.
land patent *concesión de tierras.*

paternity n. *paternidad.* **father** n. *padre.*
• The status of being a father. – Syn. fatherhood.
acknowledgment of paternity *reconocimiento de paternidad.*
declaration of paternity *declaración de la paternidad.*
denial of paternity *negación de la paternidad.*
paternity proceedings *acciones de paternidad.* – Syn. affiliation proceedings.
paternity suit *juicio de paternidad, acción de desconocimiento de la paternidad.* – Syn. paternity action.
paternity test *examen para determinar la paternidad.*
Rel: progenitorship, *relativo a un progenitor.*

patricide n. *patricidio* || *patricida.*
• The killing of a father.

pauper n. *pobre, indigente.*
See: poor.

pawn¹ n. *empeño, prenda (en casa de empeño).*
pawnee n. *persona o institución en cuyo favor se empeña, casa de empeños.* **pawnor** n. *persona que empeña.* **pawn** v. *empeñar.*
• A pledge of chattels and in most cases a deposit of personal property as security for a loan. It also means "the condition of being held on deposit as a pledge." (Black's Law Dict., 8th. ed., 1164).
Cf: **pawn • pledge.** Pawn and pledge are synonymous. A pawn is understood as a pledge made to a pawnbroker or a person in the business of small loans secured by chattels.
↪ Pawn businesses in Anglo-American and Hispanic countries show considerable differences in spite of the great similarity in legal meaning. Pawnbroker's shops in English-speaking countries are usually privately owned establishments that do business as small operators in the large loan industry dominated by banks and financial institutions. *Casas de empeño* in Hispanic countries are usually managed by government-controlled charitable establishments. Thus, in these countries, a pawnbroker is usually a government institution or a not-for-profit company and the pawnbroker's shop is often a large well-known establishment in town.

pawn ticket *papeleta o boleta de la casa de empeños.*
pawnbroker [de]*prestamista de empeños.*
pawnbroker's shop *casa de empeños, monte de piedad.*
Rel: bailment, *depósito.*

pawn² (chattel) n. *bien empeñado, prenda.*
• The item of personal property pledged or pawned.

pay v. *pagar.*
pay back *restituir.*
pay cash *pagar en efectivo.*
pay damages *pagar daños y perjuicios.*
pay in advance *pago adelantado o anticipado.*
pay in installments *pagar a plazos, pagar en abonos.*
pay off *saldar, finiquitar.*

pay n. *pago, sueldo, salario.*
rate of pay *cantidad pagada por hora, día, etc.*
take-home pay *salario neto.*

payment n. *pago.* **payee** n. *a quien se paga.*
payer or payor n. *quien paga, pagador.*
• What is to be paid, what is paid, and the act of paying.
↪ Spanish legal usage typically avoids direct reference to payee and payer, using other appropriate terms like *acreedor, deudor, beneficiario, girado, obligado, comprador, vendedor,* etc. There is no close legal equivalent term in Spanish for payee, but *pagador* is sometimes used as legal equivalent for payer.
advance payment *pago anticipado.*
balloon payment *pago final global.*
full payment *pago total.*
late payment *pago tardío, pago retrasado, pago moroso.*
lump sum payment *pago global.*
payment for honor *pago por intervención.*
payment in due course *pago a su debido tiempo.*
payment into court *pago consignado o depositado en un juzgado.*
payment on demand *pago a la vista.*
payment under protest *pago bajo protesta.*
Rel: downpayment, *pago inicial, enganche;* overpayment, *sobrepago, pago en exceso;* underpayment, *pago incompleto, pago de menos.*

payola n. *cohecho.*
payroll n. *nómina.*
payroll tax *impuesto sobre nóminas* || *impuesto deducido del ingreso neto de un trabajador o*

empleado.

payroller *trabajador que cobra pero no trabaja, aviador* (Mx).

peace n. *paz.* **pacifist** n. *pacifista.*
peace treaty *tratado de paz.*

peace officer *encargado del orden público, policía* (euph).

peccadillo n. *falta menor.*

peculation n. *peculado.*
See: embezzlement.

pecuniary loss *pérdida pecuniaria.*

pederasty n. *pederastia.*
• Anal intercourse between men, more specifically a man and a boy. – Syn. pedophilia.
See: sodomy.

pedestrian n. *peatón.*
pedestrian crossing *cruce de peatones.*

penal action *acción penal.*

penal code *código penal.*

penalty[1] **(punishment)** n. *castigo, pena.*
• Punishment imposed on those violating the law, especially criminal law offenders.
– Syn. sanction, *sanción.*
statutory penalty *castigo señalado en la ley.*

penalty[2] **(fine)** n. *multa, sanción.*
• Punishment for a civil or criminal offense, usually constrained to pecuniary punishment.
– Syn. fine.
civil penalty *multa por violación de una disposición legal.*
late payment penalty *multa de mora.*
penalty clause *cláusula penal.*
statutory penalty *multa señalada en la ley.*

pendente lite (lat.) *pendente lite, durante el juicio.* Pending the lawsuit.

penitentiary n. *penitenciaría.*
See: prison.

pension plan *plan de jubilación.*

people n. *el pueblo* (PR) || *[le]la gente.*

people's exhibit *prueba material del fiscal.*

per se (lat.) *per se, por sí mismo, en sí mismo.* By itself.

peremptory adj. *perentorio.*
peremptory challenge *descalificación sin causa de un jurado, recusación perentoria* (PR).
peremptory exception *excepción perentoria.*

performance n. *cumplimiento (de una obligación).*
• "The doing of the acts required by the agreement at the time and place therefor and in the manner stipulated." (17 Am. Jur. 2d Contract § 606)
part performance *cumplimiento parcial.*
performance bond *garantía del cumplimiento de las obligaciones adquiridas.* – Syn. completion bond.
specific performance *cumplimiento forzado de la obligación contractual.*
substantial performance *cumplimiento sustancial.*

peril n. *peligro.*
imminent peril *peligro inminente.*

perils of the sea *peligros del mar, riesgos de la navegación marítima.*

perjury n. *falsedad de declaraciones o testimonio, perjurio* (PR).
perjured testimony *testimonio declarado con falsedad.*

permanent adj. *permanente, estable, duradero.*
– Syn. endless, *sin fin.* everlasting, *eterno.* infinite, *infinito.* perpetual, *perpetuo.*
permanent alimony *alimentos vitalicios, pensión alimenticia vitalicia (entre cónyuges).*
permanent disability *incapacidad permanente.*
permanent injury *lesión permanente.*
permanent residence *residencia permanente.*

permit n. *permiso.*
gun permit *permiso para portar arma.*
judicial driving permit *permiso judicial para conducir o manejar.*
restricted driving permit *permiso con restricciones para conducir.*

perpetration n. *perpetración.* **perpetrator** n. *perpetrador.* **perpetrate** v. *perpetrar.*

person[1] **(human being)** n. *persona física.*
• A human being; a human living body.
– Syn. natural person.

person[2] **(entity)** n. *persona jurídica.*
• A legal entity recognized by law to be capable of rights and responsibilities.
artificial person *persona moral.*
– Syn. fictitious person. juristic person. legal person.
juridical person *persona jurídica.*
natural person *persona física.*
Ref: (UK) Royal Mail Steam Packet Co v Braham (1877), 2 App. Cas. 381 at 386; (US) Central Amusement Co. v. District of Columbia, D.C. Mun.App., 121 A.2d 865, 866.

persona non grata INTL.LAW *persona non grata.*

personal[1] **(individual)** adj. *personal.* – Syn. distinct, *distintivo.* particular, *particular.*

personal action *acción personal.*
personal exception *excepción personal.*
personal income *ingresos personales.*
personal knowledge *conocimiento personal.*
personal liability *responsabilidad personal.*
personal recognizance *libertad bajo palabra.*
personal[2] **(private)** adj. *privado.* – Syn. confidential, *confidencial.* restricted, *restringida.*
personal and confidential *personal y confidencial.*
personal data *generales, información personal.*
personal effects *objetos personales.*
personal information *información personal.*
personal injury TORTS *responsabilidad civil (por lesiones físicas o morales)* || *daño causado a una persona en sus derechos (por negligencia).*
personal injury case *caso de responsabilidad civil (por lesiones físicas o morales).*
Rel: earning capacity, *capacidad de ingreso;* funeral expenses, *gastos funerarios;* loss of companionship, *pérdida de la compañía (de otra persona);* loss of consortium, *pérdida de los derechos de intimidad conyugal;* medical expenses, *gastos médicos;* mental anguish, *angustia mental;* pain and suffering, *daños físicos o morales;* permanent injury, *lesión permanente;* pre-existing injuries, *lesiones preexistentes;* soft-tissue injury, *lesión de tejidos blandos;* wrongful death, *muerte resultante de actos ilícitos de otro.*
personal property [fe]*bienes muebles,* [de]*bienes que no son inmuebles.*
• Any tangible or intangible property not classified as real property. – Syn. personal estate. personalty. things personal.
intangible personal property *bienes muebles incorpóreos o intangibles.*
tangible personal property *bienes muebles corpóreos o tangibles.* – Syn. goods.
Rel: chattels, [brder]*bienes muebles;* choses in action, *derechos intangibles que pueden ejercitarse judicialmente.*
See: movable property.
personate v. *suplantar, impostura* (PR), *personificar* (Mx). **personation** n. *suplantación, impostura* (PR), *personificación* (Mx). – Syn. impersonate.
personation or misuse of papers in naturalization proceedings IMMGR. *suplantación o uso judicial indebido de documentos de naturalización.*
petition n. *petición* || *demanda (en derecho-*

equidad). **petitioner** n. *peticionario, promovente, demandante.* **respondent** n. *contraparte, demandado.*
• A request for legal relief, a formal written request made before a court. In equity procedure, the petition is the functional equivalent of a complaint at law.
filing of a petition *presentación de una petición.*
petition for divorce *petición de divorcio, juicio de divorcio.*
petition for redress *petición de resarcimiento o indemnización.*
petition in bankruptcy *declaración de quiebra o bancarrota.*
Rel: complaint, *demanda;* motion, *petición,* [nrwer]*promoción;* prayer, *petición, puntos petitorios.*
petty adj. *inferior, menor, trivial.*
petty cash *caja chica o menuda.*
petty/petit jury *jurado de un juicio ordinario.*
petty/petit larceny *hurto menor.*
petty/petit theft *robo menor, robo de menor cuantía.*
physical adj. *físico.*
continuous physical presence *presencia personal continua o continuada.*
physical appearance *apariencia física.*
physical damage to property *daño material en propiedad ajena.*
physical disability *incapacidad física.*
physical examination *examen físico.*
physical impairment *invalidez física.*
physical possession *posesión física.*
physical property *propiedad física.*
physical violence *violencia física.*
Rel: corporeal, *corporal;* flesh and blood, *de carne y hueso.*
physical evidence CRIML.LAW *pruebas materiales.*
Glossary: blood patterns, *formas de las manchas de sangre;* bloodstains, *manchas de sangre;* carpet fibers, *fibras de alfombra;* contour comparisons, *comparación de relieve;* footprints, *huellas de los pies;* hair fibers, *fibras de cabello, cabellos;* imprints, *impresiónes;* paint matching, *igualamiento de pintura;* paint specimens, *muestras de pintura;* prints, *marcas, huellas;* stains, *manchas;* tire imprints, *impresiones de la llanta o neumático.*
See: DNA. evidence. fingerprints.
physician n. *médico.*
physician-patient privilege *confidencialidad entre médico y paciente.*
picket line *cadena o fila de huelguistas.*

piercing the corporate veil [de]*invalidar la protección de la personalidad jurídica (de una empresa), corrimiento del velo societario* (Ar), [borr.]*levantamiento del velo corporativo.*

pilferage n. *hurto, ratería.*
Rel: theft, *robo.*

pillage n. *pillaje.*

pimping (crime) *vivir de una prostituta, proxenetismo.* **pimp** n. *proxeneta, alcahuete, gigoló, padrote* (slg.)(Mx).

piracy n. *piratería.*
air piracy *piratería aérea.*
piracy on the high seas *piratería en alta mar.*

plagiarism n. *plagio.* **plagiarist** n. *plagiario.*
plagiarize v. *plagiar.*

plain view doctrine CRIML.PROCED [le]*principio de "a plena vista".*
• Principle that objects falling in plain view of a police officer, lawfully in that position, are subject to seizure without a warrant and admissible as evidence. – Syn. clear view doctrine.

plaintiff n. *demandante, actora, parte actora.*
– Syn. complainant.
plaintiff in error *apelante, recurrente.*
plaintiff rests (oral expr.) *el demandante ha terminado su presentación de pruebas.*
plaintiff-respondent *contrademandado.*
third-party plaintiff *demandado que interpone una tercería.*
See: parties.

plea[1] CRIML.PROCED n. [de]*declaración formal de culpabilidad o no culpabilidad (hecha ante el juez por parte del acusado al iniciarse el proceso), alegación* (PR).
• At an arraignment, the defendant's answer of guilty or not guilty.
entering a plea *declararse culpable o inocente.*
plea of guilty *declaración de culpabilidad, alegación de culpabilidad* (PR).
plea of nolo contendere *declaración de culpabilidad penal sin responsabilidad civil.*
– Syn. no contest plea.
plea of not guilty *declaración de no ser culpable.*
Rel: arraignment, *presentación o lectura de la acusación.*

plea[2] CIVIL.PROCED n. [de]*contestación de la demanda (fundada en hechos),* [fe]*defensa o excepción, alegación* (PR).
• The answer of the defendant to the complaint setting up a factual allegation as a defense.
– Syn. answer, *contestación de la demanda.*

Cf: **plea • demurrer.** A plea introduces a matter of fact as a defense, while a demurrer interposes objections on grounds of law.
dilatory plea *excepción dilatoria.*
jurisdictional plea *excepción de falta de jurisdicción.*
negative plea *contestación negando en parte o en su totalidad los hechos (de la demanda).*
peremptory plea *excepción perentoria.*
plea in confession and avoidance [de]*admisión de los hechos de la demanda y presentación de hechos favorables no alegados.*
plea of insanity [brder][de]*defensa de demencia.* [fe]*defensa o alegatos de inimputabilidad por la enajenación mental del acusado.*
– Syn. insanity defense.
plea of self-defense *defensa basada en la legítima defensa.*
Rel: demurrer, *pedir la improcedencia de la demanda por falta de fundamento;* traverse, *negación del hecho o hechos.*
See: pleadings[1].

plea[3] COMMON LAW n. *contestación de la demanda (en derecho estricto).*
• "A defendant's answer to a plaintiff's declaration in an action at common law." (Oxford Dictionary of Law, 342)
Rel: declaration, *demanda.*

plea bargain *declaración de culpabilidad negociada.* – Syn. negotiated plea. plea agreement.

pleadings[1] **(allegations)** [de]*escritos promoviendo las pretensiones y defensas (de las partes),* [de]*demanda-contestación y escritos complementarios, alegaciones* (PR).
• The formal allegations by the parties of their respective claims and defenses.
The function of the pleading stage is to establish the issues for trial. In the United States, pleadings may consist of a complaint, an answer, a counterclaim, a cross-claim, a reply to a counter claim, an answer to a cross-claim, a third party complaint and a third party answer. In England, pleadings are generally the plaintiff's statement of a claim, the defendant's defence, and (sometimes) the plaintiff's reply. Under common law, pleadings consist of a declaration, a demurrer or plea, a replication, a rejoinder, a surrejoinder, a rebutter and so on.
⟻ In contrast with common law, civil law procedure in most countries does not designate pleadings with a single generic term, but refers rather to each pleading using specific designations, such as *demanda* and *contestación.*

pleadings

Ref: (UK) 36 Halsbury's Laws para 1; (US) Fed.R. Civil Proc.7(a).

amendment to a pleading [de]*subsanar la demanda-contestación y escritos complementarios.*

argumentative pleading [de]*demanda-contestación y escritos complementarios verbosos o redundantes.*

defect in the pleading [de]*defecto o error en la demanda-contestación o escritos complementarios.*

supplemental pleadings [de]*escrito o promoción que adiciona la demanda-contestación o escritos complementarios.*

verification of pleadings [de]*ratificación de la demanda-contestación o escritos complementarios.*

Rel: answer, *contestación de la demanda;* complaint, *demanda.*

pleadings² **(narrowing issues)** *fijación de la litis.*
• Steps in a lawsuit directed to narrowing the issues by which the parties file formal documents setting forth their claims or defenses.

plebiscite *plebiscito.*
Rel: referendum, *referendo.*

pledge n. *prenda.* **pledgee** n. *acreedor prendario.* **pledgor** n. *deudor prendario.*
• A deposit of personal property made to a creditor as security for a debt. Also, pledge refers to the item deposited under these conditions.
Much of the law of pledges has been replaced in the United States by the provisions for secured transactions in Article 9 of the Uniform Commercial Code (U.C.C.).
Rel: collateral, *garantía colateral;* hypothec, *hipoteca;* lien, *derecho preferencial;* pawn, *empeño;* secured transaction, *operación de garantía.*

plot n. *complot, conspiración.*

ploy n. *táctica, estratagema.*

plunder n. *botín, despojo.* **plunder** v. *pillar, saquear.*
Rel: booty, *botín.*

poaching v. *cazar ilegalmente.* **poacher** n. *cazador ilegal.*

police n. *policía.* **policeman** n. *policía.* **policewoman** n. *mujer policía.* **police** v. *vigilar, mantener bajo control.* – Syn. cops (slg.), *fiana* (Cu), *chota, poli* (Mx), *paco* (Ch). constable (RU), *policía.* fed (slg.), *policía federal.*
chief of police *jefe de la policía.*
police badge *placa, insignia.*

police beat *ronda de policía, patrullaje de la policía.*

police brutality *brutalidad policíaca.*

police dog *perro policía.*

police force *fuerza policíaca.*

police interrogation *interrogatorio policial o policíaco.*

police officer *policía, oficial de policía.*

police record *récord policíaco o policial, prontuario policial* (Ar). – Syn. arrest record.

police station *estación de policía.*
Rel: homicide unit, *unidad de homicidios;* vice squad, *escuadrón contra el vicio.*

police power *poderes o facultades de policía y buen gobierno.*
• "The police power gives the states broad authority to regulate private behavior in the interest of public health, safety, and general welfare. It enables states and their respective local units of government to enact and enforce policies deemed appropriate to serve the public good." (Chandler, Enslen & Renstrom, 442)

policy¹ (govmt.) n. *política.*
• The directive principles adopted by a government establishing and implementing a course of action.
foreign policy *política extranjera.*
monetary policy *política monetaria.*

policy² INSURANCE n. *póliza de seguro.* **policyholder** n. *asegurado, titular de la póliza.*
• A document containing an insurance contract.
blanket policy *póliza flotante.* – Syn. floating policy.
extended policy *póliza ampliada, póliza prorrogada.*
group policy *póliza colectiva.* – Syn. collective policy.
master policy *póliza maestra, póliza básica.*
open policy *póliza abierta.*
policy loan *préstamo garantizado por una póliza (de seguros).*
policy value *valor de rescate de una póliza.*

political asylum *asilo político.*

political party *partido político.*

political rights *derechos políticos.*

political trial *juicio político.*

pollution n. *contaminación.*
air pollution *contaminación del aire.*
international pollution *contaminación internacional.*
oil pollution *contaminación petrolera, contaminación de petróleo.*
water pollution *contaminación del agua.*

Rel: environmental law, *derecho ambiental, ley del medio ambiente.*

polygamy n. *poligamia.* **polygamist** n. *polígamo.* **polygamous** adj. *polígamo.*

polygraph n. *detector de mentiras.* – Syn. lie detector.

poor adj. *pobre.* **poverty** n. *pobreza.* – Syn. broke, *sin dinero.* destitute, *necesitado.* indigent, *indigente.* needy, *necesitado.* poverty-stricken, *pordiosero, menesteroso.*
Rel: pauper, *pobre, indigente.*
poor man's oath *juramento de pobreza.* – Syn. pauper's petition.

pornography n. *pornografía.* **pornographic** adj. *pornográfico.*

• Material is pornographic or obscene if the average person, applying contemporary community standards, would find that the work taken as a whole appeals to the prurient interest, and it depicts in a patently offensive way sexual conduct, and the work taken as a whole lacks serious literary, artistic, political or scientific value.
Cf: **pornography • obscenity.** "Although 'pornographic' and 'obscene' are often used interchangeably, they are not synonymous. Offensive or disgusting conduct of any kind may constitute an obscenity; pornographic is limited to written, graphic or spoken depictions designed to cause sexual excitement." (Ballentine's Legal Assistant, 413)
child pornography *pornografía de menores.*
Rel: obscene material, *material obsceno.*

port n. *puerto.*
home port *puerto de origen.*
port authorities *autoridades portuarias.*
port duties *derechos portuarios.*
port of arrival *puerto de llegada, puerto de destino.*
port of call *puerto de escala, puerto de arribada.*
port of departure *puerto de salida o partida.*
port of entry *puerto de entrada.*
port of registry *puerto de registro o matriculación.*

portrait parle *retrato hablado.* – Syn. composite picture.
See: *retrato hablado.*

possession[1] PROP.LAW n. *posesión.*
• Actual control of property with the intent to exclude others.
Cf: **possession • custody • control.** These related terms are usually clearly distinguished.

Possession includes custody of property plus the assertion of a right to exercise dominion and control over it. <A car owner who leaves his or her car in an automobile shop for a few days to be repaired is giving the shop possession of it, but an owner who waits in the shop while the repairs are being made is giving to the repair shop custody only.> Control, on the other hand, refers to the power or authority to direct or manage property.
☛ As contrasted with the civil law system, "the important element in the common law is not the *animus domini* or intent to deal with the thing as owner, but the intent to exclude others from the immediate use and enjoyment of the thing." (Eder, 124)
action to recover possession *acción posesoria.*
actual possession *posesión física.*
– Syn. physical possession.
adverse possession *prescripción positiva.*
constructive possession *posesión jurídica o virtual.* – Syn. effective possession.
continuous possession *posesión continua.*
direct possession *posesión directa.*
– Syn. immediate possession.
notorious possession *posesión pública y notoria.* – Syn. open possession.
peaceable possession *posesión pacífica.*
possession in law *posesión por ministerio de ley.* – Syn. constructive possession.
possession is nine-tenths of the law (max.) *la posesión es nueve décimos del derecho.*
tenant in possession *inquilino o detentador en posesión (de un inmueble), poseedor legítimo.*
undisturbed possession *posesión pacífica.*
uninterrupted possession *posesión ininterrumpida.*
wrongful possession *posesión de mala fe.*
Rel: animus possidendi (lat.), *animus possidendi, intención de poseer;* detinue, *acción reivindicatoria (de bienes muebles) en derecho estricto o "common law";* replevin, *acción reivindicatoria (de bienes muebles).*
Ref: (UK) 35 Halsbury's Laws para 1211; (US) Rice v. Frayser, C.C.Ark., 24 F. 460, 463.

possession[2] CRIML.LAW n. *posesión, portación.*
possession of a weapon *portación de arma, posesión de arma.*
possession of burglary tools *posesión de implementos o herramientas para robar, posesión de herramientas para escalar* (PR).
possession of cannabis *posesión de canabis.*
possession of controlled substances *posesión*

post facto

de sustancias ilegales.

possession of drug paraphernalia *posesión de aditamentos para el uso de drogas.*

possession of marijuana *posesión de marihuana.*

possession of stolen property *posesión de bienes robados.*

post facto (lat.) *post facto, posterior al hecho.* After the fact.

post-dated check *cheque postdatado o posfechado.*

posthumous adj. *póstumo.* – Syn. postmortem.
posthumous child *hijo póstumo.*

postmortem n. *autopsia.* – Syn. autopsy.
☞ As an adjective, postmortem means after death or *después de la muerte,* and the Spanish word *postmórtem* is frequently used. As a noun, postmortem refers to an *autopsia* or *necropsia.*
postmortem examination *examen postmórtem, autopsia.*

postnuptial agreement *contrato (entre los cónyuges) respecto de los bienes conyugales con posterioridad al matrimonio.*

postponement n. *aplazamiento.* **postpone** v. *posponer.* **postponable** adj. *aplazable.* – Syn. deferment, *diferimiento.*

post-trial evidence *pruebas sobrevinientes.*

post-trial remedies *recursos procedentes después de dictada la sentencia penal.* – Syn. postconviction relief.

power¹ (authorization) n. *poder, facultad, autoridad, atribución, autorización, derecho.*
• "The legal act or authorization to act or not to act; a person's or organization's ability to alter, by an act of will, the rights, duties, liabilities or other legal relations either of that person or of another." (Black's Law Dict., 8th. ed., 1207)
Cf: **power ● right.** When power is used to mean legal authorization, both of these terms are considered synonyms.

power² const n. *poder.*
• Legal authorization given by a constitution or a constitutional instrument or practice.
commerce powers *poderes constitucionales para regular el comercio.*
concurrent powers *poderes concurrentes.*
constitutional powers *poderes constitucionales.*
exclusive powers *poderes exclusivos.*
expressly forbidden powers *poderes expresamente prohibidos.*

inherent constitutional powers or inherent powers *poderes constitucionales implícitos, poderes constitucionales inherentes al cargo.*
taxing power *poder recaudatorio, poder impositivo fiscal.*

power³ corp. n. *facultad, atribución.*
• Legal authorization granted by a corporate charter.

power coupled with an interest [de]*poder dado con relación a bienes reales sobre los que el apoderado tiene un interés jurídico.*

power of appointment [de]*poder o facultad jurídica dada a otra persona para designar beneficiario.* **donor** n. *otorgante, donante.* **donee/appointor** n. *apoderado, facultado.* **beneficiary/appointee** n. *recipiente, beneficiario.*
• The authority conferred by one person upon another, by will or deed, to select and nominate the person or persons to receive the donor's estate or income.
Cf: **power of appointment ● agency.** "The power of appointment is not an agency. It does not create any relation of principal and agent. A usual power of appointment in gifts or testamentary dispositions is where the property is given to A for his life and, then, to succeed A, to such person or persons as he [donee] may designate." (Eder, 117-18)
appendant or appurtenant powers [de]*poder o facultad dada a otra persona que tiene un vínculo o interés jurídico en los bienes a los que se refiere el poder.*
general powers [de]*poder o facultad dada a otra persona para designar a cualquiera como beneficiario.*
particular powers [de]*poder o facultad dada a otra persona para designar beneficiario sobre bienes u objetos específicos.*
testamentary power [de]*poder o facultad dada a otra persona para designar beneficiario que solamente puede ejercitarse en un testamento.*
Rel: future interest, [de]*derecho sobre un inmueble que permite su posesión o disfrute a futuro.*

power of attorney *poder.*
• A formal document by which an agent is appointed. – Syn. letter of attorney, *carta poder.* mandate, *mandato.*
general power of attorney *poder general.*
specific power *poder especial, poder específico* (PR).
Rel: power of alienation, *poder de disposición.*

practice of law *ejercicio de la abogacía.*

precedent n. *precedente judicial.*
• A prior decision by a court furnishing the basis for deciding an identical or similar subsequent case or question of law.
Cf: **precedent ● stare decisis.** Precedent means a court decision that guides or influences the outcome of a later case that has similar facts or questions of law. Stare decisis, on the other hand, refers to the practice or rule of recognizing precedents as authority to be applied in deciding similar new cases.
⊶ While precedent has been the preeminent source of law in common law systems for centuries, it is today often considered at a par with statutory law, especially in the arena of social reform. The opposite could be said of the historical development of legislative laws and precedent in civil law systems, where the traditional preeminence of enacted legislation is being eroded by the acceptance of precedent as an equal in certain situations.

> Comment: "The legal profession [in England] was not so much interested in anticipating the adjudication of infractions of the law, such as those anticipated by statutory proscriptions, as it was in maintaining the precedent-setting value of actual controversies settled. This reliance on the value of precedent is perhaps the greatest legacy of the English common law system." (Chandler, Enslen & Renstrom, 14)

precedent condition *condición suspensiva.*

precept[1] (order) *orden judicial.*
• A writ or warrant; an order issued by a person in authority.

precept[2] (text) *precepto.*
• A rule of conduct; a moral or ethical rule.

precondition n. *condición existente previamente, prerrequisito.*

predatory pricing *precios de rapiña, precios exageradamente altos.*

predatory sexual offender *depredador sexual* (pop.), *delincuente sexual peligroso.*

preemptive right CORP. *derecho preferente de suscripción en la emisión de nuevas acciones, derecho preferente de adquisición de acciones en una nueva emisión.*
• The right given to a stockholder to keep his or her share of ownership by buying a proportionate share of any new stock issues.

preference BANKRUPTCY n. *derecho preferente.*

preferred stock *acciones preferentes.*

prejudice[1] (injury) n. *perjuicio.*
• Detriment or damage to one's rights or interests.
dismissal with prejudice *sobreseimiento precluyendo el ejercicio de cualquier acción.*
dismissal without prejudice *sobreseimiento sin precluir el ejercicio de acciones procedentes.*

prejudice[2] (preconception) n. *prejuicio.* **prejudice** v. *prejuiciar.* **prejudicial** adj. *prejuiciado.*
• An opinion formed beforehand or in disregard of the facts. – Syn. bias.
Rel: discrimination, *discriminación.*

prejudicial error *error apelable, error sobre derechos fundamentales de forma o fondo.*

preliminary adj. *preliminar, preparatorio.*
– Syn. introductory, *introductorio.* preparatory, *preparatorio.*
preliminary agreement *convenio preliminar.*
preliminary examination *interrogatorio preliminar.*
preliminary relief *medidas judiciales preliminares o precautorias.*

preliminary hearing [le]*audiencia preliminar, vista preliminar* (PR). [fe][brder]*instrucción o sumario.*
• A hearing before a judge to determine whether there is enough evidence to prosecute a person believed to have committed a crime. – Syn. preliminary examination. preliminary probable cause hearing.
⊶ The determination of probable cause in common law systems is usually made in a single hearing based on prima facie evidence; in contrast, probable cause evaluation in civil law systems is usually a long process carried on in several stages by prosecutors and judges introducing detailed evidence and culminating in a finding. In strict sense, then, there is no an exact functional equivalent in Spanish for preliminary hearing as a single event, but *instrucción or sumario*, albeit different in nature and scope, can be used to designate the action of evaluating proof of probable cause and finding or not finding probable cause to prosecute.
Rel: finding of probable cause, *determinación de existir causa probable o fundada (de que el presunto acusado ha cometido un delito);* indictment, *acusación formal (de un delito).*

preliminary inquiry DER.MILITAR *vista preliminar, exámen preliminar.*

premeditation n. *premeditación.*
• Forethought for a length of time, however short. – Syn. aforethough. prepense. machina-

premises

tion, *maquinación, artificio.*
premeditated homicide *homicidio premeditado.*
premeditated murder *homicidio agravado con premeditación.*
Rel: intent, *intención, intencionalidad;* malice aforethought, *dolo específico de homicidio, intención homicida.*
premises[1] **(hypotheses)** n. *premisas, antecedentes.*
premises[2] **(buildings)** n. *propiedad inmueble, instalaciones, construcción, edificio, local.* – Syn. dwelling, *morada.* house, *casa.* shelter, *refugio.* building, *construcción, edificio.*
premium[1] **(reward)** n. *premio o bonificación.*
• A prize won in a contest; a bonus received for doing something.
premium[2] **(insurance payment)** n. *prima.*
premium[3] **(excess value)** n. *sobreprecio.*
prenuptial *contrato prenupcial, acuerdo pre-matrimonial.* – Syn. antenuptial contract. pre-marital contract. – Other spell.: pre-nuptial agreement.
preponderance of the evidence *de mayor valor probatorio, por mayoría de pruebas.*
• Evidence of the greatest weight.
Rel: clear and convincing evidence, *prueba clara y convincente, prueba concluyente.*
presentence hearing *audiencia preparatoria de la condena.* – Other spell.: pre-sentence hearing.
presentence investigation *investigación preparatoria de la condena.* – Other spell.: pre-sentence investigation.
presidential system (govmt.) *sistema presidencial.*
presumption n. *presunción.* **presumptive** adj. *que se presume, presunto.*
• A rule of evidence that gives rise to a presumed conclusion based on the known or proven existence of another fact, until rebutted.
irrebuttable presumption *presunción que no admite prueba en contrario.* – Syn. conclusive presumption. presumption juris et de jure.
presumption of death *presunción de muerte.*
presumption of fact *presunción de hecho.*
presumption of guilt *presunción de culpabilidad.*
presumption of innocence *presunción de inocencia.*
presumption of legitimacy *presunción de legitimidad.*

presumption of paternity *presunción de paternidad.*
raise a presumption *dar lugar a una presunción, establecer o sentar una presunción.*
rebuttable presumption *presunción que admite prueba en contrario.* – Syn. prima facie presumption.
statutory presumption *presunción legal.*
Rel: burden of proof, *carga de la prueba;* inference, *inferencia, deducción.*
pretrial conference *reunión de las partes con el juez previa al juicio,* [le]*conferencia previa al juicio* (PR). – Other spell.: pre-trial conference.
pretrial evidence *desahogo de pruebas previo al juicio.* – Other spell.: pre-trial evidence.
pretrial hearing *audiencia previa al juicio.* – Other spell.: pre-trial hearing.
pretrial investigation (PTI) *investigación de información personal del acusado previa al juicio.* – Other spell.: pre-trial investigation.
Rel: plea bargain, *declaración de culpabilidad negociada.*
preventive detention *detención preventiva.*
price n. *precio.*
asking price *precio de oferta.*
fair price *precio justo.*
market price *precio de mercado.*
price discrimination *discriminación a través del ofrecimiento de precios diferenciados (a clientes).*
price earnings ratio *relación precio-beneficio, relación precio-ganancias.*
price index *índice de precios.*
price fixing *establecimiento o fijación de precios en común, colusión de precios.*
retail price *precio de venta al menudeo, precio de venta al detalle* (Esp).
Rel: charge, *cargo;* cost, *costo;* expense, *gasto.*
prima facie *prima facie, a primera vista.* At first view, on its face.
prima facie evidence *pruebas que establecen una presunción prima facie.*
prima facie case *acción probada prima facie, establecimiento de una presunción prima facie.*
principal[1] CRIML.LAW n. *autor (de un delito).*
• A chief actor or perpetrator, or an aider and abettor, actually or constructively present at the commission of a crime, as distinguished from an "accessory."
principal in the first degree *autor.*
principal in the second degree *coautor.*

152

Rel: accessory, *cómplices, delincuentes accesorios;* aider and abettor, *aquel que asiste en la comisión de un delito.*

principal² AGENCY n. *mandante, representado.*
disclosed principal *representante por nombre y cuenta del representado.*
undisclosed principal *representante por nombre y cuenta propios.*
Rel: agency, *representación.*

principal³ (finance) n. *principal.*
principal amount *cantidad o suma de principal.*
Rel: interest, *interés.*

prior conviction *haber sido encontrado culpable anteriormente.*
Rel: criminal background, *antecedentes penales.*

prison n. *prisión.* **prisoner** n. *prisionero.*
• A secured confinement center for convicted criminals, especially felons. – Syn. penal institution, *insitución penal.* penitentiary, *penitenciaría.*
maximum security prison *prisión de máxima seguridad.*
prison break *fuga o escape de una prisión.*
prison labor *trabajos en la prisión, trabajos penitenciarios.*
prison sentence *condena de prisión.*
prison term *plazo o término de prisión.*
Rel: custody, *detención;* jail, *cárcel.*

privacy n. *privacía, privacidad.*
invasion of privacy *violación del derecho de privacía, atentados a la vida privada.*
right of privacy *derecho de privacía.*
Rel: intrusion, *intrusión.*

private¹ (not public) adj. *privado, particular.*
privatize v. *privatizar.*
private adoptions *adopciones hechas por particulares.*
private property *propiedad privada.*

private² (confidential) adj. *privado, confidencial.*
private papers *papeles privados.*
Rel: secret, *secreto.*

private law *derecho privado.*
"In a civilian mind, all law is automatically divided into private law and public law....The tremendous practical importance of the dichotomy lies in its jurisdictional aspect. The jurisdiction of the ordinary civil courts in continental [and most Latin American] countries is traditionally limited to disputes governed by private law." The adjudication of public law disputes lies on separate administrative courts. In the common law, very early the "courts asserted, and through centuries of political and military struggles successfully preserved, their power to curb abusive official action. As a result of these struggles, which reached their points of climax in the days of Magna Carta and later of Lord Coke, the common law established the basic principle that the same court which decides a private dispute between two individuals also reviews the lawfulness of administrative acts." (Schlesinger, 183)

private limited company (UK) *sociedad limitada (cuyas acciones no se cotizan en la bolsa).*
– Abbr. Ltd.

privilege¹ (benefit) n. *privilegio, inmunidad.*
• A right, exception or advantage possessed by a person or class but not possessed by others. "Privilege is a slippery legal word most commonly denoting a person's legal freedom to do or not to do a given act." (Garner, 693)
absolute privilege *inmunidad absoluta.*
Crown's privilege (UK) *privilegio o prerrogativa de la Corona para revelar pruebas documentales.*
parliamentary privilege *privilegio o inmunidad parlamentaria.*
testimonial privilege *privilegio para negarse a testificar, dispensa para rendir testimonio.*

privilege² (confidence) n. *confidencialidad, privilegio* (PR).
• The right to prevent disclosure of certain facts in court. – Syn. confidential, *confidencial.*
attorney-client privilege *confidencialidad entre cliente y abogado.*
doctor-patient privilege *confidencialidad entre doctor y paciente.*
executive privilege *confidencialidad de secretos de estado por parte del ejecutivo.*
husband-wife privilege *confidencialidad entre esposos.*

privileged communication *información sujeta a confidencialidad, comunicación confidencial* (PR).

privity of contract *relación contractual entre las partes.*
• The relationship existing between parties to a contract.
☛ While civil law countries have unanimously accepted exceptions to the principle that only a party to a contract can sue and be sued on it, common law countries have been more rigid; today more flexibility is being introduced by legislation, rather than the courts, particularly in England.
Rel: vinculum juris, *vinculum juris.*

privity of estate *relación jurídica (entre partes que son titulares de derechos sobre un mismo inmueble), nexo jurídico.*

pro bono (lat.) adv.adj. *pro bono,* [le]*para el bienestar público, servicios gratuitos.* For the public good.
• Referring to unpaid legal services (for the public good). – Syn. pro bono publico (lat.).
pro bono case *llevar o tomar un caso sin pago de honorarios (por parte de un abogado).*

pro forma *pro forma.* For form.
• As a matter of form; as a formality. Also, provided in advance; perfunctory.
pro forma invoice *factura pro forma, factura provisional.*

pro indiviso *pro indiviso.* As undivided.
• Undivided property owned by several persons.

pro se (lat.) adv.adj. *pro se, por propio derecho.* On one's own behalf. – Syn. pro persona. in propia persona.

pro tempore (lat.) adv.adj. *pro tempore, por ahora.* For the time being.

probable cause *causa probable, motivos fundados.*
• A reasonable suspicion based upon trustworthy information that a person has committed a crime. – Syn. reasonable and probable cause (CA), *causa probable y razonable.* reasonable belief, *creencia razonablemente fundada.* reasonable cause, *causa razonablemente fundada.*
finding of probable cause *determinación de existir causa probable o motivos fundados (para presumir que el presunto acusado ha cometido el delito),* [le]*encontrar causa probable.*
probable cause hearing *audiencia de determinación de la existencia de causa probable o motivos fundados,* [le]*audiencia de causa probable.*
Rel: preliminary hearing, *audiencia preliminar.*

probate¹ (estate) n. *procedimiento testamentario, sucesión.*
• Probate is broadly used to refer to proceedings pertaining to estates and related matters.
probate court *corte sucesoria o testamentaria.*
probate estate *patrimonio de una sucesión testamentaria.*
probate jurisdiction *jurisdicción en materia testamentaria.*

probate² (will) n. [de]*declarar judicialmente válido un testamento.* **probate** v. *ofrecer pruebas validando un testamento.*

• The validation of a will in court. – Syn. proof of will.
probate proceeding [de]*procedimiento judicial de validación de un testamento.*

probation n. [nrwer]*condena condicional,* [nrwer] *libertad vigilada* (Ch,Co,Sp), [nrwer]*libertad a prueba* (PR), [nrwer]*sentencia suspendida* (PR). [nrwer]*reserva del fallo condenatorio* (Pe). [le]*probación.* **probationer** n. *persona bajo condena condicional,* [le]*persona bajo probación.*
• A sentence allowing a person convicted of a crime to remain free imposing several conditions to be fulfilled by the convicted person under the supervision of a probation officer.
⊷ Probation was initially a system allowing a person to remain free under supervision, after having been convicted of a crime, by suspending the sentence handed down. Such arrangement is also found in Spanish-speaking civil law systems under the terms *condena condicional, libertad a prueba* and *sentencia suspendida.* Probation, however, later evolved from being the suspension of a sentence to being a sentence in and of itself, and as such, there is no exact equivalent *condena* or *pena* in Spanish describing such conditional supervised release. *Reserva del fallo condenatorio* is an attempt by Peruvian legislators to avoid the conviction of defendants, requiring them instead to fullfil certain specific conditions; it is very similar to probation, but more limited and more directly aimed to defer the carrying out of a sentence. *Libertad vigilada o vigilancia por la autoridad* is aimed to provide custody or control over an individual who has been found guilty of a crime, for the first time, and considered especially dangerous, this in addition to the sentence. Finally *probación,* as equivalent of probation, while widely used, mostly by Hispanics in the U.S., is not a legal term adopted by Hispanic legal writings, codes or scholarly work.
probation officer *funcionario a cargo de personas en condenas condicionales,* [le]*oficial de probación.*
revocation of probation *revocación de la condena condicional,* [le]*revocación de la probación.*
violation of probation (VOP) *violación de las condiciones de la condena condicional,* [le]*violación de la probación.*
Rel: parole, *libertad condicional.*
probationary license ᴛʀᴀꜰꜰɪᴄ *licencia a prueba.*

procedural law *derecho procesal.*

procedure n. *procedimiento.*
• The mode of carrying on the enforcement of a legal right.
civil procedure *procedimiento civil.*
criminal procedure *procedimiento penal o criminal.*
rules of procedure *reglas del procedimiento.*
Rel: substantive law, *derecho sustantivo.*

> Comment: "English procedure, in the last 100 years, has been simplified a good deal ... Nevertheless, the state of mind produced by this centuries' long legal tradition is still perpetuated in various institutions and continues to be very much part of present day attitudes. For example, the procedure followed in the law courts remains largely the same as it was when it was normal to have jury trials even though at the present time the use of the jury, especially in civil matters, has become quite rare." (David & Brierley, 329)

See: civil procedure. criminal procedure.

proceeding[1] (lawsuit) n. *proceso, juicio.*
• The orderly succession of events, including all possible steps, in an action from its commencement to the execution of judgment.
– Syn. lawsuit. process.
abandonment of a proceeding *desistimiento de un proceso.*
bankruptcy proceeding *juicio de quiebra o bancarrota.*
civil proceeding *proceso civil.*
criminal proceeding *proceso penal.*
ordinary proceeding *juicio ordinario, procedimiento ordinario.*
probate proceeding *juicio sucesorio.*
summary proceeding *juicio sumario.*
testamentary proceeding *juicio testamentario.*

proceeding[2] (redress) n. *procedimiento.*
• Any procedural step brought before a court or agency requesting that rights be enforced or redress be provided.
condemnation proceeding *procedimiento de expropiación.*
enforcement proceeding *procedimiento de ejecución.*
garnishment proceeding *procedimiento de embargo de bienes en manos de un tercero.*
habeas corpus proceeding *procedimiento de hábeas corpus.*
liquidation proceeding *procedimiento de liquidación.*

proceeding[3] (court business) n. *actuación judicial.*
• Business or acts conducted by the court.

proceeds n. *ingresos, productos.*
Rel: income, *ingreso.*

process[1] (course) n. *procedimiento, proceso.*
• All of the acts forming the proceedings of a civil or criminal action.
process of law *procedimiento legal, proceso legal.*
summary process *procedimiento sumario, proceso sumario.*

process[2] (summons) n. *diligencia.*
• Writ issued by authority of law, usually to compel attendance of a defendant in court in a civil suit. – Syn. judicial process. legal process.
alias process *repetición de un acto procesal.*
service of process *diligencia de notificación.*

process[3] (patent) n. *proceso.*
• A method or way of doing or producing something.

products liability *responsabilidad civil del fabricante, responsabilidad del producto.*
• "The liability of the manufacturer or seller of an article for an injury caused to person or property by a defect in or condition of the article sold." (Ballentine's Law Dict., 1003)
– Syn. liability for defective products.
products liability action *acción de responsabilidad civil del fabricante, acción de responsabilidad del producto.*

profanity[1] (blasphemy) n. *sacrilegio, blasfemia*
– Syn. blasphemy, *blasfemia.*

profanity[2] (foul language) n. *groserías, malas palabras.*

professional association[1] (practice) *asociación en participación de profesionales, asociación de profesionales.*
• A group of professionals who practice together. – Abbr. P.A.
Rel: professional corporation, *sociedad profesional, sociedad civil;* limited liabililty partnership, *sociedad profesional organizada como comandita.*

professional association[2] (advancement) *asociación profesional.*
• A group of professionals associated to further their professional advancement, enhance their profession, protect their common interests and the like.
professional liability *responsabilidad civil de un profesionista o profesional.*

profile n. *perfil.*

profiling [de]*registros y detenciones policíacos basados en el perfil de identificación de ciertos individuos (generalmente su perfil racial o*

155

étnico), [de]*asedio u hostigamiento policial basado en el perfil racial (de los afectados)*.

• Police practice of detaining and searching certain persons based on their personal characteristics, usually race or national origin.

profit n. *ganancia*. **profit** v. *ganar*. – Syn. gain, *ganancia*. return, *utilidades*. yield, *rendimiento*.

gross profit *ganancia bruta*.

net profit *ganancia neta*.

operating profit *ganancias operativas, ganancias de explotación*.

profit and loss statement *estado de pérdidas y ganancias*.

profit sharing plan *plan de reparto de utilidades*.

undistributed profits *ganancia no distribuida, ganancia no aplicada, ganancia no asignada*.

profiteering *acaparamiento, especulación*.

profiteer v. *acaparar, especular*.

prohibition[1] **(denial)** n. *prohibición*.

prohibition[2] **(exclusion)** n. *inhibitoria, auto inhibitorio*.

• The forbidding of a lower court (by a higher court) to see a case or matters belonging to another court's jurisdiction. – Syn. writ of prohibition.

promise[1] **(offer)** CONTRACTS n. [fe]*declaración unilateral de voluntad* || *promesa*. **promisee** n. *quien acepta una declaración unilateral, aceptante*. **promisor** n. *promitente*.

• "A promise is a manifestation of intention to act or refrain from acting in a specified way, so made as to justify a promisee in understanding that a commitment has been made." (Restatement (Second) of Contracts §2)

Cf: **promise • statement of intention**. These similar terms are rarely used interchangeably. A promise is usually given in exchange for consideration, while a statement of intention is not ordinarily given for consideration.

aleatory promise *declaración unilateral de voluntad basada en un hecho aleatorio*.

conditional promise *declaración unilateral de voluntad hecha en forma condicional*.

express promise *declaración unilateral de voluntad hecha en forma expresa*.

implied promise *declaración unilateral de voluntad por ministerio de ley*. – Syn. fictitious promise.

marriage promise *promesa de matrimonio*.

naked promise *declaración unilateral de voluntad sin contraprestación*. – Syn. bare prom-ise. gratuitous promise.

Rel: bargain, *policitación, negociación contractual;* offer, *oferta, propuesta*.

See: contract.

promise[2] NEGOT.INSTR n. *promesa (de pago)*.

• "The words in a promissory note expressing the maker's intention to pay a debt." (Black's Law Dict., 8th. ed., 1249)

promise to pay *promesa de pago*.

promissory estoppel [de]*excepción o impedimento basado en una declaración unilateral (que contradice lo alegado)*.

promissory note *pagaré*. **maker** n. *suscriptor*. **payee** n. *beneficiario*. – Syn. note.

demand promissory note *pagaré a la vista*.

time promissory note *pagaré a plazo*.

See: note.

proof n. *prueba*. **prove** v. *probar*.

• The evidence or the resulting belief evidence produces in the fact-finder. – Syn. evidence.

adequate proof *prueba suficiente*.

affirmative proof *prueba directa o positiva*.

burden of proof *carga de la prueba*.

clear and convincing proof *prueba clara y convincente*.

collateral proof *prueba indirecta*.

failure of proof *sin valor probatorio*.

final proof *prueba definitiva*.

full proof *prueba plena*.

furnish proof *exhibir o presentar pruebas*.

proof beyond a reasonable doubt *prueba fuera de toda duda razonable, prueba más allá de toda duda razonable* (PR).

proof of disability *prueba de incapacidad o invalidez*.

proof of payment *prueba de pago*.

Rel: moral certainty, *certeza moral, certeza absoluta*.

property[1] **(right)** n. *propiedad*.

• One's exclusive right to possess, use and dispose of a thing. – Syn. estate.

Cf: **property • ownership**. "In the popular sense the word property is often used in reference to those tangible things, which are subject to the rights, which we designate by the term ownership. A man's property may consist of lands, buildings, furniture, cattle, wagons, automobiles and the like. In the legal sense, however, property means not the thing itself, but the rights which inhere in it. Ownership, or the right of property is, moreover, not a single indivisible concept but a collection or bundle of rights, of legally protected interests." (Brown. Legal Terminology 6)

☞ "The European civil law adopts a basically unitary view of 'property' which emphasizes 'ownership' rather than the various separate legal interests that are included in 'ownership' … The Anglo-American law adopts, at least with respect to property in land, a very different view which places much greater emphasis on the various aggregates of legal interests into which 'complete property' may be divided." (Cunningham, Steobuck & Whitman, §1.2 at 7)
absolute property *propiedad absoluta.*
acquisition of property *adquisición de la propiedad.*
disposition of property *enajenación de la propiedad.*
encumbrance on property *cargas o gravámenes de la propiedad.*
intellectual property *propiedad intelectual.*
literary property *propiedad literaria.*
private property *propiedad privada.*
property insurance *seguro inmobiliario, seguro sobre inmuebles.*
property right *derecho de propiedad.*
property tax *impuesto predial.*
public property *propiedad pública.*
transfer of property *transmisión de la propiedad.*
trust property *bienes fiduciarios.*
urban property *propiedad urbana.*
Rel: possession, *posesión.*
Ref: (US) City of Cleveland v. Village of Cuyahoga Heights, Ohio Com.Pl., 79 N.E.2d 576, 581; Todeva v. Oliver Iron Min. Co., 45 N.W.2d 782, 788, 232 Minn. 422.

property²(thing) *bienes.*
• The object, benefit or prerogative over which the rights of possession, use and enjoyment are exercised.
abandonment of property *abandono de bienes.*
intangible property *bienes intangibles.*
lost property *bienes perdidos.*
mislaid property *bienes dejados en algún lugar.*
movable property *bienes muebles.*
personal property [fe]*bienes muebles,* [de]*bienes que no son considerados inmuebles.*
real property *bienes inmuebles.*
tangible property *bienes tangibles.*
Rel: thing, *cosa.*

proposal n. *propuesta.*

proprietary rights *derechos patrimoniales.*
Rel: proprietary interest, *interés jurídico patrimonial.*

prosecution CRIML.LAW n. *el proceder penalmente,*

prosecución, el ejercicio de la acción penal, persecución (Ve) || *órgano de acusación, Ministerio Público.* **prosecute** v. *proceder penalmente, ejercer o ejercitar la acción penal.*
• To initiate a criminal action against a defendant. – Syn. criminal prosecution.
malicious prosecution [de]*ejercicio de una acción penal improcedente con un propósito indebido o ilícito.*
witness for the prosecution *testigo de cargo, testigo de la fiscalía.*

prosecutor CRIML.LAW n. *fiscal.* – Syn. crown counsel. crown prosecutor. district attorney (D.A.), [le] *fiscal de distrito.* prosecuting attorney. state's attorney, *fiscal estatal.* procurator fiscal (Scot.).
Rel: Attorney general, *Procurador federal;* Crown Prosecution Service (CPS)(Engl;), *Procuraduría o Fiscalía de la Corona;* Federal Prosecution Service (FPS)(CA), *Procuraduría o Fiscalía Federal;* Director of Public Prosecutions (DPP) (AU, Ireland), *Procurador o Fiscal General, Director de la Fiscalía.*
private prosecutor, *acusador particular o privado.*
special prosecutor *fiscal especial.*

prospectus SEC.LAW n. *prospecto.*

prostitution (crime) n. *prostitución.* **prostitute** n. *prostituta.*
house of prostitution *prostíbulo.*
prostitution of minors *prostitución de menores.*
Rel: brothel, *prostíbulo;* pandering, *proxenetismo, lenocinio.*

protection n. *protección.* **protect** v. *proteger.*
protective adj. *protector.*
consumer protection *protección al consumidor.*
order of protection *orden de protección* (DR, PR). – Syn. protection order.
protective custody *detención para la protección del afectado.*
protective tariff *tarifa protectora a la industria nacional.*
witness protection program *programa de protección de testigos.*

protectorate INTL.LAW n. *protectorado.*

protest¹(objection) n. *protesta.*
• A usually formal expression of objection or disapproval.
diplomatic protest *protesta diplomática, nota de protesta.*
under protest *bajo protesta.*

protest² NEGOT.INSTR n. *protesto de un título de crédito.*

• A formal declaration that a negotiable instrument has been neither paid nor accepted.
notice of protest *notificación del protesto.*
waiver of protest *renuncia al protesto.*
Rel: dishonor, *falta de pago o aceptación (de un título de crédito).*
protocol[1] **(minutes)** n. *acta de una asamblea.*
protocol[2] **(etiquette)** n. *protocolo.*
provisional remedies *medidas precautorias, medidas cautelares, medidas provisionales.*

• Incidental proceeding to the main action, while the action is still pending, to assure that the claimant's rights will be preserved or that he will not suffer irreparable injury. – Syn. precautionary measures.
Rel: attachment, *embargo;* claim and delivery, *petición de restitución de bienes muebles;* deposit in court, *depósito judicial;* injunction, *interdicto, mandamiento judicial prohibitorio;* receivership, *administración judicial.*

provocation n. *provocación.*
proximate cause[1] ᴛᴏʀᴛꜱ *causa suficiente para fincar responsabilidad civil.*
• Cause which is legally sufficient to establish liability. – Syn. direct cause. legal cause.
proximate cause[2] ᴛᴏʀᴛꜱ *causa directa o inmediata, causa próxima* (PR).
• It is that cause in natural and continuous sequence that produces the event and without which the event would not have occurred. – Syn. cause in fact.

proxy[1] **(power)** n. *poder, carta poder.*
• The authority given to a person to act for another.
proxy battle *disputa por el control de los votos de los accionistas de una sociedad.*
proxy vote *voto por apoderado, voto por representación.* – Syn. vote by proxy.
proxy[2] **(person)** n. *representante, apoderado.*
proxy marriage *matrimonio por apoderado.*
prudent person test [lexical exp.]*figura jurídica del hombre prudente.*
• In trust law, the rule that a trustee must make only those investments that a prudent man would make to obtain a reasonable income and preserve the principal. – Syn. prudent man rule, *regla del hombre prudente.*
psychoanalysis n. *psicoanálisis.*
psychology n. *psicología / sicología.*
psychopath n. *psicópata.*
psychopath personality *personalidad psicópata.*

psychosis n. *psicosis.*
See: mental disease.
puberty n. *pubertad.*
public adj. *público.*
public assistance *asistencia pública.*
public charge *carga pública.*
public domain *propiedad de dominio público.*
public enemy *enemigo público.*
public hearing *audiencia pública.*
public indecency *faltas a la moral, indecencia en público.*
public law *derecho público.*
public notice *aviso público.*
public nuisance *molestia pública.*
public office *cargo público.*
public safety *seguridad pública.*
public service *servicio público, función pública.*
public use *utilidad pública.*
public utilities *servicios públicos.*
public welfare *bienestar público* || *asistencia pública, beneficencia pública.*
public works *trabajos públicos.*
public defender *defensor público o de oficio.*
• An attorney appointed by the court to represent indigent defendants.
Rel: indigent, *indigente;* legal aid, *ayuda legal gratuita, asesoría legal gratuita;* right to counsel, *derecho de representación legal.*
public limited company (UK) *sociedad anónima.* – Abbr. plc.
public policy *orden público.*
• A concept indicating that the creation and application of the law needs to be directed towards "the protection and promotion of public welfare, including public health and morality" (17A Am. Jur. 2d Contract § 258). – Syn. policy of the law.
Cf: **public policy • public interest.** Terms often treated as synonyms; however, a distinction is sometimes made in that public interest is considered a more particularized application. See: *orden público.*
punishment n. *pena, castigo* (pop.).
• The sanction for a transgression of the law.
capital punishment *pena capital.*
cruel and unusual punishment [le]*pena cruel e inusual,* [de]*pena inhumana y extraordinaria.*
excessive punishment *pena desproporcionada, pena excesiva.*
punitive damages *indemnización por daños a título de pena.*
purchase n. *compra.* **purchaser** n. *comprador.*
purchase v. *comprar.*

purchase agreement *contrato de venta, compraventa.*

lay-away purchase plan *compra mediante pagos parciales anticipados, venta de mercancía apartada.*

purchase money *depósito inicial (en compra de inmueble hipotecado).*

purchase order *orden de compra.*

purchase price *precio de compra.*

QQQQ

qualification[1] **(competence)** n. *calificación.*
qualify v. *estar calificado.* **qualified** adj. *calificado.*
qualified attorney *abogado calificado.*
qualified expert witness *perito calificado.*
qualified voter or elector *votante o elector registrado o empadronado.*
Rel: competence, *competencia.*

qualification[2] **(limitation)** n. *limitación o restricción.*
qualified acceptance *aceptación condicional o condicionada.*
qualified indorsement *endoso sin mi responsabilidad.* – Syn. indorsement without recourse.
qualified privilege *inmunidad limitada.*

quash v. *dejar sin efectos.*
• "… to annul, overthrow, or vacate by judicial decision." (Wilson v. Commonwealth, 162 S.E. 1,2, 157 Va. 776.)
"In [American English] a motion to quash is usu. a motion to nullify a writ or subpoena. In [British English], by contrast, quash has broader uses. For example an indictment or a conviction may be said to be quashed." (Garner, 725)
Cf: **quash ● vacate ● set aside.** "Vacate or set aside often serves in place of quash. One or another may be used in special contexts; e.g., quash an indictment but vacate (or set aside) a judgment; e.g., quash is restricted to defects that are apparent, as opposed to a more general use of vacate and set aside. Procedure and use vary with jurisdiction." (Mellinkoff's Dict., 532)
motion to quash *petición de que se deje sin efectos, petición de que se anule.*
Rel: void, *nulo.*

quasi (lat.) *cuasi, casi, casi como.* As it were, so to speak; nearly, almost.
• Relating to or having the character of.
quasi contract *cuasicontrato.*
quasi crime *cuasidelito.*
quasi in rem *cuasi in rem.*

question[1] **(ask)** n. *pregunta.*

hypothetical question *pregunta hipotética.*
irrelevant question *pregunta irrelevante.*
leading question *pregunta tendenciosa.*
suggestive question *pregunta sugestiva.*

question[2] **(issue)** n. *cuestión.*
question of fact *cuestión de hecho.*
question of law *cuestión de derecho.*

questioning *interrogatorio.*
custodial questioning *interrogatorio bajo detención o bajo custodia, interrogatorio del detenido.*

questionnaire n. *cuestionario.*
Rel: application, *solicitud.*

quid pro quo (lat.) *quid pro quo, sustituir una cosa por otra equivalente.* "This for that", "something for something."
• A thing that is exchanged for another thing of more or less equal value.

quitclaim v. *renunciar o liberar (un derecho o una acción).*

quitclaim deed *[de]escritura de finiquito de inmuebles, [de]escritura de transmisión de derechos de propiedad sin obligarse a garantizar su legitimidad.*
• Conveying whatever interest one has in real property.

quorum n. *quórum.*
• The number of members whose presence in the meeting of a body permits the meeting to be lawfully conducted.

quota n. *cuota.*
export quota *cuota de exportación.*
import quota *cuota de importación.*

RRRR

race n. *raza.* **racism** n. *racismo.* **racist** n.adj. *racista.* **racial** adj. *racial.*
racial discrimination *discriminación racial.*
racial profiling *[de]registros y detenciones policiacos basados en el perfil racial (de ciertos individuos), [de]asedio u hostigamiento policial basado en el perfil racial (de los afectados).*
Rel: discrimination, *discriminación;* hate crime, *delito motivado por odio contra un cierto grupo de personas.*

racketeering *extorsión e intimidación organizada.*
• An organized conspiracy to commit extortion or coercion.
Rel: extortion, *extorsión;* racket, *fraude organizado.*
Ref: (US) 18 U.S.C. §§1961-68.

ransom n. *rescate.*

rap sheet (US) *hoja de antecedentes penales, ficha policíaca.*

rape (crime) n. *violación, acceso carnal violento,* (Co), *agresión sexual* (Sp). **rapist** n. *violador.*

• In common law, rape is an unlawful sexual intercourse with a female person without her consent. Today several jurisdictions have broadened rape to include sexual activity with a male victim also. – Syn. [brder]sexual battery. unlawful sexual intercourse.

Cf: **rape ● sexual assault ● statutory rape.** In many jurisdictions, rape has been abolished as a separate offense. Statutes generally have created a new crime labeled sexual assault, which usually defines rape broadly, for example, to include male victims; sexual assault also defines a lesser sexual offense when penetration is not present. Statutory rape is usually sexual intercourse by a male with a female, with or without her consent, when the female is under the age stipulated by statute.

aggravated rape *violación con agravantes, acceso carnal con agravación punitiva* (Co).

forcible rape *violación con violencia, violación mediante el uso de la fuerza.*

date rape [de]*violación por una persona con quien la víctima sale.*

statutory rape *estupro.*

Rel: carnal knowledge, *conocimiento carnal;* consent, *consentimiento;* outcry, *desahogo, desahogarse, exclamación espontánea* (PR)*;* vaginal penetration, *penetración vaginal.*

ratification n. *ratificación.* **ratify** v. *ratificar.*

• A confirmation or approval of acts needed to make them valid.

Cf: **ratification ● adoption ● confirmation.** These terms are distinguishable: adoption of a contract is accepting it as one's own; ratification is the confirmation of a contract entered into by one person on behalf of another without authority; confirmation, on the other hand, is the act of admitting something.

express ratification *ratificación expresa.*

implied ratification *ratificación tácita o implícita.*

ratification of a treaty *ratificación de un tratado.*

Rel: estoppel, *excepción o impedimento basado en las consecuencias jurídicas de actos o declaraciones anteriores.*

ready[1] **(prepared)** adj. *listo, preparado.*

defense is ready (oral expr.) *la defensa está*

lista para proceder.

prosecution is ready (oral expr.) *el fiscal está listo para proceder.*

ready willing and able buyer *el comprador está habilitado legal y financieramente.*

ready[2] **(willing)** adj. *dispuesto.*

real estate *bienes raíces.*

• Land or real property. – Syn. land. real property. realty.

Cf: **real estate ● real property.** Real estate and real property are synonyms referring to land and anything growing on, attached to or erected on it. Real estate is a mostly American term developed to designate "land and houses."

real estate agent *agente de bienes raíces.* – Syn. realtor.

real estate broker *corredor de bienes raíces.*

real estate investment trust *fideicomiso de inversión en bienes inmobiliarios.* – Abbr. REIT.

real estate law *ley de bienes raíces.*

real estate listing *listado de inmuebles en venta.*

real estate tax *impuesto inmobiliario, impuesto sobre adquisición de inmuebles.*

Rel: appraisal, *valuación;* building code, *reglamento de construcción o edificación;* developer, *urbanizador, fraccionador;* frontage, *frente;* housing development, *desarrollo habitacional;* location, *ubicación, localización;* subdivision, *fraccionamiento, subdivisión;* zoning, *regulación o planeación urbana.*

real property [fe]*bienes inmuebles, propiedad inmueble.*

• The ground and anything permanently attached to it, including land, buildings, growing trees and the airspace above the ground. – Syn. real estate, *bienes raíces.* realty.

Rel: easements, *servidumbres;* estate, *derecho que una persona tiene sobre un bien inmueble;* fixture, *inmueble por accesión o adhesión;* personal property, *bienes muebles, bienes que no son considerados inmuebles;* tenancy, *tenencia.*

See: estate[3]. tenancy.

reasonable adj. *razonable.*

reasonable belief *creencia razonable.*

reasonable care *cuidado razonable* || *diligencia razonable.*

reasonable cause *causa razonable.*

reasonable doubt *duda razonable.*

reasonable force *uso razonable de la fuerza.*

reasonable-man standard *figura jurídica del hombre razonable.*

reasonable suspicion *sospecha razonable.*

rebate n. *descuento en devolución.*

rebellion n. *rebelión.* **rebel** n. *rebelde.*

• "Violent opposition by a substantial group of persons against the lawfully constituted authority in a state, so substantial as to amount to an attempt to overthrow that authority." (Walker, 1040) – Syn. insurgency, *insurgencia.* revolt, *revuelta.* sedition, *atentados contra la autoridad.* uprising, *levantamiento, insurrección.*

rebuttal n. *refutación, prueba en contrario.* **rebut** v. *rebatir, refutar.*

rebuttable presumption *presunción que admite prueba en contrario, presunción refutable.*

rebuttal witness *testigo que contradice lo asentado por otro.*

recall[1] **(remove)** n. *destitución, retiro.* **recall** v. *destituir, retirar.*

recall a diplomat *retiro de un diplomático (de un país), retirar a un diplomático.*

recall a public official *destitución de un funcionario público, destituir a un funcionario.*

recall of a product *retiro de un producto del mercado.*

recall[2] **(revoke)** n. *revocación.* **recall** v. *revocar.*

recall a judgment *revocar una sentencia.*

recall[3] **(review)** v. *revisar nuevamente.*

recall a case *dar vista a un caso nuevamente.*

recall[4] **(remember)** v. *recordar.*

recant CRIML.LAW v. *retractarse, desdecirse.* Rel: confession, *confesión.*

receipt n. *recibo, comprobante.* – Syn. ticket, *boleta, tickete* (PR). voucher, *comprobante.*

receipts n. *ingresos, entradas.*

receivership n. *administración judicial de bienes, intervención judicial.* **receiver** n. *administrador judicial de bienes.*

• Proceeding in which a receiver is appointed for an insolvent corporation, partnership or individual.

Cf: **receiver • trustee in bankruptcy.** These terms are clearly different, but are often used as synonyms. A receiver is given control of certain property during litigation or court proceedings as an equitable court measure to preserve, manage and dispose of as the court directs. A trustee in bankruptcy takes legal title to the property of the bankrupt party and holds it "in trust" for equitable distribution among the creditors. A receiver holds property as custodian; a trustee holds it as legal owner.

receiver in bankruptcy *administrador judicial de una quiebra.*

receiver pendente lite *administrador judicial de bienes pendente lite.*

receivership in foreclosure *administración judicial de bienes en un juicio hipotecario.* Rel: bankruptcy, *quiebra.*

receiving stolen property *estar en posesión de bienes robados.* – Syn. handling stolen goods (UK). receiving stolen goods.

recess n. *receso.* Rel: adjournment, *suspensión.*

recidivist n. *reincidente.* **recidivism** n. *reincidencia.* – Syn. repeat offender.

reciprocity[1] INTL.LAW n. *reciprocidad internacional.*

• Similar mutual concessions or advantages between two states regarding their citizens. Rel: comity, *cortesía internacional.*

reciprocity[2] **(fed.system)** n. *reciprocidad.*

• Mutual concessions made between two states, within a federal system, regarding certain rights or privileges of each other's citizens.

recklessness n. *imprudencia grave, culpa consciente o con representación,* [brder]*culpa lata o grave,* **reckless** adj. *imprudente.* **recklessly** adv. *imprudentemente.*

• Conduct that is careless to the safety and rights of others or that is carried on by a person even though he or she foresees possible harm. – Syn. advertent negligence.

Cf: **gross negligence • recklessness • willful • wanton.** These terms are all used synonymously in an attempt to define conduct between intentional wrongdoing on one end, and negligence on the other. Negligence refers to lack of care as defined by reasonable standards; in turn, gross negligence refers to lack of care that even a careless person would not forgo. Recklessness is behavior that requires a conscious awareness of the risk involved. Willful means a voluntary intentional action that is not necessarily malicious. Wanton refers to behavior that manifests extreme indifference to a risk of injury to another, and it usually includes malice.

reckless conduct *conducirse con imprudencia grave, conducta con culpa consciente.*

reckless disregard *imprudencia grave y sin consideración,* [fe]*dolo eventual con representación.*

reckless driving *conducir con imprudencia grave,* [fe]*conducir en forma culposa consciente o con representación, conducción con imprudencia temeraria.*

reckless endangerment *poner en peligro injustificadamente.*

reckless homicide *homicidio culposo consciente o con representación.*
Rel: intent, *intención;* negligence, *negligencia, culpa, imprudencia.*

recognizance n. *caución judicial.*
personal recognizance *bajo palabra.*
release on own recognizance *libertad bajo palabra.*

reconvene v. *convocar o reunirse de nuevo, reanudar una sesión.*

record[1] **(entry)** n. *registro, inscripción,* [transpl.] *récord.* **recorder** n. *registrador.*
• The filing made of an instrument or document in a registry for the purpose of its preservation and retrieval. – Syn. entry. register.
lien record *inscripción de un gravamen o de un derecho preferencial de garantía.*
mortgage record *inscripción de una hipoteca.*
official record *registro oficial.*
public record *registro abierto al público.*
record date *fecha de inscripción.*
recording fees *costos de inscripción, gastos de inscripción.*
sealed record *registro o documento cerrado al público.*

record[2] **(transcript)** n. *acta.*
• A document memorializing certain acts or events.
as a matter of record *como consta en actas.*
let the record show *que se señale en actas.*
off the record *sin que se transcriba en el acta, sin que conste en actas.*
Rel: minutes, *minutas;* transcript, *transcripción.*

record[3] **(court proceedings)** n. *autos, expediente.*
• The official complete documentation in a court case.
judicial record *expediente, autos.*
– Syn. docket.
party of record *parte acreditada en autos.*
record on appeal *autos para apelación.*
Rel: file, *expediente.*

recorder n. *magistrado municipal* (UK).

recorder of deeds *jefe o director del registro de propiedad o catastro.*

recourse NEGOT.INSTR n. *acción cambiaria de regreso.*

recovery[1] **(restoration)** n. *recuperación, resarcimiento.*
• The restoration of something taken away or lost.
recovery of land *recuperación de la posesión*

de un inmueble.

recovery[2] **(judgment)** n. *sentencia favorable (especialmente ordenando un pago).*
• "[T]he establishment of a right by the judgment of a court … It also refers to the amount of the judgment as well as the amount actually collected pursuant to it." (Gifis, 393)
specific recovery *sentencia ordenando el cumplimiento de una obligación (en vez de una indemnización).*
Rel: restitution, *restitución.*

recusal n. *excusarse o abstenerse del conocimiento de una causa.*
• The removal of oneself as a judge considering a case.
Cf: **recusal • recusation • disqualification.**
Recusal is the removal of oneself as a judge for a case. Recusation is used sometimes as a synonym for recusal, but it is more properly used by countries in the civil law tradition where recusation means a motion to disqualify a judge, either for cause or without it. Disqualification, in turn, is used sometimes instead of recusal, but the opposite is not true, recusal is not used to mean disqualification.
Rel: [borr.]recusation, *recusación;* substitution of judge (SOJ), *recusación de un juez.*

red tape *papeleo* || *burocracia.*

redemption n. *recuperación, rescate, redención.*
• The recovery of possession of property, usually mortgaged or pledged, by making payment of an amount due; repurchase.
redemption of a mortgage *pago o extinción de una hipoteca en ejecución.*
redemption of collateral *rescate de una garantía colateral.*
right of redemption *derecho de rescate o recuperación.*

redress n. *remedio legal, recurso legal* || *resarcimiento.* – Syn. relief. remedy.

referee n. *árbitro.*

reentry *reposesión (de un inmueble).*

referendum n. *referendo, referéndum.*
Rel: initiative, *proyecto de ley por iniciativa popular.*

refugee n. *refugiado.*
Rel: asylum, *asilo.*

refund n. [fe]*devolución en dinero.* **refund** v. *devolver.*
Cf: **refund • reimbursement • repay.** These terms are used synonymously and interchangeably, but are sometimes differentiated. Refund

refers to a pay back in money, reimbursement means to refund in a form different than the one used to receive what is being reimbursed, while repay means to give back in the same form that the original payment was received, that is, a restoration.
Rel: discount, *descuento*; rebate, *descuento en devolución.*

register n. *registro.* **register/registrar** n. *registrador, jefe del registro.* **registration** n. *inscripción, registro.* – Other spell.: registry.
register of copyrights *registro de derechos de autor.*
register of deeds *registro de documentos legalizados sobre inmuebles.*
register of patents *registro de patentes.*
register of wills *registro de testamentos.*
register office *oficina del Registro civil.*
Rel: index, *índice;* record, *registro;* title, *título, escritura.*

regulation[1] (statute) n. *reglamentación.* **regulate** v. *reglamentar.* **regulatory** adj. *reglamentario.*
• Rules promulgated by a local government or an administrative agency exercising limited rulemaking authority. – Syn. delegated legislation, *legislación reglamentaria.* subordinated legislation, *legislación reglamentaria.*
Code of Federal Regulations (US) *Código de Reglamentos Federales.*
zoning regulations *reglamentación de zonas urbanas.*

regulation[2] (control) n. *regulación.* **regulatory** adj. *regulador.*
• Control or direction over a particular activity in accordance with specific authority given by law.
regulatory agency *órgano o entidad pública a cargo de la regulación de una actividad económica, órgano regulador.* – Syn. administrative agency.
rate regulation *regulación de tarifas.*
Rel: deregulation, *abrogación de la regulación legal de una rama o industria;* restrictions on entry, *limitantes a la entrada de nuevas empresas (a una industria);* unregulated market, *mercado sin regulación legal, mercado libre.*

rehabilitation[1] (reforming) n. *rehabilitación.*
rehabilitate v. *rehabilitar.*
• The reforming of criminals in order to become productive members of society; the recuperation from addiction of drug or alcohol addicts.
rehabilitation center *centro de rehabilitación.*
rehabilitation of offenders *rehabilitación de delincuentes.*

vocational rehabilitation *rehabilitación vocacional.*
rehabilitation[2] (credibility) n. *rehabilitación de un testigo.*
• The restoration of the lost credibility of a witness after being impeached.
rehabilitation of a witness *rehabilitación de un testigo.*

rehearing v. *reposición de la audiencia, repetición de la audiencia.*
Rel: retrial, *repetición del juicio.*

reimbursement n. *reembolso.*

reindictment CRIML.LAW n. [de]*reposición de una acusación formal.* – Syn. reinstatement of an indictment.

reinstatement n. *reposición.*
reinstatement of a case *reposición de un caso o proceso.*
reinstatement of insurance *restablecimiento o restitución de un seguro.*
Rel: expiration, *expiración;* superseded, *substituído.*

relative n. *familiar.*
• A person connected with another by blood or affinity. – Syn. relations, *pariente, allegado.*
blood relative *pariente consanguíneo.*
half-blood relative *pariente por uno de los progenitores solamente, media sangre, media casta.*
Rel: family, *familia;* kinship, *parentesco.*
See: *familiares.*

release[1] (liberation) n. *liberación,* **release** v. *liberar.* **releasee** n. *liberado.*
• Liberation from an obligation or duty. – Syn. discharge. surrender.
Cf: **release ● waiver.** These terms are usually clearly differentiated: a waiver is a voluntary relinquishment of a known right, while a release is a liberation from an obligation, duty or demand.
conditional release *liberación condicional, liberación sujeta a condición.*
partial release *liberación parcial.*
release of a claim *desistirse de una denuncia o demanda.*
release of a lien *liberación de un gravamen o un derecho preferencial.*
release of property *liberación de una propiedad.*

release[2] (document) n. *liberación, renuncia.*
• A written discharge from any claim.

release[3] (freeing) n. *libertad, descargo.* **release** v. *liberar, poner en libertad.* **releasee** n.

liberado, quien queda en libertad.
• The freeing of a detained person. – Syn. discharge.
release on bail *libertad bajo caución.*
release on bond *libertad bajo fianza, libertad caucional, libertad provisional* (Sp).
release on own recognizance *libertad bajo palabra.* – Abbr. ROR.
release on parol *libertad condicional.*
relief¹ (redress) n. *tutela jurídica o protección otorgada por los tribunales, impugnación bajo el derecho-equidad.*
• "The redress or assistance awarded to a complainant by a court, especially a court of equity." (Gifis, 428) – Syn. remedy. redress.
Cf: **relief ● remedy.** These terms are used synonymously but usually not interchangeably. Relief has traditionally been associated with the courts of equity <equitable relief>, while remedy has typically been used in connection with the courts of law <legal remedies>.
affirmative relief *tutela jurídica o protección otorgada mediante el ejercicio de una reconvención.*
equitable relief *tutela jurídica o protección otorgada a través del régimen de derecho-equidad.*
post conviction relief *derechos y recursos posteriores a la sentencia condenatoria.*
relief from forfeiture *impugnación de la pérdida de un derecho o un bien.*
relief from judgment *impugnación de una sentencia.*
temporary relief *tutela jurídica dada en forma temporal o precautoria.*
Rel: injunction, *interdicto;* rescission, *rescisión;* specific performance, *cumplimiento forzado de la obligación contractual.*
relief² (aid) n. *ayuda o asistencia.*
relinquishment n. *abandono.* **relinquish** v. *abandonar.* – Syn. abandonment, *abandono.*
relinquish a claim *desistirse de una demanda.*
remainder PROP.LAW n. [borr.]*remainder,* [de]*derecho residual (de propiedad),* **remainderman** n. *persona titular de un remainder.*
• "A future interest arising in a third person —that is, someone other than the estate's creator, its initial holder, or the heirs of either — who is intended to take after the natural termination of the preceding estate." (Black's Law Dict., 8th. ed., 1317)
contingent remainder [lexical exp.]*remainder condicional.* – Syn. executory remainder.

vested remainder [lexical exp.]*remainder ejecutado.* – Syn. executed remainder.
Rel: estate, *derecho que una persona tiene sobre un bien inmueble;* reversion, [borr.] *reversión (de un inmueble).*
remand (US) n. *devolución de los autos (por un tribunal de apelación).* **remand** v. *devolver los autos (por un tribunal de apelación)* ‖ *poner en detención (nuevamente).*
• To send back a case to the tribunal from which it was appealed or moved (usually a lower court).
remedy n. *recursos (lato sensu) bajo el derecho estricto,* [de]*medios jurídicos para ejercer o defender un derecho o para impedir su violación, remedios* (PR).
• The means employed to enforce a right or to prevent or redress a wrong.
extrajudicial remedy *recursos extrajudiciales.*
extraordinary remedy *recursos extraordinarios.*
provisional remedies *medidas preparatorias, medidas cautelares o provisionales.*
remedy at law *recursos legales (bajo el derecho estricto —en contraste con recursos bajo el derecho-equidad), remedio legal* (PR). – Syn. legal remedy.
statutory remedy *medios estipulados por la ley.*
Rel: relief, *tutela jurídica o protección otorgada por los tribunales.*
Ref: (US) U.C.C. §1-201; California Prune & Apricot Grower's Ass'n v. Catz American Co., 60 F.2d 788, 85 A.L.R. 1117.
remission n. *remisión (de deuda o de condena).*
renegotiation n. *renegociación.*
renewal n. *renovación.* **renew** v. *renovar.*
renewal of a lease *renovación de un contrato de arrendamiento.*
renewal of a license *renovación de una licencia.*
renewal of an insurance policy *renovación de una póliza de seguro.*
Rel: extension, *ampliación, extensión.*
rent¹ (lease) n. *renta, alquiler.*
• The compensation paid to the landlord in return for the tenant's right to possess and use the leased premises.
"Although rent is a normal incident of the landlord-tenant relationship, the relationship may be created without any duty on the part of the tenant to pay for the possession and use of the premises if such is the express intent of the

parties." (Hill, 257).

action for rent *acción de pago de rentas.*

assignment of rents *cesión de rentas.*

distress for rent *embargo para garantizar el pago de rentas.*

prepayment of rents *pago anticipado de rentas.*

recovery of rent *cobro judicial de rentas.*

rent in arrears *renta atrasada.*

Rel: lease, *arrendamiento;* rental building, *edificio de rentas.*

rent²(finance) n. *renta.*

• "Profit or return derived from any differential advantage in production." (Webster Encyclopedic Unabridged Dict., 1215)

reopen a case CRIML.LAW *reabrir un caso.*

reopen an investigation *reabrir una investigación.*

reorganization CORP. n. *reorganización corporativa.*

repeal n. *abrogación (de una ley).* **repeal** v. *revocar.*

• Abrogation of an existing statute by the body that originally passed it.

Cf: **repeal • abrogation • derogation**. Repeal and abrogation are often used synonymously. Abrogation is the broader term, meaning annulment of a law or an agreement. Repeal refers to the abrogation of an existing statute by the legislature, while derogation refers to the partial repeal or abrogation of a law.

express repeal *abrogación expresa.*

implied repeal *abrogación implícita.*

repeal a statute *abrogar una ley.*

Rel: statute, *ley escrita.*

replevin n. *acción reivindicatoria (de bienes muebles).*

• "An action in which the owner or one who has a general or special property in a thing taken or detained by another seeks to recover possession in specie, and sometimes the recovery in damages as an incident of the cause." (Ballentine's Law Dict., 1094)

replevin bond *caución o fianza de la acción reivindicatoria.*

Rel: detinue, *acción reivindicatoria (de bienes muebles) en derecho estricto o "common law";* ejectment, *acción reivindicatoria (de bienes inmuebles);* wrongfully detained property, *bienes retenidos ilícitamente.*

report n. *informe, parte.*

accident report *parte de un accidente, informe de un accidente.*

annual report *informe anual.*

medical report *parte médico, informe médico.*

police report *parte de la policía, parte policíaco o policial, reporte de la policía.*

to present a report *presentar un informe.*

repossession n. *recuperación de la posesión.*

repossess v. *recuperar o recobrar (un bien).* – Syn. repo.

representation¹ (presentation of facts) n. *manifestación o declaración de hechos.*

• A statement of fact.

estoppel by representation *excepción o impedimeto basado en la negación de declaraciones hechas con anterioridad.*

false representation *manifestación o declaración falsa.* – Syn. misrepresentation.

material representation *manifestación o declaración determinante o sustancial.*

Rel: material fact, *hecho fundamental o esencial.*

representation² AGENCY n. *representación.* **representative** n. *representante.*

• To act for another; to stand on behalf of another.

adequate representation *representación apropiada.*

legal representative *representante legal.*

personal representative *representante personal.*

registered representative *representante registrado.*

Rel: agent, *agente, representante.*

reprieve n. *aplazamiento.* **reprieve** v. *aplazar la ejecución de una pena.*

Rel: commutation, *conmutación;* pardon, *indulto.*

reprimand n. *reprimenda.*

reprisal n. *represalia.* – Syn. retaliation.

repudiation n. *repudio.* **repudiate** v. *repudiar.*

Rel: renunciation, *renuncia.*

reputation n. *reputación.*

• Repute in which a person is held by the people in his or her community, such as neighbors, friends and coworkers.

Cf: **reputation • character**. Character and reputation are used synonymously. Character is what a person is, as defined by his or her attributes; reputation is what others believe the person is, as defined by attributes others believe he or she possesses.

requisition¹ (purchase) n. *requerimiento, pedido.*

• A formal written order or request.

requisition² (demand) n. *requisición.* **requisition** v. *requisar.*

• The taking of private property or the making of an authoritative demand by the government, often in a situation of emergency. <demand of the government for military supplies> <the taking of private property for use by the government in the waging of a war.>

res ipsa loquitur (lat.) *res ipsa loquitur, la cosa habla por sí misma.* The thing speaks for itself.
• Rule that a presumption of negligence is raised by the mere fact of the occurrence of an injury in some circumstances.

res judicata (lat.) *res judicata, cosa juzgada.* The thing has been decided.
• Doctrine by which a final judgment by a court is conclusive and constitutes an absolute bar to a subsequent action involving the same claim.
– Syn. claim preclusion. res adjudicata.
Cf: **res judicata ● collateral estoppel.** Res judicata refers to the fact that a final judgment by a court is conclusive over the parties in any subsequent litigation, and it constitutes a "claim preclusion." Collateral estoppel refers to the conclusiveness of the set of facts or issues litigated and determined in earlier proceedings, and it constitutes an "issue preclusion."
Rel: collateral estoppel, *preclusión de cuestiones o determinaciones de hecho litigadas anteriormente;* stare decisis, *jurisprudencia obligatoria.*

res nullius (lat.) *res nullius, cosa sin dueño.*

resale price maintenance (UK) *sistema de control de precios (para asegurar un precio mínimo de ciertos artículos de consumo).*

rescission n. *rescisión.* **rescind** v. *rescindir.*
• Either a unilateral unmaking of a contract for a legal cause or a mutual agreement to discharge contract obligations.
Rescission is an ambiguous term referring to the termination of a contract that places the parties in a position similar to that one they had before concluding the agreement. This kind of termination is usually exercised only in cases where it is possible to restore the parties to their original positions or where third parties' rights will not be harmed.
Cf: **rescission ● cancellation.** Rescission is often distinguished from cancellation in that cancellation causes the termination of a contract by breach of one of the parties, while rescission is an agreement reached by the parties to discharge contractual obligations. This distinction is not generally followed and accepted, however.

Rel: breach, *incumplimiento;* default, *incumplimiento.*
See: cancellation. revocation.

reserve (finance) n. *reserva.*
bad debt reserve *reserva para cuentas malas o cuentas incobrables.*
bank reserves *reservas bancarias.*
cash reserve *reservas de capital.*
contingency reserve *reserva para gastos extraordinarios, reserva para imprevistos.*
currency reserves *reservas de divisas.*
depletion reserve *reserva de agotamiento (de un recurso, fondo, etc.).*
depreciation reserve *reserva de depreciación.*
legal reserve *reserva legal.*
sinking fund reserve *reserva para la formación de un fondo de amortización.*

residence n. *residencia.* **reside** v. *residir.* **resident** adj. *residente.*
• The place where a person lives.
The term residence is a flexible concept that denotes a temporary or even transient abode in some contexts, and a permanent and fixed one in others.
Cf: **residence ● domicile.** Both terms are often used as synonyms, but in a more strict sense residence refers to the dwelling of a person in a particular abode, a place where the person can be temporarily found. Domicile, in contrast, is the place legally recognized as a person's permanent residence, the place where a person always intends to return.
permanent residence *residencia permanente.*
resident alien *extranjero residente.*
nonresident visa *visa de no residente.*
Rel: abode, *habitación;* domicile, *domicilio.*
Ref: (CA) Citizenship Act, S.C. 1974-75-76, c.108; Re Fulford and Townshend [1970] 3 OR 493 at 500 (Surr. Ct.); (UK) 8(1) Halsbury's Laws para 703 at 705; (US) Town of Roanoke Rapids v. Patterson, 113 S.E. 603, 604, 184 N.C. 135; Robinson v. Robinson, 67 A2d 273, 275 362 Pa. 128.

resignation n. *renuncia, dimisión.* **resign** v. *renunciar, dimitir.*

resisting arrest (crime) *resistir arresto o detención, resistencia a un agente de la policía (al hacer un arresto o detención).*
• Physical efforts to oppose a lawful arrest by a police officer.
Rel: resisting an officer, *resistencia a la autoridad, resistencia a un oficial de la ley.*

respondeat superior (lat.) TORTS *respondeat superior, que el superior sea responsable.*
• A doctrine imposing liability on employers

for wrongful acts of their employees during the scope of their employment. – Syn. master-servant rule.

respondent¹ (equity) n. *demandado.*
• A party who makes an answer to a bill or other proceeding in equity. – Syn. defendant.
respondents in discovery *partes en la etapa de requerimiento y producción de pruebas.*
respondent² APPEAL n. *apelado.*
responsibility¹ (accountability) n. *responsabilidad.*
• The state of being liable or accountable. – Syn. liability.
responsibility² CRIML.LAW n. *responsabilidad penal o criminal.*
• Answerable for criminal behavior; guilty for his or her criminal actions.
criminal responsibility *responsabilidad penal, responsabilidad criminal.*

restitution n. *restitución.*
• Restoration to a person of a specific thing of which he or she has been wrongly deprived; compensation given for loss, damage or injury to another. – Syn. indemnification, *indemnización.*
order of restitution *orden de restitución.*
partial restitution *restitución parcial.*
Rel: unjust enrichment, *enriquecimiento ilegítimo.*
Ref: (UK) 40(2) Halsbury's Laws para 1310 at 1311; (US) Duffy v. Scott, 292 N.W. 273, 275, 276, 235 Wis. 142, 129 A.L.R. 487.

restraining order¹ (prevention) *interdicto o mandamiento judicial prohibitivo provisional,* [borr]*restraining order.*
• An order granted ex parte asking the adverse party to restrain from certain behavior until a permanent or temporary injunction can be issued. – Syn. temporary restraining order.
Cf: **restraining order** • **cease-and-desist order.**
These terms are clearly different. A restraining order is a provisional measure to preserve the status quo while a request for an injunction is being considered by the court. A cease-and-desist order is one issued by a court or administrative tribunal ordering a person or entity to stop engaging in a particular activity or practice in violation of the law (like an unfair labor practice, for example).
See: injunction.

restraining order² (protection) *orden de protección* (DR,PR), [borr.]*restraining order.*
• An order issued ex parte, temporarily preserv-ing the status quo, and granting the protection of the court to those requesting it by prohibit-ing others from oppressing, harassing, and even approaching them in some cases. – Syn. order of protection.
See: domestic violence.

restraint n. *restricción, limitación.*
combination in restraint of trade *asociación o acuerdo en contra del libre comercio o la libre competencia.*
judicial restraint *prohibición o limitación impuesta judicialmente.*
restraint of trade *impedimento o restricción al libre comercio o libre competencia.*
unlawful restraint CRIML.LAW [le]*restricción ilegal de la libertad.*
Rel: self-restraint, *autolimitación.*

retainer¹ (payment) n. *anticipo de honorarios profesionales, adelanto.*
• An advance payment given to an attorney to secure his or her legal services. – Syn. retaining fee.

retainer² (authorization) n. *autorización de la representación (por apoderado).*
• Authorization given to a lawyer to represent a client.

retaliation n. *represalias.*

retirement n. *jubilación.* **retire** v. *jubilarse.*
• To give up one's career, work, business, etc., especially because of advanced age.
retirement benefits *prestaciones de jubilación.*
retirement plan *plan de jubilación.*
Rel: employee benefit plan, *paquete de jubilación, plan completo de jubilación;* individual retirement account (US), *cuenta individual de retiro;* pension fund, *fondo de pensiones.*

retrial n. *repetición de un juicio, reposición de un juicio, reenjuiciar.*
Rel: mistrial, *nulidad de actuaciones.*

retribution n. *retribución.*

retroactivity n. *retroactividad.* **retroactive** adj. *retroactivo.*
Rel: ex post facto (lat.), *ex post facto, después del hecho;* retrospective, *retrospectivo.*

return TAX n. *declaración (de impuestos),planilla* (PR,Ve).
amended return *declaración enmendada, declaración modificada, planilla enmendada* (PR).

revenue n. *ingresos, percepción, renta.* – Syn. income.
general revenue *fondo general de ingresos públicos.*

public revenue *ingresos públicos.*

revenue authorities *autoridades fiscales.*

revenue law *ley fiscal o tributaria.*

reversal of judgment *revocación de una sentencia.*

reversion PROP.LAW n. [borr.]*reversión.*

• A future interest arising at the termination of an estate in land in favor of the original owner or his heirs.

See: future interest.

revocation n. *revocación.* **revoke** v. *revocar.*
revocable adj. *revocable.*

• The annulment, cancellation or recall of a power or authority, or the cancellation of an instrument previously made.

Cf: **revocation • nullification • cancellation • rescission.** All these terms refer to forms of termination of rights, powers, authority or obligations and are often used interchangeably. Nullification means the act of making something void. Revocation refers to annulment by taking back or recalling. Cancellation means to terminate or destroy the force or validity of a promise or an obligation (often by marking a text). Rescission usually means to abrogate by mutual agreement (especially a contract or transaction).

revocation of a license *revocación de una licencia.*

revocation of a will *revocación de un testamento.*

revocation of probation *revocación de la condena condicional,* [le]*revocación de la probación.*

Rel: abrogation, *abrogación;* cancellation, *cancelación;* rescission, *rescisión;* retract, *retractarse, retracto.*

reward n. *recompensa.*

Rex (lat.) n. *Rex, el Rey, la Corona.* – Abbr. R.

rider n. *suplemento, anexo.*

insurance policy rider *anexo o endoso de una póliza de seguro.*

right¹ (entitlement) n. *derecho.* **rightful** adj. *legítimo, con derecho.*

• "A power or privilege to which a person is entitled. A right confers control of action upon an individual and provides protection for that action." (Chandler, Enslen & Renstrom, 448) – Syn. jus (lat.), *jus.*

exclusive right *derechos exclusivos.*

incorporeal right *derechos inmateriales, derechos intangibles.*

marital rights *derechos maritales.*

material right *derechos materiales, derechos tangibles.*

preemptive right *derechos preferenciales.*

Rel: prerogative, *prerrogativa;* privilege, *privilegio.*

right² (claim) n. *derecho, derecho subjetivo.*

• A legally enforceable claim. – Syn. claim.

right of entry *derecho de ingreso.*

right of first refusal *derecho de preferencia, tanteo.*

right of redemption *derecho de rescate o recuperación.*

right to a jury trial *derecho de tener un juicio ante jurados.*

right to bear arms *derecho de tener armas.*

right to counsel or attorney *derecho a tener un abogado, derecho a asesoría legal.*

right to legal representation *derecho de representación legal.*

right to strike *derecho de huelga.*

right³ PROP.LAW n. *derecho (sobre una cosa).*

• The interest, claim or ownership that one has in property.

right of way *derecho de paso.*

right⁴ (moral) n. *justicia.*

• In accordance with what is considered moral and ethical.

because it is right, *porque es lo justo.*

right of privacy *derecho de privacía o privacidad.*

• "[The] right to be let alone; that is, the right to be free from unwarranted publicity, or the right to live without unwarranted interference by public in matters with which it is not necessarily concerned." (Brents v. Morgan, 221 Ky. 765, 299 S.W. 967 55 A.L.R. 964)

The English courts have not yet accepted the tort of invasion of privacy, but allow other grounds for liability arising from such invasion, especially defamation.

right-to-die laws *leyes sobre el derecho a morir dignamente.*

right to die *derecho a morir dignamente, derecho a prolongar la vida artificialmente.*

• Right to make a determination to artificially prolong one's life when gravely ill.

Rel: health care proxy, *poder (dado a un tercero) para decidir acerca de tratamiento médico adecuado (cuando la persona está imposibilitada de hacerlo);* living will, *declaración de voluntad de una persona de que no se le mantenga viva artificialmente (si sufre un quebranto irreparable en su salud).*

rights n. *derechos.*
  civil rights *derechos civiles.*
  constitutional rights *derechos constitucionales.*
  future rights *derechos futuros.*
  human rights *derechos humanos.*
  mineral rights *derechos mineros, derechos sobre minerales.*
  natural rights *derechos naturales.*
  political rights *derechos políticos.*
  preemptive rights *derechos preferenciales, derecho del tanto.*
  riparian rights *derechos de los propietarios ribereños.*
  visitation rights *derechos de visita.*
  voting rights *derecho de voto.*
  water rights *derechos sobre aguas.*
  Rel: Bill of Rights (US), *Declaración de derechos constitucionales.*
riot n. *motín, disturbio.* **rioter** n. *amotinador, amotinado.*
  • The unlawful acts or conduct of an assembly —of three or more persons— possessing a common intent which breaches the peace or brings about or threats with violence in a tumultuous manner.
  Cf: **riot • unlawful assembly • disturbance.** While riot is the commission of an unlawful act by a group in a tumultuous manner, unlawful assembly is an illegal gathering which may or may not culminate in a riot. Disturbance, on the other hand, refers to an act that causes interference with public peace or with another's lawful activities, usually without rising to the level of being tumultuous.
  inciting a riot *incitación a un motín.*
  riot police *policía antimotines.*
  Rel: demonstration, *manifestación;* disturbance, *disturbio;* unlawful assembly, *reunión ilegal.*
risk n. *riesgo, peligro.* **risky** adj. *arriesgado, peligroso.*
  • The chance of injury or loss. In an insurance policy, the harmful possibility of injury or loss to the insured protected by the policy.
  Cf: **risk • hazard • peril.** There is no commonly accepted standard usage that establishes or recognizes separate and distinct definitions for these terms. Risk and hazard are used synonymously and interchangeably. Peril, being synonymous, implies a potential physical cause of loss. In insurance law, hazard refers to a specific situation that introduces or increases the probability of occurrence of a loss arising from

a peril, or that may influence the extent of a loss.
  assumption of risk *asunción de riesgo.*
  foreseeable risk *riesgo previsible.*
  ordinary risk *riesgos ordinarios.*
  risk capital *capital de riesgo.*
  risk management (business) *administración de riesgo.*
  risk of flight CRIML.PROCED. *en riesgo de fugarse, riesgo de fuga.*
  risk of loss (sale) *riesgo, riesgo de pérdida.*
  Rel: hazard, *peligro, riesgo;* peril, *peligro.*
  See: dangerous.
robbery (crime) n. *robo, robo con violencia (en las personas).* **rob** v. *robar.* **robber** n. *ladrón.*
  • "Robbery is the felonious taking of personal property in the possession of another, from his person or immediate presence, and against his will, accomplished by means of force or fear." (Penal Code of the State of California §211) – Syn. forcible stealing. hold-up. stick-up (slg.).
  aggravated robbery *robo con agravantes.*
  armed robbery *robo a mano armada, asalto a mano armada.*
  attempted robbery *intento o tentativa de robo.*
  highway robbery *robo en carretera, robo en despoblado.*
  Rel: theft, *robo;* to be mugged, *ser asaltado.*
rogatory letters *cartas rogatorias, exhorto.*
  See: letters rogatory.
rollover TAX n. *reinversión.*
royalties n. *regalías.*
  Rel: copyright, *derechos de autor;* patent, *patente.*
rule of law[1] (society's controlling system) *estado de derecho, régimen de derecho.*
  • The supremacy of law as a controlling system and as a guarantee against arbitrariness.
rule of law[2] (legal principle) *principio de derecho, figura jurídica.*
  • "A substantive legal principle." (Black's Law Dict., 8th. ed., 1359) <parol evidence rule>
rule of law[3] (ruling) [le]*regla de derecho,* [lat.]*ratio decidendi,* [fe]*norma individualizada.*
  • The principle of law expressed in a court decision. – Syn. holding.
rule to show cause *procedimiento para fundamentar lo actuado, procedimiento para que se demuestre que el incumplimiento o lo actuado tiene justificación legal.* – Syn. show-cause proceeding.

rules of procedure *reglas del procedimiento.*

ruling *fallo, decisión.*

runaway child *niño escapado de casa* || *niño que está fuera de control.*

SSSS

sabotage n. *sabotaje.* **saboteur** n. *saboteador.*

safe deposit box *caja de seguridad.*

salary n. *salario.*
• Compensation paid on a periodic basis, usually for professional or similar type of work.
– Syn. emolument, *emolumento.* stipend, *estipendio.* wage, *sueldo.*
Cf: **salary • wage.** While salary often denotes compensation for professional or supervisory work paid weekly, biweekly or monthly, wage usually refers to compensation given to employees based on time worked or quantity produced.

sale n. *compraventa, venta.* **sell** v. *vender.* **sellable** adj. *vendible.* **seller** n. *vendedor.* **buyer** n. *comprador.* **vendor** n. *vendedor, abastecedor.* **purchaser** n. *comprador, adquirente.* **salesman** n. *vendedor.*
• Sale is a contract by which property is transferred to another for a price.
auction sale *subasta, remate.*
bill of sale *documento o instrumento translativo de propiedad.*
bulk sale *venta de los bienes de una empresa en paquete (incluyendo inventario y equipo).*
– Syn. bulk transfer.
conditional sale *venta condicional.*
installment sale *venta en abonos, venta a plazos.*
judicial sale *venta judicial.*
public sale *venta pública.*
sale agreement *contrato de compraventa.*
sale on credit *venta a crédito.*
Rel: auction, *subasta, remate;* discount, *descuento;* down payment, *enganche.*
sale of goods *compraventa de mercancías,* [fe]*compraventa mercantil.*
Cf: **law of sales • sale of goods • contract for sale.** These are all terms given to the principles regulating the sale of goods. Law of sales is an expression reflecting the origin of these principles of law as an extension of contract law. Contract for sale is the modern term used in the U.S. Uniform Commercial Code. Sale of goods is the more traditional designation that means both the law of sale of goods and

the commercial transaction it describes.
sale by sample *venta por muestra, venta sobre muestras.*
sale in gross *venta de géneros, venta a granel.*
Rel: collect on delivery (C.O.D.), *pago contra entrega;* goods, *bienes muebles tangibles, mercancía;* passing of risk, *transmisión del riesgo, traslado del riesgo;* risk of loss, *riesgo de pérdida.*
See: international trade. goods.
Ref: (CA) Sale of Goods Act , R.S.O. 1990; (UK) Sale of Goods Act (1979) Amended; (US) U.C.C. §2-106(1).

salvage[1] (rescue) n. *salvamento.*
• Rescue of property from peril. Also property remaining after a loss.
salvage loss *pérdida de salvamento.*

salvage[2] (compensation) n. *premio, compensación (de un salvamento).*
• Compensation paid to those who save a ship or its cargo.

sample n. *muestra.*

sanction[1] (penalty) n. *sanción.* **sanction** v. *sancionar.*
• The punishing measures resulting from failure to comply with a rule or order. – Syn. penalty, *castigo.*

sanction[2] (approval) n. *sanción, aprobación.* **sanction** v. *aprobar, confirmar.*
• Official approval.

sanity n. *cordura, sensatez.*

savings n. *ahorros.*
savings account *cuenta de ahorros.*
savings bank *banco de ahorros.*
savings bonds *bonos de ahorro.*

scandalous allegations *afirmaciones escandalosas o difamatorias (e irrelevantes).*

scene n. *escena.*
crime scene *escena del crimen.*
leaving the scene of an accident *abandonar la escena o el lugar de un accidente.*
scene diagram *diagrama de la escena (de un delito o accidente).*

schizophrenia n. *esquizofrenia.*

scintilla of evidence *mínimo indicio de prueba.*

sea n. *mar.*
high seas *alta mar.*
open seas *mar abierto.*
territorial sea *mar territorial.*
See: law of the sea.

seal n. *sello.* **seal** v. *sellar.*
corporate seal *sello corporativo, sello oficial*

(de una persona jurídica o moral).
public seal *sello oficial de una entidad pública.*
Rel: locus sigilli (L.S.), *el lugar del sello.*
sealed bid *oferta cerrada.*
sealed case *caso bajo sello de confidencialidad, caso cerrado al público.*
sealed indictment *acusación formal en sobre cerrado.*
sealed record *registro o documento cerrado al público.*
sealed verdict *veredicto en sobre cerrado.*
search CRIML.PROCED n. *registro, cateo* (Mx), *pesquisas* (Ar). **search** v. *registrar.*
• Examination of a person or a person's home or property to find an indication of the probability that he or she committed a crime. – Syn. examination *examen.* inspection *inspección.*
body search *cacheo.*
border search *registro fronterizo.*
cavity search *registro de cavidades (corporales).*
consent search *registro consensual.*
cursory search *registro superficial.*
custodial search *registro hecho durante una detención o un arresto.*
illegal search *registro ilegal.*
inventory search *registro para efectos de inventario.*
search incidental to an arrest *registro accesorio con motivo de una detención, registro resultante de una detención.*
search warrant *orden de registro.*
spread-leg standing search *registro estando en posición parada con las piernas abiertas.*
strip search *registro removiendo prendas de vestir.*
Rel: curtilage, *inmediaciones de un hogar;* exclusionary rule, *inadmisibilidad o improcedencia de pruebas obtenidas en forma ilegal;* fruit of the poisonous tree doctrine, *inadmisibilidad de pruebas obtenidas en registros, detenciones o confesiones ilegales;* plain view doctrine, *figura jurídica de "a plena vista."*
search and seizure *registro y secuestro, allanamiento y secuestro, registro e incautación* (PR).
• "The power exercised by public authority to enter private premises for the purpose of arresting a man or of obtaining evidence of his guilt of a crime of which he is charged." (Radin, 309)
unreasonable search and seizure *registro y secuestro indebidos.*

Rel: Fourth Amendment (US), *Cuarta Enmienda (constitucional).*
secured transactions *operaciones comerciales de garantía.* **secured party** *parte en favor de quien se ha establecido la garantía.* **creditor** n. *acreedor.* **debtor** n. *deudor.*
• A business arrangement creating a security interest to guarantee payment.
Rel: bail, *fianza;* guarantee, *garantía;* letter of credit, *carta de crédito;* lien, *derecho preferencial de garantía, gravamen;* mortgage, *hipoteca;* pledge, *prenda.*
Ref: (US) U.C.C.§-105(h)
securities n. *valores, títulos.*
• Loosely, stocks, shares, debentures, bonds or any other instruments representing a right to receive interest or dividends. More specifically, a right to share in the profits, assets or debt of a company.
convertible securities *valores convertibles.*
equity security *título representativo de capital de una sociedad.*
issue of securities *emisión de valores.*
listed security *valores listados en la bolsa de valores.*
marketable securities *valores negociables (que tienen un mercado activo), valores que pueden ser comprados y vendidos inmediatamente.*
municipal securities *valores municipales.*
public securities *valores públicos.*
sale of securities *venta de valores.*
securities broker *corredor de valores.*
securities offering *emisión de valores.*
Rel: bond, *bono;* shares, *acciones;* stock, *acciones, valores;* stock exchange, *bolsa de valores.*
security[1] **(safety)** n. *seguridad, aseguramiento.*
• Protection; safety.
maximum security prison *prisión de máxima seguridad.*
security[2] **(guaranty)** n. *obligado, fiador.*
• A person who becomes the guarantor for another.
security[3] **(collateral)** n. *colateral, garantía.*
• A collateral pledged to a creditor for payment of a debt.
real security *garantía real.*
security agreement *convenio de garantía.*
security deposit (lease) *depósito de seguridad.*
sedition n. *atentados contra la autoridad.*
seditious adj. *que atenta contra la autoridad.*

seduction

• Stirring resistance to legitimate authority or tending to cause or advocate the overthrow of the government.
seditious libel (UK) *publicaciones o escritos que atentan contra la autoridad.*
Rel: treason, *traición.*

seduction n. *seducción.* **seduce** v. *seducir.* **seductive** adj. *seductor.*

segregation n. *segregación.*
racial segregation *segregación racial.*
Rel: equal protection clause, *cláusula constitucional del derecho de igualdad.*

seisin PROP.LAW (hist.) n. *posesión efectiva de un inmueble (basada en derecho), derecho del vasallo sobre la propiedad dada por el soberano.*
• Possession of a freehold in land.
Cf: **seisin • possession • ownership • title.** Seisin and possession were traditionally considered distinct concepts since a man could be considered in possession of land but not seised of his estate. In modern statutes, however, the term seisin has survived describing the right to a freehold, and as a "synonym for one or more of the words title, ownership, and possession." (Mellinkoff's Dict., 590)
livery of seisin (obs.) *solemnidad de la transmisión de propiedad.*
seisin in fact *posesión de hecho.*
seisin in law *posesión de derecho.*
See: ownership.

seizure n. *secuestro judicial (cosas) || detención (personas).*
• The act of taking possession of property or persons by legal right or process. – Syn. levy.
search and seizure *registro y secuestro, allanamiento y secuestro, registro e incautación* (PR).
Rel: attachment, *embargo;* confiscate, *confiscar;* forfeiture, *pérdida de un derecho, decomiso;* garnishment, *embargo de bienes en manos de un tercero;* impound, *confiscar.*

self-defense n. *legítima defensa.*
• The protection of one's person or property, using reasonable force against some injury attempted by another. – Other spell.: self-defence (UK).
Rel: imminent danger, *peligro inminente;* justification, *justificantes;* reasonable force, *uso razonable de la fuerza.*

self-employment n. *trabajo por cuenta propia.*
self-employed, *que trabaja por cuenta propia, que tiene su propio negocio, cuentapropista.*

self-help n. *por sí mismo, hacerse justicia por*

propia mano.
• The obtaining of a remedy or solving of a dispute through one's own actions without recourse to legal process. <A self-help eviction is one in which the landlord removes the tenant's possessions from the property and bars the tenant from entering the premises.>
Rel: vigilantism, *hacerse justicia por sí mismo,* [borr.] *vigilantismo.*

self-incrimination n. *autoincriminación, autoincriminación.*
Rel: Fifth Amendment (US), *Quinta Enmienda (constitucional);* Miranda warnings (US), [le] *prevenciones Miranda.*

self-inflicted injury *herida autoinfligida.*

seniority LABOR n. *antigüedad.*

sentence[1] CRIML.PROCED n. *condena, sentencia* (PR).
sentence v. *condenar, sentenciar.* **sentencing** v. *dictar condena.* **sentencing** adj. *condenatorio.*
• Punishment imposed on a defendant after he or she enters a guilty plea or is found guilty by a court. – Syn. condemnation, *condena.*
Cf: **sentence • condemnation • conviction • punishment.** Condemnation and conviction are synonyms but are rarely used interchangeably; both mean the pronouncement of someone's guilt, or sometimes simply guilt. Sentence, on the other hand, refers to the punishment imposed by the condemnation or conviction issued by a court or tribunal. A sentence determines the sanction to be applied to a guilty violator, while punishment establishes the form of that sanction.
appellate review of sentence *revisión en apelación de una condena.*
concurrent sentences *condenas simultáneas.*
consecutive sentence *condena sucesiva.*
correction of sentence *corrección de una condena.*
cumulative sentence *condena acumulativa.*
excessive sentence *condena excesiva.*
indeterminate sentence *condena por un plazo sin determinación específica.*
life sentence *condena de cadena perpetua, condena de por vida.*
mandatory sentence *condena obligatoria.*
maximum sentence *condena máxima.*
minimum sentence *condena mínima efectiva.*
sentence in absentia *condena in absentia.*
split sentence *condena mixta.*
suspended sentence *condena suspendida.*
to serve a sentence *cumplir una condena.*

Rel: conviction, *sentencia condenatoria;* credit for time served, *abono por tiempo en prisión;* judgment, *sentencia;* punishment, *pena.*

sentence² CIVIL PROCED n. *sentencia.*
• The final decision by a court in a civil action. In civil law "judgment," "award" and "finding" are the preferred terms, but sentence is still often used, and in those cases the Spanish equivalent is *sentencia.*
interlocutory sentence *sentencia interlocutoria.*
sentence of nullity *sentencia de nulidad (del matrimonio).*
separate property FAM.LAW *separación de bienes.*
separation n. *separación.*
• The living apart of a husband and a wife, arranged by mutual agreement or judicial decree. – Syn. legal separation.
legal separation *separación legal.*
order of separation *orden judicial de separación.* – Syn. divorce from bed and board. limited divorce.
separation agreement *convenio de separación.*
separation by consent *separación de común acuerdo.*
separation decree *sentencia de separación.* Rel: breakup, *rompimiento;* desertion, *abandono;* divorce, *divorcio.*
separation of church and state *separación de la iglesia y el estado.*
separation of powers *separación de poderes.*
sequestration n. *secuestro, embargo.*
sequestration of assets *secuestro de bienes, embargo de bienes.*
sequestration of account *embargo de una cuenta bancaria.*
sequestration of jury *aislamiento o confinamiento de un jurado.* See: attachment.
service n. *notificación judicial.* **serve** v. *notificar judicialmente.*
• Delivery of a pleading, notice or other document in a suit to the opposite party, which constitutes a legal acknowledgment of receipt.
personal service *notificación personal.*
return of service *acta de diligenciamiento de la notificación.*
serve a notice *llevar a cabo una notificación, diligenciar una notificación.*
serve a subpoena *notificar una citación o un citatorio judicial.*
serve a summons *efectuar el emplazamiento*

de la demanda.
service by publication *notificación por edictos.*
service of process *diligencia de notificación.*
substituted service [de]*notificación hecha por una persona judicialmente autorizada para ello.*
serving a sentence *cumpliendo una condena.*
serving time *cumpliendo una condena de prisión.*
servitude n. *carga sobre un inmueble.* See: easement. equitable servitude.
session n. *sesión.*
closed session *sesión cerrada.*
joint session *sesión conjunta.*
plenary session *sesión plenaria.*
regular session *sesión ordinaria.*
special session *sesión especial, sesión extraordinaria.*
settlement¹ (agreement) n. *convenio, transacción, arreglo* (pop.).
• An agreement ending a lawsuit.
out-of-court settlement *convenio extrajudicial.*
marriage settlement *capitulaciones matrimoniales.* – Syn. marital agreement.
settlement of a dispute *transacción de una controversia.* Rel: accord and satisfaction, *transacción, convenio transaccional.*
settlement² SUCCESSION n. *administración y liquidación de una herencia.*
• The final and complete execution of an estate. – Syn. settlement of an estate.
settlement³ (termination) n. *finiquito, liquidación.*
• The payment or adjustment of an account
settlement of an account *liquidación de una cuenta.* Rel: closing, *cerrar, concluir.*
settlement⁴ (conveyance) n. *transferencia de propiedad.*
• The conveyance of property.
severance (separation) n. *escisión, separación* || *partición.*
severance of actions *escisión de acciones, escisión de procesos.*
severance pay *indemnización de salarios por despido justificado.*
severance tax *impuesto sobre la extracción de minerales y productos forestales.*
sex n. *sexo.* **sexual** adj. *sexual.* – Syn. gender, *género.*
sex discrimination *discriminación sexual.*

sex offender *convicto de delitos sexuales, delincuente sexual.*

sexual abuse *abuso sexual.*
• "An illegal sex act, esp. one performed against a minor by an adult." (Black's Law Dict., 8th. ed., 10) – Syn. criminal sexual abuse. Sexual abuse is sometimes used broadly meaning any kind of sexual wrongdoing, but it is more often used to define any kind of illegal sex act perpetrated against a minor.

sexual assault[1] (rape) *violación.*
See: rape.

sexual assault[2] (non-rape) *abuso deshonesto.*
– Syn. sexual contact. indecent assault.

sexual contact *abuso deshonesto.*
• "In accordance with a typical definition, 'sexual contact' means the touching of a person's 'intimate parts,' directly or through clothing for the purpose of 'sexual arousal, gratification or abuse'." (8 Wharton's Criminal Law, §291 at 131, 132)

sexual crimes *delitos sexuales.*
Specific types: indecent exposure, *exhibiciones obscenas;* lewdness, *faltas a la moral;* rape, *violación;* sexual abuse, *abuso sexual;* sexual assault, *violación, abuso deshonesto;* sexual battery, *violación, abuso deshonesto.*

sexual harassment *insinuaciones, acoso u hostigamiento sexuales.*
• Employment discrimination consisting in unwanted or abusive behavior of sexual nature causing distress to an employee.
Rel: hostile workplace, *ambiente de hostilidad en el trabajo.*

sexual intercourse *relaciones sexuales, cópula.*
– Syn. coitus, *coito.* carnal knowledge, *conocimiento carnal.* copulation, *copulación.* fornication, *fornicación.* fucking (vul.), *coger* (Mx, Ar,Ve), *clavar, culear.* making love, *hacer el amor.* screwing (vul.), *coger, clavar, joder.* sex, *sexo.*

sexual orientation *preferencia sexual.*
Rel: homosexuality, *homosexualismo;* lesbianism, *lesbianismo;* transsexualism, *transexualismo;* transvestism, *transvestismo.*

sexual predator *depredador sexual.* – Syn. sexually dangerous person.

sham marriage *matrimonio en fraude de la ley, matrimonio simulado.*

share[1] CORP. n. *acción.*
• The fractional equal parts into which the capital stock of a corporation or joint stock company is divided.

outstanding shares *acciones emitidas.*
preferred shares *acciones preferentes.*
share certificate *certificado de acciones.*
treasury shares *acciones de tesorería.*
Rel: securities, *valores, valores accionarios;* stock, *capital social por acciones, acciones.*
See: stock[1].

share[2] SUCCESSION n. *parte (de la herencia o haber hereditario).*
• A portion of an estate.

shareholder n. *accionista.* – Syn. stockholder, *accionista.*

controlling shareholder *accionista que tiene el control (de la sociedad), accionista que tiene suficientes acciones para controlar las decisiones corporativas.*
majority shareholder *accionista mayoritario.*
minority shareholder *accionista minoritario.*
shareholder resolution *resolución de la asamblea de accionistas.*
shareholder's derivative suit *acción entablada por un accionista contra tercero para proteger sus derechos.*
shareholder's direct suit *acción entablada por un accionista contra una sociedad para hacer valer sus derechos.*
shareholder's equity *patrimonio neto* (Sp), *capital contable* (Mx). – Syn. net worth.
shareholder's meeting *asamblea general de accionistas, junta general de accionistas* (Bo, Ch,Ec,Sp,Pe).
annual meeting *asamblea ordinaria.*
special meeting *asamblea extraordinaria.*
Rel: proxy, *poder;* quorum, *quórum;* voting, *votación;* voting trust, *cesión fiduciaria (de acciones).*
See: corporation.

sheriff[1] (US) n. [borr.]*sheriff, alguacil* (PR).
• The elected chief law enforcement officer in a county. Duties usually include keeping order within the jurisdiction, running the county jail, and providing service process and execution of court orders.
deputy sheriff *asistente del sheriff o alguacil.*
sheriff's deed *título de propiedad adquirido en venta judicial.*
sheriff's sale *venta judicial.* – Syn. execution sale. judgment sale.

sheriff[2] (UK) n. *funcionario público.*

sheriff[3] (Scot.) n. *juez penal.*

ship n. *barco, embarcación, nave, navío.*
Cf: **ship ● vessel.** Vessel is considered a broad concept that defines any kind of craft used to

navigate on water; ship, on the other hand, is usually considered a vessel capable of navigating in deep water and propelled in a form other than oars or the like.
arrest of ship *embargo de buque* || *apresamiento de embarcación o buque.*
ship broker *agente naviero.*
ship lien *privilegio marítimo.*
ship mortgage *hipoteca marítima o naval.*
ship owner *armador o propietario del buque.*
ship's registry *registro naval.*
shipwreck *naufragio.*
Rel: charter, *fletamiento;* crew, *tripulación;* master, *capitán;* pilotage, *pilotaje;* registration, *matriculación;* stowage, *estiba;* towage, *remolque.*
See: *buque.*
shipping[1] MARIT.LAW n. *embarque, transportación marítima.* **shipper** n. *embarcador, fletador.*
• The act or business of transporting goods by sea.
shipping articles *contrato de trabajo (a bordo de embarcaciones).*
shipping casualty *siniestro marítimo.*
shipping company *compañía marítima, compañía naviera.*
shipping inquiry *investigación de un siniestro marítimo.*
shipping[2] (general) n. *transportación, expedición.*
shipper n. *transportista, expedidor.*
• Transportation of goods by any type of carrier.
shipping agent *agente transportista.*
shipping documents *documentos de embarque.*
shipping order *orden de embarque.*
Rel: carrier, *transportador, porteador.*
See: *documentos de embarque.*
shoplifting v. *hurto de mercancía en una tienda o almacén.* **shoplifter** n. *ladrón, ratero.*
show cause *fundamentación de lo actuado, demostrar que el incumplimiento o lo actuado tiene justificación legal,* [le]*mostrar causa* (PR).
• To give a legally satisfactory reason (for the purpose of avoiding a judicial consequence).
motion to show cause *petición pidiendo se fundamente lo actuado (por la contraria), pedir que se demuestre que el incumplimiento o lo actuado tiene justificación legal,* [le]*moción por causa* (PR).
order to show cause *auto pidiendo se fundamente lo actuado, auto pidiendo que se demuestre que el incumplimiento o lo actuado tiene justificación legal.*
sidebar conference (trial) [de]*consulta confidencial entre abogados y juez (durante un juicio*

con jurados).
• Discussion in a trial courtroom between the judge and lawyers outside the jury's hearing.
– Syn. sidebar.
sight draft *giro a la vista.*
sight letter of credit *carta de crédito a la vista.*
sight paper NEG.INSTR *título a la vista.*
sign language *lenguaje de señas.*
• A form of communication using hand signs, body and facial movements to either reproduce another spoken, speech-based language, or to form a new sign-based one.
Rel: American sign language (ASL), *lenguaje de señas americano, lenguaje americano para sordomudos;* deaf culture, *cultura de la comunidad de personas sordas;* facial expressions, *expresiones faciales;* fingerspelling or handspelling, *deletreo digital;* hard of hearing, *audición disminuida;* hearing impairment, *defecto auditivo;* relay interpreter, *intérprete de relevo.*
signatory n. *signatario.*
signature n. *firma.*
digital signature *firma digitalizada.*
Rel: cosigner, *cofirmante.*
simulation n. *simulación.* – Syn. sham, *ficticio.*
simulated contract *contrato simulado, simulación de contrato.*
simulated fact *hecho simulado.*
simulated sale *venta simulada.* – Syn. simulated transaction.
sine qua non (lat.) *sine qua non, sin el cual no.*
A necessary condition or thing.
slander n. *difamación oral, difamación de palabra.* **slanderer** n. *difamador de palabra.*
slanderous adj. *difamatorio.*
• Oral false statements made, damaging a person's reputation or bringing him or her into disrepute.
slanderous per se *términos difamatorios per se, difamatorios en sí.*
Rel: defamation, *difamación;* libel, *difamación escrita.*
slander of title (tort) *declaración falsa acerca de la legitimidad de un título o escritura.*
slang[1] (casual speech) n. *modismo.*
• Highly informal speech outside conventional usage, often restricted to special contexts.
slang[2] (jargon) n. *jerga, argot, caló.*
• Jargon or special vocabulary of a profession or group of persons.
slush fund *fondo para actividades ilícitas o de*

smuggling

corrupción, fondo para propósitos ilegales.

smuggling v. *introducir contrabando.* **smuggler** n. *contrabandista.*

smuggling aliens *introducir extranjeros ilegalmente (al país).*

See: contraband.

sniper n. *francotirador.*

sobriety tests *pruebas para determinar la sobriedad o ebriedad (de una persona).*

balance test *prueba de equilibrio, "hacer un cuatro"(Mx).*

blood test *análisis de sangre.*

field sobriety test *prueba de sobriedad en el lugar.*

finger count test *prueba de contar con los dedos.*

finger to nose test *prueba de tocar la punta de la nariz con la punta del dedo.*

heel to toe test *prueba de la punta del pié al talón.*

walking the line test *prueba de caminar sobre la línea.*

Glossary: bleary-eyed, *con mirada cansada o apagada;* breathalyzer, *analizador de aliento, alcoholímetro;* drunk, *ebrio;* fumbling, *andar a tientas;* glassy eyes, *ojos vidriosos;* sober, *sobrio;* staggering, *bamboleándose, tambaleándose;* stumbling, *tropezando;* swaying, *ladeándose;* watery eyes, *ojos llorosos, ojos acuosos;* wobbling, *inestable, bamboleándose.*

social security *seguro social, seguridad social.*

Social Security Administration (US) *Administración del seguro social, Seguro social.*

social security benefits *servicios o prestaciones del seguro social.*

social security number *número de seguro social.*

social services *servicios sociales.*

social worker *trabajador social.*

sodomy n. *sodomía.*
• Sexual intercourse between persons of the same sex. Also copulation between a human and an animal (also known as bestiality).
– Syn. buggery. crime against nature.

sole adj. *único, sólo, solitario.* – Syn. single.

sole heir *heredero único.*

sole ownership *propietario o dueño único.*
– Syn. sole proprietorship.

sole practitioner *en práctica por sí solo.*

solicitation[1] (request) n. *petición.*

solicitation[2] (inciting) n. *invitación a la comisión de un delito, instigación para delinquir* (Co).

– Syn. incitement.

solicitation of a bribe *incitación a cometer un soborno o cohecho.*

solicitation of clients for prostitution *invitación hecha a otros para el comercio carnal, invitación para intercambiar sexo por dinero.*

solicitation of murder for hire *instigación para mandar matar a otro.*
Rel: attempt, *tentativa;* conspiracy, *acuerdo para cometer un delito;* instigation, *instigación.*

solicitor (UK) n. *abogado asesor.*

Solicitor General *Procurador general.*

solitary confinement *incomunicado, en solitario.*

solvency n. *solvencia.*

sororicide n. *sororicidio.*
• The killing of one's own sister.

sound mind *cabal juicio, (en) sano juicio.*

sound and disposing mind and memory *con capacidad testamentaria, en su sano juicio.*

sources of law *fuentes del derecho.*

sovereignty n. *soberanía.* **sovereign** adj.n. *soberano.*
• "The supreme, absolute and uncontrollable power by which any independent state is governed." (2 West's Law & Commercial Dictionary in Five Languages, 553) The supreme power in a government.

sovereign immunity *inmunidad judicial del estado (o sus representantes en ejercicio de sus funciones).*

sovereign states *estados soberanos.*

specific intent *dolo específico.*

specific performance *cumplimiento forzado de la obligación contractual, cumplimiento específico* (PR).
• The equitable remedy of compelling a party to a contract to do what was promised.
Rel: specific enforcement, *ejecución forzada de la obligación contractual.*
See: cumplimiento[1].

speech[1] (talk) n. *habla, palabra.*
Rel: hesitant, *balbuciante, vacilante;* hoarse, *ronco, ronquera;* incoherent, *incoherente;* slow, *lento;* slurred, *hablar arrastradamente;* stutter, *tartamudeo.*

speech[2] (language) n. *habla, lenguaje.*

speech[3] (address) n. *discurso.*

speedy trial *juicio expedito, juicio rápido* (PR).

split custody *custodia alternada.*

split sentence *condena mixta.*

spouse n. *cónyuge.* **spousal** adj. *relativo a los esposos o cónyuges.* – Syn. better half (idiom), *media naranja.* consort, *consorte.* mate, *pareja.*

spousal abuse *maltrato de cónyuge, abuso de esposo o esposa.*

spousal rape *violación entre esposos.*

surviving spouse *cónyuge supérstite.*

spurious charge *acusación falsa.*

spy n. *espía.* **spy** v. *espiar.* **spying** *espionaje.*

squatter n. *ocupante ilegal, intruso, paracaidista* (slg.)(Mx).

ss (abbr.) *sección (en un escrito), subscripsi (firmado abajo).*

stalking *hostigamiento y acecho de una persona.*

• Putting another in fear by following or undertaking surreptitious actions aimed to harass, annoy or commit assault or battery.

stamped paper *papel sellado.*

standard of care *tipo de cuidados considerados normales y razonables.*

standard of proof *tipo de la carga de la prueba requerido (para probar un hecho o una causa).*

standing[1] PROCEDURE n. *capacidad procesal.*

• A party's legal authority to make a claim or demand enforcement of a right from a court of law. – Syn. standing to sue.

standing[2] **(permanent)** n. *permanente.* – Opp. ad hoc, *ad hoc.*

standing committee *comité permanente.*

stare decisis (lat.) [de]*doctrina de la obligatoriedad de los precedentes judiciales,* [fe]*jurisprudencia obligatoria,* [borr.]*stare decisis.*

• To abide by, or adhere to, decided cases. Doctrine that judicial decisions applying a principle of law stand as precedents to be followed in similar cases in the future.

Today stare decisis seems to have diminished in authority in the United States, judges being empowered to disregard otherwise binding decisions for what is judged good reasons. In England, in contrast, stare decisis has still formal authority.

☞ Stare decisis is a common law creation that can be found in civil law countries playing a lesser role. Although few countries in the civil world recognize stare decisis formally, most recognize the value of precedent in the development of their legal systems and have instituted informal precedent-setting mechanisms. These are usually referred to as *precedentes, ejecutorias* or *jurisprudencia.* Those that are

deemed mandatory, like the so-called *jurisprudencia obligatoria,* can be considered equivalents of stare decisis, provided we keep in mind its diminished role as a source of law.
Rel: dicta, *obiter dicta, comentarios;* precedent, *precedente judicial;* ratio decidendi, *ratio decidendi, norma individualizada;* res judicata, *res judicata, cosa juzgada.*
See: precedent.
Ref: (CA) Reference re Canada Temperance Act, [1939] 4 D.L.R. 14 at 33, 72 C.C.C. 145, [1939] O.R. 570 (C.A.), McTague J.A.; Stuart v. Bank of Montreal (1909) 41 S.C.R. 516; (US) Monongahela Street Ry. Co. v. Philadelphia Co., 39 A.2d 909, 915, 350 Pa 603.

stash n. *dinero o bienes guardados u ocultos.*

state[1] **(condition)** n. *estado.*

state of emergency *estado de emergencia.*

state of war *estado de guerra.*

state[2] INTL.LAW n. *estado.* **statesman** n. *estadista.*

stateless n. *apátrida.*

• A body politic or society of people with the purpose of promoting their safety, occupying a territory and organized under a single government.

head of state *jefe de estado.*

state action *acción de estado.*

state secret *secreto de estado.*

Rel: neutrality, *neutralidad;* protectorate, *protectorado;* recognition, *reconocimiento;* right of self-determination, *derecho de autodeterminación;* sovereignty, *soberanía;* territory, *territorio.*

state[3] CONST n. *estado.*

• A political entity that forms part of a larger national political body.

state courts *tribunales estatales.*

state law *derecho estatal.*

state's attorney *fiscal estatal.*

Rel: Province (CA), *Provincia.*

State Department(US) *Departamento de Estado.*

state of mind *estado mental.*

statement[1] **(assertion)** n. *declaración, afirmación.*

• An assertion; a recital of facts.

inconsistent statement *declaración inconsistente.*

statement of fact *declaración de hecho.*

witness statement *declaración de un testigo.*

voluntary statement *declaración voluntaria, declaración hecha en forma voluntaria.*

statement[2] CRIML.LAW n. *declaración.*

• A declaration made to the police investigators by a person suspected of involvement in a crime.

statement[3] **(balance)** n. *estado de cuenta.*

bank statement *estado de cuenta bancaria.*
statement of condition *balance general.*
– Syn. balance sheet. statement of financial condition.

statement of claim *demanda.* – Syn. declaration.

statement of confession *allanamiento del demandado.* – Syn. confession of judgment.

statement of defence (UK) n. *contestación de la demanda.*

statement of particulars *relación detallada de cargos, escrito de particulares* (PR). – Syn. bill of particulars.

status quo (lat.) *status quo, el estado de las cosas.* The situation that currently exists.

statute n. *ley, ley escrita, estatuto* (PR).
• A law duly passed and enacted by a legislature. – Syn. [brder]act of parliament (UK), *acta del parlamento].*
↪ The word statute is used to designate the legislatively created laws as opposed to court decisions or unwritten laws. In Hispanic countries, legislatively created laws or statutes are simply referred to as *leyes*, and the term *leyes escritas* is considered to be unnecessarily redundant in most cases.
In strictly legal terms, statutes in common law systems are subordinated to the grounds or reasoning of judicial decisions or legal rulings; in fact, for a statute to become part of the national law system, it needs to be reviewed and even modified by the courts when ruling on a case within the statute. In a civil law system, the duality *ley-norma individualizada* is reversed: *normas individualizadas* (that is legal rulings) are subordinated to *leyes.*

private statute *ley privativa o especial.*
– Syn. special law, *ley especial o privativa.*

statute of distribution [de]*ley de distribución de bienes de intestados.*

statute of frauds [de]*ley para la prevención de fraudes (estableciendo formalidades escritas contractuales).*

statute of limitations [de]*ley referente a los términos de prescripción,* [de]*ley de prescripción.*

statutory adj. *por ley, señalado por la ley, reglamentario.*
• Created by statute as opposed to created by common law, case law or equity.

statutory liability *responsabilidad estipulada o reglamentada en una ley.*

statutory offense *delito tipificado en una ley.*

statutory presumption *presunción legal.*

statutory rape *estupro.*

statutory remedy *recursos estipulados o reglamentados en una ley.*

statutory summary suspension *suspensión sumaria de conformidad con la ley, suspensión automática por disposición o ministerio de la ley.*

stay n. *suspensión.* **stay** v. *suspender (un procedimiento).*

extension of stay *extensión de la suspensión.*

stay by undertaking *suspensión mediante el otorgamiento de una garantía.*

stay of deportation *suspensión de la deportación.*

stay of enforcement *suspensión del cumplimiento, suspensión de la ejecución.*

stay of execution *suspensión de la ejecución.*

stay pending appeal *suspensión pendiente de apelación.*

stay of proceedings *suspensión del procedimiento.*

stenographic record *acta taquigráfica o estenográfica.* **stenographer** n. *taquígrafo, estenógrafo.*
Rel: transcript, *acta, transcripción.*

stipulation[1] (condition) n. *estipulación.*
• A representation of factual nature made in an agreement or contract as part of the same.
– Syn. proviso.
Rel: clause, *cláusula;* provision, *cláusula.*

stipulation[2] (agreement) n. *acuerdo entre las partes, estipulación* (PR).
• An agreement between parties in a court case regarding a specific point.

by way of stipulation *mediante acuerdo entre las partes, por acuerdo entre las partes.*

stipulated damages *daños convencionales.*

stock[1] (shares) n. *acciones.* **stockholders** n. *accionistas.*
• Shares in the capital stock of a company. A proportional unit of the capital of a corporation granting its holder rights to participate in corporate decisions and capital gain and losses.
– Syn. shares.
Cf: **stock • share.** Terms used synonymously and interchangeably. Stock is a mass noun, that is, an abstract concept which cannot be enumerated. Shares is a count noun, that is, it denotes things that can be individually identified and thus enumerated.

common stock *acciones comunes.*

convertible stock *acciones convertibles.*

cumulative preferred stock *acciones preferentes o preferenciales acumulativas.*

cumulative stock *acciones cumulativas.*
par value stock *acciones de valor par, acciones a la par.*
preferred stock *acciones preferentes o preferenciales.*
redeemable stock *acciones amortizables.*
stock certificate *certificado de acciones.*
stock dividend *dividendo en acciones.*
stock issue *emisión de acciones.*
stock option *opciones financieras de valores, opciones de valores.*
treasury stock *acciones de caja.*
voting stock *acciones con voto.*
watered stock *acciones de valor real reducido indebidamente.*
Rel: securities, *valores*; stock company, *sociedad por acciones.*

stock² (capital) n. *capital social.*
• Capital or funds raised by a corporation.
– Syn. capital stock.
authorized stock *capital autorizado.*
issued stock *capital emitido.*
paid up stock *capital pagado.*

stock³ (goods) n. *existencias.*
• Total amount of goods for sale or trade in a commercial business.

stock exchange *bolsa de valores.*
• An organized and established place of "business wherein the marketing of securities is conducted and accomplished." (Fratt v. Robinson, 37 A.L.R.2d 636, 637)
Rel: finance, *finanzas;* stock market, *mercado de valores.*
See: Appendix D. Stock Exchange glossary.

stolen property *bienes robados.*

stowage n. *estiba.*

stowaway n. *polizón.*

street n. *calle.*
• "A highway or public thoroughfare in an urban community, such as a city, town, or village." (Ballentine's Law Dict., 1223)
Rel: highway, *carretera, camino;* location, *ubicación.*
Glossary: alley, *callejón, callejuela;* avenue, *avenida;* block, *cuadra;* boulevard, *bulevar,* [borr;]*boulevard;* center divider/median, *arriate, refugio, sardinel, camellón* (Mx)*;* corner, *esquina;* crosswalk, *cruce de peatones, vía de peatones, zona peatonal;* intersection, *crucero, bocacalle, intersección* (Mx)*;* lane, *carril, senda, vía, canal* (Sp)*;* one-way street, *calle de un solo sentido* (Mx)*, una vía* (Cu)*, una sola dirección* (PR)*;* sidewalk, *acera, andén, banqueta* (Mx)*;* two-way street, *calle de doble sentido* (Mx)*, de doble vía* (Cu)*, de doble dirección* (PR)*.*

strict liability *responsabilidad objetiva.*
• Liability without fault. "Liability for an injury resulting to another where no account is taken of the standard of care exercised." (Ballentine's Law Dict., 7) – Syn. liability without fault. absolute liability.
strict liability crimes *delitos de responsabilidad objetiva.*
strict liability statute *ley basada en el principio de la responsabilidad objetiva.*

strike (work stoppage) n. *huelga.* **striker** n. *huelguista.*
• The action of a substantial number of employees in a workplace to stop working for an employer until their demands for better terms of employment are considered.
Cf: **strike ● work stoppage ● walkout ● lockout.**
As distinguished from strike, which is a widespread and organized movement stopping or slowing down work, work stoppage and walkout are equivalent terms that mean a more informal, often spontaneous plan to stop working. A lockout, on the other hand, is a denial of employment by an employer as a means to coerce workers to accept work conditions.
general strike *huelga general.*
no strike clause *cláusula de prohibición de huelga.*
right to strike *derecho de huelga.*
sit down strike *huelga de brazos caídos.*
strike-breaker *esquirol, rompehuelgas.*
– Syn. scab.
sympathy strike *huelga de solidaridad.*
wildcat strike *huelga desautorizada.*
Rel: lockout, *paro patronal;* picketing, *instalar piquetes de trabajadores en huelga en el lugar de trabajo;* slowdown, *trabajar lentamente en forma intencional (como táctica de presión laboral);* walkout, *paro.*

strike¹ (invalidate) v. *invalidar, cancelar.* **struck** *cancelado, invalidado.* **stricken** *téngase por no hecha, cancélese.*
bond forfeiture be stricken *téngase por invalidada la violación de las condiciones de la fianza, téngase por revocada la pérdida de la fianza.*
motion to strike *petición pidiendo se invalide (una actuación o diligencia).*
to strike down *cancelar, invalidar, tenerse por no hecha.*
strike² (remove) v. *tachar, testar.*

strike a juror *tachar o deshabilitar a un jurado.*

strike from the record *dése por no sentado en el acta.*

strike[3] **(declare)** v. *emplazar a huelga.*

strike suit *juicio superfluo (entablado con la finalidad de obtener beneficios para su promovente).*

sublease n. *subarriendo, sublocación.*
– Syn. sublet.

subpoena n. *citación judicial, citatorio.*
• A writ issued by a court ordering the appearance of a witness, disobedience of which may be punishable as contempt of court.
alias subpoena *repetición de una citación.*
subpoena ad testificandum *citación de un testigo.*
subpoena duces tecum *citación para la presentación de documentos, libros o registros; requerimiento judicial de la entrega de documentos, libros o registros.*
Rel: summons, *emplazamiento.*

subrogation n. *subrogación.* **subrogee** n. *subrogatario.* **subrogor** n. *subrogante.*
• The substitution of one party for another regarding a claim or debt against a third party.
conventional subrogation *subrogación convencional.*
legal subrogation *subrogación legal.*

subsidy n. *subsidio, subvención.*
• A grant by the government to a business or other entity considered desirable as a matter of public policy.
subsidies and countervailing duties *subsidios y aranceles compensatorios.*

substantive law *derecho sustantivo.*

substitution of counsel *substitución de abogado.*

substitution of parties *substitución de una o varias de las partes.*

substitution of judge *recusación de un juez, substitución de un juez.* – Abbr. SOJ.

succession[1] **(hereditament)** n. *sucesión.* **successor** n. *sucesor.*
• The acquisition of property or rights upon the death of a decedent through descent or will. Succession is frequently defined by statute as the acquisition of title to the property of someone who dies without leaving a will.
hereditary succession *sucesión hereditaria.*
intestate succession *sucesión intestada, intestado.*

line of succession *línea de sucesión.*
testamentary succession *sucesión testamentaria.*
succession tax *impuesto sucesorio.*
Rel: estate, *patrimonio hereditario;* intestacy, *intestado;* probate, *procedimiento testamentario, sucesión.*

succession[2] **(replacement)** n. *sucesión.*
• A person who assumes the place of another, taking his or her place in relation to office, property or the like.
successor in interest *sucesor.*

sufferance n. *consentimiento por omisión, consentimiento tácito.*
• To consent or tolerate passively.
See: omission.

suicide n. *suicidio.* **suicidal** adj. *suicida.*
– Syn. self-killing, *matarse, morir por su propia mano.*
aiding suicide *auxilio o inducción al suicidio, incitación al suicidio.*
commit suicide *cometer suicidio.* – Syn. blow one's brains out, *volarse la tapa de los sesos.* take one's life, *quitarse la vida.*

sui generis (lat.) *sui generis, de su propio género o especie.* Of its own kind or class.

suit (court proceedings) n. *juicio, acción, procedimiento judicial.* **sue** v. *demandar.*
• Generally, any proceeding before a court in which a person pursues the remedy that the law affords. – Syn. lawsuit.
Cf: **action ● action at law ● suit.** The term suit was used to designate a proceeding in equity only, to be distinguished from an action at law. Today the term action includes both designations, although sometimes suit is still referred to as an equitable action. It is also to be noted that suit, like lawsuit, is rarely used in criminal cases.
class suit *acción colectiva, acción en beneficio de un grupo de personas.* – Syn. class action.
suit in equity *acción en equidad, acción bajo el derecho-equidad.*
Rel: nonsuit, *sobreseimiento, caducidad.*

summary n. *resumen.*

summary adj. *sumario.*
• Short, concise. Without all the steps or formalities; presented in condensed form.
summary conviction CRIML.LAW *sentencia condenatoria por delito menor en procedimiento sumario.*
summary conviction offence (CA) *delito menor, [le]delito de procedimiento sumario.*

summary judgment *sentencia dictada sumariamente.*

summary trial *procedimiento sumario (normalmente sin jurado).* – Syn. summary proceeding.

summary jury trial [de]*juicio abreviado ante un jurado informal.*
• An abbreviated trial as a form of alternative dispute resolution before a neutral third party who may issue an advisory opinion as a means to settle the case. – Syn. minitrial.

summons n. *emplazamiento.* **summonee** n. *emplazado.*
• Notice served on a party, advising an action has been commenced against him or her in a court, requiring that an appearance be filed. "The writ [of summons] includes only enough information to apprise the defendant of the nature of the action. It is unlike the earlier, strict forms of action, which required a plaintiff to choose the form correctly or face dismissal. The writ is a command in the name of the sovereign to enter an appearance before the court. The 'appearance' is accomplished by sending an acknowledgment of service to the court office which issued the writ." (Glendon, Gordon & Carozza, 237)
alias summons *repetición del emplazamiento, segundo emplazamiento.*
Rel: notification to appear, *notificación de comparecencia;* order to appear, *orden de comparecencia.*

supersede v. *invalidar, reemplazar.*

supersedeas (lat.) [borr.]*supersedeas, suspensión de un procedimiento o de la ejecución de una sentencia.* You shall forbear. – Syn. writ of supersedeas.

supervening cause (tort) *causa superveniente, causa posterior.* – Syn. intervening cause.
Rel: proximate cause, *causa directa o inmediata;* superseding cause, *causa excluyente (de responsabilidad).*

support[1] (assistance) n. *alimentos, pensión alimenticia.* **support obligor** *acreedor alimentario o alimenticio.* **support obligee** *deudor alimentario o alimenticio.*
• A source or means of living, which includes, in a broad sense, all means necessary for comfortable living.
Cf: **support • maintenance.** Both terms are synonymous and mean financial assistance or allowance given by one person to another. While support is considered broader and is usually preferred, maintenance is more often used when associated with alimony.

child support *pensión alimenticia o alimentos para un menor.*
support agreement *convenio de pensión alimenticia.*
support obligation *obligación alimenticia.*
support order *orden de pensión alimenticia.*
support payments *pago de pensión alimenticia, alimentos.*
support payor *retenedor de una pensión alimenticia.*
Rel: alimony, *alimentos (entre esposos);* non-support, *falta de pago de la pensión alimenticia.*

support[2] (construction) n. *apoyo, sustentación (de una construcción).*
• Right to have one's land held firm by the land surrounding or that lies underneath it.
lateral support *apoyo o sustentación lateral.*
right to support *derecho de sustentación de una construcción.*
subjacent support *apoyo subyacente o subterráneo.*

support[3] (assist) n. *ayuda, base.*
give support *dar apoyo, brindar apoyo.*
support group *grupo de apoyo.*

supporting documents *documentos comprobatorios.*

suppression of evidence *deshechamiento o improcedencia de la prueba.*

suppression hearing [de]*audiencia de deshechamiento o improcedencia de pruebas, audiencia de desestimación* (PR).
• A hearing requesting that certain evidence be excluded from a criminal trial on the grounds that it was illegally obtained.
Rel: motion to suppress, *petición de que no se admita la prueba, moción de supresión de evidencia* (PR).

Supreme Court *Suprema Corte de Justicia* (DR, Mx, Ur), *Corte Suprema de Justicia* (Ar,Bo,Ch, Co,CR,Gu,Ho,Ec,Ni,Pa,Pe,Py,El), *Tribunal Supremo* (Sp,PR), *Tribunal Supremo de Justicia* (Ve), *Tribunal Supremo Popular* (Cu).

surcharge n. *recargo.*

suretyship n. *fianza, garantía.* **surety** n. *fiador, garante.* **obligee** n. *acreedor.* **principal** n. *obligado principal.*
• A contractual relationship in which a person contracts to answer for the debt or default of another.
Cf: **suretyship • insurance • fidelity bond.**

Suretyship is a financial guarantee under which the surety will pay, subject to reimbursement, if the principal fails to perform its obligation. An insurer spreads the risk of losses over the population exposed to them. The insurer expects that a certain percentage of its insureds will suffer a loss during the policy period and sets premiums accordingly. Fidelity bonds are really insurance against loss through certain types of dishonesty; the premiums are based on the insured's type of business, financial performance, internal controls and other similar relevant factors.

suretyship and guaranty *garantía que responde en forma subsidiaria y solidaria.*
suretyship bond *certificado de fianza.*
See: bond.

surrender[1] PROP.LAW n. [de]*transferir derechos sobre inmuebles (para reunificar el derecho de propiedad).*
• The delivery of possession to an owner in remainder or reversion in response to a demand to consolidate the estate.
Rel: remainder, *derecho residual;* reversion, [borr.]*reversión.*

surrender[2] (giving up) n. *abandono, renuncia.*
surrender v. *abandonar, renunciar.*
surrenderee n. *persona a favor de quien se renuncia.* **surrenderer** n. *renunciante.*
• The giving up of a right or claim. – Syn. release.
final and irrevocable surrender for purposes of adoption *renuncia definitiva e irrevocable en un procedimiento de adopción.*
surrender clause INSURANCE *cláusula de rescate de primas de seguro.*
surrender of an unborn child *renuncia a los derechos de un niño concebido sin nacer.*
surrender value INSURANCE *valor de rescate de una póliza de seguro de vida.*

surrender[3] (capitulation) n. *rendición.* – Syn. capitulation, *capitulación.* submission, *sumisión.*
surrender of a criminal *entregarse un delincuente.*

surrogate adj. *sustituto.*
surveillance n. *vigilancia.*
Rel: wiretapping, *intercepción de una comunicación telefónica.*
surviving spouse *cónyuge sobreviviente, cónyuge supérstite.*
suspension n. *suspensión.*
• A temporary delay, interruption or cessation.
statutory summary suspension *suspensión*

sumaria por ministerio de ley, suspensión automática por disposición o ministerio de la ley.
suspended license *licencia suspendida.*
suspended sentence *condena suspendida.*
suspension order *orden de suspensión.*
suspicion n. *sospecha.* **suspect** n. *sospechoso.*
arouse suspicion *despertó sospechas.*
under suspicion *bajo sospecha.*
sustain v. *ha lugar, aprobar.*
sustain an objection *ha lugar la objeción, procede la objeción.*
swear v. *jurar.*
being duly sworn *habiendo prestado juramento debidamente.*
solemnly swear *jurar solemnemente.*
swearing in *prestar juramento.*
sworn affidavit *declaración jurada extrajudicial.*
sworn statement *declaración jurada.*
Rel: affirm, *protestar;* oath, *juramento.*
swindle n. *estafa, fraude.* **swindler** n. *estafador, timador.*
Rel: cheat, *engañar;* fraud, *fraude;* trickery, *trampa, embuste.*
sympathy strike *huelga de solidaridad.*
syndicate n. *sindicación, asociación o consorcio.*
• A group of individuals or entities organized to pursue a common purpose.
criminal syndicate *sindicación criminal, asociación de delincuentes.*
syndicated gambling *juego prohibido organizado, juego ilegal organizado.*
syndicated loan *préstamo sindicado.*

TTTT

take the Fifth (US) *acogerse a la Quinta enmienda (constitucional).*
take the stand *testificar, atestiguar.*
take-home pay *salario neto.*
tamper v. *manipular, alterar, adulterar.*
tamper with a commercial product *alterar o adulterar un producto comercial.*
tamper with food, drugs or cosmetics *alterar o adulterar comida, medicinas o cosméticos, corrupción de alimentos o medicinas* (Co).
tampering with the jury *intento de sobornar o cohechar a un jurado.*
tariff[1] (tax schedule) n. *tarifa arancelaria.*
• Schedule of articles on which a duty is imposed at the time of importation, including

applicable tax rates.

antidumping tariff *tarifa compensatoria.*

preferential tariffs *tarifas preferenciales.*

protective tariff *tarifa proteccionista.*

revenue tariff *tarifa recaudatoria.*

tariff² ᴛᴀx n. *arancel, impuesto de importación o exportación.* – Syn. customs duty.

tariff³ (service charge) n. *tarifa.*

tax n. *impuesto, contribución* (PR). **tax** v. *gravar, establecer un impuesto.* **taxpayer** n. *causante.* **taxable** adj. *gravable, imponible.* **taxable** adv. *gravablemente.*

• A charge, usually in money, imposed by a legislative authority on persons, entities or property to fund public purposes. – Syn. duty. exaction. impost. tax charge.

Cf: **tax ● levy ● duty.** These similar terms are often used interchangeably. Tax is the most general and widely used term, while levy refers more to the act of imposing taxes, that is, declaring the subject and rate of amount of tax ation. Duty, on the other hand, usually refers to taxes levied on commodities or transactions; in this sense duties are primarily imposed on goods as opposed to persons.

↝ Spanish-speaking countries usually use two different terms to refer to taxes: *tributo* and *impuesto. Tributo* is considered a generic term that includes *impuestos* and other tax-related charges, while *impuesto* is a specific term that refers to traditional tax payments made by tax payers to fund general public expenses.

assessment of tax *determinación del impuesto, determinación de la contribución* (PR).

estate tax *impuesto hereditario.*

excise tax *impuestos interiores, impuesto sobre artículos de uso y consumo.*

gift tax *impuesto sobre donaciones.*

income tax *impuesto sobre el ingreso, impuesto sobre la renta, contribución sobre ingresos* (PR).

property tax *impuesto predial.*

sales tax *impuesto sobre ventas.*

tax court *tribunal fiscal, tribunal tributario.*

tax evasion *evasión fiscal, evasión de impuestos.* – Syn. tax fraud.

tax law *derecho fiscal.*

tax refund *devolución o reembolso de impuestos, reintegro de contribuciones* (PR).

tax return *declaración de impuestos, planilla para la declaración* (PR.Ve).

Rel: basis, *base;* deduction, *deducción;* expense, *gasto;* income, *ingreso;* return, *declaración.*

See: income tax. *tributo.* Appendix E. Tax law glossary.

tax procedure *procedimiento fiscal.*

Glossary: administrative appeal, *apelación contencioso-administrativa;* assessment of deficiency, *determinación del saldo fiscal a deber o déficit fiscal;* delinquent penalty, *multa por mora, multa moratoria;* demand for payment, *intimación de pago, pedir pago;* fraudulent return, *declaración fraudulenta;* frivolous return, *declaración de impuestos incorrecta o inapropiada;* levy, *imposición de un impuesto;* notice of assessment, *notificación de crédito fiscal a pagar;* penalties, *multas;* protest, *protesto;* settlement, *acuerdo o arreglo fiscal;* summons power, *facultad de pedir testimonio, documentos o récords;* tax audit, *auditoría fiscal;* tax avoidance, *elusión impositiva;* tax collection, *cobro de impuestos;* tax evasion, *evasión de impuestos;* tax fraud, *fraude fiscal;* tax investigation, *investigación fiscal;* tax lien, *gravamen fiscal;* tax refund, *devolución de impuestos;* willful failure to file or pay, *no declarar o pagar impuestos en forma dolosa o intencional.*

telephone harassment *hostigamiento mediante llamadas telefónicas, intrusión en la tranquilidad personal* (PR).

temporary adj. *temporal, provisional, momentáneo.* – Syn. interim, *ínterin.* provisional, *provisional.* short-lived, *de corta duración.* transitory, *transitorio.*

temporary alimony *alimentos provisionales, pensión alimenticia provisional (entre esposos).*

temporary custody *custodia temporal.*

temporary disability *invalidez temporal.*

temporary insanity [brder][de]*demencia temporal, enajenación mental transitoria.*

temporary relief *medidas temporales o precautorias.*

tenancy n. *tenencia,* [de]*tenencia u ocupación de un inmueble (por derecho).*

• Holding or possessing lands or tenements by right or title.

Tenancy means "a tenant's right to possess or occupy an estate, whether by lease or by title, derived from the Latin 'tenere' meaning 'to hold.' Tenancy refers generally to any such right to hold property, but in a more limited sense it refers to holding in subordination to another's title, as in the landlord-tenant relationship." (Gifis, 508)

joint tenancy *copropiedad (con derecho de sobrevivencia).*

month-to-month tenancy *tenencia mensual, tenencia de mes a mes,*[nrwer]*arrendamiento renovable mensualmente.*

periodic tenancy *tenencia por periodos, tenencia renovada periódicamente.* – Syn. tenancy from period to period.

several tenancy *tenencia individual (en contraste con tenencia colectiva).*

tenancy at sufferance *tácita reconducción de un arrendamiento.* – Syn. holdover tenancy.

tenancy at will *tenencia por tiempo indeterminado,*[nrwer]*arrendamiento por tiempo indeterminado.*

tenancy by the entireties *sociedad conyugal, tenencia en copropiedad con derecho de sobrevivencia entre cónyuges.* – Syn. tenancy by the entirety.

tenancy for years *tenencia por tiempo determinado.* – Syn. estate for years. term of years.

tenancy in common *copropiedad (sin derecho de sobrevivencia).*

tenancy in partnership *bienes comunes en sociedad comanditada.*
Rel: lease, *arrendamiento;* possession, *posesión.*
See: estate[3].

tenant n. *inquilino, arrendatario.*
  objectionable tenant *inquilino indeseable.*
  tenant for life *inquilino vitalicio, usufructuario.*

tender[1] (offer) n. *ofrecimiento de pago o cumplimiento.* **tender** v. *ofrecer.*
  legal tender (bid) *postura legal.*

tender[2] (payment) n. *pago.*
  legal tender *pago legal, moneda de curso legal.*

term[1] (period) n. *duración.*
  • A period of time.
  term of imprisonment *duración de la pena de prisión.*
  term of lease *duración del contrato de arrendamiento.*
  term of office *duración del nombramiento.*

term[2] (provision) n. *condición, término.*
  • A stipulation part of an agreement.
  fundamental term CONTRACTS *elemento esencial.*
  implied term *condición tácita o implícita.*

term[3] (jargon) n. *término.*
  • A word or expression that has a specific meaning in a particular field.
  term considered served CRIML.PROCED *se da por cumplida la pena de prisión, se tiene por cumplida la pena de prisión.* – Abbr. TCS.

termination n. *terminación.* – Syn. cessation, *cesación.* expiration, *expiración.*

termination of contract *terminación de contrato.*

termination of employment *terminación de la relación de trabajo o del contrato de trabajo.*

termination of lease *terminación del arrendamiento.*

terms n. *términos, condiciones.*
  terms of payment *términos o condiciones de pago.*
  terms of sale *términos o condiciones de venta.*
  terms of shipment *términos o condiciones de embarque.*

terms of art *términos técnicos.*
  • Words having specific, precise meanings in a given specialty. <and his heirs> <replevin>
  – Syn. words of art.
  See: jargon.

territory (land area) n. *territorio.* **territorial** adj. *territorial.*
  territorial conflict *conflicto territorial.*
  territorial jurisdiction *jurisdicción territorial, competencia territorial.*
  territorial sovereignty *soberanía territorial.*
  territorial waters *aguas territoriales.*
  Rel: border, *frontera;* protectorate, *protectorado.*

terrorism n. *terrorismo.* **terrorist** n.adj. *terrorista.*
  • "The use or threat of violence to intimidate or cause panic, esp. as a means of affecting political conduct." (Black's Law Dict., 8th. ed., 1512)
  domestic terrorism *terrorismo nacional.*
  international terrorism *terrorismo internacional.*
  terrorist activity *actividades terroristas.*
  terrorist attack *ataque terrorista.*
  terrorist threat *amenaza terrorista.*
  Rel: airport security, *seguridad en aeropuertos;* counterterrorism, *antiterrorismo;* deterrence, *disuasión;* hostage-taking, *toma de rehenes;* separatist movement, *movimiento separatista;* skyjacking, *secuestro aéreo, secuestro de aeronave;* suicide bombing, *atentado suicida.*

test[1] (legal) n. *adecuación de la regla (de derecho) a los hechos.*
  legal test *comprobación de una figura jurídica (específica).*

test[2] (medical) n. *prueba, análisis, examen.*
  blood test *análisis de la sangre.*
  breathalyzer test *prueba del analizador de aliento.*
  urine test *análisis de la orina.*
  See: drug tests. sobriety tests.

testament n. *testamento.* **testator** n. *testador.*

testatrix n. *testadora.* **testamentary** adj. *testamentario.*
• The disposition of personal property by will. – Syn. will.
The term testament is seldom used now; will is preferred since it relates to both personal and real property, unlike testament, which has been traditionally associated with personal property only.
testamentary capacity *capacidad para testar.*
testamentary executor *albacea.*
testamentary gift *donación testamentaria.*
testamentary heir *heredero testamentario.*
testamentary proceeding *juicio testamentario.*
testamentary succession *sucesión testamentaria.*
testamentary trust *fideicomiso testamentario.* See: will[1].
testimony n. *testimonio.* **testify** v. *testificar.*
• Evidence given by a witness under oath or affirmation at trial or in a deposition or affidavit.
expert testimony *peritaje.*
false testimony *testimonio falso.*
impeachment of a testimony *desvirtuar o tachar un testimonio, impugnación de un testimonio.*
incompetent testimony *testimonio de una persona no competente.*
perjured testimony *declararse con falsedad, testimonio declarado falsamente.*
Rel: deposition, *testimonio extrajudicial;* examination, *examen testimonial, examen oral de un testigo;* witness, *testigo.*
theft n. *hurto, robo* (Mx). **thief** n. *ladrón.*
• The taking of property without the owner's consent with the intent to deprive the owner of its use. – Syn. [nrwer]larceny.
identity theft *robo de identidad.*
theft by deception *hurto mediante engaño.*
theft by false pretenses *hurto mediante estafa.*
theft of services [le]*robo de servicios.*
Rel: burglary, *robo de casa habitada;* looting, *saqueo;* purse snatching, *arrebatar un bolso o bolsa;* robbery, *robo con violencia;* shoplifting, *hurto de mercancía en una tienda o almacén;* shortchange artist, *timador usando el cambio (de dinero);* stealing, *robar, hurtar.*
See: larceny.
thereafter adv. *en adelante, de allí en adelante.*
thereof adv. *del mismo, de los mismos, de eso, de esto.*
thereupon adv. *acto seguido, seguidamente.*

third degree *interrogatorio causándole mal (al interrogado), interrogatorio con "mano dura."*
third party n.adj. *terceros.*
third party beneficiary *tercero beneficiado.*
third party complaint *tercería.*
third party defendant *tercero demandado.*
third party liability *responsabilidad de tercero.*
third party plaintiff *demandante promoviendo tercería.*
Rel: privity, *relación jurídica (entre partes).*
threat n. *amenaza.* **threaten** v. *amenazar.*
– Syn. menace, *amenaza.*
Rel: coercion, *coerción;* intimidation, *intimidación.*
time sharing PROP.LAW *tiempo compartido.*
– Syn. interval ownership.
tip off *informar confidencialmente,* [exp.léxica] *dar un tip.*
title[1] (right) n. *derecho de propiedad, título de propiedad, titularidad.*
• The label used for the bundle of rights in property that is commonly called ownership; a person's right of ownership. – Syn. ownership, *propiedad.*
perfect title *título válido y legítimo.*
title by adverse possession *adquisición del derecho de propiedad mediante posesión prescriptiva.*
title by prescription *adquisición del derecho de propiedad mediante prescripción.*
title insurance *seguro que garantiza la legitimidad y validez del derecho de propiedad.*
title search *verificación de la legalidad de un título.*
title[2] (document) n. *título de propiedad, título.*
• The written document evidencing ownership in land.
abstract of title *resumen de los antecedentes de un título de propiedad, compendio de los antecedentes de la propiedad, estudio de título* (PR). – Syn. brief.
chain of title *antecedentes del título de propiedad de un inmueble, cadena de títulos* (PR).
clear title *título de propiedad libre de gravámenes.*
cloud on title *defecto o irregularidad del título de propiedad de un inmueble, título turbio* (PR).
color of title *apariencia de legitimidad de un título de propiedad, título colorado* (PR).
title deed *escritura de propiedad.*
Rel: deed, *escritura o instrumento traslativo de derechos sobre inmuebles;* registry, *registro.*

title³ (distinction) n. *título.*
• Designation given as a sign of privilege, distinction or profession.

tort n. [fe]*responsabilidad civil, responsabilidad civil extracontractual.* [borr.]*responsabilidad civil delictual.* [lexical exp.]*responsabilidad civil torticera* (PR). [borr.]*tort.* **tortfeasor/tort-feasor** *responsable de un ilícito civil.* **tortious** adj. *afectado de ilicitud civil, torticero* (PR).
• A wrongful act other than a breach of contract that injures another and for which the law imposes civil liability, usually in the form of damages. – Syn. delictual liability.
Cf: **tort ● social security ● crime.** The law of tort aims to compensate victims of the commission of a wrong by entitling them to redress usually in the form of damages. "Social security affords a broader protection. It concerns only persons, not goods. But it protects them against all damage suffered whether as the result of mere sickness or of someone else's wrongful conduct. It even goes beyond damage in the normal sense of the word: it protects persons against lack of resources due to unemployment or old age. It is based on solidarity between men in a given society." (10 International Encyclopedia of Comparative Law. Torts, Part I, 19, 14) In contrast, "[t]he direct purpose in a criminal action is to inflict a sanction on someone who has committed a breach of the law, or to take some safety measures in respect to him." (10 International Encyclopedia of Comparative Law. Torts, Part I, 50, 30)
➥ It is generally acknowledged now that tort cannot be translated as *delitos y cuasidelitos* (delict and quasidelict) or its modern equivalent *actos ilícitos* (unlawful acts), since some torts or civil liabilities flow from acts or actions that are perfectly lawful. *Responsabilidad civil*, being broader, or *responsabilidad civil extracontractual*, being somewhat more precise, are usually preferred. The term *responsabilidad civil delictual*, on the other hand, is a direct borrowing from French doctrine and case law, which has not taken root in the Spanish-speaking legal systems.
It is important to keep in mind that while the common law system of torts has developed a number of specific torts, the civil law system is built around a general clause describing torts in a general and abstract form. As a result, torts are not specifically labeled in Hispanic countries, unlike torts in English-speaking jurisdictions.

intentional tort *responsabilidad civil incurrida en forma intencional.*

non-intentional tort *responsabilidad civil incurrida en forma no intencional.*

personal tort *responsabilidad civil causada por daño o lesión a una persona.*

strict tort liability *responsabilidad civil objetiva.*

tortious act *acto constitutivo del ilícito civil, acto torticero* (PR).

Specific types: assault and battery, *lesiones, agresión;* conversion, *apropiación ilícita;* deceit, *engaño;* defamation, *difamación;* false imprisonment, *privación ilegal de la libertad;* infliction of emotional distress, *aflicción emocional;* invasion of privacy, *violación del derecho de privacía, atentados a la vida privada;* libel, *difamación escrita;* malicious prosecution, *ejercicio de una acción penal improcedente con un propósito indebido o ilícito;* negligence, *negligencia, culpa, imprudencia;* product liability, *responsabilidad civil del fabricante, responsabilidad del producto;* slander, *difamación oral;* trespass, *violación de derechos, usurpación.*

Rel: damages, *daños y perjuicios;* fault, *culpa;* strict liability, *responsabilidad objetiva.*

Comment: "Both the law of contract and the law of tort entitle people to claim compensation for harm they have suffered. The law of contract does so only in a rather limited area, where the plaintiff has been disappointed in his justifiable expectation that the defendant would honor his promise. But citizens have many other interests and the law of tort deals with the cases where they have been infringed, where the plaintiff's health has been impaired, his reputation besmirched, his land adversely affected, his goods damaged, or where he has suffered some other economic loss." (Zweigert & Kotz, 596-97)
Ref: (CA) Lawson v Wellesley Hospital (1976) 9 OR (2d) 677 at 681 (Ont. CA); (US) Bennett v. Vennie, Pa., 21 Monroe L.R. 38; Hayes v. Massachussetts Mut. Life Ins. Co., 18 N.E. 322, 325, 125 Ill. 626, 1 L.R.A. 303; (UK) 45(2) Halsbury's Laws para 301.

torture n. *tortura.* – Syn. torment, *tormento.*

totality of the circumstances test *tomando en cuenta la totalidad de las circunstancias.*

trade n. *comercio.*

   in the ordinary course of trade *en el curso ordinario del comercio.*

   stock in trade *inventario de existencias.*

   trade barrier *barrera comercial.*

   trade discount *descuento comercial.*

   unfair trade *competencia desleal.*

trade name n. *nombre comercial.*

trade secrets *secretos comerciales, secretos industriales.*
Rel: nondisclosure or confidentiality agreement, *contrato de confidencialidad.*

trade union *sindicato.*
See: union.

trademark n. *marca, marca comercial.*
• A word, mark, logo, symbol or device used by a manufacturer or seller to identify a product in the marketplace and to distinguish it from products manufactured or sold by others. – Syn. mark.
certification mark *marca de certificación (de origen, calidad u otra característica).*
collective mark *marca colectiva.*
service mark *marca de servicios.*
Rel: distinctiveness, *ser distintivo, ser carácterístico;* infringement, *violación (de un derecho).*

traffic n. *tráfico.*
traffic court *tribunal de tráfico.*
traffic light *semáforo, luz de tráfico.*
traffic signs *señales de tráfico.*
traffic stop *alto, señal de alto, pare* (Sp).
traffic ticket *boleta o infracción de tráfico,* [borr.]*tickete.*
Rel: driver's license, *licencia de conducir;* road rage, *ira causada por el tráfico, cólera de automovilista.*

traffic accident *accidente de tráfico, accidente de tránsito.*
scene of a traffic accident *lugar de un accidente de tráfico.*
traffic accident report *reporte de un accidente de tráfico.*
Rel: collision, *colisión;* hit and run, *chocar y darse a la fuga, chocar y huir.*
Glossary: back up, *retroceder, ir en reversa, dar marcha atrás;* blind spot, *punto ciego, zona muerta;* blowout, *ponchadura, pinchazo, reventón;* broadside, *chocar de costado, chocar de un lado;* bus, *autobús, bus, ómnibus, camión, chiva* (Co), *guagua* (Cu); crash, *choque;* fender-bender, *choque ligero, un golpe de nada;* flat tire, *llanta ponchada, neumático pinchado, llanta desinflada;* head-on collision, *choque de frente;* rear-end collision, *choque por detrás;* sideswipe, *raspar lateralmente;* skid marks, *huellas de frenazo o patinazo;* skidding, *derrapar, patinar;* slam on the breaks, *dar un frenón o enfrenón, dar un frenazo;* spin out, *dar vueltas, hacer un trompo;* swerve, *desviarse, virar bruscamente;* tailgate, *seguir muy de cerca, no guardar su distancia;* traffic jam, *embotellamiento, con-*

gestionamiento; van, *camioneta, microbús, troca;* yield, *ceder el paso, dar el paso;* zigzag, *zigzaguear.*

traffic violations *infracciones de tráfico.*
moving traffic violations *infracciónes de tráfico (al conducir o manejar), infracciónes de circulación (de tráfico).*
parking traffic violations *infracciones de tráfico al estacionarse, infracciones de estacionamiento (de vehículos).*

trafficking in cannabis *tráfico de canabis.*

trafficking in illegal drugs *tráfico de drogas ilegales.*

trafficking in stolen property *comercio ilegal de bienes hurtados o robados.*

transcript n. *transcripción, copia o acta oficial.*
transcript on appeal *acta oficial de lo actuado para efectos de apelación.*
Rel: court reporter, *taquígrafo judicial, transcripcionista o taquimecanógrafo judicial.*

transfer n. *transmisión, transferencia.* **transfer** v. *transmitir, transferir.* **transferee** n. *recipiente.* **transferor** n. *transmisor.*
• The broadest term to describe any form of disposing of an asset or an interest in it.
transfer in contemplation of death *donación mortis causa.* – Syn. gift causa mortis.
transfer in fraud of creditors *enajenación en fraude de acreedores.*
transfer of property *transmisión de propiedad.*
transfer payments *redistribución de la percepción fiscal, redistribución fiscal del ingreso, pagos de transferencia fiscal.*
transfer tax *impuesto sobre la transmisión.*
Rel: assignment, *cesión;* conveyance, *transmisión de la propiedad inmueble;* gift, *donación.*

transgression n. *transgresión.* **transgressor** n. *transgresor.*

transient adj. *transeúnte, itinerante, sin residencia fija.*
transient merchant *comerciante ambulante.*

translation n. *traducción.* **translator** n. *traductor.* **translate** v. *traducir.*
legal translation *traducción legal.*
literal translation *traducción literal.* – Syn. verbatim translation.
literary translation *traducción literaria.*
medical translation *traducción médica.*
Rel: interpretation, *interpretación;* original text, *texto de partida, texto original;* target text, *texto de llegada, texto final.*

transmission of HIV *transmisión de SIDA.*

treason

treason (crime) n. *traición*. **traitor** n. *traidor*.
treasonable adj. *traidor, traicionero*.
• Crime consisting of adhering to the enemy
and rendering the enemy "aid and comfort."
(U.S. Constitution, Article III § 3) – Syn. high
treason, *alta traición*.
Rel: sedition, *atentados contra la autoridad*.
Ref: (US) 18 U.S.C.A.§2381.

treaty n. *tratado*.
• "A written international agreement concluded between states or other subjects of international law, governed by international law,
whether embodied in a single instrument or in
two or more related instruments and whatever
its particular designation." (Bledsoe & Boczec,
(279) at 271) – Syn. convention, *convención*.
pact, *pacto*.
Cf: **treaty ● convention ● pact ● executive agreement.** A treaty is the most formal type of agreement between nations. A convention or pact is
usually less formal and important. Executive
agreement refers to an agreement entered by
the President of the United States, without the
Senate's ratification, and another nation. An
executive agreement is also often confusingly
labeled a pact, protocol or treaty.
accession to a treaty *accesión a un tratado*.
commercial treaty *tratado comercial*.
extradition treaty *tratado de extradición*.
invalidity of a treaty *invalidez de un tratado*.
peace treaty *tratado de paz*.
Rel: adoption, *suscribir o ser parte (de un tratado);* entry into force, *entrada en vigor;* ratification, *ratificación;* registration, *registro;*
reservation, *reserva*.
Ref: (Int) Vienna Convention on the Law of Treaties;
(UK) 18(2) Halsbury's Laws para 655; (US) Louis
Wolf & Co. v. United States, Cust. & Pat. App., 107
F.2d 819, 827.

trespass[1] (injury) n. [de]*violación de derechos
(que causan daños y perjuicios)*. **trespasser** n.
*persona que viola derechos (resultando en
daños y perjuicios)*.
• The commission of an unlawful act against
another's property or person. – Syn. intrusion,
intrusión.
constructive trespass *violación de derechos
por determinación de la ley*.
willful and deliberate trespass *violación de
derechos en forma deliberada e intencional*.
Rel: encroach, *penetrar, acceder;* infringe,
infringir.

trespass[2] (wrongful entry) n. [de]*entrar u ocupar
una propiedad ajena sin autorización*.

trespasser n. *ocupante indebido de una propiedad, transgresor* (PR).
• An unauthorized interference with the possession and use of real property. – Syn. trespass to
land, *entrar u ocupar un inmueble sin derecho*.
criminal trespass *entrar o permanecer ilegalmente en una propiedad (infringiendo una disposición penal), entrada ilegal* (PR).
forcible trespass *apoderamiento de un bien
mueble sin derecho mediante intimidación*.
Rel: invitee, *invitado;* licensee, *con permiso (de
entrar o estar en el lugar)*.

trespass[3] (action) n. *acción de daños y perjuicios*.
trespass on the case (hist.)(common law) *acción
de daños y perjuicios causados en forma indirecta*.

trial n. *juicio, proceso*.
• A judicial examination of a cause deciding
legal claims before a court with jurisdiction
over the matter.
Cf: **trial ● case ● cause.** While all three terms refer to litigated actions, trial emphasizes the examination and resolution of the controversy,
case usually underlines the view of a set of
facts and the corresponding conclusion of law,
and cause implies the entire judicial proceeding. Cause is synonymous with suit.
⊷ The trial in common law systems has become "an event" in the sense that is necessary
to bring a group of ordinary citizens—the
jury—to hear the testimony of the witnesses
and observe the evidence, find the facts, and
apply the law in accordance with the instructions given by the judge—all of this at one
time. In civil law systems, there is no single,
concentrated event. A *juicio* or *proceso* is a
succession of meetings and communications
between counsel and the judge in which evidence is introduced and rendered and procedural motions are made and ruled on, leading
to a final decision or judgment as just one
more isolated procedural act.
bench trial *juicio ante un juez (sin jurado)*.
– Syn. trial by court, nonjury trial.
bifurcated trial *proceso desarrollado en dos
etapas*.
bringing a cause to trial *promover un juicio,
proceder en juicio*.
date certain for trial *fecha señalada para la
realización del juicio*.
joint trial *acumulación de procesos*.
jury trial *juicio ante un jurado, juicio ante
jurados*. – Syn. trial per pais.
political trial *juicio político*.

post-trial evidence *pruebas sobrevinientes.*
speedy trial *juicio expedito, juicio rápido* (PR).
trial court *juzgado de primera instancia, tribunal de lo contencioso (materia administrativa).*
trial de novo *juicio de novo.*
trial judge *juez del juicio, juez de la causa.*
trial lawyer *abogado litigante.*
Rel: closing arguments, *alegatos finales;* evidence, *pruebas;* judgment, *sentencia;* opening statements, *alegatos de apertura del juicio;* sentence, *condena;* testimony, *testimonio;* witness, *testigo.*
See: civil trial. criminal trial. jury trial. *procedimiento civil.*
Ref: (CA) R. v. Dennis, (1960), 30 W.W.R. 545 at 550, [1960] S.C.R. 286, 32 C.R. 210, 125 C.C.C. 321, per Ritchie J. 3.; Catherwood v Thompson [1958] OR 326 at 331, 332 Ont.; (US) Smith v. City of Los Angeles, 190 P.2d 943, 946, 84 Cal.App.2d 297.

truancy n. *faltar a la escuela injustificadamente, holgazanería.* **truant** n. *que falta a la escuela repetidamente, holgazán, tunante.*

trust[1] **(custody)** n. *fideicomiso,* [borr.]*trust.* **trustee** n. *fideicomisario.* **trustor/settlor/grantor/donor** n. *fideicomitente.* **cestui que trust/beneficiary** n. *beneficiario.* **corpus/trust res/trust fund/ trust property/trust principal** *patrimonio fiduciario, cosa del trust.*
• Property, real or personal, held by one party for the beneficial enjoyment of another.
"A trust is a right of ownership to property held by one person for the benefit of another. When a trust is established, the legal title (full, absolute ownership) in a particular item of property is separated from the equitable or beneficial title (the right to beneficial enjoyment) in the same property. The person who establishes the trust is called either the settlor, the trustor, the grantor, or the donor. The person who holds the equitable or beneficial title is known as the beneficiary. The beneficiary, also known as the cestui que trust, is the one for whom the trust is created and who receives the benefits from it. The property that is held in trust is called either the corpus, the trust res, the trust fund, the trust property, or the trust principal." (Brown, Legal Terminology, 258-59)
Cf: **trust • agency • bailment.** Both trust and agency are fiduciary relationships in which one person acts for another. An agency is terminated upon the incapacity or death of either the agent or the principal. A trust, once created, exists as long as permitted by the trust terms. The principal is liable for the acts of the agent done within the scope of employment, but neither the settlor nor the beneficiary is liable for the acts of the trustee. The agent seldom has title, while the trustee always does. A bailment is the delivery of personal property by the owner to another for the performance of some act (shipment, storage, cleaning, repair) and return to the owner, subject to a possessory lien for the reasonable charges for the service. Unlike a trust, a bailment cannot be entered into with respect to real property. Bailment refers to possession and not title. A bailment is not a fiduciary relationship. A trust tends to be longer-lasting and more formal than a bailment.
↪ "There is no civil law property institution quite like the trust. Its generality and flexibility as a device for disposing of property, together with its peculiar juridical nature, combine to make it unique ... no single analogous concept exists in the civil law, and no combination of civil legal devices to achieve substantially similar ends quite adds up to the same thing." (Merryman, The Civil Law Tradition. The Legal Systems of Western Europe and Latin America, 923-24) In the Spanish-speaking world, the trust has been adapted in a modified form, mostly as a way to transfer property to third parties or as a form of conveying or managing public property.
charitable trust *fideicomiso con fines benéficos o caritativos.* – Syn. public trust.
constructive trust *fideicomiso implícito.* – Syn. implied trust. involuntary trust.
dormant trust *fideicomiso inactivo.*
executed trust *fideicomisos ejecutados.*
execution of a trust *celebración o perfeccionamiento de un fideicomiso.*
executory trust *fideicomiso por ejecutarse.*
express trust *fideicomiso expreso.* – Syn. direct trust.
irrevocable trust *fideicomiso irrevocable.*
liquidating trust *fideicomiso de liquidación.*
living trust *fideicomiso cuyos efectos tienen lugar durante la vida del fideicomitente.* – Syn. inter vivos trust.
perpetual trust *fideicomiso de duración indeterminada.*
private trust *fideicomiso privado, fideicomiso con fines privados.* – Syn. personal trust.
revocable trust *fideicomiso revocable.*
sprinkling trust *fideicomiso que otorga pagos periódicos a sus beneficiarios.* – Syn. spray trust.

testamentary trust *fideicomiso testamentario.*

trust agreement *contrato de fideicomiso.*

trust deed *escritura del fideicomiso.*

trust fund *fondo fiduciario, patrimonio fiduciario.* – Syn. *corpus.* trust res. trust principal.

trust property *propiedad fiduciaria.*

Rel: investment trust, *fideicomiso de inversión.*

trust² (confidence) n. *relación fiduciaria.*

• A relationship in which confidence is deposited in a person who is in a position to look after property for another.

trust receipt [le]*recibo fiduciario,* [de]*recibo de la posesión de mercancías (hecho en favor del propietario, generalmente una entidad financiera, por parte del comerciante, generalmente un mayorista).*

turnkey project *proyecto de "llave en mano."*

turpitude n. *infamia, bajeza, vileza.*

crimes involving moral turpitude [ed]*delitos que requieren de bajeza moral, delitos infamantes.*

moral turpitude *vileza moral, inmoralidad, bajeza moral, torpeza moral* (PR).

UUUU

ultimatum n. *ultimátum.*

ultra vires CORP. [borr.] *ultra vires, doctrina de actos fuera del objeto social (de una sociedad), actos sobre los que se carecen de facultades (según el objeto social).*

unauthorized adj. *sin autorización, desautorizado.*

unauthorized entry of dwelling *entrar a una casa habitada sin autorización.*

unauthorized practice of law *ejercicio de la abogacía sin autorización, ejercicio ilegal de la abogacía.*

unauthorized use of a vehicle *uso de un vehículo sin autorización.*

Rel: disallowed, *indebido, que no se permite;* prohibited, *prohibido;* unlawful, *ilegal;* unlicensed, *sin registro o licencia.*

unconditional adj. *incondicional.* – Syn. unqualified. unrestricted, *sin restricciones.* without reservations, *sin reservaciones.*

unconditional discharge CRIML.LAW *dejar en libertad incondicionalmente, liberación incondicional (de un detenido o convicto).*

unconditional discharge (debt) *liberación incondicional de una obligación.*

unconscionable adj. *leonino, injusto o abusivo, viciado de lesión.* **unconscionably** adv.

leoninamente, injustamente, arbitrariamente.

unconscionableness n. *injusticia, abuso.*

• Unfair, oppressive or one-sided. <An unconscionable contract is one that is so unfair, oppressive or one-sided that a court may refuse to enforce it.> – Syn. unfair, *injusto.* unscrupulous, *inescrupuloso.*

unconscionable bargain *negociación contractual viciada de lesión.*

unconscionable contract *contrato leonino, contrato viciado de lesión.*

unconstitutional adj. *inconstitucional.*

unconstitutionality n. *inconstitucionalidad.*

unconstitutionally adv. *inconstitucionalmente.*

Rel: judicial review, *control constitucional de los actos del gobierno.*

under the influence [le]*estar bajo la influencia de alcohol u otras drogas,* [fe]*estar en estado de ebriedad o intoxicación, estar bajo los efectos del alcohol o drogas.*

See: alcohol. driving under the influence.

underage adj. *menor de edad.*

undercover agent *policía secreto, agente secreto, agente en cubierto* (PR).

underinsured motorist *conductor sin suficiente cobertura de seguro.*

understanding *entendimiento.*

memorandum of understanding *memorandum de entendimiento.*

underworld¹ (criminals) n. *hampa, el bajo mundo.*

Rel: criminal, *delincuente;* gangster, *gángster;* Mafia, *mafia;* organized crime, *crimen organizado;* underground, *clandestino.*

underworld² (otherworldly) n. *el otro mundo.*

undocumented alien IMMGR *extranjero indocumentado.*

undocumented worker IMMGR *trabajador indocumentado.*

undue influence *coerción, presión o influencia, influencia indebida* (PR).

• The exertion of influence on another destroying his or her free will and favoring the wrongdoer, who is in a position of trust. Such form of coercion creates a ground for nullifying the consent required in a contract or transaction, or the free will needed in a will or improvident gift. – Syn. coercion, *coerción.* unfair persuasion, *persuasión maliciosa.*

Rel: domination, *dominación;* pressure, *presión;*

See: duress.

Ref: (UK) 31 Halsbury's Laws para 839; (US) Long v. Long, 125 S.W.2d 1034, 1035, 133 Tex. 96.

unemployment n. *desempleo, desocupación.*
unemployed adj. *desempleado.*
unemployment benefits *prestación del seguro de desempleo.*
unemployment compensation *pensión de desempleo, subsidio de desempleo.*
unemployment insurance *seguro de desempleo.*
unemployment rate *tasa de desempleo.*
unfair adj. *injusto.* **unfairly** adv. *injustamente.*
unfairness n. *injusticia.* – Syn. biased, *parcial.* inequitable, *inequitativo.* prejudiced, *prejuiciado.* unjust, *injusto.*
unfair business practices *actividades comerciales indebidas o desleales.*
unfair competition *competencia desleal.*
unfair labor practice *prácticas laborales ilegales.*
unfair trial *juicio injusto.*
unfit[1] **(unqualified)** adj. *incapaz.* **unfitness** n. *incapacidad.*
unfit to stand trial *incapacidad procesal, incapacitado para comparecer en juicio.*
unfit[2] **(incapable)** adj. *inepto.* **unfitness** n. *ineptitud.* – Syn. inept.
unfit mother *madre inepta, mala madre.*
unfounded adj. *sin fundamento, infundado.* – Syn. baseless, *sin base.* groundless, *infundado.* unsupported, *sin apoyo, sin base.*
unfounded accusation *acusación infundada.*
unfounded claim *demanda infundada.*
unilateral adj. *unilateral.*
unilateral contract *contrato unilateral.*
uninsured motorist *conductor sin seguro, conductor no asegurado.*
union[1] LABOR n. *sindicato, unión.*
• Organization of workers formed for the purpose of negotiating with employers regarding wages and work conditions.
company union *sindicato controlado por la empresa, sindicato blanco.*
horizontal union *sindicato horizontal.* – Syn. craft union.
independent union *sindicato independiente, sindicato no afiliado.*
local union *sindicato local.*
trade union *gremio, sindicato.*
vertical union *sindicato vertical.* – Syn. industrial union.
Rel: collective bargaining, *negociación colectiva;* strike, *huelga.*
union[2] **(unity)** n. *unión, coalición.*
the Union *la Unión americana.*

Union Jack *la bandera inglesa.*
United Nations (U.N.) *Naciones Unidas* (ONU).
United Nations Food and Agriculture Organization (FAO) *Organización de las Naciones Unidas para la Agricultura y la Alimentación* (FAO).
United Nations Educational Scientific and Cultural Organization (UNESCO) *Organización de las Naciones Unidas para la Educación, la Ciencia y la Cultura* (UNESCO).
See: *Organización de las Naciones Unidas.* Appendix F. United Nations.
unjust enrichment CONTRACTS *enriquecimiento ilegítimo, enriquecimiento sin causa, enriquecimiento injusto* (PR).
• Principle by which a person is entitled to restitution based on the fact that another person has been unjustly enriched at the expense of the first person. – Syn. unjust benefit (UK).
Rel: quantum meruit, *compensación justa por servicios prestados.*
unlawful adj. *ilegal, ilícito.*
• Contrary to, prohibited by or unauthorized by law; not lawful. – Syn. illegal. illicit, *ilícito.*
unlawful act *acto ilegal, acto ilícito.*
unlawful assembly *reunión o congregación con el propósito de crear un disturbio o motín.*
unlawful detainer *retención ilegal de un inmueble.*
unlawful entry *entrada ilegal.*
unlawful imprisonment *privación ilegal de la libertad.* – Syn. false imprisonment.
unlawful possession of a controlled substance *posesión ilegal de una sustancia regulada.*
unlawful possession of a weapon *posesión ilegal de armas, portación ilegal de armas.*
unlawful restraint *restricción ilegal de la libertad.*
unlawful use of a weapon *uso ilegal de un arma.*
See: illegal.
unreasonable force *uso indebido de la fuerza.*
unrest[1] **(disturbance)** n. *disturbio.*
unrest[2] **(uneasiness)** n. *inquietud.*
unscrupulous adj. *inescrupuloso.*
unsecured loan *préstamo no garantizado, préstamo sin garantía.*
unsound mind *(estar) fuera de juicio, no estar en sus cabales, demente.*
See: insanity.
urban adj. *urbano.*
urban area *área urbana.*

urban easement *servidumbre urbana.*
urban property *propiedad urbana.*
usage n. *uso, costumbre.*
• Customary practice.
custom and usage *usos y costumbres.*
immemorial usage *uso inmemorial.*
usage of trade *usos del comercio, usos comerciales.*
use¹ (benefit) n. *uso y aprovechamiento (como beneficiario en derecho-equidad de la propiedad de otro).*
• The right to enjoy the benefits flowing from real or personal property, especially the profits from land to which another has legal title and possession.
beneficial use *uso y aprovechamiento de un bien como beneficiario (bajo el derecho-equidad),* [de]*derecho de uso y aprovechamiento efectivo de la propiedad.*
cestui que use *beneficiario del uso y aprovechamiento de un inmueble.*
Rel: enjoyment, *disfrute;* usufruct, *usufructo.*
See: beneficial owner.
use² (application) n. *uso, utilización, aplicación.*
• The application or employment of something. – Syn. application.
conforming use ZONING *utilización de tierras de conformidad con su régimen jurídico.*
exclusive use (trademarks) *uso exclusivo.*
public use *uso público.*
use tax *impuesto de uso, pago de tenencia.*
use³ (practice) n. *hábito.*
• "A habitual or common practice." (Black's Law Dict., 8ᵗʰ. ed., 1578)
usual place of abode *lugar de residencia habitual.*
usurpation n. *usurpación.*
usurpation of office *usurpación de funciones.*
usury n. *usura.*
• Any interest beyond the limit fixed by statute or law. An unconscionable or exorbitant rate of interest.
usury laws *leyes que regulan la usura.*
Rel: excessive interest, *interés excesivo;* legal interest, *interés legal;* loan sharking, *prestar usureramente.*
uxoricide¹ (crime) n. *uxoricidio, uxoricida.*
• The killing of one's own wife.

VVVV

vacant¹ (empty) adj. *vacío.*
vacant building *edificio o construcción vacía.*

Rel: unoccupied, *desocupado.*
vacant² (unattended) adj. *vacante.*
vacant land *bien inmueble vacante.*
vacant lot *terreno baldío, lote baldío.*
vacate¹ (void) v. *revocar, invalidar.*
• To make something void.
Cf: **vacate • set aside.** "Vacate and set aside are synonymously used to denote an appellate court's wiping clean the judgment slate. The effect is to nullify the previous decision, usually of a lower court, but not necessarily to dictate a contrary result in further proceedings." (Garner, 632)
vacate a judgment *revocar una sentencia.*
vacate an order *revocar una orden judicial.*
See: quash.
vacate² (leave) v. *dejar, desalojar, desocupar.*
• To leave or surrender possession.
vacate an office *desalojar un puesto, dejar una posición.*
vacate the premises *desalojar un inmueble, desalojar un edificio.*
vagrancy n. *vagancia (permanente), el vivir en la calle, el deambular sin domicilio fijo.*
vagrancy statutes or laws *leyes sobre personas de la calle, leyes sobre la vagancia.*
Rel: homeless, *persona que vive en la calle, persona de la calle;* loitering, *vagancia (en un lugar), estar de vago (en un lugar), permanecer en un lugar sin hacer nada.*
valid adj. *validez.* **validity** n. *validez.* **validly** adv. *válidamente.* – Syn. having legal force, *teniendo fuerza legal.*
valid claim *reclamación o demanda válida.*
valid contract *contrato válido.*
valid judgment *sentencia válida.*
valid statute *ley válida.*
validate v. *convalidar, confirmar* || *validar, legalizar.* **validation** n. *validación, convalidación.*
validate a sale *legalizar una venta.*
valuation n. *valuación.*
value n. *valor.* **value** v. *valorar.* – Syn. worth.
appraised value *valor de avalúo.*
book value *valor en libros.*
cash value *valor en efectivo.*
face value *valor nominal.*
intrinsic value *valor intrínseco.*
market value *valor de mercado.*
net value *valor neto.*
par value *valor par, valor a la par.*
rental value *valor de productos.*
taxable value *valor fiscal.*
vandalism n. *vandalismo.* **vandal** n. *vándalo.*

• Willful or malicious destruction or damaging of property.

vehicular manslaughter *homicidio no intencional causado con un vehículo.* – Syn. vehicular homicide.
Rel: reckless driving, *conducir con imprudencia grave.*

vendetta n. *vendetta.*

venire (lat.) n. *venire, grupo de posibles jurados.* To come. **veniremen** n. *posibles jurados.*
• A group or panel of possible jurors from whom a jury will be selected.
venire facias *venire facias, orden judicial para llamar y formar al jurado.*

venue n. *competencia territorial o espacial, lugar del juicio* (PR).
• The possible or proper place for the trial of a suit, from among several places, where jurisdiction can be exercised.
Cf: **venue ● jurisdiction.** Venue is usually distinguished from jurisdiction in that it refers to the place, out of several possible places, where jurisdiction is established, while jurisdiction refers to the authority of the court to exercise judicial power. "The distinction is sometimes blurred in that both words can refer to geographical location.... An important distinction between venue and jurisdiction remains: right to a particular venue may be waived; the parties cannot confer subject matter jurisdiction." (Mellinkoff's Dict., 672)
change of venue *cambio de competencia territorial.* – Syn. transfer of venue.
waiver of venue *renuncia de competencia territorial.*
wrong venue *competencia territorial improcedente.*
Rel: jurisdiction, *jurisdicción.*
Ref: (CA) Rex v Dunn [1945] 2 W.W.R. 495 (B.C.C.A.); (US) 28 U.S.C.A. §1391; Jones v. Brinson, 78 S.E.2d 334, 337, 238 N.C. 506.

verbal adj. *verbal.* – Syn. oral, *oral.*
verbal abuse *malos tratos (de palabra principalmente).*
verbal argument *disputa verbal, pelea de palabras.*
verbal contract *contrato verbal, contrato oral.*

verbatim adv. *palabra por palabra.* – Syn. literal, *literal.*

verdict n. *veredicto.*
• The formal decision or finding made by a jury upon the matters or questions submitted to the jury at trial.

Cf: **verdict ● judgment.** These terms are usually distinguished in that verdict is not a judicial determination but rather a finding of fact to be weighed by the court in formulating its judgment. When verdict and judgment are used loosely meaning decision, however, both terms are considered synonyms.
adverse verdict *veredicto desfavorable.*
directed verdict *veredicto dictado por el juez (en un juicio ante jurados).*
final verdict *veredicto definitivo.*
general verdict [de]*veredicto en favor o en contra de una de las partes (en vez de resolver cuestiones de hecho)* [le]*veredicto general.* – Syn. general finding.
judgment notwithstanding the verdict *sentencia no obstante veredicto en contrario, sentencia no obstante veredicto* (PR).
partial verdict [le]*veredicto parcial,* [de]*veredicto parcialmente absolutorio.*
sealed verdict *veredicto en sobre cerrado.*
special verdict [de]*determinación de hechos, veredicto que resuelve una cuestión de hecho.*
verdict of guilty *veredicto de culpabilidad.*
Comment: An important recent difference between American and British verdicts in criminal trials is the need for unanimity in the former and the introduction of majority verdicts in the latter.

verification n. *certificación, ratificación.*
verifiable adj. *certificable.* **verify** v. *certificar.* – Syn. certification, *certificación.*
verification of pleadings *ratificación de un hecho en la demanda o en la contestación.*
verified complaint *denuncia ratificada.*
verified copy *copia certificada.*
Rel: acknowledgment, *reconocimiento;* authentication, *autenticación.*

vessel n. *embarcación, buque.*
• "Anything floating in and on the water, built and used for navigation, regardless of form, rig, or motive power." (Ballentine's Law Dict., 1339)
See: ship.

vested estate *derecho adquirido sobre un inmueble.*

vested pension *derecho adquirido a una pensión o jubilación.*

vested rights *derechos adquiridos.*

veto n. *veto.* **vetoer** n. *aquél que ejerce el veto.*
override a veto *dejar sin efectos o prevalecer sobre un veto.*
veto power *poder de veto.*

vicarious liability *responsabilidad por terceros, responsabilidad subsidiaria.*

• Liability imposed upon a person because of the act or omission of another, such as the principal's vicarious liability for the acts of its agent. – Syn. vicarious responsibility.
Rel: respondeat superior, *respondeat superior, que el superior sea responsable.*

victim CRIML.LAW n. *víctima, sujeto pasivo (del delito).* **victimize** v. *victimar.* **victimizer** n. *victimario.*
• A person against whom a crime, tort or a wrong has been committed.
victim-impact statement [de]*declaración del impacto causado a la víctima o sus familiares (por la comisión del delito).*
victim's assistance program *programa de ayuda a las víctimas (de delitos).*
victim's rights *derechos de las víctimas (de delitos).*
Rel: aggrieved party, *parte agraviada;* complaining witness, *denunciante, querellante;* injured party, *parte lesionada, ofendido.*

vigilante n. *aquél que se hace justicia por sí mismo.* **vigilantism** n. [borr.]*vigilantismo.*

violation¹ (transgression) n. *violación, transgresión.*
• An infraction or breach of the law. The infringement of a right or duty. – Syn. breach *incumplimiento.* contravention *contravención.* infraction *infracción.* infringement *infringir.* transgression *transgresión.*
violation of bail bond *violación de las condiciones de la fianza.*
violation of order of protection *violación de la orden de protección.*
violation of probation (VOP) *violación de la condena condicional,* [el]*violación de la probación, infringir la condena condicional.*
violation of supervision *violación de las condiciones de la supervisión.*
violation² (rape) n. *violación.*

violence n. *violencia.* **violent** adj. *violento.* **violently** adv. *violentamente.*
to resort to violence *recurrir a la violencia.*
violent offense *delito de violencia.*

vis major (lat.) *vis major, fuerza mayor.* A greater force, superior force. – Syn. force majeure (law fr.), *fuerza mayor.*
Cf: **vis major • force majeure • act of god.** The first two terms are Law Latin and Law French synonyms. Both force majeure and vis major are broader terms than act of god because they include acts not only of nature but also of people.

Rel: act of god, *fuerza física irresistible;* vis divina (lat.), *vis divina.*

visa IMMGR n. *visa.*
business visa *visa de hombre de negocios.*
to deny a visa *negar el otorgamiento de una visa.*
to issue a visa *otorgar una visa.*
tourist visa *visa de turista.*
Rel: passport, *pasaporte.*

visitation order FAM.LAW *orden de derechos de visita.*
visitation rights FAM.LAW *derechos de visita.*
vital statistics *datos del Registro civil.* [le]*estadísticas vitales.*

void n. *nulidad.* **void** adj. *nulo.* **void** v. *anular.*
• Having no legal force, unenforceable.
Cf: **void • voidable.** Void means that an instrument or transaction is ineffectual and nothing can cure that condition. Voidable exists when a defect can be cured by ratification or confirmation. This distinction is usually of great importance in contract law, but not closely observed in other areas.
null and void *nulo y sin efecto.*
void contract *contrato nulo.*
void judgment *sentencia sin ningún efecto legal.*
void marriage *matrimonio nulo.*
Rel: annul, *anular;* cancel, *cancelar;* quash, *dejar sin efecto;* vacate, *revocar.*

voidable adj. *anulable, sujeto a nulidad.*
voidable contract *contrato anulable o sujeto a nulidad.*
voidable judgment *sentencia impugnable.*
voidable lease *contrato anulable o sujeto a nulidad.*
voidable marriage *matrimonio anulable o sujeto a nulidad.*
voidable will *testamento anulable o sujeto a nulidad.*
See: void.

voir dire (law fr.) [borr.]*voir dire,* [de]*examen preliminar de un candidato a jurado (por las partes y el juez).* To speak the truth.
"[T]he most notable distinction in the [jury] selection process in England [from that of the United States] is the absence of a voir dire examination … The rule is to accept those persons called to serve by the administrative machinery, however haphazard that process may be." (Glendon, Gordon & Carozza, 251)
voluntary adj. *voluntario.* **volunteer** n. *voluntario.* – Syn. willful, *voluntario.* deliberate, *deli –*

berado.

voluntary abandonment *abandono voluntario, abandono de hogar.*

voluntary appearance *comparecencia voluntaria.*

voluntary bankruptcy *quiebra voluntaria.*

voluntary compliance *cumplimiento voluntario.*

voluntary confession *confesión voluntaria.*

voluntary conveyance *translación gratuita de un inmueble.*

voluntary dismissal *renuncia voluntaria.*

voluntary manslaughter *homicidio intencional bajo estado pasional o emoción violenta (arrebato u obcecación).*

vote n. *voto.* **voter** n. *votante.* **vote** v. *votar.*

majority vote *voto mayoritario.*

vote of confidence *voto de confianza.*

voting *votación.*

voting block *voto en bloque.*

voting by proxy *votación por poder.*

voting by secret ballot *votación secreta.*

voting rights *derechos de voto.*

voting stock *acciones con derecho de voto.*

Rel: ballot, *cédula o boleta electoral.*

voting trust *sindicación fiduciaria de acciones (para obtener el control de una porción de votos).*

voucher n. *comprobante, recibo, vale.*

vox populi (lat.) *vox populi, de conocimiento público, voz del pueblo.*

WWWW

wage n. *sueldo, salario.*

• Compensation paid to employees usually based on hours worked or items produced. – Syn. compensation, *compensación.* earnings, *ingreso, ganancias.* pay, *paga.* remuneration, *remuneración.* salary, *salario.* stipend, *estipendio.*

minimum wage *salario mínimo.*

wage earner *asalariado.*

wage freeze *congelación de salarios.*

wage garnishment *embargo de salario, retención o deducción de salario (por orden judicial).*

Rel: bonus, *gratificación;* take-home pay, *salario neto.*

See: salary.

wager n. *apuesta.* **wagerer** n. *apostador.*

waif property *artículos robados dejados atrás (por el ladrón al huir).*

waiting period *período de espera.*

waiver n. *renuncia.* **wave** v. *renunciar.*

• An intentional and voluntary giving up, relinquishment or surrender of a right, benefit or advantage. Also the written instrument containing the waiver. – Syn. relinquishment, *renunciación.*

Cf: **waiver • estoppel.** Sometimes waiver and estoppel are incorrectly regarded as synonymous. Estoppel is a broader term than waiver, meaning "the legal abatement of a person's rights and privileges when it would be inequitable to allow that person to assert them." (Garner, 923) Waiver, on the other hand, refers to the voluntary relinquishment of a legal right.

implied waiver *renuncia tácita.*

jury waiver *renuncia al derecho de tener un juicio de jurados, renuncia de un juicio ante jurados.*

waiver clause *cláusula de renuncia.*

waiver of excludability *renuncia a la exclusión migratoria.*

waiver of extradition proceedings *renuncia al proceso de extradición.*

waiver of formal reading of the indictment *renuncia a la lectura de la acusación formal (de un delito).*

waiver of immunity *renuncia de inmunidad.*

waiver of jurisdiction *renuncia de jurisdicción.*

waiver of Miranda rights (US) [lexical exp.] *renuncia a los derechos Miranda.*

waiver of venue *prórroga de jurisdicción.*

Rel: dispensation, *dispensa;* release, *abandono;* surrender, *liberar, ceder.*

Ref: (CA) Crump v McNeill (1918), 14 Alta. L.R. 206 at 211; (UK) 16 Halsbury's Laws para 922; (US) Scherer v. Wahlstrom, 318 S.W.2d 456, 459.

wanton[1] **(careless)** adj. *indiferencia sin importar las consecuencias, culpa grave* || *mala intención.*

Cf: **wanton • reckless.** Wanton is usually acknowledged as indicating a greater degree of culpability than reckless. "In criminal law wanton usually connotes malice but reckless does not." (Garner, 924)

wanton disregard *indiferencia intencional (sin importar las consecuencias).*

wanton negligence *culpa o negligencia grave e intencional, imprudencia temeraria.*

Rel: negligence, *negligencia;* recklessness, *imprudencia grave.*

wanton[2] **(lewd)** adj. *sensual, lascivo.*

war n. *guerra.*

• The condition of mutual hostilities between two countries or among significant armed factions within a country or region. – Syn. conflagration, *conflagración.*

Cf: **war • armed conflict • hostilities • belligerency.** War and armed conflict are used synonymously, but many writers consider the former a wider term. Hostilities refers to acts of war, while belligerency indicates the status of the party waging war. A belligerent is a party to war; a combatant is a participant in hostilities who distinguishes himself or herself from the civil population, and who acts on behalf of a belligerent.

casualties of war *bajas, víctimas de la guerra.*
civil war *guerra civil.*
to wage war *hacer la guerra.*
war crimes *crímenes de guerra.*
war criminal *criminal de guerra.*
war declaration *declaración de guerra.*
– Syn. declaration of war.
war powers *facultades o atribuciones en materia de guerra (de un gobierno).*
world war *guerra mundial.*
Glossary: aggression, *agresión;* air warfare, *guerra aérea;* armed conflict, *conflicto armado;* armistice, *armisticio;* blockade, *bloqueo;* capitulation, *capitulación;* chemical and biological weapons, *armas químicas y biológicas;* combatant, *combatiente;* conventional weapons, *armas convencionales;* enemy alien, *extranjero de un país enemigo;* Geneva conventions, *Convenciones de Ginebra;* genocide, *genocidio;* hostilities, *hostilidades;* irregular forces, *fuerzas irregulares;* mercenary, *mercenarios;* neutrality, *neutralidad;* noncombatant, *no combatiente, civiles;* nuclear weapons, *armas nucleares;* prisoner of war (POW), *prisionero de guerra;* prohibited weapons, *armas prohibidas;* reprisals, *represalias;* safe-conduct, *salvo-conducto;* unconditional surrender, *rendición incondicional;* warlord, *jefe militar.*

ward of court *(estar) bajo la tutela de un tribunal, niño bajo tutela del tribunal.*

warden[1] n. *guardián, celador, vigilante.*
– Syn. jailer, *carcelero.*

warden[2] **(UK)** n. *director.*

warehouse n. *almacén.* – Syn. storage facility.
warehouse receipt *certificado de depósito en almacén.* – Syn. deposit warrant, *certificado de depósito.*

warning[1] **(announcement)** n. *aviso.*

warning[2] **(admonition)** n. *advertencia, amonesta-*

ción, prevención. – Syn. caveat.
proper warning *advertencia adecuada.*

warrant[1] **(judicial writ)** n. *orden judicial (de detención o requisición).* **warrantless** adj. *sin una orden de detención o registro.*
• "A writ issued by a court authorizing the arrest of a person, or the seizure of property." (Radin, 369)
arrest warrant *orden de detención, orden de aprehensión* (Mx).
bench warrant *orden expedida por el juez.*
distress warrant *orden de embargo.*
execute a warrant *ejecutar una orden.*
fugitive warrant *orden de detención de un prófugo.*
off a warrant *en ejecución de una orden judicial.*
search warrant *orden de registro, orden de cateo* (Mx).
warrant of extradition *orden de extradición.*
warrant recalled and quashed *la orden judicial se cancela y se deja sin efecto.*
Rel: order, *orden judicial.*

warrant[2] **(document)** n. *certificado, comprobante.*
• "A document conferring authority, esp. to pay or receive money." (Black's Law Dict., 8th. ed., 1617)
county warrant *orden de pago (emitida por un condado).*
deposit warrant *certificado de depósito en almacén.*
treasury warrant *cheque de tesorería.*

warrant[3] **(option)** n. *opción de compra de acciones.* – Syn. subscription warrant.

warrantless arrest *detención sin orden judicial.*
warrantless search *registro sin orden judicial.*
warranty[1] CONTRACTS n. *garantía contractual.*
• A promise that a proposition of fact is true.
Cf: **warranty • representation.** These terms are often used synonymously. Warranty is a written essential part of a contract that must be strictly complied with; representation, on the other hand, is often an incidental part of a contract, not always written, and substantial compliance is sufficient in most cases.
as-is warranty, *garantía limitada a la condición actual de la cosa.*
breach of warranty *violación de la garantía.*
disclaimer of warranty *falta o limitación de garantía.*
extended warranty, *garantía adicional.*
implied warranty *garantía implícita.*
limited warranty *garantía limitada.*

warranty of habitability *garantía de habitabilidad (de un inmueble), garantía de que un inmueble está en buenas condiciones para ser habitado.*
written warranty *garantía escrita.*
Rel: guaranty, *garantía;* insurance warranty, *garantía, cláusula de garantía.*
warranty[2] PROP.LAW n. *garantía del título transmitido (incluyendo el derecho de compensación con otro inmueble).*
• A covenant by which the grantor assumes the obligation before the grantee to secure the estate conveyed, and to compensate with other land of similar value in the event that eviction by another claimant be successful.
general warranty *garantía general.*
special warranty deed [de]*escritura incluyendo solamente la garantía de la legitimidad del título en el caso de acciones procedentes contra el otorgante.*
warranty deed [de]*escritura incluyendo la garantía de la legitimidad y legalidad del título de propiedad.* – Syn. general warranty deed.
warranty[3] **(sales)** n. *garantía comercial.*
• Seller's promise to buyer that a product has good title or other certain qualities.
express warranty *garantía expresa.*
full warranty *garantía de partes y servicio.*
warranty of merchantability *garantía de mercantibilidad o comerciabilidad.*
warranty of title *garantía de la legitimidad de la propiedad, garantía de propiedad legítima.*
Ref: (US) 15 U.S.C.A. §2301; U.C.C. §2-312ss.
warranty[4] INSURANCE n. *declaraciones del asegurado, garantías y representaciones del asegurado.*
• Assurance that facts and circumstances are and exist as stated.
affirmative warranty *declaración del asegurado.*
waste[1] **(harm)** PROP.LAW n. *deterioro permanente de un inmueble (causado por su poseedor o tenedor).*
• Destruction or permanent harm to real property by the person in possession to the detriment of another's interest in that property.
ameliorating waste *modificaciones sin autorización de mejoras permanentes a la propiedad.*
commissive waste *deterioro permanente por acciones del poseedor o tenedor.* – Syn. affirmative waste. voluntary waste.

impeachment of waste *responsabilidad por deterioro permanente.*
permissive waste *deterioro permanente por falta de reparaciones de mantenimiento.*
Rel: wear and tear, *uso y deterioro normal (de un bien).*
waste[2] **(trash)** n. *deshechos, desperdicios.*
• Refuse or left over material, especially from manufacturing and consumer goods.
hazardous waste *deshechos peligrosos.*
toxic waste *deshechos tóxicos.*
water n. *agua.*
high water mark *marca del nivel más alto de las aguas.*
internal waters *aguas interiores.*
low water mark *marca del nivel más bajo de las aguas.*
navigable waters *aguas navegables, vías navegables.*
private water *aguas restringidas a uso particular.*
public water *aguas navegables o de acceso al público.*
subterranean waters *aguas subterráneas.*
water pollution *contaminación de las aguas.*
watercourses *vías fluviales.*
Rel: accretion, *aluvión, crecimiento natural;* alluvion, *aluvión;* aquifer, *acuífero;* avulsion, *avulsión;* diversion, *desviación o alteración (del curso de un río);* groundwater, *agua del subsuelo;* spring, *manantial;* stream, *corriente;* well, *pozo.*
water rights *derechos sobre aguas.*
Rel: riparian rights, *derechos de los propietarios ribereños;* storage rights, *derechos de almacenaje.*
watered stock *acciones cuyo valor real ha sido reducido indebidamente.*
wealth n. *riqueza.* **wealthy** adj. *rico, acaudalado.*
Rel: affluence, *afluencia;* economic means, *medios económicos;* filthy rich, *asquerosamente rico;* fortune, *fortuna;* money, *dinero;* moneyed, *adinerado;* opulence, *opulencia;* riches, *riquezas;* well off, *próspero, acaudalado;* well-to-do, *pudiente, acomodado.*
weapon n. *arma.*
• Any instrument used to injure or attack another.
bladed weapon *arma punzo-cortante.*
carrying a concealed weapon *portación de armas, portación de armas ocultas.*
deadly weapon *arma mortífera.*
weapons of mass destruction (WMD) *armas*

de destrucción masiva.

Glossary: awl, *punzón;* baseball bat, *bate o bat de beisból;* axe, *hacha;* baton, *macana, garrote;* bayonet, *bayoneta;* billy club, *macana, garrote, porra;* black jack, *cachiporra, garrote;* bludgeon, *cachiporra;* brass knuckles, *manopla,* bóxer (Mx), *nudillera;* butcher knife, *cuchillo de carnicero;* cane, *bastón;* carving knife, *trinchador;* chisel, *cincel;* club, *garrote, porra;* crowbar, *palanca, pata de cabra* (Cu,PR); dagger, *puñal, daga;* dart, *dardo;* explosives, *explosivos;* firearms, *armas de fuego;* fixed-blade knife, *cuchillo de hoja fija;* folding blade knife, *navaja de hoja plegadiza;* harpoon, *arpón;* hatchet, *hacheta;* hoe, *azadón;* ice pick, *picahielos, punzón* (Cu); knife, *cuchillo, navaja;* machete, *machete;* machine-gun, *metralleta, ametralladora;* picklock, *ganzúa;* pincers, *tenazas;* pistol, *pistola;* pocket knife, *navaja de bolsillo;* poniard, *puñal;* revolver, *revólver;* rifle, *rifle;* scissors, *tijeras;* sickle, *hoz;* sling, *honda, tirapiedra* (Cu); spear, *lanza;* stick, *palo, garrote;* switchblade, *navaja de resorte, sevillana;* sword, *espada;* whip, *látigo.* See: gun.

wed v. *casarse.* **wedding** *boda, casamiento.*

out of wedlock *fuera de matrimonio.*

wedlock *matrimonio.*

welfare n. *bienestar público* || *beneficencia, asistencia pública.*

on welfare *recibir asistencia pública.*

welfare benefits *ayuda de la asistencia pública.*

welfare recipient *beneficiario de la asistencia pública.*

welfare state *estado de bienestar, estado benefactor, estado providencia.*

whereas n.conj. *dado el hecho que, considerandos.* Given the fact that.

whereby conj. *por lo cual, mediante lo cual.*

wherefore n.adv. *por que propósito o razón, por lo tanto.* For what purpose or reason, therefore.

whereof conj. *de que, de lo que.* Of what, of which.

whereupon conj. *por lo cual, en consecuencia de lo cual.* On which, in close consequence of which.

whistleblower n. *denunciante (generalmente en forma confidencial), soplón.*

white slave trade *trata de blancas.* – Syn. white slave traffic.

white-collar crimes *delitos cometidos por empleados de oficinas, crímenes de cuello blanco.*

will[1] **(testamentary instrument)** n. *testamento.* **testator** n. *testador.* **testatrix** n. *testadora.* **testamentary** adj. *testamentario.*

• The disposition of property made by a person to take place after his or her death. It also denotes the document embodying a person's disposition of property. – Syn. testament, *testamento.* Cf: **will • testament • codicil.** Will is an Anglo-Saxon term referring to an instrument disposing of real estate. Testament is a Latin term referring to an instrument that disposes of personal property. Today both terms are used interchangeably, will being the preferred term. Codicil is an alteration or addition to an existing will.

challenge to a will *oposición a un testamento.*

conditional will *testamento condicional.*

contested will *testamento impugnado, juicio testamentario.* – Syn. will contest.

execution of a will *celebración o perfeccionamiento de un testamento.*

gift inter vivos *donación inter vivos.*

holographic will *testamento ológrafo.*

joint will *testamento mancomunado, testamento de hermandad* (Sp-Navarra).

last will and testament *último testamento.*

living will *declaración de voluntad de una persona de que no se le mantenga viva artificialmente (si sufre un quebranto irreparable en su salud).*

mutual will *testamentos recíprocos.* – Syn. reciprocal will.

nuncupative will *testamento privado.*

revocation of a will *revocación de un testamento.*

unconditional will *testamento incondicional.*

voidable will *testamento anulable, testamento viciado de nulidad.*

Glossary: attestation clause, *cláusula o párrafo de la certificación;* curtesy (obs.), *derecho del marido sobre los bienes de la esposa a su muerte;* dower (obs.), *dote;* executor, *albacea;* no contest (in terrorem) clause, *cláusula de inimpugnabilidad, cláusula testamentaria condicionando la distribución de bienes a la aceptación de la inimpugnabilidad del testamento;* pretermitted heir, *heredero preterido, heredero excluído de un testamento;* probate, *procedimineto testamentario;* residuary estate, *remanente del patrimonio hereditario;* sound mind and memory, *en uso de sus facultades mentales, mente y memoria* (PR). See: devise. legacy. succession.

will[2] **(desire)** n. *voluntad.*

• Choice; volition; desire.

willful adj. *intencional, voluntario.*
• Intentional, deliberate or voluntary without being necessarily malicious. – Syn. deliberate, *deliberado.* intentional, *intencional.* purposeful, *con un propósito determinado.* – Other spell.: wilful.

willful and deliberate trespass *violación deliberada e intencional de derechos.*

willful and malicious injury BANKRUPTCY *perjuicio causado intencionalmente.*

willful murder *homicidio intencional, homicidio doloso.*

willful negligence *negligencia grave.*
Rel: malicious, *doloso, intencional;* neglect, *descuido, con falta de cuidado;* reckless, *imprudente;* wanton, *inexcusable, injustificable.*

wiretap n. *intercepción clandestina telefónica, intercepción de comunicaciones telefónicas.*

withdraw charges CRIML.LAW *retirar acusaciones, retirar cargos.*

withdrawal of a motion *desistimiento de una promoción, desistimiento de una petición.*

withholding evidence *supresión de pruebas, ocultamiento de pruebas.*

without due notice *sin notificación legal.*

without due process of law *sin el debido proceso legal.*

without recourse *sin recurso.* – Syn. sans recours (fr.).

witness¹ (testimony) n. *testigo.*
• Person testifying in a cause before a court to what he or she has seen, heard or observed.
adverse witness *testigo hostil, testigo desfavorable.* – Syn. hostile witness.
character witness *testigo de solvencia moral.*
coached witness *testigo aleccionado.*
competent witness *testigo competente.*
confronting a witness *confrontación (de un testigo).*
credible witness *testigo veraz.*
crown witness (UK) *testigo de cargo, testigo de la fiscalía.*
expert witness *perito.*
hostile witness *testigo hostil.*
impeachment of a witness *tacha de testigo, impugnación de lo dicho por un testigo.*
material witness *testigo de hechos importantes o relevantes.*
rebuttal witness *testigo que contradice lo asentado.*
unreliable witness *testigo no confiable.*
witness for the defense *testigo de descargo.*

witness for the plaintiff *testigo de la actora.*
witness for the prosecution *testigo de cargo.*
witness stand *banquillo o estrado de los testigos.* – Syn. witness box (UK).
witness statement (UK) *declaración de un testigo (por escrito).*
witness-protection program *programa de protección de testigos.*
Rel: deponent, *declarante, deponente.*

witness² (observer) n. *testigo.* **witness** v. *presenciar, observar.*
• One who personally sees or perceives a thing, act or event. – Syn. observer, *observador.* eyewitness, *testigo ocular.*
complaining witness *denunciante, querellante.* – Syn. complainant. prosecuting witness.
Rel: bystander, *circunstante, transeúnte;* onlooker, *espectador;* spectator, *espectador.*

witness³ (verifier) n. *testigo.*
• A person who observes the signing of a legal document. – Syn. attestant/attester, *testigo.*

witnesseth v. *testificando que, consta que.*
this agreement witnesseth that *el presente acuerdo hace constar que, por el presente acuerdo se hace constar que.*
this document witnesseth that *el presente documento hace constar que, por el presente documento se hace constar que.*

work n. *trabajo.* **work** v. *trabajar.* – Syn. employment, *empleo.* job, *trabajo.*

work for hire *trabajo contratado.*

work-release program [de]*programa de trabajo externo para reos, remisión automática.*

worker n. *trabajador.*
casual worker *trabajador eventual.*
domestic worker *trabajador doméstico.*
live-in domestic worker *trabajador doméstico residente (en el lugar de trabajo).*
longshore and harbor workers *estibadores y trabajadores de puerto.*
temporary worker *trabajador temporal.*
undocumented worker *trabajador indocumentado.*
Rel: jobber, *trabajador a destajo.*

worker's compensation *compensación o indemnización por accidentes de trabajo, compensaciones a obreros.*
• Statutes regulating benefits provided to employees injured in their employment. – Syn. workmen's compensation.
Rel: accidental injury, *lesión accidental;* arising out of and in the course of employment, *originados con motivo del trabajo y en el desem-*

peño normal del mismo; death benefits, indemnización por fallecimiento; disability, incapacidad; medical expenses, gastos médicos; occupational disease, enfermedad profesional.

World Bank Banco Mundial. – Syn. International Bank for Reconstruction and Development (IBRD).

World Court Tribunal Internacional de Justicia.
See: International Court of Justice.

World Health Organization (WHO) Organización Mundial de la Salud (OMS).

World Intellectual Property Organization (WIPO) Organización Mundial de la Propiedad Industrial (OMPI).

World Meteorological Organization (WMO) Organización Meteorológica Mundial (OMM).

World Trade Organization (WTO) Organización Mundial de Comercio (OMC).
Rel: Council for Trade in Goods, Consejo del Comercio de Mercancías; Council for Trade in Services, Consejo del Comercio de Servicios; Council for Trade-Related Aspects of Intellectual Property Rights (TRIPS), Consejo de los Aspectos de los Derechos de Propiedad Intelectual relacionados con el Comercio (ADPIC); Director-General, Director General; General Agreement on Tariffs and Trade (GATT)(obs.), Acuerdo General sobre Aranceles y Comercio; General Council, Consejo General; Ministerial Conference, Conferencia Ministerial.

wound n. herida. **wound** v. herir. – Syn. lesion, lesión. injury, lesión, daño.
through and through wound herida en sedal.
wound healing curación o cicatrización de una herida || recuperarse de una herida.
Glossary: abrasion, raspón, rozadura; bite, mordedura; bruise, moretón, magulladura; chafe, rozadura; concussion, concusión; contusion, contusión; cut, cortadura; ecchymosis, equimosis; hematoma, hematoma; incision, incisión; laceration, laceración; puncture, herida penetrante; rash, salpullido, erupción; scrape, raspadura; scratch, rasguño, raspón; sore, llaga, ulceración; tear, desgarre; trauma, trauma, traumatismo.

wreck n. naufragio. **wreck** v. naufragar.

writ n. auto, orden, mandamiento, [borr.]writ.
• A court's written order compelling a person to do or forgo a specified act.

"In [American English] writ generally applies to judicial writs, which are either extraordinary writs (e.g., mandamus, prohibition) or writs used in appellate procedure (e.g., writ of error, writ of certiorari). In [British English] by contrast, writ is usu. synonymous with original writ… as an abbreviated form of writ of summons." (Garner, 945)

writ of attachment auto de embargo.
writ of certiorari requisitoria.
writ of ejectment auto de desahucio.
writ of entry acción posesoria.
writ of error auto de admisión de la apelación basada en error.
writ of execution auto de ejecución.
writ of habeas corpus auto de hábeas corpus, habeas corpus.
writ of mandamus orden o mandamiento judicial extraordinario, [borr.]mandamus.
writ of prohibition inhibitoria.
writ of replevin acción reivindicatoria.
writ of restitution auto de restitución.
writ of summons emplazamiento.
Rel: order, orden judicial.

write-in case caso agregado (a la lista de casos).

written formalisms (legalese) formalismos escritos (legales).
Glossary: brethren, colegas (de un tribunal colegiado); by virtue of the authority vested in me, en virtud de la autoridad que se me ha conferido, en uso de mis facultades; Comes now (the plaintiff; the defendant), Comparece (el demandante; el demandado); except as otherwise provided, salvo pacto en contrario; Further affiant sayeth not, Sin que el declarante tenga nada más que decir o declarar; Further deponent sayeth not, Sin que el deponente tenga nada más que decir o declarar; hereunto set his hand and seal, firma y sella la presente; in full possession of his or her faculties, en pleno uso de sus facultades; In Witness Whereof, En fe de lo cual, En testimonio de lo cual; Know All Men By These Presents, Dése a conocer por la presente que, Hágase saber por la presente que, Conste por la presente que; knowledge and belief, a su leal saber y entender; To All To Whom These Presents, A quien la presente corresponda; to wit, a saber; Whereas, Dado el hecho que, Considerando que; witnesseth, a la vista, teniendo a la vista, visto (el acuerdo).
See: oral formalisms.

wrong (injury) n. violación de un derecho, incumplimiento de un deber jurídico. **wrongly** adv. en

violación de un derecho.
• A violation of the legal rights of another.
Rel: tort, *responsabilidad civil.*

wrong[1] **(bad)** adj. *malo, impropio.*
wrong[2] **(mistaken)** adj. *equivocado, erróneo.*
wrongdoer n. *transgresor, infractor.*
• One who violates the law. – Syn. lawbreaker, *transgresor de la ley, infractor.* offender, *infractor.* transgressor, *transgresor.*
Rel: criminal, *delincuente;* guilty party, *parte culpable;* tortfeasor, *responsable de un ilícito civil.*

wrongful adj. *ilícito, ilegal.* **wrongfully** adv. *ilícitamente, ilegalmente.*

wrongful birth action [de]*acción de responsabilidad profesional por parto,* [de]*acción de responsabilidad profesional debido al parto de un niño con defectos de nacimiento.*

wrongful discharge *despido injustificado, despido ilegal.* – Syn. wrongful dismissal (UK). wrongful termination.

wrongful imprisonment *privación ilícita de la libertad.*

wrongful invasion *transgresión ilícita (del derecho de otro).*

wrongful possession *posesión de mala fe.*

wrongful-life action [de]*acción de responsabilidad profesional por omitir información de defectos del feto,* [de]*acción de responsabilidad profesional por la falta de información a los padres de los defectos de un niño antes o después de la concepción.*
Rel: crime, *delito;* tort, *responsabilidad civil.*

wrongful act *acto ilícito.*
• An act that infringes upon the right of another. – Syn. wrongful conduct.

Cf: **wrongful act ● negligence.** Wrongful act "is occasionally equated to term 'negligent,' but generally has been considered more comprehensive term, including criminal, wilful, wanton, reckless and all other acts which in ordinary course will infringe upon rights of another to his damage." (Black's Law Dict., 5th. ed., 829)

wrongful-death action *acción de responsabilidad civil por la muerte de* una persona *(causada por un acto ilícito o imprudencial).*
• Lawsuit brought by the decedent's beneficiaries asking for compensation for the dece-

dent's death, caused by a willful act or negligence of another.

XXXX

xenophobia n. *xenofobia.* **xenophobic** adj. *xenófobo.*

YYYY

yield n. *rendimiento.*
net yield *rendimiento neto.*
nominal yield *rendimiento nominal.*
yield to maturity *rendimiento al vencimiento.*
youth n. *juventud, joven.*
youthful offenders *jóvenes delincuentes, delincuentes juveniles de mayor edad (casi adultos).*
See: juvenile.

ZZZZ

zoning *regulación del uso del suelo, regulación o planeación urbana, planeamiento urbanístico, planificación, zonificación* (PR).
• "Zoning is the process of regulating the use of land by designating specific areas for certain uses." (Brown, Legal Terminology, 336)
cluster zoning *planeación urbana que establece densidades basada en cierta proporcionalidad de áreas destinadas a servicios y recreación.* – Syn. density zoning.
contract zoning *zonificación adoptada mediante convenio.*
exclusionary zoning *zonificación excluyente de cierta clase de negocios.*
floating zoning *establecimiento de áreas urbanas diferentes a las que prevalecen en una zonificación sin determinar su ubicación en la misma.*
spot zoning *regulación de un terreno urbano sin tomar en cuenta el tipo de zonificación que lo rodea.*
zoning map *mapa de zonificación.*
zoning rules *reglamentos urbanos, regulación urbana.*
Rel: condemnation, *expropiación;* density, *densidad;* housing, *habitación, vivienda;* housing discrimination, *discriminación habitacional;* land development, *desarrollo urbano, urbanización;* nonconforming use, *utilización de un terreno en infracción del uso permitido.*

ESPAÑOL-INGLÉS

Abreviaturas
(Español-Inglés)

Abr.	abreviatura
adj.	adjetivo
adv.	adverbio
Ant.	antónimo
Ar	Argentina
Au	Australia
Bol	Bolivia
C.	Constitución Política
Ca	Canadá
CC	Código civil
CCo.	Código de comercio
CFF	Código Fiscal Federal (México)
CFPC	Código federal de procedimientos civiles
CFPP	Código federal de procedimientos penales
CGP	Código general del proceso (Uruguay)
Ch	Chile
Co	Colombia
CP	Código penal
CPC	Código de procedimientos civiles. código de procedimiento civil
CPCC	Código procesal civil y comercial (Argentina)
CPCDF	Código de procedimientos civiles del Distrito Federal (México)
CPP	Código de procedimientos penales
CR	Costa Rica
CST	Código sustantivo del trabajo (Colombia)
CT	Código del trabajo (Chile). Código de trabajo (Guatemala, Panamá)
Cu	Cuba
der rom.	derecho romano
der.	derecho
der.admvo.	derecho administrativo
der.const.	derecho constitucional
der.intl.	derecho internacional
der.intl. privado.	derecho internacional privado
der.merc.	derecho mercantil
der.proc.	derecho procesal
der.proc.civil	derecho procesal civil
der.proc.penal	derecho procesal penal
DR	República Dominicana
Ec	Ecuador
ed	equivalente descriptivo
ef	equivalente fucional
el	equivalente literal
Esco.	Escocia
ES	El Salvador
Esp	España
ET	Estatuto de los trabajadores (España)
EEUU	Estados Unidos de América
EEUU-La.	Estados Unidos de América – Luisiana
euf.	eufemismo
ext.lexico	extensión lexicográfica
fmal.	formal
fr.	francés
GB	Gran Bretaña
genrico	genérico
gob.	gobierno
gre.	griego
Gu	guatemala
hist.	histórico

Ingl.	Inglaterra
inic.	iniciales
Int.Org.	International Organizations
interp.	intepretación
LA	Ley de amparo (México)
lat.	latín
LC	Ley de compañías (Ecuador)
LCCH	Ley cambiaria y del cheque (España)
LCh	Ley del cheque-No 2859 (República Dominicana)
LEC	Ley de enjuiciamiento civil (España)
legsmo	legalismo
LF	Ley de Fideicomisos (Venezuela)
LFT	Ley federal del trabajo (México)
LGTOC	Ley general de títulos y operaciones de crédito (México)
LHRP	Ley Hipotecaria y del Registro de la Propiedad (Pueto Rico)
LJC	Ley de la Jurisdicción Constitucional (Costa Rica)
LOPJ	Ley orgánica del poder Judicial (España)
LOPJF	Ley orgánica del poder judicial federal (México)
LOT	Ley orgánica del trabajo (Venezuela)
LOTC	Ley orgánica del tribunal constitucional (España)
LN	Ley de navegación (Argentina)
LPRA	Leyes de Puerto Rico Anotadas
LSA	Ley de sociedades anónimas (Chile). Ley sobre sociedades anónimas (Panama)
LGSM	Ley general de sociedades mercantiles (Mexico)
max.	máxima
mod.	modismo
Mx	México
NCPPCh.	Nuevo código procesal penal chileno
n.	sustantivo
NZ	Nueva Zelanda
obs.	obsoleto
oral expr.	expresión oral
Pa	Panamá
Pay	Paraguay
Pe	Perú
pop	popular
PR	Puerto Rico
prest.	prestado (de otro sistema legal)
prop. ind.	propiedad industrial
prop.intelec.	propiedad intelectual
RPC	reglas de procedimiento criminal (Puerto Rico)
rtrgido	restringido
RU	Reino Unido
Sin.	sinónimo
transpl.	transplante (de otro sistema jurídico)
TRLSA	Texto refundido de la Ley de Sociedades Anónimas (España)
Ur	Uruguay
v.	verbo
Ve	Venezuela
vul	vulgar

AAAA

a continuación *hereinafter.*

a contrario sensu (lat.) *a contrario sensu, on the other hand, in the opposite sense.*

a cuenta *on account.*

a destajo *by the piece or quantity.*

a granel *in bulk.*

a instancia de parte *upon petition of a party, at the request of one of the parties.* – Sin. a petición de parte.

a la orden *to the order.*

a la vista *upon presentment.*

a largo plazo *long-term.*

a menos que se estipule lo contrario *unless otherwise specified herein, unless otherwise agreed.*

a mi leal saber y entender *to the best of my knowledge and belief.*

a quemarropa *point blank.*

a sabiendas e intencionalmente *knowingly and willfully.*

a sangre fría *in cold blood.*

a solicitud de *at the request of.*

ab intestato (lat.) *ab intestato, by intestacy.*
• Sin haber hecho testamento. – Sin. intestado, *intestacy.* sucesión intestada, *intestate succession.* sucesión legítima, *intestate succession.* intestado.

abanderamiento DER.MARÍTIMO *registration of a ship or vessel.*
• Significa tanto el acto físico de enarbolar la bandera en la nave o barco como el acto de su matriculación.
Rel: bandera de conveniencia, *flag of convenience;* pabellón, *flag.*

abandono de acción DER.PROCESAL *abandonment of action.*
• La falta de actuaciones por parte de la actora sin justificación, y por un período que la ley considera no rasonable.
Cf:**abandono de acción • abandono de la instancia.** Abandono de acción y abandono de la instancia son términos sinónimos cuando el segundo se refiere al abandono de la acción que se ejercita, pero no lo son cuando abandono de la instancia se refiere al abandono de la pretensión jurídica o derecho que se quiere hacer valer.
Rel: abandono de querella (Esp), *abandonment of complaint;* desistimiento, *voluntary dismis-*sal; perención de la instancia (Ar,Co), *lapsing of a lawsuit due to inactivity, nonsuit.*

abandono de atropellado *leaving the scene of an automobile accident with injury (with a person having been run over), hit and run (with a person having been run over by an automobile).*

abandono de bienes *abandonment of goods.*
– Sin. abandono de cosas muebles (Ar), *abandonment of chattels.* derrelicción (Esp), *dereliction.*
Cf:**abandono de bienes • renuncia de bienes • res nullius.** Abandono y renuncia de bienes son generalmente distinguidos en que en el abandono la extinción del derecho de propiedad es hecha en forma tácita o implícita, en tanto que en la renuncia la extinción es hecha en forma expresa. Por su parte *res nullius* es el vocablo latino para designar a un bien mueble que no tiene dueño.
Rel: renuncia de bienes, *relinquishment or abandonment of property;* res nullius, *thing without owner, ownerless chattel.*
Comentario: Los efectos de derecho que se atribuyen al abandono de bienes se aplican solamente a bienes muebles, ya que en el caso de bienes inmuebles el simple abandono no produce efectos jurídicos, pues se requiere además del abandono la prescripción positiva para que otra persona los adquiera.

abandono de buque DER.MARÍTIMO *abandonment of ship or vessel.*
• "Auto en virtud del cual el naviero entrega a los acreedores el buque con todas sus pertenencias y los fletes, para que los ejecuten y cobrar de esa forma sus créditos." (Dicc. ed. Comares, 1) – Sin. dejación, *abandonment of ship to insurer.*

abandono de cosas aseguradas (seguro marítimo) *abandonment of insured property.*

abandono de empleo DER.LABORAL *abandonment of employment.*
• Acción unilateral y voluntaria del trabajador ausentándose de su trabajo en forma injustificada.
Cf: **abandono de empleo • abandono de trabajo • abandono de labores.** Los dos primeros términos se usan sinónimamente excepto cuando abandono de trabajo se refiere al abandono de las tareas sin implicar la terminación del contrato de trabajo. Abandono de labores se refiere a una suspensión parcial de labores por parte del trabajador.
Rel: abandono de labores, *temporary abandon-*

ment of work; abandono de trabajo, *abandonment of work.*

abandono de hogar PERSONAS [ef]*abandonment of spouse,* [el]*abandonment of domicile.*

• Separación del hogar familiar de uno de los cónyuges en forma voluntaria y con la firme intención de romper la convivencia. – Sin. abandono conyugal (Mx). abandono del hogar conyugal. abandono voluntario, *voluntary abandonment.* separación del hogar conyugal, *desertion of spouse.*
Ref: (Ar)CC a.202-5 y 214-1; (Ec)CC a.108-11 (Esp) CC a.82-1; (Mx)CC a.267-VIII; (Pe)CC a.333-5; (Ve) CC a.185-2.

abandono de mercancías DER.ADUANAL *abandonment of goods.*

• "Cuando en forma tácita o expresa el importador cede las mercancías al fisco federal al cumplirse los requisitos legales para ello." (Mx-LA, a.19)

abandono de personas DER.PENAL *abandonment of persons, desertion.*

• "Es culpable de abandono aquel que dejare de cumplir los deberes legales de asistencia inherentes a la patria potestad, tutela, guarda o acogimiento familiar o dejare de prestar la asistencia necesaria legalmente establecida para el sustento de sus descendientes, ascendientes o cónyuges que se hallen necesitados." (CP-Esp., a.226) – Sin. abandono de hijos, *abandonment of children.* omisión de asistencia a la familia. abandono de familia (Esp), *desertion of family.*
Cf: **abandono de personas • abandono de hogar.** Abandono de personas se refiere al abandono del cumplimiento de los deberes de asistencia que la ley exige de ciertas personas (aunque en algunos países se limita al abandono de un menor solamente). Abandono de hogar, por su parte, se refiere generalmente a la salida del hogar de uno de los esposos como el hecho sobre el que se basa la causal de divorcio de abandono.
Rel: abandono de menores o incapacitados (Esp), *abandonment of minors or of the legally incompetent;* abandono de niños, *abandonment of children;* omisión de cuidados (Mx), *failure to provide due care.*
Ref: (Ar)CP a.106-108; (Bo)CP a.248; (Co)CP a.127; (Ec)CP a.474-480; (Esp) CP a.226-231; (Mx)CP a. 336; (Pe)CP a.125; (PR)CP a.158-160; (RD)CP a. 348,349; (Ve)CP a.437ss.

abandono del cargo (delito) *desertion of post or position.*

• Delito contra la administración pública que comete el funcionario que abandona su cargo sin justa causa. – Sin. abandono de funciones públicas, *desertion of public service post.*
Rel: abandono de destino (militar), *being away without leave* (AWOL); abandono de un deber, *neglect of duty.*

abdicación n. *abdication.* **abdicar** v. *to abdicate.*

• Significa la cesión o renuncia de un derecho y más particularmente del trono o la corona de un monarca. – Sin. dimisión, *resignation.* renuncia, *resignation.*
abdicación expresa *express abdication.*
abdicación tácita *implied abdication.*

abigeato n. *cattle stealing.*

abogado[1] **(profesión)** n. *attorney at law, lawyer,* [prest.]*abogado,* [rtrgido]*barrister* (RU,Au), [rtrgido]*solicitor* (RU). **abogacía** n. *practice of law.*

• Profesional del derecho, con título de licenciado en derecho, que ejerce la abogacía consistente primordialmente en la dirección y defensa de las partes en toda clase de procesos, así como en dar asesoría jurídica. – Sin. asesor legal, *legal counselor.* bachiller en leyes o derecho, [el] *bachelor in laws.* jurista, *jurist.* jurisconsulto, *legal consultant.* letrado (Esp,Cu), *lawyer.* licenciado en leyes o en derecho, [el]*licenciate in law.* patrono, *solicitor.* procurador, *solicitor, legal representative.*
Cf: **jurista • jurisconsulto • licenciado • bachiller • letrado.** Jurista es un hombre versado en la erudición del derecho y en la crítica de las leyes y códigos. Jurisconsulto legal es un erudito del derecho que da consejo o consulta. Licenciado en leyes o en derecho, es aquél que ha recibido el título académico de licenciatura en derecho. Bachiller en leyes o derecho es aquél que ha recibido el título de bachiller en derecho. El grado académico usado en la mayoría de países de habla hispana en la actualidad es la licenciatura en leyes o derecho; el grado de bachiller, que es un término antiguo académicamente equivalente, ha prácticamente desaparecido. Letrado es un término que significa en forma general hombre de conocimientos o ciencia y más específicamente abogado.

↳ Abogado y *lawyer* o *attorney* designan al profesional, debidamente acreditado, que litiga ante los tribunales y asesora a clientes que solicitan sus servicios. Mientras la palabra abogado se usa con cierta ambigüedad, extendiéndose en ocasiones a personas que no están legalmente autorizadas para ejercer el derecho (mayormente como un resabio de usos pasados), la denominación *lawyer* o *attorney* se usa solamente para designar a aquellos que han recibido autorización para ejercer la profesión a través de la agrupación profesional aprobada para ello. Por su parte, en Inglaterra aún se conserva estrictamente la distinción entre *barrister*, quien se dedica exclusivamente a litigar ante los tribunales, y *solicitor*, quien primordialmente cumple una función de asesoría legal.

abogado civilista *civil law lawyer.* – Sin. civilista.

abogado con personalidad acreditada *attorney of record.*

abogado consultor *legal adviser.*

abogado de empresas *corporate lawyer.*

abogado de la contraria *opposing counsel.*

abogado de oficio *court-appointed counsel.*

abogado de pobres *public defender.* – Sin. defensor público.

abogado defensor *counsel for the defense, defense attorney.*

abogado del estado *prosecuting attorney, state's attorney* (EEUU). – Sin. fiscal.

abogado en ejercicio *practicing attorney.*

abogado fiscal *prosecutor* || *tax attorney.* – Sin. fiscalista. tributarista.

abogado leguleyo *shyster lawyer.*

abogado litigante *trial lawyer, barrister* (RU,Au).

abogado particular *private attorney.*

abogado penalista *criminal lawyer.* – Sin. penalista.

abogado picapleitos *ambulance chaser.*

Rel: pasante, *articled clerk;* jurista, *legal expert;* jurisconsulto, *law scholar.*

Ver: licenciado en derecho. *lawyer.*

abogado² **(promotor de causas sociales)** n. *advocate,* [prest.]*abogado.*

• Persona que defiende una causa social o que instiga que se haga justicia.

<él es un abogado de las causas justas del pueblo, *he is an advocate of the people's just causes.*> – Sin. defensor *defender.* paladín *paladin, champion.*

abono a cuenta *payment on account.* – Sin. para abono en cuenta.

abono de tiempo de prisión DER.PENAL *time considered served, credit for time served.*

Rel: bonificación del tiempo en detención, *time credited while in custody;* tiempo en prisión no elegible para la pena, *dead time.*

abordaje DER.MARÍTIMO n. *collision between ships.*

• Choque o colisión entre dos buques. Por extensión se usa en el caso del choque de un buque con una estructura fija y el choque de dos aeronaves. – Sin. choque, *crash.*

abordaje culpable *negligent collision between ships.*

abordaje dudoso *collision of ships where fault cannot be determined.*

abordaje fortuito *non-negligent or unavoidable collision between ships.*

abordaje por falta común *collision of ships where both are at fault, both-to-blame collision.*

aborto (delito) n. *abortion.* **abortar** v. *to abort.* **abortivo** adj. *abortive.*

• "Expulsión prematura y violentamente provocada del producto de la concepción, o su destrucción dentro del seno de la madre." (Dicc. ed. Comares, 4) – Sin. delito de aborto, *crime of abortion.* aborto penal, *criminal abortion.*

Cf: **aborto** ● **delito de aborto** ● **malparto.** En un contexto legal aborto se refiere al delito de aborto. En un contexto no legal generalmente significa la terminación del embarazo en forma involuntaria dentro de los primeros meses del embarazo; en tanto que malparto es un término común para referirse a la terminación involuntaria del embarazo dentro de los últimos meses, (por lo general a partir del séptimo mes).

aborto consentido *consensual abortion*

aborto delictivo *criminal abortion.*

aborto espontáneo *miscarriage.* – Sin. aborto involuntario. pérdida del bebé (pop.).

aborto imprudente *abortion caused by criminal negligence.* – Sin. aborto culposo.

aborto legal *legal abortion.* – Sin. aborto despenalizado.

aborto por necesidad o necesario *abortion by medical necessity, therapeutic abortion.* – Sin. aborto terapéutico. aborto indirecto. aborto despenalizado.

aborto provocado *induced abortion.* – Sin. aborto procurado. aborto de propósito.

Rel: embarazo, *pregnancy;* feto, *fetus;* malogro, *fail, abort;* malparto, *miscarriage;* parto prematuro, *premature delivery;* pro vida, *pro life;* viabilidad, *viability.*

Comentario: Los sistemas más comunes en países hispanos permiten el aborto en los casos en que existen razones o motivos importantes (llamados también indicaciones en España) que justifiquen su realización. Tales razones se refieren a poner en peligro la salud de la mujer, a los casos de abrogación

violación y a otras circunstancias especialmente graves de índole social, económica o personal.
Ref: (Ar)CP a.85-88; (Bo)CP a.263-269; (Ch)CP a.342-345; (Co)CP a.122-124; (Ec)CP a.444-447; (Esp)CP a.144-146; (Gu)CP a.133; (Mx)CP a.329-334; (Pa)CP141ss.; (Pe)CP a.114ss.; (PR)CP a.91, 92, 33 LPRA 4010, 4011; (RD)CP a.317; (Ur)CP a.325ss.; (Ve)CP a.432-436.

abrogación n. *repeal,* [amplio]*abrogation.* **abrogar** v. *to repeal, to abrogate.* **abrogatorio** adj. *abrogative.* **abrogable** adj. *repealable.*
• Permite que una ley anterior quede sin efecto legal por otra posterior. – Sin. abolición, *abolition.*
Cf: **abrogación • revocación • derogación.**
Revocación es el término más amplio, ya que tiene aplicación en materias tanto civiles como administrativas, y significa dejar un acto sin efectos por voluntad de su autor o de las partes. Abrogación se refiere exclusivamente a la revocación o anulación de una ley mediante la promulgación de otra que la substituye, en tanto que derogación se refiere solamente a la revocación o anulación parcial de una ley.
Rel: derogación, *derogation;* revocación, *revocation;* supresión, *suppression.*

absolución DER.PROCESAL n. *acquittal, dismissal with prejudice.* **absolutorio** adj. *acquitting.*
• "Supone la terminación de un proceso mediante sentencia favorable al reo o al demandado." (Dicc. UNAM, 21) – Sin. exculpación, *exculpation.*
absolución con reserva *dismissal without prejudice.*
absolución de la demanda *dismissal of the complaint.*
absolución de la instancia DER.PROCESAL *dismissal with prejudice, dismissal of the case.*
– Sin. libertad por desvanecimiento de datos, *acquittal for lack of evidence.* sobreseimiento, *dismissal.*
Rel: suspensión del proceso penal, *suspension of criminal procedure.*
absolución de posiciones DER.PROC.CIVIL *answering interrogatories.*
• Actuación judicial en la que el declarante, bajo juramento, afirma o niega preguntas preparadas con anticipación por la otra parte. – Sin. absolver posiciones, *to answer interrogatories.* interrogatorio.
↦ La absolución de posiciones se refiere al interrogatorio que se lleva a cabo normalmente en la audiencia de desahogo de pruebas de un procedimiento civil. Consiste en la lectura

de preguntas sobre los hechos controvertidos, elaboradas con anticipación a través del pliego de posiciones, hechas al declarante generalmente en forma oral y a las que se deberá contestar con un sí o no. *Interrogatories,* por su lado, es un concepto similar en forma pero lleva a cabo una función diferente: la de obtener o encontrar pruebas en la etapa preliminar al juicio. La figura jurídica más cercana a la absolución de posiciones y que desahoga la testimonial en el proceso oral de la *common law* es la llamada *witness examination,* que sólo se da en forma restringida en el juicio penal y que es inexistente en el juicio civil del sistema romano-germánico.
Rel: confesión judicial, *judicial admission;* pliego de posiciones, *list of written questions.*

abstención¹ (inacción) n. *abstention.* **abstenerse** v. *to abstain.* **abstinente** adj. *abstinent.* **abstencionismo** n. *nonparticipation.* **abstencionista** adj. *abstaining.* **abstencionista** n. *abstainer.*
abstención² (omisión) n. *forbearance, failure.*
abstencionismo electoral *electoral abstentionism, non-participation in an election.*

abuso n. *abuse.* **abusar** v. *to abuse.* **abusador** n. *abuser.* **abusivo** adj. *abusive.* **abusivamente** adv. *abusively.* – Sin. atropello, *outrage, abuse.*
abuso de armas (Ar) *unlawful use of arms.*
abuso de menores *child abuse.*
Rel: arbitrariedad, *arbitrariness.* exceso, *excess. highhandedness.* injusticia, *injustice.*
abuso de autoridad (delito) *abuse of authority.* – Sin. abuso de cargo (Esp). abuso de poder.
abuso de confianza¹ (delito) *embezzlement, criminal breach of trust (Ca).*
• Abuso de confianza es la apropiación, ya en beneficio propio ya de otro, de una cosa ajena que se le haya entregado o confiado a una persona con la obligación de restituirla o hacer de ella un uso determinado, causando un perjuicio. – Sin. apropiación indebida. desfalco.
El abuso de confianza no es considerado delito en todos los países hispanos. En muchos de ellos se le considera una circunstancia agravante de otros delitos; en esos casos, abuso de confianza se refiere generalmente al aprovechamiento de las facilidades dadas por una relación interpersonal.
Cf: **abuso de confianza • peculado.** Delitos similares que se conforman por los mismos elementos, con la distinción por parte del peculado de tratarse de un funcionario o servidor público como sujeto activo, el ser generalmente mayor

la punición, y el perseguirse de oficio. En contraste, el abuso de confianza se distingue por cometerlo cualquier persona a quien se han confiado bienes, por ser el castigo menor para el infractor y por no perseguirse de oficio en la mayoría de las legislaciones.

Rel: administración fraudulenta, *fraudulent administration;* peculado, *peculation.*
Ref: (Ar)CP a.172; (Bo)CP a.346; (Co)CP a.249; (Mx)CP a.382-385; (RD)CP a.408; (Ve)CP a.468.

abuso de confianza² (conducta) *breach of trust.*

• El rompimiento de una relación, basada en la expectativa de lealtad y buena fe mutuas, existente entre dos personas.
En España abuso de confianza es primordialmente un agravante del delito de hurto.

abuso del derecho [prest.]*abusive exercise of rights.* [el][prest.]*abuse of rights.*

• Es el ejercicio de un derecho por parte de un particular en forma tal que primordialmente persiga el causar un daño o el desconocer la función social de las normas que expresan tal derecho. – Sin. abuso de derecho.

Cf: **abuso del derecho ● fraude de la ley ● fraude procesal.** Abuso del derecho se refiere al uso abusivo de un derecho, esto es, al uso que causa daño sin beneficio a su titular, el que se ejercita sin interés o con un objeto diferente a aquel al que originalmente se otorgó, o el que va en contra de la justicia. Fraude de la ley tiene aplicación primordialmente en derecho internacional privado y es el acogimiento a la palabra de la ley eludiendo su sentido, finalidad u objeto; por ejemplo, se presenta como un remedio que permite la aplicación de una ley extranjera a la que las partes se han sometido, evadiendo de esa manera la ley nacional. Finalmente, fraude procesal se refiere a actos procesales efectuados en forma artificiosa o engañosa para obtener un beneficio indebido o lograr un objetivo que no podría obtenerse siguiendo puntualmente la ley.

↪ En virtud de su amplitud y generalidad, abuso del derecho no encuentra un concepto equivalente en inglés que comprenda el concepto de abuso de derecho en su totalidad, por lo que las expresiones *abusive excercise of rights* y *abuse of rights* han sido tomados directamente de la tradición romano-germánica; sin embargo, se pueden encontrar varios términos que podrían considerarse como aplicaciones concretas del mismo, tales como: *abuse of process, malicious prosecution, abuse of right in detriment of others and the tort of nuisance.*

Rel: fraude de la ley, [ed]*fraudulent evasion of applicable law;* fraude procesal, *abuse of process,* [ed]*fraud committed by the use of legal procedure.*

abuso deshonesto (delito) *criminal sexual contact,* [amplio]*sexual battery,* [amplio]*sexual assault.*

• Delito que consiste en realizar actos obscenos con personas de uno u otro sexo sin que haya acceso carnal, cuando se usare de fuerza o intimidación o cuando se trate de un menor o incapacitado. – Sin. [amplio]abuso sexual. atentados al pudor. atentados contra el pudor (Ec). atentado violento al pudor. ultrajes al pudor. acto sexual violento (Co).

abuso deshonesto con agravantes *aggravated criminal sexual contact.*

Rel: estupro, *statutory rape;* violación, *rape.*
Ref: (Ar)CP a.127; (Bo)CP a.312; (Co)CP a.206, 209; (Ec)CP a.505; (Esp)CP a.181-183; (Gu)CP a.179ss.; (Mx)CP a.260; (Pa)CP a.220; (Pe)CP a.176; (RD)CP a.333; (Ur)CP a.273.

acaparamiento n. *hoarding.* **acaparar** v. *to hoard, monopolize.* **acaparador** n. *hoarder, profiteer.*

acaparar el mercado *cornering the market.*
acaparamiento de artículos de primera necesidad *hoarding necessities.*
Rel: monopolio, *monopoly.*

Comentario: Acaparamiento es un término usado comúnmente en el ámbito civil, mercantil y administrativo. En algunas legislaciones aparece también como delito cuando su objeto es el sustraer artículos de primera necesidad, o esenciales para la economía, de su disponibilidad en el mercado.

Ver: especulación.

accesión n. *accession.*

• Forma de adquirir la propiedad mediante la titularidad de un bien que produce otros o al que se le unen o incorporan natural o artificialmente.

Cf: **accesión ● aluvión ● avulsión ● edificación ● adjunción.** La accesión es el concepto genérico que incluye a todos los demás. Aluvión es adquisición por accesión mediante el acrecentamiento de terrenos ubicados a las márgenes de una corriente de agua por sedimento, arena, etc. Avulsión es similar a aluvión excepto que el acrecentamiento se efectúa en forma súbita o violenta. La edificación es un término genérico al que también frecuentemente se le denomina plantación, siembra o construcción, y que se refiere a la accesión mediante la adhesión de lo plantado, sembrado o construído en terreno inmueble ajeno. Finalmente la adjunción se

refiere a la accesión de un bien mueble a otro.
adquisición por accesión *acquisition (of ownership) by accession.*
Rel: adjunción, *acquisition by uniting two chattels into one (belonging to different owners);* aluvión, *accretion;* avulsión, *avulsion;* edificación, *acquisition by planting or constructing on another's property.*
Ver: adquisición de la propiedad.

accesorio adj. *accessory, ancillary.*
– Sin. auxiliar, *auxiliary.* incidental, *incidental.* subsidiario, *ancillary.* secundario, *secondary.*

accidente n. *accident.* **accidentar** v. *to have an accident.* **accidental** adj. *accidental.* **accidentado** n. *victim of an accident.* **accidentalmente** adv. *accidentally.*
• Es una acción o suceso eventual de la que inesperadamente, y sin intención del causante, resulta un daño para las personas o cosas.
– Sin. siniestro. *casualty, accident.* desgracia, *misfortune, disgrace.* percance, *mishap.*
Cf: **accidente • desgracia • eventualidad • percance.** Términos usados sinónimamente. Accidente es el término más usado y es normalmente considerado amplio en su significado y neutro en su dirección. Siniestro se refiere a un daño, pérdida o destrucción fortuita y es el término preferido en materia de seguros. Desgracia es un suceso adverso en el que destaca el elemento de aflicción. Eventualidad pone énfasis en la incertidumbre de la realización. Percance enfatiza la idea de contratiempo o estorbo.
accidente de circulación *moving traffic accident.*
accidente de trabajo o laboral *occupational accident.*
accidente de tránsito o tráfico *traffic accident.*
accidente in itinere *accident while commuting to work.*
accidentes del mar *perils of the sea.*
prevención de accidentes *accident prevention.*
Rel: eventualidad, *eventuality, contingency;* negligencia, *negligence.*

acción[1] DER.PROCESAL n. *action,* [lat.]*actio, lawsuit.*
accionar v. *to sue.*
• Acción procesal es el derecho, potestad, facultad o actividad, mediante la cual una persona autorizada para ello por la ley provoca la actividad de juzgamiento de un tribunal para decidir un litigio o dilucidar un derecho.
Cf: **acción • pretensión • demanda.** Estos tres términos se usan frecuentemente como sinóni-

mos siendo distinguibles. Acción se refiere al poder jurídico de acudir ante los órganos jurisdiccionales o jueces pidiendo se acepte o confirme la pretensión del promovente. La pretensión, a su vez, es la reclamación específica que el demandante formula contra el demandado, basada en la convicción de que se tiene un derecho válido, sea esto cierto o no. El promovente puede accionar aun si su pretensión es infundada. La demanda, por su parte, es el documento formal en el que se plasma la pretensión ante el juzgador conforme las reglas establecidas por la ley para tal efecto.
acción cambiaria de regreso *collection action against secondary endorsers (of a negotiable instrument), legal action in reversion.* – Sin. acción de regreso.
acción cambiaria *right of recourse, collection action based on a negotiable instrument.*
acción causal *personal action on a negotiable instrument.*
acción colectiva *class action.*
acción conjunta *joint action.*
acción constitutiva *action which attempts to establish, modify or abolish a legal right.*
acción de alimentos *action for payment of support.*
acción de daños y perjuicios *action for damages.*
acción de desahucio *eviction, unlawful detainer action, summary ejectment.*
acción de divorcio *action for divorce.*
acción de enriquecimiento indebido *action for unjust enrichment.*
acción de estado civil *action to establish or modify someone's marital status.*
acción de indemnización *action for indemnity or compensation.*
acción de nulidad *action to declare a contract or transaction null and void.*
acción de pago de salarios *action for recovery of wages.*
acción de petición de herencia *probate proceeding brought by legitimate or testamentary heir to divide estate.*
acción de reclamación de paternidad *paternity action.* – Sin. acción de paternidad.
acción de saneamiento *action against buyer to cure legal defects of the thing purchased.*
acción de simulación *action to invalidate an agreement which appears to be a fraudulent transaction with a third party.*
acción declarativa *action for a declaratory judgment.*

acción ejecutiva *action for summary proceedings, special summary procedure for enforcing bills of exchange.*

acción hipotecaria *action of foreclosure.*

acción pauliana *action to void prior acts by debtor intended to defraud his o her creditors.*

acción penal *penal or criminal action.*

acción personal *personal action, action in personam.*

acción popular, [ed]*criminal action prosecuted by complainant* || *proceeding declaring unconstitutional a law or other regulations.*

acción posesoria *possessory action.*

acción precautoria *action for a provisional remedy.*

acción real [obs.]*real action, action in rem.*

acción redhibitoria *redhibitory action.*

acción reivindicatoria *replevin (chattels), ejectment (land).* – Sin. acción de reivindicación.

acción rescisoria *action to rescind.*

acción sin respuesta de la contraria *uncontested action.*

acción sumaria *summary proceeding.*

ejercicio de la acción *to bring an action, to file a legal action.*

Rel: pretensión jurídica, *claim;* demanda, *complaint.*

Comentario: No hay un concepto de acción unánimemente aceptado. Las doctrinas al respecto pueden dividirse en dos grandes grupos: aquellas que se basan en el derecho romano y que identifican a la acción con el derecho substantivo, de tal manera que la acción es considerada el derecho de perseguir en juicio lo que nos es debido o lo que nos pertenece; y aquellas que se suscriben a la doctrina moderna que sostiene que la acción es algo distinto y diverso al derecho substantivo, y que puede definirse ya como un "acto provocatorio de la jurisdicción", ya como un poder o potestad para permitir la actuación del órgano jurisdiccional, ya como "un derecho abstracto de obrar", entre otras posibles definiciones.

Ver: demanda.

Ref: (Ch)CPP a.10ss.; (Esp)C a.24; (Mx)CPCDF a.1ss.

acción² SOCIEDADES n. *stock, share.*

• "Parte alícuota del capital social de las Sociedades Anónimas y las Comanditarias por acciones." (Dicc. ed. Comares, 9)

acciones al portador *bearer shares.*

acciones amortizables *redeemable shares.*

acciones de goce *certificates giving limited rights to holders of retired stock.*

acciones de tesorería *treasury stock.*

– Sin. acciones en caja. acciones rescatadas.

acciones de trabajo *shares payable with work or services.* – Sin. acciones de premio (Ar). acciones laborales.

acciones de voto limitado *shares with limited voting rights.*

acciones emitidas *outstanding shares.* – Sin. acciones en circulación.

acciones exhibidas *paid-up shares.*

acciones fraccionadas *fractional shares.*

acciones liberadas *paid-up shares.* – Sin. acciones desembolsadas (Esp). || *bonus shares.*

acciones nominativas *nominative or registered shares.*

acciones ordinarias *common stock.*

acciones pagadoras *unpaid shares, called-up capital stock.*

acciones preferentes *preferred shares.*

acciones provisionales *temporary share certificates.*

acciones redimibles *callable shares.*

acciones sin derecho a voto *non-voting shares.* – Sin. acciones neutras.

acciones sin valor nominal *non-par-value stock.* – Sin. acciones sin valor a la par.

título de las acciones *certificate of stock.*

Rel: aportaciones de capital, *capital contributions;* capital social, *capital stock, capital of a company.*

accionista n. *shareholder, stockholder.* – Sin. socio.

accionista mayoritario *majority shareholder.*

accionista minoritario *minority shareholder.*

aceptación n. *acceptance.* **aceptar** v. *to accept.* **aceptante** n. *acceptor.* **proponente** n. *offeror.*

• Manifestación de consentimiento concorde con un ofrecimiento o propuesta. Aprobación, asentimiento. – Sin. admisión, *admission.* consentimiento, *consent.*

aceptación a beneficio de inventario *acceptance under benefit of inventory.*

aceptación bancaria *banker's acceptance.*

aceptación condicional *qualified acceptance.*

aceptación de la herencia *acceptance of estate by heir.*

aceptación de la letra *acceptance of a bill of exchange.*

aceptación de un cheque *acceptance of a check.*

aceptación de una licitación *acceptance of an offer.*

aceptación en blanco *blank acceptance.*

aceptación lisa y llana *unconditional accep-*

tance. – Sin. aceptación pura y simple.

aceptación por determinación de la ley *constructive acceptance.* – Sin. aceptación por ministerio de ley.

aceptación por intervención *acceptance by a third party.*

aceptación por omisión *acceptance by omission, sufferance.*

aceptación sujeta a condición *conditional acceptance.*

aceptación tácita *implied acceptance, acceptance by conduct.*

Rel: acuerdo, *agreement.*

aclaración de sentencia *clarification of judgment.*

acoso sexual (Esp) *sexual harassment.* – Sin. hostigamiento sexual.

acreditar v. *to prove, to establish.*

acreditar la personalidad *to furnish evidence of one's authority to represent another person.*

acreedor n. *creditor.*

• Sujeto de una obligación que está facultado para exigir su cumplimiento por parte del deudor.

acreedor alimentario *support obligor, person entitled to support.*

acreedor cambiario *holder of a bill of exchange.*

acreedor común *general creditor.*

acreedor hereditario *creditor of the deceased person's estate.*

acreedor hipotecario *mortgagee.*

acreedor mancomunado *joint creditor.*

acreedor prendario *pledgee, holder of a chattel mortgage.*

acreedor privilegiado *preferred creditor.* – Sin. acreedor preferente.

acreedor quirografario *unsecured creditor.* – Sin. acreedor común.

acreedor solidario *joint and several creditor.*

Rel: deudor, *debtor;* obligación, *obligation.*

acta n. *written record, certificate,* [fr.]*acte.*

• "Instrumento o pieza escrita en la cual el redactor de la misma refiere circunstanciadamente un hecho o acto jurídico, relatando las formas de su acontecimiento, el estado de las cosas o las manifestaciones de voluntad de las personas que participaron en él." (Couture, 70) – Sin. certificado, *certificate.*

Cf: **acta ● certificado.** Términos que tienen coincidencia y se usan sinónimamente con frecuencia. Ambos se refieren a un documento que formaliza un acto o evento, pero mientras

el acta es un término genérico que se refiere a cualquier relación escrita autorizada por el redactor o los participantes en el acto o suceso relatado, el certificado es un término que se refiere por lo general a un documento autorizado por una autoridad pública o administrativa y que en ocasiones, usado como adjetivo, describe el proceso de autorización mismo. <traductor certificado>

acta circunstanciada *detailed certificate.*

acta constitutiva *articles of incorporation.*

acta de adopción *adoption decree.*

acta de defunción *death certificate.*

acta de divorcio *divorce decree.*

acta de la asamblea *minutes of the meeting.*

acta de matrimonio *marriage certificate.*

acta de nacimiento *birth certificate.*

acta del tenor siguiente *record that reads as follows.*

acta electoral *election certificate.*

acta judicial *court transcript (duly certified by the clerk).*

acta notarial *notarial certificate.* – Sin. acta legalizada por notario.

acta taquigráfica *stenographic record.*

actas del estado civil *legal status certificate, marital status certificate.*

actas del registro civil *vital records.*

como consta en actas *as a matter of record.*

levantar un acta *to produce a written record.*

Rel: documento, *document;* testimonio, *notarial document;* transcripción, *transcript.*

activismo judicial *judicial activism.*

activo (cont.) n. *assets.*

activo circulante *current assets.* – Sin. activo corriente.

activo contable *book assets.*

activo de fácil realización *liquid assets.*

activo en circulación *working capital.*

activo fijo *fixed assets.*

activo físico *tangible assets.*

activo intangible *intangible assets.* – Sin. activo inmaterial.

activo neto *net assets.*

activo real *tangible assets.*

activo realizable *quick assets, liquid assets.*

Rel: pasivo, *liabilities.*

acto n. *act, action,* [lat.]*actus.*

acto administrativo *act carried out by an administrative body of government.*

acto de autoridad *action by an authority.*

acto de dominio *act of acquiring or selling property.*

acto de gobierno *a political question* || *action*

by the authorities.
acto ilegal *illegal act.*
acto ilícito *illicit act, wrongful act.*
acto legislativo *legislative action.*
acto manifiesto *overt act, express act.*
acto mercantil *mercantile act.*
acto procesal *act done as part of a judicial procedure, procedural step.*
acto punible *a criminal punishable action.*
acto seguido *thereupon, immediately next.*
acto voluntario *wilful act.*
acto solemne *solemn act.*

acto de comercio *act regulated by commercial law, [el]commercial act.*
• Los actos de comercio son aquellos que las legislaciones mercantiles señalan como tales, ya por su naturaleza mercantil, ya por ser efectuados por comerciantes, ya por razones de índole práctico.
Rel: comerciante, *merchant, trader, businessman.*

Comentario: La aplicación de la legislación mercantil se basa en la determinación de si la actividad a ser regulada es realizada por un comerciante o se trata de un acto de comercio. Para darle contenido a la ley mercantil los códigos de comercio de los países hispanos enumeran lo que se considera acto de comercio describiendo y, cuando es posible reduciendo a tipos generales, lo que se ha llegado a considerar tradicionalmente como actividad comercial.
Ref: (Ar)CCo a.8; (Ch)CCo a.3; (ES)CCo a.3; (Mx) CCo a.75; (Esp)CCo a.2; (PR)CCo. a.2, 10 LPRA Sec. 1002; (Ve)CCo. a.2.

acto jurídico *juridical transaction, [el]juristic act, [ed]act which has legal effects, voluntary legal act.*
• Es la manifestación de voluntad de una o más personas, cuyo fin es el producir efectos de derecho. – Sin. negocio jurídico.
Rel: consecuencias jurídicas, *legal result;* hecho jurídico, *legal fact, [ed]legally significant phenomenon, event or situation;* manifestación de voluntad, *declaration of intent, manifestation of volition.*

Comentario: El acto jurídico es uno de los conceptos básicos sobre el que se ha construído el sistema de generalizaciones sistematizadas que constituyen el fundamento del derecho civil en la tradición jurídica romano-germánica. No se trata de un acto individualizado y concreto sino de una abstracción que define la expresión de las posibles conductas en una forma ordenada y general, permitiendo la asignación sistematizada de consecuencias de derecho.
Ver: hecho jurídico.

actor DER.PROCESAL n. *plaintiff, claimant, complainant.* – Sin. demandante, *plaintiff, petitioner.* peticionario, *petitioner.*
Rel: acusador, *accuser, complaining witness;* fiscal, *prosecutor;* litigante, *litigant.*
Ver: partes.

actuaciones judiciales[1] (procedimientos) *judicial or court proceedings.*
• Toda diligencia, trámite o procedimiento que se lleva a cabo con motivo de un proceso.
actuaciones superfluas *frivolous proceedings.*
actuaciones urgentes (Esp) *emergency proceedings.*

actuaciones judiciales[2] (registros) *court records.*
• Las constancias escritas y autorizadas que resultan de las actividades llevadas a cabo en un procedimiento judicial. – Sin. autos.

actuario[1] (juzgado) n. [ed][rtrgido]*process server,* [ed][rtrgido]*court executor,* [ed]*officer of the court in charge of summons and execution of court orders and judgments.*
• Auxiliar judicial que da fe en las actuaciones procesales, normalmente a cargo de hacer las notificaciones y llevar a cabo la debida ejecución de las sentencias. <el embargo se traba o constituye por el actuario del juzgado, *the court executor executes the attachment.*> <el actuario entregó personalmente la notificación, *the court process server served notice in person.*> – Sin. [rtrgido]notificador, *process server.* secretario notificador y ejecutor.
Cf: **actuario • secretario.** El secretario es el asistente principal del juez llevando a cabo múltiples tareas que van desde la redacción de autos y proyectos de sentencias, hasta cuestiones propiamente administrativas. El actuario por su parte, tiene una función más específica: el ser el fedatario judicial de las actuaciones autorizadas o pedidas por el juez y el ejecutar ciertas diligencias.
Rel: secretario del juzgado, [el]*court clerk,* [ed]*court's assisting attorney.*

actuario[2] (seguros) n. *actuary.*
• Persona especializada en estadística que calcula las primas de un seguro basándose en el riesgo al que se encuentran asociadas.

acuerdo[1] (coincidencia) n. *agreement, understanding, accord.* **acordar** v. *to agree upon.* **acordado** adj. *agreed upon.*
• Es una coincidencia de intención de las partes relativas a un objeto común o "el concierto de dos voluntades o inteligencias de personas que llevan a un mismo fin." (I Cabanellas, 151)

acuerdo de las partes *agreement between the parties* || *stipulation.* – Sin. acuerdo entre las partes.

acuerdo de voluntades *mutual assent, meeting of the minds.*

acuerdo extrajudicial *out-of-court settlement.*

acuerdo judicial *stipulation, agreement ratified before the court.*

llegar a un acuerdo *to reach an agreement.*

Rel: aceptación, *acceptance;* consentimiento, *consent, mutual assent;* convenio, *agreement.*

acuerdo[2] (decisión) n. *resolution, disposition.* **acordar** v. *to resolve, to decide.* **acordado** adj. *decided.*

• Resolución tomada por un órgano o grupo organizado de personas, en especial un tribunal o juzgado.

acuerdo plenario *decision handed down by the full court (or full body involved).*

Rel: decisión, *decision.*

acumulación n. *joinder.*

• El unir uno o varios autos o acciones con un propósito de ahorro procesal.

acumulación de acciones *joinder of actions.* – Sin. acumulación de pretensiones.

acumulación de autos *joinder of claims.* – Sin. acumulación de causas.

acumulación de delitos *joinder of offenses.*

acumulación de partes *joinder of parties.* – Sin. litisconsorcio.

Rel: litispendencia, *lis pendens.*

acusación DER.PENAL n. *accusation.* **acusar** v. *to accuse.* **acusador** n. *accuser.* **acusatorio** adj. *accusing, accusatory.*

• "Cargo que se formula ante un juez contra una persona determinada, por considerarla responsable de un delito o falta, con el objeto de que se le aplique la sanción prevista por la ley." (Ramírez Gronda, 39) – Sin. denuncia, *criminal complaint.* querella de parte, *aggrieved-party complaint.* incriminación, *incrimination.* inculpación, *inculpation.* imputación, *imputation.* queja, *complaint.*

Cf: **acusación • imputación.** Términos similares y usados sinónima e indistintamente con frecuencia. Acusación se refiere al señalamiento ante la autoridad respectiva de que una persona ha realizado un acto presumiblemente delictuoso. La imputación, por su parte, se refiere primordialmente a una adscripción o atribución a un sujeto, resultando directamente ligada a los conceptos de responsabilidad tanto penal como civil.

acusación falsa *false accusation.*

acusación maliciosa (PR) *malicious accusation.*

acusador particular (Ar, Esp) *private prosecutor.*

acusador privado (Ar,Esp) *private prosecutor (for cases involving close personal relationships).*

Rel: denuncia, *criminal complaint;* imputación, *imputation.*

Ver: denuncia. querella.

acusado DER.PENAL n. *defendant, the accused.* – Sin. culpado. encausado, *sued, on trial.* enjuiciado, *on trial.* inculpado, *inculpated.* indiciado, *suspect.* procesado, *on trial.*

Cf: **acusado • indiciado • inculpado • encausado • procesado • enjuiciado • condenado.** Acusado es el término más usado y de connotación más amplia. Indiciado significa sospechoso o presunto autor. Inculpado se refiere a alguien a quien se considera participante en la comisión de un delito. Por su parte encausado, procesado o enjuiciado significa que la persona ha sido acusada formalmente y que se sigue un procedimiento judicial en su contra. Finalmente, condenado describe a alguien que ha sido encontrado culpable y a quien se le ha impuesto una pena.

Rel: culpable, *guilty,* sospechoso, *suspect.*

acusar recibo *to acknowledge receipt.*

adicción n. *addiction.*

adicción a las drogas *drug addiction.*

adicción al juego *addiction to gambling.*

Rel: dependencia, *dependence.*

adicto n. *addict, hype, hophead, junkie.*

adicto a la heroína *heroin addict, sleepwalker.*

adicto a LSD *LSD addict, acid freak.*

Rel: marihuano, *doper, pothead, weed head;* alcohólico, *alcoholic.*

adjudicación n. *award,* **adjudicar** v. *to award.* **adjudicatario** n. *awardee.* **adjudicador** n. *awarder.*

• Es el acto por el cual se reconoce el derecho a una persona de gozar de un bien mediante el reconocimiento que hace una autoridad calificada para ello.

adjudicación de contrato *award of contract.*

adjudicación de herencia *award of inheritance.*

adjudicación de quiebra *adjudication in bankruptcy.*

adjudicación en almoneda pública *award in public auction.*

administración[1] (gestión) n. *administration,*

management. **administrar** v. *to manage, administrate.* **administrador** n. *manager, administrator.* **administrativo** adj. *administrative.* – Sin. dirección, *direction, management.* gestión, *manejo.*
administración de justicia *administration of justice* || *law enforcement.* – Sin. función jurisdiccional.
administración de la herencia *estate administration.*
administración de la quiebra *bankruptcy receivership.*
administración de la sociedad *company management.*
administración de negocios *business administration.*
administración fiduciaria *trusteeship.*
administración judicial *judicial administration, court administration.*
administración pública *public administration.*
administración² (**institución**) n. *government.* – Sin. gobierno. régimen, *regime.*
administración central *central government.*
administración de justicia *court system.*
administración fiscal *tax authorities.*
admisión n. *admission.* **admitir** v. *to admit.* – Sin. aceptación, *acceptance.*
admisión de culpabilidad *admission of guilt.*
admisión de la demanda [ed]*acknowledgement by the court that a complaint has been filed and allowed.*
admisión tácita *incidental admission.* Ver: confesión.
admonición n. *admonition, warning.*
adopción FAMILIA n. *adoption.* **adoptar** v. *to adopt.* **adoptivo** adj. *adoptive.* **adoptante** n. *adopter.* **adoptado** n. *adoptee.*
• Acto judicial por el que se constituyen vínculos análogos al de hijos y padres entre personas que no tienen tal parentesco.
adopción de agencia *adoption made through an agency.*
adopción internacional *international adoption.*
adopción legal *legal adoption.*
adopción plena *full adoption.*
adopción póstuma *posthumous adoption.*
adopciones hechas por particulares *private adoptions.*
agencia de adopción *adoption agency.*
padres adoptivos *adoptive or foster parents.*
Rel: familia, *family;* filiación, *filiation.*

Ref: (Ec)CC a.332-348; (Mx)CC a.399; (Pe)CC, a. 377; (RD)CC a.343; (Ur)CC a.243-251; (Ve)CC a.246-260.
adoptar medidas necesarias *to take appropriate measures or action.*
adquisición n. *acquisition.* **adquirir** v. *to acquire.*
adquirente o adquisidor n. *acquirer, transferee.*
• El obtener o el hacer propio un bien o un derecho por recibirlo originalmente, como en el hallazgo, o por transmisión lucrativa, como en la compraventa, o por prescripción adquisitiva.
adquisición a título gratuito *acquisition by gift or donation.*
adquisición a título oneroso *purchase for value.*
adquisición de buena fe *good faith acquisition.*
adquisición de derechos *acquisition of rights.*
adquisición de la nacionalidad *naturalization.* – Sin. adquisición de la ciudadanía.
adquisición de mala fe *bad faith acquisition.*
adquisición del dominio *acquisition of ownership.*
adquisición original *original acquisition.*
adquisición de la propiedad (formas o modos de) *methods of acquiring ownership (over property).*
Consiste en incorporar un bien al patrimonio de una persona mediante la realización de un hecho o acto jurídico.
Rel: accesión, *accession;* ocupación, *occupation;* prescripción adquisitiva o usucapión, *prescription (if personalty)* || *adverse possession (if realty);* sucesión, *succession.*
adscrito adj. *assigned.*
aduana¹ (**función**) *customs.* **aduanero** adj. *pertaining to customs.* **aduanal** adj. *pertaining to customs.*
• Lugar donde se establece el control administrativo de la entrada y salida de mercancias de un país.
aduana de entrada *entry customs.*
aduana de salida *departure customs.*
agente aduanal *customs agent, customs official.* – Sin. agente de aduanas.
arancel de aduanas *customs duties.* – Sin. arancel aduanal. derechos arancelarios.
declaración aduanal *customs declaration.*
despacho aduanero o aduanal *customs clearance.*
resguardo aduanal *customs control.*
tarifa aduanera *customs duty, tariff.*

Rel: comercio internacional, *international trade.*

aduana[2] **(estructura)** *custom-house.* – Sin. garita aduanal, *custom-house.* edificio aduanal, *customs building, customs edifice.* recinto aduanal, *customs facilities, custom-house.*

adulteración de alimentos (delito) *adulteration of food.* – Sin. alteración de alimentos. corrupción de alimentos.

adulteración de documentos *falsification of documents.*

adulterio n. *adultery.* adúltero n. *adulterer, adulteress.* **adúltero** adj. *adulterous.* **adulterino** adj. *adulterine, adulterous.* – Sin. infidelidad, *infidelity.*

adulto n. *adult.*

• Adulto es una persona que ha alcanzado la pubertad.

Rel: adolescente, *adolescent, teenager, juvenile.*

mayoría de edad, *age of majority.*

Comentario: Desde el punto de vista jurídico, la mayoría de edad raramente coincide con el advenimiento de la pubertad. Al igual que en otros países, en hispanoamérica y España la edad requerida para establecer responsabilidad legal varía según la materia y la localidad. Por ejemplo, la mayoría de edad civil se obtiene entre los 18 y 21 años según el lugar, pero en materia de delincuencia juvenil la legislación para menores se aplica solamente a aquellos entre los 8 y 18 años en la mayoría de los países.

advertencia n. *warning.* **advertir** v. *to warn.*

aeronave n. *aircraft, airship.* – Sin. avión, *aircraft, airplane.* aeroplano, *airplane.*

Rel: piloto, *pilot;* tripulación, *crew.*

afidávit (prest.) n. *affidavit.*

afianzadora n. *bonding company.* **afianzar** v. *to guarantee.*

afinidad n. *affinity.*

• "Parentesco que se contrae en virtud del matrimonio entre el marido y los parientes de la mujer y entre ésta y los de su cónyuge." (De Pina, 65)

parentesco por afinidad *relationship by affinity.*

Rel: matrimonio, *marriage.*

agencia[1] **(contrato)** n. [ed]*procuration of business for another.* [prest.][lat.]*procuratio negotiorum.*

agente n. *agent.* **principal** n. *principal.*

• Contrato mercantil por el que el agente se obliga a promover y concluir contratos en nombre de otro mediante pago de una cantidad.

agencia en exclusiva *exclusive agency.* – Sin. **agencia con exclusiva.**

agente comercial *commercial agent.*

agente de ventas *sales representative.*

agente viajero *traveling representative.*

Rel: comisión mercantil, *mercantile agency, commercial agency;* concesión, *franchise;* intermediación, *intermediation.*

Comentario: "Es un contrato mercantil atípico que contiene elementos del contrato de comisión y del de arrendamiento de servicios. La agencia es concertada entre dos comerciantes independientes: uno de ellos llamado principal, encarga a otro llamado agente, que represente sus intereses coordinándolos con la industria independiente que ejerce el último. La representación de dichos intereses se materializará promocionando contratos en interés del principal al que representa; en este sentido, el agente hace de mediador. Pero a diferencia de éste, que se limita a indicar la ocasión de concluir un contrato, el agente se compromete a ejercer esa función de forma continuada en una pluralidad de negocios que se celebran sucesivamente. El agente debe seguir las instrucciones del principal, que suelen concretarse a las condiciones contractuales y a las medidas de publicidad; debe informar al principal sobre las condiciones de la zona asignada para la agencia y sobre los negocios en curso..." (Ribó Durán, 37)

agencia[2] **(negocio)** n. *agency, office.*

agencia de adopción *adoption agency.*

agencia de bienes raíces *real estate agency.*

agencia de cobranzas *collection agency.*

agencia de empleos *employment agency.* – Sin. agencia de colocaciones. oficina de empleos.

agente de bolsa *stockbroker.*

agente de seguros *insurance agent.*

agencia[3] **(sucursal)** n. *branch, office.* **agente** n. *representative.*

• Parte de la organización administrativa de una negociación. – Sin. oficina de representación, *representative's office.* sucursal. *branch.*

agencia foránea *foreign branch, out-of-town agency.*

agiotaje n. *speculation.* **agiotista** n. *profiteer.* – Sin. especulación, *speculation.*

agravantes DER.PROC.PENAL n. *aggravating circumstances.*

• Son circunstancias que agravan la responsabilidad criminal de quien comete un delito. – Sin. circunstancias agravantes. circunstancias de agravación.

Tipos: abuso de confianza, *breach of trust;* abuso de superioridad, *abuse of authority;* alevosía, *surreptitiously or by surprise;* en cuadrilla, *in a gang;* ensañamiento, *aggravated brutality;* nocturnidad o de noche, *at night;* premeditación, *premeditation;* traición, *treachery;* ventaja, *undue advantage.*

agravio[1] **(ofensa)** n. *injury, offense, grievance.* **agraviar** v. *to injure or wrong.* **agraviado** n. *aggrieved or wronged party.*

• La lesión u ofensa causada a una persona, en especial la causada mediante una resolución judicial. – Sin. afrenta, *affront.* insulto, *insult.* lesión, *injury.* ofensa, *offense.* ultraje, *offense, outrage.*

agravio[2] **(apelación)** n. [ed]*error or injury upon which an appeal is based, grounds for appeal.* **agraviado** n. *appellant.*

• "[C]ada uno de los motivos de impugnación expresados en el recurso de apelación contra una resolución de primera instancia." (Dicc. UNAM, 125)

escrito de agravios *appellate brief.*

agresión[1] n. *aggression, attack, battery* (PR). **agredir** v. *to assault, to attack.* **agresor** n. *aggressor.* **agresivo** adj. *aggressive.* **agresivamente** adv. *aggressively.*

• Ataque contra una persona para lesionarla, especialmente sin justificación. – Sin. acometida, *attack, assault.* acometimiento, *attack, assault.* asalto, *assault.* ataque, *attack.* violencia física, *physical violence.*

agresión física *physical aggression.* **agresión sexual (Esp)** *sexual assault.*

Rel: hostilidad, *hostility.* lesiones, *battery.*

agresión[2] DER.INTL n. *aggression.*

• Ataque armado en estado de ejecución o cuya realización es inminente, llevado a cabo por grupos combatientes de otro país.

aguas n. *water.*

aguas nacionales *public waters.* – Sin. aguas propiedad de la nación.

aguas propiedad de los particulares *private waters.*

aguas interiores DER.INTL *internal waters.*

ajustarse a derecho *to conform to law.*

ajusticiar v. *to execute.*

albacea n. *executor, executrix.* **albaceazgo** n. *executorship.*

• Albacea es la persona designada en un testamento para llevar a cabo las disposiciones de última voluntad hechas por el testador. – Sin. ejecutor testamentario.

albacea accidental *acting executor.* – Sin. albacea de hecho.

albacea dativo *dative executor, court-*

appointed temporary executor.

albacea especial *special executor.* – Sin. albacea particular.

albacea testamentario *testamentary executor.*

albacea universal *general executor.*

albaceas mancomunados *joint executors, coexecutors.*

Rel: administrador, *administrator.*

Comentario: El término albacea se usa frecuentemente para designar no sólo al ejecutor testamentario sino también a aquel que se encarga de la ejecución de una sucesión intestada. Tal es el caso de la legislación mexicana.

alcaide (Ar) n. *governor or warden of a prison.*

alcalde n. *mayor, provost* (Esco.). **alcaldía** n. *city hall, mayor's office.* **alcaldesa** n. *mayoress.*

• Alcalde es el Presidente del Ayuntamiento y jefe de la administración municipal. – Sin. corregidor.

Rel: concejales, *board members, aldermen;* Ayuntamiento, *county or city Board.*

alcohol n. *alcohol.* **alcoholizar** v. *to add alcohol, to alcoholize.* **alcohólico** *drunkard, alcoholic.* **alcoholismo** n. *drunkenness, alcoholism.* **alcoholero** adj. *maker or seller of alcohol.*

Alcohólicos Anónimos (AA) *Alcoholics Anonymous* (AA).

bebida alcohólica *liquor, distilled spirits.*

beber alcohol en la vía pública *drinking in public.*

síndrome de abstinencia de alcohol *alcohol abstinence syndrome.*

Rel: alcoholemia, *alcoholemia;* alcoholímetro, *alcoholometer;* conducir en estado de ebriedad, *drunk driving, driving under the influence;* ebriedad, *drunkenness, inebriation;* licor, *liquor.*

aleatorio adj. *aleatory, uncertain.* – Sin. dudoso, *doubtful.* fortuito, *fortuitous.* incierto, *uncertain.*

contrato aleatorio *hazardous or aleatory contract.*

alegación n. *argument* || *pleading.* **alegar** v. *to argue.*

• Presentación de hechos y argumentación de derecho dadas por las partes para apoyar sus pretensiones. – Sin. alegatos.

Cf: **alegación** ● **alegatos.** Ambos términos son sinónimos e intercambiables cuando se refieren a discursos de persuasión presentados ante el juez. La preferencia en su uso varía según el país pero en términos generales ambos, alegación y alegatos, se usan indistintamente con este significado. Es de señalarse, sin embargo, que este mismo par de términos tiene un significado diferente que no es coincidente: alegación también se usa como una afirmación de hechos, y en particular aquella que fija la litis; en tanto que alegatos también se puede referir a la argumentación final de las partes en un juicio.

alegaciones conclusivas *closing arguments.* – Sin. alegatos.

alegaciones de fijación *pleadings.*

alegaciones de introducción *arguments made in the complaint.*
Rel: fijación de la litis, *pleadings.*

alegación (PR) n. *pleadings.*

alegatos¹ (alegaciones) n. *argument.*
• Los argumentos que presentan las partes ante el juez para persuadirlo del mérito de sus pretensiones. – Sin. alegación.

alegatos² (discurso final) DER.PROC n. *closing argument.*
• Afirmaciones finales estableciendo las partes el fundamento y las razones de sus pretensiones.

alevosía n. [ed]*surreptitiously or by surprise.*
alevoso adj. *surreptitious.* **alevosamente** adv. *surreptitiously.*
• La alevosía es toda cautela que asegura la comisión del delito y elimina el riesgo de reacción del sujeto perjudicado en contra del delincuente.
Comentario: Alevosía está constituída por dos elementos principales que son: la presencia de medidas de aseguramiento de la acción delictiva y la eliminación del riesgo.

alguacil (Esp,Ar) *sheriff, bailiff.*

alias n. *alias.* – Sin. apodo, *nickname.* sobrenombre, *nickname.* mote, *nickname.*

alienable adj. *alienable.* **alienar** v. *to alienate.* – Sin. enajenable, *alienable, transferable.*

alimentos FAMILIA n. *support payments.* **alimentante** n. *provider of support.* **alimentista** n. *recipient of support.*
• Es la prestación en dinero, hecha en forma periódica, que los obligados por la ley entregan a aquellos designados como recipientes para su sustento, habitación, vestido y asistencia médica. – Sin. obligación de alimentos, *obligation to pay support.* pensión alimenticia o alimentaria.

acreedor alimentista *support obligor.* – Sin. acreedor alimentario.

alimentos provisionales *support pendente lite.* – Sin. alimentos pendente lite.

deudor alimentista *support obligee.* – Sin. deudor alimentario.

inasistencia alimentaria (delito) *nonsupport, criminal nonsupport.*
Ref: (Ar)CC a.367ss; (Ch)CC a.321 y 323; (Ec)CC a.369; (Esp)CC a.142ss.; (Mx)CC a.308ss; (Pay)CC a.256; (Pe)CC a.472; (PR)CC a.142 31 LPRA 561; (RD)CC a.208,209; (Ve)CC a.282ss.

allanamiento n. *legal search (of premises by the authorities).*

allanamiento a la demanda DER.PROC.CIVIL *acceptance of the complaint (by defendant), acquiescence to the complaint (by defendant).*
• Manifestación de voluntad de la parte demandada expresando su conformidad con lo pedido en la demanda por la parte actora. – Sin. reconocimiento de la acción.
Ver: autocomposición.

allanamiento de morada (delito) *home invasion, illegal entry in another's home.*
• Penetración furtiva o con engaño o violencia, o sin permiso de la persona autorizada a una vivienda habitada sin orden de autoridad competente o ilegalmente. – Sin. violación de domicilio (Ar). violación de habitación (Co). violación de morada (PR).
Rel: allanamiento de domicilio de personas jurídicas (Esp), *illegal entry of a business address;* allanamiento de propiedad ajena, *criminal trespass, unlawful entry;* allanamiento policial (Co), *lawful police entry without a warrant.*
Ref: (Ar)CP a.150-152; (Bo)CP a.298; (Esp) CP a.202; (Mx) CP a.285; (Pe)CP a.159,160; (Ur)CP a.294-295.

almoneda n. *public auction.* – Sin. remate, *auction, closing sale.* subasta, *auction.*

alquiler n. *rental, rent.*

alta mar *high seas.* – Sin. mar abierto, *open seas.*

alteración del orden público *breach of the peace.* – Sin. alteración a la paz (PR).

aluvión PROPIEDAD n. *alluvion, accession by alluvial deposits.*
• Incremento de un predio ribereño en virtud de la acumulación paulatina de materiales arrastrados por la corriente.
Rel: accesión, *accession.*

alzada n. *appeal.* **alzamiento** n. *appeal.*

alzamiento de bienes *concealment of assets.*

alzamiento de embargo *release of an attachment, discharge of an attachment.* – Sin. levantamiento de embargo.

ámbito de validez de la norma jurídica *applicability of the law.*

ámbito espacial de validez [fe]*territorial prescriptive jurisdiction, spatial applicability of the law.*

ámbito temporal de validez *period of time during which a law is in effect.*

amenazas[1] **(intimidación)** n. *threat.* **amenazar** v. *to threaten.* **amenazador** adj. *threatening.* **amenazante** adj. *threatening.* **amenazadoramente** adv. *threateningly.*

• Manifestación hecha por una persona de causarle daño a otra ocasionando desasosiego y aprensión. – Sin. amago, *menace.* intimidación, *intimidation.* violencia moral, *intimidation.*

amenazas de lesiones *threats to cause harm or injury,* [ef]*assault.*

amenazas de muerte *death threats.*

Rel: conminación, *commination;* injurias, *affronting wrong, insults;* miedo, *fear.*

amenazas[2] **(delito)** n. *threat, uttering threats* (Ca).

• Comete este delito el que amenazare con causar un daño grave en otra persona, en su familia, o en su honra o propiedad.

amenaza condicional *conditional threat.*

amenaza simple *unconditional threat.*

amigable componedor [ed]*mediator appointed by mutual agreement (between the parties),* [prest.][fr.]*amiable compositeur.* – Sin. árbitro de conciencia. árbitro de equidad.

Rel: arbitraje, *arbitration;* mediación, *mediation.*

amnistía n. *amnesty.* **amnistiar** v. *to grant amnesty.* **amnistiado** adj. *granted amnesty.*

• Acto del poder legislativo por el cual se concede perdón a ciertas personas aboliendo los procesos y las penas que les correspondan por la comisión de delitos, generalmente de tipo político.

Rel: conmutación, *commutation (of sentence);* indulto, *pardon.*

Comentario: Este acto debe estar basado en razones de conveniencia pública y debe ser de aplicación general a todo acusado que caiga en los supuestos legales.

Ver: perdón.

amonestación[1] **(reprimenda)** n. *admonition, reprimand.*

• "Corrección disciplinaria. Represión para que no se reitere un comportamiento indebido dentro del procedimiento." (Dicc. UNAM, 153) – Sin. apercibimiento, *admonition.* represión, *reprimand.* reprimenda, *reprimand.*

Rel: censura, *censure, condemnation;* regaño, *scolding, reprimand;* reproche, *reproach.*

amonestación[2] **(aviso)** n. *warning.*

• Exhortación para que no se repita una conducta delictuosa. – Sin. advertencia. aviso, *notice, warning.*

amonestaciones matrimoniales *banns of matrimony.*

amortización[1] **(reducción)** n. *amortization, redemption.* **amortizar** v. *to amortize.*

• "[E]xtinción gradual de un activo, de un pasivo o de una cuenta nominal, por medio de la división de su importe en cantidades periódicas durante el tiempo de su existencia." (Mancera Hermanos, 20)

amortización constante *straight-line method of amortization.*

amortización de títulos de crédito *cancellation of negotiable instruments.*

amortización de una hipoteca *amortization of a mortgage.*

amortización fiscal *tax write-off.*

amortización variable *declining balance method of amortization.*

Ver: depreciación.

amortización[2] **(pago)** n. *repayment of a loan.* **amortizar** v. *to pay back (a loan).*

amortización de acciones *repurchase of a company's own stock (by the company itself).*

ampliación de la demanda *amendment of a complaint.*

ampliación del embargo *adding property in attachment or garnishment.* [ed]*extension of attachment or garnishment.*

amparo n. [prest.]*amparo.* **amparar** v. *to file an amparo writ or suit.*

• Procedimiento judicial impugnatorio, generalmente extraordinario o constitucional, que procura la protección de los derechos fundamentales o garantías constitucionales de los particulares cuando son violados por actos de las autoridades. – Sin. juicio de amparo, [exp.léxica]*writ of amparo,* [exp.léxica]*amparo suit.*

⤶ Amparo es un término típicamente hispanoamericano que no tiene una equivalencia clara en las instituciones de países de habla inglesa. Tradicionalmente se usa la expresión "amparo" para referirse a esta institución en inglés. En términos generales amparo se diferencia del *hábeas corpus,* con el que se le asocia a veces, en que el amparo es un juicio que protege a todos y cada uno de los derechos considerados fundamentales, mientras que el hábeas corpus normalmente se refiere solamente a la protección de la libertad corporal.

amparo directo *direct amparo,* [ed]*one-step amparo.*

amparo indirecto *indirect amparo,* [ed]*two-step amparo.*

improcedencia del juicio de amparo *inadmissibility of amparo suit.*

sobreseimiento del juicio de amparo *dismissal of amparo suit.*

Rel: acto reclamado, *act complained of;* actos de autoridad, *acts or actions of government authorities;* autoridad responsable, *responsible authority;* garantías individuales, *civil rights, constitutional guarantees;* informe previo, *preliminary answer (by the corresponding government authorities);* parte agraviada, *injured party;* suspensión del acto reclamado, *suspension of the act complained of;* tercero perjudicado, *injured third party.*

Comentario: Esta institución ha sido adoptada por un gran número de legislaciones de países hispanos, apareciendo en diferentes modalidades y con grandes variantes en su detalle. En Argentina, por ejemplo, el amparo nació como un reconocimiento directo de los tribunales argentinos (caso Siri, Angel) estableciendo una acción para la protección de ciertas garantías constitucionales. En México, país en el que el amparo ha sido ampliado y cuidadosamente desarrollado, es un juicio constitucional que no solamente protege a los particulares de actos violatorios de sus garantías por parte de la autoridad, sino que también asegura el respeto de la legalidad mediante la realización de la garantía de la exacta aplicación del derecho.

Ver: casación.

Ref: (Ar)C a.43 Ley 16.986, CPCN a.321-2; (Bo)C a.19; (CR)C a.48. LJC a.29; (Ec)C a.95; (Gu)C 265; (Ho)C 183; (Mx)C a.103 y 107, Ley de Amparo.; (Esp)C a.53.2, LOTC a.41; (Pa)C a.50; (Pay)C 134; (Pe)C 200; (Ve)C a.27.

anatocismo n. *anatocism, compound interest.*
• Los intereses producidos por la acumulación del interés pactado. Esto es interés sobre interés.

anatomía forense *forensic anatomy.*

animus domini (lat.) *animus domini, the intent to own something.*

animus donandi (lat.) *animus donandi, the intention to give.*

animus possidendi (lat.) *animus possidendi, the intent to possess a thing.*

ante mí *before me.*

antecedentes¹ DER.PENAL n. *prior record, background.*
• Registro de las sentencias condenatorias impuestas a una persona asentadas en un registro

conservado y administrado por una entidad pública, normalmente el Ministerio de Justicia o su equivalente.

antecedentes penales *criminal record.*

antecedentes penales de un menor *juvenile record.*

antecedentes policiales o policíacos *police records.*

sin antecedentes penales *without a criminal record.*

tener antecedentes penales *to have prior convictions, to have a criminal record.*

antecedentes² CONTRATOS n. *recitals, preamble, whereas.*
• Narración de los hechos sobre los que se basan los elementos principales de un contrato.
– Sin. considerandos.

anteriormente adv. *heretofore, above.*

anticipo de honorarios *retainer.*

anticipo en efectivo *cash advance.*

anticonstitucional adj. *unconstitutional.*
• Que es contrario a un precepto constitucional.

anticresis CONTRATO n. [prest.][lat.]*antichresis.*
• Por este contrato el acreedor adquiere el derecho de percibir los frutos de un inmueble propiedad de su deudor, con la obligación de aplicarlos al pago de los intereses primero y al del capital después.

antigüedad DER.LABORAL n. *seniority.*

antijuridicidad DER.PENAL n. *contrary to law, unlawful.*
• Lo contrario a derecho.
"La voz antijuridicidad representa un intento de traducir el vocablo alemán Rechtswidrigkeit. Significa 'lo contrario a derecho'. Por este motivo se consideró preferible construir ese feo neologismo, en lugar de reemplazarlo por la voz ilicitud." (I Cury Urzua, 347)

antijurídico adj. *unlawful.*

anulación n. *annulment.* **anular** v. *to annul, to quash.*
Ver: nulidad.

año n. *year.*
año bisiesto *leap year.*
año calendario *calendar year.* – Sin. año civil. año natural.
año en curso *current year.*
año fiscal *fiscal year.*
año judicial *court calendar year.*
año legal *statutory year.*
Rel: tiempo, *time.*

apalancamiento *leverage.*

aparcería rural *sharecropping.* **aparcero** n. *sharecropper.*

• Consiste en la cesión temporal del uso y disfrute de una finca rústica para que otro lleve a cabo su explotación o aprovechamiento, con la participación en efectivo, ganado o maquinaria del cedente, debiendo ser divididas las ganancias en proporción a sus aportaciones.

apátrida adj.n. *stateless.*

apelación[1] **(revisión judicial)** n. *appeal.* **apelar** v. *to file an appeal.* **apelante** n. *appellant.* **apelado** n. *appellee.*

• "Mediante [la apelación] la parte vencida en la primera instancia obtiene un nuevo examen y fallo de la cuestión debatida por un órgano jurisdiccional distinto … jerárquicamente superior…" (De Pina, 88) – Sin. alzada.

"Apelación posee dos acepciones procesales muy distintas: en significado amplio es toda reclamación formulada contra un juez o tribunal, con la pretensión o esperanza de mejorar la situación de una parte en la misma causa; pero estrictamente, como se considera de modo especial ahora, apelación es la segunda instancia o recurso de alzada, a diferencia de los recursos extraordinarios, como el de casación..." (I Cabanellas, 326)

↝ *Appeal* se reduce normalmente a una revisión del fallo basado en los autos del juicio y los agravios de la parte apelante expresados oralmente. Apelación, por su parte, comprende un examen más amplio, generalmente haciendo un examen *de novo*, esto es una revisión de la cuestión litigiosa sin tomar en cuenta la decisión emitida por el juez de primera instancia, que incluye la totalidad del procedimiento, desahogando pruebas nuevas si es necesario e incluso supliendo agravios en materia penal.

apelación adhesiva *appeal joined by all or some other parties (of the case).*

apelación con efecto devolutivo *devolutive appeal,* [fe]*appeal which does not enjoin enforcement of judgment.*

apelación con efecto suspensivo *suspensive appeal,* [de]*appeal suspending enforcement of judgment.*

apelación en ambos efectos [ed]*appeal requesting that all statutory favorable consequences be granted (to appellant).*

apelación extraordinaria *appeal on procedural grounds.*

apelación ordinaria *appeal on the merits.*

declarar desierta la apelación *declaration (made by the court) that the term for appeal*

has expired.
Rel: agravios, *grounds for appeal.*

apelación[2] **(impugnación)** n. *appeal.*

• Cualquier reclamación de una resolución judicial que puede modificarla. – Sin. impugnación. recurso.
Rel: casación, *cassation;* remedios, *relief, remedy.*
Ver: recurso.

apeo y deslinde (inmuebles) *survey and demarcation of boundaries.*

apercibimiento[1] **(amonestación)** n. *admonition.* – Sin. amonestación. admonición.
Ver: amonestación.

apercibimiento[2] **(prevención)** n. *warning.*

• Prevención o anuncio formal hecho a una persona citada, emplazada o requerida, de las consecuencias que se seguirán de determinados actos u omisiones suyos. – Sin. prevención, *prevention.*

apersonarse v. *to enter an appearance (in court).* – Sin. comparecer.

apertura de crédito *opening of a line of credit.*
apertura de crédito en cuenta corriente *line of credit in current account.*
apertura de crédito garantizada *guaranteed line of credit.*

apertura de testamento. *reading or opening of a will.*

apertura de la prueba *opening of the phase of presentation of evidence (in a lawsuit).*

apertura de la sucesión *initiation of an inheritance case (in court).*

aplazamiento n. *postponement, deferment, stay.*

• Diferimiento de un acto o actuación judicial. – Sin. demora, *stay.* diferimiento, *deferment.* prórroga, *extension.*
aplazamiento de la ejecución *stay of execution.*
aplazamiento de pago *deferment of a payment.*

aplicación de fondos *application of funds, allocation of funds.*

aplicación de la ley *law enforcement.* – Sin. administración de justicia.

apoderado n. *attorney-in-fact, legal agent.*
– Sin. abogado, *attorney, private attorney.* mandatario, *agent, mandatary.* procurador, *agent, attorney.* representante, *agent, representative.*
apoderado especial *special agent.*
apoderado general *general agent, universal agent.*

apoderado judicial *judicial representative, court representative.*

apoderamiento de datos informáticos (Esp) *theft of computer data.*

apología del delito (delito) *advocating criminal behavior.*
• "La exposición, ante una concurrencia de personas o por cualquier otro medio de difusión, de ideas, o doctrinas que ensalcen el crimen o enaltezcan a su autor." (Dicc. ed. Comares, 49) – Sin. apología del crimen.

apología del delito de genocidio *advocating genocide (by supporting its commission or authors).*

apología del delito de terrorismo *advocating terrorism (by expressing approval).*
Ref: (Ar)CP a.213; (Co)CP a.102; (Ec)CP a.387; (Esp)CP a.18; (Mx)CP a.209; (Pe)CP a.316; (Ur)CP a.148.

aportación n. *contribution.* – Sin. aporte.

aportación de capital *capital contribution.*

aportación en efectivo *cash contribution.*
– Sin. aportación en numerario.

aportación en especie *contribution in kind.*

apostilla (fr.) *apostille.*
• Nota o acotación haciendo un comentario o completando un texto.

aprehensión¹ (detener) n. *apprehension, arrest.* **aprehender** v. *to arrest.*
• La detención o captura de una persona con motivo de una pesquiza criminal. – Sin. detención, *detention.*

orden de aprehensión (Mx) *arrest warrant.*
– Sin. orden de detención. orden de arresto (PR).

aprehensión² (capturar) n. *apprehend, seize.* **aprehender** v. *to apprehend.*
• Coger o asir a una persona o a un bien. También es equivalente de secuestro o embargo en algunas jurisdicciones.

apremio¹ (orden judicial) n. *judicial order to enforce compliance.*
• Vía sumaria de ejecución. – Sin. ejecución.

apremio tributario (Esp) *tax collection in execution.*

vía de apremio *action to enforce compliance || collection in execution.*

apremio² (coerción) n. *pressure, coercion.*

apropiación indebida o ilegal (delito) *embezzlement || fraudulent conversion.*
• Aplicación, en beneficio propio o de otro, de dinero, valores o bienes muebles recibidos en depósito, administración o con otro destino, causando perjuicio a tercero. – Sin. abuso de confianza. apropiación ilícita.
Esta figura es usada en ocasiones en forma restringida refiriéndose solamente a la aplicación de los bienes a una finalidad diferente a aquella a la que están legalmente afectados, excluyendo el otro elemento del delito, que es la disposición que se hace de los mismos causando un perjuicio a otro. En esta modalidad restringida el concepto equivalente en países de habla inglesa es *fraudulent conversion,* usándose en español en ocasiones, además de apropiación indebida, términos como desvío de fondos o similares. Es de notarse que en Puerto Rico la denominación apropiación ilegal describe el llamado delito de hurto.
Ver: abuso de confianza. peculado.
Ref: (Bo)CP a.345; (Ch)CP a.470-1; (Esp)CP a.252-254; (Pe)CP a.190; (Ur)CP a.351; (Ve)CP a.468.

apuesta n. *bet, betting.* **apostar** v. *to bet.* **apostador** n. *bettor.*

arancel¹ (impuestos) n. *tariff.*
• Tarifa de impuestos applicable a la importación o exportación de mercancías.

arancel aduanal o aduanero *tariff, schedule of customs duties.*

arancel de exportación *export tariff.*

arancel de importación *import tariff.*

aranceles compensatorios *countervailing duties.* – Sin. derechos compensadores.
Rel: ad valorem, *ad valorem.*

arancel² (tarifa) *fee.*
• Tarifa establecida para el pago de ciertos derechos o servicios, por ejemplo costas judiciales.

arancel judicial *schedule of court fees.*

arancel notarial *schedule of notary's fees.*

arbitraje¹ (intermediación) n. *arbitration.* **árbitro** n. *arbitrator.*
• Es la actividad desarrollada fuera de los tribunales por terceros imparciales, nombrados por las interesados en una controversia, para seguir un procedimiento y dictar una decisión tendiente a resolverla.
Cf: **arbitraje • mediación.** Términos diferenciables y claramente separados que se refieren a la intermediación en un conflicto o diferencia. Arbitraje es la forma de tratar de resolver el conflicto usando un árbitro como juzgador, quien generalmente sigue un procedimiento más o menos formal, y emite un laudo o dictamen que las partes se han comprometido a acatar. Por su parte, la mediación trata de resolver el conflicto a través de un mediador que participa directamente en las ne-

gociaciones de las partes haciendo propuestas que éstas pueden o no aceptar.

arbitraje comercial *commercial arbitration.*

arbitraje forzoso u obligatorio *compulsory arbitration, mandatory arbitration.*

arbitraje internacional *international arbitration.*

arbitraje laboral *labor arbitration.* – Sin. arbitramento obligatorio (Co).

arbitraje voluntario *voluntary or consensual arbitration.*

cláusula de arbitraje *arbitration clause.* – Sin. cláusula arbitral. cláusula compromisoria.

compromiso arbitral *arbitration agreement (as a means to settle an existing controversy).* – Sin. compromiso. sumisión a arbitraje.

contrato arbitral *arbitration agreement.* – Sin. contrato de arbitraje. contrato preparatorio de arbitraje. contrato de compromiso.

laudo arbitral *arbitration award.*
Rel: conciliación, *conciliation;* ex aequo et bono, *ex aequo et bono;* homologación de un laudo, [exp.léxica]*homologation of an arbitration award,* [ed]*judge's approval of an arbitration award;* mediación, *mediation.*

arbitraje² (valores) n. *arbitrage.*

arbitrio judicial *judicial discretion.*
• "Facultad que se deja a los jueces para la apreciación circunstancial a que la ley no alcanza." (Martínez Marín y otros, 36)
Rel: integración, [ed]*judge's law-making authority (by way of interpretation);* interpretación, *interpretation.*

archivos *archives, records.* **archivar** v. *to file (in an archive or registry), to archive.* **archivista** n. *archivist, file clerk.* – Sin. registro, *registry.*

arma de fuego *firearm.*
• Arma que dispara un proyectil mediante el uso de una carga detonante, normalmente hecha a base de pólvora.

arma de fuego recortada *sawed-off shotgun.*

arma de fuego registrada *registered firearm.*
Glosario: alza o mira, *sight;* ametralladora, *machine gun;* ánima o alma, *bore;* boca del cañón, *muzzle;* botador, *ejector;* cañón, *barrel;* carabina, *carbine;* cargador, *clip, magazine;* cerrojo, *bolt;* cilindro o tambor, *cylinder;* culata, *butt;* escopeta, *shotgun;* extractor, *extractor;* fusil de cerrojo, *bolt action rifle;* gatillo, *trigger;* guardamonte, *thumbs latch;* magnum, *magnum;* martillo o percutor, *hammer;* metralleta, *submachine gun;* pistola de perdigón o postas, *pellet gun;* pistola, *handgun, pistol;* recámara,

breech; revólver automático, *automatic revolver;* rifle de asalto, *assault rifle;* rifle de repetición, *repeating rifle;* rifle o fusil automático, *automatic rifle;* rifle o fusil, *rifle;* rifle recortado, *sawed-off rifle;* seguro, *lock;* silenciador, *silencer;* semiautomática o escuadra, *semi-automatic.*
Ver: cartucho. disparo de arma de fuego.

armas n. *weapons.*
• Instrumento destinado a atacar o defenderse.

arma automática *automatic weapon.*

arma blanca *weapon with a blade, bladed weapon.*

arma portátil *portable weapon.*

arma prohibida *illegal weapon.*

arma punzocortante *bladed weapon.*

arma reglamentaria *service weapon.*

arma semiautomática *semi-automatic weapon.*

armisticio n. *armistice.* – Sin. suspensión de hostilidades, *suspension of hostilities.* tregua, *truce.*

arraigo DER.PROC.CIVIL n. [ed]*order to restrict movement of persons (out of the court's jurisdiction),* [ef]*ne exeat order.*
• Medida precautoria, a petición de parte con el objeto de que el arraigado no abandone el lugar del juicio sin dejar apoderado que responda por él.

arraigo del demandado *court order restricting movement out of the jurisdiction.*

arraigo penal *order to place bond or guarantee || order to be confined (to a place)*(Mx).

arraigo del juicio *order to place bond or guarantee.*
• Es una orden contra extranjero demandante pidiendo el otorgamiento de fianza en garantía como resultado de haberse excepcionado el demandado. – Sin. arraigo en juicio.
Ref: (Ar)CPCC a.348; (Mx)CPP a.271.

arras n. *pledge, earnest money.*

arreglo extrajudicial *out-of-court settlement.*

arrendamiento (contrato) n. *lease.* **arrendar** v. *to lease.* **arrendador** n. *lessor, landlord.* **arrendatario** n. *lessee, tenant.* **casero** n. *landlord.* **inquilino** n. *tenant.*
• En el contrato de arrendamiento una de las partes se obliga a conceder el uso o goce temporal de una cosa y la otra a pagar por ese uso o goce un precio cierto. – Sin. alquiler. arriendo. En la República Dominicana se usa el término alquiler para designar al arrendamiento y, a su vez, arrendamiento es el término usado para designar el goce por precio de una hacienda

rural.

arrendamiento de buque *charter, leasing of a ship.*

arrendamiento de cosas *lease of a thing.*

arrendamiento de servicios *service contract.*

arrendamiento de un predio *lease of land.*

arrendamiento de vivienda *housing lease, lease of a dwelling construction or house.*
– Sin. arrendamiento de casa habitación. arrendamiento urbano.

arrendamiento financiero o leasing *lease with option to purchase.*

arrendamiento por tiempo determinado *lease for specified term.*

arrendamiento rústico *lease of rural property.*

subarrendamiento *sublease.*

Rel: renta, *rent;* depósito en garantía, *security deposit.*

Ref: (Ar)CC a.1493ss; (Ch)CC a.1915; (CR)CC a.1124ss.; (Ec)CC a.1883; (Mx)CC a.2398ss.; (Pe)CC a.1666-1712; (PR)CC a.1432, 31 LPRA sec. 4011; (RD)CC a.1711; (Ur)CC a.1776ss.; (Ve)CC a.1,579ss.

arresto n. *detention, arrest.* **arrestar** v. *to detain, arrest.* **arrestado** n. *arrestee.*

• Arresto se refiere a la detención provisional de un presunto inculpado. Asimismo define la reclusión, por un período breve, que se impone a una persona culpable de la violación de una disposición administrativa o de una falta menor.

Cf: **arresto ● detención.** Detención es el término usado para expresar la privación de libertad llevada a cabo en forma legal por la sospecha de la comisión de un delito. Arresto significa una detención provisional y generalmente se aplica en situaciones no penales. Su uso es común en el derecho militar y el derecho administrativo. Algunas legislaciones, como la española y la colombiana por ejemplo, usan o han usado arresto como equivalente de pena de prisión, mientras otras, como la puertorriqueña lo usan como equivalente de detención.

arresto administrativo *administrative arrest.*

arresto domiciliario *home confinement, house arrest.*

arresto menor (Esp) *minimum-term imprisonment.*

arresto preventivo *preventive detention.*

arresto sustitutorio (Esp) *substitution of a fine for time in jail or community service.*
– Sin. arresto policivo.

Rel: aprehensión, *arrest;* detención, *arrest.*

arribada forzosa n. *unscheduled stop at a port, emergency call (at a port).*

artículo de previo y especial pronunciamiento [ef]*dilatory defense,* [ed]*incidental matter to be disposed of before judgment is issued.*

artículos básicos *basic commodities.*

artículos de primera necesidad *staple products.*

artículos terminados *finished goods.*

asalto¹ (robo) n. *robbery, hold-up, stick-up.*

asaltador o asaltante n. *robber, assailant.*
– Sin. atraco.

asalto a mano armada *armed robbery.*

asalto en carretera *highway robbery.*

asalto en despoblado *robbery in a rural area.*

asalto² (ataque) n. *assault, attack.* **asaltar** v. *to assault, to attack.* **asaltador o asaltante** n. *assailant.* – Sin. agresión, *aggression.*

asalto y agresión (PR) *assault and battery.*

tomar por asalto *take by storm.*

asamblea constituyente *constitutional convention.*

asamblea de acreedores *creditor's meeting.*

asamblea general de accionistas *general shareholder's meeting.* – Sin. junta general de accionistas, reunión de accionistas.

asamblea general extraordinaria de accionistas *special shareholder's meeting,* [el] *extraordinary shareholder's meeting* – Sin. junta general extraordinaria.

asamblea general ordinaria de accionistas *regular shareholder's meeting,* [el]*ordinary shareholder's meeting.*

Rel: convenios de voto, *voting or pooling agreements;* convocatoria, *notice of a meeting;* orden del día, *agenda;* quórum, *quorum.*

asamblea legislativa *legislative assembly, legislature.*

asentimiento n. *assent.* **asentir** v. *to assent.*
– Sin. anuencia. aquiescencia, *acquiescence.* asenso.

Rel: consentimiento, *consent.*

asentar en el expediente *to make part of the record.*

asesinato n. *murder,* [rtrgido]*assassination.* **asesinar** v. *to assassinate, kill.* **asesino** n. *assassin, killer.*

• Matar a una persona con alevosía, por precio o recompensa, con ensañamiento o con otras circunstancias especialmente graves señaladas por la ley. – Sin. homicidio calificado. homicidio con agravantes.

En lenguaje popular asesinato es el término preferido frecuentemente para referirse a un homicidio.
Cf: **asesinato ● homicidio calificado.** Asesinato y homicidio son términos que se usan sinónima e indistintamente con frecuencia a pesar de que homicidio es reconocido como un término más amplio que incluye al asesinato como una de sus modalidades. Estrictamente hablando asesinato implica un homicidio calificado o agravado por ciertas circunstancias específicamente reconocidas por la ley; a su vez, un homicidio calificado describe a aquel homicidio cuya agravación es dada por cualquiera de las agravantes tradicionalmente aceptadas por la doctrina (generalmente alevosía, premeditación, ventaja y traición).

↦ Asesinato es generalmente un término más amplio que su equivalente inglés *assassination* en su connotación legal. Ambos son similares cuando describen un homicidio llevado a cabo por recompensa o motivos políticos, pero son diferentes cuando se efectúa en otras circunstancias y, en tales casos, es muy probable que a un delito descrito como asesinato deba identificársele como *murder* u *homicide*.

asesinato a sangre fría *cold-blooded murder,* [el]*cold-blooded assassination.*
asesinato en primer grado *murder in the first degree.*
asesinato piadoso *mercy killing.*
asesinato premeditado *premeditated murder,* [amplio]*assassination.*
asesino a sueldo *hired killer.*
asesino en serie *serial killer,* – Sin. multiasesino.
asesoría legal *legal advice.* – Sin. asesoría jurídica. asesoramiento jurídico.
aseveración n. *assertion.*
asiento CONT. n. *entry.*
asiento contable *accounting entry.*
asiento de abono *credit entry.*
asiento de cargo *debit entry.*
asilo[1] **(refugio)** n. *asylum.* **asilar** v. *to give asylum.*
asilado n. *refugee.*
• Protección dada a nacionales de otro estado que son perseguidos por motivos políticos.
– Sin. santuario, *sanctuary.* refugio, *refuge.*
asilo diplomático *diplomatic asylum.*
asilo político *political asylum.*
asilo[2] **(casa de ancianos)** n. *home for the aged, retirement home.*
hacer ingresar al asilo *to commit (someone) to a retirement home.*

asociación n. *nonprofit organization, nonprofit association, nonprofit* || [amplio]*association.*
• Grupo de personas que constituyen una persona jurídica con nombre, patrimonio y órganos propios que persiguen un fin común de carácter no económico.
Cf: **asociación ● sociedad.** Considerados en forma genérica la asociación y la sociedad se distinguen fundamentalmente por la finalidad perseguida y las formalidades a que se someten. En términos generales los socios de una asociación persiguen una finalidad común que no es preponderantemente económica, mientras los socios de una sociedad persiguen una finalidad que lo es. Los requisitos formales son en general mayores en el caso de una sociedad.
↦ Consideradas ampliamente, una asociación y una *association* son entidades similares, sin embargo cuando se les considera en forma más específica, estos términos tienen diferencias jurídicas importantes que inciden en su equiparación: la asociación es una persona jurídica, y como tal releva de responsabilidad a sus miembros, lo que no sucede con la *association* que hace responsables a sus *associates* de las obligaciones sociales.
Ver: sociedad.
asociación delictuosa *criminal association, criminal affiliation.*
• Grupo u organización que persigue como fin la comisión de delitos o que persiguiendo objetivos lícitos lo hace en forma violenta, intimidante o engañosa. – Sin. asociación ilícita. asociación delictiva. concierto para delinquir (Co).
asociación u organización terrorista *terrorist organization.*
Rel: banda, *ring, gang;* cabecilla, *ring leader;* guerrilla, *guerrillas.*
asociación en participación *joint venture,* [el]*participation association* || [rtrgido] *partnership.*
• Organización mercantil mediante la cual un grupo de asociados aportan bienes o servicios a una (o varias personas) a cargo de la consecución de un fin mercantil, consistente en obtener y repartir utilidades mediante la realización de uno o varios negocios individualmente especificados. – Sin. sociedad accidental. sociedad o asociación momentánea.
↦ La asociación en participación se acerca al concepto de *joint venture* cuando se trata de una empresa única, temporal o no permanente y el socio principal o asociante actúa por su cuenta

y se responsabiliza mayormente de la operación. Se asemeja más a la figura de *partnership* cuando se trata de una empresa permanente y continua y el asociante hace del conocimiento de terceros la existencia de la asociación y comparte el manejo y la responsabilidad del proyecto.

Comentario: La asociación en participación es una figura ambigüa que se caracteriza por ser una asociación de personas que persiguen un fin principalmente económico e incluso especulativo, que carece de personalidad jurídica, y en la que el asociante responde con su patrimonio por las deudas y realiza las operaciones de la asociación en su propio nombre pudiendo mencionar o no la existencia de la asociación.

asociación profesional *professional association or trade organization,* || *worker or employer association* (Ar).

asonada n. *tumultuary demonstration, mutinous demonstration.*

• "Reunión más o menos numerosa realizada tumultuariamente con propósito de obtener por medio de la violencia una finalidad de tipo social, económico o político." (De Pina, 113)
Rel: atentados contra la autoridad, *attacks against the authorities, resisting authorities;* movilización, *demonstration;* rebelión, *rebellion;* sedición, *uprising, revolt.*
Ver: rebelión.

asunción de deuda *assumption of debt.*
– Sin. cesión de deuda, *assignment of credits or debts.* substitución de deudor, *substitution of creditor.*

asunción de riesgo *assumption of risk.*

ataque n. *attack, assault.* **atacar** v. *to attack, to assault.* **atacante** n. *assailant.* – Sin. acometida. asalto. agresión, *aggression.*

ataque a mano armada *armed assault.*

ataque peligroso [ed]*assault with a dangerous or deadly weapon* || *dangerous attack.*

ataques a las vías de comunicación *attack against the transportation system.*

ataque colateral (PR) *collateral attack.*

atentado[1] **(crimen)** *crime* || *criminal assault or attack.* – Sin. delito, *crime.* golpe.

atentado terrorista *terrorist attack.*

atentado[2] **(tentativa)** *criminal attempt.* – Sin. tentativa, *attempt.*

atentado a la vida *attempt to kill.*

atentado contra la seguridad del estado *threat to national security.*

atentado[3] **(resistencia)(Esp)** *resisting authority.*

atentados al pudor (delito) *criminal sexual contact.*
Ver: abuso deshonesto.

atenuante adj. *mitigating.* **atenuar** v. *to mitigate.* **atenuación** *mitigation.* – Sin. mitigante, *mitigating.*

circunstancias atenuantes *mitigating circumstances.* – Sin. circunstancias de atenuación.
Rel: arrebato pasional, *in the heat of passion;* confesión espontánea, *spontaneous confession;* duelo, *duel;* riña, *quarrel, fight.*

atraco n. *robbery, hold-up.*

audiencia[1] **(actuación judicial)** *hearing.*
• "[C]omplejo de actos de varios sujetos, realizados con arreglo a formalidades preestablecidas, en un tiempo determinado, en la dependencia de un juzgado o tribunal destinados al efecto, para evacuar trámites precisos para que el órgano jurisdiccional resuelva sobre las pretensiones formuladas por las partes, o por el Ministerio Público, en su caso." (De Pina, 114) – Sin. vista.
↝ Audiencia y *hearing* son términos equivalentes formalmente ya que se refieren a la actuación de las partes ante el juez hecha en forma personal, oral y en un solo evento o diligencia. Las diferencias provienen del papel dado a la audiencia y *hearing* en sus respectivos sistemas legales. Audiencia se usa en el procedimiento para tramitar y resolver cuestiones de gran importancia como desahogar pruebas, presentar alegatos y para tramitar cuestiones preliminares al juicio; *hearing*, en cambio, se usa casi exclusivamente para decidir cuestiones legales o de hecho incidentales o preliminares a la realización de un juicio, cualquier otra cuestión, incluyendo el desahogo de pruebas y los alegatos, se lleva a cabo normalmente durante la realización del juicio oral o *trial.*

audiencia de conciliación [ed]*pre-trial settlement hearing, settlement hearing.*

audiencia de pruebas *evidentiary hearing.*

audiencia de vista *closing arguments.* [ed]*session for closing arguments.* – Sin. audiencia final. audiencia de juicio. audiencia de alegatos.

audiencia preliminar al juicio *pre-trial hearing.*

audiencia preliminar *preliminary hearing.*

audiencia pública *public hearing.*
Rel: garantía de audiencia, *due process of law.*

audiencia[2] **(tribunal)(Esp)** *tribunal, court.*

Audiencia Nacional [el]*National Audiencia,*

National Court.

audiencia provincial [ext.lexico.]*provincial audiencia, provincial court.*

audiencia territorial [ext.lexico.]*territorial audiencia, territorial court.*

audiencia³ (juicio)(PR) *trial.* – Sin. vista.

auditoría (contab.) n. *audit.* **auditar** v. *to audit.* **auditor** n. *auditor.*

auditoría externa *external audit.*

auditoría fiscal *tax audit.*

practicar una auditoría *to perform an audit, carry on an audit.* – Sin. llevar a cabo una auditoría.

ausencia (personas) n. *absence.* **ausentismo** n. *absenteeism.*

• La falta de presencia de una persona en su domicilio sin explicación y por un período considerable de tiempo. También expresa, en ocasiones, la falta de comparecencia de una persona en un procedimiento judicial.

declaración de ausencia *court order recognizing someone as being absent.*

estado de ausencia *legal status of being absent.*

en ausencia [lat.]*in absentia, in someone's absence.*

juicio en ausencia [ext.lexico.]*proceedings in absentia.*

Rel: desaparecido, *missing;* presunción de muerte, *presumption of death;* rebeldía, *in default, non-appearance.*

autentificación n. *authentication.* **autentificar** v. *to authenticate.* **autentificador** n. *authenticator.* – Sin. autenticación, *authentication.*

auto (actuación) n. *court order or decree* || *writ.* || *interlocutory order.*

• Es una resolución dictada por la autoridad judicial en un proceso impulsando el procedimiento que pueda producir a las partes un perjuicio irreparable, no siendo de mero trámite ni tratándose de la sentencia.

Cf: **auto • resolución judicial.** Auto es reconocidamente una de las posibles resoluciones judiciales que puede dictar un juez en un proceso; en otras palabras, el concepto de resolución judicial es el género y el auto es una de sus especies. Específicamente se considera auto a una resolución que decide algún punto dentro del proceso, diferenciándose de las simples determinaciones de trámite, llamadas decretos, y de las resoluciones que deciden el fondo del litigio, conocidas como sentencias.

↳ Mientras auto y *court order* (también llamada *judicial order*) son equivalentes casi exactos, el listado de los autos y las *court orders* específicos no refleja esta situación automáticamente, ya que cada sistema ha desarrollado su propia terminología para identificar a ciertos autos y *court orders* dentro de ciertas materias o circunstancias. Por ejemplo, un auto de ejecución de una sentencia civil no es una *court order* sino un caso especial de orden o mandamiento denominado *writ,* o un auto reconociendo el divorcio de los cónyuges no es una *order* sino un *decree* por estar regido por los principios de *equity.*

auto de declaratoria de herederos [ed]*court order acknowledging the legal heirs (in an intestate succession).*

auto de detención *issuance of arrest warrant.*

auto de ejecución *writ of execution.*

auto de embargo *writ of attachment or garnishment.*

auto de libertad por falta de méritos [ef] *court order dismissing charges (for lack of evidence).* – Sin. auto de libertad. auto de no sujeción a proceso.

auto de nombramiento de albacea *letters testamentary.*

auto de procesamiento (Esp) [ef]*indictment and order to stand trial.* – Sin. auto de sujeción a proceso. auto de formal prisión (Mx). auto de declaratoria de reo (Ch). resolución de acusación (Co).

auto de radicación [ef]*court order establishing jurisdiction,* [ed]*judicial admission of a criminal cause (by the court).* – Sin. auto de cabeza de proceso.

auto para mejor proveer [ed]*order requiring parties to provide additional evidence.* Ver: resolución judicial.

autocomposición n. [ed]*non-adversarial settlement of a controversy,* [ed]*non-litigious settlement.*

• Es el arreglo a una controversia proveniente de las mismas partes en conflicto.

Cf: **autocomposición • avenencia • conciliación • transacción • allanamiento • desistimiento.** La autocomposición es un término genérico que tradicionalmente incluye: la conciliación, que es el resultado del acuerdo entre las partes para resolver amigablemente un conflicto; la avenencia, que es el acuerdo mismo que resuelve el conflicto reconociendo una de las partes cierta razón a la otra y la que sin rendirse se conviene o aviene; la transacción, en la que ambas partes aceptan, pero no siempre acuerdan voluntariamente; y el allanamiento y desistimiento en los que sólo una de las partes puede desistirse o allanarse.

Rel: allanamiento a la demanda, [ed]*acceptance of the complaint by defendant;* avenencia, *settlement, compromise;* conciliación, *conciliation;* desistimiento de la acción, *voluntary dismissal;* transacción, *accord and satisfaction.*

autodefensa¹ (excluyente de responsabilidad) n. *self-defense.* – Sin. defensa propia.

autodefensa² (defensa) n. *pro se representation.*

autodeterminación DER.INTL n. *self-determination.*

autoincriminación *self-incrimination.*

automóvil n. *automobile, car.* – Sin. auto, *auto.* carro, *car.* coche, *car.*

desmantelamiento de un automóvil *car stripping.*

seguro de un automóvil *car insurance, automobile insurance.* – Sin. seguro automovilístico.

autonomía de la voluntad [ef]*contractual freedom.* [ef]*autonomous legal ordering.*
• La libertad que tienen las partes en un contrato para acordar su contenido.

autopsia n. *autopsy.*
• "Es el examen médico de un cadáver para determinar las causas y circunstancias de la muerte." (Ribó Durán, 64) – Sin. examen postmortem, *post-mortem examination.* necropsia, *necropsy.*

autopsia de ley *autopsy required by law.*
practicar una autopsia *to perform an autopsy.*

Rel: médico forense, *medical examiner, specialist in forensic medicine;* muerte, *death.*

Glosario: cavidad abdominal, *abdominal cavity;* cavidad craneal, *cranial cavity, skull cavity;* cavidad toráxica, *thoracic cavity;* examen bacteriológico, *bacteriological examination;* examen externo, *external examination;* examen interno, *internal examination;* examen radiológico, *radiological examination;* examen toxicológico, *toxicological examination;* exámenes complementarios, *supplementary examinations;* exámenes de alcohol en líquidos orgánicos, *test of body fluids for alcohol;* exámenes histopatológicos, *histopathological examinations;* sistema cardiovascular, *cardiovascular system.*

autor intelectual DER.PENAL *mastermind (behind a crime).*

autor material DER.PENAL *perpetrator (of a crime).*

autoridad¹ (poder político) n. *authority.*
autoritario adj. *authoritarian.*
autoritariamente adv. *authoritatively.*

• Esfera de poder político ejercido por una entidad pública o un grupo debidamente reconocido por la ley. – Sin. potestad.

autoridad competente *competent authority*
autoridad hacendaria *tax authority.*
autoridad pública *public authority.*
autoridades militares *military authorities.*

autoridad² (facultad) n. *power.*
• Facultad o poder que una persona o entidad tienen para actuar legalmente. – Sin. facultad.

autorización n. *authorization.* **autorizar** v. *to authorize.* **autorizable** adj. *able to be authorized.* – Sin. permiso, *permit, leave.* venia, *leave.*

autos (expediente) *court file, judicial records.*
• "Es el cuerpo de escritos en que se refleja el desarrollo de un determinado proceso, formándose con los documentos aportados por los litigantes y los documentos en que ha quedado constancia de las sucesivas actividades procesales...." (Ribó Durán, 65) – Sin. actuaciones. diligencias. expediente judicial. legajo.

Rel: piezas, *sections (of the court file).*

aval TÍTULOS DE CRÉDITO n. *accommodation indorsement,* [ed]*surety for a negotiable instrument,* [ed]*guarantee by endorsement.* **avalado** n. *accommodated party.* **avalista** n. *accommodation party, guarantor, surety.*
• "Consiste en la firma que se consigna en un título para garantizar su pago total o parcial, en caso de no realizarlo la persona principalmente obligada a ello." (Mx-LGTOC, a.109)

aval ilimitado *unrestricted accommodation indorsement.*
aval limitado *restricted accommodation indorsement.*

Rel: endoso, *indorsement;* firma, *signature.*

avalúo n. *appraisal, valuation, assessment.* – Sin. estimación. tasación.

avalúo catastral *assessment of real estate (made by the authorities).*
avalúo fiscal *appraisal for tax purposes.*

avenimiento n. *settlement, compromise.* **avenir** *to conciliate.* **avenencia** n. *settlement, compromise.*
• "Conciliación, entendimiento o acuerdo dirigido a remitir un juicio eventual o poner fin al juicio pendiente, ya sea mediante allanamiento, renuncia o transacción." (Couture, 121) – Sin. arreglo, *settlement.* conciliación, *conciliation.*

Rel: allanamiento, [ed]*admission of the complaint by defendant;* transacción, *accord*

and satisfaction.
Ver: autocomposición.

avería DER.MARÍTIMO n. *average.*

• Se da el nombre de avería a los daños que sufren las mercaderías u otros objetos durante el transporte, y a los gastos extraordinarios e imprevistos que en beneficio de la nave o de la carga deban llevarse a cabo.
avería común *gross average.* – Sin. avería gruesa.
avería general *general average.*
avería particular *simple average.* – Sin. simple average.
Rel: abordaje, *collision between ships;* arribada forzosa, *unscheduled stop at a port, emergency call (at a port);* daño, *damage;* detrimento, *detriment;* merma, *diminution;* naufragio, *shipwreck;* pecio, *flotsam.*

averiguación previa DER.PROC.PENAL *preliminary investigation.*

• Período de preparación de la acción penal consistente en la práctica de las diligencias necesarias para averiguar y hacer constar la perpetración del delito y la culpabilidad del presunto autor. Fase que normalmente lleva a cabo el Ministerio Público. – Sin. instrucción preliminar (Esp).

aviador (Mx) *phantom employee, ghost payroller.*

avío¹ (intangible) n. *goodwill.* – Sin. aviamiento.

avío² (préstamo) n. [ed]*loan made to farmers and cattlemen.* – Sin. préstamo de avío.

aviso n. *notice.*
aviso al público *public notice.*
aviso comercial PROP.INTELEC *commercial slogan.*
aviso de alta DER.LABORAL *notice of new hires (given to the authorities).*
aviso de baja DER.LABORAL *notice of terminated employees (given to the authorities).*
aviso de señalamiento DER.PROCESAL *notice of date and time and place (for judicial proceedings).*
aviso legal *legal notice.*

ayuntamiento¹ (institución) [fe]*county or city board.*
Rel: alcalde, *mayor;* cabildo, *town council;* municipio, *municipality.*

ayuntamiento² (lugar) *town hall, city hall.*

BBBB

bajo fianza *on bail or bond.*

bajo juramento *under oath.*
bajo mundo *underworld.*
bajo palabra *on one's own personal recognizance.*
bajo protesta *under protest.*
bajo protesta de decir verdad (Mx) *under affirmation.*
bajo supervisión *under supervision.*

bala n. *bullet.* **balear** v. *to shoot.* – Sin. balín, *small bullet, pellet.* munición, *munition, ammunition.* proyectil, *projectile.*
a prueba de balas *bulletproof.*
bala de expansión *expanding bullet.*
bala de goma *rubber bullet.*
bala explosiva *explosive bullet.*
bala perdida *astray bullet.*
Rel: blindaje (camisa), *jacket;* calibre, *caliber;* cartucho, *cartridge.*
Ver: cartucho.

balance general (contab.) *balance sheet.*
balance general dictaminado *audited balance sheet.*

balanza comercial *balance of trade.*
balanza de divisas *balance of foreign exchange.*
balanza de pagos *balance of payments.*

balazo n. *shot* || *bullet* || *wound.* – Sin. plomazo (mod.).

balear v. *to shoot.* **baleo** n. *shooting.* – Sin. balacear (Mx,Cu,Sa,Ho).
Rel: balacera, *shootout;* tiro, *shot.*

balística n. *ballistics.*
• La balística se ocupa del estudio de las armas de fuego, de los proyectiles o balas, de su trayectoria y de los efectos de su impacto.
balística de arribada o efecto *terminal ballistics.*
balística exterior *exterior ballistics.*
balística forense *forensic ballistics.*
balística interior *interior ballistics.*
Rel: arma de fuego, *firearm;* bala, *bullet;* cartucho, *cartridge;* disparo de arma de fuego, *gunshot.*
Glosario: análisis de partículas, *particle analysis;* ángulo de caída, *angle of descent;* ángulo de elevación, *angle of elevation;* ángulo de salida, *angle of departure;* camisa metálica, *jacket;* casquillo, *cartridge case;* cromatografía, *chromatography;* estriación, *groove;* impacto, *impact;* indicio, *trace;* magnificación, *magnification;* marcas del extractor, *extractor marks;* micrómetro, *micrometer;* microscopio electrónico de análisis, *scanning electron microscope;* morfo-

logía, *morphology;* plano horizontal del cañón, *cannon horizontal plane;* pólvora, *powder;* rayado del arma, *a gun's groove lands;* rayos x, *x-rays;* residuo, *residue;* retrodispersión, *backscatter;* trauma hidrostática, *hydrostatic shock;* trayectoria, *trajectory;* velocidad inicial, *initial velocity.*

banca n. *the banking system, banking.*
banca electrónica *electronic banking.*
banca múltiple *full-service banking, universal banking.* – Sin. banca universal.

bancarrota n. *bankruptcy.*
Ver: quiebra.

banco n. *bank.* **banquero** n. *banker.* **bancario** adj. *banking.*
• Banco es una empresa intermediadora del crédito.
Crédito, a su vez, en términos generales se refiere a la transferencia de bienes que se hacen en un momento dado por una persona a otra, para ser devueltos a futuro, en un plazo señalado, y generalmente con el pago de una cantidad por el uso de los mismos.
banco central *central bank.*
banco comercial *commercial bank.*
banco corresponsal *correspondent bank.*
banco de ahorros *savings bank.* – Sin. banco de depósito y ahorro.
banco de capitalización *capitalization bank.*
banco de crédito agrícola *farm or agricultural bank.*
banco de fomento *development bank.*
banco de inversión *investment bank.*
banco de primer piso *first-tier bank.*
banco de segundo piso *wholesale bank.*
banco fiduciario *trust company.*
banco hipotecario *mortgage bank.*
banco industrial *industrial development bank.*
cuenta bancaria *bank account.*
derecho bancario *banking law.*
giro bancario *bank draft.*
estado de cuenta bancario *bank statement.*
intervención de un banco *takeover of a bank by regulators.*
Rel: caja de ahorro, *savings and loan;* cajero automático, *automated teller machine* (ATM); cámara de compensación, *clearing house;* encaje legal, *reserve requirement;* unión de crédito, *credit union.*
Ver: crédito[1].

Banco Internacional de Reconstrucción y Fomento (BIRF) *International Bank for Reconstruction and Development* (IBRF).

– Sin. Banco Internacional para la Reconstrucción y Desarrollo (BIRD).

bandido n. *robber, bandit* || *wanted fugitive* (Esp). – Sin. bandolero, *bandit.* salteador, *highwayman, highway robber.*

bando n. *decree, proclamation.*

barco n. *boat, ship.*
Ver: buque.

barra de abogados *Bar association.* **barrista** n. *bar member.* – Sin. colegio de abogados.

> Comentario: En contraste con los países de la tradición jurídica de la *common law,* en los países hispanos la membresía en la Barra o Colegios de abogados no es obligatoria, ni se requiere para poder ejercer la profesión.

barreras arancelarias *tariff barriers.*
barreras no arancelarias *non-tariff barriers.*
base gravable *tax base.*

beligerancia DER.INTL n. *belligerence.* **beligerante** n. *belligerent.*
Rel: armisticio, *armistice;* capitulación, *capitulation.*

beneficencia n. *charity, welfare institution.*
beneficencia pública *public welfare.*
institución de beneficencia *charitable institution.* – Sin. establecimiento de beneficencia.
Rel: benevolencia, *benevolence;* caridad, *charity;* limosna, *charity, alms.*

beneficiario n. *beneficiary.* **beneficiar** v. *to benefit.*
beneficiario de un fideicomiso *beneficiary,* [amplio]*cestui que trust.*
beneficiario de una herencia *beneficiary.*

beneficio de inventario [prest.]*benefit of inventory.*
• Es el beneficio por el que el heredero responde a los cargos de la herencia hasta la cuantía de los bienes que hereda.

beneficio de orden y excusión [prest.]*benefit of priority and discussion.*
• Es el beneficio por el que el fiador no puede ser compelido a pagar hasta que se le ha pedido pago al deudor y se han agotado todos sus bienes.

beneficio de pobreza *right to proceed in forma pauperis.* – Sin. beneficio de litigar sin gastos.

bienes n. *property, assets, goods.*
• Se entiende por bien todo aquello que puede ser objeto de apropiación. A su vez son objeto de apropiación todos los bienes que no están excluidos del comercio ya sea por su natura-

leza, ya por disposición de la ley.

Cf: **bien ● cosa.** Ambos términos se usan como sinónimos e indistintamente. En estricto sentido se hace una diferenciación entre ellos, considerando a una cosa como una entidad u objeto que es valorable por representar un beneficio para alguien, en tanto que un bien es una cosa que puede ser objeto de apropiación.

⮡ Bienes y *property* expresan conceptos equivalentes en virtud de que ambos utilizan la apropiación como uno de los elementos definitorios. Sin embargo el término bienes tiene un ámbito de aplicación más amplio, en virtud de la generalización con que se usa este término en el sistema romano-germánico. *Property* por su parte es una palabra que significa, no solamente bienes, sino también propiedad lo que contribuye, en ocasiones, a cierta confusión en su uso. Cuando no es posible usar *property* en su significación de bienes, los términos más frecuentemente utilizados son *assets*, cuando el término bienes se considera desde el punto de vista económico o contable; *goods*, como bienes muebles, principalmente aquellos en el comercio, y en ocasiones *estate*, como bien inmueble (especialmente con una servidumbre).

bienes abandonados *abandoned property.*
bienes alodiales *allodial property.*
bienes comunales *communal property.*
bienes corporales *tangible assets.*
bienes de capital *capital assets, capital goods.*
bienes de consumo *consumer goods.*
bienes de dominio público *property in the public domain.*
bienes duraderos *durable goods.*
bienes en tránsito *goods in transit.*
bienes fungibles *fungible things.*
bienes futuros *futures.*
bienes gananciales *property earned by husband and wife during marriage.*
bienes incorporales *intangible property.*
– Sin. bienes incorpóreos. bienes intangibles.
bienes inembargables *unattachable property.*
bienes inmuebles *real property.*
bienes litigiosos *property in dispute before the court.*
bienes mostrencos *lost property, unclaimed personal property.*
bienes parafernales *paraphernal property.*
bienes patrimoniales *a person's net worth.*
bienes raíces *real estate.*
bienes semovientes *livestock.*
bienes vacantes *real estate without known*

owner or proprietor.
Ver: cosa.
Ref: (Ar)CC a.2312; (Ch)CC a.565; (Esp)CC a.333; (Mx)CC a.747ss.; (Pe)CC a.885-895; (PR)CC a.252, 31 LPRA sec. 1021; (Ur)CC a.461; (Ve)CC a.525.
bienes inmuebles *real property, real estate, realty,* [lat.]*bona immobilia.*
• Son bienes inmuebles aquellos que por su forma fija no pueden ser trasladados de un lugar a otro. También lo son ciertos bienes que, siendo muebles originalmente, la ley los considera inmuebles por el fin a que se destinan o el objeto al cual se aplican.
– Sin. bienes raíces, *real estate.* inmuebles.
inmuebles por determinación de la ley *property that is immovable by operation of law.*
bienes muebles *movable property,* [amplio]*chattels, personal property,* [lat.]*bona mobilia.*
• Son "bienes muebles aquellos que pueden trasladarse de un lugar a otro ya sea por sí mismos, … ya por efecto de una fuerza exterior." (II Rojina Villegas, 70) – Sin. bienes mobiliarios, *movables.* muebles.
Cf: **bienes muebles ● cosas ● mercaderías o mercancías.** Bienes muebles es la designación genérica que incluye a todo aquello que puede ser apropiado y puede ser trasladado. Cosas designan aquello que es físico o material, esto es, algo tangible, mientras mercaderías o mercancías son la designación preferida en el ámbito comercial para referirse a bienes muebles tangibles.
⮡ *Movables* se refiere solamente a aquello que puede trasladarse y equivale al término bienes muebles por su naturaleza, siendo por lo tanto un término más restringido que el de bienes muebles en general. *Personal property* y *chattels* son términos sinónimos equivalentes a bienes muebles con una importante diferencia: *chattels* incluye a inmuebles constituidos bajo el régimen de *leasehold* mientras *personal property* no incluye ningún inmueble.
muebles por determinación de la ley *property that is movable by operation of law.*
bigamia n. *bigamy.* **bígamo** n. *bigamist.*
• El hecho de contraer nupcias estando aún casado con otra persona. – Sin. matrimonio ilegal (Esp,Ar).
bilateral adj. *bilateral.*
acuerdo bilateral *bilateral agreement.*
contrato bilateral *bilateral contract.*
Rel: sinalagmático, [prest.]*synallagmatic.*

blanqueo de dinero *money-laundering.*
Ver: lavado de dinero.

blasfemia n. *blasphemy.* **blasfemar** v. *to blaspheme.* **blasfemo** n. *blasphemer.* **blasfemo** adj. *blasphemous.*
• Injuria grave contra una persona. Su connotación original es la de una injuria contra Dios. – Sin. injuria, *insult, slander.* ultraje, *offense, outrage.*

bloqueo económico *embargo.*

bloqueo de fondos *freezing of assets.*

boicot n. *boycott.* **boicotear** v. *to boycott.*

boletín oficial *official bulletin or newspaper, gazette.* – Sin. diario oficial, gaceta oficial.

boleta n. *ticket, slip.* – Sin. billete. boleto. cédula. papeleta.

boleta de depósito *deposit slip.*

boleta de empeño *pawn ticket.*

boleta predial *property tax notice.*

bolsa de valores *stock exchange.*
Ver: Apéndice D. Glosario de la Bolsa de Valores.

bolsa de trabajo *employment agency, employment office.* – Sin. agencia de empleo. agencia de locaciones.

bonificación n. *allowance.* **bonificar** v. *to give an allowance.*

bonificación tributaria *tax credit.*

bono[1] **(título)** n. *bond.* **tenedor** n. *bondholder.* **titular** n. *registered bondholder, holder of record.* **emisor** n. *issuer.*
• Títulos representativos de deuda, que incorporan la promesa de pagar interés en forma periódica por la duración de un plazo establecido, y al final devolver la cantidad original prestada.

bono basura *junk bond.* – Sin. bono chatarra.

bono convertible *convertible bond.*

bono de ahorro *savings bond.*

bono de fundador *founder's shares.*

bono de interés variable *floating rate bond.*

bono de prenda [ed]*note issued for a loan against goods in a warehouse, collateral certificate,* [rtrgido]*warrant.*

bono de renta perpetua *perpetual bond.*

bono del tesoro *treasury bond.* – Sin. bonos de tesorería.

bono financiero *general lien bond.*

bono hipotecario *mortgage bonds.*

bono inmobiliario *real estate bond.*

bono nominativo *registered bond.*

bono redimible *callable bond.*

bono[2] **(additional)** n. *bonus.*

bono anual *annual bonus.*

botín n. *loot, booty.* – Sin. despojos.

bracero (obs.)(Mx) *agricultural worker under contract.*

brutalidad policíaca *police brutality.*

buen padre de familia [el]*good family man standard,* [ef]*reasonable and prudent man standard.*

buena conducta *good behavior, good conduct.*

buena fe [rtrgido]*good faith,* [lat.]*bona fide.*
• "Calidad jurídica de la conducta, legalmente exigida, de actuar ... con probidad, en el sincero convencimiento de hallarse asistido de la razón." (Couture, 127)
actuar de buena fe *in good faith.*
↪ Buena fe y *good faith* tienen el mismo origen y significado, el actuar honrada y concienzudamente en la formación y ejecución de un negocio jurídico; sin embargo, *good faith* es un término más restringido ya que excluye el elemento de negligencia que el término buena fe incluye en su modalidad de negligencia grave.

buena salud *sound health.*

buenas costumbres *good morals, public morality.* – Sin. boni mores (lat.).
Al igual que el orden público, las buenas costumbres tienen una doble acepción: una simple que es la de el estar bien educado o conducirse apropiadamente, y una estrictamente jurídica, que es la expresión de moralidad que se considera tiene una comunidad o sociedad dada.
↪ En su acepción de buena conducta, el término equivalente de buenas costumbres que se usa generalmente en inglés es el de *good manners*, mientras que en su significado de moralidad normalmente se usan las expresiones *good morals* o *public morality.*
Ver: orden público.

buenos oficios *good offices.*
• Los buenos oficios se limitan a buscar una aproximación entre partes en conflicto, tratan de favorecer la negociación sin intervenir en ella.
Rel: mediación, *mediation.*

bufete jurídico *law firm, law office.* – Sin. despacho jurídico. oficina de abogados. estudio de abogados (Ar).

buque n. *ship, vessel.*
• Es una construcción flotante adecuada para navegar por agua y dedicada al tráfico maríti-

mo. – Sin. barco. embarcación, *vessel.* nave. navío.

Cf: **buque • barco • embarcación • navío.** Todos estos términos son usados sinónimamente, sin embargo es posible hacer ciertas distinciones: buque es la palabra tradicional usada en los textos legales y normalmente se refiere a un barco que realiza travesía marítima; barco es un término más amplio, tanto de uso popular como técnico, y que se refiere a cualquier estructura diseñada para la navegación; navío o nave es normalmente un término antiguo para designar a un barco, que aparece frecuentemente en la legislación hispanoamericana; finalmente, embarcación es un concepto general e impreciso que incluye cualquier estructura construida con la finalidad de ser usada en la navegación.

arrendamiento del buque *charter, leasing of a ship.* – Sin. arrendamiento de nave.

buque armado *ship that is ready-to-sea.*

buque comercial *commercial ship.*

buque de cabotaje *ship to navigate coastal waters.*

buque de carga o carguero *freighter.*

buque extranjero *foreign ship.*

buque mercante *merchant ship.*

buque pirata *pirate boat or ship.*

buque portacontenedores o de contenedores *full container ship.*

buque sin ruta fija *tramps.*

buque tanque o cisterna *tanker.*

embargo de *buque arrest of ship* || *attachment of ship.*

pérdida de buque *loss of ship.*

Rel: abordaje, *collision between ships;* avería, *average.*

Glosario: aparejos, *rigging;* armador, *ship's husband (if not ship owner), ship owner (if owner), person in charge of supplying and readying a ship;* arqueo, *tonnage;* capitán, *captain, shipmaster;* casco, *hull;* encalladura, *stranding;* estiba, *stowage;* matrícula, *registration;* naviero, *charterer;* piloto, *first mate;* polizón, *stowaway;* práctico, *pilot;* quilla, *keel;* tara, *tare;* tonelaje, *tonnage.*

Ref: (Ar)LN, a.2; (Ch)CCo. a.826-830; (Ec)CCo, a. 724; (Esp)CCo, a.573ss.; (Ve)CCo. a.612.

burdel n. *brothel, bordello, whorehouse.* – Sin. casa de citas. casa de tolerancia. casa de prostitución, *house of prostitution.* casa non sancta. casa pública. lenocinio. lupanar. prostíbulo.

burocracia¹ (trabajador) n. *bureaucracy.*
burócrata n. *civil servant, bureaucrat.*

burocracia² (work) n. *red tape.*

CCCC

cabal juicio *sound mind.*

cabildo n. *municipal council.* **cabildear** v. *to lobby.*

cabotaje DER.MARÍTIMO n. *coastal sailing, cabotage.*
• Comercio o tráfico costero, sin perder de vista la costa.

cacheo n. *frisk.* **cachear** v. *to frisk.*

cacique n. [prest.]*cacique, political boss.*

cadáver n. *corpse, cadaver.*

cadena de título *chain of title.* – Sin. cadena de títulos.

cadena perpetua *life sentence, life imprisonment.*

caducidad n. *lapse, extinction.* **caducar** v. *to lapse, expire.* **caduco** adj. *lapsed, expired.*
• "Por caducidad debe entenderse una sanción que se pacta, o se impone por la ley, a las personas que en un plazo convencional o legal, no realizan voluntaria y conscientemente los actos positivos para hacer nacer, o para mantener vivo, un derecho sustantivo o procesal, según sea el caso." (Gutiérrez y González, 866) – Sin. extinción, *extinction.* preclusión, *extinction of a procedural right.*
Fuera del campo procesal, a la caducidad por lo general se le asigna el significado de no tener efecto, o no tener validez.

Cf: **caducidad • prescripción.** Ambos términos se confunden frecuentemente. Son similares en cuanto extinguen derechos mediante la intervención de un plazo, pero no son considerados términos sinónimos. La prescripción es un medio de defensa y debe, por lo tanto, ser alegado por el interesado. La caducidad, por lo contrario, opera ipso jure y puede ser declarada oficiosamente por el juez. La prescripción es renunciable, la caducidad no lo es por ser de orden público.

caducidad de la fianza *bond forfeiture.*

caducidad de patentes *lapse of patent registration.*

Rel: prescripción, *prescription.*

Ver: preclusión.

caducidad de la instancia *nonsuit,* [rtrgido]*laches.*
• "Extinción anticipada del proceso debido a la inactividad procesal de las dos partes, y en ocasiones, de una de ellas, durante un período

calidad migratoria

amplio, si se encuentra paralizada la tramitación." (Dicc. UNAM, 372)
– Sin. abandono de la instancia, *abandonment of the lawsuit.* perención de la instancia.

☛ En tanto que *nonsuit* describe la caducidad de la instancia en forma amplia, poniendo de relieve el desistimiento de la acción y la extinción del proceso sin una resolución de fondo, *laches* la describe en forma restringida, refiriéndose principalmente a la inactividad procesal de una de las partes como el fundamento para pedir proceda la excepción de *equitable estoppel.*

promover la caducidad de la instancia *motion for nonsuit,* [ed]*motion for involuntary or voluntary dismissal.*
Rel: sobreseimiento, *dismissal.*

calidad migratoria *immigrant status.*

calidad moral *moral character.*

alta calidad moral *good moral character.*

calificación[1] CONFLICTO DE LEYES n. *characterization.*
• Determinación del concepto o categoría jurídica usada por la ley para designar la norma de conflicto aplicable.
Ver: conflicto de leyes.

calificación[2] **(evaluación)** n. *determination or classification (of facts),* **calificar** v. *to determine, to classify.* **calificado** adj. *classified.*

calificación del delito *determination of the specific crime committed by the accused.*

calificación fiscal. *determination of amount of tax payable, tax assessment.*

calificación de elecciones *approval of election results.*

calumnia n. *slander.* **calumniar** v. *to slander.*

calumniador n. *slanderer.* **calumnioso** adj. *slanderous.*
• La calumnia es el acusar falsamente a otro de la comisión de un delito, en forma maliciosa.
Cf: **calumnia • injuria • difamación.** Estos tres delitos atentan contra el honor o buen nombre de las personas, pero no son sinónimos. La calumnia es el acusar falsamente a otro de la comisión de un delito con la finalidad de dañarlo. La injuria es el atacar el honor o reputación de una persona con la intención de ofenderlo (animus injuriandi). La difamación, por su parte, es el desacreditar a una persona o exponerla al desprecio de alguien mediante la divulgación o comunicación hecha a una o varias personas, esto es en forma pública. Modernamente el delito de injuria o injurias ha ido desapareciendo discretamente de la práctica

forense y de las legislaciones de los países hispanoparlantes.
Rel: difamación, *defamation;* injurias, *affronting wrong,* insults.

cámara n. *chamber, assembly, office.*
Cámara de Comercio e Industria *Chamber of Commerce and Industry.*
Cámara de Comercio Internacional *International Chamber of Commerce.*
cámara de compensación *clearing house.*
Cámara de diputados o representantes *House of Representatives, Chamber of Deputies.* – Sin. Cámara baja.
cámara de origen [ed]*chamber or assembly where a Bill is first brought for consideration.*
Cámara de Senadores *Senate.* – Sin. Cámara alta.
cámara revisora [ed]*Chamber or assembly voting on final approval of a Bill.*

cambio n. *change, exchange.* **cambiar** v. *to change, exchange.* cambista n. *money changer,* money **broker.** **cambiario** adj. *exchangeable.*
cambio de calidad migratoria *change of immigrant status.*
cambio de domicilio *change of address.*
cambio de jurisdicción *change of venue.*
cambio oficial *official rate of exchange.*
tipo de cambio *rate of exchange.*

camino n. *road, way.* – Sin. carretera, *highway.* pista, *road.* ruta, *route.* vía, *way.*
camino de cuota *toll road.*
camino público *public road.*
Rel: supercarretera, *multilane highway;* vía rápida, *expressway.*

canabis n. *cannabis.* – Sin. hasish/haschich, *hashish, hash.* marihuana, *marijuana.*
– También: cannabis.

cancelación *cancellation.* **cancelar** v. *to cancel.* **cancelado** adj. *cancelled.*
• "Anulación o acto de dejar sin efecto un documento privado, un instrumento público, una inscripción registral o una obligación. Supone la extinción de un derecho…" (II Cabanellas, 43) – Sin. anulación, *annulment.*
cancelación de antecedentes delictivos *expungement of criminal record.* – Sin. cancelación de antecedentes penales.
cancelación de asientos del registro civil *cancellation of entries in the civil registry.*
cancelación de un título de crédito *cancellation of a negotiable instrument.*
cancelación de una cuenta *closing an account.*

cancelación de una deuda *abatement of a debt.*
cancelación de una hipoteca *cancellation of a mortgage.*
cancelación de una póliza de seguro *cancellation of an insurance policy.*
Rel: abrogación, *repeal abrogation;* extinción, *discharge;* rescisión, *rescission;* revocación, *revocation.*
canciller[1] **(Ministro)** n. *Chancellor, Minister of Foreign Affairs.* **Cancillería** *Ministry of Foreign Affairs.*
canciller[2] **(diplomático)** n. *ambassador, diplomat.*
candidatura n. *candidacy, nomination.*
candidato n. *candidate.*
capacidad n. *capacity* || *competence.* **capaz** adj. *competent.*
• "Aptitud legal de una persona para ser sujeto de derechos y obligaciones o como la facultad, o posibilidad de que esta persona pueda ejecutar sus derechos y cumplir sus obligaciones por sí misma." (Dicc. UNAM, 397) – Ant. incapacidad, *incapacity.* – Sin. capacidad jurídica.
↦ Capacidad y *capacity* son conceptos similares que se refieren a la determinación legal de si una persona está facultada o no para ejercer sus derechos y si es responsable por sus obligaciones. En el campo procesal, el término capacidad frecuentemente es equivalente de *competence* o *competency*, sobre todo en materia de pruebas. <capacidad de un testigo, *competence of a witness.*>
capacidad contractual *capacity to contract.*
capacidad de ejercicio *legal capacity to act.* – Sin. capacidad de obrar.
capacidad de goce [ed]*minimum legal capacity, legal capacity, standing.* – Sin. capacidad jurídica.
capacidad mental *mental capacity.*
capacidad plena *full authority, full competency.*
capacidad procesal *legal capacity to sue, competency to stand trial.*
capacidad testamentaria *testamentary capacity.* – Sin. capacidad para testar.
Rel: emancipación, *emancipation.*
Ref: (Ar)CC a.31 y 32; (Bol)CC a.3; (Ch)CC a.1446-1447; (Ec)CC a.1488,1489; (Esp)CC a.29y37; (Mx)CC a.450 y 23; (Pay)CC a.73; (Pe)CC a.42-46; (Ve)CC a.18,19.
capacidad contributiva *taxpaying capacity.*
capital n. *capital.* **capitalizar** v. *to capitalize.*
capitalismo n. *capitalism.* **capitalista** adj. *capitalist.* – Sin. caudal.

capital de inversión *investment capital.*
capital de riesgo *venture capital.*
capital extranjero *foreign capital.*
capital privado *private capital.*
capital público *government capital.*
huída de capitales *capital flight.*
capital social (sociedades) n. *capital of a company, capital of a corporation or partnership.*
• Fondo constituido por las aportaciones de los socios que se estipula en una cantidad fija en los estatutos de la sociedad, y que sólo puede modificarse de conformidad con el procedimiento señalado en los mismos.
capital autorizado *authorized capital.*
capital contable *net worth.* – Sin. capital en giro. patrimonio neto. capital neto.
capital en acciones *capital in issued stock.*
capital inicial *initial capital.*
capital pagado *paid-up capital.* – Sin. capital cubierto. capital exhibido.
capital suscrito *subscribed capital.*
capital variable *variable capital.*
Rel: acciones, *stock shares;* haber social, *corporate assets;* patrimonio social, [ed]*totality of corporate assets and liabilities.*
capitán de buque *captain, shipmaster.*
capitulaciones matrimoniales *articles of marriage.*
• Contrato entre los cónyuges por el que establecen el régimen jurídico aplicable a los bienes del matrimonio. – Sin.convenciones nupciales.
Ver: régimen económico del matrimonio.
cárcel n. *jail, cooler* (mod.), *slammer* (mod.).
carcelero n. *warden, jail-keeper.*
• Centro de detención en donde permanecen recluídos aquellos que han sido acusados de un delito o que están siendo juzgados por ello, sin el beneficio de libertad bajo fianza o palabra. – Sin. correccional, *correctional facility.* mazmorra, *dungeon.* calabozo, *dungeon, cell.* galeras, *gaol.*
Ver: prisión.
careo DER.PROC.PENAL n. *confrontation.* **carear** v. *to confront.* – Sin. confrontación.
• "Es la confrontación del acusado con los testigos de cargo, así como entre las personas que formulan declaraciones contradictorias en un proceso penal, con el objeto de establecer la veracidad de los testimonios." (Dicc. UNAM, 416) – Sin.confrontación de testigos, *witness's confrontation.*
↦ El careo o confrontación y la *confrontation,*

provenientes de la constitución de los Estados Unidos de América, son conceptos equivalentes en su definición, pero de diferente amplitud en su detalle. El careo consiste en enfrentar al acusado con sus acusadores, o a testigos en contradicción entre sí, mediante la exhortación hecha a los declarantes por el juez o secretario (a petición de la parte interesada) de ratificar o modificar la declaración que aparece en discordia. *Confrontation* sigue un procedimiento más estricto ya que se exige que el acusador no sólo comparezca a declarar frente al acusado en juicio, sino que éste tiene el derecho de hacer un examen detallado, o *cross-examination*, de las contradicciones del testimonio dado por el denunciante.

diligencia de careo *confrontation proceedings.*

carga[1] **(obligación)** n. *burden.*
carga de la prueba *burden of proof.*
carga de trabajo *workload.*
carga impositiva *tax burden.*
carga pública *civic duty.*
carga tributaria *tax burden.*

carga[2] PROPIEDAD n. *encumbrance.* – Sin. gravamen. servidumbre, *easement.*
Cf: **gravamen • carga.** En español las palabras gravamen y carga se usan generalmente en forma sinónima; sin embargo en ocasiones se hace una distinción al considerar gravamen como un término amplio, que incluye tanto bienes reales como personales, en tanto que carga se entiende referida más frecuentemente sólo a bienes reales.

carga[3] **(responsabilidad)** n. *charge.*
carga pública *public charge.*
carga social (compañía) *social security contributions (made by employer).*

carga[4] **(peso)** n. *freight.* **cargar** v. *to load.*
cargador n. *loader, shipper.* **cargamento** n. *load, cargo, shipment.* – Sin. cargamento.
carga general *general cargo.*
carga parcial *partial cargo.*
transporte de carga *freight carrier.*

cargo[1] **(acusación)** n. *charge, count.*
• Una acusación concreta o el delito específico del que se acusa; asimismo el acto o circunstancia sobre la que una acusación está basada. – Sin. acusación, *accusation.*
cargo penal *criminal charge.*
probar los cargos *to substantiate charges.*
testigo de cargo *witness for the prosecution.*

cargo[2] **(costo.)** n. *debit, charge.*

cargos diferidos *deferred charges.*
cargo[3] **(posición)** n. *post, office.* – Sin. posición, position. puesto, *post.*
cargo de confianza *supervisory position, post held on discretionary basis.*
cargo directivo o de responsabilidad *senior post.*
cargo honorario *honorary position.*
cargo político *political office.*
cargo público *public office.*
desempeñar el cargo *discharge the duties (of office).*
ejercer un cargo *to hold office.*

carnet n. *card.* – También: carné.
carnet de conducir *driver's license.* – Sin. licencia de conducir o manejar.
carnet de identidad *identification card (ID card).* – Sin. cédula de identidad.
carnet electoral *voter registration card.* – Sin. credencial de elector.

carta[1] **(documento)** n. *document.*
carta de despido (Esp) *dismissal letter, dismissal statement.*
carta de fletamiento *charter.*
carta de intención *letter of intent.*
carta de naturalización *naturalization certificate, naturalization papers.* – Sin. carta de ciudadanía.
carta de porte aéreo *air waybill, bill of lading.*
carta de porte *waybill, bill of lading.* – Sin. guía de embarque.
carta patente *letters patent, public grant.*
carta poder *power of attorney* || *proxy (securities).*
carta rogatoria *letters rogatory, letter of request.*

carta[2] **(writing)** n. *letter.* – Sin. correspondencia, correspondence. misiva, *missive, letter.*
carta certificada *certified letter.*
carta de recomendación *letter of recommendation.*

carta[3] **(estatuto)** n. *charter.*
Carta de las Naciones Unidas *Charter of the United Nations.*
carta constitucional *constitution, constitutional charter.*

carta de crédito *letter of credit.*
• "Es un documento por cuyo medio la persona que la expide suplica a otra que le entregue a una tercera, una cantidad fija o varias cantidades indeterminadas, comprendidas en un máximo cuyo límite se debe señalar." (Dicc.

UNAM, 421)
carta de crédito a la vista *sight letter of credit.*
carta de crédito bancaria *bank letter of credit.*
carta de crédito confirmado irrevocable *confirmed irrevocable letter of credit.*
carta orden *written order (given to a lower court by a higher court), writ.*
• Es la comunicación hecha por un tribunal superior a uno inferior ordenándole la realización de diligencias o actos procesales, así como transmitirle alguna noticia de la que deba ser informado. – Sin. despacho.
Rel: requisitoria, [ed]*request made to a judge by another to execute a sentence;* suplicatorio, [ed]*request made to a higher court by a lower court.*
Ver: comunicación procesal.

cartas credenciales *diplomatic credentials.*
• Documento oficial que acredita solemnemente a un representante diplomático de primer nivel, como un embajador o nuncio.
Rel: cartas patentes (lettres de provision), *letters of credence;* exequatur, *exequatur.*

cartera n. *portfolio.*
cartera de créditos *loan portfolio.*
cartera de valores *portfolio of securities.*
cartera vencida *nonperforming loans.*

cartucho n. *cartridge.*
• Es la unidad completa necesaria para realizar un disparo e incluye normalmente la vaina o casquillo, la cápsula detonante, la carga fulminante, la carga impulsora, y el proyectil o bala, o las postas o perdigones. – Sin. carga, *charge.*
Cf: **cartucho ● munición ● bala.** Munición es el nombre genérico dado al conjunto de tiros o cartuchos con que se carga un arma de fuego. Cartucho es la unidad que corresponde a cada tiro incluyendo todos los elementos necesarios para el disparo. Bala o proyectil es la parte del cartucho que es proyectada al exterior hacia el blanco durante el disparo.
Rel: arma de fuego, *firearm;* bala, *bullet;* balística, *ballistics.*
Glosario: cápsula detonante, *detonating cap;* carga fulminante, *explosive charge;* carga impulsora, *propelling charge;* pólvora negra, *black powder;* pólvora sin humo, *smokeless powder;* postas o perdigones, *pellets, shots;* proyectil o bala, *projectile or bullet;* vaina o casquillo, *cartridge case.*

casa n. *house, office.*
casa de cambio *money-exchange office.*

casa de empeño *pawnshop.* – Sin. monte de piedad.
casa de gobierno *presidential house* || *main government building.*
casa de moneda, *mint.*
casa habitación *residence.*
casa habitada *residence, inhabited house.*
casa matriz *main office, headquarters.*

casación n. [prest.]*cassation,* [ed]*quashing of court decisions by the highest court (on grounds of error of interpretation or application of the law)* || [rtrgido][fe]*reversal.*
• "Es un recurso procesal que la ley otorga a las partes para obtener la invalidación de una sentencia cuando ésta ha sido dictada en un procedimiento vicioso o cuando el tribunal ha infringido la ley decisoria del conflicto al resolverlo." (Alessandri Rodriguez, 217).
– Sin. nulidad de un proceso.
Cf: **casación ● apelación.** La casación es un recurso extraordinario promovido ante un tribunal de última instancia, que "casa" o invalida una sentencia judicial cuando se ha violado la debida observancia de la ley o se discrepa con la jurisprudencia establecida por el tribunal de casación. La apelación, por su parte, es el recurso ordinario procedente ante el juez jerárquico superior para su revisión con motivo de cualquier decisión que cause perjuicio, sea ésta un auto o una sentencia.
↳ La casación, como una forma de invalidar sentencias judiciales característica de los sistemas romano-germánicos, se expresa preferentemente en inglés usando el término francés *cassation.* Cuando se prefiere subrayar el efecto jurídico de la casación, se usa frecuentemente la expresión *reversal* o *quashing (of a decision or judgment)* indicando que la sentencia ha sido invalidada y deberá dictarse una nueva por el tribunal de jurisdicción original. La nueva sentencia, según el sistema seguido en el país de que se trate, puede ser a su vez invalidada nuevamente *(reversed or quashed)* o aceptada *(remanded)* por el tribunal de casación. En cualquier caso este último órgano dictará la resolución final correspondiente.
casación por infracción de fondo *reversal on the merits.*
casación por infracción de forma *reversal on a procedural matter.*
corte de casación *cassation court.*
recurso de casación *cassation.*
Rel: apelación, *appeal;* impugnación, *chal-*

lenge, impugnment.

> Comentario: En México el recurso de casación "se eliminó totalmente con ese nombre, pero en realidad, quedó subsistente incorporada en el juicio de amparo contra resoluciones judiciales, por lo que la doctrina predominante ha reconocido las similitudes tan estrechas entre ambas instituciones, de manera que a este sector del amparo se le ha calificado con toda justificación como 'amparo-casación'..." (Dicc. UNAM, 430)

Ref: (Ch)CPC a.764ss.; (Co)CPP a.205ss; (Esp)LEC a.477, LPL a.202; (Ve)CPC a.312-326.

casamiento n. *wedding, marriage.* **casar** v. *to wed, to marry,* [idiom]*to tie the knot.*

casamentero n. *matchmaker.* – Sin. matrimonio, *marriage.* boda, *wedding.* enlace, *marriage, to tie the bow.*

caso[1] **(suceso)** n. *case, event.* – Sin. ocurrencia, *occurrence.* suceso, *event.*

caso de fuerza mayor *event of force majeure.*
caso fortuito *unforeseen circumstance, fortuitous event.*

caso[2] **(causa)** n. *case.* – Sin. causa.
caso civil *civil case.*
caso penal *criminal case.*
caso pendiente *pending case.*

castigo n. *punishment.* **castigar** v. *to punish.*
castigador adj. *punishing.* – Sin. punición. penalidad. sanción, *sanction, punishment.*
castigo capital *capital punishment.*
castigo corporal *corporal punishment.*
castigo cruel e inusitado (PR) *cruel and unusual punishment.*
Ver: pena. condena.

catastro n. *real estate registry, cadastre.*
catastral adj. *pertaining to cadastre.* – Sin. censo, *census.* padrón, *registry.*

cateo (Mx) n. *search (executing a search warrant).* **catear** v. *to search.*
• "Registro y allanamiento de un domicilio particular por la autoridad con el propósito de buscar personas u objetos que están relacionados con la investigación de un delito." (Dicc. UNAM, 433) – Sin. registro. pesquisa.

cateo y secuestro de bienes *search and seizure.* – Sin. registro y secuestro.

orden de cateo *search warrant.* – Sin. orden de registro.

> Comentario: Las diligencias se practicarán por el tribunal que las ordene a través de su secretario o actuario, o por los funcionarios o agentes de la policía judicial, y podrá asistir al propio cateo la autoridad que lo hubiese solicitado de parte de la fiscalía o Ministerio Público. En la práctica la diligencia requiere de la presencia de un fedatario

que normalmente es el agente de la fiscalía o Ministerio Público, aunque pueden actuar como tales tanto el secretario como el actuario del juzgado.

caución n. *surety, bond.* **caucionar** v. *to guarantee, to bond.* **caucionable** adj. *bailable.*
• "Seguridad que da una persona a otra de que cumplirá lo pactado, convenido u ordenado. Puede darse caución presentando fiadores, ofreciendo bienes o prestando promesa jurada." (Ramírez Gronda, 75) – Sin. garantía, *guarantee.*

caución de arraigo en juicio [ed]*bond or surety to guarantee defendant will not leave the jurisdiction.* – Sin. fianza de arraigo.

caución de buena conducta *bail bond.* – Sin. caución de conducta. fianza penal.

caución de licitación *bid bond.*

caución de no ofender [ed]*bond posted to guarantee defendant will refrain from certain behavior.*
Rel: prenda, *pledge.*
Ver: fianza.

caudal hereditario *estate of a deceased person, decedent's estate.* – Sin. acervo hereditario. patrimonio hereditario.

causa[1] CONTRATOS n. [ef]*consideration,* [el]*cause,* [lat.]*causa.* **causal** adj. *causal.* **causalidad** n. *causality.*
• Modernamente se considera a la causa contractual como el móvil o motivo determinante de la voluntad, esto es, la razón que lleva a alguien a contratar. Es exterior al contrato y es diferente para cada persona y contrato.
☞ Tanto causa como *consideration* tienen una amplia literatura en la que se pone de relieve su diferenciación. A pesar de ello, tanto causa como *consideration* son equiparados en la función que frecuentemente se les asigna: la de dar nacimiento a una obligación contractual. De esta manera ambos términos se consideran equivalentes cuando causa se refiere a la contraprestación contractual, o como aquello que se hace, da, o deja de hacer. Son por otro lado diferenciados cuando causa es expresada, no como una contraprestación, sino como una motivación, propósito o fuente de obligaciones y es descrita mayormente en forma diferente para cada tipo de contrato, por ejemplo, obtener la renta para el arrendatario, adquirir la propiedad de la cosa para el vendedor, etc.

causa[2] **(razón)** n. *cause.* **causar** v. *to cause.*
causante n. *one who causes.* – Sin. origen, *origin.* razón, *reason.*

causa de la muerte *cause of death.*

causa inmediata *proximate cause.*

causa petendi (lat.) *causa petendi, cause of action.*

causa probable *probable cause.*

causa sobreviniente *supervening cause.* – Sin. causa superveniente.

causa³ (juicio) n. *lawsuit, case.* – Sin. litigio, *litigation.* pleito, *suit.* caso, *case.* proceso, *proceeding.*

causa civil *civil case.* – Sin. pleito civil. juicio civil.

causa criminal *criminal case.* – Sin. juicio penal.

causas de justificación DER.PENAL *justification.*

• "[C]ada una de las circunstancias eximentes en que el sujeto no incurre sino en la apariencia del delito; pues no existe infracción del ordenamiento jurídico general o de las normas de cultura predominantes..." (II Cabanellas, 110) – Sin. causas de incriminación.

Tipos: cumplimiento de un deber, *fulfillment of a duty;* estado de necesidad, *necessity or necessity defense;* impedimento legítimo, *legal excuse;* legítima defensa, *self-defense;* obediencia jerárquica, *hierarchical obedience.*

causahabiente n. *assignee, successor.*

causales de divorcio *grounds for divorce.*

causales de terminación *grounds for dismissal.*

causante (der.fiscal) n. *taxpayer.*

causante mayor *major taxpayer.*

causante menor *minor taxpayer.*

cédula de empadronamiento *registration certificate.*

cédula de emplazamiento *certificate of service.*

cédula de notificación *official court notice form.*

cédula hipotecaria *mortgage bond.*

censo¹ (enumeración) n. *census.*

censo² (contrato) n. [prest.]*censo,* [ed]*an annuity or periodic payment for the use of land.*

• "[Derecho] real inmobiliario que consiste en el poder jurídico que se otorga a su titular de exigir una prestación periódica del propietario del bien sujeto al gravamen." (Dicc. ed. Comares, 91)

censo consignativo [ed]*a transferable annuity guaranteed by debtor's real property.*

censo enfitéutico *emphyteutic annuity.*

censo redimible *redeemable annuity.*

censo reservativo [prest.]*censo reservatio,* [ed]*annuity payable by a grantee of land to a*

grantor *(reserved when land in grantee's possession).*

censura n. *censorship.* **censurar** v. *to censure.* **censurador** n. *censor.* **censurador** adj. *censorious.* **censurable** adj. *censurable.* – Sin. crítica, *criticism.* reproche, *reproach.*

certificación n. *certification* || *jurat.* Ver: legalización.

certificado n. *certificate.* **certificar** v. *to certify.* **certificación** n. *certification.* **certificador** n. *certifier.* **certificativo o certificatorio** adj. *certifiable.*

• "Documento público expedido por persona competente, destinado a hacer constar la existencia de un hecho, acto o calidad, para que surta los efectos jurídicos en cada caso correspondiente." (De Pina, 150)

certificado catastral *certificate of real estate registration.*

certificado de acciones *stock certificate.*

certificado de buena conducta *statement of good behavior.* – Sin. certificado de no tener antecedentes penales.

certificado de buena salud *clean bill of health.*

certificado de defunción *death certificate.*

certificado de depósito bancario *bank certificate of deposit, certificate of deposit.*

certificado de depósito en almacén *warehouse receipt.*

certificado de libertad de gravámenes *certificate acknowledging certain real property is free and clear of encumbrances.*

certificado de nacimiento *birth certificate.*

certificado de nacionalidad *certificate of naturalization.*

certificado de no adeudo *certificate of no indebtedness.*

certificado de origen *certificate of origin.*

certificado de participación (Mx) *certificate of investment.*

certificado fitosanitario *phytosanitary certificate.*

certificado sanitario *certificate of approval of sanitation (from health authorities).*

certificados provisionales de acciones *provisional stock certificates.*

copia certificada *attested copy, certified copy.* Rel: documento, *document;* título, *document, certificate.* Ver: acta.

cesión n. *assignment.* **cesionario** n. *assignee.* **cedente** n. *assignor.*

• La transferencia por acuerdo entre vivos de bienes, derechos o créditos a favor de otra persona. – Sin. transmisión. traspaso.

cesión de acciones *transfer of shares.*

cesión de activos *assignment of assets.*

cesión de bienes *general assignment, voluntary assignment.*

cesión de créditos *assignment of credits or debts.* – Sin. asunción o cesión de deudas.

cesión de derechos *assignment of rights.*

cesión de derechos litigiosos *assignment of claims in litigation.*

cesión de rentas *assignment of rents.*

cesión en beneficio de acreedores *assignment for the benefit of creditors.*

chantaje n. *blackmail.* **chantajear** v. *to blackmail.* **chantajista** n. *blackmailer.* Rel: extorsión, *extortion.*

cheque TÍTULOS DE CRÉDITO n. *check.* **librador** n. *drawer.* **librado** n. *drawee.*

beneficiario/tomador n. *payee.*

• Título de crédito por el que se da una orden incondicional a una institución de pagar a la vista una suma determinada de dinero tomándola de una cuenta previamente establecida con tal institución.

cheque a la orden *check paid to the order of.*

cheque al portador *bearer check.*

cheque antedatado *antedated check.*

cheque certificado *certified check.* – Sin. cheque visado. cheque conformado.

cheque cruzado *check for deposit only.* – Sin. cheque para abono en cuenta.

cheque de caja *cashier's check.*

cheque de plaza *local check.*

cheque de ventanilla *counter check.*

cheque de viajero *traveler's check.*

cheque documentado *documentary check.*

cheque en descubierto *check kiting, check issued without sufficient funds.* – Sin. cheque al descubierto.

cheque postal *postal money order.*

cheque postdatado *postdated check.*

cheque sin fondos *check with insufficient funds, bad check, rubber check.* – Sin. emisión ilegal de cheque.

girar un cheque *to draw a check, write a check.*

Rel: chequera, *checkbook;* títulos de crédito, *negotiable instruments.*

Ref: (ES)CCo a.793ss.; (Esp)LCCH a.106-107; (Mx)LGTOC a.175ss.; (RD)LCh a.1; (Ve)CCo. a.489ss.

chicano n. *chicano, Mexican-American (person).*

– Sin. pocho (mod.)(Mx).

choque n. *crash, collision.* **chocar** v. *to crash.* – Sin. colisión, *collision.* encontronazo, *crash.* impacto, *impact.*

choque automovilístico *car crash, automobile crash.*

choque de frente *head-on collision.*

choque por atrás *rear-end collision.*

circuito judicial *judicial circuit.*

circular (Mx) n. *administrative order or regulation* || *notice.*

circunstancias agravantes *aggravating circumstances.* Ver: agravantes.

circunstancias atenuantes *mitigating circumstances, extenuating circumstances.* Ver: atenuantes.

circunstancias excluyentes de responsabilidad *excuse, exculpatory circumstances.* – Sin. circunstancias eximentes. eximentes. Ver: excluyentes de responsabilidad.

citación a comparecer *subpoena, summons to appear.*

citación a juicio *summons.* – Sin. citación del demandado. emplazamiento.

citación para sentencia [ed]*notice of sentencing hearing.*

citatorio n. *citation.*

ciudadanía n. *citizenship.* **cuidadano** n. *citizen.*

carta de ciudadanía *certificate of naturalization, letter of citizenship, certificate of citizenship.*

ciudadano naturalizado *naturalized citizen.* – Sin. ciudadano por naturalización.

ciudadano por nacimiento *native-born citizen.*

Rel: nacionalidad, *nationality, citizenship.*

civil adj. *civil.* – Sin. cívico.

acción civil *civil action.*

código civil *civil code.*

derechos civiles *civil rights.*

estado civil *civil status.*

juzgado civil *civil law court.*

matrimonio civil *marriage as a civil contract.*

registro civil *civil registry.*

sociedad civil *civil society.*

civil n. *civilian.*

cláusula n. *clause, stipulation,* [lat.]*clausula.*

• "Cada una de las disposiciones de un contrato, tratado, testamento o cualquier otro documento análogo, público o particular." (I Dicc.

REA, 487) – Sin. disposición, *decree, stipulation.* estipulación, *stipulation.*

cláusula arbitral *arbitration clause.*
– Sin. cláusula compromisoria.

cláusula de admisión *admission clause.*

cláusula de escala móvil *indexing clause.*

cláusula de exclusión *exclusion clause.*

cláusula de nación más favorecida *most-
favored-nation clause.*

cláusula de no competencia *non-competition
clause.*

cláusula de pago de intereses *interest-
payment clause.*

cláusula de tanteo *right of first refusal
clause.*

cláusula de vencimiento anticipado
acceleration clause.

cláusula jurisdiccional *jurisdictional clause.*

cláusula penal *penalty clause.* – Sin. cláusula
conminatoria.

cláusulas de estilo *customary clauses.*
– Sin. cláusulas de cajón.

Rel: artículo, *article;* párrafo, *paragraph,
section.*

clausura¹ (terminar) n. *closing of a session,
closing of an event.*

Cf: **clausura • levantamiento.** Una sesión se
clausura cuando los asuntos motivo de la misma
se dan por terminados. El levantamiento de una
sesión significa la conclusión final de la sesión,
mas no necesariamente de las materias a
ventilarse.

clausura² (cerrar) n. *closure of a business or
operation.* **clausurar** v. *to close a business or
operation.* – Sin. cierre, *shutdown, closing
down.*

coacción n. *coercion, force.* **coaccionar** v. *to
coerce.* **coactivo** adj. *coercive.*

• Uso de la fuerza física o moral contra una
persona para obligarla a realizar una acción u
omisión. – Sin. coerción, *coercion.* compulsión,
compulsion. conminación, *commination.*

coacciones (delito)(Esp) *intimidation.*

coacusado n. *co-defendant.*

coalición n. *coalition.* – Sin. alianza, *alliance.*
unión, *union.*

coartada n. *alibi.* – Sin. defensa, *defense.*

coautor n. *co-author.*

cobertura n. *coverage.*

cobertura de cambio (money) *exchange
cover.*

cobertura médica *medical coverage.*

cobranza n. *collection.* **cobrar** v. *to collect.*
cobro n. *collection.* **cobrador** n. *collector.*
cobrable adj. *collectable.* – Sin. cobro.
percepción.

agencia de cobranzas *collection agency.*

cobranza de créditos *debt collection.*
– Sin. cobro de adeudos.

oficina de cobro de impuestos *tax collection
office.*

Rel: recaudación, *collection, tax collection.*

cobro de lo indebido [ef]*unjust enrichment,*
[ed]*receipt of payment by error.* [ef]*wrongful
payment (causing unjust enrichment of
recipient).*

Ver: pago de lo indebido.

cocaína n. *cocaine.* **cocainómano** n. *cocaine
addict.* – Sin. coca, *coke.*

adicción a la cocaína *cocaine addiction.*
– Sin. cocainomanía.

cocaína crack *crack cocaine.*

cocaína roca *rock cocaine.*

Rel: adicción, *addiction.*

codeína n. *codeine.*

codicilo n. *codicil.*

código n. *code.*

• Recopilación de normas legales que normalmente contienen los principios generales
aplicables a una materia, ordenadas en forma
metódica y sistemática.

Cf: **código • recopilación • compilación.** Un
código conjunta principios jurídicos vigentes
en una materia dada sin especificar la fuente
de cada uno de ellos. Una recopilación conjunta varias leyes vigentes respetando su
estructura e identificando cada una de ellas
dentro de la recopilación. Una compilación,
por otro lado, es una acumulación de leyes que
no tiene carácter oficial y su valor no es de
derecho vigente sino de conocimiento práctico o histórico.

código civil *civil code.*

código de comercio *commercial code.*

código de Justiniano (hist.) *Justinian code.*

código de procedimientos civiles *code of
civil procedure.* – Sin. código de procedimiento
civil. ley de enjuiciamiento civil (Esp). código
procesal civil.

código de procedimientos penales *code of
criminal procedure.* – Sin. código de procedimiento penal o criminal. ley de enjuiciamiento
penal (Esp). código procesal penal.

código napoleónico (hist.) *Napoleonic code*
– Sin. código de Napoleón.

código penal o criminal *criminal code.*
código tributario *tax code.* – Sin. código fiscal.
Rel: compilación, *compilation;* recopilación, *compilation of laws in effect.*
Ver: *code.*

coerción n. *coercion.* **coercibilidad** n. *coercion.*
coercitivo adj. *coercive.* **coercible** adj. *coercible.*
• Amenaza del uso de la fuerza para lograr el cumplimiento de una orden o mandato.
– Sin. coacción, *coercion.*

cofirmante n. *cosigner.*

cogestión n. *co-partnership, participation of employees in the management of the company.*
• La participación de los trabajadores, conjuntamente con los propietarios y directivos, en la dirección y administración de una empresa.

cohecho (delito) n. *bribery (of a public official), payola.* **cohechar** v. *to bribe.*
• Este delito se configura cuando un funcionario oficial acepta, para sí u otra persona, prebenda en cualquier forma para el cumplimiento de las funciones inherentes al cargo ocupado.
– Sin. soborno, *bribery.*
Ver: soborno.

colegio de abogados *bar association.*
Ver: barra de abogados.

colegio profesional *professional association.*
– Sin. asociación profesional.

colindante adj. *adjoining, adjacent.* **colindante** n. *adjoining property.* **colindar** v. *to adjoin.*
colindancia n. *boundary.* – Sin. colindante. contiguo. vecino, *neighboring.*
predio colindante *adjoining lot or tenement.*

colisión n. *collision.* – Sin. choque, *crash.*

colusión n. *collusion.* **coludir** v. *to collude.*
• El llevar a cabo un acuerdo en perjuicio de tercero.

comercio n. *trade, commerce.* **comerciar** v. *to trade, do business.* **comerciante** n. *merchant, trader.* **comercializar** v. *to commercialize, to market.*
comercio al por mayor *wholesale trade.*
comercio al por menor *retail trade.*
comercio bilateral *bilateral trade.*
comercio de exportación *export trade, exports.*
comercio de importación *import trade, imports.*
comerciante mayorista *wholesaler.*
comerciante minorista *retailer.*
comerciante sin autorización *interloper.*

prácticas comerciales *customary business practices.*
Rel: derecho mercantil, *business law.*
Ver: actos de comercio.

comercio internacional *international trade.*
– Sin. comercio exterior, *foreign trade.*
Rel: aduana, *customs;* carta de embarque, *bill of lading;* exportaciones, *exports;* importaciones, *imports;* incoterms, *incoterms;* transporte, *transportation.*

comicios n. *elections.*

comisario de la quiebra *trustee in bankruptcy.*

comisario de policía *commissioner, police inspector, police superintendent.* – Sin. jefe de la policía, *police chief.*

comisario de una sociedad *stockholder's auditor.* – Sin. auditor, *auditor.* síndico.

comisión¹ (retribución) n. *commission, fee.*
comisionista n. *commission agent, on commission.*
• Cantidad retribuida a una persona por sus servicios o cierta actividad o derecho comercial basada en un porcentaje. – Sin. a comisión. retribución, *retribution.*
comisión bancaria *banking fee.*
comisión de compra *purchaser's fee.*
comisión de gestión *management fee.*

comisión² (organismo) n. *commission, board.*
• Grupo de personas dentro de una organización encargado de un cierto asunto o negocio, o de cierta actividad específicamente definida.
– Sin. comité.
comisión asesora *consulting or advisory board.*
comisión de control de cambios *foreign exchange control board.*
comisión parlamentaria *parliamentary commission, congressional or legislative committee.*
comisión permanente *standing committee.*

comisión³ (perpetrar) n. *commission.*
• Acción de cometer.
comisión de un delito *commission of a crime.*

comisión mercantil (contrato) n. [ed]*mercantile agency.* **comisionista** n. [ed]*mercantile agent.*
comitente n. *principal.*
• Mandato para actos de comercio. – Sin. mandato mercantil.

contrato de comisión *mercantile agency agreement.*

comodato (contrato) n. [prest.][lat.]*commodatum,* [ef]*gratuitous bailment.* **comodante** n. *bailer, lender.* **comodatario** n. *bailee, borrower.*

• Contrato por el cual el comodante entrega gratuitamente al comodatario una cosa no fungible para que use de ella y se la devuelva dentro de cierto tiempo. – Sin. préstamo de uso.
Rel: fungible, *fungible;* mutuo, *mutuum, loan.*
Ver: préstamo.
compañía *company.* – Sin. empresa, *business firm.* firma, *firm.*
Compañía es un término impreciso que se usa generalmente para designar a entidades comerciales, especialmente cuando no se quiere poner de relieve su forma jurídica específica. Es por ello que en la mayoría de los países hispanoparlantes compañía se usa normalmente como un sinónimo de sociedad mercantil.
compañía controladora *holding company.*
– Sin. compañía tenedora o matriz.
conglomerados (Ch).
compañía de fianzas *bonding company.*
– Sin. compañía afianzadora o fiadora.
compañía de seguros *insurance company.*
compañía de transporte *transportation company.*
compañía fiduciaria *trust company.*
compañía filial *subsidiary.*
compañía multinacional *multinational corporation.*
compañía mutualista de seguros *mutual insurance company.*
compañía privada *private corporation.*
compañía sin afán de lucro *nonprofit organization.*
ley de compañías (Ec) *corporate law.*
Ver: sociedad.
comparecencia n. *appearance.* **comparecer** v. *to enter an appearance.* **compareciente** n. *one who attends.*
• Acto de presentarse personalmente, por medio de representante o escrito, ante una autoridad judicial o administrativa. – Sin. presentación (en un proceso o trámite).
La comparecencia de parte puede obedecer a que se le haya citado, esto es, que se le haya señalado fecha cierta para su presentación, o a que se le haya emplazado, esto es, que se le haya dado un plazo para que comparezca.
comparecencia de testigos *appearance of witnesses.*
comparecencia personal *physical appearance, personal appearance.*
comparecencia voluntaria *voluntary appearance.*
comparecer en juicio *to file an appearance in court.*

falta de comparecencia *nonappearance.*
– Sin. incomparecencia.
Rel: concurrir ante un juez, *to appear before a judge.*
compensación¹ (balance) n. *compensation, balancing.*
• Extinción de una obligación cuando dos personas son acreedor y deudor, el uno del otro, por la cantidad concurrente correspondiente.
– Sin. equivalencia, *equivalence.*
compensación bancaria *bank clearing, check clearing.*
compensación de deudas *offsetting debt.*
compensación de impuestos *offsetting taxes.*
compensación por accidentes de trabajo *worker's compensation.*
compensación por el costo de la vida *cost-of-living adjustment.*
compensación² (sueldo) n. *compensation.*
compensar v. *to compensate.* **compensatorio o compensativo** adj. *compensatory.* – Sin. remuneración, *remuneration.*
compensación extraordinaria *overtime pay.*
competencia¹ (jurisdicción) n. [ed]*court's jurisdictional authority,* [ed]*court's jurisdictional limits,* [amplio]*jurisdiction.*
• Competencia es la medida de distribución de controversias entre los diferentes órganos jurisdiccionales; la esfera dentro de la "cual una autoridad puede desempeñar válidamente sus atribuciones y funciones." (Gómez Lara, 127)
competencia en razón de la cuantía *jurisdiction based on the amount in dispute.* [ed]*court's jurisdictional authority based on the amount in dispute.*
competencia en razón de la materia *subject-matter jurisdiction,* [ed]*court's jurisdictional power based on subject-matter.*
competencia originaria *original jurisdiction,* [ed]*original court's jurisdictional authority.*
competencia territorial *venue, territorial jurisdiction.*
tribunal competente [ed]*court having jurisdictional authority (to issue a decision in a case), court of proper jurisdiction.*
Rel: incompetencia, *lack of jurisdiction or venue,* [ed]*lack of jurisdictional authority.*
Comentario: "Si bien la jurisdicción, como facultad de administrar justicia, incumbe a todos los jueces y magistrados, es indispensable reglamentar su ejercicio para distribuirla, en cada rama jurisdiccional, entre los diversos jueces. Y es ésta la función que desempeña la competencia. La competencia es, por tanto, la facultad que cada juez o magistrado de una rama jurisdiccional tiene, para ejercer la

competencia

jurisdicción en determinados asuntos y dentro de cierto territorio." (I Devis Echandía, 135)
Ver: jurisdicción.
competencia² (concurso) *competition.* **competir** v. *to compete.* **competidor** n. *competitor.*
– Sin. concurrencia.
competencia desleal *unfair competition.*
competencia ilícita *illegal competition.*
libre competencia *free competition.*
complemento salarial *supplemental salary.*
cómplice n. *accessory,* [rtrgido]*accomplice.*
complicidad n. *complicity.*
Cf: **cómplice • participante.** Ambos términos se usan sinónimamente y en forma intercambiable. Participante es el término más general significando simplemente aquél que participa, connotando neutralidad. Cómplice en cambio se refiere a aquél que participa, pero implicando criminalidad o ilicitud.
cómplice encubridor *accessory after the fact.*
cómplice instigador *accessory before the fact.*
Rel: autor del delito, *offender, criminal, perpetrator.*
complot n. *plot.* **complotar** v. *to plot.*
compras públicas *government purchasing.*
compraventa (contrato) n. *sale contract, sale.*
comprador n. *buyer.* **vendedor** n. *seller.*
• Es un contrato por el que el vendedor se obliga a transferir la propiedad de una cosa o la titularidad de un derecho al vendedor, quien se obliga a pagar un precio cierto y en dinero.
– Sin. venta, *sale.*
compraventa a plazos *credit or installment sale.* – Sin. compraventa a crédito.
compraventa al contado *cash sale.*
– Sin. compraventa a la vista.
compraventa con pacto de retracto *sale with repurchase clause, sale with right of redemption.* – Sin. compraventa con pacto de retroventa.
compraventa con reserva de dominio *purchase-lease agreement,* [ed]*purchase-lease agreement under which seller keeps legal title until final payment,* [el]*sale with reservation of title.*
compraventa de cosa esperada *conditional sale of future goods.*
compraventa de esperanza *sale of future goods, sale of hope* (EEUU-La).
compraventa de futuro *futures contract.*
– Sin. compraventa de cosa futura.
compraventa en abonos *retail installment sale.* – Sin. venta en abonos. venta a plazos.

compraventa internacional *international sales.*
compraventa mercantil *commercial sale.*
compraventa sobre muestras *sale by sample.*
contrato de compraventa *contract of sale.*
Comentario: "Distinto es, por lo general el punto de vista del Derecho moderno. Si antes –dice Planiol– el objeto de la venta era la transmisión de una cosa considerada en su realidad material, hoy es la transmisión de la propiedad la que los pueblos, de común acuerdo, le asignan como fin." (IV Castan Tobeñas, 67)
Ref: (Ar)CC a.1323ss.; (Ch)CC a 1793; (CR)CC a. 1049ss.; (Ec)CC a.1759-1863; (Esp)CC a.1445; (Mx) CC a.2248ss.; (Pe)CC a.1529ss.; (PR)CC a. 1334, 31 LPRA sec. 3741; (RD)CC a.1582; (Ur)CC a.1661 ss.; (Ve)CC a1.474ss.
comprobante¹ (proof) n. *proof, receipt.* **comprobar** v. *to prove.* **comprobatorio** adj. *probatory.* – Sin. recibo.
comprobante de adeudo *proof of debt.*
comprobante de pago *proof of payment.*
comprobante² (accounting) n. *voucher.*
compromiso¹ (avenencia) n. *arbitration agreement.* **compromisorio** adj. *pertaining to an arbitration agreement.*
• Acuerdo por el que terceros a una controversia se avocan a resolverla con la anuencia de las partes en conflicto. – Sin. compromiso arbitral.
cláusula compromisoria *arbitration clause.*
compromiso² (obligación) *commitment.*
comprometer v. *to commit.* – Sin. obligación.
compromiso formal *formal commitment.*
compromiso matrimonial *engagement.*
comunicación procesal *judicial communication,* [ed]*written communication between the court and all the parties (involved in a case).*
• Comunicación procesal se refiere al intercambio escrito entre jueces, partes y terceros con motivo de un proceso.
Las comunicaciones procesales pueden clasificarse según se trate de las efectuadas entre tribunales entre sí (suplicatorio, carta orden o despacho), entre tribunales y autoridades no judiciales (oficio, exposición), entre tribunales y los particulares (notificaciones, emplazamiento, requerimiento y citación), y entre tribunales y autoridades y tribunales extranjeros (exhorto y carta o comisión rogatoria).
Rel: carta orden o despacho, *writ (issued by a higher court to a lower court);* citación, *subpoena;* emplazamiento, *summons;* exhorto, *letter of request, requisitory letter;* exposición,

246

[ed]*court's written communication to high government authorities;* notificación, *service of notice, notice;* oficio, [ed]*court's written official communication to other government authorities or institutions;* suplicatorio, [ed] *communication issued to a higher court (by a lower court).*

comunidad n. *community* || *similarity.* – Sin. agrupación, *group.*

comunidad de intereses *common interest.*

comunidad indígena *indigenous community, indian community.*

comunidad internacional *international community.*

comunidad de bienes[1] (matrimonial) *community property.*

• La masa común de bienes formada por la totalidad, o sólo una parte, de aquellos bienes que les pertenecen a los cónyuges.

régimen de comunidad de bienes *community property system.*

Ver: régimen económico del matrimonio.

comunidad de bienes[2] (copropiedad) *tenancy in common.*

• El caso en que una cosa o un derecho pertenece pro indiviso a dos o más copropietarios.

comunidad de bienes[3] (comunal) *communal property.*

• Bienes que están afectos a su pertenencia a una entidad productiva y comunitaria, generalmente se trata de tierras y equipo para labores agrícolas o ganaderas de una comunidad.

Comunidad Europea *European Community, European Union* (EU). – Sin. Comunidad Económica Europea (CEE), *European Economic Community.* Unión Europea, *European Union* (EU).

Ver: derecho comunitario.

con mayor razón [lat.]*a fortiori, with stronger reason.*

concesión[1] DER.ADMVO n. *grant.* **concesionario** n. *grantee.* **otorgante de una concesión** *grantor, franchisor.*

• Otorgamiento en favor de un particular por parte de la administración pública de la gestión de servicios públicos que deberá tomar bajo su cuenta y riesgo.

concesión administrativa *government grant, franchise or license.*

concesión minera *mineral lease.*

concesión[2] (privilegio) n. *franchise.* **concesionario** n. *franchisee.* **otorgante de una conce-**

sión *franchiser, franchisor.* – Sin. franquicia, *franchise.*

Ver: franquicia.

concesión[3] (ceder) n. *concession.*

conceder la elección *to concede the election.*

concesión de uso de nombre comercial *trade name license.*

conciliación n. *conciliation.* **conciliar** v. *to conciliate.* **conciliador** adj. *conciliable.* **conciliativo o conciliatorio** adj. *conciliatory.*

• "Acuerdo de dos personas en litigio que se realiza con el objeto de poner fin a un juicio o pleito." (Ramírez Gronda, 85)

Rel: avenencia, *settlement, compromise;* transacción, *accord and satisfaction.*

Comentario: "La conciliación tiene amplia aplicación jurídica. Forma parte importante del derecho procesal del trabajo, pero también del derecho civil y del derecho internacional público, en donde ha alcanzado también categoría de instancia obligatoria; [también tiene aplicación] en controversias que se presentan en una amplia gama de actividades relacionadas con instituciones bancarias, instituciones de seguros, defensa del consumidor o protección de personas y menores." (Dicc. UNAM, 568)

Ver: autocomposición.

conclusión[1] (disposición) *conclusion, finding.* – Sin. resolución, *resolution.*

conclusión de derecho *conclusions of law.*

conclusión de hecho *findings of fact.*

conclusiones de la sentencia *findings on the judgment.*

conclusiones del fiscal o Ministerio Público *prosecutor recommendations* || *prosecutor closing arguments.*

conclusión[2] (celebración) *closing.* – Sin. consumación, *completion.*

conclusión de un contrato *closing of a contract.*

conclusión de un tratado *signing of a treaty.*

conclusión[3] (terminación) *conclusion, termination.*

conclusión de la relación laboral *termination of employment.*

concordato[1] (insolvencia) n. *debtor reorganization plan.*

concordato[2] (acuerdo) n. *treaty between the Holy See and another State.*

concordato fiscal *stipulated tax settlement.*

concubinato n. *concubinage, common law marriage.* **concubina** n. *concubine.* **compañera** n. *live-in girlfriend.* **compañero** *live-in* *boyfriend.* – Sin. amancebamiento. amasiato. contubernio. barraganería. pareja de hecho. Rel: amante, *lover;* manceba, *concubine.*

concurrencia mercantil *market competition.*

concurrente adj. *concurrent.* **concurrencia** n. *concurrence.* – Sin. simultáneo, *simultaneous.*

concurrencia de acciones *joinder of lawsuits.*

concurrencia de créditos [ed]*debt held jointly by several creditors.*

concurso n. *tender.* **concursar** v. *to tender.*

concursante n. *participant in a tender, bidder.*

• Forma de adjudicar una licitación considerando ganadora a aquella que deposita la mejor oferta. – Sin. licitación.

concurso público *public tender.*

concurso comercial *bankruptcy proceedings,*

concurso de acreedores *liquidation of insolvent's assets by a court.*

concurso de delitos *joinder of offenses.* – Sin. concurrencia de delitos. pluralidad de delitos.

concurso de derechos [prest.]*concurrent rights.*

concurso de leyes *conflict of laws.* – Sin. conflicto de leyes.

condena n. *sentence.* **condenar** v. *to sentence.* **condenado** n. *convict.* **condenable** adj. *condemnable.*

• Resolución judicial dictada por el juez imponiendo la pena correspondiente al procesado que ha encontrado culpable.

Con frecuencia, sobretodo en el habla popular, se tiende a usar indistintamente los términos condena y sentencia —se le sentenció a cadena perpetua, por ejemplo. La condena se distingue claramente de la sentencia ya que la primera se refiere a la imposición por parte del tribunal de un castigo al autor de un delito, una vez que se le ha encontrado culpable. La sentencia por su parte, se refiere precisamente a esa declaración previa por el juez de la culpabilidad o no culpabilidad del acusado.

Cf: **condena • pena • sanción.** Estos tres términos se usan como sinónimos en ocasiones, significando castigo. Más frecuentemente condena se refiere a la declaración impositiva de un castigo con motivo de una sentencia de culpabilidad, mientras que pena y sanción definen el castigo específico y concreto que se le ha impuesto al condenado.

condena a pagar costas *order to pay legal costs.* – Sin. condena en costas. condena de costas.

condena anterior *prior sentence.*

condena civil *non-criminal punishment, penalty.*

condena cumulativa *cumulative or accumulative sentence, consecutive sentence.*

condena penal *sentence, sentencing.*

condena suspendida *suspended sentence.*

reos condenados a muerte *death row inmates.*

sentencia condenatoria *conviction.* Rel: castigo, *punishment;* pena, *punishment;* sanción, *sanction.*

condena condicional [brder]*probation,* [ed]*a suspended sentence allowing the conditional supervised release (of a convicted person).*

• Consiste en la suspensión de la pena condicionada a la no comisión de otra infracción durante el período de duración de tal pena. – Sin. condenación condicional (Ar). libertad a prueba (PR). sentencia suspendida. Rel: arresto de fin de semana, *weekend confinement;* servicio a la comunidad, *community service;* suspensión de condena, *suspended sentence;* suspensión de la pena, *suspension of carrying out the sentence.* Ref: (Ar)CP a.26-28; (Bo)CP a.59; (Co)CP a.63; (Ec)CP a.82; (Esp)CP a.80-87; (Mx)CP a.90 (Pe)CP a.57-61; (Ur)CP a.126. Ver: libertad vigilada. *probation.*

condición[1] **(depender)** *condition.* **condicional** adj. *conditional.* **condicionado** adj. *conditional.* **condicionalmente** adv. *conditionally.*

• Es el acontecimiento futuro e incierto del cual depende el nacimiento o resolución de una obligación o un derecho.

condición pre-existente *precondition.*

condición resolutoria *subsequent condition.*

condición sine qua non *sine qua non condition, without which not.*

condición suspensiva *precedent condition.*

condición tácita *implied condition.* Rel: término, *term, period.*

condición[2] **(forma)** n. *terms, conditions.*

• Términos de un contrato o subasta.

condiciones de pago *terms of payment.*

condiciones de trabajo *conditions of employment.*

condiciones de venta *terms of sale.*

condominio PROPIEDAD n. *condominium.*

condómino n. *condominium owner.*

• Régimen de propiedad en el que un inmueble u otro bien se encuentra dividido en partes o secciones que pertenecen a cada condómino en forma exclusiva y partes o secciones que pertenecen a todos los condóminos en forma conjunta e indivisible. La designación condominio también se aplica con frecuencia solamente al inmueble mismo <venta de condominios>. – Sin. propiedad horizontal, *horizontal property.*

condonación n. *remission.* **condonar** v. *to remit.* **condonante** adj. *condoning.*
• Acto de liberación, perdón o remisión de una deuda por el acreedor. – Sin. perdón, *pardon.* remisión, *remission.*

conducir[1] **(manejar)** v. *to drive.* **conductor** n. *driver.* **conducción** n. *driving.*
conducción temeraria *reckless driving.*
conducir bajo el efecto de enervantes *driving under the influence.*
conducir en estado de ebriedad *driving under the influence.* – Sin. conducir bajo el efecto de bebidas alcohólicas. conducir bajo la influencia.
conducir en exceso de velocidad *speeding.*

conducir[2] **(dirigir)** v. *to guide, to direct.*

conducta n. *behavior, conduct.*
– Sin. comportamiento. proceder, *to proceed, behave.*
conducta antijurídica *unlawful action.*
conducta criminal o delictiva *criminal behavior.*
Rel: acción, *act, action;* omisión, *omission, abstention.*

confesión[1] DER.PROC.CIVIL n. [el]*confession,* [ef]*admission.* **confesar** v. *to confess.* **confeso** adj. *self-confessed, having confessed.*
• "La declaración judicial o extrajudicial, espontánea o provocada, mediante la cual una parte capaz de obligarse, y con ánimo de proporcionar a la otra una prueba en perjuicio propio, reconoce total o parcialmente la verdad de un hecho susceptible de producir consecuencias jurídicas a su cargo (Lessona)." (Ramírez Gronda, 89) – Sin. admisión, *admission.* reconocimiento, *admission, recognition.*
En materia procesal civil la confesión se efectúa mediante declaración de la parte confesante durante el interrogatorio de la contraria. Esta declaración puede ser hecha reconociendo la verdad de lo afirmado por la contraria (confesión llana) o evadiéndola (confesión ficta).
Cf: **confesión • admisión • reconocimiento.**
Admisión y confesión se usan con frecuencia sinónimamente pero raramente en forma intercambiable. Confesión parece identificarse mayormente con el campo penal que con el civil modernamente. Admisión, por su parte,

se identifica casi exclusivamente con la materia civil, ya que cuando se usa en materia penal generalmente su significado se reduce a reconocer la participación del declarante en los hechos alegados, y raramente se hace en forma judicial. El reconocimiento es la admisión de un hecho, normalmente ajeno, y la aceptación de las consecuencias jurídicas, para sí y para otros, que hace una persona o un estado en forma voluntaria. <reconocimiento de paternidad> <reconocimiento de hostilidades>
confesión ficta *admission by silence.*
confesión judicial *judicial admission.*
confesión llana *admission of facts alleged by the opposing party.*
confesión tácita *implied admission, tacit admission.* – Sin. confesión implícita.
retractación de la confesión *recantation.*
Rel: declaración, *declaration, statement;* interrogación, *questioning.*

confesión[2] DER.PROC.PENAL n. *confession.*
En materia penal la confesión se hace cuando el acusado se declara culpable de haber cometido el delito del que se le acusa. Se le denomina entonces acusado o procesado confeso.
confesión a golpes *confession by beating.*
confesión extrajudicial *out-of-court confession.*
confesión judicial *judicial confession.*
confesión voluntaria *voluntary confession.*
– Sin. confesión espontánea.

confidencial n. *confidential.* **confidencialidad** n. [ef]*privileged communication, confidentiality.*

confinamiento n. *confinement.* **confinar** v. *to confine.* **confinado** adj. *confined.* **confinación** n. *confinement.* – Sin. reclusión. encerramiento, *locking up, confining.*
confinamiento domiciliario *house confinement, house arrest.* – Sin. restricción domiciliaria.

confirmación n. *confirmation.* **confirmar** v. *to confirm.* **confirmante** adj. *confirming.* **confirmatorio** adj. *confirmatory.* **confirmativo** adj. *confirmatory.* – Sin. corroboración, *corroboration.*
confirmación de la sentencia *affirmance of judgment.*
Rel: autenticación, *authentication;* ratificación, *ratification;* reconocimiento, *acknowledgment.*

confiscación n. *confiscation, forfeiture.* **confiscar** v. *to confiscate.* **confiscable** adj. *confiscable.*
• La privación de bienes de un particular en

favor del Estado, generalmente como sanción por la comisión de delitos o infracciones. – Sin. comiso (Co).
Rel: decomiso, *seizure of instruments of crime;* incautación, *seizure.*
Ver: decomiso.

conflicto n. *conflict.* **conflictivo** adj. *conflicting.* – Sin. disputa, *dispute.*
conflicto de competencias *conflict of venue.*
conflicto de intereses *conflict of interest.*
conflicto de jurisdicción *conflict of jurisdiction.*
conflicto laboral *labor dispute.*
conflicto de leyes *conflict of laws.*
• Se presenta un conflicto de leyes cuando una relación o situación jurídica contiene elementos que la vinculan con dos o más sistemas jurídicos que pretenden o rehusan regirla. – Sin. concurrencia de leyes.
Rel: calificación, *characterization;* estatutos, [ed]*law and rules to be applied to resolve conflict of laws;* puntos o elementos de conexión, *connecting factor;* reenvío, *renvoi.*

conforme a derecho *in accordance with the law* || *in all justice.*
conforme a lo establecido en el código *in accordance with the provisions of the Code.*
confrontación[1] **(careo)** n. *comparing testimony face to face, confrontation.* **confrontar** v. *to compare testimony face to face.* – Sin. careo, confrontación de testigos.
confrontación[2] **(identificación)** n. *personal identification of a suspect.* **confrontar** v. *to identify a suspect.*
• El reconocimiento o la identificación de un sospechoso realizada por un testigo en un proceso penal. – Sin. identificación.
confrontación en fila *line-up.*
confrontación en rueda de presos *personal identification in a line-up.*
Rel: reconocimiento, *identification of items or property.*

confusión de derechos *confusion, confusion of rights, merger.*
• Forma de extinción de las obligaciones por reunirse en una sola persona las calidades de deudor y acreedor.

conminación n. *admonition.* **conminar** v. *to warn.* **conminativo o conminatorio** adj. *warning.* – Sin. apercibimiento.
conmutación de la pena *commutation of sentence.*

• Substitución de una pena por otra menos rigurosa, a modo de indulto parcial. – Sin. substitución, *substitution.*
Rel: indulto, *pardon;* perdón, *pardon.*

conocimiento carnal *carnal knowledge.*
conocimiento de embarque *bill of lading.*
• Es el documento en el que las compañías de navegación estipulan las condiciones del transporte marítimo de mercaderías. Es un contrato de adhesión en el que se fijan los derechos y obligaciones del fletante, del capitán y del fletador, acreditando el hecho de la carga y estableciendo las obligaciones de restituirla al término del viaje. – Sin. carta de porte, *waybill, bill of lading.* guía de embarque. póliza de cargamento.

Cf: **conocimiento de embarque • carta de porte.** Términos sinónimos que se refieren al documento o título que designa la mercancía a ser transportada y las condiciones de dicha transportación. En algunas legislaciones se distingue el conocimiento de embarque de la carta de porte en virtud de que el primero se aplica únicamente a la transportación marítima mientras que el segundo tiene aplicación general.

conocimiento de embarque a la orden *negotiable bill of lading.*
conocimiento de embarque con anotaciones *unclean bill of lading.*
conocimiento de embarque directo *through bill of lading.*
conocimiento de embarque limpio a bordo *clean bill of lading.*
conocimiento de embarque nominativo *straight bill of lading.*
conocimiento de embarque recibido a bordo *on board bill of lading.*
conocimiento de embarque recibido para embarque *received for shipment bill of lading.*
conocimiento personal *personal knowledge.*
consanguíneo adj. *consanguineous.* **consanguinidad** n. *consanguinity.*
consanguinidad colateral *collateral consanguinity.*
consanguinidad en línea directa *lineal consanguinity.*
consejero[1] **(asesor)** n. *advisor, counselor.* – Sin. asesor. mentor, *mentor.*
consejero[2] **(consejo de admon.)** n. *director (member of a board of directors).* – Sin. administrador. director.

consejo de administración *board of directors.*
– Sin. directorio. junta directiva. junta de
directores.

consejo de guerra *court martial.*

Consejo de Seguridad de las Naciones Unidas
United Nations Security Council.

consejo de vigilancia *stockholder's auditing
representatives.*

consentimiento¹ (aprobación) n. *consent.*
consentir v. *to consent.*
• El aprobar afirmativamente un acto, una
acción o una omisión.
consentimiento expreso *express consent.*
consentimiento por omisión *sufferance,*
[el]*consent by omission.*
consentimiento presuntivo *implied consent.*
– Sin. consentimiento implícito.
consentimiento tácito *implied or constructive
consent.*

consentimiento² (aceptación) CONTRATOS *consent,
mutual assent.* **oferente** n. *offeror.* **aceptante**
n. *offeree.*
• "[E]s la manifestación de voluntad conforme
entre la oferta y la aceptación, y uno de los requisitos esenciales exigidos por los códigos
para los contratos." (II Cabanellas, 308)
– Sin. acuerdo de voluntades, *meeting of the
minds.* consenso.
Cf: **acuerdo • consentimiento.** Acuerdo se refiere a un entendimiento en su sentido más
amplio, significando una coincidencia de intención en cuanto a una misma finalidad <un
acuerdo para contratar>. Consentimiento, por
su parte, se refiere a la aceptación de una o-
ferta concreta en forma indudable constituyendo uno de los elementos esenciales de los
contratos <dar su consentimiento para comprar dicho inmueble>.
vicios del consentimiento *defects of
contractual mutual assent, defects of
contractual consent.*
Rel: aceptación, *acceptance;* oferta o propuesta, *offer.*
Ref: (Ar)CC a.1144-1159; (Ch)CC a.1445,1451; (CR)
CC a.1008-1021; (Ec)CC a.1488-2; (Esp)CC a.1262;
(Mx)CC a.1794, 2224; (Pe)CC a.1373; (PR)CC a.
1214,12 31 LPRA sec. 3401; (Ur)CC a.1262ss.; (Ve)
CC a.1141-1.

considerandos¹ (legal instrument) n. *preamble,
recitals, whereas.*

considerandos² (sentencia) *points of law, applicable law.*
• Es la parte de la sentencia que incluye el fun-

damento jurídico sobre el que se basa.
Rel: resultandos, *the facts (of a sentence).*

consignación¹ (depósito) n. *deposit.* **consignar** v.
to deposit. **consignador** n. *depositor.* **consignatario** n. *depositary, trustee.*
• Depósito efectuado por el deudor a título liberatorio, como pago o como garantía. – Sin. depósito, *deposit, bailment.*
consignación de salario *deposit of salary in
payment.*
consignación de una suma de dinero *deposit
of money (intended as legal performance).*
consignación en pago *deposit in payment of a
debt, tender and deposit* (EEUU-La).
consignación judicial *judicial deposit.*
Ver: depósito.

consignación² (venta) n. *consignment.* **consignar**
v. *to consign.* **consignatario** n. *consignee.*
consignador n. *consignor.*
• Modalidad de la venta consistente en la entrega de mercancía a un vendedor o distribuidor
para que la exhiba o promueva por el dueño o
fabricante, sin tomarla en propiedad y devol-
viéndola si no es adquirida en compra.

consignación³ (Mx) DER.PROC.PENAL n. *charge,
accusation, information, indictment.*
– Sin. procesamiento.
• Es el acto procesal a través del cual el estado,
por conducto del agente del Ministerio Publico
o su equivalente, ejercita la acción penal.

conspiración¹ (rebelión) n. *seditious conspiracy.*
conspirar v. *to conspire.* conspirador n.
conspirator.
• Actividad encaminada a cometer delitos
contra la seguridad de la nación. – Sin. complot,
plot.

conspiración² (acuerdo) n. *conspiracy.* **conspirar**
v. *to conspire.* **conspirador** n. *conspirator.*
– Sin. confabulación criminal.
Cf: **conspiración • acuerdo para cometer un
delito.** Conspiración en su acepción más común
se refiere a un complot con la intención de de-
rribar a la autoridad constituida; en lenguaje
común y corriente y usada en forma esporádica,
significa un acuerdo para cometer un delito.
En algunos países de habla hispana, principalmente en España y Puerto Rico, esta segunda
acepción es el significado legal principal.

constancia n. *written proof.* – Sin. prueba documental, *documentary evidence.*
constancia de deuda *evidence of
indebtedness.*
constancia escrita *written record of evidence.*

constancia notarial *notarial attestation.*
constancias judiciales *judicial records.*
dejar constancia *to furnish proof, to have the record reflect.*
constar v. *to be established or stated.* conste *be it known, for the record.*
hacer constar por escrito *to write down, to reduce to writing.*
constitución n. *constitution.* constitucional adj. *constitutional.* constitucionalismo n. *constitutionalism.* constitucionalmente adv. *constitutionally.*
• "Conjunto de normas consuetudinarias o escritas que en un estado regulan la forma y organización del poder público, los derechos de los asociados y la manera como se concilian la autoridad y la libertad." (I Madrid-Malo, 119) – Sin. carta fundamental.
asamblea constitucional *constitutional assembly.*
constitución no escrita *unwritten constitution.*
derecho constitucional *constitutional law.*
garantías constitucionales *constitutional rights, constitutional guarantees.*
Rel: garantías individuales, *civil rights, constitutional guarantees;* inconstitucional, *unconstitutional.*
consuetudinario adj. *customary.*
derecho consuetudinario *common law, law based on custom.*
consulado n. *consulate.* cónsul n. *consul.* consular adj. *consular.*
consumidor n. *consumer.* consumir v. *to consume.*
contabilidad n. *accounting.* contador o contable *accountant.* – Sin. contaduría.
contabilidad a base de efectivo *cash accounting.*
contabilidad de costos *cost accounting.*
Rel: contador público recibido, *certified public accountant.*
Ver: Apéndice B. Términos contables.
contaminación n. *pollution, contamination.*
contaminar v. *to pollute, contaminate.*
contaminador adj. *polluting, contaminating.* – Sin. polución.
contaminación ambiental *environmental pollution.*
contaminación del mar *sea pollution.*
contaminación de la prueba *evidence contamination.*

contencioso adj. *contentious, litigious, adversarial.*
contencioso-administrativo *court administrative proceeding,* [ed]*adversarial administrative proceeding.* – Sin. proceso administrativo, *administrative proceeding.* Rel: procedimiento administrativo, *administrative procedure.*
contestación de la apelación *cross-appeal.*
contestación de la demanda *answer to a complaint, answer.*
contestación improcedente *inadmissible answer, answer improperly brought or filed.*
contrabando n. *smuggling.* contrabandear v. *to smuggle.* contrabandista n. *smuggler.* – Sin. matute (mod.).
contrademanda n. *cross-complaint, cross-claim.* contrademandado *plaintiff-respondent.* Rel: reconvención, *counterclaim.*
contraparte en juicio *opposing party in a lawsuit.*
contraprestación n. *consideration.* contraprestación real *bargained-for-consideration.* Ver: causa.
contratista n. *contractor.*
contrato n. *contract,* [amplio]*agreement.* contratar v. *to contract.* contratante n. *contracting party.* contractual adj. *contractual.* contractualmente adv. *contractually.*
• Es un acuerdo de voluntades que produce la creación de derechos y obligaciones. – Sin.acuerdo contractual, *contractual agreement.* pacto, *pact.*
Cf: contrato • convenio. En la tradición romano-francesa que siguen los códigos civiles latinoamericanos y español, el contrato es una especie del género convenio. Mientras el convenio es un acuerdo de dos o más personas para crear, transferir, modificar o extinguir derechos y obligaciones, el contrato es el convenio que crea y transfiere derechos y obligaciones solamente.
↪ Contratos y *contracts* son, en términos generales, instituciones afines tanto en estructura como en funcionamiento. Sus diferencias importantes se refieren al papel que cada uno de ellos juegan en el sistema jurídico al que pertenecen y, naturalmente las consecuencias que ello les provoca. A grandes rasgos se puede mencionar que los contratos expuestos en los códigos civiles de países hispanos tienen

vigencia supletoria e interpretativa, se basan en la autonomía de la voluntad y constituyen un área protegida de la regulación de la administración pública. Por su parte los *contracts* del *common law*, en cambio, desconocen la supletoriedad y son interpretados en forma estricta y restrictiva, se basan igualmente en la autonomía contractual pero invaden todas las áreas del derecho ya que la dicotomía derecho público-derecho privado no es relevante. En la práctica el término contrato puede referirse no sólo a *contracts* estrictamente hablando, sino también a ciertos *agreements* que no son considerados *contracts* en el derecho anglosajón, como *executed sales, gifts,* y otros *transfers of property.*

contrato accesorio *accessory contract.*
contrato administrativo *administrative contract.*
contrato aleatorio *aleatory contract.*
contrato bilateral *bilateral contract.*
contrato colectivo de trabajo *collective bargaining agreement.* – Sin. convención colectiva de trabajo. convenio colectivo. acuerdo colectivo.
contrato consensual *consensual contract.*
contrato de adhesión *adhesion contract, contract of adhesion.*
contrato de aparcería *sharecropping agreement.*
contrato de apertura de crédito *opening of credit agreement, credit contract.*
contrato de arrendamiento *contract to lease, lease agreement.*
contrato de carga *freight contract.*
contrato de compraventa de bienes inmuebles *land contract.*
contrato de compraventa *sales contract, sales agreement.*
contrato de crédito de habilitación o avío *loan secured with inventories.*
contrato de depósito *deposit agreement.*
contrato de donación *gift, donation.*
contrato de fianza *contract of suretyship.*
contrato de fideicomiso *trust deed.*
contrato de fletamiento *contract of affreightment, freight contract.*
contrato de hospedaje *lodging contract.*
contrato de mandato *agency.*
contrato de matrimonio *marriage contract.*
contrato de mutuo *loan agreement.*
contrato de obra "llave en mano" *turn key contract.*
contrato de obra *construction agreement.*

contrato de permuta *barter or exchange.*
contrato de prenda *pledge.*
contrato de prestación de servicios *service contract.*
contrato de préstamo *loan contract.*
contrato de seguro *insurance contract, contract of insurance.*
contrato de transporte *transportation contract.*
contrato gratuito *enforceable donative promise.*
contrato ilegal *illegal contract.*
contrato innominado *contract not specifically regulated by the civil code, innominate contract* (EEUU-La). – Sin. contrato atípico.
contrato leonino *unconscionable contract, one-sided contract.*
contrato nominativo *contract specifically regulated by the civil code, nominate contract* (EEUU-La).
contrato nulo *void contract.*
contrato obligatorio *binding contract.*
contrato oneroso *a contract bargained for with consideration, contract for valuable consideration.*
contrato prenupcial *prenuptial agreement.*
contrato preparatorio *preliminary contract.*
contrato sujeto a condición *conditional contract.*
contrato unilateral *unilateral contract.*
Rel: consentimiento, *consent, mutual assent;* convenio, *agreement;* cumplimiento, *performance;* obligaciones, *obligations.*
"El derecho contractual angloamericano moderno está basado en un enfoque comercial, la idea de que se requiere de una negociación como el elemento esencial, por su parte la consideration expresa la idea de un quid pro quo. En contraposición, el sistema de derecho civil empieza con la presunción de la validez del consentimiento como el elemento esencial." (DeVries, 378)
Ref: (Ar)CC a.1197; (Ch)CC a.1438; (Ec)CC a. 1481; (Esp)CC a.1254ss.; (Mx)CC a.1793ss.; (Pe)CC a. 1351; (RD)CC a.1101ss.; (Ur)CC a.1247; (Ve)CC a. 1133ss.

contrato-ley *union contract made mandatory for an entire industry.*

contrato de trabajo *employment contract, contract of employment.*
contrato de trabajo marítimo *marine labor contract, marine work contract.* – Sin. contrato de ajuste.
Rel: relación de trabajo, *master and servant;* período de prueba, *probationary period.*

contravención

contravención n. *offense, violation.* **contravenir** v. *to violate, breach.*

contribución DER.FISCAL n. *tax, assessment.*

contribuyente n. *taxpayer.*

• "La prestación obligatoria debida en razón de beneficios individuales o de grupos sociales, derivados de la realización de obras públicas o de especiales actividades del Estado." (I Giuliani Fonrouge, 295) – Sin. derecho (Mx).

contribución de mejoras *assessment for improvements.* – Sin. contribuciones especiales.

contribución especial *extraordinary tax.*

contribuciones parafiscales *contributions allocated to social goals.*

controversia n. *controversy.* **controvertir** v. *to controvert.* **controvertible** adj. *controvertible.* – Sin. disputa, *dispute.*

contumacia n. *nonappearance, default.*

contumaz n. *a person in default.* – Sin. rebeldía, *default.*

convalidación n. *validation.* **convalidar** v. *to validate.*

• "Acción y efecto de subsanar los vicios de los actos jurídicos, ya sea por el transcurso de tiempo, por la voluntad de las partes o por una decisión judicial." (Couture, 179)

convalidación del matrimonio *validation of marriage.*

Rel: confirmación, *confirmation;* ratificación, *ratification.*

convención[1] **(reunión)** n. *convention.*

convención[2] **(acuerdo)** n. *agreement.* – Sin. acuerdo, *agreement.* pacto, *pact.*

convención internacional *international agreement.*

Convención para la Protección de los Derechos Humanos y las Libertades Fundamentales (Unión Europea) *Convention for the Protection of Human Rights and Fundamental Freedoms.* Rel: Corte Europea de Derechos Humanos, *European Court of Human Rights.*

convenio n. *agreement.* **convenir** v. *to agree.*

• Es el acuerdo de dos o más personas para crear, transferir, modificar o extinguir derechos u obligaciones.

convenio accesorio *accessory agreement.*

convenio de garantía *security agreement.*

convenio de separación *separation agreement.*

convenio extrajudicial *out-of-court settlement.*

convenio transaccional *accord and satisfaction.*

Rel: compromiso, *settlement;* estipulación, *stipulation, provision.*
Ver: contrato.

convenio colectivo DER.LABORAL *collective bargaining agreement.* – Sin. contrato colectivo de trabajo. convenio colectivo de trabajo.

convenio internacional *international convention.*

convicción (PR) *conviction.* – Sin. sentencia condenatoria.

convicto n. *convict.*

convocatoria n. *notice of a meeting.* **convocar** v. *to convene.*

• Anuncio formal de llamamiento para una reunión a una hora y fecha específica.

cónyuge n. *spouse.* **conyugal** adj. *spousal, marital.*

• Cada una de las personas que forman un matrimonio y se encuentran legalmente unidas como esposos. – Sin. consorte, *consort.* esposo, *spouse.* [mod.]media naranja, *better half.*

cónyuge supérstite *surviving spouse.* – Sin. cónyuge sobreviviente.

cooperativa n. *cooperative, co-op.*

cooperativismo n. *cooperative movement.*

cooperativo adj. *cooperative, pertaining to cooperatives.*

• "Sociedad económico-social constituida sobre el principio de que la riqueza no debe producirse para el cambio [o comercio], sino para la satisfacción de las necesidades, es decir, su producción debe ser gobernada por los consumidores asociados." (Machado Schiaffino, 83)

cooperativa de consumo *consumers' cooperative.*

cooperativa de crédito *credit cooperative.*

cooperativa de productores *producer's cooperative.*

sociedad cooperativa *cooperative corporation.*

copia n. *copy.* **copiar** v. *to copy.* – Sin. duplicado, *duplicate.* réplica, *replica.* reproducción, *reproduction.*

copia certificada *certified copy.*

copia fiel *true copy.*

copia legalizada *authenticated copy.*

copia simple *uncertified copy.*

copias notariales *notarial copies.*

copropiedad n. *joint ownership.* **copropietario** n. *joint owner.*

• Situación en la que un bien le pertenece a

varios propietarios conjuntamente en forma pro indivisa.

corporación n. *corporation, legal entity.*
• Entidad o cuerpo de personas reconocidas por la ley que persiguen la representación y protección de sus intereses comunes.
– Sin. entidad, *entity.* instituto, *institute.* organismo, *body, organization.*
Cf: **corporación • fundación.** Modernamente ambos términos tienden a confundirse refiriéndose en foma amplia a una persona moral o jurídica, sin embargo ambos tienen un orígen común, diferenciándose en que mientras corporación enfatizaba a las personas que la constituían, la fundación ponía de relieve la finalidad perseguida. En materia administrativa se entiende por corporación cualquier entidad pública que no sea parte del gobierno central, sobre todo en España.
En cuanto a Puerto Rico, corporación es también el término usado para designar el concepto de *corporation* que ha sido transplantado del derecho anglosajón.

corrección disciplinaria *disciplinary measure.*
– Sin. medida disciplinaria.

correccional n. *department of corrections.*

corredor DER.MERC n. *broker.* **correduría** n. *brokerage.* **corretaje** n. *brokerage, broker's fee.*
corredor de apuestas *bookmaker.*
corredor de bolsa *stockbroker.*
corredor de cambio *exchange broker.*
corredor de comercio *commission merchant.*
corredor público *commercial notary.*
Rel: agente, *agent;* comisionista, *commission agent.*

correo n. *mail.* **cartero** n. *mail carrier.*
correspondencia n. *correspondence, mail.*
correo certificado *certified mail.*
correo con acuse de recibo *mail with acknowledgment of receipt.*
correo registrado *registered mail.*
oficina de correos *post office.*

corrupción n. *corruption.* **corruptible** adj. *corruptible.* **corruptibilidad** n. *corruptibility.* **corruptor** adj. *corrupting.* **corruptor** n. *corruptor, perverter.*
• Sobornar o cohechar a una persona mediante dádivas, favores o acciones similares.
Rel: integridad, *integrity;* soborno, *bribing.*

corrupción de menores (delito) *corruption of minors.*

corrupción oficial (delito) *graft.* – Sin. corrup-

ción de funcionarios públicos.
Rel: cohecho, *bribing;* colusión, *collusion;* concusión, *graft;* mangoneo (mod.), *graft;* mordida (pop.)(Mx), *bribe;* soborno, *bribing.*

corte n. *court.*
La palabra corte refiere a tribunales de apelación o casación generalmente; sin embargo, también se ha usado indistintamente en ocasiones para designar juzgados de primera instancia, <cortes penales> juzgados de jurisdicción especial <corte marcial> juzgados internacionales, <corte internacional de justicia> e incluso a una asamblea legislativa <Cortes Generales Españolas>.

Corte Suprema de Justicia *Supreme Court* (EEUU,CA,NZ), *High Court* (Au), *House of Lords/Court of Appeal* (UK). – Sin. Suprema Corte de Justicia. Tribunal Supremo. Tribunal Supremo de Justicia (Ve). Tribunal Supremo Popular (Cu).
Ver: *Supreme court.*

corte de circuito *circuit court.*
corte marcial *martial court.*
Ver: juzgado, court.

Corte Internacional de Justicia *International Court of Justice.*

cortesía judicial *comity.*

cortesía internacional *comity of nations.*

cosa n. *thing, chose, res.*
• Sustancia corporal, material, susceptible de ser aprehendida que pueda ser valorada.
cosa ajena *abandoned thing.*
cosa cierta *thing certain.*
cosa determinada *specified thing.*
cosa inmueble *real property.* – Sin. bien inmueble.
cosa mueble *chattel, movable thing.* – Sin. cosa mueble.
cosa perdida *lost property.*
cosa sin dueño *res nullius, thing without an owner.*
Ver: bienes.

cosa juzgada DER.PROCESAL [lat.]*res judicata.*
• "Autoridad y eficacia que adquiere la sentencia judicial cuando no proceden contra ella recursos ni otros medios de impugnación, y cuyos atributos son la coercibilidad, la inmutabilidad y la irreversibilidad en otro proceso posterior." (Couture, 184) Como tal, la cosa juzgada es frecuentemente entendida y usada como la excepción que establece que una cierta cuestión individualizadamente considerada ha sido resuelta en definitiva y puede oponerse a

un demandante.

Cf: **res judicata • cosa juzgada • preclusión.**
Res judicata y cosa juzgada son términos sinónimos e intercambiables. Res judicata es la expresión en latín, cosa juzgada es la expresión en español. La cosa juzgada se distingue de la preclusión en que la primera pone fin al proceso y sus efectos se proyectan fuera del mismo, en tanto que la segunda se manifiesta exclusivamente dentro del proceso cerrando una de sus etapas, permitiendo que siga adelante.
cosa juzgada formal *claim preclusion.*
cosa juzgada material *issue preclusion.*
Rel: ejecutoria, [ed]*final sentence or judgment in a case (when sustained after appeal or when non-appealed), final judicial decision;* preclusión, *preclusion;* sentencia firme, *final unappealable judgment or sentence.*
Ref: (Co)CPP a.19; (Mx)CPP a.443.

cosas n. *goods.*

coseguro n. *co-insurance.*

costas n. *court costs.*

• Aquellos gastos, normalmente a cargo de las partes, que son directamente necesarios para la tramitación de un proceso. – Sin. costas judiciales. costas procesales.
planilla de costas *schedule of court costs.*
– Sin. pliego de costas.
Rel: gastos procesales, *expense of litigation;* cuotas o contribuciones de tramitación judicial, *court fees.*

costo n. *cost.* – Sin. coste.
costo de reposición *replacement cost.*
costo histórico *historical cost.*
costo ponderado promedio *average weighted cost.*
costo seguro y flete (CSF) *cost, insurance and freight* (CIF).

costumbre *custom, custom and usage.*

• "Modo de conducta que al reiterarse durante cierto tiempo adquiere valor normativo por su uso inveterado y su generalización." (I Madrid-Malo, 134)
costumbre contra legem [ed]*custom operating against an applicable statute.*
costumbre jurídica *customary or consuetudinary law.* – Sin. norma consuetudinaria.
costumbre praeter legem [ed]*applicable custom when statute does not regulate a given case.*
costumbre secundum legem [ed]*custom operating concordantly with applicable statute.*

costumbres locales *local custom.*
costumbres mercantiles *commercial usage.*
Rel: hábito, *habit;* uso, *usage.*
Comentario: La costumbre en países con derecho de tradición romanista, como los países hispano-americanos, se define en un contexto en el que el derecho legislado, esto es la ley, es la fuente primordial y de mayor autoridad, al grado que normalmente es ella la que define y controla la aplicación de normas nacidas de la costumbre mediante principios generales plasmados en las leyes, como por ejemplo la máxima de que contra la ley no puede alegarse uso o práctica en contrario.

cotejo de documentos *comparison of documents, collation of documents.*

cotejo de firmas *expert comparison of signatures.*

cotización¹ (price) *quotation, price.* **cotizar** v. *to quote.*

cotización² (participación) *contribution.* **cotizar** v. *to contribute.*

coyote (Mx) *smuggler of illegal aliens ‖ unlicensed legal facilitator (of filings, court proceedings, applications and similar formalities),* [amplio] *shark.* – Sin. pollero (Mx) *alien smuggler.*

coyuntura *circumstances.*

crédito¹ (derecho) n. *credit.* **crediticio** adj. *pertaining to credit.* **acreditante** n. *creditor, debtee.* **acreditado** n. *debtor.*

• En el ámbito jurídico, "crédito no sólo se aplica al derecho que tiene el acreedor para exigir del deudor la cantidad prestada y los intereses convenidos, sino también al documento con que se justifica ese derecho." (II Cabanellas, 406)
⌐ La palabra crédito en el ámbito jurídico se usa con frecuencia indistintamente con dos significados cercanos: el de un derecho para exigir una cantidad prestada, así como el del préstamo mismo que da origen a tal derecho. En su conversión al inglés, en el primer caso se usa la palabra *credit* significando tanto una disponibilidad de fondos a favor de un sujeto como la obligación implícita de su devolución, mientras que en el segundo normalmente se usa la palabra *loan* en su significado amplio de préstamo.
carta de crédito *letter of credit.*
crédito confirmado *confirmed credit.*
crédito documentario *documentary credit.*
crédito fiscal *tax credit.*
crédito hipotecario *mortgage-backed credit, mortgages receivable.*
crédito respaldado (Esp) *back to back credit.*

crédito revolvente *revolving credit.* – Sin. crédito rotativo.
tarjeta de crédito *credit card.*
Rel: interés, *interest.*
crédito² (disponibilidad de fondos) n. *credit.*
abrir una cuenta de crédito *to open a credit account.*
compañía de crédito *credit bureau.* – Sin. bureau de crédito. buró de crédito.
crédito bancario *credit given by a bank (to a person or business).*
crédito en cuenta corriente *credit on current account.*
establecer crédito *to establish credit.* – Sin. sentar crédito.
otorgar crédito *to grant credit.*
sujeto de crédito *creditworthy.*
Rel: capacidad de pago, *ability to pay.*
crédito³ (préstamo) n. *loan, credit.* **prestador** n. *lender.* **prestatario** n. *borrower.* – Sin. préstamo, *loan.*
crédito garantizado *secured loan.*
– Sin. préstamo garantizado.
crédito hipotecario *mortgage loan.*
– Sin. préstamo hipotecario.
crédito puente *bridge loan.* – Sin. préstamo puente.
crédito quirografario *unsecured loan.*
– Sin. préstamo quirografario.
crédito refaccionario *bank loan secured with capital assets, equipment loan.* – Sin. préstamo refaccionario.
Rel: banco, *bank.*
crédito⁴ (contab.) n. *credit.*
créditos incobrables *bad debts.*
créditos vencidos *past due loans.*
Rel: débito, *debit.*
crimen n. *crime, criminal offense.* **criminal** n. *criminal.* **criminal** adj. *criminal.* **criminalidad** n. *criminality.* **criminalista** n. *criminologist.*
Cf: **crimen • delito.** Crimen y delito son usados como sinónimos comúnmente. Con mayor rigor jurídico, los autores hispanoparlantes se han inclinado por la denominación delito para identificar a la violación de la ley penal, mientras que el término crimen se usa frecuentemente para señalar un delito grave por un lado <crimen de guerra>, o simplemente la designación de la conducta antisocial en general <es un crimen no participar en la vida ciudadana>. En Chile los delitos graves se denominan crímenes, los de menor gravedad simples delitos y aquellos que son delitos menores son designados como faltas.

crimen contra la humanidad *crimes against humanity.*
crimen organizado *organized crime.*
crímenes de guerra *war crimes.*
criminal peligroso *dangerous criminal.*
Ver: delito.
criminalística n. *criminalistics.*
• Es la rama de las ciencias criminales que aplica conocimientos y métodos de las ciencias naturales en el examen de la evidencia física auxiliando la administración de justicia.
criminología n. *criminology.* **criminólogo** n. *criminologist.* **criminológico** adj. *criminological.*
• Disciplina que estudia el delito, sus causas y su posible represión.
crueldad n. *cruelty.* **cruel** n. *cruel.* **cruelmente** adv. *cruelly.* – Sin. atrocidad, *atrocity.*
crueldad extrema *extreme cruelty.*
crueldad mental *mental cruelty.*
cuantía n. *value, amount.* – Sin. suma, *sum, amount.*
cuasicontrato n. *quasi-contract.*
• Hecho puramente voluntario y lícito del hombre del que se derivan obligaciones para con un tercero. <pago de lo indebido>
cuasidelito n. *quasi-crime.*
• Acto dañoso del derecho ajeno sin intención de producir un mal, pero del que se deriva responsabilidad civil.
cuenta n. *account.*
cuenta bancaria *bank account.*
cuenta bancaria bloqueada *blocked account.*
– Sin. cuenta congelada.
cuenta bancaria mancomunada *joint bank account.*
cuenta corriente *current account.*
cuenta corriente de cheques *checking account.*
cuenta corriente de crédito *current credit account.*
cuenta de ahorros *savings account.*
cuenta en participación *joint accounts.*
cuenta saldada *closed account.* – Sin. cuenta cerrada.
cuenta sin movimiento *inactive account.*
cuentas por cobrar *accounts receivable.*
cuerpo¹ (presencia física) n. *body.* **corporal** adj. *corporal.*
cuerpo del occiso *body of the deceased, corpse.* – Sin. cuerpo del muerto.
cuerpo humano *human body.*

cuerpo[2] **(organización)** n. *team, body.*
– Sin. corporación, *corporation.* órgano, *organization, agency.*
cuerpo consular *consular representative.*
cuerpo de rescate *rescue squad.*
cuerpo diplomático *diplomatic corps.*
cuerpo electoral *electoral body.*
cuerpo policíaco *police force.*
cuerpo del delito [lat.]*corpus delicti, proof of crime.*
• "El conjunto de elementos objetivos o externos que constituyen la materialidad de la figura delictiva descrita concretamente por la ley penal." (Dicc. UNAM, 786)
El concepto de cuerpo del delito se refiere con frecuencia a los instrumentos u objetos o medios para la perpetración del delito, incluyendo el cuerpo de la víctima. En una acepción más técnica se refiere a los elementos objetivos externos que constituyen la comisión del delito y que son considerados por sí mismos para efectos probatorios.
se da por constituido del cuerpo del delito *proof exists that a crime has been committed.*
se levantó el cuerpo del delito *the corpse was analyzed at the crime scene.*
cuestión n. *question, issue.*
cuestión de derecho *question of law.*
cuestión de hecho *question of fact.*
cuestión previa *preliminary issue.*
cuestionario n. *questionnaire.*
cuidado n. *care.* **cuidadoso** adj. *careful.*
– Sin. atención, *attention.* supervisión, *supervision.*
cuidado paterno *parental care.*
cuidados intensivos *intensive care.*
cuidados médicos *medical care.*
Rel: asistencia, *assistance;* custodia, *custody.*
culpa[1] DER.CIVIL n. [lat.]*culpa,* [rtrgido]*negligence, fault.*
• Falta de diligencia o cuidado en el cumplimiento de una obligación. – Sin. imprudencia, *imprudence, negligence.*
Cf: **culpa • negligencia • imprudencia • custodia.** Culpa es el género y los términos de imprudencia y negligencia son sus especies, siendo usados intercambiablemente con frecuencia. Culpa equivale a una falta de diligencia, entendida como el deber que tienen todos los hombres de evitar el daño usando todos los medios posibles. Negligencia e imprudencia son el no poner tales medios en práctica sin intención de perjudicar. Negligencia equivale

a descuido, es la falta de cuidado, aplicación o exactitud, mientras que imprudencia es la falta de una conducta prudente. Custodia, por su parte, es una forma especial de diligencia que consiste en el cuidado que debe de ponerse en conservar la cosa ajena.
☞ El término culpa se presta a confusión fácilmente ya que tiene un doble significado en materia civil: por un lado, en su acepción amplia, es un concepto genérico que incluye como especies tanto al dolo civil o *intentional fault,* como a la culpa en sentido restringido o *non-intentional fault.* Por el otro lado, en su acepción restringida, sólo se refiere a la culpa sin intención, y no a ambas, y es entonces cuando aparece como culpa causada por imprudencia, negligencia o descuido.
culpa grave *gross fault,* [lat.]*lata culpa.*
culpa leve *ordinary fault,* [lat.]*levis culpa.*
culpa levísima *slight fault,* [lat.]*levissima culpa.*
Rel: dolo, [lat.]*dolus, fraud or deceit.*
culpa[2] DER.PENAL n. *criminal negligence.*
• "Se produce cuando obrando sin intención y sin la diligencia debida se causa un resultado dañoso, previsible y penado por la ley" penal. (Dicc. ed. Comares, 150).
Rel: dolo, *criminal intent.*
Ref: (Bo)CP a.15; (Co)CP a.22; (Esp)CP a.12; (Gu) CP a.12; (Mx)CP a.8,9.
culpabilidad DER.PENAL n. *culpability, guilt.*
culpable adj. *culpable, guilty.*
• La culpabilidad se da cuando un sujeto actúa contrariamente a la ley, pudiendo y debiendo actuar en otra forma, debido a que su voluntad está consciente por un juicio de reproche de su actitud culpable.
"Aunque la palabra culpabilidad se ha impuesto ya en el Derecho penal, su significación jurídica no ha logrado unidad conceptual en la doctrina ni en la jurisprudencia, y, como es natural, tampoco en los códigos. Las opiniones varían desde una concepción escuetamente psicológica del fenómeno hasta una posición que sólo ve en él un puro ente normativo." (Reyes Echandía, 4)
Rel: inculpabilidad, *lack of culpability.*
cumplimiento[1] **(implementar)** n. *performance.*
• Es la realización de la prestación que prometió el obligado. – Sin. observancia, *action, implementation.*
cumplimiento contractual *contractual performance.*
cumplimiento de la ley *compliance with the*

law, obeying the law.
cumplimiento de las obligaciones
performance of obligations.
cumplimiento de un contrato *performance of a contract.*
cumplimiento en ejecución forzosa o forzada *specific performance.*
cumplimiento específico (PR) *specific performance.*

Comentario: "La idea de que el cumplimiento de un contrato de conformidad con sus términos es la solución deseable, y que daños, rescisión y restitución se constituyen en el mejor de los casos en substitutos de segunda clase del cumplimiento, prevalece fuertemente en los sistemas de derecho civil; es tan fuerte, verdaderamente, que incluso después de haber sido puesto en rebeldía, y habiendo sido demandado mediante una acción pidiendo la restitución o los daños por falta de cumplimiento, el obligado normalmente puede desvirtuar la acción dando cumplimiento junto con intereses (y otros daños por el retraso) y costas." (Schlesinger, 120. Traducción del editor)

cumplimiento² (terminación) n. *expiration, completion.* – Sin. conclusión, *conclusion.* descargo, *discharge.*
cumplimiento de una condena *completion of a sentence.*
cumplimiento de una pena *completion of punishment or sanctions.*

cumplimiento³ (ejecución) n. *execution.*
– Sin. ejecución, *execution.*
cumplimiento de una sentencia *execution of a judgment.*
cumplimiento judicial *judicial enforcement.*
cumplimiento de un deber n. *fulfillment of a duty.*
• Eximente de culpabilidad consistente en que el acusado actuó en estricto cumplimiento de sus atribuciones o deberes.

cuota n. *quota, fee.*
cuota compensatoria *countervailing duties.*
cuota obrera *worker's contribution (to a fund).*
cuota patronal *employer's contribution (to a fund).*
cuota sindical *union fees.*

curatela FAMILIA n. [prest.]*curatorship, special guardianship.* **curador** n. *curator.*
• Institución que permite la administración judicial de bienes o patrimonios que requieren ser administrados o vigilados por no poder hacerlo su titular. – Sin. curaduría.
Ver: tutela.

custodia¹ (cuidado) *duty of care.* **custodiar** v. *to care for.* **custodio** n. *depositary.* – Sin. cuidado,

care.
custodia de bienes *property being cared for.*
custodia² FAMILIA *custody.* **custodiar** v. *to have custody over.* **custodio** n. *custodial person, custodian.* – Sin. cuidado, *care.* protección, *protection.*
custodia alternada *split custody.*
custodia dividida *divided custody.*
Ver: patria potestad.

custodia³ DER.PENAL *custody.* – Sin. bajo arresto, *under arrest.* en detención, *in detention.* privado de su libertad, *to be incarcerated, not free.*
custodia de presos *prisoners in custody.*
estar bajo custodia *to be in custody.*

DDDD

dación en pago OBLIGACIONES [ed]*discharge of obligation by performance other than the one agreed upon,* [ed]*something given in lieu of payment.*
• Extinción de una obligación mediante la realización de una prestación distinta a la inicialmente establecida, con el consentimiento del acreedor.
Rel: cumplimiento, *performance.*

dactiloscopia n. *dactyloscopy.*
Ver: huellas digitales.

daño n. *damage, harm.* **dañar** v. *to damage.* **dañino** adj. *damaging.* **dañoso** adj. *damaging.*
• "Lesión, detrimento o menoscabo, causado a una persona, en su integridad física, reputación o bienes." (Couture, 197)
– Sin. deterioro, *impairment.* detrimento, *detriment.* lesión, *lesion.* menoscabo, *damage, reduction.* pérdida, *damage, loss.*
Cf: **daño • perjuicio • lucro cesante.** Daño y perjuicio son dos conceptos íntimamente relacionados en las legislaciones modernas. Ambos son claramente diferenciables en la mayoría de los casos. En lenguaje común, mientras daño es la lesión o menoscabo en las cosas o personas, perjuicio es la medida patrimonial de tal lesión o menoscabo. En su acepción jurídica, sin embargo, daño se refiere primordialmente a la compensación que cuantifica el menoscabo directo, en tanto que perjuicio se refiere a la utilidad lícita que dejó de obtenerse. Lucro cesante, por su lado, es la ganancia de cualquier tipo, no percibida, con motivo del daño.
daño corporal *bodily harm.*

daño emergente *actual loss.*

daño fortuito *accidental damages.*

daño moral *emotional distress, mental suffering, mental anguish.*

daños compensatorios *compensatory damages.*

daños irreparables *irreparable damages.*

daños materiales *property damage.*
– Sin. daños patrimoniales.

daños y perjuicios *damages.*

estimación de daños *assessment of damages.*

reparación del daño [ef]*restitution,* [el]*indemnification for damage caused (in the commission of a crime).*

Rel: indemnización, *indemnity;* lucro cesante, *loss of lawful gains (due to damage or harm);* perjuicios, *profit loss or undue expense (due to damage or harm).*

daño en propiedad ajena (delito) *criminal damage to property.*

• Delito consistente en la destrucción o menoscabo de bienes ajenos, o bienes propios cuando resultan en perjuicio de un tercero. – Sin. daño penal.

Rel: estrago, *major destruction or damage;* daños maliciosos, *malicious mischief.*

dar conocimiento *to serve notice.*

dar de alta *admission, enrollment, registration.*

dar de baja *discharge, cancel.*

dar en prenda *to pledge.*

dar fe *to certify, attest.*

dar muerte *killing, to kill.*

dar parte *make a report.*

dar vista *notify, to serve notice.*

darse de alta *enroll, register.*

darse por notificado *to accept service.*

darse por recibido de *to acknowledge receipt of.*

datos n. *data.*

de acuerdo o conformidad con lo aquí dispuesto *in accordance with the provisions hereof.*

de buena fe *bona fide.*

de conocimiento público *of public knowledge.*

de común acuerdo *by mutual agreement.*

de cujus (lat.) *decedent.*

• Autor de una sucesión. La persona fallecida cuyo patrimonio será transmitido a aquellas que la sobrevivan. – También: de cuius.

de derecho *de jure, legally.*

de hecho *de facto.*

de mayor valor probatorio *preponderance of the evidence.*

de mi conocimiento *personally known to me.*

de oficio *sua sponte power, on its own motion.*

de pleno derecho *by operation of law, as a matter of law.*

deber n. *duty.*

• El deber jurídico es el comportamiento exigido por el ordenamiento jurídico. La necesidad de obrar de conformidad con la norma jurídica. Todo lo que se considera jurídicamente obligatorio constituye un deber jurídico.

deber de socorro *duty to aid or assist.*

deber jurídico *legal duty.*

deber moral *moral duty.*

Rel: obligación, *obligation;* responsabilidad, *responsibility.*

Comentario: Deber "posee en la esfera jurídica la excepcional y amplísima acepción que proviene de constituír el reverso de derecho, entendido subjetivamente como potestad, atribución o facultad; en cuyo sentido, el deber integra obligación (legal, natural o convencional), constreñimiento, subordinación, necesidad jurídica." (III Cabanellas, 18)

deber v. *to owe.*

debidamente jurado *duly sworn.*

debido proceso legal *due process of law.*
– Sin. procedimiento legal debidamente establecido. principio de legalidad.

declaración¹ (exposición) n. *declaration, statement.* **declarar** v. *to declare, make a statement.* **declarante** n. *declarant.*
declaratorio o declarativo adj. *declaratory.*
• Manifestación pública de un hecho, acto o intención. – Sin. afirmación, *affirmation.* manifestación, *manifestation.*

declaración de bienes *disclosure of assets.*

declaración de guerra *war declaration.*

declaración de neutralidad *neutrality proclamation.*

declaración de última voluntad *last will and testament.*

declaración de voluntad *manifestation of intent.* – Sin. manifestación de voluntad.

declaración previa *prior statement.*

declaración² (discurso formal) n. *sworn statement, representation.* **declarar** v. *to declare, make a statement.* **declarante** n. *deponent.*
• Testimonio o deposición jurada o bajo protesta de decir verdad. – Sin. deposición, *deposition.* testimonio, *testimony.*

declaración aduanera *custom declaration.*

declaración bajo protesta *statement under affirmation.*

declaración de culpabilidad *guilty plea (from defendant)* || *finding of guilt (ruling from court).*

declaración de inocencia *plea of not guilty.*

declaración de testigos *witnesses' testimony.*

declaración falsa *misrepresentation, false statement.*

declaración informativa [ed]*statement made before a policeman or an out-of-court investigator.* – Sin. averiguación previa.

declaración jurada *sworn statement.*

declararse culpable o inocente *entering a plea.*

tomar una declaración *to depose (someone), to take a statement (from someone).*

declaración[3] **(determinación judicial)** n. *finding, determination.* **declarar** v. *to declare, find, determine.*
• Resolución judicial normalmente estableciendo una conclusión. – Sin. declaratoria.

declaración de ausencia *judicial determination of a person being absent or missing.*

declaración de derechos *declaration of rights.*

declaración de divorcio *divorce decree.*

declaración de incapacidad *determination of incompetency.*

declaración de inconstitucionalidad *finding of unconstitutionality.*

declaración de muerte *judicial determination of presumptive death,* [prest.] *declaration of death* (EEUU-La).

declaración de nulidad *annulment.*

declaración de paternidad *declaration of paternity.*

declaración de quiebra *determination of bankruptcy.*

declaración de rebeldía *finding of default or non-appearance.*

Declaración de derechos *Bill of Rights.*

declaración de impuestos *tax return.*
– Sin. declaración fiscal. manifestación de impuestos.

presentación de la declaración (de impuestos) *to file a tax return.*

prórroga para la presentación de la declaración (de impuestos) *extension of time to file a tax return.*

declaración preparatoria [ed]*first statement made by defendant before a judge (regarding the facts of the case).*
Ver: indagatoria.

declaración unilateral de voluntad *express promise,* [ed]*unilateral intent to bind.*
• Exteriorización de la voluntad expresa o tácita, dirigida a producir efectos jurídicos determinados. – Sin. voluntad unilateral.
Rel: estipulación a favor de tercero, *independent promise made in favor of a third party beneficiary;* promesa de recompensa, *promise to pay a reward.*

Declaración Universal de los Derechos del Hombre *Universal Declaration of Human Rights.*

declarar que ha lugar *admit, grant, uphold, sustain.*

declarar que no ha lugar *dismiss, overrule.*

declaratoria n. *finding, determination.*
– Sin. declaración.

declaratoria de culpabilidad *finding of guilt.*

declaratoria de herederos *determination of heirship, acknowledgment of heirship.*
– Sin. declaración de herederos.

declaratoria de inocencia *acquittal.*

declaratoria de pobreza [ed]*approval of poverty affidavit,* [ed]*admission of pauper's status.*

declinatoria n. *jurisdictional plea, plea or demurrer to the jurisdiction.* – Sin. declinatoria de jurisdicción.
• Es una cuestión de competencia que se pide ante el juez que haya empezado a conocer de la causa, pidiéndole que se separe del conocimiento del asunto, y remita los autos al juez considerado competente.
Rel: inhibitoria, *motion to determine proper jurisdiction.*

decomiso n. *seizure of instruments of a crime or other assets (as punishment).* **decomisar** v. *to seize.*
• Es la privación de los bienes de una persona, aplicada a título de pena o sanción por la violación de una disposición legal. – Sin. comiso.
Cf: **decomiso • confiscación.** Decomiso se refiere a una incautación parcial con motivo de la comisión de un ilícito sobre todo incluyendo los instrumentos usados, en cambio la confiscación puede recaer sobre la totalidad de los bienes y sin que éstos tengan relación alguna con la infracción.

decomiso fiscal *customs seizure.*
Rel: confiscación, *confiscation;* incautación, *seizure;* secuestro, *seizure.*

decreto[1] **(der.admvo.)** n. *executive order, resolution.* **decretar** v. *to decree, to order.*
• Resolución del Poder Ejecutivo o del jefe del Estado en uso de sus facultades reglamentarias o administrativas. – Sin. edicto. bando.
decreto reglamentario [ed]*an executive order regulating a specific matter (as outlined in a statute).*
decreto[2] DER.PROCESAL n. *resolution.* **decretar** v. *to order.*
• Resolución dictada por el juez en un procedimiento que es de mero trámite.
– Sin. resolución. decisión.
decreto-ley *executive proclamation.*
• "Disposición legislativa de carácter general dictada por el gobierno en caso de extraordinaria y urgente necesidad." (Dicc. ed. Comares, 160)
Comentario: "Casi podría decirse que este tecnicismo, situado en verdad en zona intermedia, es más militar que jurídico en la práctica; por cuanto la historia prueba que la mayoría de los decretos-leyes llevan la firma de militares, por corresponder con frecuencia a gobiernos provisionales o excepcionales, en que las fuerzas armadas han asumido, de una forma u otra, el ejercicio expeditivo del gobierno." (III Cabanellas, 39)
deducción n. *deduction.* **deducir** v. *to deduct.*
deducible adj. *deductible.* – Sin. substracción, *subtraction.*
deducción fiscal *tax deduction.*
defecto n. *fault, defect.* **defectuoso** adj. *faulty.*
– Sin. vicio, *defect.*
defecto oculto *latent defect.* – Sin. vicio oculto.
defecto del título *cloud on title.*
defensa[1] DER.PROC n. *defense.* **defender** v. *to defend.*
defensor adj. *defending.* **defensor** n. *defender.*
defendible adj. *defensible.*
• Argumento o razón aducido en un juicio contra la pretensión del demandante o acusador.
– Sin. excepción. oposición, *opposition.*
defensa procesal *defense in legal proceedings.*
– Sin. oposición procesal.
defensa putativa [ed]*defense based on allegations of the defendant's false perception or belief, putative defense.*
legítima defensa *self-defense.*
Ver: excepción.
defensa[2] **(abogado)** *defense, defense attorney.*
defensa[3] **(protección)** *defense.*
defensa civil *civil defense.*
defensor de oficio *public defender.* **defensoría** n. *public defender's office.*

• Abogado a cargo de la defensa de personas indigentes acusados de delitos, generalmente en forma gratuita. – Sin. defensor de pobres.
defraudación[1] **(delito)** n. *fraud.* **defraudar** v. *to defraud.* **defraudador** adj. *defrauding.*
• En materia penal es la denominación común generalmente dada a un grupo de delitos que tienen como característica el referirse al apoderamiento de la propiedad ajena mediante fraude. – Sin. fraude (Mx).
La mayoría de los países en donde el español es el idioma oficial usan este término con la notable excepción de México, en donde el término fraude se usa para designar tanto al delito específico de estafa como al genérico de defraudación. Hay consenso en la mayoría de los países, sin embargo, en cuanto a la denominación defraudación cuando se trata de delitos fiscales. <defraudación fiscal>
defraudación a la seguridad social *social security fraud.*
defraudación de fluido eléctrico *theft of utility service.* – Sin. defraudación de energía eléctrica.
Rel: insolvencia fraudulenta o punible, *fraudulent insolvency;* quiebra fraudulenta, *fraudulent bankruptcy;* suplantación o uso de nombre fingido, *impersonation or use of false name;* venta de cosa ajena, *sale of property of another.*
Ver: fraude. estafa.
defraudación[2] **(conducta)** n. *fraud.*
• En general defraudación se refiere a cualquier fraude o engaño en las relaciones con otro.
– Sin. fraude.
defraudación fiscal *tax fraud, tax evasion.*
• "Comete el delito de defraudación fiscal quien haga uso de engaños o aproveche errores para omitir total o parcialmente el pago de algún impuesto." (Mx-CFF, a.71) – Sin. defraudación tributaria. evasión fiscal, *tax evasion.*
defunción n. *death.* **difunto** n. *deceased.*
– Sin. fallecimiento.
delación n. *accusation, delation.* **delatar** v. *to inform against.* **delator** n. *informer.*
– Sin. denuncia, *criminal complaint.*
delegación administrativa *administrative delegation.*
delegación de facultades *delegation or transfer of authority.*
delegado sindical *union representative.*

delincuencia n. *delinquency*. **delinquir** v. *to commit crimes, to be delinquent*. **delincuente** adj. *delinquent*. – Sin. criminalidad, *crime*.
delincuencia juvenil *juvenile delinquency*.
delincuente n. *offender, criminal*. – Sin. autor del delito, *offender, criminal, perpetrator*. criminal, *criminal*. malhechor, *wrongdoer*.
delincuente habitual *habitual offender*.
delincuente juvenil *juvenile delinquent*.
delincuente ocasional *casual criminal*. – Sin. delincuente por necesidad.
delincuente profesional *professional criminal, career criminal*.
delincuente reincidente *repeat offender*.
delincuente sexual *sex offender*. – Sin. delincuente de delitos sexuales.
delito n. *crime, offense*. **delinquir** v. *to be delinquent, to commit a crime*.
• Delito es una acción u omisión en contravención al derecho que es culpable y sancionada con pena. – Sin. crimen. falta. ilícito penal, *crime, criminal wrong*. infracción penal, *crime, criminal infringement of the law*.
"En donde hay concepto tripartita de las infracciones punibles, el delito es la intermedia, superado en gravedad por el crimen y superior a la venialidad de la falta. En los códigos penales dualistas, como el español, el delito constituye la conducta reprimida más severamente, en oposición a las faltas. Donde impera el monismo criminal, como en la legislación argentina, delito son todas las figuras reprimidas, aunque en una escala muy variada de severidad." (III Cabanellas, 59)
Cf: **delito • infracción • ilícito penal o punible.** Delito e ilícito penal o punible son expresiones sinónimas que son usadas indistintamente. Infracción se usa frecuentemente también como sinónimo cuando se adiciona el adjetivo penal o criminal, pero la palabra infracción por sí sola generalmente sugiere la violación de disposiciones administrativas o, en ocasiones, faltas penales de menor gravedad.
delito calificado *aggravated crime or offense*.
delito capital, *capital felony*.
delito común *state crime (as opposed to federal crime), local crime (as opposed to national crime)*.
delito conexo *related crime or offense*.
delito continuo *continuing crime*.
delito contra la propiedad *crime against property*.
delito contra la salud *drug-related crime*.
delito criminal *criminal offense*.

delito culposo o delito imprudencial, [ed]*crime caused by negligent or imprudent action or behavior*.
delito de sangre *violent crime*.
delito doloso o intencional *intentional crime*.
delito en grado de tentativa *attempted crime*.
delito federal *federal crime*.
delito flagrante *in flagrante delicto, in the act of committing a crime*.
delito grave *felony*. – Sin. delito mayor.
delito infamante *infamous crime*.
delito menor *misdemeanor*. – Sin. delito menos grave. delito leve.
delito militar *military crime*.
delito oficial *crime committed by government officials*.
delito pasional *crime of passion, crime in the heat of passion*. – Sin. delito emocional. crimen cometido en estado de emoción violenta (Gu).
delito político *political crime*.
delito preterintencional [ed]*crime causing an injury greater than the one initially intended*. Rel: antijuridicidad, *contrary to the law, unlawful;* culpabilidad, *culpability;* denuncia, *criminal complaint;* excluyentes de responsabilidad, *excuse;* punibilidad, [ed]*punishability,* [el]*punitiveness;* tipicidad, [ed]*fit between the facts and the legal description of a crime;* víctima, *victim.*
Comentario: "En la doctrina penal se suele definir el delito como una acción u omisión típica, antijurídica y culpable. A partir de esta definición, se distinguen tres elementos diferentes ordenados de tal forma que cada uno de ellos presupone la existencia del anterior. Estos son la tipicidad, la anitijuridicidad y la culpabilidad. Esta fórmula es conocida genéricamente como el sistema Liszt-Beling en referencia a los autores a quienes, con razón a pesar de pertenecer a escuelas diferentes, se les atribuye el mérito de haber puesto las bases fundamentales de la moderna teoría del delito. En términos generales, la tipicidad es la adecuación de un hecho concreto con la definición abstracta y genérica que hace un tipo legal; la antijuridicidad, la contravención de ése hecho típico con todo el ordenamiento jurídico; y la culpabilidad, es el continente de todo lo que dice relación con el sujeto responsable e implica, por tanto, la capacidad del Estado para exigirle al sujeto responsabilidad por ese hecho. Estos tres conceptos de la definición y sus contenidos conforman lo que en derecho penal se conoce como la teoría del delito." (Bustos Ramírez y Hornazábal, 15)
Ref: (Ch)CP a.1; (Co)CP a.9,19; (ES)CP a.18; (Esp) CP a.10; (Mx)CP a.7; (Pe)CP a.11; (PR)CP a. 9, 33 LPRA sec 3041; (Ur)CP a.1.

demanda

demanda DER.PROCESAL n. *complaint, petition.*
demandante n. *plaintiff, petitioner.* **demandado** n. *respondent.* **demandar** v. *to file suit, to bring suit.*

• Escrito inicial con el que la parte actora ejercita la acción y plantea su pretensión concretamente ante la autoridad judicial.

allanamiento a la demanda *acceptance of the complaint by defendant, acquiescence to the complaint by defendant.*

ampliación de la demanda *supplemental complaint.*

contestación de la demanda *answer of the complaint.*

demanda de amparo (Mx) [el]*petition of amparo, petition for constitutional relief.*
demanda de apelación *bill of appeal.*
demanda fiscal *tax claim.*
demanda temeraria *frivolous claim or complaint.* – Sin. demanda infundada.

desistimiento de la demanda *voluntary dismissal of the complaint, abandonment of the action or claim.*

emplazamiento de la demanda [ed]*service of the complaint or petition, summons.*

presentación de la demanda *filing of the complaint.* – Sin. deducción de la demanda (Ar).

procede la demanda *the complaint will be allowed (by the court).*

traslado de la demanda *to serve notice of complaint or petition (to the opposing party in a lawsuit).*

Rel: acción, *action;* contrademanda, *counterclaim;* pretensión, *claim.*
Ver: acción. petición.

Comentario: "Presentada la demanda con tantas copias como partes, se da traslado a la persona o personas contra las cuales se propone, con emplazamiento improrrogable para personarse en autos. De no efectuar esa comparecencia dentro del plazo, se acusará la rebeldía y se daría por contestada la demanda. El contestar ésta tiene el trascendente sentido procesal de trabar la litis, de impugnar las pretensiones; pues, de aceptarlas en tal escrito, se produciría el allanamiento y, por tanto, el final del pleito en su comienzo." (Cabanellas, III-75)
Ref: (Ar)CPC a.330; (Ch)CPC a.253, 254; (Ec)CPC a.70ss.; (Esp)NLEC a.399; (Mx)CPC a.255; (Ur) CGP a.117ss.; (Ve)CPC a.338-343.

demencia n. *dementia.* **demente** n. *insane, unsound mind.*
• Enfermedad consistente en la disminución o pérdida de las capacidades mentales de una persona. – Sin. locura.
demencia senil *senile dementia.*

democracia n. *democracy.* **democratizar** v. *to make democratic, to democratize.* **demócrata** n. *democrat.* **democrático** adj. *democratic.*
democracia directa *direct democracy.*
democracia popular *popular democracy.*
democracia representativa *representative democracy.*

demora n. *delay.* **demorar** v. *to delay.*
– Sin. atraso. retraso. morosidad, *delay in payment.* dilación, *undue delay.*
demora en pago *overdue payment.*
recargo por demora *late payment penalty.*

denegación de justicia DER.INTL *denial of justice, lack of due process, refusal to apply due process.*

denegada apelación (Mx) [ed]*motion presented in the form of an appeal protesting the denial of appeal (or the denial of the type of appeal requested).* – Sin. recurso de hecho (Ve), recurso de queja, [ed]*motion presented in the form of an appeal protesting court decisions that are not appealable.*
Ref: (Mx)CFPC a.259-266 CPP a.435-442 CFPP a.392-398.

denuncia[1] **(acusación)** DER.PROC.PENAL n. *criminal complaint, accusation.* **denunciante** n. *complainant, complaining witness, accuser.* **denunciado** n. *defendant, accused.*
• Acto por medio del cual una persona pone en conocimiento del órgano de la acusación la comisión de hechos que pueden constituir un delito perseguible de oficio. – Sin. delación, *accusation.*
Cf: **denuncia ● querella ● acusación ● delación.**
Términos separadamente identificables que se refieren a la acción de poner en conocimiento de la autoridad la comisión de un hecho delictivo. Acusación es el término más amplio y se usa generalmente sin especificidad alguna. La delación implica que se desconoce el autor de la información dada. La denuncia es aquella que hace el órgano de acusación, esto es la fiscalía o el Ministerio Público en la mayoría de los casos, encargado de iniciar la acción penal de oficio. La querella es la que hace un particular, ya iniciando la acción, ya instigando a que la inicie el órgano de acusación correspondiente.
denuncia falsa (delito) *false accusation.*
denunciar un delito *to file a complaint.*
– Sin. hacer una denuncia.
Rel: acusación, *accusation;* querella de parte, *aggrieved-party complaint.*
Ref: (Ch)NCPCh a.173, CPP a.82; (Esp)LECr a.259 -269; (Mx)C a.16; (PR)RPC r.5; 34 LPRA Ap. II R 5.

denuncia² (repudiación) n. *denouncement.*
denunciar v. *to denounce.*
denuncia de un tratado internacional *to denounce a treaty.*
denuncia³ (reclamación) n. *claim.*
denuncia de un intestado *petition made to the court to initiate intestate proceedings.*
departamento¹ (inmueble) *department.*
Cf: **departamento • apartamento • piso.** Términos sinónimos e intercambiables. Departamento que significa parte de una unidad habitacional es el término preferido en Sudamérica, apartamento es la designación preferida en Centroamérica, y piso es la palabra normalmente usada en España.
departamento² (sección) n. *department.*
departamental adj. *departmental.*
departamento de quejas *complaint department.*
departamento fiduciario *trust department.*
departamento jurídico *legal department.*
departamento³ (división política) *county, municipalidad* || *departamento o territorio.*
dependencia¹ (office) n. *office.*
dependencia oficial *government office.*
dependencia² (relación) n. *dependence.*
depender v. *to depend.* **dependiente** adj. *dependent.*
dependencia alcohólica *alcohol dependence.*
dependencia económica *economic dependence.*
fármacodependencia *drug addiction.*
– Sin. drogadicción.
Rel: adicción, *addiction.*
dependiente (comercio) n. *employee, agent.*
– Sin. factor. empleado, *employee.* auxiliar, *business help.*
deportación n. *deportation.* **deportar** v. *to deport.* **deportado** n. *deported.*
Rel: desterrado, *exiled, banished.*
deposición n. *deposition.* **deponente** n. *deponent.* – Sin. declaración, *statement, representation.* testimonio, *testimony.*
depósito n. *deposit,* [amplio]*bailment.* **depositante** n. *depositor, bailee.* **depositario** n. *custodian, bailor.*
• El contrato de depósito se constituye por la entrega de la cosa ajena con la obligación de guardarla y restituirla.
Cf: **depósito • consignación.** El elemento fundamental que caracteriza al depósito es la custodia de un bien que ha sido entregado, y

que debe ser restituido al depositante. La consignación es una institución muy parecida que consiste en la entrega de un bien en custodia, pero con la finalidad de que se considere como pago o como el cumplimiento de una obligación previamente existente en favor de un tercero y, que en consecuencia, no se restituirá al sujeto que lo entregó.
depósito a la vista *demand deposit.*
depósito a plazo *time deposit.*
depósito bancario *bank deposit.*
depósito de personas *placement of individuals in protective custody.*
depósito de valores *custody of securities.*
depósito en almacenes generales *storage in a government-approved warehouse.*
depósito en cuenta de cheques *deposit in a checking account.*
depósito en garantía (arrendamiento) *security deposit.* – Sin. depósito de garantía.
depósito judicial *court-ordered deposit.*
depósito mercantil [ed]*commercial deposit, bailment.* – Sin. depósito comercial.
Rel: consignación, *consignment;* custodia de un bien, *custody (of chattels).*
depósito de cadáveres *mortuary, morgue.*
– Sin. morgue, *morgue.*
depreciación n. *depreciation.* **depreciar** v. *to depreciate.*
• Pérdida o disminución de valor de una cosa, ocasionada entre otras causas, por el uso normal de la misma o por el simple transcurso del tiempo.
Cf: **depreciación • amortización.** Depreciación y amortización se usan ocasionalmente como sinónimos, pero generalmente se reconoce que se trata de dos conceptos diferenciables. La depreciación es normalmente la disminución o pérdida de valor de un bien o activo fijo tangible debido, fundamentalmente, al uso o desmejoramiento de la propiedad. Amortización por su lado, denota la extinción gradual de un activo, de un pasivo o de una cuenta nominal, por medio de la división de su importe en cantidades periódicas durante el tiempo de su existencia o aprovechamiento. Así un préstamo se amortiza, mientras un automóvil se deprecia.
depredación n. *depredation.* **depredador** n. *plunderer, pillager.*
Rel: pillaje, *pillaging;* saqueo, *ransacking.*
derecho¹ (orden jurídico) *law,* [lat.]*jus.*
• El derecho como orden jurídico es un complejo de normas e instituciones que imperan coac-

tivamente en una sociedad estatal. Tal complejo está constituido por un conjunto de normas bilaterales, externas, generalmente heterónomas y coercibles, que tienen por objeto regular la conducta humana. – Sin. derecho objetivo. orden jurídico. sistema jurídico.

La palabra derecho tiene varias acepciones. En primer lugar se le puede concebir en forma objetiva como un conjunto de normas, esto es, de reglas de conducta que imponen deberes y confieren derechos. Al mismo tiempo, se le puede concebir subjetivamente como la facultad que tiene una persona para exigir el cumplimiento de lo señalado por la norma. Desde otro punto de vista derecho es identificado como aquellas normas que se encuentran efectivamente en vigor en una jurisdicción determinada, en este caso se habla de derecho positivo o derecho vigente. Finalmente derecho frecuentemente se identifica con la justicia, esto es, derecho se entiende como un conjunto de normas que son naturalmente justas independientemente de su aplicación, entonces nos referimos al llamado derecho natural.

Cf: **derecho • moralidad • convencionalismo.** Términos claramente diferenciados por la doctrina. El derecho implica que frente a la persona obligada existe otra facultada para exigir el cumplimiento en forma forzada, si es necesario, del deber establecido por la norma jurídica. A diferencia la moralidad, por su parte, implica normas de conciencia que no pueden ser exigidas en forma coercible. A su vez, los convencionalismos sociales son reglas aceptadas por la persona con motivo de la convivencia social cuya sanción persigue el castigo del infractor y no el cumplimiento de la regla.

⌐ El derecho románico-germano y la *common law* se refieren a conceptos diferentes cuando se especifica la regla de derecho que propone solución a casos concretos y específicos. El primero se refiere a la norma jurídica considerada como una regla general que impone deberes o establece derechos, mientras el segundo habla de *rule of law* entendida como el *ratio decidendi* sobre el que se basa una sentencia en un caso dado. Aunque ambos conceptos realizan una función similar en cuanto representan la base sobre la que se dan soluciones jurídicas a casos concretos, se trata de términos que no son equivalentes en virtud de la naturaleza diferente de los sistemas de los que son parte. La norma jurídica es un concepto parte de una construcción sistematizada que usa la interpretación pa-

ra su localización y aplicación al caso concreto. La *rule of law* es un concepto más flexible parte de un sistema basado en la casuística y que usa la técnica de *distinctions* para identificar y aplicar la regla.

derecho agrario [prest.]*agrarian law,* [ed]*agriculture law.* – Sin. derecho rural. derecho de la tierra.

derecho ambiental *environmental law.* – Sin. derecho del ambiente.

derecho bancario *banking law.*

derecho comparado *comparative law.*

derecho comunitario (Esp) *community law.* – Sin. derecho de la comunidad europea.

derecho consuetudinario *customary law.*

derecho corporativo *corporate law.*

derecho de autor *copyright law.* – Sin. derecho de propiedad literaria.

derecho de extranjería [ed]*law regulating alien status,*[ed]*body of law dealing with foreigners.* – Sin. extranjería.

derecho de familia *domestic law, family law, domestic relations law.* – Sin. derecho familiar.

derecho de guerra *law of war.*

derecho de petición *right to petition government authorities.*

derecho económico *economic law.*

derecho electoral *voting law.*

derecho fiscal *tax law.*

derecho foral (Esp) *local civil law.*

derecho hereditario *law of inheritance.* – Sin. derecho sucesorio.

derecho internacional privado *international private law.*

derecho marcial o militar *military law.*

derecho marítimo *maritime law.*

derecho minero *mining law.*

derecho municipal *municipal law.*

derecho natural *natural law.*

derecho notarial [ed]*law regulating notaries public.*

derecho parlamentario *parliamentary law.*

derecho penitenciario *corrections law, correctional facilities regulation.*

derecho positivo *positive law.*

derecho procesal *procedural law.* – Sin. derecho adjetivo.

derecho público *public law.*

derecho sustantivo *substantive law.*

derecho supletorio *suppletive law,* [ed]*law applied in absence of legally applicable statute or code.*

derecho vigente *law in effect.*

derecho² (facultad) n. *right,* [lat.]*jus.*

• Permisiones o facultades, así como exigencias o reclamos que se consideran jurídicamente justificados. – Sin. derecho subjetivo.
derecho adquirido *vested right.*
derecho de asilo *right of asylum.*
derecho de audiencia *due process of law.*
– Sin. garantía de audiencia.
derecho de huelga *right to strike.*
derecho de paso inocente *right of innocent passage.*
derecho de paso *right of way.*
derecho de patente *patent right.*
derecho de propiedad *property right.*
derecho de retención DER.MARÍTIMO *maritime lien,*
– Sin. privilegio.
derecho de reunión *right of assembly.*
derecho del tanto *right of first refusal.*
– Sin. tanteo. derecho de tanteo.
derecho inalienable *inalienable right.*
derecho ripario (PR) *riparian rights.*
por mi propio derecho *having legal standing.*
derecho³ (disciplina) n. *law.*
• Disciplina o conjunto de conocimientos jurídicos. – Sin. leyes. <escuela de leyes>
fuentes del derecho *sources of law.*
lagunas del derecho *gaps in the law.*
principios generales del derecho *general principles of law.*
derecho administrativo *administrative law.*
• "Totalidad de normas positivas destinadas a regular la actividad del Estado y de los demás órganos públicos, en cuanto se refiere al establecimiento y realización de los servicios públicos, así como a regir las relaciones entre la administración y los particulares y los de las entidades administrativas entre sí." (De Pina, 228)
Rel: concesión, *concession, franchise;* nacionalización, *nationalization;* servicio público, *public service.*
Comentario: "La esencia diferencial del derecho administrativo radica en la nota de preeminencia que favorece a la Administración pública situándola en un nivel superior al administrado en cuanto aquella realiza actividades de interés general." (Ribó Durán, 202)
Ver: *administrative law.*
derecho canónico *canon law.*
• Conjunto de normas que rigen la conducta de los miembros de una fe religiosa; en particular la codificación de la iglesia católica romana.
– Sin. derecho eclesiástico.
Glosario: abogado, *advocate;* apostolado, *apostolate;* bautismo, *baptism;* canonización, *canonization;* clérigos, *clerics;* Colegio de Cardenales,

College of Cardinals; Colegio de Obispos, *College of Bishops;* confirmación, *confirmation;* defensor del vínculo, *defender of the bond;* Dióceses, *Dioceses;* dispensa, *dispensation;* El Papa, *The Pope;* El Pontífice Romano, *The Roman Pontiff;* eucaristía, *eucharist;* excomunión, *excommunication;* La Curia Romana, *The Roman Curia;* La Rota Romana, *The Roman Rota;* La Santa Sede, *The Holy See;* Legados Pontificios, *Papal Legates;* Parroqias, *Parishes;* penitencia, *penance;* procurador, *procurator;* promotor de justicia, *promoter of justice;* sacramentos, *sacraments;* Sínodo de Obispos, *Synod of Bishops;* tribunal de primera instancia, *tribunal of first instance;* tribunal de segunda instancia, *tribunal of second instance.*
derecho civil *civil law.*
• Conjunto de normas, técnicas y doctrina que se refieren a las relaciones jurídicas de la vida ordinaria del ser humano, considerada como persona.
Rel: bienes, *property law;* contratos, *law of contracts;* familia, *family law;* obligaciones, [ed] *law of obligations;* personas, [ed]*law of status (of a person's legal personal rights),* [ed]*law of personal legal condition;* sucesiones, [ed] *law of successions, law of descent and distribution.*
Comentario: Esta rama tradicionalmente incluye los conceptos de persona, patrimonio y familia como núcleo central, así como normas que regulan principios generales de la aplicación e interpretación de las leyes. En cuanto a su distinción con otras ramas de derecho privado, el derecho civil se puede identificar por exclusión como la disciplina que regula todas las relaciones entre particulares que no sean mercantiles, agrarias u obreras.
derecho común *civil law, national law.*
• Es el derecho civil, en contraste con el derecho mercantil, o el derecho nacional, en contraste con el derecho foral en España o el derecho local en otros países.
Rel: jus commune (hist.)(lat.), *jus commune.*
derecho común (PR) *common law.*
derecho comunitario (Esp) *European Community law.*
• "Es el conjunto de normas, doctrinas y técnicas jurídicas que determinan la organización, las competencias y el funcionamiento de la Comunidad europea." (Ribó Durán, 202)
Glosario: Tratado de la Unión Europea (TUE), *European Union Treaty* (TEU), *Maastricht Treaty;* Unión Europea (UE), *European Union;* Comunidad Económica Europea (CEE),

European Economic Community; Comunidad Europea del Carbón y del Acero (CECA), *European Coal and Steel Community* (ECSC)*;* Comunidad Europea de Energía Atómica o EURATOM (CEEA), *European Atomic Energy Community (Euratom);* Política Exterior y de Seguridad Común (PESC), *Foreign and Security Policy;* Cooperación en Asuntos de Justicia e Interior (CASAI), *Cooperation in the fields of Justice and Home affairs;* Unión Económica Monetaria (UEM), *European Economic and Monetary Union;* Parlamento Europeo, *European Parliament;* Defensor del Pueblo, *European Ombudsman;* Tribunal de Cuentas, *European Court of Auditors;* Comité de las Regiones, *Committee of the Regions;* Banco Central Europeo (BCE), *European Central Bank;* principio de subsidiariedad, *subsidiarity principle;* principio de proporcionalidad, *proportionality principle;* El Consejo, *Council;* La Comisión, *Commission;* Tribunal de Justicia, *Court of Justice;* Comité de Representantes Permanentes (COREPER), *Committee of Permanent Representatives* (COREPER)*;* Sistema Europeo de Bancos Centrales, *European Systems of Central Banks;* Banco Europeo de Inversiones, *European Investment Bank;* Tribunal de Primera Instancia, *Court of First Instance;* Procedimiento de Cooperación, *cooperation procedure;* Procedimiento de codecisión, *co-decision procedure;* Derecho primario u originario, *primary legislation;* Derecho secundario, *secondary legislation;* Directiva, *directive;* Reglamento, *regulations;* Decisión, *decision;* Unión aduanera, *Customs Union.*

derecho constitucional *constitutional law.*
• "Rama del Derecho Político que estudia la estructura del Estado, los derechos fundamentales de los individuos y de los grupos frente al Estado y la organización y relaciones de los poderes públicos." (Ramírez Gronda, 119)
Rel: constitución, *constitution;* división de poderes, *separation of powers;* garantías individuales, *civil rights, constitutional guarantees.*

derecho de autor *copyright.* – Sin. derechos autorales. propiedad literaria, *literary property.*
Convención Universal sobre Derecho de autor *Universal Copyright Convention.*
Registro Público del Derecho de autor *Registry or Register of Copyright.*
violación de los derechos de autor *copyright infringement.*

Rel: artistas, intérpretes o ejecutantes, *artists, interpreters* or *performers;* autor, *author;* dominio público, *public domain;* obra literaria, *literary work;* obra, *work;* piratería de obra, *copyright piracy.*
Ver: *copyright.*

derecho del mar *law of the sea.*
Ver: law of the sea.

derecho-equidad, *equity.*
Ver: equity[1].

derecho fiscal *tax law.*
• "Conjunto de normas que regulan la relación jurídico tributaria y los procedimientos administrativos de aplicación, gestión y control de los tributos." (Martínez Marín y otros, 140) – Sin. derecho tributario.
Rel: fisco, *tax administration;* impuesto, *tax;* tributo, *tax.*
Ver: Apéndice E. Glosario de Derecho Fiscal.

derecho internacional público *international law.*
• Es el conjunto de normas jurídicas que regulan las relaciones de los Estados entre sí y las que resultan con las organizaciones o sujetos internacionales. – Sin. jus gentium (lat.), *jus gentium.* derecho de gentes (lat.), *jus inter gentes.* derecho internacional.
Rel: agentes diplomáticos, *diplomats;* comunidad internacional, *international community;* derecho del mar, *law of the sea;* organizaciones internacionales, *international organizations;* soberanía, *sovereignty;* tratado, *treaty.*

derecho internacional privado *international private law.*
Es aplicable en casos en los cuales no se sabe que ordenamiento nacional debe regir una determinada situación, o bien, cuando se pretende conocer la situación jurídica de una persona en país extraño o la forma de atribución y modalidades de determinada nacionalidad. Al primer aspecto se le ha denominado conflicto de leyes, a los otros dos: condición jurídica del extranjero o extranjería y nacionalidad, respectivamente.
Rel: conflicto de leyes, *conflict of laws;* extranjería, [ed]*law regulating alien status,* [ed]*body of law dealing with foreigners;* nacionalidad, *immigration and citizenship.*

derecho laboral *labor law.*
• "Es la parte del ordenamiento jurídico que regula las relaciones laborales individuales y colectivas, así como la organización y funcionamiento de la previsión social y de los

organismos administrativos y jurisdiccionales especializados en las referidas materias." (Ribó Durán, 208) – Sin. derecho del trabajo. derecho obrero.

Rel: contrato de trabajo, *contract of employment;* derecho procesal del trabajo, *procedure applicable to labor matters;* seguridad social, *social security;* sindicato, *trade union.*

derecho mercantil *commercial or business law.*

• Es el campo jurídico cuyas normas determinan su campo de aplicación asignando el calificativo de mercantiles a ciertos actos, y regulando éstos y las actividades de aquellas personas que los realizan.

↪ Mientras la distinción entre derecho civil y mercantil es importante en los sistemas de origen romano-germánico, no lo es en el derecho anglosajón. El *law merchant*, habiendo sido desarrollado separadamente del *common law* inicialmente, es ahora parte de éste y consiste en una extensión de los principios generales de los contratos aplicados a las transacciones de carácter mercantil. Por ello normalmente no se habla de *mercantile law*, que es un equivalente literal de derecho mercantil, sino de *commercial* o *business law*, que es una creación fundamentalmente académica, consistente en la agrupación de varias materias diversas referentes a los negocios sin constituir una disciplina autónoma. Es común, en consecuencia, que se haga referencia en inglés frecuentemente a las materias específicas que componen la llamada *business law*, tales como *agency, sale of goods, bankruptcy, business entities, insurance*, etc.

Rel: actos de comercio, *acts of commerce;* sociedades mercantiles, *mercantile companies, business entities;* títulos de crédito, *negotiable instruments.*

derecho militar *military law.*

Glosario: baja del servicio, *discharge from service;* consejo de guerra, *court martial;* correctivo disciplinario, *disciplinary measure;* delito militar, *military crime or offense;* disciplina militar, *military discipline;* ejército, *army;* fuero militar o de guerra, *military jurisdiction;* fuerza aérea, *air force;* fuerzas armadas, *armed forces;* guardia nacional, *national guard;* infracción militar, *military infraction, military violation;* Jefe del estado mayor, *chief of staff;* mandos operativos, *operative commands;* protección civil, *civil protection;* región militar, *military region;* servicio activo, *in active duty;* servicio militar, *military service;* tiempo de guerra, *war time;* tiempo de paz, *peacetime;*

tribunal militar, *military court;* zona militar, *military zone.*

derecho penal *criminal law.*

• Conjunto de normas destinadas a la definición de los delitos y la fijación de las sanciones aplicables. – Sin. derecho criminal.

Rel: acusación, *accusation;* agravantes, *aggravation;* atenuantes, *mitigation;* causas de justificación, *justification;* delito, *crime;* dolo, *criminal intent;* medidas de seguridad, *non-custodial sentencing measures (handed down as punishment);* pena, *punishment.*

derecho privado *private law.*

• "[E]s el que rige los actos de los particulares cumplidos por su iniciativa y en su propio nombre y beneficio. Por su origen y finalidad se ve dominado por el interés individual, frente al bien general que se asigna a la especie opuesta" y que constituye el derecho público (Cabanellas, III-146).

Comentario: La dicotomía de Derecho público-Derecho privado es característica del sistema romano-germánico. En los sistemas de *common law* la dicotomía Derecho público-Derecho privado nunca llegó a adoptarse como división fundamental. Los tribunales que en la evolución histórica del derecho inglés presidían sobre litigios de índole privada perdieron importancia y cedieron ante los tribunales cuya jurisdicción se concentraba en los intereses del Reino y la Corona. De esta manera el aspecto "público" del Derecho inglés quedó plenamente establecido. Cuando se emite un *writ*, por ejemplo, no se trata de una simple orden del tribunal, técnicamente es un mandato del rey, que en caso de ser desobedecido coloca a aquél que desobedece en oposición directa a la administración. El derecho privado tradicionalmente incluye al derecho civil y al derecho mercantil. Por su parte el derecho público, que es un desarrollo más reciente, incluye al derecho administrativo, al constitucional, al penal y al internacional público. Otras disciplinas de derecho se consideran ya parte del derecho privado, ya del derecho público, ya disciplinas de naturaleza mixta. Estas clasificaciones abarcan todo el derecho del sistema romano-germánico y permiten un mejor entendimiento de conceptos jurídicos fundamentales como por ejemplo la jurisdicción, la administración de justicia, los recursos judiciales, etc.

derecho procesal civil *civil procedure.*

• "Es el conjunto de normas, técnicas y doctrinas que tratan de la presentación, desarrollo y solución de las reclamaciones planteadas ante los tribunales fundadas en la aplicación de normas de derecho privado." (Ribó Durán, 212)
Ver: procedimiento civil.

derecho procesal penal *criminal procedure.*

• "Conjunto de normas internas y públicas, que regulan y determinan los actos, las formas y formalidades que deben observarse para hacer factible la aplicación del Derecho Penal sustantivo." (Colín Sanchez, 5)
Ver: procedimiento penal.

derecho real [prest.]*real right*, [ed]*rights in a thing*, [ef]*right in rem*.

• Poder jurídico que una persona ejerce en forma directa e inmediata sobre un bien específico para su aprovechamiento, siendo ese poder oponible a terceros. Por ejemplo, el derecho de propiedad o el derecho de servidumbre son considerados derechos reales.

Comentario: "La función básica del Derecho de cosas consiste en la atribución de los bienes a personas determinadas. Como consecuencia de esta atribución se otorga a dichas personas derecho sobre las cosas (de aquí el nombre de derechos reales) que les permiten actuar lícitamente sobre ellas e implican ciertos poderes para imponer el respeto a dicha atribución como consecuencia de los que pueden surgir relaciones con otras personas. El derecho real se caracteriza por la relación directa e inmediata del titular con el objeto y la protección absoluta frente a todos. El poder que atribuye sobre la cosa es independiente de una relación con otra persona y se conserva cualquiera que sea su poseedor y propietario." (II Enciclopedia Cívitas, 2366)

derecho romano *Roman law*.
Rel: familia romano-germánica, *Romano-Germanic family*.

derecho subjetivo [el]*subjective right, right*.

• Es la facultad jurídica derivada de una norma para exigir de otro una conducta consistente en una acción o una omisión.
Rel: derecho objetivo, *objective law, law*.

derechohabiente *beneficiary, successor*.
– Sin. causahabiente.

derechos[1] **(privilegio)** *rights*.
derechos civiles *civil rights*. – Sin. derechos individuales. derechos constitucionales, *constitutional rights*. garantías individuales, *constitutional guarantees*.
derechos constitucionales *constitutional rights, civil rights*.
derechos humanos *human rights*.
derechos inmateriales *incorporeal rights*.
derechos maritales *marital rights*.
derechos patrimoniales *proprietary rights, pecuniary rights*.
derechos sindicales *union rights*.

derechos[2] **(tributo)** *duties, charges, assessments*.
– Sin. contribución, *tax, assessment*. tasas, *taxes, charges*.

derechos aduaneros *custom duties*.
derechos antidumping (Esp) *antidumping duties*.
derechos arancelarios *custom duties, legal fees*.
derechos consulares *consular fees*.
derechos de exportación *export duties*.
derechos de importación *import duties*.
derecho de inscripción *registration fees*.
derechos del timbre *stamp taxes*.

derogación n. *derogation*. **derogar** v. *to derogate*. **derogatorio** adj. *derogative*.
Ver: abrogación.

derrocamiento n. *overthrow*. **derrocar** v. *to overthrow*.
Rel: golpe de estado, *coup d'état*.

desacato n. *contempt*. **desacatar** v. *to be in contempt*. **desacatamiento** n. *contempt*.
– Sin. desobediencia, *disobedience*.

desacuerdo n. *disagreement*. – Sin. desavenencia, *lack of agreement*. disconformidad, *difference, nonconformity*. discrepancia, *discrepancy*. divergencia, *divergence*.
estar en desacuerdo *to be in disagreement*.

desafuero n. *deprivation of a legal privilege*.
desaforar v. *to deprive of a legal privilege or right*. **desaforado** n. *one deprived of a legal privilege or right*.

• Privar del fuero, esto es, de las leyes o privilegios concedidos a ciertas personas, grupos, regiones o comunidades.

desahucio n. *eviction, dispossession of a tenant*.

• "Acto de despedir el dueño de una casa o el propietario de una heredad a un inquilino o arrendatario, por las causas expresadas en la ley o convenidas en el contrato." (III Cabanellas, 163) – Sin. desalojo, *ejection*. lanzamiento, *eviction, dispossession*. desocupación, *dispossession*.

juicio de desahucio *eviction proceedings*.

desaparición de poderes (Mx) [ed]*legislative act declaring a local government illegitimate*.

desarme n. *disarmament*. **desarmar** v. *to disarm*. **desarmado** adj. *disarmed*.

desarrollo habitacional *housing development*.

desarrollo urbano *urban development*.

descanso laboral *rest period (at work)* ‖ *leave*.

descargo[1] **(defensa)** n. *defense*.
testigo de descargo *witness for the defense*.
Rel: cargo, *charge*.

descargo[2] **(concluir)** n. *release, acquittal*.

descendiente n. *descendant*. **descendencia** n.

descendants || descent. **descend** v. *to descend.*
descendiente en línea recta *lineal descendant.*
Rel: familiares, *relatives.*

descentralización (der.admvo) n. *decentralization.* **descentralizar** v. *to decentralize.* – Sin. desconcentración, *a breaking up, divergence.*

desconocimiento de paternidad *denial of paternity.*

descripción (persona) n. *description (of a person).*

descuento n. *discount.* **descontar** v. *to discount.* – Sin. rebaja, *reduction, markdown.* reducción, *reduction.*

descuido n. *neglect, carelessness.* **descuidar** v. *to neglect.* **descuidado** adj. *careless, negligent.* **descuidadamente** adv. *carelessly.* – Sin. desatención, *carelessness.* negligencia, *neglect.*
descuido absoluto *gross neglect.*

desechamiento de la demanda *court's dismissal of a complaint, nonsuit.*
• Auto dictado por el juez negando la admisión de la demanda por no reunir los requisitos mínimos o por ser claramente infundada o temeraria. – Sin. desestimación de la demanda.

desechamiento de la prueba *exclusion or suppression of evidence.*

desempleo n. *unemployment.* **desemplear** v. *to discharge.* **desempleado** adj. *unemployed.* **desempleado** n. *unemployed person.*
prestaciones de desempleo *unemployment compensation.*
seguro de desempleo *unemployment insurance.*
taza de desempleo *unemployment rate.*
Rel: empleo, *employment, job.*

deserción n. *desertion.* **desertar** v. *to desert.* **desertor** n. *deserter.* – Sin. defección, *defection.* abandono, *abandonment.*
deserción militar *military desertion.*
desertar un recurso *to abandon a legal recourse.*

desestimar v. *to deny, to dismiss.* **desestimación** n. *denial, nonsuit.* – Sin. denegar. desechar.
desestimación de la demanda *dismissal of the complaint, nonsuit (involuntary dismissal).*
desestimación de la denuncia (CR) *nolle prosequi.*

desfalco (delito) n. *embezzlement, defalcation.* **desfalcar** v. *to embezzle.* **desfalcador** n.

embezzler.
• "Substracción, retención indebida o uso privado de caudales o valores por la persona que tiene la obligación de custodiarlos, de devolverlos o de servirse de ellos para fines específicos." (III Cabanellas, 190) – Sin. abuso de confianza. apropiación indebida.

desgravación[1] DER.FISCAL n. *tax credit, tax relief, tax reduction.* **desgravar** v. *to exempt from taxes.*
• Reducción de los tributos en el caso de que el contribuyente satisfaga los supuestos legales.

desgravación[2] **(garantía)** n. *lien removal.*
desgravar v. *to remove a lien.*
• Liberar de un gravámen.

desheredar v. *to disinherit.* **desheredación** n. *disinheritance.* **desheredamiento** n. *disinheritance.* **desheredado** adj. *disinherited.*

desintoxicación n. *detoxification, detoxication.* **desintoxicar** v. *to detoxicate, detoxify.*

desistimiento DER.PROCESAL n. *voluntary dismissal, abandonment.* **desistirse** v. *to dismiss.*
• "Modo anormal de conclusión del juicio, por virtud del cual uno de los dos litigantes se aparta de él en forma expresa, renunciando a su demanda o a su oposición." (Couture, 222) – Sin. renuncia, *renunciation.* abandono, *abandonment.* retractación, *retraction.*
El desistimiento de la acción produce la inexistencia del juicio y retrotrae los efectos al momento inmediato antes del ejercicio de la acción; el desistimiento de la instancia crea la suspensión del procedimiento; y el desistimiento del derecho produce la abdicación de la pretensión jurídica.
desistimiento de la acción *voluntary dismissal of a case, abandonment of action.*
desistimiento de la instancia *abandonment of the instance.*
desistimiento del derecho *abandonment of a right.*
Ver: autocomposición.

deslindamiento n. *delimitation.* **deslindador** n. *one who sets limits.*

deslinde n. *demarcation or delimitation of property.* **deslindar** v. *to delimit, to delimitate.*
• Identificar y distinguir delimitando claramente un lugar o heredad. – Sin. delimitación, *delimitation.* demarcación, *demarcation.*
deslinde y amojonamiento *survey and demarcation of boundaries.*
Rel: mojonera, *boundary mark.*

desmembramiento de la propiedad [ed]*the dividing up of the right of property over a thing.*

– Sin. modalidades de la propiedad.

↦ Desmembramiento de la propiedad es el término frecuentemente usado por la doctrina para expresar la posible división del derecho de propiedad en la tradición jurídica proveniente del derecho romano. En principio el concepto mismo de propiedad se entiende como único y a su división se le trata como un desarrollo excepcional y limitado. El número y la naturaleza de tales divisiones han sido rígidamente establecidas (tradicionalmente usufructo, habitación y uso). En contraste, el derecho angloamericano, menos preocupado por el derecho de propiedad, permite la creación sin limitaciones de múltiples derechos sobre la propiedad de un bien.
Ver: *property.*

desnacionalización[1] **(nacionalidad)** n. *denationalization, to lose citizenship.*

desnacionalización[2] **(sociedades)** n. *privatization of public companies.*

desobediencia civil *civil disobedience.*

desorden público *breach of the peace* || *disturbance.*

despacho[1] **(oficina)** n. *office.* – Sin. bufete, *office (of certain professionals).*
despacho jurídico *law office.* – Sin. bufete jurídico.
despacho privado *office, chambers.*

despacho[2] **(mensaje)** n. *message, order, dispatch.* – Sin. comunicación, *communication.*

despacho[3] **(resolver)** n. *conclusion of a matter, resolution.* **despachar** v. *to settle.* – Sin. resolución, *resolution.*
encargado del despacho del juzgado *in charge of the resolutions or dispositions of the court.*

despacho aduanal *customhouse clearance.*

despido DER.LABORAL n. *firing, dismissal.* **despedir** v. *to fire, to dismiss.* **despedido** *fired.*
• Terminación de la relación de trabajo por parte del patrono o empleador en forma unilateral y voluntaria. – Sin. destitución, *discharge.* echar a la calle, *to show (a person) the door.* recorte de personal, *employee cutback.* ser corrido de un trabajo, *to be fired from a job.*
carta de despido *letter of dismissal, pink slip.*
despido colectivo *mass firing.*
despido injustificado *dismissal without legal justification, wrongful discharge.* – Sin. despido improcedente.
despido justificado *dismissal with legal*

justification. – Sin. despido por justa causa.

despojo n. *dispossession.* **despojar** v. *to despoil, rob.* **despojador** adj. *despoiling.*
• Usurpar de otro o deshacerse uno mismo de la posesión de un bien. – Sin. desposeimiento, *dispossession.* usurpación, *usurpation.*
acción de despojo *forceful eviction, dispossession.*

destierro n. *exile.* **desterrar** v. *to exile.*
desterrado adj. *banished.* **desterrado** n. *exile, outcast.*
• Prohibición de residir en cierta jurisdicción o lugares especificados a título de pena.
– Sin. exilio, *exile.*

destitución[1] **(remover)** n. *removal.* **destituir** v. *to remove.* **destituible** adj. *removable.*
• Apartar o separar de un cargo o posición.
– Sin. despido, *dismissal.* remoción, *removal.*
destitución de albacea *removal of an executor.*
destitución de funcionario *dismissal of a public official.*

destitución[2] **(quitar bienes)** n. *deprivation.*

desviación sexual *sexual deviation.*
Rel: exhibicionismo, *exhibitionism;* fetichismo, *fetishism;* masoquismo, *masochism;* pedofilia, *pedophilia;* sadismo, *sadism;* sadomasoquismo, *sadomasochism;* travestismo, *transvestism;* voyerismo, *voyeurism;* zoofilia, *zoophilia.*

detector de mentiras *lie detector.*

detención n. *arrest* || *detention.* **detenido** n. *arrestee, detainee.* **detener** v. *to arrest, to detain.*
• "La detención significa la privación judicial, gubernativa o disciplinaria, de la libertad personal, como medio de contribuir a la investigación de un delito o como sanción discrecional de una falta o contravención." (III Cabanellas, 223)
– Sin. aprehensión. captura. detenimiento.
detención arbitraria *illegal detention.*
– Sin. detención ilegal.
detención del acusado *arrest of the accused.*
orden de detención *arrest warrant.*
detención por un particular *citizen's arrest.*
detención preventiva *arrest.*
Rel: bajo custodia, *in custody;* confinamiento, *confinement;* encarcelamiento, *incarceration.*
Ver: *arrest.*

detentación n. *detainer.* **detentador** n. *person who detains or holds property, deforciant.*
• "Retener uno lo que no le pertenece." (Martínez Marín y otros, 147)

Rel: apropiamiento, *appropriation;* retención, *retain;* usurpación, *usurpation.*
Ver: posesión. tenencia.

deuda n. *debt.* – Sin. débito, *debit.* pasivo, *liabilities.*
deuda a corto plazo *short-term debt.*
deuda a largo plazo *long-term debt.*
deuda civil *civil debt.*
deuda de dinero *money debt.*
deuda exigible *debt due.*
deuda exterior *foreign debt.*
deuda flotante *floating debt.*
deuda líquida *liquid debt.*
deuda pública *public debt.*
saldar la deuda *to discharge a debt.*
– Sin. solventar la deuda.

deudor n. *debtor.* **deudor** adj. *indebted.*
• El sujeto pasivo de una obligación jurídica.
deudor alimentario *support obligee.*
deudor hipotecario *mortgagor.*
deudor judicial *judgment debtor.*
deudor solidario *joint and several debtor.*
Rel: codeudor, *joint debtor.*

devolución¹ (return) n. *return ‖ refund.* **devolver** v. *to return.* **devolutivo o devolutorio** adj. *returnable.* – Sin. reembolso, *reimbursement.* reintegración, *restoration.* remisión, *remission.*
Cf: **devolución•devolución en dinero•reembolso.** Términos sinónimos. Devolución es la entrega de regreso de la cosa inicialmente dada. Devolución en dinero implica la corrección de un sobrepago mediante regreso de fondos o numerario. Reembolso, a su vez, hace referencia a que la devolución no es hecha en términos idénticos a los efectuados al hacerse la entrega original.
devolución de impuestos *tax refund.*
devolver en pago *to repay.*

devolución² (apelación) n. *remand.*
devolución de los autos *remand.*
efecto devolutivo *remand, remanded.*

día n. *day.*
día de fiesta *holiday.* – Sin. día festivo. día de asueto.
día feriado o de descanso *legal holiday.*
día hábil *workday.*
día inhábil *non-business day.*
día natural *natural day.*
días calendario *calendar days.*

dialecto n. *dialect.*
Rel: lengua, *tongue.*

diario oficial *official bulletin, gazette or*

newspaper. – Sin. boletín oficial (Esp).

dictamen¹ (decisión) n. *decision, judgment.*
dictaminar v. *to issue a decision or judgment.*
dictaminador adj. *adjudicating, judging.*
– Sin. decisión, *decision.*
dictamen judicial *decision of the court.*

dictamen² (reporte) n. *opinion.* **dictaminar** v. *to render an opinion.* – Sin. informe, *report.* opinión, *opinion.*
dictamen jurídico *legal opinion.*
dictamen pericial *expert opinion.*

difamación (delito) n. *defamation.* **difamar** v. *to defame.* **difamatorio** adj. *defamatory.*
• Desacreditar a uno respecto a terceros.
difamación escrita *libel.*
Rel: afrenta, *affront;* calumnia, *slander;* descrédito, *discredit;* desprecio, *contempt, scorn;* oprobio, *opprobrium.*

difunto n. *defunct, deceased.*
difunto esposo *late husband.*

dilatorio adj. *dilatory.*
• "Que prorroga o extiende un término judicial o la tramitación de un asunto." (I DRAE, 751)
– Sin. retardado, *delayed.*
excepción dilatoria *dilatory defense.*

diligencia¹ (ejecución) n. *execution of a court order.* **diligenciar** v. *to execute a court order, to serve process.* **diligenciamiento** n. *service, execution of a court order.*
• Diligencia se refiere a la ejecución de una resolución judicial. – Sin. ejecución de una resolución judicial.
Diligencia es un término cuyo significado es difícil de precisar en ocasiones ya que, aunque su significado más importante es el de la ejecución de una resolución judicial, también se le usa en su significación de un procedimiento o secuencia de actos e incluso, en menor grado, simplemente en su acepción de un expediente o los autos.
Cf: **diligencia • actuación judicial.** Diligencia es una especie del género actuación judicial cuando se le considera como una forma procesal de ejecución de disposiciones judiciales <diligencia de embargo>. Pero a diligencia también se le identifica y confunde con actuación judicial cuando se le define como un procedimiento y se le otorga la significación dual de actos procesales y autos. <diligencias preliminares>
diligencia de embargo *execution of attachment.*
diligencia de pruebas *taking of evidence.*

diligencia judicial *execution of a judicial order.*

diligencia o providencia para mejor proveer [ed]*court-ordered actions to facilitate adjudication or to complete and clarify evidence.*

diligencia²(procedimiento) n. *proceeding.*
• "Conjunto de actuaciones que conforman el procedimiento." (Dicc. ed. Comares, 192)
– Sin. actuaciones judiciales, *court proceedings.* procedimiento, *proceeding.* trámite, *formality, step, negotiation.*
diligencia de reconocimiento *line-up proceedings.*
diligencia judicial *judicial proceeding.*
diligencias preliminares *pre-trial proceedings, pre-trial.* – Sin. diligencias preparatorias.
practicar una diligencia *to carry out a procedural act.*

diligencia³(solicitud) n. *diligence.*
• Cuidado; exactitud. – Sin. celo, earnestness.
diligencia de buen padre de familia *reasonable and prudent man standard of diligence.* – Sin. buen padre de familia.
diligencia razonable *reasonable diligence, reasonable care.*
diligenciamiento de emplazamiento *service of summons.*
diligenciamiento de notificación *service of notice.*

dinero n. *money.*
dinero bancario *banking money.*
dinero en efectivo *cash.*
dinero falsificado *counterfeit money.*
dinero falso *bogus money.*
dinero lavado *laundered money.*
dinero legal o de curso legal *legal tender.*
dinero marcado *bait money.*
Rel: capital, *capital;* caudal, *wealth;* efectivo, *cash;* fondos, *funds;* fortuna, *fortune;* moneda, *currency;* plata (mod.), *dough;* riqueza, *wealth.*

diplomacia n. *diplomacy.* **diplomático** adj. *diplomatic.* **diplomático** n. *diplomat.*
valija diplomática *diplomatic pouch.*
– Sin. [fr.]valise diplomatique.

diputado n. *congressman* || *deputy.* **diputación** n. *congressional delegation* || *legislative body.*
– Sin. representante, *representative.*
Cámara de diputados *House of Representatives.* – Sin. Asamblea de representantes.
Rel: Congreso, *Congress.*

director¹ (funcionario) n. *manager.* **dirigir** v. *to manage.* **dirección** n. *management.*
director de mercadotecnia *marketing manager.*
director de ventas *sales manager.*
director ejecutivo *chief executive.*

director² (consejo de admon.) n. *director (member of the board).* – Sin. administrador. consejero.
director propietario *legally appointed director.*
director suplente *alternate director.*

directorio n. *board of directors.*
Ver: consejo de administración.

discreción n. *discretion.* **discrecional** adj. *discretionary.*
discreción absoluta *absolute discretion.*
discreción judicial *judicial discretion.*

discriminación n. *discrimination.* **discriminar** v. *to discriminate.* **discriminatorio** adj. *discriminatory.* **discriminador** adj. *discriminating, discriminative.*
delito de discriminación (Esp) *hate crime.*
discriminación racial *racial discrimination.*

disidente n. *dissenter, dissident.* **disidente** adj. *dissenting.*

disolución n. *dissolution.* **disolver** v. *to dissolve.*
– Sin. rompimiento, *breaking, breakdown.*
disolución de la sociedad conyugal *separation of community property.*
disolución de matrimonio *dissolution of marriage.*
disolución de una sociedad *dissolution of a corporation.*

disparo (de arma de fuego) *gunshot, discharge of a firearm.*
disparo a quemarropa *point blank gunshot.*
disparo contra un vehículo *firing at a vehicle.*
disparo mortal de un arma *deadly gunshot.*
Rel: prueba de dermotest o de la parafina, *paraffin test;* prueba de rodizonato de sodio, *sodium rhodizonate test.*
Ver: balística.

dispensa n. *dispensation, exemption.*

disposiciones n. *provisions.*
• Preceptos o reglas legales o reglamentarias.
– Sin. mandato, *rule.* precepto. *precept.*
disposiciones discrecionales *discretionary provisions.*
disposiciones sustantivas *substantive law provisions.*
disposiciones transitorias *transition provisions.*

disposiciones tributarias *tax rules.*

distrito judicial *judicial district.*

disturbio n. *disturbance, riot.* – Sin. borlote. trastorno, *upheaval.* desorden, *disorder, turmoil.* tumulto, *tumult, mob.*
Rel: asonada, *tumultuous demonstration;* motín, *riot, mutiny;* revuelta, *revolt.*

dividendo n. *dividend.*
dividendo acumulativo *cumulative dividend.*
dividendo en acciones *stock dividend.*
dividendo en especie *dividend in kind.*
– Sin. dividendo de bienes.
dividendo extraordinario *extraordinary dividend.*
dividendo ordinario *regular dividend.*
dividendo preferente *preferred dividend.*
– Sin. dividendo preferencial. dividendo preferido.
dividendos decretados *declared dividends.*
dividendos distribuidos *dividends paid.*
dividendos ganados *dividends earned.*
dividendos por pagar *dividends payable.*

divisas n. *foreign currency.* – Sin. moneda extranjera.

división de bienes comunes *partition of property held in common.*

división de la herencia *distribution of a decedent's estate.*
Rel: por partes iguales, *share and share alike.*

división de poderes DER. CONST *separation of powers.*

divorcio n. *divorce.* **divorciar** v. *to divorce.*
divorciado n. *divorced.* **divorciada** n. *divorcée.*
• Disolución de un matrimonio válido mediante resolución judicial fundada en una causal debidamente probada.
Cf: **divorcio ● separación.** El Derecho canónico introdujo el divorcio-separación, actualmente conocido simplemente como separación judicial, en el que el vínculo matrimonial persiste a pesar de la separación física de los cónyuges. El divorcio por su lado, de origen secular, da por resuelto el vínculo matrimonial ordenando la separación como consecuencia lógica de su terminación.
causales de divorcio *grounds for divorce.*
– Sin. causas de divorcio.
divorcio administrativo (Mx) *uncontested divorce.*
divorcio contencioso *contested divorce.*
– Sin. divorcio necesario.

divorcio voluntario *divorce by mutual agreement, no-fault divorce.* – Sin. divorcio no contencioso. divorcio por mutuo consentimiento.
Rel: disolución, *dissolution;* reconciliación, *reconciliation;* ruptura, *break up;* separación, *separation.*
Ref: (Ar)CC a.214; (Ec)CC a.105ss.; (Mx)CC a.266ss.; (Pe)CC a.348-360; (PR)CC a.96, 31 LPRA sec 321; (Ve)CC a.185ss.

doble exposición (PR) *double jeopardy.*

doble nacionalidad *double nationality.*

doble tributación *double taxation.* – Sin. doble contribución. doble imposición.

doctrina¹ (ciencia jurídica) *legal science.*
doctrinal adj. *doctrinal.*
• Conjunto de ideas y conceptos que formulan los juristas y transmiten en la enseñanza del derecho. – Sin. dogmática jurídica.
En esta acepción doctrina es sinónimo de ciencia del derecho o dogmática jurídica.

doctrina² (opinión docta) n. *theses and opinion of legal scholars.*
• Opiniones y tesis de juristas y estudiosos del derecho respecto de cuestiones y tópicos legales específicamente definidos. – Sin. escuela.
doctrina Calvo DER.INTL *Calvo doctrine.*
doctrina Estrada *Estrada doctrine.*
se ha sentado doctrina *a thesis or opinion has been adopted.*

documento n. *document.* **documentar** v. *to document.* **documental** adj. *documental, pertaining to documents.* **documentado** adj. *well documented.* **documentación** n. *documentation.*
• "Instrumento escrito que contiene la relación o constatación de un hecho o circunstancias relativas a hechos o personas." (Dicc. ed. Comares, 197) – Sin. instrumento, *instrument.*
documento auténtico *certified or notarized document.*
documento constitutivo *incorporation papers.* – Sin. escritura constitutiva.
documento ejecutivo [ed]*document which grants right to execute on property by means of a summary proceeding.* – Sin. título ejecutivo.
documento nacional de identidad (Esp) *National identity card.*
documento oficial *official document.*
documento original *source document.*
documento privado *private document, document not recorded by a public notary.*
documento público *public document.*
documentos falsos *false documents.*

documentos por cobrar (contab.) *notes receivable.*

documentos por pagar (contab.) *notes payable.*

documentos probatorios *supporting documents, evidentiary documents.*
Rel: acta, *act;* certificado, *certificate.*

documentos de embarque *shipping documents.*
Tipos: certificado de origen, *certificate of origin;* certificado fitosanitario, *phytosanitary certificate;* conocimiento de embarque, *bill of lading;* contrato de transporte, *transportation contract;* factura comercial, *commercial invoice;* factura consular, *consular invoice;* factura pro-forma, *pro-forma invoice;* flete aéreo, *air freight;* guía aérea, *airbill;* lista de empaque o embalaje, *packing list.*

dolo[1] DER.CIVIL n. [lat.]*dolus,* [rtrgido]*fraud or deceit,* [rtrgido]*malicious fraud.* **doloso** adj. *fraudulent.*
• Dolo civil se refiere a una conducta por acción u omisión que usando artificio, astucia o maquinación afirma lo que es falso o disimula lo verdadero.
Cf: **dolo ⚊ mala fe.** Aunque dolo es frecuentemente confundido con la mala fe se ha considerado que se diferencia de ésta, en que mientras el dolo provoca el error en otro, la mala fe la tiene el que se aprovecha del error una vez conocido.
⌐ Dolo es un concepto amplio que se refiere a "la deliberada intención de causar injustamente un mal a alguien ..." (Dicc. UNAM, 1204). En derecho civil aparece como un vicio de la voluntad en la formación de los contratos, y como un elemento en la responsabilidad civil. *Fraud,* entendido como una manifestación a sabiendas falsa de la verdad que al motivar la actuación de otro le causa un perjuicio, es un concepto más restringido en su definición y en su aplicación apareciendo casi exclusivamente en el ámbito de la responsabilidad civil o *torts.*
Malicious fraud describe apropiadamente el engaño intencional del concepto de dolo pero sin referirse a sus consecuencias como vicio de los contratos, siendo por lo tanto también un término más restringido. Por su parte, aunque *dolus* es el término latino equivalente original, raramente se usa en inglés.
contrato afectado de dolo [ed]*contract made under fraud or deceit,* [ed]*contract made under malicious fraud.*
vicio de dolo [ext.lexico]*defect of dolus (in a contract).*
Ver: fraude.

Ref: (Ar)CC a.931ss.; (Ch)CC a.1451,1458 y 1459.; (Ec)CC a.1501,1502; (Esp)CC a.1269 y 1270; (Mx) CC a.1815; (Ur)CC a.1276; (Ve)CC a.1154.

dolo[2] DER.PENAL n. *criminal intent.* **doloso** adj. *intentional, with intent.*
• El dolo penal se refiere al propósito o intención de cometer el delito. – Sin. intencionalidad. Es un concepto que incluye tanto el saber o conocimiento, como el querer o volición de lo que se realiza.
delito doloso *intentional crime.*
dolo con intención ulterior *ulterior intent.*
dolo de consecuencias necesarias *constructive intent.*
dolo directo *criminal intent.*
dolo eventual [ed]*constructive intent when result may or may not occur.*
Rel: culpa, *criminal negligence.*

domicilio n. *domicile.* **domiciliar** v. *to domicile.* **domiciliario** adj. *domiciliary.*
• Lugar donde una persona reside con intención de permanecer allí. – Sin. dirección, *address.* morada, *dwelling, abode.* residencia, *residence.*
Domicilio es un concepto al que se le ha dado considerable flexibilidad para permitir su adaptación a las necesidades de la vida moderna. La legislación moderna permite diferentes definiciones de domicilio, dependiendo de la materia y las circunstancias de la persona; así mientras en derecho civil el domicilio es considerado uno de los atributos de la personalidad y definido como el lugar de residencia habitual, en materia tributaria frecuentemente se le considera como el lugar en el que se genera el crédito fiscal o el determinado por la legislación en la materia, y en derecho procesal se entiende por domicilio el que señalen las partes o el que se presume legalmente para efectos de comunicación judicial.
domicilio convencional *elected domicile.*
domicilio conyugal *matrimonial domicile.*
domicilio desconocido *unknown whereabouts.*
domicilio fiscal *domicile for tax purposes.*
domicilio legal *legal domicile.*
domicilio para notificaciones *elected domicile.*
domicilio procesal *address for purposes of a lawsuit.*
domicilio real *actual address.*
domicilio social *place of business.*

dominio n. [prest.][lat.]*dominium,* [ef]*ownership.*
• "Derecho real que atribuye a su titular el po-

der o señorío más amplio posible sobre una cosa corporal dentro de límites institucionales." (Dicc. ed. Comares, 198) – Sin. imperio. propiedad. señorío.
"A nuestro juicio, entre la propiedad y el dominio no hay diferencia de extensión y contenido, sino simplemente de punto de vista. La propiedad es un concepto económico-jurídico. La palabra dominio tiene un sentido predominantemente subjetivo, pues implica, como dice Ruggiero, la potestad que sobre la cosa corresponde al titular; la palabra propiedad lo tiene predominantemente objetivo, acentuando la relación de pertenencia de la cosa a la persona." (II Vol. I Castan Tobeñas, 95)
dominio absoluto [fe]*fee simple,* [lat.]*dominium plenum.* – Sin. dominio pleno.
dominio aéreo *air space.*
Rel: poder, *power;* potestad, [lat.]*potestas.*
Ver: propiedad.

donación n. *gift, donation,* [lat.]*donatio.* **donar** v. *to donate.* **donante** n. *donor.* **donatario** n. *donee.* **receptor** *recipient.*
• "La donación es un acto de liberalidad por el cual una persona dispone gratuitamente de una cosa, en favor de otra, que la acepta." (CC-Esp., a.618) – Sin. dádiva. donatio (lat.). donativo, *gift, contribution.* obsequio. regalo.
donación antenupcial *premarital gift.*
donación inter vivos *inter vivos gift.*
donación mortis causa *gift causa mortis.*
donación revocable *revocable gift.*
donación testamentaria *testamentary gift.*
donante de embriones *embryo donor.*
donante de órganos *organ donor.*
Ref: (Ar)CC a.1789-1868; (Ch)CC a.1386ss.; (CR) CC a.1393-403; (Esp)CC a.618; (Mx)CC a.2332; (Pay)CC a.1202; (Pe)CC a.1621-1647; (RD)CC a. 894ss.; (Ur)CC a.1613; (Ve)CC a1.431.

dote n. *dowry.* **dotal** adj. *dotal.*

droga¹ (deuda) n. *money owed.* **endrogarse** v. *to go into debt.*
estar endrogado *to owe money.*

droga² (sustancia) n. *drug.* **drogarse** v. *to drug oneself.* **drogadicción** n. *drug addiction.*
Rel: estupefacientes, *narcotics and similar substances;* tráfico de drogas, *drug traffic.*
Glosario: acetona, *nail polish remover;* aerosoles, *aerosols;* alcohol, *alcohol;* analgésicos, *analgesics;* anfetaminas, *amphetamines;* barbitúricos, *barbiturates;* barniz, *varnish;* bencedrina, *benzedrine;* cemento, *glue;* cloroformo, *chloroform;* cocaína, *cocaine;* codeína, *codeine;* depresivos, *depressants, downers;* DMT, *DMT;* DOM, *DOM;* estimulantes, *stimulants;* gasolina, *gasoline;* alucinógenos, *hallucinogens;* hashish, *hashish;* heroína, *heroin;* inhalantes, *inhalants;* lacas, *lacquer;* LSD, *LSD;* mariguana, *marijuana;* MDA, *MDA;* mezcalina, *mescaline;* metadona, *methadone;* morfina, *morphine;* narcóticos, *narcotics;* opiatos, *opiates;* PCP, *PCP;* peyote, *peyote;* píldoras para dormir, *sleeping pills;* psicotrópicos, *psychotropics;* psilocibina, *psilocybin;* sedativos, *sedatives;* thiner, *thinner;* tranquilizante, *tranquilizer;* valium, *valium.*

drogadicto n. *drug addict.* – Sin. adicto, *addict, user, glass eyes, hophead, hype, junkie.*
adicto a anfetaminas *speed freak.*
adicto a la heroína *sleep walker.*
adicto a la mariguana (marihuano) *doper, pothead, weed head.*
adicto a LSD *acid freak.*
adicto a píldoras (píldoro) *pill freak.*
Rel: adicción, *addiction;* dosis para uso personal, *amount (of drug) for personal consumption;* síndrome de abstinencia de droga, *withdrawal syndrome.*

duelo n. *duel.* **duelista** n. *dueler.*

dueño n. *owner.*

dumping (prest.) n. *dumping.*

duración n. *duration.* **durar** v. *to last.* **duradero** adj. *durable, lasting.* – Sin. vigencia, *effect, force.*
duración de la pena de prisión *term of imprisonment.*
duración de la relación laboral *duration of employment.*
duración del contrato de arrendamiento *term of lease.*

EEEE

ebriedad n. *drunkenness, inebriation.* **ebrio** n. *drunk, inebriate.* – Sin. embriaguez. borrachera.
ebriedad habitual *habitual drunkenness, habitual drunkards.*

echazón DER.MARÍTIMO n. *jettison.*
• Arrojar al mar la carga total o parcialmente para aligerar el buque.
Rel: avería, *average.*

edad n. *age.*
edad avanzada *old age.*
edad biológica *biological age.*
edad cronológica *real age, actual age.*

edad civil *age of majority.* – Sin. mayoría de edad. edad legal.

edad mental *mental age.*

edad penal *age of criminal responsibility.*
Rel: ancianidad, *old age;* juventud, *youth;* madurez, *maturity;* mocedad, *youth;* niñez, *childhood;* vejez, *old age.*

edicto¹ (notificación) n. *legal notice.*

notificación por edictos *service by publication.*

edicto² (proclamación) n. *decree, proclamation.*
– Sin. bando. decreto. proclama, *proclamation.*

edificio n. *building.* **edificar** v. *to build.*

edificación n. *construction.* **edificador** adj. *constructing.* – Sin. construcción. inmueble.

edificio de departamentos o apartamentos *apartment building.*

edificio de rentas *rental building.*

efectivo n. *cash.* – Sin. numerario, *cash, coins.*

dinero en efectivo *cash.*

descuento en efectivo *cash discoount.*

flujo de efectivo *cash flow.*

efectivo disponible *cash on hand.*

pago en efectivo *cash payment.*

efectivo en caja *cash on hand.*

efecto n. *effect.*

efecto constitutivo [ed]*creating a legal status or new legal consequences.*

efecto devolutivo DER.PROCESAL *without a stay of execution.*

efecto retroactivo *retroactive effect.*

efecto suspensivo *staying effect.*

efectos legales a que haya lugar *resulting legal consequences, corresponding legal consequences.*

surtir efecto *legally binding, to be effective.*

efectos personales *personal effects.*

ejecución¹ (llevar a cabo) n. *execution.* **ejecutar** v. *to execute.* **ejecutable** adj. *executable.*

ejecutor n. *executor.*

ejecución de la ley *law enforcement.*
– Sin. aplicación de la ley.

ejecución de las penas *execution of a criminal sentence, carrying out a criminal sentence.*

ejecución de una sentencia *enforcement of a judgment.*

ejecución forzada de un contrato *court enforcement of a contract.*

ejecución hipotecaria *foreclosure of a mortgage.*

mandamiento de ejecución *writ of execution.*

traer aparejada ejecución *coupled with summary execution proceedings, to be enforceable on its face.* – Sin. traer aparejada ejecución.
Rel: cumplimiento, *performance;* realización, *fulfillment.*

ejecución² (pena de muerte) n. *execution.*

ejecutar v. *to execute.* **ejecutado** adj. *executed.*

verdugo n. *executioner.*

ejecución de la pena de muerte *carrying out the death penalty.* – Sin. ejecución de la pena capital.

ejecución de un reo *execution of an inmate.*

ejecutoria n. [ed]*final sentence or judgment in a case (when sustained after appeal or when not-appealed), final judicial decision.*

ejecutoriar v. *to become final (a sentence).*
• Una sentencia que no puede ser impugnada.
– Sin. sentencia ejecutoriada. sentencia firme.

ejercicio de la abogacía *practice of law.*
– Sin. ejercicio del derecho.

ejercicio de un derecho *exercise of a right.*

ejercicio presupuestario *budget year.*

ejercicio fiscal *fiscal year, tax year.*

ejército n. *army.* – Sin. fuerzas armadas, *armed forces.*

ejército aliado *allied forces.*

ejército de reserva *reserves.*

ejército mercenario *mercenary army.*

ejército regular *regular army.*
Rel: consejo de guerra, *court martial.*
Ver: derecho militar.

ejido [prest.]*ejido,* [ed]*land used in common by inhabitants of a town.* **ejidatario** n. [prest.] *ejidatario.* **ejidal** adj. *pertaining to the ejido.*
• El ejido es tradicionalmente una tierra común para pastura y entretenimiento de una población. En México, sin embargo, el ejido se refiere normalmente a una dotación de tierras, bosques y aguas comunales que se trabajan conjuntamente por un grupo organizado de campesinos llamados ejidatarios, y a la que se le ha dado una regulación especial cuyos principios básicos han sido consagrados en la constitución.

comisariado ejidal (Mx) *ejido's executive board.*

derecho ejidal (Mx) *ejido law.*

terreno ejidal *ejido land.*

elecciones n. *elections.* **elegir** v. *to elect.* **elector** n. *elector, voter.* **electoral** adj. *electoral.*

electorado n. *electorate.* **electivo** n. *elected.*

electivo adj. *elective.*

- Ejercicio del derecho de sufragio.
- – Sin. comicios, *elections.* sufragio, *suffrage.* votación, *vote.*

"[E]xpresa también el período de la campaña proselitista o de propaganda y las actividades relacionadas con la designación de candidatos, actos públicos de éstos y nombramientos de los representantes de los partidos ante las mesas electorales, entre otras." (III Cabanellas, 398)

abstencionismo electoral *electoral abstentionism.*

campaña electoral *election campaign.*

cargo electivo *elective office.*

colegio electoral *election board* || [el]*electoral college* (EEUU).

elecciones federales *federal election.*

elección general *general election.*

empadronamiento electoral *voter's roll, voter's list.*

fraude electoral *electoral fraud.*

ley electoral *electoral law.*

urna electoral *ballot box.*

tribunal electoral [ed]*electoral court, election court* (GB).

Rel: encuesta de salida, *exit poll;* escrutinio (de votos), *vote count;* plebiscito, *plebiscite;* voto, *vote.*

embarcación n. *vessel, ship.*

apresamiento de embarcación *arrest of a vessel.*

decomiso de embarcaciones *seizure of vessels (as punishment for a major violation of the law).*

Ver: buque.

emancipación n. *emancipation.* **emancipar** v. *to emancipate.* **emancipado** n. *emancipated minor.*

- La emancipación consiste en la extinción de la patria potestad o tutela que personas mayores tienen sobre los menores, ya por haber llegado a la mayoría de edad, ya por otras razones permisibles por la ley, confiriéndoles un grado de capacidad similar a la mayoría de edad.
- – Sin. manumisión, *manumission.*

emancipación judicial *court-ordered emancipation.*

emancipación legal *emancipation by operation of law.*

emancipación por mayoría de edad *age of majority emancipation.*

emancipación voluntaria *emancipation by parent's agreement.*

Rel: mayoría de edad, *age of majority;* patria potestad, [lat.]*patria potestas.*

embajada n. *embassy.* **embajador** n. *ambassador.*

Rel: legación, *legation;* misión diplomática, *diplomatic mission.*

embargo DER.PROCESAL n. *attachment, garnishment.* **embargar** v. *to attach, to garnish.* **embargado** n. *one who is subject to attachment, garnishee.* **embargable** adj. *susceptible to be attached or garnished.*

embargante/embargador n. *party requesting attachment or garnishment.*

- El embargo es la afectación de bienes a un proceso dictada por un juez para facilitar al tribunal la satisfacción de la pretensión de ejecución que debe atender al pedírsele que haga efectiva la sentencia. – Sin. secuestro, *seizure.*

Cf: **embargo • secuestro • requisa • decomiso.** Embargo y secuestro se usan sinónimamente con frecuencia. En estricto rigor el término secuestro es más amplio, ya que se refiere al apoderamiento no sólo de bienes, sino también de personas. Asimismo, secuestro puede tener un propósito diferente al del embargo, que consiste exclusivamente en satisfacer la pretensión del promovente de la acción. El decomiso se refiere a una apropiación de bienes, decretada por la autoridad judicial, primordialmente como una sanción por la comisión de un ilícito, generalmente sobre los bienes o instrumentos del delito. La requisa, por su parte, es una incautación de carácter extraordinario y general que se lleva a cabo cuando así lo demanda la necesidad pública urgente como lo es el caso de guerra o similar.

auto de embargo *writ of attachment.* – Sin. auto de exequendo.

diligencia de embargo *attachment proceeding.*

embargo de armas DER.INTL *arms embargo.*

embargo de propiedad en manos de un tercero *garnishment.*

embargo ejecutivo *judgment execution.*

embargo precautorio *provisional attachment.* – Sin. embargo preventivo.

levantamiento de un embargo *release of an attachment or garnishment.*

trabar embargo *to attach or garnish, to levy an attachment or garnishment.*

Rel: decomiso, *seizure;* retención, *withholding;* señalamiento de bienes, *indication of attachable property.*

Comentario: "El auto o resolución que ordena el embargo, o auto de exequendo (ejecutando, literalmente), como

también se le llama no sin cierta impropiedad, puede dictarse según el caso, antes del juicio, al iniciarse éste o durante él ... también puede dictarse ... para tratar de lograr la ejecución coactiva de la sentencia de condena o de algún otro título ejecutorio. En este caso el embargo tendrá carácter definitivo, ejecutivo o apremiativo." (Dicc. UNAM, 1250-251)
Ver: *attachment*. secuestro.
Ref: (Ar)CPCC a.531; (Co)CPP a.60; (Esp)NLEC a.727; (Mx)CPC a.543ss.; (Ve)CPC a.534ss., 591-598.

embarque n. *shipment*. **embarcar** v. *to ship*.
emabarcador n. *shipper*. **remitente** *sender*.
destinatario n. *addressee, consignee*.
embarques parciales *partial shipments*.
Rel: transportación, *transportation*.

emboscada n. *ambush*. **emboscar** v. *to ambush*.
– Sin. celada, *ambush, trap*. trampa, *trap*. zalagarda, *ambush, trap*.

emigración n. *emigration*. **emigrar** v. *to emigrate*. **emigrante** adj. *emigrating*.
emigrante n. *emigrant*, [fr.]*emigré*. **emigrado** n. *emigrant*.

emisión de acciones *issue of stock*.

emisión de bonos *bond issue*.

empadronar v. *to register, roll*.
empadronamiento n. *registration*. **padrón** n. *register*. – Sin. censo, *register*.

emplazamiento n. [ed]*court's request to the parties in a lawsuit to act within a certain period of time*, [prest.] *emplazamiento*, [rtrgido] [ef]*summons*. **emplazar** v. *to request the parties to act within a certain period of time, to summon*.
• Es el acto por el cual el juez comunica la fijación de un espacio de tiempo para la ejecución de un acto procesal ante él, a llevarse a cabo por una o ambas partes.
Cf: **emplazamiento • citación**. Aunque usados sinónimamente en ocasiones, son términos claramente distinguibles: emplazamiento es la notificación de un plazo dado a una o ambas partes para que realicen un acto procesal, mientras que citación, a diferencia, es un requerimiento para que la parte o partes se presenten en un momento cierto a realizar un acto o diligencia.
↝ Emplazamiento y *summons* son frecuentemente equivalentes, pero emplazamiento es un concepto más amplio por definición. Mientras emplazamiento se usa en ocasiones con motivo de cualquier diligencia o acto procesal, *summons* generalmente se refiere a la notificación de la demanda hecha al demandado exigiendo su comparecencia y contestación dentro de cierto plazo. En este sentido, *summons* coincide con emplazamiento cuando éste es usado con ese mismo significado, como frecuentemente lo es. Por ejemplo, en México éste es el significado exclusivo de emplazamiento. Contrastantemente, cuando ambos términos no coinciden no son equivalentes.

emplazamiento de la demanda [ef]*summons*.
emplazamiento de huelga *strike call*.
– Sin. emplazamiento a huelga.
Rel: citación, *subpoena;* comparecencia, *appearance*.
Ver: comunicación procesal.
Ref: (Esp)LEC a.270,274 y 276; (Mx)CPCDF a.114 y 117; (Ve)CPC a.344-345.

empleo n. *employment, job*. **emplear** v. *to employ*. **empleado** n. *employee*. **empleador** n. *employer*. **empleable** adj. *employable*.
– Sin. cargo, *post*. ocupación, *occupation*. puesto, *position*. trabajo, *job*.
agencia de empleo *employment agency*.
empleado de confianza *employee in a supervisory capacity*.
empleado público *government employee*.
tasa de empleo *employment rate*.

empresa[1] **(negocio)** n. *business*. **empresario** n. *businessman*.
• La unidad económica organizada y encaminada a la producción o distribución de bienes o servicios. – Sin. giro mercantil, *commercial business*. negociación, *business*.
Cf: **empresa • sociedad**. Ambos términos se usan indistintamente con frecuencia. Empresa se refiere primordialmente a la organización de capital, trabajo y tecnología encaminada a la producción de bienes y servicios, mientras sociedad define primordialmente a un "orden jurídico particular" creado por el derecho para darle existencia a un ente ficticio diferente de las personas físicas que la constituyen.
administración de empresas *business administration*.
comité de empresa *committee made up of employees or workers (of a company)*.
empresa comercial *commercial business*.
– Sin. empresa mercantil.
empresa multinacional *multinational company, multinational corporation*.
– Sin. compañía multinacional.
empresa pública *government-owned company*.
empresa transnacional *transnational company*. – Sin. compañía transnacional.

empresas agropecuarias *agribusiness.*
empresas vinculadas *related companies.*
Rel: compañía, *company;* sociedad, *business entity.*
empresa²(proyecto) n. *enterprise, undertaking.*
empresario n. *entrepreneur.*
• Una obra, proyecto o designio emprendido especialmente por varias personas. – Sin. iniciativa, *undertaking.* proyecto, *project.*
empréstito DER.ADMVO n. *government loan, public debt.*
• Empréstito es un préstamo público a largo o mediano plazo, generalmente para satisfacer una finalidad extraordinaria, aunque en la actualidad se le considera frecuentemente como un recurso ordinario de obtención de crédito.
en caso contrario *otherwise, on the contrary.*
en el fondo *on the merits.*
en especie *in kind.*
en fe de lo cual *in witness whereof.*
en igualdad de circunstancias *all other things being equal.*
en rebeldía *by default.*
en su cabal juicio *of sound mind.*
en testimonio de lo cual *in witness whereof.*
en vigor *in force, in effect.*
enajenación n. *transfer of ownership.* **enajenar** v. *to transfer ownership* **enajenado** adj. *transferred or alienated property.* **enajenante** n. *transferor, alienor.* **enajenador** n. *transferor, alienor.*
• "Acción y efecto de transferir a otro a título legítimo y por acto entre vivos, la propiedad de una cosa o la titularidad de un derecho." (Couture, 254) – Sin. alienación, *alienation.*
enajenación de bienes *conveyance of property, transfer of property.*
enajenaciones de bienes de menores *alienation of minor's property, transfer of minor's property.*
enajenación en fraude de acreedores *transfer to defraud creditors.*
Rel: disposición, *disposal;*
enajenación mental *insanity || mental derangement.* – Sin. incapacidad mental. trastorno mental permanente.
Ver: *insanity.*
encaje legal o bancario *bank reserves.*
encarcelar v. *to put in jail, incarcerate.*
encarcelamiento n. *incarceration, imprisonment.* **encarcelación** n. *incarceration, imprisonment.* **encarcelador** adj. *incarcerating.*

– Sin. aprisionar, *to imprison.* encerrar, *to lock up.* poner en la sombra (mod.), *to put in the slammer, to incarcerate.*
encubrimiento n. *accessory after the fact, harboring.* **encubrir** v. *to harbor.* **encubridor** n. *accessory after the fact.*
• Acción de ocultar a los culpables del delito, los efectos de éste, o los instrumentos o indicios con la intención de sustraerse de la justicia. – Sin. ocultamiento.
Rel: autor del delito, *offender, criminal, perpetrator;* cómplice, *accomplice.*
endoso TÍTULOS DE CRÉDITO n. *indorsement, endorsement.* endosar v. *to indorse, endorse.* **endosante** n. *endorser.* **endosatario** n. *indorsee, endorsee.*
• "La fórmula inscripta, generalmente al dorso de una letra de cambio o pagaré por la cual se transmite su propiedad." (Ramírez Gronda, 141)
endoso condicional *limited indorsement.*
endoso en administración *indorsement granting business management authority.*
endoso en blanco *blank indorsement.*
endoso en garantía *guarantor's indorsement.*
endoso en prenda *indorsement pledging instrument as collateral.*
endoso en procuración *indorsement creating an agency relationship, indorsement for collection purposes.*
endoso en propiedad *indorsement transferring title.*
endoso fiduciario *trust indorsement.*
endoso irregular *irregular indorsement, anomalous indorsement.*
endoso pleno *unrestrictive endorsement.*
Rel: aval, *accommodation indorsement;* títulos de crédito, *negotiable instruments.*
enemigo público *public enemy.*
enfermedad n. *disease, illness.* – Sin. achaque, *ailment.* afección, *affection, disease.* padecimiento, *ailment.*
enfermedad contagiosa *contagious disease.*
enfermedad de trabajo *occupational disease.*
enfermedad profesional *occupational disease.*
enfermedad mental *mental disease.*
Rel: impulsividad criminal, *uncontrollable impulse;* imputabilidad disminuida, [el] *diminished imputability, diminished competency to be charged.*
Ver: *mental disease.*
enfiteusis (obs.) n. [prest.][grk.]*emphyteusis.*
enfiteuta n. [prest.]*emphyteuta.*
• Derecho real o contrato por el que se cede el

goce de una cosa mueble a perpetuidad o por largo plazo con la obligación por parte del recipiente de pagar una pensión o canon. – Sin. censo enfitéutico, *emphyteusis*.

enganche (Mx) n. *down payment.*

engaño n. *deception.* **engañar** v. *to deceive.* **engañoso** adj. *deceitful.* **engañado** adj. *deceived, tricked.* **engañador** adj. *deceiving.* **engañador** n. *deceiver.*

• Hacer creer a otra persona algo que no es. Falta de verdad, falsedad. – Sin. embaucamiento, *tricking.* embuste, *trick.*

enjuiciamiento¹ (procedimiento) n. *legal procedure.* – Sin. procedimiento, *procedure.*
enjuiciamiento civil *civil procedure.*
enjuiciamiento criminal *criminal procedure.*

enjuiciamiento² (sustanciación) n. *lawsuit, trial.* **enjuiciar** v. *to prosecute, sue.* **enjuiciado** n. *defendant, convicted.* **enjuiciado** adj. *on trial.* – Sin. encausamiento.
Rel: sustanciación, *proceeding.*

enriquecimiento ilegítimo OBLIGACIONES *unjust enrichment, enrichment without cause.*

• El que una persona obtiene a expensas del empobrecimiento de otra, sin haber razón jurídica para justificar el desequilibrio entre los patrimonios de ambas. – Sin. enriquecimiento injusto. enriquecimiento sin causa. enriquecimiento torticero (PR).

Comentario: Establece el principio de que nadie puede enriquecerse sin derecho en perjuicio o detrimento de otro.

enriquecimiento ilícito (delito) [ed]*illicit enrichment of a public official.*

• Existe cuando un servidor público no puede acreditar el legítimo aumento de su patrimonio o la legítima adquisición de bienes.

entablar una demanda *to file a lawsuit, to bring a suit.*

entrampamiento (delito)(PR) *entrapment.*

entrar subrepticiamente *surreptitious entry.*

entrega¹ (dar una cosa) n. *delivery.* **entregar** v. *to deliver.*

• La entrega de una cosa se da cuando se pone en posesión y dominio del que la recibe. – Sin. tradición.

entrega de cosa vendida *delivery of goods or property sold.*

entrega jurídica *constructive delivery.*

entrega real *actual delivery.* – Sin. entrega material.

entrega² (capitulación) *submission, capitulation.* **entregarse** v. *to surrender.* – Sin. sumisión, *submission.*

equidad n. *equity, fairness.* **equitativo** n. *fair, just.*

• Atributo de la justicia, que cumple la función de corregir y enmendar el derecho escrito, restringiendo unas veces la generalidad de la ley y otras extendiéndola para suplir sus deficiencias, con el objeto de atenuar el excesivo rigor de la misma. – Sin. epiqueya. justicia, *justice.* En la práctica su aplicación se define como el ámbito de discrecionalidad que tiene el juez para aplicar la justicia al caso concreto o particular, atemperando el rigorismo de la ley.

☞ Equidad y *equity* son términos equivalentes cuando se les usa en su significado amplio de justicia o de aplicación equitativa de un principio o una regla. En la mayoría de los casos, sin embargo, equidad se refiere al principio que puede usar el juez para interpretar la norma en su aplicación a un caso concreto, basándose en su entendimiento de lo que la justicia es en ese caso en particular. *Equity* por su lado, se refiere a un cuerpo de principios y de reglas que se consideran separados del *common law*, pero que son igualmente parte del derecho cuya finalidad es el complementar y mejorar su aplicación.

erogación n. *expenditure.* **erogar** v. *to spend.*

error n. *error, mistake.*

• Apreciación equivocada de la realidad que vicia la voluntad y constituye una causal de nulidad de los contratos. – Sin. equívoco. yerro.
error apelable *harmful error, prejudicial error.*

error de derecho *error of law, mistake of law.*

error de hecho *error of fact, mistake of fact.*

error en el golpe *mistake in the attempt.* – Sin. aberratio ictus (lat.).

error en el nombre *misnomer.* – Sin. error nominis (lat.).

error en el objeto [lat.]*error in corpore.*

error en la persona *mistake of person,* [lat.]*error de persona.*

error enmendable *harmless error, technical error.* – Sin. error indiferente. error subsanable.
Rel: vicios del consentimiento, *defects in the formation of contractual consent.*
Ref: (Ch)CC a.1451-1455; (Ec)CC a.1495-1498; (Esp)CC a.1266; (Mx)CC. a.1813-14; (Ur)CC a. 1271; (Ve)CC a.1146-1149.
Ver: *mistake.*

escalafón (der.trabajo) *seniority list.*

escalamiento (entrada) n. *breaking and entering, burglary* (PR).

escándalo público *scandalous action or event.*
• "Conmoción en sentido moral suscitada en el público por un hecho concreto." (Dicc. ed. Comares, 216)

escape n. *escape.* **escapar** v. *to escape.*
escapatoria n. *escape.* – Sin. evasión, *flight, escape.* fuga, *flight, escape.* huída.

escisión de procesos *separation of trials.*

escisión de sociedades *spin-off.*

esclavitud n. *slavery.* **esclavizar** v. *to enslave.*
esclavo n. *slave.* **esclavo** adj. *enslaved.*
Rel: abolición, *abolition;* emancipación, *emancipation;* sumisión, *submission.*

escondite n. *hideout.* **esconder** v. *to hide.*
– Sin. escondrijo, *hiding place.* guarida, *hideout, den.*

escrito n. *written statement, brief.*
escrito de agravios *brief on appeal.*
escrito de contestación de la demanda
answer. – Sin. contestación.
escrito de la demanda *complaint.* – Sin. demanda.
ponerse por escrito *to reduce to writing.*
– Sin. constar por escrito.
Rel: acta, *act;* documento, *document;* manuscrito, *manuscript;* texto, *text.*

escritura n. *legal instrument.* **escriturar** v. *to notarize or witness.*
• Es todo escrito hecho con el objeto de que se deje constancia de un acto o negocio jurídico y se llenen las formalidades que la ley requiera según el tipo de acto o negocio de que se trate. – Sin. instrumento, *instrument.*
escritura constitutiva *corporate charter.*
escritura de propiedad *title deed.*
escritura privada *private document.*
escritura pública *notarial instrument.*
– Sin. escritura notarial.
Rel: documento, *document.*

espacio aéreo *air space.*
Rel: espacio exterior o ultraterrestre, *outer space.*

especulación[1] **(comercio)** n. *speculation, venture.*
especular v. *to speculate.* **especulativo** adj. *speculative.*
• "Operación comercial que se practica con mercancías, valores o efectos públicos, con ánimo de obtener lucro." (I Dicc. REA, 893)

especulación[2] **(agio)** n. *profiteering.* **especular** v. *to profit.* **especulador** n. *profiteer.*
• Realización de operaciones primordialmente financieras asumiendo un riesgo mayor y con la expectativa de una ganancia o pérdida desproporcionada.

Cf: **especulación** ● **agio** ● **acaparamiento.**
Especulación y agio son términos sinónimos que se usan indistintamente, la preferencia en su uso conserva su distinción de origen: especulación es más general y se refiere a la actividad y beneficio proveniente de operaciones comerciales mientras que agio es más restringido a aquélla actividad y beneficio resultante de operaciones relacionadas con el dinero. El beneficio obtenido en la especulación y el agio tiene generalmente una connotación de ilicitud o ilegalidad. El acaparamiento, por su lado, es la sustracción de bienes del mercado por una persona con la intención de provocar su escasez y el alza de su precio. El beneficio obtenido es en contravención a una ley prohibitiva.

espionaje n. *espionage.* **espiar** v. *to spy.* **espía** n. *spy.*
Rel: seguridad nacional, *national security;* servicios de inteligencia, *intelligence services.*

esponsales n. *engagement to marry, betrothal agreement.*
• La promesa hecha formalmente de contraer matrimonio.

esposos n. *husband and wife, married couple.*
esposo n. *husband.* **esposa** n. *wife.*
– Sin. consorte, *consort.* cónyuge. *spouse.* pareja, *couple.*

esquirol (huelga) n. *strike-breaker.*

esquizofrenia n. *schizophrenia.* **esquizofrénico** adj. *schizophrenic.*

establecimiento mercantil *business address, business location.*
• Lugar o local en el que se instala la empresa mercantil realizando las actividades propias de su giro. – Sin. [rtrgido]comercio. giro comercial.

estado[1] **(condición financiera)** *state.*
estado de aplicación de fondos *statement of funds received and applied.*
estado de cuentas *statement of account.*
estado de ingresos y gastos *income statement.*
estado de pérdidas y ganancias *profit and loss statement.*
estado en pro-forma *pro-forma statement.*

estado[2] **(entidad)** *state.* **estatal** adj. *pertaining to the state.*
• La entidad político-jurídica constituída por una población asentada en un territorio concretamente delimitado y un poder soberano con reconocida autoridad.
estado benefactor *welfare state.* – Sin. estado

de bienestar.

estado constitucional *constitutional state.*

estado democrático *democratic state.*

estado federal *federal state.*

estado gendarme *police state.*

estado libre asociado (PR) *Commonwealth of Puerto Rico.*

estado civil *marital status, legal status.*

• Estado de una persona que se refiere a la posición que ésta guarda en relación con la familia.

Rel: casado, *married;* divorciado, *divorced;* separado, *separated;* soltero, *single;* viudo, *widow.*

estado de emergencia *disaster proclamation, emergency conditions.* – Sin. estado de excepción.

estado de derecho *government of laws.*

estado de guerra *state of war.*

estado de indivisión *state of indivision.*

estado de necesidad DER.PENAL *necessity or necessity defense.*

• El salvar bienes o personas de un peligro grave e inminente lesionando un derecho existente, o la persona o bienes de otro, cuando no hay otro medio practicable de hacerlo.

estado de sitio *state of siege,* [ed]*proclamation of the existence of grave threat to public order.*

estado mental *mental state, state of mind.*

estafa¹ (delito) *false pretenses,* [rtrgido]*deceptive practices.* **estafar** v. *to swindle, defraud.* **estafador** n. *swindler, defrauder.*

• Comete estafa el que induciendo o manteniendo a otro en el error por medio de artificios, engaños o falsedades obtiene provecho ilícito, para sí o para otro, con perjuicio ajeno. Cf: **estafa – defraudación.** La estafa y la defraudación pertenecen al grupo de delitos que se realizan mediante fraude. La defraudación es generalmente considerado un delito genérico, esto es, una denominación que incluye diferentes conductas delictuosas en las que se da el fraude, mientras que la estafa es en la mayoría de los casos considerado un delito específico, esto es, un delito definido mediante una conducta única (el inducir o mantener en el error mediante maquinación o engaño). Esta situación ha permitido que ambos conceptos se usen sinónima e indistintamente en ocasiones.

estafa de fluido *theft of power supply or electricity, theft of utility service.*

– Sin. defraudación de fluido eléctrico. defraudación de energía eléctrica.

estafa por ardid o engaño *false pretenses.*

Rel: artificio, *artifice, ruse;* engaño, *deceit;* error, *error.*

Ver: fraude. *false pretenses.*

Ref: (Ar)CC a.172; (Bo)CP a.335; (Co)CP a.246; (Ec)CP a.560; (Esp)CP a.248; (Gu)CP a.263; (Pe)CP a.196; (RD)CP a.405; (Ur)CP a.347; (Ve)CP a.464.

estafa² n. *swindle, deceit.*

estatuto¹ (ley) n. [genrico]*statute, regulations.*

• En sentido general, toda ley, reglamento u ordenanza, pero más frecuentemente se le asigna el significado de reglas de aplicación reducida, por ejemplo las dadas para una región (como sucede en España), o las aplicables a una organización o cuerpo.

↦ Estatuto y *statute* raramente coinciden en su significado. Mientras estatuto es un término que se refiere principalmente a normas de aplicación reducida y raramente expresa la idea de una norma de aplicación general o una ley, *statute* se refiere a la ley escrita, promulgada por una asamblea legislativa y aplicable a amplios sectores de la población o del estado de que se trate. Normalmente estatuto es equivalente de *regulations* u *ordinances* y excepcionalmente de *statute.*

Ver: *statute.*

estatuto² (regla) n. *rule, bylaws.*

• "En lo civil, laboral y mercantil, los pactos, convenciones, ordenanzas o estipulaciones establecidos por los fundadores o por los miembros o socios de una entidad, para el gobierno de una asociación, sociedad, corporación, sindicato o club." (III Cabanellas, 583-84)

estatutos de un sindicato *union bylaws.*

estatutos de una asociación *bylaws of the association.*

estatutos de una sociedad *corporate bylaws.*

estatutos (conflicto de leyes) [ed]*laws and rules under consideration —applicable to either persons or property— to resolve conflict of laws, rules to resolve a case involving choice of law.*

• Cuando dos entidades jurídicas nacionales diferentes compiten para regir una controversia o una cuestión dada, las reglas a las que se recurre para encontrar la solución, según se trate de actos jurídicos, personas o cosas, se denominan estatutos.

Se entiende por estatuto el conjunto de leyes o reglas que constituyen un régimen jurídico al que está sometida una materia jurídica determinada; por ejemplo, al régimen jurídico al que están sometidas las personas se le denomina estatuto personal, al que se aplica a las cosas se le llama estatuto real.

estatuto formal *law of procedure,* [ed]*laws and rules applicable to the conduct of legal proceedings,* [ed]*the machinery for carrying on the suit.*

estatuto personal *law of persons,* [ed]*laws and rules applicable to persons.*

estatuto real *law of property,* [ed]*laws and rules applicable to property.*

estatutos sociales SOCIEDADES *by-laws.*

estímulos fiscales *tax incentives.*

estipulación[1] (disposición) n. *stipulation, clause.*
• Cada una de las disposiciones de un documento público o particular. – Sin. cláusula, *clause.* disposición, *provision.* precepto, *rule.*

estipulación[2] (acuerdo) n. *agreement.* **estipular** *to agree, stipulate.* – Sin. acuerdo, *agreement.* pacto, *pact.*

estipulación en favor de tercero *independent promise made in favor of third party beneficiary.*

estorbo (PR) *nuisance.*

estorbo legal *legal nuisance.*

estorbo público *public nuisance.*

estragos (delito) n. *major destruction or damage.*
• Destrucción mayor y catastrófica por medios explosivos o similares, como la destrucción de aeropuertos, puertos, edificios, medios de transporte, etc. – Sin. destrozos, *damage, destruction.* devastación, *devastation.*

estupefacientes n. *narcotics and similar substances.*
Rel: dosis de uso personal, *drug amount for personal consumption;* narcótico, *narcotics;* soporífero, *soporific.*
Ver: tráfico de drogas.

estupro (delito) n. *statutory rape.*
• El estupro se produce cuando hay cópula con una mujer honesta mediante la seducción o engaño y cuya edad o condiciones físicas o intelectuales no le permiten discernir la trascendencia de su aceptación. – Sin. acceso carnal abusivo (Co).
Rel: violación, *rape.*
Ref: (Ar)CP a.120; (Bo)CP a.309; (Ch)CP a.363; (Co)CP a.208; (Ec)CP a.509; (ES)CP 143-164; (Esp)CP a.163; (Gu)CP a.176; (Mx)CP a.262; (Pa)CP a.219; (Ur)CP a. 275.

etnocentrismo n. *ethnocentrism.* **etnocéntrico** adj. *ethnocentric.*
• El considerar la cultura propia el criterio exclusivo para juzgar otras culturas o grupos sociales.

eutanasia n. *euthanasia.*

evaluación n. *evaluation.* – Sin. apreciación.

evaluación de la prueba *weighing of the evidence.*

evasión[1] (evitar) n. *evasion.* **evadir** v. *to evade, avoid.* **evasor** adj. *evading.*

evasión[2] (huír) n. *escape.* **evadir** v. *to escape.* – Sin. escape. fuga.

evadirse de la justicia *abscond.*

evasión de presos (crime) *escape of prisoners, escape of inmates.* – Sin. quebrantamiento de condena (Esp).

evasión fiscal *tax evasion, tax fraud.*
• Incumplimiento de las obligaciones fiscales que le corresponden a los causantes, especialmente la falta o reducción de pago de un tributo. – Sin. elusión fiscal. fraude o defraudación fiscal, *tax fraud.*
Cf: **fraude fiscal • evasión fiscal • alusión fiscal.** Fraude y evasión fiscal se usan sinónimamente y no han sido diferenciadas claramente por la doctrina. Algunos autores consideran al fraude el género y a la evasión la especie, mientras otros toman la posición opuesta. En cualquier forma, la evasión fiscal y la defraudación fiscal, como también se le conoce al fraude, parecen estar íntimamente relacionadas, ya que mientras la evasión pone de relieve la eliminación o reducción de una obligación fiscal mediante el uso de conductas fraudulentas u omisiones violatorias de disposiciones fiscales legales, el fraude o defraudación fiscal se refiere primordialmente a la existencia de engaño o falsedad en la reducción fraudulenta de la carga fiscal. La alusión fiscal, por su parte, se refiere a la eliminación o reducción de impuestos sin infringir el texto de la ley, pero usando estructuras jurídicas atípicas o anómalas.
Rel: alusión fiscal, *tax avoidance;* fraude fiscal, [ed]*tax fraud, tax evasion.*

evicción n. *dispossession of purchased property.*
• "La evicción consiste en la privación judicial de la propiedad de la cosa entregada al comprador y en virtud del mejor derecho que se reconoce a un tercero sobre la misma cosa." (Ribó Durán, 564)

prestar la evicción to make the guarantee of quiet enjoyment effective, to quiet title.
saneamiento para el caso de evicción covenant of warranty and quiet enjoyment, warranty against dispossession or conversion. Rel: saneamiento, warranty against risk of harm.

evidencia n. evidence. **evidenciar** v. to make evident. **evidente** adj. evident. **evidentemente** adv. evidently. Ver: prueba. evidence.

ex post facto (lat.) ex post facto, after the fact, retroactively.

ex-presidiario n. ex-convict.

ex tempore (lat.) ex tempore, late in time.

examen n. examination. **examinar** v. to examine. **examinador** n. examiner. **examinado** n. examinee. – Sin. escrutinio, scrutiny. inspección, inspection.
examen de los libros books inspection.
examen de testigos examination of witnesses. – Sin. examen oral de testigos. desahogo de la (prueba) testimonial.

excepción DER.PROC n. defense, plea, [lat.]exceptio. **excepcionarse** v. to deny, demur, defend.
• Medio legal de defensa que expone la razón jurídica que el demandado alega para hacer ineficaz la pretensión del demandante. – Sin. defensa.
Cf: **excepción • defensa.** Ambos términos se usan generalmente en forma sinónima e indistinta, sin embargo la doctrina ha tratado de diferenciarlos sin que haya unanimidad al respecto. Según aquellos que encuentran una distinción, la excepción se dirige a poner un obstáculo temporal o permanente a la actividad del órgano jurisdiccional, mientras que la defensa es una oposición, no a la actividad del órgano jurisdiccional, sino al reconocimiento del derecho material pretendido en la demanda.
excepción de cosa juzgada defense of res judicata.
excepción de derecho demurrer, motion to dismiss based on law.
excepción de falta de personalidad defense of lack of authority to represent the opposing party.
excepción de incompetencia jurisdictional plea.
excepción de litispendencia [ext.lexico.]lis pendens defense, [ed]defense based on claim being already litigated in another court.

excepción dilatoria dilatory plea.
excepción para efectos de apelación objection.
excepción perentoria peremptory plea, plea in bar.
oponer excepciones to assert a defense, to plead a defense.
Ver: objection.

excluyentes de responsabilidad excuse.
– Sin. circunstancias eximentes de responsabilidad. eximentes.
Cf: **excluyentes de responsabilidad • justificantes.** Las excluyentes de responsabilidad son el género y las justificantes o causas justificantes son una de las especies. Cualquier causa que impida la configuración de un delito al afectar a cualquiera de sus elementos se le considera una excluyente de responsabilidad. Dentro de las excluyentes de responsabilidad se distinguen: las causas de justificación (la legítima defensa, estado de necesidad, cumplimiento de un deber, obediencia jerárquica, impedimento legítimo); las causas de inimputabilidad (la locura, la minoría de edad); las de inculpabilidad (obediencia debida o caso fortuito); y las de inpunibilidad (parentesco próximo en el encubrimiento o en el hurto). Rel: causas de inculpabilidad, [ed]grounds of lack of culpability; causas de inimputabilidad, [el]grounds of lack of imputability, [ed]grounds of lack of capacity to be charged; causas de inpunibilidad, [ed]grounds of lack of punishability.

excusa n. excuse. **excusarse** v. to excuse oneself.
• Manifestación de un impedimento por parte del juez, los defensores o la fiscalía para continuar su función en el proceso. – Sin. disculpa.

excusa absolutoria [ed]excuse resulting in absolution of the accused.
• Se refieren a las circunstancias que determinan la inpunibilidad o posibilidad de dejar sin punición o castigo una conducta delictuosa. – Sin. exculpación, exculpation.
La razón aducida para dejar sin castigo a un delincuente es generalmente la protección dada a ciertos valores sociales, considerados de mayor jerarquía que la aplicación de la pena al caso concreto de que se trate. Por ejemplo el no castigar el hurto recíproco entre cónyuges, o la asonada con respecto de conspiradores por motivos de seguridad nacional.

excusión de bienes application of all debtor's assets to payment.

exención n. *exemption.* **exencionar** v. *to exempt.*
exentar v. *to exempt.* **exento** adj. *exempt.*
– Sin. dispensa, *dispensation.*
exención fiscal *tax exemption.*
exento de derechos *duty free.*
exento de impuestos *tax exempt.*
exequátur[1] **(diplomacia)** n. *exequatur.*
• Reconocimiento de un cónsul extranjero por parte de un gobierno después de haber recibido las correspondientes cartas patentes (lettres de provision).
exequátur[2] **(ejecución de sentencias)** n. [ef]*request for execution of foreign judgments.*
• Procedimiento judicial por el que un estado admite la fuerza obligatoria de fallos o laudos arbitrales pronunciados en un país extranjero.
exhibición de pruebas *presentation of evidence, production of evidence.*
exhibición de documentos *production of documents.*
exhibicionismo (delito)(Esp) n. *public indecency.*
exhorto n. *letter of request, requisitory letter.*
juez o tribunal exhortante *requesting judge or court.* **juez o tribunal exhortado** *court or judge requested.*
• "Comunicación escrita que un juez dirige a otro de igual o superior jerarquía, o a un juez extranjero, requiriéndole la colaboración necesaria para el cumplimiento de una diligencia del proceso que debe realizarse fuera del lugar del juicio." (Couture, 275)
– Sin. carta rogatoria, *rogatory letter.*
diligenciación de exhorto *delivery of letter of request.*
girar un exhorto *issuance of letter of request.*
Rel: exequátur, *exequatur;* legalización de firmas, *authentication or attestation of signatures.*
Ver: comunicación procesal.
exhumación n. *exhumation.* **exhumar** v. *to exhume.*
• Desenterramiento de un cadáver. – Sin. desenterrar, *disinterment.*
exigibilidad n. *enforceability.*
exilio n. *exile.* **exiliar** v. *to exile.* **exiliado** adj. *exiled.* **exiliado** n. *exile.* – Sin. destierro, *banishment.*
eximente adj. *exculpatory, excusing.*
– Sin. circunstancias eximentes de responsabilidad, *exculpatory circumstances.* exculpación.
Ver: excluyentes de responsabilidad.
exoneración n. *exoneration.* **exonerar** v. *to*
exonerate. **exonerado** n. *exonerated.*
exonerativo adj. *exonerative.*
• Liberación de una carga, deber o acusación.
– Sin. descargo, *acquittal.*
expatriación n. *expatriation.* **expatriar** v. *to expatriate.* **expatriado** n. *expatriate.*
expediente n. [fr.]*dossier, file.*
• Constancia escrita de las actuaciones o diligencias practicadas en un negocio administrativo. Por extensión también los escritos y documentos pertenecientes a un juicio, caso en el que se le denomina más propiamente expediente judicial. – Sin. [fr.]dossier.
expediente administrativo *file, administrative file, business file.*
expediente en apelación *the record on appeal.*
expediente judicial *court file.* – Sin. autos.
toca del expediente *docket.*
Rel: foja, *page;* por pieza o cuerda separada, *separate file within same docket.*
explosivos n. *explosives.* – Sin. detonante, *detonator.*
explosivos plásticos *plastic explosives.*
Rel: dinamita, *dynamite;* nitroglicerina, *nitroglycerine;* pólvora, *gunpowder.*
exportación n. *export.* **exportar** v. *to export.*
exportador n. *exporter.*
licencia de exportación *export license.*
Rel: importación, *import.*
exposición (judicatura) [ed]*court's written communication (to high government authorities regarding important and broad issues).*
exposición de motivos (de una ley) *preamble, preliminary recitals (of a statute).*
expresión de agravios *brief of appeal.*
expropiación n. *condemnation, expropriation* (UK). **expropiar** v. *to condemn.* **expropiado** n. *party whose property was condemned.*
• La expropiación es la adquisición de la propiedad de un particular por parte del gobierno, mediante el pago de una indemnización, por motivos de utilidad pública.
Cf: **expropiación • confiscación • requisa.** Se trata de tres figuras distintas: la expropiación se efectúa por utilidad pública y mediante indemnización; la confiscación de bienes generalmente se aplica como sanción y no requiere de indemnización al afectado; la requisa o requisición es una incautación que se aplica a bienes muebles solamente, y bajo una situación

general en la que el interés público requiere de una acción urgente o inmediata.
Rel: confiscación, *confiscation;* incautación, *seizure;* requisa, *requisition;* reversión, *reversion.*
Ver: *eminent domain.*
expulsión n. *expulsion.* **expulsar** v. *to expel.* – Sin. echamiento. remoción, *removal.*
expulsión de extranjeros *expulsion of aliens.*
extensión del plazo *extension of deadline, extension of the term.*
extensión de la duración de la calidad migratoria *extension of immigrant status.*
extinción de una obligación *termination of an obligation.* – Sin. terminación de una obligación.
extinción de la acción penal *termination of right to bring a criminal action.*
extorsión (crime) n. [rtrgido]*extortion.* **extorsionar** v. *to extort, blackmail.* **extorsionador** n. *extortioner.* **extorsionista** n. *extortionist.*
• Comete extorsión aquél que obligare a otro, con violencia o intimidación, a hacer u omitir alguna cosa con el propósito de obtener provecho ilícito, para sí o para un tercero.
Rel: chantaje, *blackmail;* soborno, *bribery.*
extradición n. *extradition.* **extraditar** v. *extradite.* **extraditado** n. *extradited.* **extraditable** adj. *extraditable.*
• "Es el acto mediante el cual un Estado hace entrega de una persona refugiada en su territorio a otro Estado que la reclama, por estar inculpada, procesada o convicta en éste de la comisión de un delito del orden común, a fin de que sea sometida a juicio o recluida para cumplir con la pena impuesta." (Dicc. UNAM, 1395)
extradición internacional *international extradition.*
petición de extradición *request for extradition.*
tratado de extradición *extradition treaty.*
extrajudicial adj. *out of court.*
extranjería[1] (status) n. *status of being a foreigner.*
extranjería[2] (regulation) n. *body of law dealing with foreigners || foreign nationals.*
extranjero n. *alien, foreigner.* **extranjero** adj. *foreign.*
extranjero en tránsito *alien in transit.*
extranjero ilegal *illegal alien.*

extranjero indocumentado *undocumented alien.*
extranjero no residente *nonresident alien.*
extranjero residente *resident alien.*
Rel: inmigración, *immigration;* deportación, *deportation;* nacionalidad, *citizenship.*
extraterritorialidad n. *extraterritoriality.*

FFFF

fabricación de moneda falsa *manufacturing of counterfeit money.*
fabricación de sustancias tóxicas *manufacturing of toxic substances.*
factor n. *agent, commercial agent.*
factoring *factoring.*
factura n. *invoice, bill.* **facturar** v. *to invoice.* **facturista** n. *invoice clerk.* **facturación** n. *invoicing.*
• Documento que contiene la relación detallada de una transacción comercial, en especial la compraventa de mercancías. – Sin. nota. cuenta, *account, bill.*
factura comercial *commercial invoice.*
factura consular *consular invoice.*
factura de venta *bill of sale.*
factura pro forma *pro forma invoice.*
facultad n. *power, authority.* **facultar** v. *to grant power.* **facultado** adj. *having power.* **facultativo** adj. *pertaining to a power or authority.*
• "Facultad jurídica es la aptitud o potestad de una persona para modificar la situación jurídica existente de uno mismo o de otros." (Dicc. UNAM, 1406) – Sin. autoridad, *authority.* poder, *power.*
facultad discrecional *incidental powers, discretion.*
facultad para testar *testamentary capacity.*
facultades delegadas *delegated authority.*
facultar plenamente *to grant full powers.*
Rel: derecho, *right;* inmunidad, *immunity;* privilegio, *privilege.*
Comentario: Facultad es la aptitud o potestad para crear actos jurídicos válidos que el derecho concede a una persona por encontrarse dentro de una situación jurídica dada. El concepto de facultad jurídica presupone la posesión de una potestad o capacidad jurídica para modificar válidamente la situación jurídica. Lo opuesto a la facultad es la incapacidad o ausencia de potestad y es correlativa con la responsabilidad.

fallecimiento n. *death.* **fallecer** v. *to die.*
fallecido n. *deceased.* **falleciente** adj. *dying.*

– Sin. muerte. perecimiento. fenecimiento. defunción, *decease.*

fallo[1] **(decisión)** n. *ruling, decision* || *judgment, finding.* **fallar** v. *to judge, pass judgment, hand down a ruling.*
• Decisión que decide una controversia pronunciada por un juez, magistrado o árbitro.
– Sin. sentencia, *judgment.* laudo, *award.* decisión, *decision.*
Cf: **determinación judicial • decisión judicial • fallo.** Términos usados en forma sinónima e intercambiable. Decisión judicial es el término más amplio, refiriéndose a cualquier resolución judicial, normalmente incluyendo a la determinación y al fallo. Determinación judicial es más restringida y normalmente se aplica solamente a la decisión que emite un juez sobre cuestiones de hecho o de derecho. Fallo o sentencia, a su vez, es una determinación que decide un litigio judicial.
↳ Cuando fallo es usado como sinónimo de decisión, se le entiende usado genéricamente y fallo entonces se refiere a los equivalentes en inglés *decision, ruling* u *opinion.* Por lo contrario, cuando su uso es específico, su equivalencia es la de los términos ingleses *judgment, finding or verdict.*
emitir un fallo *to render a judgment, to hand down a judgment.*
fallo arbitral *arbitration award.*
fallo definitivo *final judgment.*
fallo del jurado *jury verdict.*
fallo judicial *judicial decision or ruling.*
Ver: sentencia.

fallo[2] **(conclusión)** n. *holding (of a sentence).*
• Parte dispositiva de la sentencia. "Parte de la [sentencia] que contiene el mandato, el pronunciamiento jurídico sobre la cuestión debatida." (Dicc. ed. Comares, 237) – Sin. puntos resolutorios.
Rel: considerandos, *points of law, applicable law (of a sentence);* resultandos, *the facts (of a sentence).*

falsedad n. *falsehood, falsity.* **falso** adj. *false.*
– Sin. mentira, *lie.* impostura, *imposture.*
declararse con falsedad *to make false statements.*
falso testimonio *false testimony, perjury.*

falsificación n. *falsification.* **falsificar** v. *to falsify.* **falsificador** n. *forger, counterfeiter.*
falsificación de documentos *falsification of documents.*
falsificación de moneda *forgery or counterfeiting of money.*

Rel: adulteración, *forgery.*
falta[1] **(violación)** n. *infraction, offense.*
• Las acciones u omisiones voluntarias castigadas por la ley con pena leve.
– Sin. contravención, *breach.* infracción, *infraction.* transgresión, *transgression.* violación, *violation.*
Cf: **falta • delito • infracción.** Términos normalmente distinguibles que se usan indistintamente con frecuencia. Falta es un concepto general que se refiere a una violación normalmente menor, en tanto que delito se aplica a ilícitos de mayor importancia, y exclusivamente a ilícitos penales. Infracción es una violación menor, generalmente de disposiciones administrativas. Falta en Derecho mexicano se emplea como sinónimo de contravención o infracción. En derecho español, chileno y uruguayo su acepción principal es la de un delito menor.
falta disciplinaria *disciplinary infraction.*
faltas militares *military violations, military infractions.*
Ver: delito.

falta[2] **(omisión)** n. *lack.* **faltar** v. *to be lacking.*
faltante n. *lack.* **faltante** adj. *lacking.*
falta de capacidad *lack of capacity.*
falta de cumplimiento *noncompliance, nonperformance, nonfeasance.*
falta de méritos para consignar [ef]*finding of no probable cause.*
falta de pago *default of payment.*
falta de personalidad *lack of legal authority.*
– Sin. falta de personería.
falta de pruebas *lack of evidence.*

falta[3] **(culpa)** n. *fault.*

familia n. *family.* **familiar** n. *relative.* **familiar** adj. *familiar.* – Sin. parentela, *relations.*
cabeza de familia *head of the family.*
familia adoptiva *adoptive family.*
familia política *relatives-in-law.*
lazos familiares *family ties.*
Rel: familiares, *relatives;* filiación, *filiation;* parentesco, *kinship;* progenie, *progeny;* prole, *progeny.*

familia romano-germánica (tradición jurídica) *Romano-Germanic family.*
La familia romano-germánica se identifica por ser la tradición legal heredada del derecho romano, las costumbres germanas y locales continentales europeas, y más modernamente, por la importancia dada a la codificación y la ciencia legal. En la actualidad la familia romano-germánica se ha extendido a la mayor parte de

Europa, casi la totalidad de Latinoamérica, Japón y partes de Asia y África.

familiares n. *relatives, family members.*
• Grupo de personas unidas por parentesco o por matrimonio. – Sin. parientes, *relatives, relations.*
Rel: allegados, *relations;* familia, *family;* parentesco, *kinship.*
Glosario: abuela, *grandmother;* abuelo, *grandfather;* abuelos, *grandparents;* bizabuela, *great-grandmother;* bizabuelo, *great-grand father;* bizabuelos, *great-grandparents;* biznieta, *great-granddaughter;* biznieto, *great-grandson;* biznietos, *great-grandchildren;* cuñada, *sister-in-law;* cuñado, *brother-in-law;* godchild, *ahijado;* godfather, *padrino;* godmother, *madrina;* hermana, *sister;* hermano, *brother;* hija, *daughter;* hijastra, *stepdaughter;* hijastro, *stepson;* hijo, *son;* madrastra, *stepmother;* madre, *mother;* nieta, *granddaughter;* nieto, *grandson;* nietos, *grandchildren;* nuera, *daughter-in-law;* padrastro, *stepfather;* padre, *father;* padres, *parents;* primo, *cousin;* sobrina, *niece;* sobrina nieta *grandniece;* sobrino, *nephew;* sobrino nieto *grandnephew;* suegra, *mother-in-law;* suegro, *father-in-law;* tía, *aunt;* tío, *uncle;* yerno, *son-in-law.*

fe de bautismo *certificate of baptism.*

fe de conocimiento *attestation of the identity of the parties.*
Rel: dar fe, *to certify, to attest.*

fe notarial *notarial authority.*

fe pública *legal authority (to authenticate and certify documents).*
Rel: hacer fe, *to be deemed authentic.*

fecha n. *date.* **fechar** v. *to date.*
fecha cierta *specific date.*
fecha de alta *discharge date, starting date.*
fecha de cierre CONTRATOS *date of execution.*
fecha de comparecencia *court date.*
fecha de entrada en vigor *effective date, date of enforceability.*
fecha de entrega *delivery date.*
fecha de expiración *expiration date.*
fecha de fallecimiento *date of death.*
fecha de inscripción *date of record.*
fecha de nacimiento *date of birth.*
fecha de presentación *filing date.*
fecha de vencimiento *due date, date of maturity.*
fecha límite *deadline.*
señalar fecha y lugar *to set date and place.*
Ver: tiempo.

fechoría *misdeed, malfeasance.*

fedatario n. [ed]*person authorized to authenticate documents,* [ed]*person having legal authority to authenticate documents.*

federación n. *federation.*
Rel: asociación, *association;* coalición, *coalition;* confederación, *confederation;* liga, *league.*
Ver: *federalism.*

federal adj. *federal.* **federalizar** v. *to federalize.*
federar v. *to federate.* **federalismo** n. *federalism.* **federal** n. *federal.*

fehaciente *attesting, certifying.*
fehacientemente adv. *attesting, that attests.*
• Que hace fe en juicio.

felonía n. *treachery.*

fianza n. *bond, surety, bail.* **fiar** v. *to guaranty, to bail.* **fiador** n. *guarantor, bondsman, bailsman.* **fiado** n. *person under bond or bail.*
• Obligación que acepta una persona a pagar o cumplir por otra si ésta incumple. También se entiende por fianza el contrato por el cual el fiador queda obligado. – Sin. caución, *surety, bond.*
fianza aduanal *customs bond.*
fianza civil *bond posted on civil law transactions.*
fianza de apelación *appeal bond.*
fianza de averías *average bond.*
fianza de cumplimiento *performance bond.*
– Sin. fianza de contratista.
fianza de embargo *attachment bond.*
fianza de licitación *bid bond.*
fianza de postura *bid bond (in an auction).*
fianza excesiva *excessive bail.*
fianza judicial *judicial bond.*
fianza mercantil [ed]*performance bond of commercial transactions.*
fianza penal *bail bond.* – Sin. caución de buena conducta.
prestar una fianza *posting bond, posting a bond.*
Rel: garantía, *security, guarantee.*

ficha antropométrica *anthropometric or anthropometrical chart.*

fichar (policía) v. *to book.*
Rel: ficha policial, *police record;* antecedentes penales, *criminal background, criminal record.*

ficción jurídica *legal fiction, artificial legal entity or concept.*

fideicomiso n. [amplio]*trust.* **fideicomisario** n. *trustee.* **fideicomitente** n. *trustor, settlor.*

fiduciario n. *fiduciary* || [ed]*representative of*

debenture holders. **beneficiario** n. *cestui que trust, beneficiary.*

• Contrato mediante el cual una persona física o moral transfiere la propiedad sobre parte de sus bienes a otra persona o institución fiduciaria, para que con ellos se realice un fin especificado en el contrato por la persona que lo constituye.

☞ El fideicomiso, derivado del *trust* anglo sajón, ha sido aceptado en varios países hispano-americanos con adaptaciones que hacen difícil el uso de una terminología generalizada, y que requieren normalmente un análisis más a fondo de su naturaleza jurídica. En Colombia y Chile, por ejemplo, el término fideicomiso se usa para definir la constitución de un gravamen sobre un bien, consistente en transmitir dicho bien si se verifica una condición; sin embargo, la figura jurídica más próxima al trust en derecho colombiano se denomina fiducia mercantil y presenta restricciones importantes, sobre todo en cuanto a las facultades dadas al fiduciario. En España se le considera un mandato irrevocable por el que se transmiten determinados bienes a una persona para que disponga de ellos conforme lo ordene la persona que los transmite. En México el fideicomiso se usa principalmente en transacciones en que se otorga el uso o goce de una propiedad inmueble en las que el fideicomisario es una institución bancaria.

contrato de fideicomiso *trust agreement.*
departamento fiduciario *trust department.*
escritura del fideicomiso *trust deed.*
fideicomiso forzoso *trust required by law.*
fideicomiso irrevocable *irrevocable trust.*
fideicomiso privado *private trust.* – Sin. fideicomiso particular.
fideicomiso público *public trust.*
fideicomiso revocable *revocable trust.*
propiedad fiduciaria *trust property.*
Rel: contratos fiduciarios (Esp), *sales with right of redemption.*

Comentario: Las legislaciones latinoamericanas que mencionan el fideicomiso lo conciben como una adaptación del *trust* en la que los derechos del beneficiario se tutelan en forma minuciosa por la ley, lo que reduce la posibilidad de abuso por parte del fiduciario, pero también desvirtúa la naturaleza del *trust* en sentido estricto. La mayoría de la doctrina considera que tal vez el obstáculo más importante para la aceptación del *trust* en los sistemas de derecho romano-germánico es el diferente concepto de propiedad, que a diferencia de la posibilidad de escisión en diferentes derechos de la *property* del *common law*, se concibe en forma autónoma e indivisible.

Ref: (Ar)Ley 34.441; (Ch)CC a.733; (Ec)CC a.767; (ES)CCo a.1234ss.; (Mx)LGTOC a.381ss.; (Ve)LF a.1.

fijación de la litis DER.PROC.CIVIL *pleadings.*
– Sin. traba de la litis.

• Es la determinación de las cuestiones controvertidas en un litigio, mediante la exposición que las partes hacen de sus pretensiones y alegatos iniciales.

Ver: procedimiento civil.

filiación[1] **(procedencia)** n. *filiation.*

• Procedencia de los descendientes respecto de los ascendientes, por ejemplo los hijos respecto de los padres.

filiación legítima *legitimate filiation.*
filiación materna *maternal filiation.*
filiación natural *natural filiation.*
filiación paterna *paternal filiation.*
Rel: adopción, *adoption;* paternidad, *paternity.*

filiación[2] **(señas)** n. *personal description.*

finanzas n. *finances.* **financiar** v. *to finance.*
financiero n. *financier.* **financiero** adj. *finance, financial.* **financiamiento o financiación** n. *financing.*
finanzas públicas *public finances.*
recursos financieros *financial resources.*

finiquito n. *release.* **finiquitar** v. *to release, to pay off.*

• Acto o documento por el que se declara cumplida y terminada la gestión hecha por una persona respecto de un negocio jurídico ajeno.

firma[1] **(rúbrica)** n. *signature.* **firmar** v. *to sign.*
– Sin. rúbrica. signatura, *filing mark, signature.*
firma a ruego *signing on behalf of another.*
firma comercial *business signature.*
firma de puño y letra *handwritten signature.*
firma en blanco [ed]*signing leaving blank the rest of form or document.*
firma legítima *authentic signature.*
muestra de una firma *specimen signature.*
recabar una firma *to obtain a signature, to get someone to sign.*
Rel: antefirma, *title before a signature.*

firma[2] **(empresa)** *firm.*
firma comercial *commercial firm, commercial company.*

firme en apelación *affirm on appeal.*

fiscal n. *prosecutor, prosecuting attorney.*
fiscalía n. *government attorney's office, state's attorney office.* – Sin. Ministerio Público. acusador.
fiscal general *attorney general.*

fiscalía del estado *government's attorney, state's attorney* (EEUU), *prosecution.*

fiscal adj. *fiscal.*

asesoría fiscal *tax advise.*

auditoria fiscal *tax audit.*

código fiscal *tax code.*

crédito fiscal *tax payable, tax credit.*

deducción fiscal *tax deduction.*

delito fiscal *tax crime.*

ejercicio fiscal *tax year.*

elusión fiscal *tax avoidance.*

evasión fiscal *tax evasion.*

incentivo fiscal *tax incentive.*

juicio fiscal *tax suit, tax petition* || *tax trial.*

legislación fiscal *tax legislation.*

paraíso fiscal *tax heaven.*

pérdida fiscal *tax loss.*

recinto fiscal *bonded warehouse.*

responsabilidad fiscal *tax liability, tax responsibilities.*

tribunal fiscal *tax court.*

fisco n. *tax administration.*

• Se denomina fisco el Estado considerado como titular de la Hacienda pública. – Sin. Hacienda pública, *public treasury, public funds.* tesoro público, *public treasury.*

Rel: erario, *fiscal Exchequer, National Treasury.*

flagrante adj. *flagrant.* **flagrancia** n. *flagrancy.* – Sin. con las manos en la masa, *red-handed.*

flagrante delito *in the act of committing a crime,* [lat.]*in flagrante delicto.* – Sin. delito in flagranti.

fletamento n. *charter, freight charter.* **fletar** v. *to charter.* **fletador/naviero** n. *charterer, freighter.* **fletante/propietario** n. *ship owner who charters.*
– También: fletamiento.

• Contrato por el cual un naviero cede el uso, parcial o total, de un buque a un sujeto para el transporte marítimo de mercancías, en los términos pactados y mediante el pago de un precio denominado flete.

fletamento total o por entero *chartering entirely (as opposed to by compartment).*

fletamento por viaje redondo *voyage charter.*

fletamento por tiempo determinado *time charter.* – Sin. fletamiento a plazo.

Rel: tarifa de carga, *freight rate;* transportación, *transportation.*

flete¹ (carga) *cargo, shipment.*

flete² (tarifa) *freight.*

fobia n. [gre.]*phobia.*

• Un miedo persistente, desproporcionado e irracional a un objeto, un animal, una actividad o una situación en particular. – Sin. temor, *fear.*

fondo n. *fund.*

fondo común de inversión *mutual fund.* – Sin. fondo de inversión. fondo mutuo de inversión. fondo mutual de inversiones.

fondo de amortización *sinking fund.*

fondo de estabilización de cambios *exchange stabilization fund.*

fondo de garantía *guaranty fund.*

fondo de previsión *pension fund, contingency fund.*

fondo de rescate *redemption fund.*

fondo de reserva *reserve fund.*

fondo de retiro *retirement fund, pension fund.* – Sin. fondo de jubilación.

Fondo Monetario Internacional (FMI) *International Monetary Fund* (IMF).

fondos n. *funds.*

fondos congelados *blocked accounts, frozen funds.*

fondos públicos *public funds.*

forense adj. *forensic.*

médico forense *medical examiner.* – Sin. médico legista.

forma jurídica *form, legal formalities.*

formalizar v. *to observe legal formalities.*

formalidad n. *formal requirements.*

formalidades n. *legal formalities.*

• Requisitos de forma o solemnidad que deben observarse para la formación válida de los negocios o actos jurídicos.

formalizar un contrato en escritura pública *to formalize a contract as a notarized instrument.*

Rel: consensualidad, *without legal formalities;* solemnidad, *solemnity.*

formulario n. *boilerplate form.*

foro¹ (tribunales) n. *forum.*

• El lugar en donde los tribunales llevan a cabo su función de administrar justicia.

foro² (abogados) n. *trial attorneys (as a whole).*

• Denominación que se refiere a los abogados y a la práctica del derecho en los tribunales. – Sin. curia.

fortuito adj. *fortuitous.* – Sin. aleatorio, *aleatory.* accidental, *accidental.* imprevisto, *unforeseen.* Ver: fuerza mayor.

franquicia¹ (exención) n. *exemption from payment* || *franchise.*

• Exención fiscal concedida a cierto tipo de

operaciones, principalmente relacionadas con la importación de mercancías o la extracción de bienes.

franquicia aduanera *tariff tax exemption.*
franquicia arancelaria *customs tax exemption.*
franquicia de correos *exemption from postal charges* || *reduction of postal fees.*
franquicia[2] **(explotación comercial)** n. *business franchise.*

• Contrato por el que un comerciante se obliga a comercializar los productos que en exclusividad le otorga otro comerciante en una zona determinada y por un tiempo especificado, frecuentemente transmitiéndose además instrucciones sobre promoción, venta y administración.

Cf: **franquicia ● concesión.** Ambos términos se usan frecuentemente en forma sinónima e indistinta, sin embargo el término franquicia se identifica modernamente cada vez más con *franchising*, que implica una explotación en paquete de patentes, marcas y modelos comerciales. Concesión, por su parte, se puede referir a un acuerdo de distribución exclusiva, al derecho de explotación de un bien o servicio otorgado por el gobierno, o a la explotación de una patente o marca en exclusividad.

fratricidio n. *fratricide.* **fratricida** adj.n. *fratricide.*
Ver: *fratricide.*

fraude n. *fraud.* **fraudulento** adj. *fraudulent.*
fraudulentamente adv. *fraudulently.*
• "Calificación jurídica de la conducta, consistente en una maquinación o subterfugio insidioso tendiente a la obtención de un provecho ilícito." (Couture, 295)
Fraude es la calificación dada a una conducta y como tal se le puede concebir en forma amplia y general. Cuando se le concibe en forma más específica, fraude destaca en materia penal, civil y procesal. En materia penal se le considera un delito, pero su definición varia en los diferentes países hispanoparlantes: en España es el cometido por funcionarios públicos quienes usando su autoridad, y en concierto con otros, defraudan a la administración pública; en México fraude es la designación usada para definir el delito de defraudación. En materia civil el fraude se destaca como causal de nulidad de los actos y contratos aunque su designación como tal no se ha generalizado. Finalmente, en materia procesal el concepto de fraude aparece principalmente en la figura jurídica del fraude procesal.

Cf: **fraude ● engaño.** Engaño es la forma o medios de que uno se sirve, hablando u obrando insidiosamente en forma falsa o con artificio, para burlar la ley; fraude por su parte, se refiere a la calificación de engañosa dada a una conducta cuando produce un perjuicio. De esta manera el engaño puede considerarse como el medio o la manera de arribar al fraude, o dicho en otra forma, es uno de los elementos que constituyen al fraude.
en fraude de acreedores *acts made with the intent to defraud creditors.*
fraude electoral *electoral fraud.*
fraude fiscal *tax fraud.*
fraude procesal *abuse of process,* [ed]*fraud committed by use of legal procedure.*
Rel: ardid, *ruse;* declaración falsa, *misrepresentation;* dolo, [lat.]*dolus;* engaño, *deception;* estafa, *swindle, deceit;* hacer trampa, *to cheat;* impostor, *impostor;* maña, *guile, deceit;* truco, *trick.*
Ver: defraudación. *fraud.*
fraude a la ley *fraudulent evasion of applicable law.*
• "[S]on las maniobras destinadas a frustrar la finalidad de la ley. Consisten en utilizar una norma para amparar un resultado prohibido o contrario al ordenamiento jurídico." (Ribó Durán, 292) – Sin. actos en fraude a la ley. fraude de ley. fraudem legis (lat.).
frontera n. *border.* **fronterizo** adj. *border, frontier.* – Sin. límite, *limit.*
border control *control de las fronteras.*
zona fronteriza *border zone.*
porous borders *fronteras fácilmente penetrables.*
patrulla fronteriza *border patrol.*
frutos n. [prest.]*fruits, products,* [lat.][rtrgido] *fructus.*
• "Son los productos o utilidades que la cosa o bien genera conforme a su destino económico y sin alterarse su substancia." (Ribó Durán, 293) – Sin. productos. *yield, rent.* utilidades, *profit, earnings.*
frutos civiles *return from leases* || *financial investments and similar,* [prest.]*civil fruits.*
frutos industriales *industrial products.*
frutos naturales [prest.]*natural fruits, products of the land or of animals.*
función pública *public service.* – Sin. servicio público.
fuentes jurídicas *sources of the law.*
• Las fuentes del derecho son los diferentes

procesos a través de los cuales se elaboran las normas jurídicas. – Sin. fuentes del derecho.
Rel: costumbre, *custom;* jurisprudencia, *judicial precedents;* ley, *statute;* principios generales del derecho, *general principles of law.*

fuero[1] **(jurisdicción)** *jurisdiction, forum.* **foral** adj. *pertaining to forums or jurisdictions.*
• Jurisdicción específica a la que están sometidas las partes de conformidad con la ley. – Sin. jurisdicción, *jurisdiction.*
de fuero *de jure, in law.*
fuero civil *civil jurisdiction.*
fuero comercial *commercial jurisdiction.*
fuero común *general jurisdiction.*
fuero militar *military jurisdiction.*

fuero[2] **(privilegio)** *legal privilege.*
• Leyes y privilegios otorgados a personas, grupos, regiones o ciertas comunidades dentro de un orden jurídico. – Sin. privilegio, *privilege.*
fuero constitucional *constitutional immunity.*
fuero eclesiástico *privilege given to members of the church.*
fuero militar *military privilege.*
fuero parlamentario *parliamentary privilege.*
fuero sindical *privilege given to members of unions.*

fuerza n. *force.* **forzar** v. *to force.*
forzadamente adv. *forcibly.* **forzoso** adj. *obligatory.* – Sin. violencia, *violence.*
fuerza bruta *brute force, sheer force.*
fuerza en las cosas *force against objects or property.*
fuerza física irresistible *irresistible force.* – Sin. fuerza irresistible.
fuerza pública *public force.*
uso irracional de la fuerza *unreasonable force.*
uso o empleo de la fuerza *use of force.*
uso o empleo excesivo de la fuerza *excessive use of force.*
Rel: a las malas, *by all means;* por las malas, *by force.*
fuerza legal, *enforceable.*
carecer de fuerza legal *to be unenforceable.*
fuerza mayor *force majeure.*
• Es un acontecimiento insuperable, imprevisible o inevitable causado por la naturaleza o los hombres y que resulta en la creación de un daño o el incumplimiento de un deber o una obligación. – Sin. caso fortuito, *unforeseen circumstance.*
Cf: **fuerza mayor • caso fortuito • fuerza física irresistible.** Caso fortuito y fuerza mayor son

términos equivalentes, ambos se refieren a un acontecimiento inevitable causado por fuerzas naturales o por la intervención humana. Fuerza física irresistible, en cambio, es un acontecimiento inevitable causado enteramente por fuerzas naturales, sin incluir la interferencia de la actividad o acción humana.
Rel: fuerza física irresistible, *irresistible force.*

fuerzas armadas *armed forces.*
fuga n. *escape, flight.* **fugarse** v. *to flee, escape.*
fugitivo n. *fugitive.* – Sin. escapatoria. evasión, *evasion.* huida.
fuga de capitales *capital flight.*
fuga de cerebros *brain drain.*
fuga de prisioneros *prisoner's escape.*

fulana de tal *Jane Doe.* – Sin. mengana. zutana.
fulano de tal *John Doe.* – Sin. mengano. zutano.

funcionario[1] **(gobierno)** n. *official, civil servant.* – Sin. oficial, *official.*
funcionario corrupto *corrupt official.*
funcionario judicial *judicial official, officer of the court.*
funcionario público *public official.*

funcionario[2] **(compañía)** n. *officer of a company.*
fundación *foundation, nonprofit organization.*
• Organización constituida con personalidad jurídica y patrimonio propios afectos a una finalidad altruista o de interés público y regulada por la ley o el acto jurídico de su constitución.
Rel: dotación, *endowment;* patronato, *board of trustees.*
Ver: corporación.

fundamento de la acción *cause of action.* – Sin. causa petendi (lat.).

fundamentos de derecho *legal grounds, legal foundation.*

fungible adj. *fungible.* **fungibilidad** n. *fungibility.*
• Algo que tiene la cualidad de consumirse al usarse; algo que puede ser substituído por otro bien de la misma cantidad o calidad.
bienes fungibles *fungible goods.*

fusión de sociedades *corporate merger.*
fusionada *merging company.* **fusionante** *surviving company.*
• La fusión de sociedades consiste en la incorporación extintiva de una sociedad a otra que adquiere el patrimonio total de la incorporada, o la conjunción de los patrimonios de dos sociedades que crean una nueva que en ella se fusionan.
fusión horizontal *horizontal merger.*

fusión por incorporación *corporate merger.*
– Sin. fusión por absorción. fusión-absorción.
fusión pura *consolidation.* – Sin. fusión por creación. fusión-creación.
fusión vertical *vertical merger.*
Rel: disolución, *dissolution;* unión de sociedades, *union of corporations, amalgamation* (UK).

GGGG

gananciales n. *property earned by husband and wife during marriage.*
• Ganancias, rentas o bienes adquiridos por los cónyuges durante el matrimonio y que les pertenecen a ambos en común. – Sin. bienes gananciales.
régimen de gananciales [ed]*community of property earned by husband and wife during marriage.*
Rel: régimen económico del matrimonio, *marital property system.*
ganancias n. *profit, gain.* – Sin. frutos, *fruits, return.* rendimiento. utilidad.
ganancias brutas *gross profit.*
ganancia de capital *capital gain.*
ganancias netas *net profit.*
garantía *guaranty, warranty, security.*
garantizar *to guarantee.* **garantizador** adj. *guaranteeing.* **garantizador** n. *guarantor.*
garantizado n. *object of a guarantee.*
garantizado adj. *guarantied.*
• Seguridad ofrecida para el cumplimiento de una obligación, ya por tercera persona (por ejemplo una garantía personal como la fianza) o mediante una cosa (por ejemplo una garantía real como la hipoteca).
dar en garantía *to pledge, to grant a security interest.*
garantía colateral *collateral.*
garantía de cumplimiento *performance bond.*
garantía hipotecaria *mortgage security,*
– Sin. hipoteca.
garantía mancomunada *joint guaranty.*
garantía personal *personal guaranty.*
garantía prendaria *pledge security.*
– Sin. prenda.
garantía real *security, guaranty by security interest in property.*
garantía solidaria *joint and several guaranty.*
garantizar el interés fiscal (Mx) *to guarantee payment of taxes due.*

violación de la garantía DER.MERC *breach of warranty.*
Rel: aval, *endorsement;* caución, *surety, bond;* fianza, *bond, surety;* hipoteca, *mortgage;* prenda, *pledge.*
garantías constitucionales *constitutional guarantees, constitutional protections.*
– Sin. garantías individuales.
gasto público *public spending, government spending.*
gastos n. *expenses.* **gastar** v. *to spend.*
– Sin. egreso. desembolso, *expenditure.*
gasto corriente *operating expense.*
gasto de capital *capital expense.*
gastos bancarios *bank charges.*
gastos de investigación y desarrollo *research and development expenses.*
gastos de operación *operating expenses.*
gastos de representación *expense account.*
gastos deducibles *deductible expenses.*
gastos funerarios *funeral expenses.*
gastos generales *overhead.* – Sin. gastos indirectos.
gastos judiciales *court expenses.* – Sin. costas.
gastos médicos *medical expenses.*
gastos personales *personal expenses.*
gastos por intereses *interest expense.*
generales n. *personal data, personal identifying data.*
• Nombre dado a la información que identifica al testigo o a cualquier persona en una solicitud o similares, tales como el nombre, la edad, el estado civil, la profesión, el domicilio, y otros datos igualmente pertinentes. – Sin. generales de ley. generales de la ley.
genocidio n. *genocide.* **genocida** n.adj. *genocide.*
• Actos encaminados a la destrucción total o parcial de un grupo nacional, étnico, racial o religioso.
gestión de negocios [ed]*the unauthorized management of the affairs of another,* [lat.]*negotiorum gestio.* **gestor** n. *manager of the affairs of another,* [prest.]*gestor.*
• Hay gestión cuando una persona se encarga de uno o varios asuntos de otra sin tener mandato o poder legal o convencional, pero con el ánimo de obligar a éste. – Sin. gestión de negocios sin mandato. agencia oficiosa.
gastos de la gestión *expenses of managing another's affairs.*
gestor oficioso *unauthorized manager of another's affairs, officious intermeddler.*
Rel: ratificación, *ratification.*

Ref: (Ar)CC a.2288-2310; (CR)CC a.1295-1300; (Ec)CC a.2213-2221; (Esp)CC a.1888ss.; (Mx)CC a.1897ss.; (Pe)CC a.1950-1953; (PR)CC a.1788, 31 LPRA sec. 5101; (RD)CC a.1372; (Ur)CC a.1309; (Ve)CC a.1173-1177.

gestor judicial *attorney, legal representative.*

giro[1] **(money transfer)** n. *transfer of money, remittance.* **girar** v. *to transfer.*
giro telegráfico *wire transfer.*

giro[2] TÍTULO DE CRÉDITO n. *draft.* **girar** v. *to draw, send.*
girador n. *drawer, maker.* **girado** n. *drawee.*
– Sin. letra de cambio, *bill of exchange.*
giro a la vista *sight draft.*
giro a plazo *time draft.*
giro bancario *bank draft.*
giro postal *mail money order.*
Ver: letra de cambio.

giro[3] **(tipo de negocio)** n. *line of business.*
giro comercial *commercial business.*

gobierno n. *government.* **gobernar** v. *to govern.*
gobernador n. *governor.* **gobernante** adj.
• Es el órgano supremo de la jerarquía de la administración del Estado. – Sin. autoridad pública, *public authorities.* régimen, *regime.*
Cf: **gobierno ● administración.** El término gobierno generalmente se refiere a las instituciones que dirigen a una sociedad, y que con motivo de ello, toman las decisiones fundamentales y establecen sus áreas de autoridad política. El término administración, en cambio, generalmente describe a la actividad cotidiana que el gobierno despliega ininterrumpidamente para implementar sus políticas y lograr fines de interés general, y a la que en la práctica se le relaciona íntimamente con los términos burocracia y administración pública.
gobierno de facto *de facto government.*
– Sin. gobierno de hecho.
gobierno de jure, *de jure government, legal government.*
gobierno en el exilio *government in exile.*
gobierno estatal *state government.*
gobierno federal *federal government.*
gobierno municipal *municipal government.*
Rel: administración pública, *public administration;* burocracia, *bureaucracy;* estado, *estate;* servidor público, *public servant.*

golpe n. *blow.*
golpe de estado [fr.]*coup d'état.* **golpista** n. *a person in favor of coup d'état.* **golpismo** n. *belief in the need of a coup d'état.*
• Violación de las normas constitucionales de un país por un grupo, generalmente de milita-

res, con la intención de substituir al gobierno establecido mediante la toma del poder.
grado de parentesco *degree of kinship.*
grados militares *military rank.*
graduación de créditos *order of preference of creditor's claims.* – Sin. prelación de créditos.
gran jurado (Mx) *impeachment jury.*
• Jurado formado por diputados y senadores para determinar la imputabilidad de delitos a ciertos funcionarios públicos. – Sin. jurado de sentencia.
gravamen (carga) n. *encumbrance, lien.* **gravar** v. *to encumber.* **gravado** adj. *encumbered.*
• Carga u obligación que pesa sobre alguien, que ha de ejecutar o consentir una cosa o beneficio ajeno. Como gravámenes pueden citarse principalmente los censos, hipotecas, prendas y servidumbres. – Sin. carga, *encumbrance, liability.* obligación, *obligation.*
Gravamen es un término genérico usado en forma amplia para referirse a las cargas u obligaciones provenientes de una garantía, de daños o perjuicios, o de costos. Se le usa frecuentemente como sinónimo de carga, de la cual no puede ser claramente separado. Por ejemplo, el código civil mexicano incluye dentro del género gravamen a las cargas, los derechos reales y todas las limitaciones de la propiedad. En el ámbito del derecho fiscal, sin embargo, gravamen se usa exclusivamente como sinónimo de tributo e impuesto.
gravamen en garantía *lien.*
gravamen hipotecario *mortgage lien.*
gravamen sobre bienes muebles *chattel lien.*
gravamen (tax) n. *tax.* – Sin. gravamen fiscal.
gravamen sucesorio *inheritance or estate tax.*
guardia civil (Esp) [el]*civil guard,* [amplio]*police force,* [prest.]*guardia civil.*
guerra n. *war.* **guerrear** v. *to wage war.*
guerrero n. *fighter.* **combatientes** *combatants.*
• "La guerra es una lucha armada entre Estados, destinada a imponer la voluntad de uno de los bandos en conflicto, y cuyo desencadenamiento provoca la aplicación del estatuto internacional que forma el conjunto de las leyes de guerra." (Seara Vazquez (1998), 385) – Sin. batalla, *battle.* combate, *combat.*
crímenes de guerra *war crimes.*
declaración de guerra *declaration of war.*
guerra civil *civil war.*
guerra fría *cold war.*
guerra internacional *international war.*

leyes de guerra *laws of war.*
ocupación de guerra *war occupation.*
prisionero de guerra *prisoner of war.*
Glosario: armisticio, *armistice;* beligerancia, *belligerence;* bloqueo, *blockade;* capitulación, *capitulation;* casus belli (lat.), *casus belli;* derecho de presa o captura, *wartime maritime capture;* hostilidades, *hostilities;* mercenarios, *mercenaries;* neutralidad, *neutrality;* rendición incondicional, *unconditional surrender;* tregua, *truce.*
Ver: *war.*

guerrilla n. [transpl.]*guerrilla.* **guerrillero** n. *guerrilla fighter.*
• Una organización de milicias con mandos reconocidos que se identifican como grupos de combatientes hostiles al gobierno en su área de operaciones.
guerrilla urbana *urban guerrilla.*

guía aérea *airbill.*

guía de embarque *bill of lading.*
Ver: documentos de embarque.

HHHH

ha lugar *sustained.*
Rel: no ha lugar, *overruled, denied.*

hábeas corpus (prest.) *habeas corpus.*
• "Que se tenga el cuerpo". Que se ponga al detenido en presencia del juez para que examine la causa de la detención y se disponga su detención o libertad, de acuerdo con la ley. – Sin. acción de hábeas corpus, auto de hábeas corpus[PR].
procedimiento de hábeas corpus *habeas corpus procedure.*
solicitud de hábeas corpus *writ of habeas corpus.*
Comentario: Esta institución jurídica proveniente del derecho anglosajón ha sido adoptada por la mayoría de los países latinoamericanos y España. En el derecho mexicano se considera que existe como parte del derecho de amparo, sin usarse la denominación hábeas corpus.
Ref: (Ar)C a.43; (Bo)C a.18; (Ch)C a.21; (Co)C a.30; (CR)C a.48 LJC a.15; (Ec)C a.93; (ES)C a.247; (Esp)C a.17.4; (Ho)C a.84; (Mx)C a.107, Ley de Amparo a.17,18; (Pa)C a.23; (Pay)C a.133; (Pe)C a.200-201; (RD)C 8.g Ley de Hábeas Corpus; (Ur) C a.17.

hábil adj. *competent.*
día hábil *working day.*
persona legalmente hábil *legally competent person.*

habilitación[1] **(financiamiento)** n. *financing.*
préstamo de habilitación o avío *loan to industrial enterprises secured with inventories.*
habilitación[2] **(autorización)** n. *authorization, qualification.*
• "Acción y efecto de declarar judicialmente la habilidad o validez de lo que no poseía tales características, en razón de impedimento o limitación legal." (Couture, 307) – Sin. permiso, *permission.*
habilitación de día *judicial authorization to treat a non-business day as a business day.*
habilitación de hora *judicial authorization to treat non-business hours as business hours.*
habilitación del día feriado *judicial authorization to treat a holiday as a business day.*

habitación n. [prest.]*right of habitation, habitation.* **habitacionista** n. *holder of right of habitation.*
• Es el derecho real de ocupar una casa o habitaciones en ella en forma gratuita. – Sin. derecho real de habitación.

Hacienda pública *national wealth, public treasury || public finances.* – Sin. fisco, tax administration.

hallazgo n. *acquisition of res nullius.*
• Apropiación de un bien mueble sin dueño (res nullius). – Sin. invención (Co).
Ver: ocupación.

hampa n. *criminals, underworld.* **hampón** n. *thug, gangster, criminal.*
• Los personajes y el estilo de vida que forman el bajo mundo de los delincuentes. – Sin. el bajo mundo, *underworld.*
Rel: crimen organizado, *organized crime;* gángster, *gangster;* mafia, *Mafia.*
Ver: delincuente.

hecho n. *fact, event.* – Sin. acontecimiento, *event,* happening. evento, *event.* suceso, *event.*
hecho consumado *fait accompli.*
hecho delictuoso *criminal action.*
hecho ilícito *unlawful act or action.*
hecho imponible *taxable event.* – Sin. hecho gravable.
hecho notorio *well known fact, judicial notice.*
hechos ajenos a su voluntad *events beyond his or her control.*
hechos base de la acción *cause of action.*
– Sin. causa petendi.

hechos probados *facts in evidence, proven facts.*

hechos incontrovertidos *undisputed facts.*

hecho jurídico *legal* fact*;* [ed]*legally significant phenomenon, event or situation;* [el]*juridical fact,* [ed]*event caused by men or nature creating, modifying or extinguishing rights.*

• "Evento constituido por una acción u omisión humana, involuntaria o voluntaria (en cuyo caso se le denomina acto jurídico), o por una circunstancia de la naturaleza, que crea, modifica o extingue derechos." (Couture, 309)

Cf: **hecho jurídico** • **acto jurídico.** El hecho jurídico, "[e]n sentido general, es el acontecimiento, suceso o hecho natural al que el ordenamiento legal otorga una determinada trascendencia jurídica. Si en la producción de tal hecho ha intervenido la voluntad del hombre, estaremos ante un hecho voluntario que, si es valorado por el Derecho como generador de consecuencias jurídicas, recibe el nombre de acto jurídico. Pero si, aún interviniendo la voluntad humana, las consecuencias jurídicas del mismo están previstas con independencia de dicha intervención, seguiremos estando ante un hecho jurídico. El acto jurídico es la unidad mínima del actuar humano que tiene relevancia jurídica…" (Ribó Durán, 309)

Rel: acto jurídico, *juridical transaction,* [el] *juristic act;* negocio jurídico, *legal transaction which creates, changes or terminates legal rights.*

heredero n. *heir.*

• La persona o personas que reciben los bienes del de cujus a título universal substituyéndose en sus derechos y obligaciones. – Sin. sucesor, *successor.*

Cf: **heredero** • **legatario.** Conceptos claramente diferentes. El heredero tiene vocación al todo de la herencia, mientras que los legatarios no tienen más derecho que aquel que se les ha legado. El heredero puede tener responsabilidad ultra vires si ha aceptado la herencia sin beneficio de inventario, el legatario nunca responde más allá de la transmisión que se produjo en su favor.

heredero a título universal *universal heir.*

heredero forzoso *forced heir.*

heredero legítimo *legal heir, statutory heir.* – Sin. heredero legitimario.

heredero testamentario *testamentary heir.*

heredero único *sole heir.*

heredero universal *heir to the entire estate.*

herencia[1] **(sucesión)** *inheritance, succession.* **heredar** v. *to inherit.* **hereditario** adj. *hereditary.* **hereditable** adj. *inheritable.*

• Significa sucesión universal o sea la transmisión de la totalidad de los bienes, derechos y obligaciones del causante dándole continuidad a su haber. – Sin. sucesión universal, *succession.* asignación (Co).

heredar por partes iguales *share and share alike inheritance.*

partición de la herencia *partition of the estate.*

petición de herencia *probate proceeding (brought by legitimate or testamentary heir to divide estate).* – Sin. acción de petición de herencia.

repudiación de herencia *repudiation of inheritance.* – Sin. renuncia de la herencia.

Rel: sucesión, *succession;* testamento, *will.*

herencia[2] **(patrimonio)** *estate, decedent's estate.*

• Es el conjunto de bienes derechos y obligaciones, cosiderados como un todo, que no se extinguen a la muerte de su titular.

En contraste con esta definición, la palabra herencia es usada en lenguage común para referirse a los bienes y derechos que quedan disponibles a los herederos después de haber descontado las deudas y obligaciones del haber sucesorio. – Sin. bienes hereditarios. patrimonio hereditario.

bienes de la herencia *assets of the estate.*

herencia vacante *escheat, inheritance without heirs,* [lat.]*bona vacantia.*

herencia yacente *inheritance in which the heir has not taken possession.*

masa de la herencia *corpus of the estate.*

herida n. *wound.* **herir** v. *to wound.* **herido** adj. *wounded.* **herido** n. *wounded or injured person.* – Sin. lesión, *lesion, injury.* lastimadura, *injury.*

herida autoinfligida *self-inflicted injury.*

herida en sedal *through and through wound.*

herida penetrante *deep wound, puncture.*

hermenéutica n. *hermeneutics.* – Sin. interpretación jurídica.

heroína n. *heroin.*

hijos n. *sons and daughters, children.* **hijo** n. *son, child.* **hija** n. *daughter.* **hijastros** n. *stepchildren.* **hijastro** n. *stepson.* **hijastra** n. *stepdaughter.*

hijo adoptivo *adopted son.*

hijo de crianza *foster child.*

hijo extramatrimonial *child born out of wedlock.* – Sin. hijo extramarital.
hijo legitimado *legitimated child.*
hijo legítimo *legitimate child.*
hijo natural *natural child.*
hijo póstumo *posthumously-born child.*
ocultación de hijo *concealment of child.*
Rel: familia, *family;* padre, *father;* primogénito, *first-born.*

hipoteca n. [prest.]*hypothec, mortgage.* **hipotecar** v. *to hypothecate, mortgage.* **acreedor hipotecario** *mortgagee.* **deudor hipotecario** *mortagor.* **hipotecado** *mortgaged.* **hipotecario** adj. *hypothecary, pertaining to mortgage.* **hipotecable** adj. *mortgageable, able to be mortgaged.*
• Derecho real de garantía que se constituye en cosas que no salen de la posesión de su dueño, y que pueden venderse en caso de incumplimiento de la obligación. – Sin. hypotheca (lat.). Cf: **hipoteca ● prenda.** Ambos son derechos reales de garantía, que han sido claramente diferenciados por la doctrina: el bien sobre el que se traba la hipoteca no sale de la posesión del titular, en tanto que el bien sujeto a prenda se entrega al acreedor como esencia de la constitución de la prenda. La hipoteca se constituye fundamentalmente sobre bienes inmuebles, mientras que la prenda se constituye exclusivamente sobre bienes muebles.
La acepción principal de hipoteca se refiere a su descripción como derecho real de garantía, sin embargo también se denomina hipoteca a la garantía constituida así como, en ocasiones, al bien objeto de la hipoteca.
amortización de una hipoteca *amortization of a mortgage.*
cédula hipotecaria *mortgage certificate.*
constituir una hipoteca *to create a mortgage.*
crédito hipotecario *mortgage loan.* – Sin. préstamo hipotecario.
ejecución de una hipoteca *foreclosure of a mortgage.*
hipoteca mobiliaria (Ven,Esp) *chattel mortgage.*
hipoteca naval *ship mortgage.*
hipoteca necesaria *legal mortgage.*
inscripción de una hipoteca *recording of a mortgage.*
segunda hipoteca *second mortgage.*
– Sin. hipoteca de segundo grado.
Rel: garantía, *guaranty, surety;* gravamen, *encumbrance, lien.*
Ref: (Ar)CC a.3108ss; (Ch)CC a.2407; (CR)CC a.

409; (Ec)CC a.2333-2360; (Esp)CC a.1874-1880, Ley Hipotecaria.; (Mx)CC a.2920ss.; (Pe)CC a.1097-1122; (PR)LHRP a.155, 30 LPRA 2551; (RD) CC a.2114ss.; (Ur)CC a.2322-2348; (Ve)CC a.1877.

homicidio (delito) n. *homicide.* **homicida** n. *killer, murderer, homicide.* **homicida** adj. *homicidal.*
• Homicidio consiste en privar de la vida a otro. – Sin. asesinato, *murder, assassination.*
homicidio accidental involuntario *involuntary manslaughter.*
homicidio calificado *murder.* – Sin. homicidio con agravantes.
homicidio con justificantes *excusable homicide.*
homicidio doloso *murder, intentional homicide.*
homicidio en riña tumultuaria *homicide committed in a brawl (the killer being unknown).*
homicidio en riña *homicide in a fight, homicide in mutual combat.*
homicidio eugenésico *ethnic cleansing.*
homicidio imprudente o imprudencial *manslaughter.* – Sin. homicidio no intencional. homicidio culposo.
homicidio por piedad *mercy killing.* – Sin. homicidio consentido.
homicidio premeditado *premeditated homicide.*
Rel: fratricidio, *fratricide;* infanticidio, *infanticide,* genocidio, *genocide;* matricidio, *matricide;* parricidio, *parricide, patricide;* uxoricidio, *uxoricide.*
Ref: (Ar)CP a.79; (Bo)CP a.251; (Ch)CP a.390-393; (Co)CP a.103-110; (Ec)CP a.449; (Esp)CP a.138; (Gu)CP a.123; (Mx)CP a.302; (Pe)CP a.106ss.; (PR) CP a.85, 33 LPRA sec. 4004; (RD)CP a.295,302, 319; (Ur)CP a.310ss.; (Ve)CP a.407-413.

homologación n. [prest.]*homologation.*
homologar v. *to homologate.*
homosexualidad n. *homosexuality.* **homosexual** n.adj. *homosexual.*
• Homosexual es el concepto genérico para designar a personas que tienen preferencia sexual por miembros de su mismo sexo. Incluye el lesbianismo y la sodomía. – Sin. sodomía, *sodomy.*
honorarios n. *fees.*
honorarios de abogado *attorney's fees.*
Rel: costas, *court costs;* iguala, *retainer fee;* pacto de cuotalitis, *contingency fee.*
hora n. *time, hour.*
horas de trabajo *work hours.*
horas extra o extraordinarias *overtime.*

horas hábiles *office hours.*

hospedaje (contrato) n. *lodging.* **hospedar** v. *to lodge.* **huésped** *guest.* **hospedero u hotelero** *host, innkeeper.*

• Contrato por el que una persona se obliga a prestar alojamiento a otra y a suministrarle habitación mediante un precio. – Sin. alojamiento. albergue, *lodging, shelter.*
Rel: hostería, *hostel;* hotel, *hotel;* parador, *inn;* posada, *inn.*

hostigamiento n. *harassing, harassment.*
hostigar v. *to harass.* – Sin. acoso. persecución, *persecution, harassment.*
hostigamiento sexual *sexual harassment.*
– Sin. acoso sexual.

hostilidades n. *hostilities.* **hostilizar** v. *to antagonize.* **hostil** adj. *hostile.*
hostilidades bélicas *war hostilities.*
inicio de hostilidades *initiation of hostilities.*
Rel: guerra, *war.*

huelga DER.LABORAL n. *strike.* **huelguista** n. *striker.*
• "La suspensión temporal de trabajo llevada a cabo por una coalición de trabajadores." (LFT-Mx., a. 440)
El derecho de huelga de los trabajadores y el derecho de paro de los patrones son principios establecidos por la mayoría de las legislaciones de los países hispanoparlantes.
comité de huelga *strike committee.*
emplazamiento de huelga *legal notice of intention to strike.* – Sin. aviso de huelga.
huelga de brazos caídos *sit-down strike.*
huelga de solidaridad *sympathy strike.*
huelga desautorizada *wildcat strike.*
huelga general *general strike.*
huelga patronal *lock-out.*
Rel: esquirol, *strikebreaker, scab;* paro laboral, *work stoppage;* paro patronal, *lockout;* sindicato, *union.*
Ref: (Ch)CT a.370; (Co)CST a.429; (Gu)CT a.239; (Esp)C a.28.2 ET a.4.1c.; (Mx)LFT a.440; (Pa)C a.65 CT a.475; (RD)CT a.401; (Ve)C a.97 LOT a.494.

huelga de hambre *hunger strike.*

huella n. *print.*
huella de la mano *handprint.*
huellas biológicas *biological fingerprints.*
huellas de la palma de la mano *palm prints.*
huellas de los pies *footprints.*
huellas latentes *latent prints.*
revelado de una huella *print development.*
Rel: impresión, *print, impression;* rastro, *trace.*
Ver: huellas digitales.

huellas digitales *fingerprints.*

• Son los dibujos dactilares, tomados de las yemas de los dedos, que describen patrones sobre los que se basan sistemas de clasificación y reconocimiento de personas. – Sin. huellas dactilares. impresiones digitales o dactilares. rostros papilares.
Los sistemas de clasificación de huellas digitales modernos se usan para identificación de personas tanto en los países de habla inglesa como en los de habla española. En los países angloparlantes el sistema está basado en los trabajos de Sir Edward Richard Henry (también conocido como sistema Galton-Henry o sistema Bengalés), que agrupa los dibujos dactilares en cuatro tipos fundamentales: *arch, loop, whorl and composite.* En la mayoría de los países hispanoparlantes se sigue el sistema de clasificación desarrollado por Don Juan Vucetish, que está basado también en cuatro tipos fundamentales, pero diferentes, a saber: arco, presilla interna, presilla externa y verticilo. Es de hacerse notar, además, que la adopción del sistema Vucetish ha desarrollado modificaciones en algunos países hispanos. Por ejemplo España ha adoptado el llamado sistema Oloriz, cambiando los nombres de los tipos básicos (llamándolos adelto, dextrodelto, sinistrodelto y bidelto).
Rel: identificación, *identification;* marcas, *marks.*

Glosario: arco, *arch;* cámara de vapores de yodo, *iodine fuming cabinet;* cinta celulosa, *cellulose tape;* compuesto, *composite;* conteo de crestas, *ridge count;* cresta, *ridge;* delta, *delta;* ficha dactiloscópica, *fingerprint card;* horquilla, *fork;* huellas latentes, *latent fingerprints;* nitrato de plata, *silver nitrate;* papilas, *papillae;* polvo para huellas digitales, *fingerprints powder;* poros, *pores;* presilla externa, *external loop;* presilla interna, *internal loop;* punto central, *core;* punto déltico, *delta;* puntos característicos, *characteristics;* revelado de huellas latentes, *development of latent fingerprints;* sistema bacilar, *bacillary system;* sistema marginal, *marginal system;* sistema nuclear, *nuclear system;* surco, *furrow;* verticilo, *whorl;* yodo metálico, *metallic iodine.*

hurto (delito) n. *larceny, theft.* **hurtar** v. *to steal.* **ladrón** *thief, robber.*
• Tomar con ánimo de lucro cosas muebles ajenas sin la voluntad de su dueño. – Sin. latrocinio. robo simple (Mx).
hurto agravado *aggravated larceny.*
hurto de mercancías *shoplifting.* – Sin. ratería o hurto de mercadería (PR).

hurto de uso de vehículo (Esp) *joy ride, unauthorized use of vehicle.*
hurto famélico *larceny caused by hunger.*
hurto mayor *grand larceny.*
hurto menor *petty larceny.*
Ver: robo.
Ref: (Ar)CP a.162-63; (Bo)CP a.326-330; (Ch)CP a. 432, 446-448; (Co)CP a.239; (Ec)CP a.547-549; (Esp)CP a.234; (Gu)CP a.246; (Mx)CP a.367; (Pe) CP a.185; (PR)CP a.165, 33 LPRA sec. 4271; (RD) CP a.379; (Ur)CP a.340; (Ve)CP a.453.

I I I I

identidad n. *identity.*
identificación n. *identification.* **identificar** v. *to identify.* **identificable** adj. *identifiable.*
• El establecimiento de la identidad de una persona. La determinación de que una persona es indubitablemente aquella que pretende ser o que se busca. – Sin. reconocimiento.
identificación de cadáver *identification of the deceased, identification of the body.*
identificación de los comparecientes *identification of the parties present.*
identificación del autor del delito *identification of the offender or perpetrator.*
Rel: antropometría, *anthropometry;* color de la piel, *color of the skin, complexion;* confrontación, *line up;* diligencia de reconocimiento, *identification proceeding;* filiación, *description;* huellas digitales, *fingerprints;* retrato hablado, *portrait parle;* señas personales, *particulars, personal description.*
ignorancia de la ley [el]*ignorance of the law,* [ef]*ignorance of the law is no excuse.*
• Expresa el principio de que la ignorancia de la ley no excusa su falta de cumplimiento.
– Sin. ignorancia del derecho no excusa su falta de cumplimiento. ignorantia iuris non excusat (lat.). ignorancia inexcusable, [lat.]*ignorantia juris.*
igualdad ante la ley *equality under the law.*
– Sin. igualdad jurídica.
ilegal adj. *illegal.* **ilegalidad** n. *illegality.*
ilegalmente adv. *illegally.*
• Lo que es contrario a la ley. – Sin. antijurídico, *unlawful.*
Ver: ilícito.
ilegitimidad n. *illegitimacy.* **ilegitimar** v. *to make illegitimate.* **ilegítimo** adj. *illegitimate.*
– Sin. bastardo, *bastard.* espurio, *spurious.*
hijo ilegítimo *illegitimate child.*
ilegitimidad del título *defective title.*

ilícito adj. *illicit.* **ilicitud** n. *illicitness.*
ilícitamente adv. *illicitly.*
• La ilicitud se da cuando el sujeto omite los actos ordenados o ejecuta los actos prohibidos.
– Sin. antijurídico, *unlawful.* ilegal, *illegal.*
Cf: **ilícito • ilegal • antijurídico.** Ilícito e ilegal se usan en forma sinónima e intercambiable. Ambos términos expresan una conducta en contra de la ley, pero mientras ilegal es usado primordialmente cuando se habla de una violación de un mandato legal o de una ley, ilícito se prefiere cuando se habla, además de una acción de rompimiento de la ley, de una infracción moral también. Antijurídico, por su parte, se usa en ocasiones en vez de ilegal, pero más frecuentemente se le entiende como una acción violatoria de un derecho de naturaleza penal.
ilícito civil *illicit act, unlawful act.*
ilícito penal *crime.*
impedimento n. *impediment.*
• Circunstancias que impiden la celebración de un matrimonio en forma válida. También una circunstancia que afecta la imparcialidad de jueces y otros funcionarios judiciales obligándolos a inhibirse del conocimiento del caso en cuestión. – Sin. imposibilidad, *impediment, disability.*
impedimentos del matrimonio o matrimoniales *impediment to marriage.*
impedimento dirimente *diriment impediment.*
impedimento impediente *prohibitive impediment.*
imperio de la ley *the rule of law.*
importación n. *imports.* **importar** v. *to import.*
importador n. *importer.* **importable** adj. *importable.*
licencia de importación *import license.*
Rel: exportaciones, *exports.*
imprescriptibilidad n. *imprescriptibility.*
imprescriptible adj. *imprescriptible.*
• Que no puede prescribir.
Rel: prescripción, *prescription.*
improcedencia n. *inadmissibility, denial.*
improcedente adj. *inadmissible.*
improcedencia de un recurso *denial of appeal or legal recourse.*
improcedencia de una petición *denial of a motion, denial of a petition.*
improrrogable adj. *final, without further continuance, unextendible.*
improrrogabilidad n. *that cannot be extended.*

Rel: inaplazable, *undeferrable, unpostponable.*

imprudencia¹ (sin prudencia) n. *imprudence.*
imprudente n. *imprudent.* **imprudencial** adj.
imprudent.
• Falta de prudencia.
conducta imprudente *imprudent behavior,
unwise behavior.*

imprudencia² (negligencia) n. *negligence.*
imprudencial adj. *negligent.* **imprudente** n.
negligent. – Sin. negligencia, *negligence.*
• Falta de una conducta prudente que conduce
a un resultado lesivo que el causante no quiere
y que el derecho sanciona.
delito imprudencial *crime caused by
negligent or imprudent action.* – Sin. delito
culposo.
imprudencia criminal *criminal negligence.*
imprudencia grave *gross negligence.*
imprudencia inexcusable *contributory
negligence.* – Sin. imprudencia concurrente
(Esp).
imprudencia leve *slight negligence.*
imprudencia profesional *professional
negligence.*
imprudencia temeraria *reckless negligence,
gross negligence.* – Sin. imprudencia crasa.
Ver: culpa¹. culpa².

impuesto DER.FISCAL n. *tax.* **causante** n. *taxpayer.*
sujeto pasivo *taxpayer.* **contribuyente** n.
taxpayer. **fisco** n. *tax administration.*
• "Contribución económica requerida por el
Estado con carácter obligatorio y general para
todos aquellos que se hallen en una situación
jurídica determinada, y destinada normalmente
al sostenimiento de los servicios públicos de la
actividad gubernamental y a los fines de política
económica del gobierno." (Couture, 323)
abatimiento de impuestos *abatement of taxes,
tax reduction.* – Sin. reducción de impuestos.
base del impuesto *tax base.*
cálculo del impuesto *tax computation.*
causar impuesto *to be subject to tax.*
cuota del impuesto *tax rate.*
declaración de impuestos *tax return.*
determinación del impuesto *assessment of
tax.*
devolución del impuesto *tax refund.*
impuesto aduanal *customs duty.* – Sin. derecho
aduanal.
impuesto al comercio exterior *foreign trade
tax.*
impuesto al valor agregado (IVA) *value
added tax* (VAT). – Sin. impuesto al valor
añadido.

impuesto de sucesión *inheritance tax.*
impuesto de traslación de dominio *transfer
tax.* – Sin. impuesto de traspaso.
impuesto de ventas *sales tax.* – Sin. impuesto a
las ventas. impuesto a la compraventa.
impuesto del timbre *stamp tax.* – Sin. impuesto
de timbres.
impuesto directo *direct tax.*
impuesto indirecto *indirect tax.*
impuesto predial *property tax, land tax.*
impuesto progresivo *progressive tax.*
impuesto proporcional *proportional tax, flat
tax.*
impuesto retenido *withholding tax.*
impuesto sobre donaciones *gift tax.*
impuesto sobre ingresos *income tax.*
impuesto sobre inmuebles *capital gains tax
(on sale of real estate property), real estate
tax.* – Sin. impuesto sobre adquisición de
inmuebles. impuesto de inmuebles.
impuesto sobre la renta *income tax.*
– Sin. impuesto a la renta. impuesto sobre
ingresos.
impuesto sobre patrimonio *net worth tax.*
– Sin. impuesto al patrimonio. impuesto
patrimonial.
impuesto sobre productos del trabajo *tax on
earned income.*
impuesto suntuario *luxury tax.* – Sin. impuesto
de lujo. impuesto sobre el lujo. impuesto sobre
artículos suntuarios.
impuestos atrasados *back taxes.*
impuestos interiores *excise tax.* – Sin. impuestos especiales. impuestos internos.
**impuestos sobre las utilidades de las empre-
sas** *corporate income tax.*
libre de impuestos *tax exempt.*
pago del impuesto *to pay taxes.* – Sin. entero
del impuesto.
recaudación de impuestos *tax revenues, tax
receipts.*
retención del impuesto *tax withholding.*
tarifa del impuesto *tax rate.*
traslación de impuestos *tax shifting.*
Rel: contribución, *tax, assessment;* derechos,
duties, charges, assessment; exención, *exemption;* gravamen fiscal, *tax;* productos, *yield,
rent;* tasa, *tax, charge.*
Ver.: tributo.

impugnación¹ (atacar) n. *challenge, impugnment.*
impugnar v. *to impugn.* **impugnador** n.
impugner. **impugnativo** adj. *impugning.*
impugnatorio adj. *impugning.*
• "Acción y efecto de atacar, tachar o refutar un

acto judicial, documento, disposición testimonial, informe de peritos, etc, con el objeto de obtener su revocación e invalidación." (Couture, 323) – Sin. objeción, *objection.*
impugnación de documentos *to challenge the validity of documents.*
impugnación de honorarios *to take exception to a professional fee.*
impugnación de un testamento *to contest or challenge a will.*
impugnación de un testimonio *impeachment of testimony.*
impugnación²(revisar decisiones) *challenging a court decision.* **impugnar** v. *to challenge a court decision.*
• La interposición de un recurso contra una resolución judicial. – Sin. oposición, *opposition.*
medios de impugnación *legal means to challenge a court decision.*
Rel: apelación, *appeal;* recurso, *legal recourse.*
Ver: recursos.

impunidad n. *impunity.* **impune** adj. *unpunished.*
impunemente adj. *with impunity.*
Rel: castigo, *punishment;* responsabilidad, *responsibility.*

imputabilidad DER.PENAL n. [prest.]*imputability, competency to be charged.*
• Capacidad condicionada por la madurez y salud mentales de una persona para comprender la antijuridicidad de su conducta y para regularla de conformidad con esa comprensión.
Rel: incapacidad, *incapacity;* madurez, *maturity;* responsabilidad penal, *criminal liability.*

imputación n. *imputation, accusation.* **imputar** v. *to impute, charge.* **imputado** n. *imputed, accused.* **imputador** n. *accuser.*
• Atribución de culpa o negligencia.
Ver: acusación.

in absentia (lat.) *in absentia, absent.*

in articulo mortis (lat.) *in articulo mortis, at the point of death.*

in dubio pro reo (max.) *in dubio pro reo. If in doubt favors the defendant.*

in forma pauperis (lat.) *in forma pauperis, in the manner of a pauper or indigent.*

in fraganti (lat.) *in fraganti, as it is occurring.*
• En el mismo momento que se está cometiendo el delito.

in limine litis (lat.) *in limine litis, preliminarily to litigation or lawsuit.*

inadmisible adj. *inadmissible.* **inadmisibilidad** n. *inadmissibility.*

inapelable adj. *without appeal, unappealable.*
inapelabilidad n. *unappealableness.*

inalienabilidad n. *inalienability.* **inalienable** adj. *inalienable.*
• Que no puede enajenarse; que se encuentra fuera del comercio.

incapacidad¹ (aptitud legal) n. *incapacity.*
incapacitar v. *to take away legal capacity.*
incapacitado n. *legally incapacitated or unqualified.*
• "La falta de aptitud jurídica para realizar, gozar o ejercer derechos o contraer derechos por sí mismo." (Ramírez Gronda, 179) – Ant. capacidad, *capacity.*
incapacidad para suceder *legal incapacity to inherit.* – Sin. incapacidad para heredar. indignidad (Pe).
incapacidad procesal *legal incapacity to sue.*
Rel: curatela, *curatorship;* tutela, *guardianship.*
Ver: interdicción.

incapacidad² (discapacidad) n. *disability.* **incapacitarse** v. *to become disabled.* **incapacitado** n. *disabled person.* **incapacitado** adj. *disabled.*
• Calidad de estar incapacitado físicamente con motivo de una lesión o defecto, adquirido o de nacimiento. – Sin. discapacidad. invalidez. minusvalidez.
incapacidad física *physical disability.*
incapacidad laboral *work disability.*
– Sin. incapacidad para trabajar.
incapacidad permanente *permanent disability.*
incapacidad temporal *temporary disability.*

incautación *seizure.*
• La toma de bienes o valores por parte de una autoridad.

incendio (delito) n. *arson.* **incendiar** v. *to set fire, burn.* **incendiario** n. *arsonist.*
• Causar en forma intencional la destrucción o deterioro de un bien ajeno mediante el fuego.
– Sin. incendio intencional. incendio provocado. incendio voluntario.
incendio agravado *aggravated arson.*
incendio forestal *forest fire.*
Rel: conflagración, *conflagration;* prender fuego, *to start a fire;* quemazón, *burning;* siniestro, *fire, disaster.*

incentivos fiscales *tax incentives.* – Sin. estímulos fiscales.

incesto (delito) n. *incest.* **incestuoso** adj. *incestuous.*

incidente DER.PROC n. *incidental proceeding, motion.*

• "Litigio accesorio que se suscita con ocasión de un juicio, normalmente sobre circunstancias de orden procesal, y que se decide mediante una sentencia interlocutoria." (Couture, 326) – Sin. artículo, *incidental proceeding.* Cf: **incidente ● artículo.** Incidente y artículo son términos sinónimos cuando se refieren a un procedimiento especial para resolver una cuestión incidental o accesoria dentro de un proceso. El término artículo, usado en este sentido, se le encuentra con mayor frecuencia en España que en los países latinoamericanos.

incidente de costas [ed]*incidental proceeding to settle court costs.*

incidente de nulidad *motion to annul the proceedings.*

incidente de previo y especial pronunciamiento [ed]*incidental proceeding to stay the main litigation.* – Sin. artículo de previo y especial pronunciamiento. Ref: (Ar)CPCC a.175ss.; (Bol)CPC a.149ss.; (Ch) CPC a.82; (Mx)CPC a.88.

incitación al delito *solicitation.* – Sin. incitación a la comisión del delito.

incomparecencia n. *nonappearance, failure to appear.*

incompetencia¹ (descalificación) n. *lack of jurisdiction or venue,* [ed]*lack of court's jurisdictional authority.* **incompetente** adj. *lacking jurisdiction or venue.*

• Es la falta de jurisdicción de un juez para conocer de una determinada causa. – Ant. competencia, [ed]*court's jurisdictional authority.*

incompetencia² (ineptitud) *incompetence.* **incompetente** adj. *incompetent.* **incompetente** n. *incompetent person.*

• Falta de la habilidad, conocimientos o experiencia necesarios para la realización de una tarea determinada. – Sin. ineptitud, *ineptitude.*

incomunicación DER.PENAL n. *isolation, solitary confinement.* **incomunicar** v. *to isolate, to place in solitary confinement.* **incomunicado** adj. *incommunicado.* – Sin. aislamiento penitenciario, *solitary confinement.* confinamiento, *confinement.*

incondicional adj. *unconditional.* **incondicionalmente** adv. *unconditionally.*

inconformidad n. *dissent* || *appeal.* **inconforme** adj. *dissenting.* **inconforme** n. *dissenter.*

inconstitucional adj. *unconstitutional.* **inconstitucionalidad** n. *unconstitutionality.*

incorregible adj. *incorrigible.* **incorregibilidad** n. *incorrigibility, incorrigibleness.* **incorregiblemente** adv. *incorrigibly.*

incorruptible adj. *incorruptible.* **incorruptibilidad** n. *incorruptibility.* **incorrupto** adj. *uncorrupted.* – Sin. íntegro, *honest, upright.* honrado, *honest.* probo, *upright, honest.*

incoterms (int.) *incoterms.*

• "[U]n conjunto de reglas internacionales de carácter facultativo que determina la interpretación de los principales términos utilizados en los contratos de compraventa internacional." (International Chamber of Commerce) Glosario: Costo/Coste y Flete, *Cost & Freight* (C&F)*;* Costo/Coste, Seguro y Flete, *Cost, Insurance and Freight* (CIF)*;* en fábrica, *ex works; libre/franco al costado del buque/vapor, *free alongside ship* (FAS); libre/franco a bordo (LAB), *free on board* (FOB)*;* franco factoría /libre fábrica, *ex factory;* franco vagón o franco camión, *free on rail, free on truck* (FOR-FOT)*;* entregada en frontera, *delivered at frontier* (DAF)*;* entregada libre de derechos, *delivered duty paid* (DDU)*;* flete o porte pagado hasta, *freight or carriage paid to;* en fábrica, *ex work;* sobre buque, *ex ship;* sobre muelle, *ex quay.*

incriminación n. *incrimination.* **incriminar** v. *to incriminate.* **incriminante** adj. *incriminating, incriminatory.* **incriminatorio** adj. *incriminating.*

• La imputación hecha a una persona de un delito o falta grave. – Sin. inculpación, *inculpation.*

inculpabilidad n. *lack of culpability.*

• Falta o ausencia de culpabilidad. – Sin. exclusión de la culpabilidad. Ver: excluyentes de responsabilidad.

inculpado *defendant, accused.* **inculpar** v. *to inculpate.* **inculpación** n. *inculpation.* Rel: procesado, *on trial;* sospechoso, *suspect;* Ver: acusado.

incumplimiento n. *breach.* **incumplir** v. *to breach.* – Sin. inobservancia, *nonobservance.* **incumplimiento de contrato** *breach of contract.* **incumplimiento de una obligación** *breach of an obligation, failure to fulfill an obligation.* **subsanar el incumplimiento (de un contrato)** *to cure a breach (of contract).*

indagatoria DER.PROC.PENAL [ed]*first statement made by defendant before a judge (regarding the facts of the case).*

• El primer interrogatorio del presunto delincuente llevada a cabo ante el órgano jurisdiccional con el propósito de indagar o averiguar detalladamente las circunstancias del delito así como la conducta del delincuente. – Sin. declaración indagatoria. declaración preparatoria (Mx). declaración previa. primera declaración del imputado (Esp).
Rel: declaración informativa, *statement made before a policeman or out-of-court investigator.*

indefensión n. *defenselessness, helplessness.*
estado de indefensión *lacking defense.*

indemnización n. *indemnity, compensation.*
indemnizar v. *to indemnify.* **indemnizado** n. *indemnified person.* **indemnizado** adj. *indemnified.*

• El resarcimiento de un daño o un perjuicio. – Sin. compensación, *compensation.* reparación, *reparation, indemnity.* resarcimiento.

indemnización de guerra *war reparation.*
indemnización pecuniaria *money damages.*
indemnización por daños a título de ejemplo *exemplary damages.*
indemnización por daños a título de pena *punitive damages.*
indemnización por daños indirectos *consequential damages.*
indemnización por daños y perjuicios *damages.*
indemnizaciones laborales *indemnification given to workers or employees.* – Sin. indemnización obrera.
indemnización por accidente de trabajo *workmen's compensation, worker's compensation.*
indemnización por despido justificado *severance pay.*
indemnización por despido colectivo *indemnification for mass firing.*
indemnización por despido injustificado o improcedente *indemnification for unjustified firing.* – Sin. indemnización por cesantía.
indemnización por antigüedad *severance pay based on seniority.*
indemnización por enfermedad *sick pay.*
indemnización por muerte del trabajador *death benefits.*

índice de criminalidad *crime rate.*

indiciado n. *suspect.*

indicios[1] n. *traces, clues, circumstantial evidence.*

• "Elemento o circunstancia que permite presumir la existencia de algún hecho." (Ramírez Gronda, 179) – Sin. conjetura, *conjecture.* señal, *trace.* pista, *clue.*

indicios[2] n. *presumption.*
Ver: presunción.

indigente n. *indigent.* **indigencia** n. *indigence.* – Sin. pobre, *poor.*

indivisibilidad n. *indivisibility.* **indivisible** adj. *indivisible.* **indivisiblemente** adv. *indivisibly.*
Rel: copropiedad, *joint property.*

indivisión n. [prest.]*indivision, undivided ownership of property.* **indiviso** adj. *undivided.*
• Estado en que se encuentra un bien o cosa que pertenece a dos o más personas en común. Rel: pro indiviso (lat.), *pro indiviso, as undivided.*

in situ (lat.) *in situ, in its place of origin.*

indulto n. *pardon,* [prest.]*indulto.* **indultar** v. *to pardon.* **indultado** n. *person pardoned.* **indultado** adj. *pardoned.*

• "En sentido amplio, el indulto es la remisión o perdón, total o parcial, de las penas judicialmente impuestas, por acto del Poder ejecutivo o del Poder legislativo." (XV Enciclopedia Omeba, 589) – Sin. condonación, *condoning, forgiveness.*
Cf: **indulto • perdón • amnistía.** Indulto y perdón se usan intercambiable y sinónimamente. Indulto generalmente se usa en el ámbito penal mientras que perdón se usa en forma más amplia y en ocasiones más informalmente. Amnistía es un término que se puede aplicar a una serie de delitos y en generalidades a ciertos delincuentes o condenados, el indulto en cambio, constituye una manifestación individual. La amnistía vuelve al pasado y destruye todos los efectos causados, el perdón va hacia el futuro y conserva en el pasado todo lo que lo provocó. El perdón es más judicial que político, la amnistía por lo contrario es una absolución general con más tintes políticos que judiciales.
indulto necesario [ed]*necessary pardon.*
indulto por gracia *pardon as an act of grace, pardon as a discretionary power.*
Rel: amnistía, *amnesty;* conmutación de pena, *commutation of punishment;* remisión, *remission.*
Ver: perdón.

ineficacia n. *lack of legal effect,* [prest.]*inefficacy.*

• Carencia de efectos jurídicos.
La ineficacia se entiende modernamente como un concepto genérico que comprende tanto la rescisión, esto es, la terminación de los efectos

legales de un negocio jurídico válido mediante una declaración de voluntad, como la nulidad, esto es, la terminación de los efectos legales de un acto jurídico viciado o inválido debido a la existencia de un defecto en su formación. Rel: nulidad, *nullity;* rescisión, *rescission.*

ineligibilidad *ineligibility.*

inexcusable *inexcusable, wanton.*

inexistencia n. *absolutely null, void.*
• Inexistencia es la resultante de la falta de alguno de los elementos esenciales para la formación de los contratos.
Rel: nulidad, *nullity.*

infamia n. *infamy.* **infamante** adj. *defamatory.* **infamación** n. *defamation.* – Sin. deshonor, *dishonor.* deshonra, *disgrace.* ignominia, *ignominy.* oprobio, *opprobrium.*

infancia n. *infancy.* **infante** n. *infant.*

infanticidio n. *infanticide.* **infanticida** n. *infanticide.* **infanticida** adj. *infanticidal.*

información n. *information.* **informar** v. *to inform.* **informativo** adj. *informative.*

informante n. *informant.* **informador** n. *informer.* – Sin. delator, *informer.* chivato (mod.), *stool pigeon.*
Rel: cantar (mod.), *to squeal;* soplón (mod.), *whistleblower.*

informe n. *report.* **informar** v. *to inform.* **informe pericial** *expert's report.* – Sin. dictamen pericial.

infracción n. *infraction, violation.* **infringir** v. *to infringe.* **infractor** n. *offender, infringer.*
• Quebrantamiento de lo que se manda o prohíbe en una norma y por extensión en un compromiso. – Sin. incumplimiento, *breach.* quebrantamiento, *breach.* transgresión, *transgression.* violación, *violation.*
Infracción en sentido amplio significa un quebrantamiento de la ley, y por extensión de un convenio o un tratado. En su sentido más restringido infracción se refiere, las más de las veces, principalmente a un incumplimiento de las disposiciones de índole administrativa y penal.
Cf: **infracción • contravención.** Ambos términos se usan sinónima e indistintamente, sin embargo la doctrina los considera dos términos distintos. La palabra infracción proviene de fracturar, hacer pedazos, romper, esto es una fractura del mandamiento público, de la ley. Contravención proviene de volver de donde se ha venido, desandar lo andado, des-hacer lo hecho, esto es contradecir lo mandado, contravenirlo. En la infracción nos oponemos al mandato, en la contravención lo ignoramos.

infracción de la ley *violation of law.*
infracción de tráfico *traffic violation.*
infracción del derecho de autor *copyright infringement.*
infringir una patente *infringement of patent.*
Rel: contravención, *contravention;* incumplimiento, *breach;* inobservancia, *in observance, nonobservance.*
Ver: falta. delito.

ingreso n. *income, revenue.* – Sin. entrada, *revenue, receipt.* renta.
ingreso actual *current income.*
ingreso bruto *gross income.*
ingreso de las personas físicas *income of individuals.*
ingreso estimado *estimated income.*
ingreso gravable *taxable income.*
ingreso mundial *worldwide income.*
ingreso neto *net income.*
ingreso real *actual income.*
ingresos no declarados *no reported income.*
ingresos por intereses *interest income.*
nivel de ingresos *income level.*
Rel: beneficio, *benefit;* ganancia, *profit;* productos, *yield, rent.*

inhabilitación n. *disqualification* || *disability* (Ve). **inhabilitar** v. *to disqualify.* **inhabilitado** n. *disqualified.*
• Descalificación para tener un puesto o aceptar una distinción como pena o sanción. – Sin. incapacitación. ineligibilidad, *ineligibility.*
inhabilitación absoluta *full disqualification.*
inhabilitación especial *partial disqualification.*
Ref: (Bo)CP a.33-36; (Co)CP a.43-46; (Esp)CP a. 33, 40,42,44-46,50,55; (Mx)CP a.212-225, 231; (Pe) CP a.36-40; (Ur)CP a.75-77; (Ve)CC a.409-412.

inhibitoria n. *motion to determine proper jurisdiction,* [ed]*motion to issue order to a judge to refrain from hearing a case for which he or she lacks jurisdiction.*
• Cuestión de competencia que se pide ante el juez que la parte tenga por competente, ante quien no se sigue la causa, pidiéndole que expida oficio a aquél ante quien se haya promovido para que se inhiba y remita los autos. – Sin. inhibitoria de jurisdicción.
Rel: declinatoria, *jurisdictional plea, plea or demurrer to the jurisdiction.*

iniciativa de la ley *bill.* – Sin. iniciativa de ley. iniciativa legislativa. proyecto de ley.

iniciativa privada *private enterprise, private companies.*
Rel: libre empresa, *free enterprise.*

inimputabilidad n. [el]*lack of imputability,* [ed]*lack of capacity to be charged.*
• Caso en el que no puede imputarse la comisión de un delito a una persona por carecer de los requisitos mentales para entender y querer una conducta.
Ver: excluyentes de responsabilidad.

injurias (delito) n. [ed]*affronting wrong, insults* (pop.). **injuriar** v. *to insult, offend.*
• Comete este delito "el autor de toda expresión proferida o acción ejecutada en deshonra, descrédito o menosprecio de otra persona." (Ribó Durán, 336)
Cf: **injurias • malos tratos • sevicia.** Términos usados frecuentemente en conjunción considerándose sinónimos. Injurias es el delito que sanciona la expresión o acción que deshonra a otro. Malos tratos y sevicia se refieren a maltrato verbal o físico, generalmente con motivo de una relación familiar o de convivencia. Sevicia normalmente hace alusión a una crueldad excesiva.
En la actualidad el delito de injurias ha prácticamente desaparecido de la legislación penal de los países hispanos, siendo un delito del que se acusa cada vez más raramente. En contraste, en el ámbito civil injurias es usado frecuentemente como equivalente de lesión o daño, en vez del significado romano original de un ilícito que afrenta o causa ofensa al honor de una persona.
injurias graves *serious offense.*
injurias leves *minor offense.*
Rel: afrenta, *affront;* blasfemia, *blasphemy;* denuesto, *insult, affront;* difamación, *defamation;* insulto, *insult;* ofensa, *offense;* ultraje, *offense, wrongfulness.*
Ver: calumnia.
Ref: (Ar)CP a.109ss.; (Bo)CP a.287; (Co)CP a.220; (Ec)CP a.489; (Esp)CP a.208; (Mx)CP 348; (Pe)CP a.130; (RD)CP a.372.

injurias[2] **(daño)** *injury, damage.*

injusticia n. *unjust.* **injusto** adj. *unjust, unfair.*
injustamente adv. *unjustly, unfairly.* – Sin. iniquidad, *iniquity.*

inmigración n. *immigration.* **inmigrar** v. *to immigrate.* **inmigrante** n. *immigrant.*
inmigrado n. *landed immigrant.*
• Inmigración se refiere a la internación y establecimiento de personas extranjeras en un país

distinto de aquél en el que habitan permanentemente o del que son naturales.
Rel: deportación, *deportation;* refugiado, *refugee;* residente, *resident.*

inmoralidad n. *immorality.* **inmoral** adj. *immoral.*
– Sin. falta de ética, *lack of ethics.* venalidad, *venality.*

inmueble n. *real estate, immovable, realty.*
Ver: bienes inmuebles.

inmunidad n. *immunity.* **inmune** adj. *immune.*
– Sin. fuero, *legal privilege.* inviolabilidad, *immunity.*
inmunidad diplomática *diplomatic immunity.*
inmunidad parlamentaria *parliamentary immunity.*
Ver: indulto.

inocencia[1] **(candor)** n. *innocence.* **inocente** adj. *innocent.* – Sin. candor, *candor.* ingenuidad, *ingenuousness.*

inocencia[2] **(no culpable)** n. *innocence.* **inocente** adj. *innocent.*
• La falta o ausencia de culpa o dolo por parte del acusado de un delito.
Rel: inculpabilidad, [ed]*lack of culpability.*

inpunibilidad [ed]*lack of punishability.*
• La falta de aplicación del castigo o la pena al delito cometido por razones de justicia o equidad. – Sin. exclusión de la punibilidad. excusas absolutorias.
Ver: excluyentes de responsabilidad.

insaculación n. *balloting.* **insacular** v. *to ballot, choose by ballot.*

inscripción[1] **(registro)** n. *registration, recording.*
inscribir v. *to register.* **inscrito** adj. *registered.*
inscripción de una hipoteca *registration of a mortgage.*
inscripción en el registro civil *registration in the vital statistics registry.*
inscripción en registro de la propiedad *registration in a real estate registry.*

inscripción[2] **(partida)** n. *record, entry.*
inscripción registral *entry in a registry.*

inseminación artificial *artificial insemination.*

insolvencia n. *insolvency.* **insolvente** n. *insolvent.*
• La condición de no poder pagar las deudas a su vencimiento durante el transcurso normal de los negocios. Cesación de pagos por incapacidad de hacer frente a las deudas.
insolvencia culpable *negligent bankruptcy.*
insolvencia fraudulenta *fraudulent insolvency.*

insolvencia punible (crime) *criminal insolvency.*
Rel: concurso civil, *bankruptcy proceeding regulated by civil code;* liquidez, *liquidity;* quiebra, *bankruptcy;* suspensión de pagos, *proceeding of suspension of payments.*

inspección n. *inspection.* **inspeccionar** v. *to inspect.* **inspector** n. *inspector.* – Sin. examen. reconocimiento. verificación, *verification.*

inspección judicial *judicial inspection.*

inspección ocular *on-site inspection.*

instancia n. *instance, jurisdictional level.*
• "Cada una de las etapas o grados jurisdiccionales del proceso destinado al examen de la cuestión debatida y a su decisión." (De Pina, 323)

en última instancia *court of last resort.*

juzgado de primera instancia [ef]*trial court, court of first instance.*

segunda instancia *second instance, appeal.*

instigación n. *instigation.* **instigar** v. *to instigate.*

instigador n. *instigator.* – Sin. incitación, *incitation.*

instigación al delito *solicitation.* – Sin. inducción al delito. instigación a delinquir.

instigación al suicidio *aiding and abetting a suicide.* – Sin. auxilio e inducción al suicidio.

institución de asistencia privada *private charity institution.*

institución de crédito *financial institution.*

instrucción DER.PROC.PENAL n. [prest.]*instruccion,* [ed]*preliminary stage (of criminal proceedings).* [ef]*probable cause phase (of a criminal cause).* – Sin. sumario.
Ver: sumario.

instrumento[1] **(escrito)** n. *instrument.*
– Sin. documento. escritura, *legal document.*
En su sentido legal tiene la connotación de referirse a toda clase de prueba, si se le considera en forma amplia, y a la de documento cuando se le considera en forma restringida.

instrumento público *certified document.*

instrumento privado *private document.*

instrumentos de crédito *negotiable instruments.*

instrumentos comerciales *commercial paper.*

instrumento[2] **(objeto)** n. *device.*

instrumentos de trabajo *tools of the trade.*

instrumentos del delito *instruments of the crime.*

insubordinación n. *insubordination.*

insubordinado adj. *insubordinate.* **insubordinado** n. *insubordinate person.*

– Sin. indisciplina, *indiscipline.* rebeldía, *rebellion.*

insurrección n. *insurrection.* **insurreccionar** v. *to instigate insurrection.* **insurrecto** n. *insurrectionist, insurgent, rebel.* **insurrecto** adj. *insurrectional, insurgent.* – Sin. alzamiento, *uprising.* insurgencia, *insurgency.* levantamiento, *uprising, revolt.* rebelión, *rebellion.* revuelta, *revolt.* sublevación, *uprising, revolt.*

insustancial adj. *immaterial.* – Sin. irrelevante, *irrelevant.* – También: insustancial.

integración del derecho [ed]*judge's law-making authority (by way of interpretation of enacted law).*
• Función del juzgador quien usando su poder discrecional debe proveer una norma aplicable al caso bajo consideración cuando no exista una ley que le sea aplicable directamente.
Ver: interpretación. lagunas del derecho.

integración económica *economic integration.*
Rel: mercado común, *common market.*

intención[1] **(propósito)** n. *intent, intention.* **intencional** adj. *intentional.*
• El dirigir la voluntad a sabiendas hacia un fin determinado. – Sin. propósito. designio.

intención de las partes *intent of the parties.*

intención del legislador *legislative intent.*

intención[2] DER.PENAL n. *intent.*
• El orientar la voluntad consciente a la ejecución de un delito. – Sin. deliberadamente, *deliberately.* intencionalidad, *with intent, intentionally.*

intención delictuosa *criminal intent.* – Sin. dolo. intención delictiva.

intención criminal *felonious intent.*

intención homicida *with intent to kill, malice aforethough.*
Rel: imprudencia, *imprudence, negligence;* premeditación, *premeditation.*

intento n. *attempt.* **intentar** v. *to attempt.*
– Sin. tentativa, *attempt.*

intento de suicidio *suicide attempt.*

inter vivos (lat.) *inter vivos, among the living.*

intercepción clandestina telefónica *wiretapping.* – Sin. interceptación telefónica.
Rel: escuchas ilegales (Esp), *illegal eavesdropping;* interceptación de comunicación inalámbrica, *electronic eavesdropping of wireless communication.*

intercepción de conversaciones *bugging.*

intercepción de correspondencia *mail tampering.* – Sin. interceptación de correspondencia.

violación de correspondencia.

interdicción n. [ed]*legal deprivation of civilian rights*, [rtrgido]*civil commitment*, [prest.]interdiction (EEUU-La)(Esco.).

• "El estado de la persona a quien se declara total o parcialmente incapaz para ejercer actos de la vida civil." (Ramírez Gronda, 184)

Cf: **interdicción • incapacidad • inhabilitación.** Términos distinguibles que se refieren a la falta de capacidad de las personas. La incapacidad, que es el estado de ausencia de capacidad de una persona, y la interdicción, que es la declaración judicial de estar incapacitado, se dictan para proteger a las personas que no pueden actuar legalmente por sí mismas, en cambio la inhabilitación se dicta como una sanción judicial.

"El derecho mexicano se aparta de otros regímenes extranjeros, como el derecho español, que conocen la interdicción civil como una pena pública, a consecuencia de ciertos delitos de orden patrimonial.... [En México] la declaración de interdicción tiene por objeto la protección de la persona y los bienes del mayor de edad que ha caído en estado de incapacidad por ... estar privado de inteligencia, por locura, idiotismo o imbecilidad, [por ser] sordomudo y no saber leer ni escribir o [por ser] ebrio consuetudinario o drogadicto." (Dicc. UNAM, 1773)

Rel: demente, *insane;* pródigo, *spendthrift.*

interdicto n. [amplio][ef]*injunction*, [ed]*a possessory order or a temporary restraining order*, [prest.]*interdict.*

• Juicios posesorios de carácter sumario que tienen por objeto adquirir, retener o recobrar la posesión o tenencia, e impedir una obra nueva. – Sin. acciones posesorias.

"(Del latín interdicto, ere, prohibir. Originalmente interdictum designa una prohibición y luego un decreto dado por el magistrado que puede contener una prohibición o una orden de exhibición o restitución de una cosa.) Los interdictos son juicios sumarios por los que se decide transitoriamente una controversia sobre la posesión de un bien, a favor de aquella de las partes que parezca ser la que de hecho posee, pero sin resolver ni prejuzgar la cuestión de la propiedad de tal cosa." (Dicc. UNAM, 1774)

↦ "El recurso preventivo del injunction puede equipararse por su origen y efectos al interdicto de nuestro derecho civil [mexicano]; pero mientras que el interdicto romano está destinado exclusivamente a retener y recuperar la

'posesión' de un bien inmueble contra el perturbador y el despojador, respectivamente, y a suspender, demoler o modificar la 'obras nuevas' y las 'peligrosas' que sean perjudiciales al poseedor de una propiedad contigua o cercana, el injunction anglosajón es una acción ilimitada que cualquiera puede promover ante los tribunales de 'equidad', en contra de otro individuo particular, para impedir en la vía civil 'toda clase de violaciones' de los derechos subjetivos por actos u omisiones ilícitas, prohibiendo la ejecución de los primeros, caso en el cual el recurso se denomina prohibitory injunction o interdicto prohibitorio, o mandando que se cumpla la prestación omitida, en la segunda hipótesis, y entonces se llama mandatory injunction o interdicto mandatorio." (Rabasa, 50)

interdicto de obra nueva *injunction to stop new construction.*

interdicto de obra peligrosa *injunction to stop dangerous or deteriorated construction.* – Sin. interdicto de obra ruinosa.

interdicto de recobrar *injunction restoring possession.*

interdicto de retener *injunction to prohibit interference with possession.*

interdicto interlocutorio *interlocutory injunction.*

Ver: *injunction.*

Ref: (Ar)CPC a.6064ss.; (Ch)CC a.930ss.; (Ec)CC a.994,996; (Mx)CPC a.16-20; (Pe)CC a.921,2019-2043; (Ur)CC a.658ss.; (Ve)CPC a.697-719.

interés¹ (rédito) *interest.*

• Renta, beneficio o lucro producido por el capital. – Sin. rédito.

capitalización de intereses *compounding of interest.*

interés compuesto *compound interest.*

interés convencional *contractual interest.*

interés legal *legal interest.*

interés moratorio *interest for late payment.*

interés simple *simple interest.*

intereses devengados *accrued interest.*

intereses financieros *interest income.*

intereses moratorios *late fee, late charge.*

intereses por pagar *interest payable.*

cuenta que produce interés *interest-bearing account.*

interés² (pretensión) *interest.*

• Pretensión que se encuentra reconocida o protegida por la norma jurídica.

interés adquirido *vested interest.*

interés asegurado *insured interest.*

interés común *common interest.*

interés jurídico *juridical interest.*
interés legal *legal interest.*
interés privado *private interest.*
interés público *public interest.*
interinato n. *temporary position.* **interino** adj. *temporary, interim.* **interino** n. *replacement, stand-in.* **interinamente** adv. *temporarily.* – Sin. provisional, *provisional.* suplente, *replacement.* temporal, *temporary.* transitorio, *transitory.*
intermediación n. *intermediation.* **intermediar** v. *to intermediate, mediate.* **intermediario** n. *intermediary, middleman.*
internación de enfermos mentales *commitment of the mentally disabled.*
interpelación n. *questioning, demand, interpellation.*
interpósita persona *mediator, intermediary.*
interpretación[1] (idiomas) *language interpretation.* **interpretar** v. *to interpret.* **intérprete** n. *interpreter.*
• Expresar oralmente el equivalente a lo dicho en otro idioma.
interpretación consecutiva *consecutive interpretation.*
interpretación oral de un texto *sight interpretation, sight translation.*
interpretación simultánea *simultaneous interpretation.*
Ver: traducción.
interpretación[2] (normas) *interpretation of the law.* **interpretar** v. *to interpret.* **interpretativo** adj. *interpretative.*
• Se entiende por interpretación el discernir o determinar el sentido o significado de una norma jurídica. – Sin. hermenéutica, *hermeneutics.* Cf: **interpretación • integración.** La interpretación se da al aplicar el juzgador la ley al caso concreto, desentrañando el significado de las normas o leyes aplicables. Cuando la ley o norma jurídica no pueda aplicarse a un caso concreto, el juez, quien está obligado a dar una solución, deberá ir más allá de la interpretación y crear una norma nueva, o cuando menos una aplicación nueva de la norma aplicable al caso, lo que constituye la llamada integración del derecho (que algunos consideran todavía una forma de interpretación).
⌐ La interpretación de la norma juega un papel fundamental en los sistemas de derecho romano-germánico. La generalidad de la ley concede al juez que la aplica un margen de discreción, definida como la esfera propia del juzgador, que éste debe llenar mediante una labor de interpretación que adecue la norma al caso concreto. Dicha interpretación se dirige esencialmente, como se dijo, a desentrañar el significado de la ley, incluso a suplementarla si ambigua o carente, a diferencia del juzgador en el sistema de derecho angloamericano en el que la *rule of law* está definida concretamente, y ante la que éste debe hacer una *distinction* clara de sus diferencias con otros casos ya decididos, para justificar la adopción de una decisión que modifique a la ya sentada y, por ende, considerada obligatoria o determinante.
interpretación auténtica *legislator's interpretation, legislative interpretation.*
interpretación constitucional *constitutional interpretation.*
interpretación de los contratos *interpretation of contracts.*
interpretación de tratados *interpretation of treaties.*
interpretación doctrinal *doctrinal interpretation.*
interpretación estricta *strict interpretation.* – Sin. interpretación restrictiva.
interpretación exegética *exegetical interpretation.*
interpretación extensiva *broad interpretation.*
interpretación histórica *historical interpretation.*
interpretación literal *literal interpretation.*
interpretación penal *interpretation of criminal laws.*
interpretación por analogía *interpretation by analogy.* – Sin. interpretación analógica.
Rel: analogía, *analogy;* equidad, *equity;* integración, *judge's law-making authority (by way of interpretation);* lagunas del derecho, *gaps in the law;* principios generales del derecho, *general principles of the law.*
interrogatorio[1] DER.PROC.PENAL n. *interrogation.* **interrogar** v. *to interrogate.* **interrogado** n. *person under interrogation.* **interrogado** adj. *interrogated.* **interrogador** n. *interrogator.* **interrogación** n. *questioning.*
• Actividad probatoria por la que el juez y las partes hacen preguntas a un testigo para establecer los hechos en una causa, normalmente durante el sumario o su equivalente.
interrogatorio de testigos *witness examination* || *interrogation of witnesses.*
interrogatorio del detenido *interrogation of the detainee.*

interrogatorio[2] DER.PROC.CIVIL n. *reply to interrogatories.*

• Lista de preguntas por escrito hechas a una de las partes, quien deberá contestarlas desahogando la testimonial correspondiente. – Sin. absolución de posiciones.

intervención[1] DER.PROC.CIV n. *intervention.* **intervenir** v. *to intervene.*

intervención de tercero *third party intervention.*

intervención forzosa *compulsory intervention.*

Rel: tercería, *third party.*

intervención[2] DER.MERC n. *intervention, mediation.*

intervención bancaria *takeover of a bank by regulators.*

intervención en la letra de cambio *voluntary acceptance and payment of a bill of exchange by a third party.*

intervención[3] DER.INTL n. *intervention.* **intervenir** v. *to intervene.* **intervencionismo** n. *interventionism.*

intervención armada *armed intervention.*

intervención[4] SOCIEDADES n. *inspection, audit.*

interventor n. *inspector.*

intestado n. *intestate.* – Sin. ab intestato (lat.), *ab intestato.* juicio intestado, *intestate proceedings.* sucesión intestada, *intestate succession.* sucesión legítima, *intestate succession.*

Este término es generalmente usado para indicar que la persona no dejó testamento, así como para referirse al procedimiento legal que debe seguirse.

Rel: sucesión testamentaria, *testate succession.*

Ref: (Ar)CC a.3545-3548 y 3565-3590; (Ch)CC a. 980ss.; (Ec)CC a.1043ss.; (Esp)CC a.912ss.; (Mx) CC a.1599-1637; (Pe)CC a.815ss.; (PR)CC a.875, 31 LPRA sec. 2591; (Ur)CC a.1011; (Ve)CC a.808ss.

intimidación n. *intimidation.* **intimidar** v. *to intimidate.* **intimidado** n. *intimidated person.* **intimidado** adj. *intimidated.* – Sin. atemorizar, *to terrify, frighten.* asustar, *frighten.*

intoxicación n. *intoxication.* **intoxicar** v. *to intoxicate.* **intoxicado** v. *intoxicated person.* **intoxicado** adj. *intoxicated.*

intrusismo (delito)(Esp) *acts of usurpation of professional status.*

intuitu personae (lat.) *intuitu personae, in consideration of the person.*

invalidez[1] **(discapacidad)** n. *disability.* **inválido** n. *invalid.*

• "La inhabilidad o decadencia física permanente, con pérdida o disminución considerable de las energías naturales y de la capacidad para el trabajo." (IV Cabanellas, 489) – Sin. discapacidad. incapacidad.

invalidez absoluta *total disability.* – Sin. invalidez total.

invalidez parcial *partial disability,* – Sin. invalidez relativa.

invalidez permanente *permanent disability.* – Sin. invalidez definitiva.

invalidez provisional *temporary disability.* – Sin. invalidez transitoria.

invalidez[2] **(ineficacia)** CONTRATOS n. *invalidity.* **invalidar** v. *to invalidate.* **inválido** adj. *invalid.* **invalidación** n. *invalidation.*

• La falta de efectos jurídicos de un contrato por la ausencia de algún elemento necesario para su eficacia. – Sin. falta de validez, *invalidity.*

causas de invalidez *causes of contract invalidation.*

Rel: nulidad, *nullity;* vicio, *defect.*

invasión n. *invasion* || *infringement.* **invadir** v. *to invade.* **invasor** n. *invader.*

invasión de derechos *infringement of rights.*

invasión de tierras *invasion of lands, encroachment of lands.*

Rel: intrusión, *intrusion;* transgresión, *transgression.*

invenciones y marcas *patent and trademark laws.* – Sin. propiedad industrial, *industrial property.*

Rel: aviso y nombre comercial, *tradename.* denominación de origen, *certification mark of origin;* marca, *trademark;* patente, *patent.*

inventario n. *inventory.* – Sin. bienes de cambio (Ar). existencias.

inventario constante *perpetual inventory.*

inventario final *closing inventory.*

rotación de inventario *inventory turnover.*

inversión n. *investment.* **inversionista** n. *investor.*

inversión a corto plazo *short term investment.*

inversión a largo plazo *long term investment.*

inversión extranjera *foreign investment.*

inversión extranjera en el capital de una empresa *foreign investment in the capital stock of a company.*

monto de la inversión extranjera *amount of foreign investment.*

participación extranjera en la administración de una empresa *foreign* *participation in the management of a company.* Rel: cláusula de exclusión de extranjeros, *exclusion of foreigners clause;* sociedad o empresa coligada (Ch), *company with minority participation in capital or management from another company.*

investidura n. *investiture.*

investigación n. *investigation.* **investigar** v. *to investigate.* **investigador** n. *investigator.* – Sin. averiguación, *inquiry.* escrutinio, *scrutiny.* indagación. pesquisa, *inquiry, investigation.*

investigación a fondo *full investigation.*

investigación de la paternidad *investigation of paternity.*

investigación de un delito *criminal investigation.*

investigador privado *private investigator.*

inviolabilidad n. *inviolability.* **inviolable** adj. *inviolable.* **inviolado** adj. *inviolate.* – Sin. inmunidad, *immunity.*

inviolabilidad de la correspondencia *inviolability of the correspondence by mail.*

inviolabilidad de un domicilio *inviolability of the domicile.*

inviolabilidad parlamentaria *parliamentary immunity.*

ipso facto (lat.) *ipso facto, by the fact itself.*
• Producido por el hecho mismo.

ipso jure (lat.) *ipso jure, by operation of the law.*
• Por disposición o ministerio de la ley.

irretroactividad n. *nonretroactivity.*
• Es el principio de derecho que establece que las leyes o disposiciones jurídicas no deben ser aplicadas a hechos anteriores a la entrada en vigencia de dichas leyes o disposiciones. – Ant. retroactividad, *retroactivity.*

irrevocable n. *irrevocable.* **irrevocabilidad** n. *irrevocability.* **irrevocablemente** adv. *irrevocably.* – Ant. revocable, *revocable.*

carta de crédito irrevocable *irrevocable letter of credit.*

iter criminis (lat.) *iter criminis, the steps or journey of the crime.*
La fase de concepción de un delito, desde la aparición de la idea en la mente del delincuente hasta el acto material de su ejecución. – Sin. camino del crimen.

ius ad bellum (lat.) *ius ad bellum, right to war.*

JJJJ

jactancia n. *slander of title* || *jactitation.*

jefe de estado n. *head of state.*

jefe de gobierno n. *head of government.*

jornada de trabajo *day's work* || *work shift.* **jornalero** n. *day laborer.* **jornal** n. *day's wage.* – Sin. jornada laboral.

jornada nocturna *night shift.*

jornada semanal de 40 horas *40-hour week.*

jubilación *retirement.* **jubilar** v. *to retire.* **jubilado** n. *pensioner, retiree.* **jubilarse** v. *to retire voluntarily.*
• Retiro concedido a un trabajador al cumplir cierto numero de años de servicio, con pagos periódicos basados en el salario percibido. – Sin. retiro.

jubilación anticipada *early retirement.*

jubilación forzosa *mandatory retirement.*

jubilación voluntaria *voluntary retirement.*

judicatura n. *judicature, judiciary.*

judicial adj. *judicial.* **judicialmente** adv. *judicially.*

proceder judicialmente *to take legal action.*

juego n. *gambling.* **jugador** n. *gambler.*

casa de juego *gambling house.*

juego de azahar *game of chance.* – Sin. juego de suerte.

juego y apuesta (contrato) *betting and gambling.*

juegos prohibidos (delito)(Mx) *illegal gambling.*
Rel: bolita, *lottery;* lotería, *lottery.*

juez n. *judge.* **juzgar** v. *to judge.*
• Es la persona designada por el estado para administrar justicia, estando dotada de jurisdicción para decidir litigios y de poder para ejecutar sus decisiones. – Sin. juzgador, *judge, person adjudging.* magistrado, *judge, justice.*
Cf: **juez • magistrado.** Términos sinónimos que son diferenciados frecuentemente sin existir consistencia en tal diferenciación. Cuando se les usa genéricamente ambos se usan indistintamente, usados en forma más restringida, sin embargo, juez es considerado el titular de un juzgado, mientras magistrado frecuentemente se aplica al titular de un tribunal colegiado y en la mayoría de las ocasiones de superior jerarquía.

juez a quo (lat.) *ad quo judge, judge to whom.* Desde el (juez) que (se apela).

juez ad quem (lat.) *ad quem judge, judge before whom.* Para el cual (ante el juez que se apela).

juez civil *civil judge.* – Sin. juez de lo civil.

juez competente *judge of competent jurisdiction.*

juez de apelación *appellate judge.* – Sin. juez de alzada.

juez de carrera *professional judge.*

juez de circuito *circuit judge.*

juez de distrito *district judge.*

juez de instrucción *investigating judge,* [ed]*judge of the preliminary stage of criminal proceeding, examining magistrate* (UK). – Sin. juez instructor. funcionario de instrucción.

juez de paz *justice of the peace.*

juez de primera instancia *trial judge, judge of first instance.* – Sin. juez de la causa.

juez de turno *sitting judge.*

juez federal *federal judge.*

juez lego *lay judge.*

juez letrado [ed]*judge who is an attorney.* – Sin. juez de letras.

juez menor *magistrate, justice of the peace.*

juez mixto [ed]*judge who hears both civil and criminal matters.*

juez municipal *municipal judge.*

juez penal *criminal judge.* – Sin. juez de lo criminal.

juez ponente [ed]*judge who writes the court's opinion.*

recusación de un juez *recusal of a judge.*

remoción de un juez *removal of a judge.*

Rel: amigable componedor, *mediator appointed by mutual agreement (between the parties),* [fr.]*amiable compositeur;* árbitro, *arbiter;* mediador, *mediator.*

> Comentario: "En el sistema romano-germánico la justicia es dictada por jueces profesionales e inamovibles que consideran la función judicial como una carrera y el cuerpo judicial como un cuerpo autónomo respecto de la administración, del Estado y de los mismos prácticos del Derecho." (David, 102)

juicio¹ (proceso) *proceedings, lawsuit, trial.*

actor n. *plaintiff.* **demandado** n. *defendant.*

• El término juicio puede ser concebido en forma amplia y se dice que consiste en la presentación y sustanciación de una controversia ante un juez, quien la resuelve mediante una sentencia o fallo; pero también puede ser entendido en forma restringida y se dice entonces que es el conjunto de actuaciones o etapas procedimentales mediante las cuales se desenvuelve un proceso. – Sin. proceso. causa, *cause, trial.* pleito, *lawsuit.*

Cf: **juicio ● proceso ● procedimiento.** Juicio es un término que es usado frecuentemente como sinónimo de proceso y de procedimiento, con los que generalmente se confunde. Juicio generalmente se usa como sinónimo de proceso cuando se le entiende en forma amplia, y con procedimiento cuando se le considera en forma restringida. Procedimiento es la manera de hacer una cosa o realizar un acto, más específicamente, la secuencia de actos o etapas para llevar a cabo un proceso. Proceso es el objetivo al que se dirige el procedimiento, o sea concretamente el dirimir una controversia mediante la toma de una decisión por parte de un órgano jurisdiccional. Para aquellos que juicio es un término diferenciable se señala que a diferencia del proceso y del procedimiento, el juicio se refiere al conocimiento de una causa concreta en la cual el juez se ha de pronunciar. La tendencia moderna, pero de ninguna manera aceptada por unanimidad, es hablar de juicio al referirse a la etapa de juzgamiento (o plenario) en el proceso penal, y hablar de proceso o procedimiento al referirse a casos de índole administrativo, civil o laboral.

⊷ Juicio y *trial* son a veces equivalentes, y a veces no lo son. Son equivalentes cuando juicio es usado en forma amplia, esto es con el significado de la presentación de una controversia ante el juez, quien debe resolverla; asimismo, lo son cuando juicio se refiere a la etapa final del procedimiento penal (o plenario). No son equivalentes cuando juicio tiene un significado restringido, esto es el significado de una sucesión de pasos o etapas concretas dirigidas a formar un expediente que el juez utilizará para tomar su decisión. En tal caso *proceedings* o *cause* son generalmente equivalentes más apropiados.

iniciar juicio *to bring a lawsuit.*

juicio arbitral *arbitration proceedings* || *arbitration.*

juicio civil ordinario *plenary civil action.*

juicio civil *civil suit.*

juicio con jurados *jury trial.* – Sin. juicio ante jurados.

juicio de alimentos *support proceedings or alimony proceedings.*

juicio de amparo *amparo suit, amparo writ.*

juicio de consignación *judicial deposit of property or money.*

juicio de desahucio *eviction proceedings.*

juicio de divorcio *divorce, divorce proceedings.*

juicio de mayor cuantía *major or valuable claim proceedings.*

juicio de menor cuantía *small claim proceedings.*

juicio en rebeldía *action in default.*

juicio expedito *speedy trial.*

juicio hipotecario *mortgage foreclosure proceedings.*

juicio intestado *intestate proceedings.*

juicio laboral *labor law action or proceedings.*

juicio mercantil *mercantile proceedings.*

juicio militar *court martial proceedings.*

juicio oral *oral trial or proceedings.*

juicio penal *criminal trial.* – Sin. juicio criminal.

juicio político *political trial.*

juicio posesorio *possessory action.*

juicio sucesorio *probate proceedings.*

juicio sumario *summary proceeding.* – Sin. proceso abreviado (CR).

juicio sumarísimo *expedited summary proceeding.*

juicio testamentario *testamentary proceeding.*

juicio² DER.PROC.PENAL *trial.* – Sin. juicio penal. plenario.
Ver: plenario.

juicio ejecutivo [prest.]*executory process,* [ed]*summary process based on a document (usually a negotiable instrument).*

• Es un juicio especial que se funda en un documento que constituye, por sí solo, prueba eficaz de la existencia de un derecho de crédito que se reclama, permitiendo la vía sumaria y el inmediato embargo, y posterior remate de bienes necesarios para cubrir el adeudo y las costas ocasionadas.

juicio ejecutivo hipotecario *foreclosure proceeding.*
Rel: auto de exequendo, *writ of attachment.*

juicio ordinario *plenary action,* [ed]*full regular proceedings.*

• Es el proceso tipo contencioso que se aplica a cualquier contienda judicial que no quede comprendida en los casos de procedimiento especial. – Sin. juicio ordinario civil.

juicio universal [ed]*proceeding including all assets of a person.*

• Es aquel proceso judicial que se refiere a la totalidad de los bienes y derechos que consti-

tuyen el patrimonio de una persona. Se clasifican en inter vivos (concurso civil, quiebras) y mortis causa (intestados y testamentarias).

junta¹ (reunión) n. *meeting.* – Sin. asamblea, *assembly.* reunión, *meeting.*

junta de accionistas *stockholders' meeting.*

junta de acreedores *creditor's meeting.*

junta de propietarios *owner's meeting.*

junta de reconciliación (divorcio) *reconciliation meeting.* – Sin. junta de avenencia.

junta de socios *partner's meeting.*

junta² (estructura) n. *board.* – Sin. comité, *committee.* consejo, *council.*

junta de apelación *board of appeals.*

junta consultiva *advisory board.* – Sin. junta asesora.

junta de administración *board of administration.*

junta de conciliación *arbitration board.*

junta electoral *electoral board.*

Junta de Conciliación y Arbitraje (Mx) *labor board, labor court,* [el]*Labor Arbitration and Conciliation Board.*

jurado n. *jury.* **jurado** n. *juror.*

• Tribunal compuesto por juzgadores no profesionales o legos, que tiene como función emitir un veredicto con base en el cual el juez debe emitir la sentencia. – Sin. juzgador lego, *lay judge.*

⮡ La importancia fundamental que el *jury* juega en el sistema procesal de la *common law* no existe en los sistemas de derecho romano-germánico. Su presencia en éstos es aún débil y tentativa, y a diferencia del derecho anglosajón la existencia del jurado no ha resultado en el desarrollo de formas procedimentales, como las reglas detalladas de exclusión de pruebas, por ejemplo, que permitan y procuren su mejor funcionamiento.

jurado de conciencia *jury formed to hear of high crimes, special jury.*

jurado dividido *hung jury.*

jurado popular *jury, lay jury.*

jurado suplente *alternate juror.*

seleccionar un jurado *impaneling a jury.*
Ref: (Mx)LOPJF a.52-63 CFPP a.308-350; (Esp)C a.125.

juramento n. *oath.* **jurar** v. *to swear.*

juramentar v. *to swear in.* **jurado** adj. *sworn.*

• Pronunciamiento de que lo aseverado o afirmado es verdadero invocando a Dios, especialmente aquel hecho ante una autoridad o un juez. – Sin.protesta, *affirmation*.

bajo juramento *under oath.*

habiendo prestado juramento *being duly sworn.*

perito jurado *sworn expert witness.*

prestar juramento *to take an oath.*

Ver: protesta[1].

juridicidad n. *lawfulness, legality.*

juris et de jure (lat.) *juris et de jure, of law and of right.*

• De pleno derecho. Que está basada en derecho y no admite prueba en contrario.

juris tantum (lat.) *juris tantum, of law until controverted.*

• Algo que es evidente y convincente tomando en cuenta las circunstancias, pero que admite y puede ser desvirtuado por prueba en contrario. – Sin. iuris tantum.

jurisconsulto n. *jurist, jurisconsult.*

jurisdicción[1] **(potestad)** n. *jurisdiction.*

jurisdiccional adj. *jurisdictional.*

• "La jurisdicción es la potestad conferida por el Estado a determinados órganos para resolver, mediante la sentencia, las cuestiones litigiosas que les sean sometidas y hacer cumplir sus propias resoluciones." (II Alsina, 414) – Sin. poder, *power*. potestad.

El término jurisdicción es usado frecuentemente sin la precisión que le otorga tradicionalmente la doctrina. Así en ocasiones jurisdicción se identifica con el conjunto de negocios sometidos ante un juez, con la autoridad requerida para gobernar o ejecutar las leyes, o con el territorio dentro del cual un funcionario ejerce sus atribuciones.

Cf: **jurisdicción ● competencia.** Ambos términos se usan indistintamente con frecuencia, sin embargo son claramente identificables jurídicamente, ya que jurisdicción se refiere a la potestad o poder que tiene atribuido un órgano judicial para dirimir controversias, mientras que competencia es la medida de distribución de controversias que se otorga concretamente a cada órgano judicial. La jurisdicción es una función del estado, mientras que la competencia es el límite de esa función, el ámbito de validez de la misma.

jurisdicción civil *civil jurisdiction.*

jurisdicción concurrente *concurrent jurisdiction.*

jurisdicción contenciosa-administrativa *administrative suits.*

jurisdicción de primera instancia *jurisdiction in the first instance, original jurisdiction.*

jurisdicción federal *federal jurisdiction.*

jurisdicción militar *military jurisdiction.*

jurisdicción prorrogada *ancillary or pendent jurisdiction.*

Rel: competencia, [ed]*court's jurisdictional authority.*

jurisdicción[2] **(órganos)** n. *jurisdiction.*

• Organización jurisdiccional. Conjunto de órganos que tienen atribuida jurisdicción.

jurisdicción militar *military court jurisdiction.*

jurisdicción religiosa *religious jurisdiction.*

jurisdicción voluntaria *voluntary jurisdiction proceedings.*

jurisprudencia[1] **(doctrina)** n. *jurisprudence, case law.*

• Es la doctrina que establece un criterio uniforme de interpretación y aplicación de las leyes a través de las decisiones emitidas por los tribunales. – Sin. doctrina legal (Esp), *jurisprudence.*

↦ A pesar de la mayor importancia que ha recibido la jurisprudencia en los sistemas romano-germánicos, aún se encuentra lejos de alcanzar la preponderancia y eficacia que la *jurisprudence* tiene en los sistemas de derecho anglosajón. Mientras el sistema anglosajón está basado en una larga tradición de la aplicación obligatoria de sentencias que reúnen ciertos requisitos, el sistema romanogermánico no otorga a los precedentes, en la mayoría de los casos, la obligatoriedad necesaria para permitir la construcción de un número importante de nuevas reglas de derecho. En consecuencia, en países hispanos siempre es posible una alteración de la jurisprudencia establecida sin una adecuada explicación, ya que normalmente ello no interfiere con la permanencia del esquema sistematizado de derecho, que es el fundamento de la tradición romano-germánica.

jurisprudencia obligatoria *judicial precedent, judge-made law.*

jurisprudencia sentada *established legal precedent.*

Rel: ejecutoria, [ed]*final sentence or judgment in a case (when sustained after appeal or when non-appealed), final judicial decision;* usus fori, *rule of court.*

Ref: (Mx)LA a.94-V,192-197 LOPJF; (Esp)CC a.1.

Ver: *precedent.*

jurisprudencia[2] **(ciencia)** n. *jurisprudence, the science of law.*

jurista n. *jurist.*

jus sanguinis (lat.) *jus sanguinis, right of blood.*
• La nacionalidad de la persona se establece por la nacionalidad que tienen los padres.

jus soli (lat.) *jus soli, right of the soil.*
• La nacionalidad de la persona se establece por el lugar de nacimiento.

justicia[1] **(equidad)** n. *justice.* – Sin. equidad.

justicia[2] **(organización)** n. *courts, judiciary.*
  justicia federal *federal courts.*
  justicia militar *military courts.*

justificantes *justification.*
Ver: causas de justificación.

juzgado n. *court.* **juzgador** n. *judge, person adjudging.* **juzgamiento** n. *action of judging, judgment.*
• Organo judicial cuya titularidad la ostenta el juez. También se entiende por juzgado el lugar en donde actúa el juez. – Sin. corte, *court.* tribunal, *tribunal.*
Cf: **juzgado • tribunal • corte.** Términos usados sinónimamente con frecuencia, pero que pueden diferenciarse, y que no son intercambiables en ciertos casos. Juzgado es el término común para describir el órgano judicial de primera instancia constituido por un solo juez y sus auxiliares. Tribunal normalmente se refiere a un órgano colegiado o pluripersonal y en la mayoría de las ocasiones superior en jerarquía. Por su parte corte ha sido usada en forma imprecisa, refiriéndose en ocasiones a un juzgado de orden común, en otras a un tribunal supremo o a uno de jurisdicción especial, e incluso a una Asamblea legislativa.

juzgado civil *civil court.* – Sin. juzgado de lo civil.

juzgado de circuito *circuit court.*

juzgado de distrito *district court.*

juzgado de guardia *night court* || *holiday court.*

juzgado de lo contencioso-administrativo [ed]*administrative law court.*

juzgado de lo familiar *court of domestic relations, family court.* – Sin. juzgado de relaciones familiares. juzgado de familia.

juzgado de lo social (Esp) *labor court, labor board.* – Sin. junta de conciliación y arbitraje (Mx).

juzgado de paz *court of the justice of peace.*

juzgado de primera instancia *court of original jurisdiction, court of first instance.*

juzgado municipal *municipal court.*

juzgado penal *criminal court.* – Sin. juzgado de lo penal.

secretaría del juzgado *clerk's office.*
Rel: oficialía de partes, *filing desk;* sala, *division of a court or tribunal.*
Ver: personal de un juzgado, *court.*

LLLL

ladrón n. *thief.* **ladronear** v. *to go about stealing or shoplifting.* **ladronzuelo** n. *petty thief.*
Rel: asaltante, *robber, assailant;* atracador, *hold up man;* bandido, *bandit;* caco (mod.), *thief;* carterista, *pickpocket;* cleptómano, *kleptomaniac;* hurtador, *thief;* rata (mod.), *sneak thief;* ratero, *petty thief, shoplifter;* robacasas, *burglar;* robachicos, *child kidnapper.*

lagunas del derecho [ed]*gaps in the law, lacunae.*
• Se da una laguna del derecho cuando el derecho, considerado como un orden jurídico total y completo en una jurisdicción determinada, no contiene la solución jurídica explícita para una controversia dada.
Cf: **laguna del derecho • laguna de la ley.** Términos usados intercambiablemente con frecuencia debido a su ambigüedad. En estricto sentido jurídico se hace una distinción de grado, ya que mientras laguna de derecho se refiere al caso en el que no hay ley o norma aplicable al caso concreto, laguna de la ley se aplica para la situación en la que un caso concreto no encuentra regulación por parte de una ley que debiera hacerlo, como por ejemplo cuando dos ordenamientos se contradicen, anulándose entre sí y creando la laguna.
↳ Según la tradición romano-germánica, en principio todas las normas requeridas para resolver casos concretos están contenidas en un orden jurídico dado en forma implícita. Se trata de un orden completo, total y al que frecuentemente se le refiere como "la plenitud hermética del derecho". Cuando se da una laguna, la solución se busca mediante la interpretación de las normas que, expresadas en forma general y abstracta, permiten encontrar la regla concreta aplicable al caso. Se trata de un proceso interpretativo fundamentalmente (aunque algunos consideren que es también "creativo," si bien en forma limitada). El sistema anglosajón no pretende consistir en una estructura normativa totalizadora, sus normas son en efecto reglas de derecho que provienen de casos concretos expresadas en

forma individualizada y aplicables solamente a casos similares. En consecuencia, el derecho angloamericano al encontrarse ante la falta de reglas de derecho aplicables a un caso concreto, prefiere referirse a la creación de reglas de derecho nuevas, ya que al no existir un precedente que sea aplicable al caso concreto el juzgador deberá crear una nueva regla, de la misma manera que está facultado para modificar una regla existente si así lo considera necesario. La falta de una regla de derecho aplicable al caso concreto es un *gap of the law*, similar a la laguna del derecho, pero mientras en el primer caso se trata de un evento común y esperado, en el segundo se trata de una situación excepcional y problemática.

Rel: integración, [ed]*judge's law-making authority (by way of interpretation);* lagunas de la ley, *gaps in the legislation, legal loophole;* plenitud hermética del derecho, [el] *hermetic completeness of the juridical order.*

lanzamiento n. *eviction or dispossession.* **lanzar** v. *to evict or dispossess.*

latifundio *large-landed estate,* [lat.]*latifundium.* **latifundismo** n. *ownership of large landed estates.* **latifundista** n. *owner of a latifundio.*

• Propiedad rural de gran extensión dedicada a actividades agropecuarias asociada con sociedades tradicionales y una clase predominante de propietarios terratenientes.

latinismos *Latin expressions, Latin terms.* Ver: Apéndice C. Latinismos.

latu sensu (lat.) *latu sensu, broadly.*

laudo n. *award.*

• Fallo o decisión que emite un árbitro o un amigable componedor.

Las Juntas de Conciliación y Arbitraje en México emiten los llamados "laudos", aunque su naturaleza jurídica es la de una decisión judicial en materia laboral.

Cf: **laudo • sentencia • veredicto.** Términos claramente diferenciados por la doctrina y la legislación: laudo es el término normalmente usado para referirse a una decisión emitida por un árbitro, sentencia es el término preferido para referirse a una decisión judicial emitida por un juez, y veredicto es el nombre dado a un fallo dictado por un jurado.

laudo arbitral *arbitration award.*

Rel: decisión, *decision;* fallo, *ruling.*

lavado de dinero *money-laundering.*

• La operación de hacer aparecer como legítimo dinero proveniente de transacciones ilega-

les, especialmente el adquirido en el tráfico de drogas. – Sin. blanqueo de dinero. blanqueo de capitales. reciclaje de dinero.

leasing (transpl.) n. *leasing.* – Sin. arrendamiento financiero.

legación DER.INT n. *legation.* – Sin. delegación, *delegation.* embajada, *embassy.* representación, *delegation.*

legado SUCESIONES n. *testamentary gift,* [rtrgido] *legacy,* [rtrgido]*devise.* **legar** v. *to bequeath, leave.* **legatario** n. *beneficiary, legatee, devisee.*

• Constituye legado la asignación de un bien o bienes, parte de una masa hereditaria, en favor de una persona hecha por el autor de un testamento o de otro acto de última voluntad. – Sin. manda (Esp) (old).

⌐ Los términos usados para referirse a disposiciones testamentarias de bienes son legado en español y *legacy* y *devise* en inglés. Mientras los legados se refieren a uno o varios bienes sin importar su naturaleza, *legacy* se aplica a bienes muebles solamente, en tanto que *devise* es el término usado para designar la disposición testamentaria de bienes inmuebles exclusivamente.

la cosa legada correrá a riesgo del legatario *the thing bequeathed shall be at the risk of the legatee.*

legado alternativo *alternative testamentary gift.*

legado causal *testamentary gift in which the reason for the gift is specified.*

legado condicional *conditional testamentary gift.*

legado de alimentos *legacy of necessities.*

legado de cantidad *testamentary gift by reference to specific amount or quantity of a class of things.*

legado de cosa ajena *testamentary gift of another's property.*

legado de cosa específica o especificada *specific testamentary gift.* – Sin. legado de cosa cierta. legado de cosa determinada.

legado de cosa genérica *testamentary gift of property specified in generic terms.*

legado de cosa gravada *testamentary gift of encumbered property.*

legado de crédito *legacy of the right to monies owed to the testator.*

legado de educación *testamentary gift for the purpose of providing education to certain persons.*

legado de liberación *legacy forgiving a debt.*

legado de menaje de casa *legacy of household furnishings.*
Rel: sucesión, *succession;* testamento, *will.*

legal adj. *lawful, legal.* **legalizar** v. *to legalize.*
legalidad n. *legality.* **legalístico** *legalistic.*
legalmente adv. *legally.* **legalismo** n. *legality, legal technicality.* – Sin. lícito, *licit.*
Rel: ilegal; *illegal;* legítimo, *legitimate.*

legalización n. *authentication or attestation of signatures and legal capacity (of signing parties of a document).*
"Legalización [es] la 'comprobación y confirmación de la verdad de un documento', y legalizar es 'dar fuerza legal a un instrumento, autorizarlo del modo más conveniente para que tenga fe y valga en cualquier lugar y en todas las circunstancias.' En sentido estrictamente notarial, legalización es certificación dada por uno o más notarios o funcionarios que aseguran la autenticidad de una firma." (Dicc. ed. Comares, 315)
Cf: **legalización • certificación.** La legalización se dirige al establecimiento de la legitimidad legal de un documento mediante la comprobación de la capacidad legal de las partes y la verificación de sus firmas; la certificación por su parte, se dirige al establecimiento de la existencia de un registro o de un hecho hecha por la autoridad o persona legítimamente facultada para ello.
Rel: certificación, *certification, jurat;* cotejo, *comparison, collation;* tener a la vista, *before me;* suscrito ante mi, *signed before me.*
Ver: visa.

legislación n. *legislation.* **legislar** v. *to legislate.*
legislador n. *legislator.* **legislativo** adj. *legislative.* **legislable** adj. *able to be regulated by legislation.* – Sin. ley, *statute.*
legislación de urgencia *emergency legislation.*
legislación delegada *delegated legislative authority.*
Ver: proceso legislativo.

legislatura n. *legislature.* **legislador** n. *legislator.* **legislativo** adj. *legislative.*

legítima SUCESIONES n. [prest.]*legitime/legitim, legal portion (of an estate).*
• "Parte de la herencia que corresponde a los herederos por la ley y de la que no puede disponer quien hace testamento." (Martínez Marín y otros, 259) – Sin. herencia legítima.
fijación de la legítima [ed]*determination of the portion (of an estate) set aside by law,* [ext.lexico]*determination of the legitime.*

legítima de ascendientes [ed]*portion (of an estate) set aside for ascendants,* [ext.lexico] *legitime of ascendants.*
legítima de cónyuge supérstite [ed]*portion (of an estate) set aside for a widowed spouse,* [ext.lexico]*legitime of the widowed spouse.*
legítima de descendientes [ed]*portion (of an estate) set aside for descendants,* [ext.lexico] *legitime of descendants.*
Rel: heredero forzoso, *forced heir.*
Ref: (Ar)CC a.3591ss.; (Ch)CC a.1181; (CR)CC a. 571-576; (Ec)CC a.1227ss.; (Esp)CC a.806ss.; (Mx) CC a.1368 (Pe)CC a.723-733; (Ur)CC a.884-895; (Ve)CC a.883-887.

legítima defensa *self-defense.*
• Defensa necesaria para rechazar una agresión actual, inminente e injusta en contra de la persona o derechos, propios o ajenos, mediante un acto apropiado contra el agresor.
– Sin. defensa propia.
legítima defensa putativa *putative self-defense, believed self-defense.* – Sin. legítima defensa imaginaria.

legitimación n. *legitimation, making (something or someone) legitimate,* **legitimar** v. *to legitimize.* **legitimado** n. *legitimated person.*
legitimado adj. *legitimated.* **legítimamente** adv. *legitimately.*
• La capacidad que tiene una persona para ser parte de una causa y poder actuar legítimamente en el proceso. También la situación jurídica en la que se encuentra una persona que le permite afectar un derecho de otro.
legitimación de firmas *authentication of signatures.*
legitimación de hijos *legitimation of a child.*
legitimación procesal *acknowledgment of legal standing in court.* – Sin. legitimación en causa.
Rel: autentificación, *authentication;* certificación, *certification, jurat;* habilitación, *authorization, qualification.*

legitimidad n. *legitimacy.* **legítimo** adj. *legitimate.*
legitimidad de un heredero *an heir's lawfulness.*
legitimidad de un título *legitimacy of an instrument.*

lenguaje n. *language.* **lengua** *tongue.*
– Sin. dialecto, *dialect.* idioma, *idiom.* lengua, *tongue.*
lenguaje materno *mother tongue.* – Sin. lengua materna.

lenocinio (delito) n. *pandering, procuring.* **lenón**

n. *panderer.* – Sin. alcahuetería. rufianería. proxenetismo.
Ver: proxenetismo.

leonino adj. *unconscionable, unfair.*
• Situación en la hay una desproporción o desventaja excesiva en perjuicio de una de las partes cuando la naturaleza de la operación exige la existencia de equilibrio o equivalencia.
– Sin. abusivo, *abusive.* arbitrario, *arbitrary.* injusto, *unfair.*
contrato leonino *unconscionable contract, one-sided contract.*
Rel: lesión², *lesion.*

lesión¹ (perjuicio) n. *injury, prejudice,* [prest.]*lesion.* **lesionar** v. *to cause injury, prejudice.* **lesionado** n. *injured person.* **lesionado** adj. *injured.*
• En sentido amplio, se entiende por lesión un "…[p]erjuicio, disminución o menoscabo deparado por un acto o hecho jurídico." (Couture, 380) – Sin. detrimento, *detriment.* menoscabo, *reduction.* pérdida, *loss.* perjuicio, *prejudice.*

lesión² contratos n. [ed]*contractual loss due to undue advantage (of one of the parties when entering into a contract).* [prest.]*lesion.*
En el ámbito contractual se entiende por lesión la merma patrimonial injusta sufrida por una de las partes, con motivo del daño causado por la explotación de su ignorancia, notoria inexperiencia o extrema miseria, por la otra parte contractual.
contrato viciado de lesión [ed]*undue advantage of one of the parties in the formation of a contract.*
Rel: vicios del consentimiento, *defects in the formation of mutual assent (in contracts).*

lesiones¹ (delito) [amplio]*battery.*
• Lo comete el que causa daño a otro en el cuerpo o la salud. – Sin. agresión (PR). golpes. violencias físicas.
Bajo lesión se comprende normalmente las heridas, escoriaciones, contusiones, fracturas, dislocaciones, quemaduras, y cualquier otra alteración de la salud o daño que deje huella en el cuerpo producida por una causa externa.
➥ En derecho anglosajón tradicional el delito de *battery* es comúnmente definido como el uso ilegal de la fuerza en contra de otro, sin requerir necesariamente de una lesión física. Sin embargo, modernamente nuevas disposiciones legislativas han introducido consistentemente la lesión física como elemento constitutivo del delito de *battery.* En los sistemas jurídicos hispanos, el delito de lesiones considera como criterio principal el causar una marca o provocar una lesión física. Aunque no exactamente equivalentes, *battery* y lesiones son generalmente equiparables, las diferencias entre ambos son meramente de énfasis, con la excepción de la existencia de la denominada "*offensive touching*" en el delito de *battery*, la que no existe en el delito de lesiones.
lesiones al feto *harm to the fetus, harm to the unborn child.*
lesiones con agravantes *aggravated battery.*
lesiones simples *simple battery.*
– Sin. violencias físicas. golpes.
Ref: (Ar)CP a.89ss.; (Bo)CP a.270-276; (Ch)CP a.395-403; (Co)CP a.111ss.; (Gu)CP a.144; (Ec)CP a.463ss.; (ES)CP a.142; (Esp)CP a.147ss.; (Mx)CP a.288; (Pe)CP a.121-124; (Ur)CP a.316ss.; (Ve)CP a.415.

lesiones²(corporales) *injury, harm.*
– Sin. contusión, *contusion.* herida, *wound.* lastimadura, *injury, bruise.*
lesiones físicas *physical injuries.*
lesiones mortales *fatal injuries.*
lesiones sufridas en el trabajo *on the job injuries, job-related injuries.*

letra de cambio títulos de crédito *bill of exchange, draft.* **librador** n. *drawer.* **librado** n. *drawee.*
beneficiario n. *beneficiary.* **tomador** n. *payee.*
• Es la "orden escrita mercantil, revestida de las formalidades que establece la ley, por la cual una persona (librador), encarga a otra (librado) que pague una suma de dinero a un tercero (tomador)." (Ramírez Gronda, 202) – Sin. giro, *draft.*
Cf: **letra de cambio** ● **giro** ● **cheque.** Letra de cambio y giro son considerados términos sinónimos, pero no intercambiables. El giro es un concepto genérico que se aplica tanto a la letra de cambio como al cheque, y que se refiere a una orden de pago normalmente con motivo de una operación comercial (cambio trayecticio). A su vez la letra de cambio, considerada como una de las especies del concepto giro, es claramente diferenciable del cheque tanto por su estructura, en la que no participa un banco, como por la regulación que se le aplica.
letra de cambio a día fijo *bill of exchange payable at a designated date, time bill.*
letra de cambio a días fecha *bill of exchange payable x days from the date of issue.*
– Sin. letra a cierto tiempo fecha. letra a plazo desde la fecha.
letra de cambio a días vista *bill of exchange payable x days from presentment.* – Sin. letra a

cierto tiempo vista. letra a un plazo desde la vista.

letra de cambio a la vista *bill of exchange payable on sight, sight draft, bill of exchange payable on demand.*

letra de cambio al portador *bearer bill of exchange.*

letra de cambio documentada *documentary bill of exchange, documentary draft.*

letra de cambio domiciliada *domiciled bill of exchange.*

letra de resaca *redraft.*

Rel: cheque, *check;* títulos de crédito, *negociable instruments.*

Ref: (Ch)Ley 18.092 a.1-2; (Co)CCo. a.671ss.; (ES) CCo a.702ss.; (Esp)LCCH a.2; (Mx)LGTOC a.1; (Ve)CCo. a.410ss.

letrado n. *attorney, learned.*

leva n. *military draft.* – Sin. alistamiento, *levy.* reclutamiento, *recruitment.*

levantamiento de cadáver *forensic inspection of a homicide scene.*

levantamiento de embargo *release of an attachment.*

levantar cargos *to press charges.*

levantar un acta *to draw up a written record.*

ley[1] **(norma general)** n. *law.*

• Norma jurídica obligatoria y general, proveniente de fuentes jurídicas, para regular la conducta de los hombres. – Sin. derecho.

aplicar la ley *to enforce the law.*

con todas las de la ley *in compliance with the law.*

ley aplicable *governing law.*

ley comentada *annotated law.*

ley de orden público [ef]*public policy law,* [el]*law of public order,* [ed]*statutes considered to benefit the public at large.*

ley dispositiva *dispositive law.*

ley escrita *written law.*

ley federal *federal law.*

ley orgánica *organic law.*

ley prohibitiva *prohibitive law.*

ley retroactiva *retroactive law.*

ley supletoria [prest.]*suppletive law,* [ed]*statute to be applied in the absence of other applicable statute or code, replacing statute.*

ley vigente *law in effect.*

Rel: norma, *legal rule;* regla, *rule.*

ley[2] **(norma legislativa)** n. *statute, act,* [lat.]*lex.*

• Regla de derecho o norma de carácter general sancionada por el órgano legitimado para

ello y debidamente publicada para su debido cumplimiento y obediencia. – Sin. estatuto. ordenanza, *ordinance.*

⤶ **ley** ● **norma jurídica.** Aunque estos dos términos se usan en forma indistinta con frecuencia, sobre todo cuando se les refiere en forma amplia, normalmente se les distingue en la doctrina y la literatura jurídica. La norma es un concepto genérico básico que consiste en un deber ser que puede imponerse coactivamente, en tanto que la ley es una norma o conjunto de normas emanadas del órgano legitimado para expedirlas. Así vista, la ley es una de las formas o "fuentes", entre otras, que generan o crean las normas jurídicas.

ley antimonopolio *antitrust law.*

ley de enjuiciamiento civil *law of civil procedure, civil procedure.*

ley de enjuiciamiento criminal *law of criminal procedure, criminal procedure.*

ley electoral *election statute.*

ley impositiva *tax law.*

ley marcial *martial law.*

ley notarial *notarial statutes.*

Rel: derogación, *derogation;* promulgación, *promulgation.*

liberación de un gravamen *discharge or release of a lien or encumbrance.*

libertad[1] **(independencia)** n. *freedom, liberty.* **libertar** v. *to free, liberate.* **libertador** n. *liberator.* **libertador** adj. *liberating.* – Sin. independencia, *independence.*

libertad[2] **(privilegio)** n. *privilege, release.* – Sin. privilegio, *privilege.* prerrogativa, *prerogative.*

libertad bajo fianza *release on bail, release on bond.* – Sin. libertad bajo caución. libertad caucional. libertad provisional.

libertad bajo palabra *release on own recognizance.* – Sin. libertad bajo protesta.

libertad condicional *parole,* [ed]*early conditional release.*

• Libertad provisional otorgada al reo que ha cumplido parte de su condena y que reune los otros requisitos exigidos por la autoridad respectiva, que generalmente incluyen el haber tenido un buen comportamiento en prisión. – Sin. libertad preparatoria (Mx), libertad anticipada (Ur).

Ref: (Ar)CP a.13; (Bo)CP a.66-69; (Co)CP a.64; (Mx)CP a.84; (Ec)CP a.87; (Esp)CP a.90.; (Ur)CP a.131.

libertad vigilada DER.PENAL [ed]*reporting release (of a convicted defendant).*

• Es una medida tutelar generalmente dictada en forma complementaria o adicional a la condena o pena aplicable al delincuente culpable, consistente en la vigilancia del sujeto por las autoridades. Su aplicación se basa en la peligrosidad del delincuente (Colombia, Chile y Guatemala) o en las características especiales del reo (minoría de edad en España).

libertades individuales *civil rights, civil liberties.* – Sin. derechos individuales. garantías individuales.

libertad de asociación *freedom of assembly.*

libertad de expresión *freedom of speech.*

libertad de imprenta *freedom of press.*

libertad de prensa *freedom of press.*

libertad de reunión *freedom of assembly.*

libertad de trabajo *freedom of employment.*

libertad religiosa *freedom of religion.* – Sin. libertad de cultos.

libertad sindical *freedom to unionize.*

libre a bordo (LAB) *free on board* (FOB).

libre bajo fianza *free on bail.*

libre de gravámenes *free and clear (land).*

libro de actas *minute book.*

licencia¹ (autorización) n. *license, permit.* **licenciar** v. *to license.* **licenciante** n. *licensor.* **licenciatario** n. *licensee.* – Sin. permiso, *permit.* concesión, *franchise.* autorización, *authorization.*

licencia de armas *gun permit.* – Sin. permiso de armas. licencia para portar armas.

licencia de construcción *construction permit.*

licencia de exportación *export license.*

licencia de importación *import permit.*

licencia² (permiso de ausencia) *leave.* – Sin. pase, *pass.*

dar licencia *to grant a leave of absence.*

gozar de licencia *to be entitled to a leave of absence* || *to be on leave.*

licencia de maternidad *maternity leave.* – Sin. licencia por maternidad.

licencia de conducir *driver's license.* – Sin. carnet de conducir, licencia de conductor. licencia de guiar. licencia de manejo. licencia para manejar. permiso de conducción.

licencia expirada *expired license.*

licencia revocada *revoked license.*

licencia suspendida *suspended license.* Rel: permiso para manejar, *driver's permit.*

licenciado n. *licentiate, licensed member of the professions.*

licenciado en derecho [el]*licentiate in law,* [amplio][ef]*lawyer.*

"En nuestro medio [México] es necesario distinguir la figura del licenciado en derecho de la figura del abogado propiamente dicho. La licenciatura en derecho no es sino un grado universitario que permite, posteriormente, obtener una autorización gubernamental para ejercer alguna de las diversas ramas de la actividad jurídica. El abogado es, en nuestro sistema, desde luego, un licenciado en derecho que se dedica a asesorar y a representar, ante los tribunales, a sus clientes. Es decir, en nuestro sistema, en rigor, no todo licenciado en derecho viene a ser un abogado, aunque todo abogado, debe ser licenciado en derecho." (Gómez Lara C., 244-45) Rel: abogado, *lawyer.*

licitación¹ (oferta) n. *bid, tender.* **licitar** v. *to bid.* **licitador o licitante** n. *bidder.* – Sin. puja.

licitación internacional *international tender.*

licitación² (concurso) n. *auction, bidding.* – Sin. concurso. subasta.

sujeto a licitación *auctioned, at auction.* Rel: fianza de participación, *bid bond;* pliego de condiciones, *terms of tender;* pliego de especificaciones, *bid documents.*

lícito adj. *licit, lawful.* **licitud** n. *lawfulness.* **lícitamente** adv. *legally, lawfully.* – Ant. ilícito, *illicit.* – Sin. legal, *legal.* permitido, *allowed.*

lindero n. *boundary.* – Sin. linde.

línea de crédito *line of credit.*

línea de crédito revolvente *revolving line of credit.*

línea de parentesco *line of descent.*

línea ascendiente *ascending line.*

línea de sucesión *line of succession.*

línea descendiente *descending line.*

línea transversal *collateral line.* – Sin. línea colateral.

liquidación de la herencia *distribution of the assets of the decedent's estate.*

liquidación de una sociedad *liquidation of a company, winding up of a company.* La liquidación "tiene como finalidad concluir las operaciones sociales pendientes al momento de la disolución, realizar el activo social, pagar el pasivo de la sociedad y distribuir el remanente, si lo hubiere, entre los socios, en la proporción que les corresponda, de acuerdo con lo convenido o lo dispuesto por la ley." (Dicc. UNAM, 2040)

liquidación tributaria *assessment of tax.* – Sin. determinación del impuesto.

literal adj. *literal.* **literalidad** n. *literalness.*

literalmente adv. *literally.* – Sin. textual, *textually, literally.* al pié de la letra, *to the letter.*

traducción literal *verbatim translation, literal translation.*

litigio n. *litigation, suit.* **litigar** v. *to litigate.*

litigante n. *trial lawyer.* **litigioso** adj. *litigious.*

• Litigio se refiere al conflicto de intereses caracterizado por la pretensión jurídica de una de las partes y la resistencia de la otra. – Sin. pleito. pendencia. controversia, *controversy.*

Cf: **litigio • proceso • procedimiento.** Litigio es un estado de conflicto intersubjetivo y de intereses en el que hay un sujeto pretensor y otro que resiste, el proceso es el instrumento jurídico para la composición o solución del conflicto, y el procedimiento es la forma y orden de desarrollo del proceso. En la práctica es común que litigio sea usado con la significación de juicio, proceso o pleito.

litisconsorcio DER.PROC.CIVIL n. *joinder of parties, joint litigants.* **litisconsorte** n. *joint litigant.*

• Litisconsorcio es la denominación dada a la situación en un litigio en la que hay una pluralidad de actores (litisconsorcio activo), o una pluralidad de demandados (litisconsorcio pasivo), o una pluralidad de ambos (litisconsorcio mixto). – Sin. acumulación de partes.

litisconsorcio activo *joinder of plaintiffs.*

litisconsorcio necesario *necessary joinder.*

litisconsorcio pasivo *joinder of respondents.*

litisconsorcio voluntario *permissive joinder.*

Rel: acumulación de acciones, *consolidation of actions.*

litispendencia DER.PROC.CIVIL n. [lat.]*lis pendens,* [ed]*a pending lawsuit.*

• La litispendencia se refiere al hecho de que al ejercitarse la acción nace el derecho, para el demandado, de poder excepcionarse si se abre la misma causa por segunda vez por estar la misma aún pendiente, ya ante el mismo juez ya ante uno diferente.

excepción de litispendencia *lis pendens defense.*

locura n. *madness, mental derangement.* **loco** n. *mad, insane.* – Sin. demencia, *dementia.* insania, *insaneness.* enajenación mental, *mental derangement.*

Rel: manía, *mania;* psicosis, *psychosis.*

locus regit actum (lat.) *locus regit actum, the place rules the act.*

• La ley aplicable al acto es aquella del lugar de su celebración.

lucro cesante *loss of lawful gains (due to damage or harm).*

lucro indebido *undue profit.*

lugar de trabajo *workplace.*

lugar de residencia habitual *usual place of abode.*

lugar del crimen *scene of a crime.*

MMMM

mafia n. *Mafia.* **mafioso** n. *mafioso.*

magistrado[1] **(gobierno)** n. *head, chief, minister.*

magistrado[2] **(juez)** n. [amplio]*judge.*

magistratura n. *judgeship.*

• Funcionario judicial que forma parte de un tribunal colegiado.

Se denomina magistrado, generalmente, al juez de rango superior (incluyendo en algunos casos a los miembros de la Suprema Corte) que revisa las actuaciones de los jueces inferiores sujetos a su jurisdicción. Aunque no existe conformidad en el uso del término magistrado, en la mayoría de los países hispanos se usa para designar al juez miembro de un tribunal o juzgado colegial (esto es en el que hay varios jueces).

↳ En términos generales magistrado y *magistrate* no son términos equivalentes. Magistrado se refiere a un juez de segunda instancia e incluso a un miembro del tribunal supremo de una jurisdicción o de un país, en tanto que *magistrate* designa generalmente a un juez de primera instancia, esto es, un juez inferior al de apelación.

magistrado de la Suprema Corte *Supreme Court Justice.*

magistrado del tribunal de apelación *appellate court judge.*

magistrado ponente *judge who writes the court's opinion.*

magistrado suplente *judge pro tempore.*

Rel: juez, *judge;* tribunal, *tribunal.*

mala conducta *misconduct.*

mala fama *ill fame.*

mala fe *bad faith.*

• Estado de ánimo de proponerse una ventaja injusta en perjuicio de otro al realizar un acto jurídico.

posesión de mala fe *mala fide possession, possession in bad faith.*

proceder de mala fe *to act in bad faith.*

mala reputación *bad reputation, disrepute.*

malas costumbres *bad habits.*

maleante *hoodlum.*

malentendido *misunderstanding.*

malhechor n. *wrongdoer, hooligan.*

malicia n. *badness, malice.* **malicioso** adj. *malicious.*
• Maldad, lo que tiene la cualidad de ser malo. En materia penal malicia es usado frecuentemente como sinónimo de dolo. – Sin. maldad, *wickedness.* perversidad, *perverseness.* Rel: dolo, *criminal intent.*
Glosario: asquerosidad, *filth;* bajo, *low;* decadencia, *decadence;* degeneración, *degeneration;* depravación, *depravity;* desprecio, *despicableness;* inmoralidad, *immorality;* maldad, *wickedness;* perversión, *perversion;* sin escrúpulos, *unscrupulous;* suciedad, *dirt;* venal, *bribable;* vicio, *vice;* vil, *vile.*

malos tratos *abuse, mistreatment.*

maltrato n. *maltreatment, ill-treatment, abuse.*
maltratar v. *to maltreat, ill-treat.* **maltratamiento** n. *maltreatment, ill-treatment.*
maltrato de esposa, *spouse abuse.*
maltrato de menores *child abuse.*
Rel: abuso, *abuse.*

malversación (delito) n. *misappropriation of public funds.* **malversar** v. *to misappropriate public funds.* **malversador** n. *public official who misappropriates public funds.*
• La distracción o sustracción de los fondos o efectos públicos, ya por sí, ya permitiéndoselo a otro, con ánimo de lucro por parte del funcionario público encargado de ellos. – Sin. distracción de fondos públicos. malversación de caudales públicos.
Cf: **malversación • defraudación • peculado.**
Malversación y peculado se usan frecuentemente como sinónimos cuando malversación es expresada en forma amplia, incluyendo la idea de apropiación o distracción de fondos del erario. No lo son cuando malversación se refiere a la aplicación de fondos públicos a destinos o fines diferentes a los establecidos legalmente, sin ocurrir una apropiación propiamente. Por lo que se refiere a la defraudación, se trata de un delito genérico que se basa en el concepto de una apropiación de bienes en manos de particulares mediante el uso de fraude, en contraste con la malversación o el peculado, los que frecuentemente implican una conducta fraudulenta, pero siempre refiriéndose a bienes públicos.
Rel: abuso de confianza, *embezzlement;* defraudación, *fraud;* desfalco, *defalcation;* peculado,

peculation.
Ref: (Ar)CP a.260; (Bo)CP a.144; (Ch)CC a.233; (Co)CP a.259; (Ec)CP a.257; (Esp)CP a.432-435; (Mx)CP a.217 y 223-IV; (Pe)CP a.389; (RD)CP a.171.

malversación de caudales públicos *misapplication of public funds.*
• Aplicación dada a fondos o caudales públicos por el funcionario público a su cargo en contravención con el destino que tienen legalmente asignados. – Sin. desvío de fondos. malversación de fondos públicos (Mx).

manchas de sangre *blood stains.*

mancomunidad n. *joint liability.* **mancomunado** n. *object of joint liability.* **mancomunado** adj. *joint.* **mancomunadamente** adv. *jointly.*
• Se dice que hay mancomunidad cuando en una misma obligación existe una pluralidad de deudores o de acreedores.
cuenta mancomunada, *joint account.*
mancomunada y solidariamente *jointly and severally.*
Rel: solidaridad, *jointly and severally.*

mandamiento DER.PROC.CIVIL n. *court order, writ.*
• "Orden o imposición que el juez emite en ejercicio de sus facultades, para asegurar cumplimiento de una decisión, o la eficacia de un acto del proceso." (Couture, 398) – Sin. mandamiento judicial. orden judicial. orden.
mandamiento de desalojo *ejectment court order.*
mandamiento de ejecución *writ of execution.*
mandamiento de embargo *writ of attachment.*

mandatario n. *high public official.*
primer mandatario *highest public official, President, Prime Minister.*

mandato[1] **(contrato)** n. *agency agreement,* [prest.]*mandate.* **mandatario** n. *agent,*[prest.] *mandatary,*[lat.] *mandatarius.* **mandante** n. *principal,* [prest.] *mandator,* [lat.]*mandant.*
• Contrato por medio del cual una persona denominada mandatario se obliga a llevar a cabo actos jurídicos por encargo y a cuenta de otra denominada mandante. – Sin. comisión mercantil, *agency agreement (for business matters).* poder, *power of attorney.* procuración, *power of attorney, representation.*
Cf: **mandato • representación.** Mandato y representación se confunden con frecuencia. Mientras el mandato es un contrato, o acuerdo de dos partes, por el que una de ellas se obliga a realizar ciertos actos jurídicos por cuenta de la otra, la representación implica simplemente

la actuación a nombre de otro, ya por la voluntad unilateral del representado, ya por disposición de la ley.

mandato especial *agency for specific matter.* – Sin. mandato particular.

mandato general *general agency.*

mandato irrevocable *irrevocable agency.*

mandato judicial *power of attorney (to represent in court).*

mandato mercantil *agency agreement for business purposes.*

mandato revocable *revocable agency.*
Rel: caucionar su manejo, *to guarantee the faithful performance of his or her duties;* encargo, *commission;* representación, *representation.* Ref: (Ar)CC a.1.869; (Ch)CC a.2116; (CR)CC a. 1251ss.; (Ec)CC a.2047-2103; (Esp)CC a.1709ss.; (Mx)CC a.2555ss.; (Pay)CC a.880ss.; (Pe)CC a. 1790-1813; (PR)CC a 1600 31 LPRA sec. 4421; (RD)CC a.1984ss.; (Ur)CC a.2051ss.; (Ve)CC a. 1684.

mandato² DER.INTL n. *mandate.*

mandato³ (orden) n. *order.* – Sin. mandamiento, *order.*

manía n. *mania.*
• Enfermedad mental que se caracteriza por una exaltación y emoción que se manifiesta en delirios y obsesiones. – Sin. fijación, *fixation.* obsesión, *obsession.*
Ver: *mania* (in the English-Spanish section).

manifestación¹ (declaración) n. *manifestation, statement.* – Sin. expresión, *expression.* declaración, *statement.*

manifestación de voluntad *manifestation of volition, declaration of intent.* – Sin. declaración de voluntad.

manifestación² (multitud) n. *demonstration, manifestation.* – Sin. mitin.

mano de obra *labor.*

manos muertas [fr.]*mortmain, deadhand control.*

manutención n. *support.* – Sin. alimentos. mantenimiento. sostenimiento.

maquiladora n. *in-bond plant,* [prest.]*maquiladora.* **maquilar** v. [ed]*to assemble or manufacture parts off-site (away from the main production facility).* **maquila** n. [ed] *parts or materials to be assembled or manufactured off the main plant* || [ed]*operations carried on by a maquiladora* || [ed]*price paid to have parts and materials assembled or manufactured.*

• Operación de producción que consiste en ensamblar las partes constitutivas de un producto provenientes de otras empresas o unidades (frecuentemente ubicadas en otros países), sujetándose generalmente a un régimen jurídico y fiscal especial.

mar libre *open sea.*

mar territorial *territorial sea, territorial waters.*
• Espacio marítimo sobre el que se extiende la soberanía del Estado. – Sin. mar adyacente. mar jurisdiccional. mar litoral.
Rel: derecho de paso en tránsito, *transit passage rights;* derecho de paso inocente, *innocent passage;* derecho de registro, *right to search;* derecho de visita, *right of inspection;* persecución continua, *hot pursuit.* Ref: (Ar)CC a.2340, Ley 17.711; (Ch)CC a.593; (Co) C a.101; (CR)C a.6; (Esp)Ley 10/1977, 4 enero.; (int. Org.)Conv. de las N.U. sobre el Derecho del Mar (1982) a.2; (Mx)C a.42-V; (Pa)C a.3; (RD)C a.5; (Ve)C a.11.

marca PROP. IND n. *trademark, brand.*
• "Signos utilizados por los industriales, fabricantes o prestadores de servicios, en las mercancías o en aquellos medios capaces de presentarlos gráficamente, para distinguirlos, singularizarlos, individualizarlos; denotar su procedencia y calidad, en su caso, de otros idénticos o de su misma clase o especie." (Dicc. UNAM, 2079) – Sin. marca comercial, *trademark.*

marca colectiva *collective mark.*

marca de productos *manufactured product trademark or brand name.*

marca de servicios *service mark.*

marca registrada *registered trademark.*
Rel: nombre comercial, *tradename.*

mariguana n. *marijuana, pot.* **mariguano** n. *doper, pothead.* – Sin. hashish. – También: marihuana.

marina n. *navy.* **marinero** n. *sailor, seaman.*

marina de guerra *navy.*

marina mercante *merchant marine.*

márshal (PR) n. *marshal (EEUU).*

masa de la quiebra *bankruptcy estate.*

masa hereditaria *decedent's estate, corpus of the estate.*

matricidio n. *matricide.* **matricida** n.*adj. matricide.*

matrícula de aeronave *aircraft registration.*

matrícula de buque *ship registration.*

matrimonio n. *marriage, wedlock.* **matrimonial** adj. *matrimonial.* **matrimonialmente** adv. *matrimonially.*
• Unión estable de hombre y mujer de conformidad al derecho vigente. – Sin. casamiento, *marriage, wedding.*
impedimentos para contraer matrimonio *marriage impediments.* – Sin. matrimonios prohibidos.
inexistencia del matrimonio *absolutely null marriage.*
matrimonio aparente *common law marriage.* – Sin. matrimonio putativo.
matrimonio canónico *religious marriage, church marriage.*
matrimonio consumado *consummated marriage.*
matrimonio de hecho *de facto marriage.*
matrimonio en fraude de la ley *sham marriage.*
matrimonio ilícito *void marriage.*
matrimonio in artículo mortis *marriage in articulo mortis, marriage under fear of imminent death.*
matrimonio por comportamiento *common law marriage.* – Sin. matrimonio consensual.
matrimonio por poder *proxy marriage.*
matrimonio religioso *marriage performed by a clergyman, church wedding.*
nacido fuera de matrimonio *born out of wedlock.*
nulidad de matrimonio *nullity of marriage.*
sentencia de nulidad de matrimonio, *annulment of a marriage.*
vínculo matrimonial *bond of marriage, bonds of matrimony.*
Rel: concubinato, *concubinage, common law marriage;* convivencia marital, *living as husband and wife;* divorcio, *divorce;* segundas nupcias, *remarriage;* sociedad conyugal, *community property, marital property.*
matrimonio civil *civil marriage, civil matrimony.*
• Es el matrimonio celebrado siguiendo los lineamientos establecido por la legislación civil.
En países hispanos el matrimonio es considerado fundamentalmente una institución civil. En la mayoría de los países de habla hispana se consideran válidos legalmente solamente aquellos matrimonios que se celebran ante las autoridades civiles; aquellos que se celebran ante autoridades religiosas surten, por lo general, solamente efectos para la comunidad

religiosa de que se trate. Como notables excepciones España, Colombia y Chile equiparan el matrimonio religioso al civil.
mayoría absoluta *absolute majority.*
mayoría de edad *legal age.*
mayoría de razón *more likely than not.*
mayoría de votos *majority of votes.*
mayoría parlamentaria *parliamentary majority.*
mediación[1] **(composición)** n. *mediation.* **mediar** v. *to mediate.* **mediador** n. *mediator.*
• En la mediación el mediador interviene directamente en la negociación proponiendo soluciones a las partes. – Sin. intercesión.
mediación internacional *international mediation.*
mediación[2] **(contrato)** n. *middleman work, agency.* **mediador** n. *intermediary.* – Sin. comisión.
contrato de mediación o comisión *commission contract.*
medianería n. *co-ownership of partition walls and properties.* **medianero** n. *owner of partition wall or properties.*
• "Titularidad conjunta de dos dueños de fincas o pisos distintos sobre un elemento común de separación: (tapia, seto o zanja en las fincas rústicas; pared divisoria compartida entre dos casas)." (Valletta, 284)
Rel: copropiedad, *joint property.*
médico forense *medical examiner, specialist in forensic medicine.*
medicina forense *forensic medicine.* – Sin. medicina legal.
Rel: autopsia, *autopsy.*
Ver: coroner.
medidas cautelares o precautorias DER.PROC.CIVIL [el]*precautionary measures,* [ef]*provisional remedies.*
• "Son los instrumentos que puede decretar el juzgador, a solicitud de las partes o de oficio, para conservar la materia del litigio, así como para evitar un grave e irreparable daño a las mismas partes o a la sociedad, con motivo de la tramitación de un proceso." (Dicc. UNAM, 2091) – Sin. medidas conservativas. providencias precautorias, *provisional relief.*
Rel: arraigo del demandado, *writ of ne exeat, civil arrest;* secuestro de bienes, *sequestration of assets.*
Ver: medios preparatorios del juicio.
medidas de apremio *court enforcement*

measures.

medidas de aseguramiento del acusado
measures to secure the defendant's appearance in court.

medidas de seguridad DER.PROC.PENAL *non-custodial sentencing measures (imposed on a guilty defendant as punishment).*

• Medidas especiales de control o guarda, con carácter preventivo, impuestos por las autoridades autorizadas para ello a determinados delincuentes con el propósito de procurar su readaptación, su separación de la comunidad o el impedir la repetición de su conducta delictiva. Cf: **medidas de seguridad • pena.** Comparada con la pena, las medidas de seguridad son una privación de derechos que persiguen una finalidad tutelar y son consecuencia de "un estado peligroso" del delincuente que resulta en su duración indeterminada. La pena por su parte, tiene un contenido expiatorio y consecuentemente una duración determinada. Mientras la pena está supeditada a la culpabilidad, las medidas de seguridad están supeditadas a la peligrosidad del autor.
Tipos: custodia familiar, *family custody or supervision;* inhabilitación profesional, *professional disqualification;* internamiento en centro educativo especial, *commitment to a special education center;* internamiento en centro psiquiátrico, *commitment to a psychiatric center;* obligación de residir en cierto lugar, *obligation to reside in an specified place or jurisdiction;* prohibición de conducir vehículos, *prohibition to drive vehicles;* prohibición de estancia y residencia en cierto lugar, *prohibition to stay and reside in a specified place or jurisdiction.*
Ver: pena.
Ref: (Ar)CP a.80; (Bo)CP a.79; (Co)CP a.69; (Esp) CP a.95,96 y 101-105; (Mx)CP a.24; (Pe)CP a.71-77; (PR)CP a.66ss., 33 LPRA 3351ss.; (Ur)CP a.92-103.

medidas disciplinarias *disciplinary measures.*

medidas para mejor proveer [ed]*court-ordered actions to facilitate adjudication or to complete and clarify evidence.* – Sin. diligencias para mejor proveer. providencias para mejor proveer.

medidas provisionales *provisional measures.*

medio ambiente *environment.*

ley del medio ambiente *environmental law.*

protección del medio ambiente *environmental protection, protection of the environment.*

Glosario: áreas naturales protegidas, *protected natural areas;* biodiversidad, *biodiversity;* contingencia ambiental, *environmental contingency;* desequilibrio ecológico, *ecological imbalance;* ecosistemas, *ecosystems;* emergencia ecológica, *ecological emergency;* equilibrio ecológico, *ecological balance;* especie amenazada, *endangered species;* especie en peligro de extinción, *species in danger to become extinct;* especie sujeta a protección especial, *species under special protection;* fauna silvestre, *wild fauna, wild animal life;* flora silvestre, *wild flora;* hábitat, *habitat;* impacto ambiental, *environmental impact;* preservación, *conservation;* recursos naturales, *natural resources.*

medios de prueba *evidence.*

• "Es medio de prueba el instrumento, cosa o circunstancia en los que el juez encuentra los motivos de su convicción." (III Alsina, 230)
– Sin. medios probatorios.
Son los medios de ataque y de defensa que poseen las partes en un litigio para demostrar sus alegaciones. Se consideran como tales: la confesión, los documentos públicos y solemnes, documentos privados y correspondencia, libros de los comerciantes, dictamen de peritos, reconocimiento o inspección judicial, testigos e informes de autoridades.
Ver: prueba.

medios preparatorios del juicio *preparatory measures (to prosecute or to sue).*

• "Son los actos o requisitos jurídicos que puede o debe realizar una de las partes, generalmente el futuro actor [en materia civil o mercantil] o el Ministerio Público (MP) en materia penal, para iniciar con eficacia un proceso posterior." (Dicc. UNAM, 2108)
Cf: **medios preparatorios • medidas cautelares.** Ambos términos se confunden y son usados indistintamente. En estricto rigor, los medios preparatorios se refieren a las medidas pedidas o hechas por una de las partes para poder conservar sus derechos o la procedibilidad de su acción antes de iniciarse el proceso <reconocimiento de firma cuando así se requiera para proceder>; las medidas cautelares, por su parte, se refieren a las acciones decretadas por el juez con el objeto de preservar la materia del litigio y evitar daño a las partes después o al mismo tiempo que se ejercita la acción. <embargo precautorio>
Rel: medidas cautelares, *provisional remedies.*

mejora n. *improvement.*

mejora a la propiedad arrendada *leasehold improvement.*

mejora de embargo *extension of attachment.*

membresía n. *membership.* **miembro** n. *member.*

memorandum de entendimiento *memorandum of understanding.*

menaje de casa *house furnishings and wares.*

menor de edad *minor.* **minoría de edad** *underage.*

maltrato de menor *child abuse.*

menor emancipado *emancipated minor.*

menor infractor *minor delinquent.*

menor trabajador *underage worker.*

mercado n. *market.* **mercadear** v. *to trade, deal.*

mercader n. *merchant.* **mercaderías** n. *goods, merchandise.* **mercancía** n. *merchandise.*

mercante adj. *merchant, mercantile.* **mercantil** adj. *mercantile.*

mercado cambiario *foreign exchange market.*

mercado común *common market.*

mercado de capitales *capital market.*

mercado de crédito *lending market, credit market.*

mercado de dinero *money market.*

mercado de futuros *futures market.*

mercado de trabajo *labor market.*

mercado de valores *securities market.*
– Sin. mercado bursátil.

mercado financiero *financial market.*

mercado nacional *domestic market.*

mercado negro *black market.*

mercadotecnia o mercadeo *marketing.*
Rel: consumidor, *consumer;* distribución, *distribution;* publicidad, *advertising.*

merino n. *judge* (PR).

mes n. *month.* **mensualidad** n. *monthly payment or allowance.* **mensual** adj. *monthly.* **mensualmente** adv. *monthly.*

miedo n. *fear.* **miedoso** adj. *cowardly.* – Sin. aprensión, *apprehension.* temor. amedrentamiento, *fright, scare.*

miedo grave *exceptional fear.*

miedo insuperable *uncontrollable fear.*

ministerio DER.ADMVO n. *ministry, department.*

ministro n. *minister.* **ministerial** adj. *ministerial.* **ministerialmente** adv. *ministerially.*
– Sin. secretaría. cartera.

Ministerio de Agricultura *Ministry of Agriculture.*

Ministerio de Comercio *Ministry of Commerce.*

Ministerio de Comunicaciones *Ministry of Communications.*

Ministerio de Defensa Nacional *Ministry of National Defense.* – Sin. Ministerio de Guerra.

Ministerio de Economía *Ministry of the Economy.*

Ministerio de Finanzas *Ministry of Finance.*

Ministerio de Hacienda *Treasury Department.*

Ministerio de Industria y Comercio *Ministry of Industry and Trade.*

Ministerio de Justicia *Ministry of Justice.*

Ministerio de Obras Públicas *Ministry of Public Works.*

Ministerio de Relaciones Extranjeras *Ministry of Foreign Affairs, State Department* (EEUU), *Foreign Office* (RU).

Ministerio de Salud *Health Ministry.*
– Sin. Ministerio de Sanidad o Salubridad.

Ministerio de Trabajo *Ministry of Labor.*

Ministerio del Interior *Department of the Interior, Home office* (RU).

ministerio de la ley *by operation of law or statute.* – Sin. ministerio de ley.

Ministerio Público *prosecution, Crown Prosecution* Service (Ingl.), *District or State's attorney* (EEUU), *Federal Prosecution Service* (Ca), *Procurator Fiscal* (Esco.), *Director of Public Prosecutions* (Au).

• "[Ó]rgano encargado de cooperar en la administración de justicia, velando por el interés del Estado, de la sociedad y de los particulares mediante el ejercicio de las acciones pertinentes, haciendo observar las leyes y promoviendo la investigación y represión de los delitos." (V Cabanellas, 424) – Abr. MP – Sin. fiscalía. Ministerio Fiscal (Esp). Procuraduría.

agente del Ministerio Público *prosecutor.*

ministro de cultos *minister (religious).*

ministro de la Suprema Corte *Supreme Court justice* (Au,Ca,NZ,EEUU). – Sin. magistrado de la Suprema Corte.

ministro sin cartera *minister without portfolio.*

minutas n. *minutes.* **minutario** n. *minutes book.*
minutas de la junta *minutes of the meeting.*

moción[1] **(promoción)(PR)** n. *motion.*

moción[2] **(parlamento)** *motion.*

• Propuesta o proposición que un participante de una reunión hace para que sea considerada por la persona o grupo que la dirige, especialmente tratándose de una asamblea legislativa.

moción de censura *motion of censure, no confidence vote.*

moción de levantar la sesión *motion to adjourn the session.*

moción de orden *motion to come to order.*

modalidades de la propiedad [ed]*the dividing up of the right of property over a thing.* Ver: desmembramientos de la propiedad.

modalidades de las obligaciones *obligation subject to a contingency.*

modificación n. *amendment.* **modificar** v. *to modify.* **modificable** adj. *modifiable.* **modificativo** adj. *modifying.* **modificatorio** adj. *modifying.* – Sin. cambio, *change.* corrección, *correction.* enmienda, *amendment.* reforma, *amendment.*

modificación de un contrato *amendment of a contract.*

modificación de un testamento *amendment of a will.*

modificación de una promoción *amendment to a pleading.*

modismo n. *idiom, idiomatic expression.*

modus operandi (lat.) *modus operandi, a manner of operating, the means of accomplishing an act.*

modus vivendi (lat.) *modus vivendi, means of living, a way of living or getting along.*

monarquía n. *monarchy.* **monarca** n. *monarch.* **monárquico** adj. *monarchical, monarchic.* **monarquista** adj.n. *monarchist.* – Sin. realeza, *royalty.* la corona, *the Crown.*

monarquía constitucional *constitutional monarchy.*

monarquía parlamentaria *parliamentary monarchy.*

moneda n. *money, currency.* **monetario** adj. *monetary.* **monedaje** n. *coinage.* – Sin. dinero, *money.*

acuñar moneda *to mint currency.*

moneda de curso legal *legal tender.* – Sin. moneda legal.

moneda extranjera *foreign currency.*

moneda falsa *fake money.*

moneda fraccionaria *coins, change.*

patrón monetario *monetary standard.*

monogamia n. *monogamy.* **monógamo** adj. *monogamous.* **monogámico** adj. *monogamic.* **monogamista** adj. *monogamist.*

monopolio n. *monopoly.* **monopolizar** v. *to monopolize.* **monopolista** n. *monopolist.* **monopolístico** adj. *monopolistic.* **monopólico** adj. *monopolistic.* **monopolización** n. *monopolization.* **monopolizador** n. *monopolizer.*

• Situación en la que un oferente de bienes o servicios puede controlar los precios en uno o varios de ellos debido a su dominación del mercado.

Rel: cártel, *cartel;* libre competencia, *open competition.*

mora (lat.) OBLIGACIONES n. *delay* || *delinquency.* **morosidad** n. *delay, delinquency.* **moroso** adj. *late, delinquent.* **morosamente** adv. *with delay, tardy.*

• Atraso o tardanza en el cumplimiento de una obligación.

"Se produce cuando el deudor no cumple la prestación en el momento debido, pero todavía puede hacerlo por tratarse de una obligación que permite cumplimiento retrasado..." (Ribó Durán, 397) – Sin. demora. dilación. retraso. tardanza, *tardiness.*

constituirse en mora *delay in performing an obligation.*

moral n. *morality.* **moralidad** n. *morality.* **moral** adj. *moral.* **moralmente** adv. *morally.* – Sin. ética, *ethics.*

alta calidad moral *good moral character.*

calidad moral *moral character.*

deber moral *moral duty.*

moral pública *public morals.*

moratoria n. *moratorium, grace period.* – Sin. prórroga, extension (of time).

morfina n. *morphine.* **morfinómano** n. *morphine addict, morphinist, morphinomaniac.* **morfinómano** adj. *morphinic, morphinomaniacal.* **morfinomanía** *morphinomania, morphinism.* – Sin. morphia.

mortis causa (lat.) *mortis causa, done or made in contemplation of one's own death.* – También: causa mortis.

mostrenco n. *ownerless.*

bien mostrenco *lost property.*

motín n. *riot* || [rtrgido]*mutiny.* **amotinarse** v. *to mutiny, riot.* **amotinado** adj. *mutinous.* **amotinado** n. *mutineer.* **amotinador** adj. *mutinous, seditious.* – Sin. amotinamiento.

Cf: **motín** • **asonada.** Ambos términos son usados como sinónimos en ocasiones, en virtud de referirse los dos a la conducta de una asamblea o grupo de personas que rompe con el orden público, pero mientras motín enfatiza la formación de un disturbio principalmente, asonada es un concepto más amplio con frecuencia, poniendo de relieve no sólo el disturbio multitudinario, sino los fines perseguidos que pueden ser sociales, económicos y sobre todo de índole política.

Rel: asonada, *tumultuary demonstration, mutinous demonstration.*
Ver: rebelión.

motivo n. *motive, reason.* **motivar** v. *to motivate.* **motivación** n. *motivation, reasoning.* **motivado** adj. *motivated.* **motivadamente** adv. *with motivation.*
• Causa o razón para hacer o dejar de hacer algo. – Sin. motivación. causa, *cause.*
motivación de la sentencia *reasoning supporting a judgment.*

móvil del delito *criminal motive.*

muchedumbre n. *crowd.* – Sin. multitud, *multitude.*
muchedumbre enardecida *active crowd.*

mueble n. [amplio]*chattel, personal property.*
Ver: bienes muebles.

muerte n. *death.* **morir** v. *to die.* **moribundo** adj. *moribund.* **moribundo** n. *dying person.*
• La terminación de la vida humana.
– Sin. finamiento. fatalidad, *casualty, death.* fallecimiento, *decease, death.* defunción, *demise, death.*
causa de muerte *cause of death.*
condenado a muerte *death row inmate, sentenced to death.*
muerte accidental *accidental death.*
– Sin. muerte causada accidentalmente. muerte imprudencial.
muerte aparente *apparent death.*
muerte civil *civil death.*
muerte por causas naturales *death by natural causes, natural death.* – Sin. muerte natural.
muerte por negligencia de otro *wrongful death.*
muerte presunta *presumptive death.*
– Sin. presunción de muerte. presunción de fallecimiento.
muerte sospechosa *death where fowl play is suspected, suspicious death.*
muerte súbita *sudden death, unexpected death.*
muerte violenta *violent death.*
pena de muerte *death penalty.* – Sin. condena de muerte. pena capital.
Rel: acta de defunción, *death certificate;* autopsia, *autopsy;* cadáver, *corpse;* homicidio, *homicide;* suicidio, *suicide;* tanatología, *thanatology.*

muerto n. *dead person.* **muerto** adj. *dead.*
– Sin. difunto, *deceased.* finado, *deceased.*

mujer n. *woman.* **mujeriego** n. *womanizer.*
– Sin. hembra, *female.*
mujer casada *married woman.*
mujer embarazada *pregnant woman.*
– Sin. mujer encinta.
mujer pública *public woman, prostitute.*
– Sin. mujer de la vida alegre (euph.). mujer de la vida airada (euph.).
mujer soltera *single woman.*

multa n. *fine.* **multar** v. *to fine.*
• Pena que consiste en el pago de dinero. Su aplicación se extiende al derecho penal, civil y administrativo. – Sin. sanción, *sanction, punishment.*
imponer una multa *to impose a fine.*
monto de la multa *fine amount.*
multa convencional *contractual penalty.*
multa disciplinaria *disciplinary fine.*
multa fiscal *tax penalty.*
reducción de multas *fine reduction.*

múltiple imposición DER.FISCAL *multiple taxation.*

municipio n. *municipality.* **municipalizar** v. *to municipalize.* **municipalidad** n. *municipality, town, city hall.* **municipal** adj. *municipal.*

mutatis mutandis (lat.) *mutatis mutandis, all necessary changes having being made.*
• Cambiando lo que se ha de cambiar.

mutilación n. *mutilation.* **mutilar** v. *to mutilate.* **mutilado** n. *crippled or disfigured person.* **mutilado** adj. *mutilated.* – Sin. corte, *cut.* ablación, *ablation.* amputación, *amputation.*

mutualidad n. *mutuality.* **mutualismo** n. *mutualism.*
• Régimen de prestaciones mutuas sobre el que se han desarrollado organizaciones o asociaciones que, en forma similar a los seguros, cubren ciertos riesgos para sus miembros.
sociedad mutualista *mutual-benefit association.*
sociedad mutualista de seguros *mutual-benefit insurance.*

mutuo (contrato) n. [prest.]*mutuum, loan.*
mutuante n. *creditor, lender.* **mutuatario** n. *debtor, borrower.* **mutuatario** adj. [prest.] *mutuary.*
• Es el contrato por el cual una de las partes entrega a la otra dinero u otra cosa fungible, con condición de devolver otro tanto de la misma especie y calidad. – Sin. préstamo de consumo.
↪ *Mutuum* es mayormente considerado como el término más apropiado en inglés, sin embargo es común que al mutuo, cuando se trata de dinero, se le refiera como *loan*, en especial el

otorgado por una institución financiera.
También, en ocasiones, mutuo puede ser considerado como un *exchange* cuando se trata de mercancías o bienes muebles fungibles que no sean dinero.
mutuo con intereses *mutuum with interest.*
– Sin. mutuo a intereses.
mutuo gratuito *gratuitous mutuum.*
mutuo mercantil *mutuum regulated by commercial law.*
mutuo oneroso *onerous mutuum.*
Ver: préstamo.
Ref: (Ar)CC a.2240; (Bol)CC a.895; (Ch)CC a.2196 ss.; (Ec)CC a.2126-2142; (Esp)CC a.1740; (Mx)CC a.2384, 2393; (Pe)CC a.1648-1665; (Ur)CC a.2197-2215; (Ve)CC a.1735.
mutuo disenso *mutual termination of a contract or juridical act.*

NNNN

nacimiento n. *birth, childbirth.* **nacer** v. *to be born.* **nacido** adj. *born.* – Sin. alumbramiento, birth. natividad, *nativity.*
nacido fuera de matrimonio *born out of wedlock.*
nacimiento de un niño muerto *stillbirth.*
nacimiento simultáneo *multiple birth.*
Rel: nonato, *unborn, not born naturally.* viabilidad, *viability.*
nacionalidad n. *nationality, citizenship.* **nación** n. *nation.* **nacional** n.adj. *national.*
• Nacionalidad es el vínculo jurídico que une a una persona con el Estado al que pertenece.
nacionalidad extranjera *foreign citizenship.*
nacionalidad originaria *nationality of origin.*
Rel: ciudadanía, *citizenship;* naturalización, *naturalization.*
Ver: *citizenship.*
nacionalismo n. *nationalism.*
nacionalización[1] **(cosas)** n. *nationalization.* **nacionalizar** v. *to nationalize.* **nacionalizado** n. *nationalized.*
nacionalización[2] **(personas)** n. *naturalization.* **nacionalizar** v. *to naturalize.* **nacionalizado** n. *naturalized.* – Sin. naturalización, *naturalization.*
Naciones Unidas *United Nations.*
Ver: Organización de las Naciones Unidas.
narcóticos n. *narcotics.*
• Sustancias que producen sopor, relajación muscular y embotamiento de la sensibilidad.

– Sin. estupefaciente. somnífero, *somniferous.* soporífero, *soporific.*
naturalización n. *naturalization.* **naturalizarse** v. *to become naturalized.* **naturalizado** n. *naturalized.*
navegación aérea *air navigation, air transportation.*
navegación marítima *sea navigation.*
ne bis in idem (lat.)(max.) *non bis in idem, no one can be judged twice for the same facts.*
negativa ficta [ed]*petition presumed denied by the authorities when unanswered.*
negligencia n. *negligence.* **negligente** adj. *negligent.* **negligente** n. *negligent person.* **negligentemente** adv. *negligently.*
• Negligencia es el descuido, falta de atención o diligencia en el cumplimiento de las obligaciones o en el ejercicio de los derechos.
– Sin. culpa sin representación (der. penal). descuido (pop.), *carelessness.* imprudencia, *lack of prudent care.*
negligencia grave *gross negligence.*
– Sin. negligencia crasa.
negligencia inexcusable *contributory negligence.* – Sin. negligencia contribuyente.
negligencia leve *slight negligence.*
negligencia profesional *malpractice.*
Rel: proceder de un buen padre de familia, *reasonable and prudent man standard.*
Ver: culpa[1].
negociación[1] **(transacción)** n. *commercial transaction, business.* **negociar** v. *to negotiate.* **negociador** n. *negotiator.* **negociador** adj. *negotiating.* <acordar la negociación de la maquinaria, *to agree on the sale of the machinery*>
negociación[2] **(giro)** n. *business.* – Sin. negocio, *business.* <una negociación de ropa usada, *a second-hand clothing business*>
negociación[3] **(pláticas)** n. *negotiation, talks.* **negociar** v. *to negotiate.* **negociador** n. *negotiator.* **negociador** adj. *negotiating.* **negociable** adj. *negotiable.*
negociación del contrato colectivo *colective bargaining agreement talks or negotiations.*
negocio jurídico [ed]*legal transaction which creates, changes or terminates legal rights.*
• Puede entenderse el negocio jurídico como la declaración de voluntad a la que el derecho le atribuye efectos coincidentes con tal declaración. – Sin. acto jurídico, *juridical act.*
La denominación "negocio jurídico" es una construcción doctrinal europea equivalente en

la mayoría de los países latinoamericanos al término "acto jurídico," entendido como un acto voluntario lícito hecho con la intención de crear, modificar o extinguir un derecho o relación jurídica, a diferencia de los llamados "simples actos voluntarios lícitos," en los que el autor se desentiende de los efectos jurídicos al efectuar el acto, aunque la ley les dé consecuencias jurídicas. En contraste, en España el término "negocio jurídico" es entendido también por varios autores como el equivalente a varios actos jurídicos coordinados para producir efectos.

Rel: contrato, *contract;* hecho jurídico, *legal fact,* [ed]*legally significant phenomenon, event or situation;* obligación, *obligation.*

negocios n. *business.*
administración de negocios *business administration.*
en el curso normal de los negocios *in the ordinary course of business.*
hacer negocios *doing business.*
negocio en marcha *going concern.*
Rel: gestión de negocios, [ed]*the unauthorized management of the affairs of another.*

nepotismo n. *nepotism.*
• Preferencia o favoritismo dado a familiares al contratar personal, especialmente para cargos públicos, o para otorgar otros favores generalmente relacionados con el trabajo.

neutralidad n. *neutrality.* **neutral** n. *neutral state.*

niño n. *child.* **niñería** n. *childish action.* – Sin. criatura. chiquillo.
niño abandonado *abandoned child, foundling.* – Sin. niño expósito.
niño callejero *street children.* – Sin. niño de la calle.
niño descuidado *neglected child.*
niño escapado de casa *runaway child.*
niño maltratado *abused child.*
Rel: bebé, *baby;* crío, *nursing baby;* chamaco, *kid;* chaval (Esp), *lad;* chico, *boy, youngster;* infante, *infant;* menor, *minor;* muchacho, *boy, youngster;* nene, *baby.*

no exigibilidad de otra conducta DER.PENAL *defense based on the absence of other course of action.* – Sin. no exigibilidad.

no ha lugar la demanda *dismissal of complaint.*

no hay pena sin ley (max.) *No punishment without a law authorizing it,* [lat.]*nulla poena sine lege.*

no intervención DER.INTL *nonintervention.*

nolo contendere (lat.) *nolo contendere, I do not wish to contend.*

nombre n. *name.* – Sin. apelativo, *appellation.*
↪ Las personas físicas en países hispanos usan uno o varios nombres de pila y dos apellidos: el apellido del padre en primer término y el apellido de la madre en segundo lugar. Normalmente la mujer al casarse deja de usar su apellido materno y lo substituye por el apellido del marido usando la preposición "de" antes del mismo. <María Gonzalez de Rubio> Las personas en países de habla inglesa en cambio usan uno o varios nombres de pila seguido del apellido del padre solamente. Cuando la mujer casada adopta el apellido del marido lo hace reemplazándolo por el suyo propio. <Jane Paterson, née Smith> La tendencia moderna es, sin embargo, tanto para los países de habla hispana como de habla inglesa, la de modificar estas prácticas en favor de usos que pongan de relieve la igualdad de las mujeres para con los hombres.
nombre civil *legal name.*
nombre comercial *tradename.*
nombre de cariño *nickname.*
nombre de pila *given name.*
nombre propio *given name.*
nombre social *company name.* – Sin. razón social.
nombre supuesto *assumed name.*
Rel: alias, *alias;* apodo, *nickname;* denominación social, *company name;* homónimo, *homonym;* mote, *nickname;* seudónimo, *pseudonym;* sobrenombre, *nickname.*

nominativo adj. *registered.*
acciones nominativas, *registered shares.*

norma n. *norm, rule of conduct.* **normativo** adj. *normative.*
• Toda regla de comportamiento. Regla que impone deberes o confiere obligaciones. – Sin. regla, *rule.*
norma de seguridad *safety rule.*
norma individualizada [el]*individualized norm,* [ed]*application of a statutory rule to an individual case.* [ef]*legal rule.*
norma moral *moral rule.*
norma social *social norm.*

norma jurídica [el]*juridical norm,* [ed]*legal norm,* [ef]*legal rule.*
• "Todo precepto jurídico con eficacia general impuesto por una fuerza social con poder de organización." (Dicc. ed. Comares, 364)

"La norma ordena la conducta humana prescribiendo determinados comportamientos o señalando determinados efectos a los actos humanos. Para ello, la norma se compone de dos elementos fundamentales: el supuesto de hecho y la consecuencia jurídica. Mediante el primero, la norma enuncia en que caso o situación fáctica operará; con la segunda señala el efecto o resultado de la voluntad del Estado." (Ribó Durán, 405)

norma dispositiva [ed]*dispositive norm.*

norma imperativa [ed]*mandatory norm.*

norma supletoria *suppletive norm,* [ed]*applicable norm in the event that no other can be applied, replacing norm.*

Rel: consecuencia de derecho, *legal consequences (as part of a norm);* supuesto jurídico, [ed] *factual hypothesis (as part of a norm).*

Ver: derecho[1].

nota n. *note, memorandum.*

nota de cargo *debit memorandum.*

nota de crédito *credit memorandum.*

notario público *notary public.* **notarización** *attestation of a notary.* **notarial** adj. *notarial.* **notariado** n. *profession of a notary.* **notariado** adj. *notarized.* **notaría** n. *notary's office.*

• Funcionario público, licenciado en derecho que está autorizado para dar fe de los contratos y demás actos jurídicos según lo señale la ley. ↪ "En los Estados Unidos el notario anglosajón o [notario] privado sólo autentica firmas, sin que su actuación se refiera al fondo del documento de que se trate.... su firma y sello sólo paralizan la acción de falsedad de firmas del documento. [En] el notariado de tipo latino ... el notario es al mismo tiempo un funcionario dotado de fe pública y un abogado que ilustra a las partes, redacta el documento, lo autoriza, expide copias certificadas y conserva el original. La actuación del notario no tiene más límites que los que marcan las leyes." (Dicc. UNAM, 2217-218)

elevar a escritura notarial *to notarize, to put into the form of a notarial instrument.*

ley del notariado *notarial statutes.*

ocurrir ante notario público *to appear before a notary public.*

testimonio notarial *notarial instrument.*

Rel: documento privado, *documents not recorded by a notary, private document;* fedatario público, *person authorized to authenticate documents, person having legal authority to authenticate documents.*

notificación[1] **(información)** n. *service, service of process, notice.* **notificar** v. *to serve.*

notificador n. *process server.* **notificado** adj. *notified.* **notifíquese** *be it served.*

• Hacer saber a un litigante una providencia judicial u otro acto del procedimiento o tenerlo por enterado formalmente de ellos, así como la constancia escrita de tal acto de información. – Sin. notificación judicial.

↪ Notificación es un término amplio que incluye tanto *notice* como *service of notice.*

notificación de apelación *notice of appeal.*

notificación personal *personal service.*

notificación por cédula *notice by written service, substituted service.*

notificación por conducta concluyente *notice implied by behavior that demonstrates receipt of notice.*

notificación por edictos *service by publication.*

notificación por estrados *notice by written service posted at the courthouse.*

Rel: citación, *subpoena;* emplazamiento, *summons;* exhorto, *letter of request.*

Ver: comunicación procesal.

notificación[2] **(documento)** n. *notice.*

novación OBLIGACIONES n. *novation.* **novar** v. *to novate.* **novatorio** adj. *novatory.*

• La extinción de una obligación mediante su transformación al cambiar la deuda, o substituir al deudor o al acreedor.

Cf: **novación • subrogación • cesión de derechos.** Hay novación de una obligación cuando las partes la extinguen creando una nueva que difiere de la extinguida en un elemento esencial. Hay subrogación cuando, por ministerio de ley, el acreedor es substituido por otro ante el deudor sin que se altere la obligación original. Y finalmente, hay cesión de derechos cuando el acreedor tramsmite su derecho a un tercero, en forma gratuita o por precio, quedando el deudor original obligado en los mismos términos aún si no consintiere en la cesión.

Rel: cesión de créditos, *assignment of credits or debt;* cesión de derechos, *assignment of rights;* subrogación, *subrogation.*

Ref: (Ar)CC a.724,801ss.; (Ch)CC a.1628; (CR)CC a.814-20; (Ec)CC a.1671; (Esp)CC a.1203ss.; (Mx) CC a.2213; (Pe)CC a.1277-1287; (Ur)CC a.1525-1543; (Ve)CC a.1.314.

nudapropiedad n. *bare ownership.*

nudopropietario n. *bare owner.*

• Es el derecho que le queda al propietario al conceder el usufructo de su propiedad, esto es, la propiedad separada del goce de la cosa.

Rel: usufructo, *usufruct.*

nulidad n. *nullity.* **nulo** *null, void.*

• La nulidad, que es la destrucción total o parcial de efectos jurídicos, se presenta cuando el acto jurídico se ha realizado imperfectamente en uno de sus elementos básicos, aunque éstos se presenten completos.
Cf: **nulidad • anulabilidad • rescisión.** La nulidad tiene como resultado el dejar sin efecto los actos o negocios afectados. Cuando un acto que está afectado de nulidad perdura y puede convalidarse, se dice que se trata de un caso de nulidad relativa o, más comúnmente, de anulabilidad. Esta posibilidad de sobrevivencia va a depender naturalmente de la gravedad de la carencia o imperfección del acto de que se trate. La rescisión también extingue los efectos derivados de un acto bilateral, pero en este caso no hay imperfección en la formación como en la nulidad, sino en la ejecución debido a la existencia o advenimiento de circunstacias que impiden o hacen impráctico el cumplimiento de las obligaciones pactadas.
nulidad absoluta *absolute nullity, without any legal force or effect, void,* [prest.]*absolutely null* (EEUU-La).
nulidad de actuaciones *nullity of proceedings, mistrial.*
nulidad de matrimonio *nullity of the marriage.*
nulidad relativa *voidable,* [prest.]*relatively null* (EEUU-La).
nulo de derecho *having no legal force.*
nulo y sin efecto *null and void.*
Rel: acto inexistente, [ed]*absolutely null and void act;* caducidad, *lapse;* invalidez, *invalid;* revocación, *revocation.*
Ref: (Ar)CC a1037ss.; (Ch)CC a.1681ss.; (Ec)CC a.1724-1741 CPC a.353ss.; (Esp)CC a.1300-314; (Mx)CC a.2224, 2226-2228; (PR)CC a.1252 ss.; (Ve)CC a.1146 CPC a.206-214.
Ver: revocación.

nunc pro tunc (lat.) *nunc pro tunc, now for then, having retroactive legal effect.*

OOOO

obcecación n. *obfuscation, blindness (confusion) || blind obstinacy.*

obediencia jerárquica *hierarchical obedience.*
• Defensa del acusado de un delito que excluye la responsabilidad penal por encontrarse el autor bajo un deber jurídico legítimo de obediencia, respecto de un superior jerárquico.
– Sin. obediencia debida, *obligational obedience.*

objeción n. *objection.* **objetar** v. *to object.*
objetante n. *objector.* **objetante** adj. *objecting.*
objetable adj. *objectionable.* – Sin. impugnación, *impugnation, challenge.* oposición, *opposition.* tacha, *challenge.*
objeción de conciencia *conscientious objection.*
Ver: objection.
objeto de la obligación *subject matter of the obligation.*
objeto jurídico del delito *social value to be protected.*
objeto material del delito [lat.]*corpus delicti, body of the crime.*
objetos personales *personal effects.*
obligación[1] **(deber)** n. *obligation, duty.*
obligación[2] DER.CIVIL n. [amplio]*obligation,* [prest.][lat.]*obligatio.* **obligaciones** *law of obligations.* **acreedor** *debtor, obligor.* **deudor** *creditor, obligee.*
• Es la relación jurídica que se establece entre una persona, que puede exigir (acreedor), a otra, que debe cumplir (deudor), una prestación consistente en un dar, un hacer o un no hacer.
– Sin. derecho personal. derecho de crédito.
↳ El término obligación en su connotación técnico-legal dentro del sistema romano-germánico no tiene un equivalente exacto en inglés, sin embargo *obligation*, que es un término usado en forma más laxa e informal, ha sido aceptado en forma unánime como un equivalente apropiado debido principalmente a la amplitud del término y a su sinonimia con la palabra deber.
obligación a plazo *obligation to be performed or to terminate on a date certain.* – Sin. obligación a término.
obligación accesoria *accessory obligation.*
obligación alimenticia *support obligation, obligation to provide support,* [prest.]*alimentary obligation* (EEUU-La).
obligación alternativa *alternative obligation.*
obligación condicional *conditional obligation.*
obligación contractual *contractual obligation.*
obligación de dar *obligation to turn over (property, use, etc).*
obligación de hacer *obligation to act.*
obligación de no hacer *obligation not to act.*
obligación facultativa *obligation which allows substitution of performance.*
obligación fiduciaria *fiduciary obligation.*

obligación

obligación mancomunada *joint obligation.*
obligación principal *principal obligation.*
obligación solidaria *joint and several obligation.*
obligación tributaria *tax obligation.*
obligación unilateral *unilateral obligation.*
Rel: compromiso, *compromise;* deber, *duty;* deuda, *debt.*
Ver: *obligation.*

obligación³ (deuda) n. *debenture.* **obligacionista** n. *obligee, holder of debentures.*

• "Son valores de financiación, con los que el emisor pretende allegar recursos financieros para su empresa a título de crédito, que deberá restituir en el momento de su vencimiento."(III Enciclopedia ed. Cívitas, 4536) – Sin. bono, *bond.*
obligación convertible *convertible debenture.*
obligación hipotecaria *mortgage-backed bond.*
obligaciones municipales *municipal bonds.*
obligaciones quirografarias *unsecured debt instruments, unsecured bonds.*
obligaciones subordinadas *subordinated debentures.*
Rel: fiduciario, *representative of debenture holders.*

obligación real PROPIEDAD [prest.]*real obligation* (EEUU-La).

• Es aquella que constituye el deber correlativo de un derecho real, como por ejemplo la obligación de costear la reconstrucción de una pared común. – Sin. obligación propter rem.

obligatorio adj. *obligatory, mandatory, compulsory.* **obligatoriedad** n. *being obligatory or mandatory.* – Sin. imperativo, *imperative.*
contrato obligatorio *binding contract.*
Rel: coactivo, *coactive;* coercitivo, *coercive.*

obras públicas *public works.*

observancia n. *observance, compliance.* **observar** v. *to comply.* **observante** n. *observant, compliant.*
dejar de observar una disposición *failing to comply with a provision.*

obstrucción a la justicia (delito) *obstruction of justice.*

ocultación n. *concealment.* **ocultar** v. *to conceal.*
ocultamente adv. *hidden from view.* – Sin. ocultamiento. encubrimiento. escondimiento, *hiding.*
ocultación de documentos *concealment of documents.*
ocultación de hijo (delito) *concealment of child.*

ocultación de un delito *misprision.*
ocultación u ocultamiento de bienes *concealment of assets.*
ocultación u ocultamiento de pruebas *withholding evidence.*
Rel: secreto, *secret.*

ocultarse furtivamente *to sneak.*

ocupación¹ (adquisición) n. *occupation.*

• Forma de adquisición de propiedad por la aprehensión o toma de posesión de una cosa que no pertenece a nadie, con intención de apropiársela. – Sin. apropiación.
Las modalidades de la ocupación son la caza y pesca, los animales y el hallazgo.
Rel: accesión, *accession;* hallazgo, *acquisition of res nullius;* invención, *invention;* tesoro, *treasure trove.*
Ver: adquisición de la propiedad.

ocupación² (posesión) n. *occupation, occupancy.* **ocupar** v. *to occupy.* **ocupacional** adj. *occupational.* **ocupador** adj.n. *occupant.* **ocupante** adj.n. *occupant.*

• Posesión de hecho sobre un territorio o un bien inmueble.
ocupación de guerra *war occupation.*
ocupación de territorios *occupation of territories.*
ocupante ilegal *squatter, illegal occupant.*
Rel: posesión, *possession;* tenencia, *tenancy;* usurpación, *usurpation.*

ocupación³ (trabajo) n. *occupation.* **ocupar** v. *to occupy.* **ocupacional** adj. *occupational.* **ocupador** adj.n. *occupant.* – Sin. actividad, *activity.*
ocupación remunerada *gainful employment.*
Rel: cargo, *position;* empleo, *employment;* profesión, *profession;* carrera, *career;* oficio, *trade;* trabajo, *job.*

ocurso (Mx) n. *written petition.* – Sin. escrito, *written statement, brief.*

ofendido n. *injured party, victim.* – Sin. víctima, *victim.*

oferta¹ (propuesta) *offer.* **proponente** adj.n. *offeror.* **aceptante** *offeree.*

• Invitación hecha por una persona a otra para la celebración de un contrato o el cumplimiento de una obligación. – Sin. propuesta, *proposal, proposition.* licitación, *offer.*
oferta contractual *offer.*
oferta de pago *payment offer.* – Sin. ofrecimiento de pago.
oferta de trabajo *employment offer || labor demand.*

oferta irrevocable *irrevocable offer.*
oferta unilateral *unilateral offer.*
Rel: aceptación, *acceptance.*

oferta² (venta) *bid, tender.* **ofertar** v. *to offer, bid.* **ofertante** adj.n. *offeror, bidder.*

• Propuesta o cotización hecha por la parte vendedora indicando su disposición para realizar la operación de venta así como los términos y plazos que está dispuesta a aceptar.

oficial n. *official.* – Sin. funcionario público, *public official.*
oficial de la administración de justicia (Esp) *judicial or court administrative worker.*
oficial de policía *police officer.*
oficial del ejército *military officer.*

oficial adj. *official.* **oficialía** n. *clerkship (in a public office).* **oficialmente** adv. *officially.*
documentos oficiales *official documents.*

oficio n. *government's written official communication.*

oficio judicial *court's written official communication (to other government authorities or institutions).* – Sin. exposición (Esp).
librar un oficio judicial *to issue a court's written official communication.*

ofrecimiento de pago *payment offer.*

ofrecimiento de pruebas *presentation of evidence.*

oligopolio n. *oligopoly.* **oligopólico** adj. *oligopolistic.*

ológrafo adj. *holograph.*
• Lo escrito por propia mano. Autógrafo.
– Sin. autógrafo, *autographic.* – También: hológrafo.
testamento ológrafo *holographic will.*

ombudsman n. *ombudsman.*
• Personaje político cuya función primordial es el recibir quejas de los particulares acerca de arbitrariedades y abusos por parte de órganos gubernamentales, y efectuar las investigaciones correspondientes. – Sin. defensor del pueblo (Sp).

omisión n. *omission, forbearance.* **omitir** v. *to omit.* **omisible** adj. *able to be omitted.*
• Una manifestación de voluntad mediante la inactividad del sujeto.
☞ Aunque omisión y *omission* se usan generalmente como equivalentes, el término *omission* es, estrictamente hablando, más reducido ya que frecuentemente se le da la significación de ausencia de conducta dada en forma involuntaria, en tanto que omisión normalmente incluye tanto ese significado como aquél que describe a la falta de conducta dada en forma voluntaria, que en inglés es generalmente expresado por la palabra *forbearance.*

omisión de asistencia a la familia (Esp) *failure to provide support.*

omisión de impedir delito (Esp) *failure to stop a crime to be carried out.*

omisión del deber de socorro *failure of duty to provide aid.* – Sin. omisión de ayuda (Co).

oneroso¹ (gravoso) adj. *onerous.*

oneroso² CONTRATOS adj. *supported by consideration,* [prest.]*onerous.*
• Conmutativo o de prestaciones recíprocas, en contraste con lo adquirido a título gratuito.
– Sin. conmutativo, *commutative.*
contrato oneroso *onerous contract.*

opción n. *option.* **opcional** adj. *optional.* **optar** v. *to elect.* – Sin. alternativa, *alternative.* disyuntiva, *disjunctive.* elección, *election.*

opciones financieras *options.*

operaciones comerciales *commercial transactions.*

operaciones de crédito *credit transactions.*

operaciones internacionales de negocios *international business transactions.*
Rel: exportaciones, *exports;* importaciones, *imports;* incoterms, *incoterms.*

opinión n. *opinion.* **opinar** v. *to give an opinion.*
opinión consultiva *advisory opinion.*
opinión pública *public opinion.*

oponer resistencia *to put up a fight, to resist.*

orden constitucional *constitutional order.*

orden de cateo (Mx) *search warrant.* – Sin. orden de registro.

orden de detención *arrest warrant.* – Sin. orden de aprehensión (Mx). orden de captura. oficio de captura. orden de arresto (PR).

orden de extradición *warrant of extradition.*

orden de pago *money order.*

orden jurídico *legal order.*
Ver: ordenamiento.

orden público [rtrgido]*public policy* || *public order.*
• El orden público se entiende, en su sentido más simple, como la necesidad que tiene una sociedad o comunidad de guardar la seguridad de sus instituciones o el buen orden de la cosa pública; en contraste, en su sentido plenamente jurídico, el orden público se refiere a la existencia de una cultura jurídica fundamental que define a las instituciones políticas y sociales

de una comunidad incluyendo sus tradiciones, ideales, e incluso dogmas y mitos sobre su derecho y su historia institucional.

⌐ Aunque *public policy* ha sido el equivalente tradicionalmente usado para expresar el concepto jurídico de orden público, se trata de un concepto más restringido, sinónimo de *public interest*, que se distingue por tratarse de una aplicación aún más paricularizada, aunque cada vez de uso menos frecuente en la actualidad. Por lo que se refiere al orden público como la ordenación de la paz pública, el término usado generalmente en inglés es el de *public order*.

Rel: buenas costumbres, *good morals, public morality;* derecho público, *public law.*

Comentario: "Los principios generales de buenas costumbres y orden público juegan un papel mayor en el derecho continental [europeo] que aquél que se le asigna a morality y public policy en el common law. Ambos no han sido usados solamente en forma negativa o restrictiva, sino que han servido para alcanzar un propósito creativo, siendo los medios que han permitido a los jueces continentales romper con los principios técnicos de interpretación establecidos y moldear la ley adecuándola a las condiciones sociales y económicas actuales." (Gutteridge, 99. Traducción del editor)

ordenamiento¹ (conjunto de leyes) n. *body of laws.*

• "Conjunto de normas que en un determinado momento histórico rigen en una comunidad." (Dicc. ed. Comares, 378)
Rel: orden jurídico, *legal order.*

ordenamiento² (ley específica) n. *statute, act.*
Rel: código, *code;* ley, *statute.*

ordenanza n. *ordinance, statute.* – Sin. ley, *statute.* estatuto, *rule, regulations.* reglamento, *regulations.*
Generalmente creada para aplicarse a los militares, a la organización de ciudades, gremios, corporaciones o comunidades.

Organización de Aviación Civil Internacional (OACI) *International Civil Aviation Organization* (ICAO).

Organización de las Naciones Unidas (ONU) *United Nations Organization* (UN).
Organos: Asamblea General, *General Assembly;* Consejo de Seguridad, *Security Council;* Consejo de Administración Fiduciaria, *Trusteeship Council;* Consejo Económico y Social, *Economic and Social Council;* Secretario General, *Secretary-General;* Corte Internacional de Justicia, *International Court of Justice.*
Ver: Apéndice F. Naciones Unidas.

Organización de las Naciones Unidas para la Agricultura y la Alimentación (FAO) *Food and Agriculture Organization* (FAO).
Rel: Conferencia, *Conference;* Consejo, *Council;* Director General, *General Director.*

Organización de las Naciones Unidas para la Educación la Ciencia y la cultura (UNESCO) *United Nations Educational, Scientific and Cultural Organization* (UNESCO).

Organización de los Estados Americanos (OEA) *Organization of American States* (OAS).
Organos: Asamblea general, *General Assembly;* Consejo permanente, *Permanent Council;* Consejo interamericano de desarrollo integral, *Inter-American Council for integral development;* Comité jurídico interamericano, *Inter-American Juridical Committee;* Comisión interamericana de derechos humanos, *Inter-American Commission on Human Rights;* Secretaría general, *General Secretariat.*

Organización Internacional de Policía Criminal *International Criminal Police Organization.* – Abr. Interpol.

Organización Internacional del Trabajo (OIT) *International Labor Organization* (ILO).
Rel: Conferencia Internacional del Trabajo, *International Labor Conference;* Consejo de Administración, *Executive Council;* Oficina Internacional del Trabajo, *International Labor Office.*

Organización Meteorológica Mundial (OMM) *World Meteorological Organization* (WMO).

Organización Mundial de Comercio (OMC) *World Trade Organization* (WTO).
Ver: *World Trade Organization.*

Organización Mundial de la Propiedad Industrial (OMPI) *World Intellectual Property Organization* (WIPO).

Organización Mundial de la Salud (OMS) *World Health Organization* (WHO).
Rel: Asamblea, *Assembly;* Consejo Ejecutivo, *Executive Board;* Secretaría, *Secretariat.*

organización no gubernamental (ONG) *non-governmental organization* (NGO).

organización no lucrativa *nonprofit organization.*

organización sindical *labor organization.*

órgano de acusación *prosecution.* – Sin. Ministerio Público. fiscalía.

órgano de gobierno *agency or branch of the government.*

órganos jurisdiccionales *adjudicative bodies, courts.*

origen nacional *national origin.*

otorgamiento n. *grant.* otorgar v. *to grant, award.* otorgante/otorgador n. *grantor.* – Sin. conferimiento, *to award, grant.*

otorgamiento de fianza *furnishing or posting bail.*

otorgamiento de un préstamo *granting of a loan, giving a loan.*

otorgamiento de una franquicia *granting of a franchise.*

otorgamiento de una visa *issuance of a visa.*

otorgamiento de escritura pública *execution of a notarial instrument.* – Sin. otorgamiento de instrumento público.

PPPP

pabellón DER.MARÍTIMO n. *flag of nationality.*

pacta sunt servanda (lat.)(max.) *pacta sunt servanda, agreements must be carried out.* Pacta sunt servanda se refiere al principio de que los acuerdos, contratos y pactos deben ser cumplidos por las partes que los celebraron; esto es, la realización de un acuerdo o contrato establece la obligación de su cumplimiento como una de sus premisas fundamentales.

pacto[1] (acuerdo) n. *pact, agreement.* pactar v. *to make a pact or agreement.*
• Acuerdo obligatorio de voluntades.
– Sin. acuerdo, *agreement.* convenio, *agreement.*
Pacto se refiere generalmente a un acuerdo que es accesorio o adicional a un contrato o convenio principal. En ocasiones un pacto está desprovisto de acción judicial. En materia internacional pacto es usado principalmente como sinónimo de convención, esto es, un acuerdo considerado un tanto menos importante y menos formal que un tratado. En tanto que en materia constitucional frecuentemente significa un acuerdo o convenio general.

pacto de exclusiva *exclusivity agreement.*

pacto de no agresión *nonaggression pact.*

pacto federal *interstate agreement creating a federal system.*

pacto leonino *one-sided agreement.*

pacto suicida *suicide pact.*

pacto[2] (cláusula) n. *clause, stipulation.*
– Sin. cláusula, *clause.* estipulación, *stipulation.*

pacto compromisorio *arbitration clause.*

pacto comisorio *clause of rescission for breach of contract.*

pacto de mejor comprador *stipulation to sell to best offer.*

pacto de cuotalitis *contingent fee clause.*

pacto de retroventa *repurchase clause, repurchase agreement.*

pacto de no competencia *nonconcurrence clause, clause or covenant not to compete, non-competition clause.*

pacto de preferencia *preferential right to purchase (given to a potential buyer if goods are to be offer for sale).*

pacto de reserva de dominio [ed]*reservation of right of ownership clause.*

salvo pacto en contrario *unless otherwise agreed, unless there is an stipulation or agreement to the contrary.*

Pacto Andino DER.INTL *Andean Pact.*

padres n. *parents.* padre n. *father.* – Sin. progenitores, *progenitors.*

padres adoptivos *adoptive parents.*

padres biológicos *biological parents.*

padres de crianza *foster parents.*

buen padre de familia [ed]*good family man,* [ef]*reasonable and prudent man standard.*

padrón electoral *voter's register, list of voters.* – Sin. censo electoral.

pagaré TÍTULOS DE CRÉDITO n. *promissory note, note.*
librador n. *drawer.* suscriptor n. *maker.*
beneficiario n. *payee.* tenedor n. *holder.*
firmante n. *maker.*
• Título valor que contiene una promesa incondicional de una persona llamada librador o suscriptor de pagar una cantidad determinada a otra, denominada beneficiario o tenedor, o a su orden, una cantidad cierta y determinada de dinero, en un lugar y fechas especificados.
– Sin.vale (pop.).

emisión de un pagaré *issuance of a promissory note.*

pagaré domiciliado *promissory note specifying place of payment.*

suscripción de un pagaré *signing of a promissory note.*

Rel: cantidad cierta y determinada de dinero, *sum certain (of money);* promesa incondicional de pago, *unconditional promise to pay.*
Ver: letra de cambio.
Ref: (Ch)Ley 18.092 a.102-103; (ES)CCo a.788ss.; (Esp)LCCH a.94ss.; (Mx)LGTOC a.170ss.; (Ve) CCo a.486ss.

pago n. *payment.* pagar v. *to pay.* pagado n.*adj. paid.* pagador n. *payor, paymaster.* pagadero adj. *payable.*

• Por pago se entiende el cumplimiento de la prestación de una obligación (consistente en dar, hacer o no hacer). También se entiende por pago la entrega de una cantidad de dinero debida, así como el abono de una deuda. – Sin. paga, *pay.*

capacidad de pago *ability to pay.*

comprobante de pago *proof of payment, receipt.*

dación en pago [ed]*something given in lieu of payment.*

falta de pago *nonpayment.*

lugar de pago *place of payment.*

pagadero a la orden *payable to order.*

pagadero a la vista *payable at sight.*

pagadero al portador *payable to bearer.*

pagar bajo protesta *pay under protest.*

pago a cuenta *payment on account.*

pago a un abogado *compensation of attorney.*

pago al contado *payment upon delivery.*

pago anticipado *prepayment, advance payment.*

pago de impuestos *tax payment.*

pago de pensión alimenticia *support payments.*

pago diferido *deferred payment.*

pago en efectivo *cash payment.*

pago en especie *payment in kind.* – Sin. pago en bienes.

pago extemporáneo *late payment.*

pago global *lump-sum payment.*

pago liberatorio [ed]*payment which extinguishes the obligation.*

pago parcial *partial payment, installment.*

pago por intervención *payment made by a third party (outside party).*

pago provisional *provisional payment.*

pago total *payment in full.*

pagos atrasados *payment in arrears.*

Rel: consignación, *consignment;* cumplimiento, *performance.*

Ref: (Ar)CC 725ss.; (Ch)CC a.1568ss.; (CR)CC a. 764ss.; (Ec)CC a.1611; (Esp)CC a.1157; (Mx)CC a.2062-2096; (Pe)CC a.1220; (Ur)CC a.1448-1467; (Ve)CC a.1283ss.

pago de lo indebido *wrongful payment (causing unjust enrichment of recipient).*

• Pago de una obligación en forma errónea que resulta en la obligación del que cobra de restituír o devolver. – Sin. cobro de lo indebido. pago de lo no debido.

páguese a la orden de *pay to the order of.*

pandilla n. *gang.* **pandillero** n. *gang member.*

pandillerismo n. *gangs.* – Sin. [prest.]*ganga* (principalmente EEUU).

Rel: banda, *band.*

papel n. *paper.* **papeleta** n. *slip of paper.*

papel moneda *bill, paper money.*

papel seguridad *safety paper.*

papel sellado *stamped paper.* – Sin. papel timbrado.

paradero n. *whereabouts.*

paraestatal adj. *state owned or controlled.*

• Organizaciones controladas por el gobierno central que proveen principalmente servicios públicos, sin ser parte de la administración pública.

Rel: empresas de participación estatal, *company in which the government owns stock;* empresas estatales o del estado, *wholly owned government companies.*

paranoia n. *paranoia.* **paranoico** n. *paranoiac, paranoid person.* **paranoico** adj. *paranoid.*

parcela n. *plot, lot.* **parcelar** v. *to parcel, to divide into lots.*

parentesco n. *kinship, parentage.* **pariente** n. *relative.* **parentela** n. *relations.*

línea y grado de parentesco (sucesiones) [ed]*a person's position in the line of ascent or descent traced through any relatives.*

parentesco íntimo *close kinship.*

parentesco por adopción *relationship by adoption.* – Sin. parentesco civil.

parentesco por afinidad *relationship by affinity.* – Sin. parentesco de afinidad.

parentesco por consanguinidad *relationship by blood, relationship by consanguinity.*

pariente cercano *close relative.*

pariente consanguíneo *blood relative.*

pariente político *in-law relative.*

Rel: allegados, *relations;* consanguinidad, *consanguineous;* familiares, *relations.*

parlamento n. *parliament.* **parlamentario** n. *member of parliament.* **parlamentario** adj. *pertaining to parliament.*

• El órgano legislativo y de control político de los países con un sistema parlamentario cuyos representantes son elegidos popularmente y tienen carácter representativo.

Cf: **asamblea legislativa • parlamento.** El término asamblea legislativa implica fundamentalmente la creación de leyes, mientras que la denominación parlamento se refiere a un concepto más amplio que incluye todas aquellas otras funciones que realiza el poder legislativo, incluyendo las políticas.

comisión parlamentaria *legislative committee.*

régimen parlamentario *parliamentary system of government.*
Rel: asamblea legislativa, *legislative assembly;* mesa (Esp), *parliamentary assembly;* sesión plenaria, *plenary session.*

paro n. *work stoppage.*
paro laboral *walkout, stoppage.* – Sin. paro obrero.
paro patronal *lockout.*
Rel: huelga, *strike;* suspensión de labores, *shut down.*

parricidio n. *parricide.* **parricida** adj.n. *parricide.*

parte alícuota PROPIEDAD *aliquot or fractional share.*
• Calificativo que indica que un todo está dividido en porciones iguales. En el caso de copropiedad la parte alícuota de cada propietario divide al derecho de propiedad y no a la cosa sujeta a propiedad.

parte de accidente *accident report.*
– Sin. reporte policíaco o policial.

parte de fundador *founder's capital share or shares.* – Sin. bono de fundador.

parte de guerra *war communiqué, dispatch during wartime.*

parte ofendida *injured party.*

parte policíaco *police report.*

parte social [prest.]*share of a sociedad de responsabilidad limitada,* [amplio]*share of partnership.* – Sin. cuota social (Ar,Ven). participación social (Pe).

partes¹ (proceso) *parties.*
• Las partes en un proceso civil son los enfrentados en un litigio. La parte reclamante se denomina demandante o actor, la parte reclamada, demandada. En un proceso penal las partes son el acusado, el órgano de acusación estatal (normalmente el fiscal o el Ministerio Público) y en algunos casos especiales querellantes y acusadores privados o particulares. – Sin. litigantes, *litigants.* partes procesales, *parties in a lawsuit.*
parte actora *plaintiff, petitioner.* – Sin. actor. demandante.
parte contraria *opposing party.*
parte culpable *guilty party.*
parte demandada *respondent, defendant.*
– Sin. demandado.
parte demandante *plaintiff.*
parte recurrente *petitioner, appellant.*
– Sin. recurrente.

parte recurrida *appellee.* – Sin. recurrido.
Rel: terceros, *third parties.*

partes² (actos jurídicos) *parties.*
partes contractuales *contractual parties.*

partición de la copropiedad *partition of joint property.*

partición de una herencia *partition of a succession.*

participación en las utilidades *profit sharing.* – Sin. participación en los beneficios o ganancias.

partida n. *entry, record.* – Sin. anotación, *annotation, note.* asiento, *entry.* registro, *record.*
partida de defunción *record of death || death certificate.*
partida de matrimonio *record of marriage || marriage certificate.*
partida de nacimiento *record of birth || birth certificate.*

partido judicial *judicial district.*

partido político *political party.*

pasantía n. *law clerkship.* **pasante** n. *law clerk.*

pasaporte n. *passport.*
pasaporte diplomático *diplomatic passport.*
pasaporte familiar *family passport.*
pasaporte oficial *official passport.*
pasaporte ordinario *regular passport.*
Rel: salvoconducto, *safe-conduct.*

pasivo (cont.) n. *liabilities.*
pasivo acumulado *accrued liabilities.*
pasivo circulante *current liabilities.*
– Sin. pasivo exigible.

patente¹ PROP.IND n. *patent.* **patentar** v. *to patent.*
patentado adj. *patented.* **patentable** adj. *patentable.*
• Derecho de explotación en forma exclusiva de un invento o sus mejoras, así como el documento en el que consta tal derecho. "En la actualidad, hay unanimidad legislativa y doctrinal sobre la atribución de la palabra patente en exclusiva al campo de la protección jurídica de las invenciones." (III Enciclopedia ed. Cívitas, 4796)
caducidad de patente *forfeiture or abandonment of a patent.*
concesión de la patente *license of a patent, grant of a patent.*
derechos de patente *patent royalties.*
explotación de patentes *exclusive benefit (of a patent).*
Oficina de Patentes y Marcas *Patent and*

Trademark Office.
patente de diseño *design patent.*
patente de invención *patent of invention.*
patente de proceso *process patent.*
violación del derecho de patente *infringement of a patent.*
Rel: invención, *invention;* licencia de explotación, *license (of exclusive benefit);* mejora, *improvement.*
patente² (**autorización**)(**obs.**) n. *license, grant.*
• "Autorización expedida por autoridad competente para el ejercicio de alguna actividad o función, hecha constar en documento auténtico." (De Pina, 398) – Sin. concesión.
patente de comercio *business license.*
patente de corso *letters of marque.* – Sin. carta de marca.
paternidad FAMILIA n. *paternity.*
  acción de desconocimiento de la paternidad *paternity suit.* – Sin. impugnación de la paternidad.
  reconocimiento de la paternidad *acknowledgment of paternity.*
  presunción de la paternidad *presumption of paternity.*
Rel: filiación, *filiation.*
patria potestad FAMILIA *parental rights and duties,* [prest.][lat.]*patria potestas.*
• "Posición jurídica caracterizada por el conjunto de deberes y derechos que el padre y la madre tienen sobre sus hijos legítimos o sobre los naturales reconocidos o dados por reconocidos." (Couture, 448) – Sin. patria potestas.
Cf: **patria potestad ● custodia.** Términos usados indistintamente que tienen origen y alcance diferentes. La patria potestad proviene del latín "patria potestas" y significa modernamente la autoridad y obligaciones que los padres tienen para con los hijos hasta su mayoría de edad; originalmente enfatizaba el poder que el padre tenía sobre los hijos. La custodia es un término igualmente latino, "custos", del que derivó el significado guardar o cuidar y se refiere a la obligación de dar sustento, manutención y protección a un menor, poniendo de relieve el aspecto de los cuidados requeridos por un buen padre. Con frecuencia a custodia se le asigna el significado aún más reducido de convivencia o cuidados solamente, destacando aún más la mayor amplitud y generalidad del término patria potestad.
↪ Patria potestad es un término que comprende o intenta incluir todas las relaciones que los padres tienen para con los hijos; en consecuencia, incluye el cuidado, la manutención, la protección y educación de los menores, así como el ejercicio de autoridad y las facultades de representación y administración (con limitantes) de sus bienes. No existe en derecho anglosajón un término genérico equiparable, en ocasiones se usa el latinismo *patria potestas* para expresar éste término con precisión. Más comúnmente se usan los diferentes términos que expresan los derechos y obligaciones que componen la relación de los padres con respecto de los hijos, como *parental rights, parental authority, support, etc.*
  ejercicio de la patria potestad *exercise of parental rights and duties.*
  pérdida de la patria potestad *loss of parental rights and duties.*
  suspensión de la patria potestad *suspension of parental rights and duties.*
  terminación de la patria potestad *termination of parental rights and duties.*
Rel: emancipación, *emancipation;* hijos, *children;* medidas correctivas, *corrective measures.*
Comentario: Como una excepción discordante el código civil chileno considera a la patria potestad como los derechos y deberes que corresponden al padre o a la madre sobre los bienes de sus hijos no emancipados.
Ref: (Ar)CC a.264; (Ch)CC a.243-268; (Ec)CC a. 300-325; (Esp)CC a.154, 156; (Mx)CC a.412ss.; (Pa)C a.55; (Pe)CC a.418ss.; (PR)CC a.152 31 LPRA sec 591; (Ur)CC a.252ss.; (Ve)CC a.261-63.
patrimonio de familia *family property,* [ef]*homestead.* – Sin. bien de familia (Ar). hogar seguro (PR), patrimonio familiar.
patrimonio hereditario *estate, patrimony.* – Sin. acervo hereditario. caudal hereditario.
patrimonio jurídico [prest.]*patrimony, totality of assets and liabilities.*
• Conjunto de bienes y deudas, apreciables en dinero, que pertenecen a una persona física o jurídica y que constituyen una universalidad jurídica.
  déficit patrimonial [ed]*debt outstanding after applying totality of assets to pay liabilities, patrimonial deficit.*
  haber patrimonial *totality of assets.*
  patrimonio de destino (**doctrina**) [ed]*considering totality of assets and liabilities when applied to a specific goal.* – Sin. patrimonio afectación.
  patrimonio social (**organizaciones**) [ed]*totality of corporate assets and liabilities.*

Rel: bienes, *property, assets, goods;* deudas, *debts, liabilities;* universalidad jurídica, [lat.] *universitas juris,* [ed]*totality of a person's legal relations.*

patrimonio nacional [el]*national patrimony, state property.*

patrón n. *employer.* **patronal** adj. *pertaining to employment.* – Sin. empleador. empresario. patrono.

peculado (delito) n. *peculation.*

• Comete peculado el funcionario público que substrae o usa indebidamente los fondos o caudales públicos. – Sin. malversación.
Rel: fondos o caudales públicos, *public funds;* funcionario público, *public official.*
Ver: abuso de confianza. malversación.

pedimento n. *petition, request, claim.*

• Solicitud, petición o requerimiento, sobre todo aquellos hechos ante una autoridad judicial.
Pedimento es un término que tiene un significado amplio pudiendo significar un reclamo judicial, una petición o promoción hecha ante el juez o, incluso, una solicitud específica hecha en un escrito presentado ante un tribunal.

pedimento aduanal (Mx) *customs entry petition* || *customs entry form.*

pedimento o promoción unilateral *ex parte motion.*
Ver: *motion.*

pelea[1] **(combate)** n. *fight, quarrel.* **pelear** v. *to fight.* **peleador** n. *fighter.* **peleador** adj. *fighting.* – Sin. contienda, *fight, battle.* refriega, *brawl,* ataque, *attack.* agresión física, *battery.* encuentro, *bout.* riña, *fray.* disputa, *dispute.* encuentro a puñetazos, *fist fight.*
Rel: agarrar, *to grab, to hold;* apalear, *beating;* dar empujones, *to shove;* forcejeo, *scuffle;* meterse con alguien, *to pick a fight with someone;* oponer resistencia, *to put up a fight.*

pelea[2] **(esfuerzo)** n. *struggle.* – Sin. lucha. esfuerzo, *effort.*

peligro n. *danger, peril, hazard.* **peligroso** adj. *dangerous.* **peligrosamente** adv. *dangerously.* **peligrosidad** n. *dangerousness.* – Sin. riesgo, *risk, hazard.*

peligros del mar *perils of the sea.*
peligro inminente *imminent danger.*

pena[1] **(castigo)** n. *punishment* || *sentence.* **penalidad** n. *punishment.* **penal** adj. *penal.* **penalista** n. *criminal lawyer.* **penalmente** adv. *criminally.*

• Sanción fijada por la ley para quien comete un delito o falta. – Sin. castigo (pop.), *punishment.* correctivo, *corrective.* penitencia, *penitence.*

Cf: **pena • sanción • castigo.** Términos usados sinónimamente con frecuencia. Pena es considerado el término técnico penal exclusivo para designar la sanción que se le impone al acusado culpable. <pena de muerte> Sanción es el concepto genérico que designa retribución o compensación por actos de los que se deriva algún tipo de responsabilidad, su aplicación se extiende normalmente a otras ramas del derecho. <sanciones administrativas> Castigo, por su parte, es considerado generalmente el equivalente del término sanción en el habla popular.

aplicación de la pena *sentencing.* – Sin. fijación de la pena.
pena capital *capital punishment, death penalty.* – Sin. pena de muerte.
pena corporal *corporal punishment.*
pena de prisión *punishment by incarceration, prison term.* – Sin. pena privativa de libertad, pena de reclusión.
pena militar *military punishment.*
pena pecuniaria *fine.* – Sin. multa.
purgar una pena *to serve one's sentence.* – Sin. cumplir una pena.
remisión de la pena *remission of an offense.*
suspensión de la pena *suspension of carrying out the sentence.* – Sin. [amplio]suspensión de la condena.
terminación de la pena *completion of a sentence.*
Rel: amonestación, *admonition;* confinamiento, *confinement;* multa, *fine;* pérdida de los instrumentos del delito, *destruction of the instruments of the crime;* reclusión, *internment, imprisonment;* reparación del daño, *restitution;* retribución, *retribution.*
Ref: (Ar)CP a.5ss.; (Bo)CP a.25,26; (Ch)CP a.18, 21; (Co)CP a.34-53; (Esp)CP a.32ss.; (Mx)CP a.24; (Pe)CP a.28; (PR)CP a.38, 33 LPRA sec. 3191; (RD)CP a.6-8; (Ur)CP a.66ss.; (Ve)CP a.8ss.
Ver: condena.

pena[2] **(sanción)** n. *penalty.* – Sin. sanción, *sanction.*

pena convencional *contractual penalty.* – Sin. pena contractual.

penal adj. *penal, criminal.* – Sin. criminal. punible, *punishable.* punitivo, *punitive.*
código penal *penal or criminal code.*
derecho penal *penal law, criminal law.*

penal n. *prison.* – Sin. prisión, *prison.*
institución penal *prison.*
ir al penal *to go to prison.*
pendente lite (lat.) *pendente lite, while the action is pending, pending the lawsuit or litigation.*
penitenciaría n. *penitentiary.*
penología *penology.*
pensión n. *pension,* **pensionar** v. *to grant a pension.* **pensionado/pensionista** n. *pensioner.* – Sin. renta, *rent.*
pensión de jubilación *retirement pension.*
pensión de viudedad *widow pension.* – Sin. pensión de viudez.
pensión militar *military pension.*
pensión perpetua *permanent pension.*
pensión por invalidez *disability pension.*
pensión vitalicia *annuity, life pension.*
Rel: jubilación, *retirement.*
pensión alimenticia *support payments.* – Sin. alimentos. obligación alimenticia, *alimentary obligation.* pensión alimenticia.
pensión alimenticia para un menor *support payments.*
pensión alimenticia provisional para el cónyuge *temporary alimony.*
Ver: alimentos.
pequeña propiedad *small rural tract.*
per diem (lat.) *per diem, (calculated) per day.*
per se (lat.) *per se; of, in or by itself.*
pérdida n. *loss.* – Sin. mengua, *lessening.* merma, *shrinkage.* quebranto, *loss.*
deducción de pérdidas *deduction of losses.*
diferimiento de pérdidas *loss deferral.*
pérdida fiscal *tax loss.*
pérdida pecuniaria *pecuniary loss.*
pérdida real *actual loss.*
pérdida total *total loss.*
pérdidas y ganancias *profit and loss.*
perdón n. *pardon.* **perdonar** v. *to pardon.* **perdonable** adj. *pardonable.*
• "Remisión de la pena merecida, de la ofensa recibida o de alguna deuda u obligación pendiente." (I Dicc. REA, 1573) – Sin. indulto, *pardon.*
Cf: **perdón ● remisión.** Perdón es un término más amplio que remisión, refiriéndose a la extinción de una pena o de una deuda u obligación mediante declaración voluntaria del facultado para perdonar. La remisión significa alzar la pena, eximir o liberar de una obligación y es una especie del género renuncia en materia civil, definiéndose como una renuncia

de derechos de crédito solamente; mientras en materia penal, generalmente se refiere al perdón parcial de una pena con motivo de la realización de cierta actividad o la satisfacción de ciertos requisitos, como la buena conducta o la realización de trabajo.
perdón de la deuda *forgiveness of the debt.*
perdón del ofendido *injured party's pardon.*
perdón judicial *criminal pardon.*
Rel: amnistía, *amnesty;* clemencia, *mercy, leniency;* condonación, *condone, forgive;* conmutación, *commutation;* gracia, *grace;* remisión, *remission.*
Ver: indulto.
perención de la instancia [ed]*lapsing of a lawsuit due to inactivity of the parties,* [prest.] *peremption.* – Sin. abandono del proceso.
perentorio adj. *peremptory.* **perentoriamente** adv. *peremptorily.*
• Aquel plazo o término que es fatal. El último plazo que se concede en cualquier asunto. También se entiende como algo concluyente o decisivo. – Sin. apremiante, *pressing.*
plazo perentorio *peremptory term.*
perfeccionar un contrato *conclusion of a contract.*
pericia n. *expert knowledge.* **perito** n. *expert.* **pericial** adj. *expert.* **peritaje/peritazgo** n. *expert's report.* **peritación** n. *expert's research.* – Sin. destreza, *skill, dexterity.* habilidad, *ability.*
dictamen pericial *expert's report.*
peritaje médico *medical expert's report.*
perito calígrafo/caligráfico *handwriting expert.*
perito testigo *expert witness.*
prueba pericial *expert evidence.*
período de gracia *grace period.*
período de prueba DER.LABORAL *trial or test period* || *evidentiary period.*
perjuicio (daño) *profit loss or undue expense* || *damage.*
• En sentido estricto, ganancia lícita que deja de percibirse o gastos ocasionados por la acción u omisión de otro que debe indemnizar.
Cf: **daños ● perjuicios.** En su acepción amplia ambos términos implican pérdida o merma y en ese sentido ambos términos son usados sinónimamente. <el accidente les causó perjuicio> Por otro lado, en su sentido técnico-jurídico los daños se refieren al menoscabo patrimonial que se sufre y que debe ser reparado al procederse judicialmente, en tanto que los perjuicios son el lucro lícito perdido con motivo del acto

u omisión ilícita y cuya exigencia procede por la vía de la indemnización. <demanda de daños y perjuicios>
daños y perjuicios *damages.*
perjuicios materiales *property damage.*
perjuicios morales *emotional distress, mental suffering.*
Rel: daño, *damages;* lucro cesante, *loss of lawful gains (due to damage or harm).*
perjurio n. *perjury, false swearing.* **perjurar** v. *to perjure.* **perjurador/perjuro** adj. *perjurios.*
• Declarar con falsedad estando bajo protesta o juramento de decir verdad. – Sin. falso testimonio. declarar con falsedad. juramento falso, *false swearing.* quebrantar un juramento, *breach of an oath.*
bajo la pena de perjurio *under the penalty of perjury.*
permiso¹ (licencia) n. *permit, authorization.*
– Sin. autorización, *authorization.* licencia, *license.* permisión, *permission.*
permiso de armas *gun permit.* – Sin. permiso de portación de armas. licencia de armas.
permiso de conducir *driving permit.*
permiso de exportación *export permit.*
permiso judicial para conducir *judicial driving permit.*
permiso² DER.MILITAR n. *leave, furlough.*
– Sin. licencia, *leave.* pase, *pass.*
permuta (contrato) n. *exchange,* [lat.]*permutatio.* **permutar** v. *to exchange property.* **permutación** n. *bartering.* **permutante** n. *barterer.* **permutable** adj. *exchangeable.*
• Trueque o cambio de una cosa por otra. – Sin. cambio. trueque, *barter.* permutación (Ar).
permuta mercantil *barter agreement.*
Ref: (Ar)CC 1485; (Ch)CC a.1897; (Esp)CC a.1.538; (Mx)CC a.2327; (Pe)CC a.1602; (PR)CC a.1428, 31 LPRA sec. 3981; (Ur)CC a.1779-1775; (Ve)CC a.1558-1564.
perpetración n. *perpetration.* **perpetrar** v. *to perpetrate.* **perpetrador** n. *perpetrator.*
persecución n. *persecution, pursuit.* **perseguir** v. *to persecute.* **perseguidor** n. *pursuer.*
– Sin. perseguimiento.
persona¹ (entidad) PERSONAS n. *artificial person, juristic person.* – Sin. persona artificial, *artificial person.* persona ficticia, *fictitious person.* persona jurídica. persona moral, *moral person.*
"La condición de sujeto de derecho o de relaciones jurídicas está no sólo atribuida a la persona humana (persona física o persona natural), sino también a las organizaciones o agrupacio-

nes de personas físicas a las que la ley reconoce personalidad independiente de los sujetos que las integran. Son las denominadas personas jurídicas, personas morales o personas ficticias." (Ribó Durán, 447)
persona jurídica pública *public corporation.* Rel: capacidad, *capacity;* nacionalidad, *nationality, citizenship;* sujeto de derecho, *legal entity or being,* [ef]*legal person.*
Ref: (Ar)CC a.30; (Ch)CC a.545; (CR)CC a.33; (Ec) CC a.583; (Mx)CC a.22,25; (Pe)CC a.76-79; (PR) CC a.27, 31 LPRA sec 101; (Ur)CC a.21; (Ve)CC a.19.
persona² (individuo) n. *individual.* **personal** adj. *personal.* **personalmente** adv. *personally.*
– Sin. individuo, *individual.* prójimo, *fellow man.* semejante, *fellow man.*
persona física *natural person.* – Sin. persona natural.
persona desaparecida *missing person.*
personal de seguridad *security personnel.*
personal de un juzgado *court personnel.*
personalidad¹ PERSONAS n. [ed]*(quality of) being a legal entity.*
• Concepto abstracto que se refiere a la cualidad de una persona en virtud de la cual se le considera sujeto de derecho y obligaciones. – Sin. personalidad jurídica.
Rel: capacidad, *capacity.*
personalidad² DER.PROCESAL n. *legal authority to sue, legal standing.*
• En el ámbito procesal se entiende por personalidad la capacidad para comparecer en juicio así como el tener representación legal y bastante para litigar. – Sin. personería.
falta de personalidad *lack of authority to sue, lack of standing.* – Sin. falta de personería.
personalidad³ (psicología) n. *personality.*
– Sin. identidad, *identity.*
personalidad múltiple *multiple personality.*
personalidad psicópata *psychopath personality.*
personería¹ (mandato) n. *function of agent.*
personería² (personalidad) n. *legal authority to sue* || *to be legally registered (as a legal entity).* – Sin. capacidad procesal.
personificación n. *impersonation.* **personificar** v. *to personify.* – Sin. encarnación (fig.).
perturbación mental *mental defect.*
petición n. *petition, request, motion.* **peticionario** n. *petitioner or petitionist.* **petitorio** adj. *petitionary.* – Sin. solicitud, *application.*

Al término petición se le asignan generalmente dos acepciones principales en materia jurídica, una amplia significando cualquier reclamo hecho a la autoridad, y otra restringido, refiriéndose a aquél reclamo que se hace siguiendo un procedimiento debidamente especificado, generalmente ante la autoridad judicial. Por otro lado, cuando se habla del derecho de petición generalmente se está haciendo alusión a aquél que tienen los particulares para requerir una respuesta escrita de la administración pública con relación a la esfera de sus funciones.

derecho de petición *right to petition public officials.*

petición de divorcio *petition for divorce.*

petición de herencia *probate proceeding brought by legitimate or testamentary heir to divide estate.*

petición de quiebra *filing for bankruptcy.*
Rel: demanda, *claim, complaint;* promoción, *motion.*
Ver: promoción.

petición de mano *request of a woman's hand in marriage.*

piratería n. *piracy.* **piratear** v. *to practice piracy.*
pirata n. *pirate.* – Sin. corso, *privateering.*
piratería aérea *air piracy.*
Rel: pillaje, *pillage;* saqueo, *plundering.*

pistola n. *pistol.* **pistolero** n. *gunman, gunslinger.*
pistola de aire *air gun.*
pistola de perdigón *pellet gun.*
Ver: arma de fuego.

plagio[1] **(apropiación)** n. *plagiarism.* **plagiar** v. *to plagiarize.* **plagiario** n. *plagiarist.*
• La utilización con ánimo de lucro, y en perjuicio de tercero, de parte o del todo de una obra literaria, artística o científica sin la autorización de su autor. – Sin. imitación, *imitation.* apropiación, *appropriation.*

plagio[2] **(secuestro)** *n kidnapping.* – Sin. secuestro.

plan de jubilación *pension plan.*

plan de reparto de utilidades *profit sharing plan.*

plataforma continental *continental shelf.*

plazo[1] **(period)** n. *time period, term.*
plazo contractual *contract term.*
plazo de arrendamiento *term of lease.*
plazo de gracia *grace period.*
plazo de vigencia de una ley *period a statute is in effect.*
plazo legal *legal term.*

plazo[2] **(término)** n. *term, deadline.*

plazo de vencimiento *expiration term.*
plazo final *final term or deadline.*

plazo[3] OBLIGACIONES n. *date certain, term.*
• "Plazo es un acontecimiento de realización cierta, del cual depende la exigibilidad o la resolución de derechos y obligaciones." (Gutiérrez y González, 653) – Sin. término.
Cf: **plazo • término.** Términos generalmente usados sinónimamente al aplicarse a las obligaciones, pero que han sido distinguidos por la doctrina. El término es el momento o instante en que ha de cumplirse o extinguirse una obligación, mientras que el plazo es el lapso o período de tiempo durante el cual puede cumplirse o extinguirse.

obligación a plazo *obligation to be performed or to terminate on a date certain.* – Sin. obligación a término.

plazo judicial *judicially prescribed term.*
– Sin. término judicial.
cómputo de plazos *term calculation.*
plazo improrrogable *deadline which cannot be extended.*
plazo perentorio *peremptory term.*
plazo procesal [ed]*period to file a motion or complete other procedural step.*
Rel: vencimiento, *due, expiration.*

plebiscito n. *plebiscite.*
• "Acto extraordinario e independiente, en el que se consulta al electorado sobre una cuestión vital del Estado." (Fernández Vázquez, 570) – Sin. consulta popular. referéndum, *referendum.*
Cf: **plebiscito • referéndum.** Ambos términos se usan en forma sinónima e indistinta. La doctrina distingue ambos conceptos considerando que el plebiscito se refiere a cuestiones de hecho, actos políticos y medidas de gobierno, esto es cuestiones esencialmente de índole política, mientras que el referéndum es una consulta popular dirigida a aprobar leyes o decidir cuestiones normativas, esto es cuestiones esencialmente de índole jurídica.

pleito[1] **(proceso)** n. *suit.* – Sin. juicio. proceso, *proceeding.*
pleito civil *civil suit.*
pleito judicial *lawsuit.*

pleito[2] **(litigio)** n. *litigation, judicial action.*
– Sin. controversia, *controversy.* litigio, *litigation.*

plenario n. [prest.]*plenario,* [ed]*trial stage of criminal proceedings.*
• Etapa del procedimiento penal que sigue a la

instrucción durante el cual se formulan los cargos, se presenta la defensa, las pruebas y alegatos, y se emite la sentencia. – Sin. juicio penal. proceso principal o debate.
Ver: procedimiento penal.

plica n. [ed]*document in a sealed envelope to be opened under specified conditions.*

pliego de posiciones DER.PROC.CIVIL *interrogatories.* – Sin. pliego de preguntas.
Rel: absolvente, *deponent, witness;* articular y absolver posiciones, *to submit and answer interrogatories;* calificación (de preguntas), *approval (of questions);* objeción, *objection.*

pluralidad de delitos *joinder of offenses.* – Sin. concurso de delitos.
Rel: delito conexo, *related crime.*

plusvalía n. *appreciation, goodwill.*

población n. *population.* – Sin. habitantes, *inhabitants.*

pobre n. *poor.* **pobreza** n. *poverty.* **pobremente** adv. *poorly.* **pobretón** adj. *very poor.* **pobrete** adj. *poor, unfortunate.* – Sin. indigente, *indigent.* menesteroso, *needy.* necesitado, *needy.*
declaración o declaratoria de pobreza *approval of poverty affidavit || admission of pauper's status.*
demanda de pobreza *poverty affidavit, pauper's affidavit, pauper's petition.*
Rel: mendigo, *beggar;* miserable, *miserable;* paupérrimo, *very poor, poverty-stricken;* pordiosero, *beggar.*

poder¹ (política) n. *power || branch.* – Sin. autoridad, *authority.*
poder constituido *constitutional power.*
poder constituyente *constitutional assembly.*
poder de policía *police powers.*
poder ejecutivo *the executive, executive branch.*
poder judicial *the judiciary, judiciary branch.* – Sin. rama judicial.
poder legislativo *the legislature, legislative branch.*
poder político *political power.*
poder público *government power, state power.*

poder²(representación) n. *power, agency. || power of attorney.* **apoderado** n. *agent.* **poderdante** n. *principal.*
• Facultad de representar a otro o de celebrar negocios jurídicos en su representación.
aceptación de poder *acceptance of power, acceptance of power of attorney, acceptance of agency.*

poder de disposición *power to convey property.*
poder especial *special power.* – Sin. *poder específico* (PR).
poder general para actos de administración [ed]*general power for managerial or administrative functions.*
poder general para actos de dominio [ed] *general power for transfer of ownership and conveyance.*
poder general para pleitos y cobranzas. [ed] *general power for litigation and collection.*
Rel: mandato, *agency agreement;* representación, *representation.*

poder³ (atribución) n. *power.* – Sin. facultad.
poder de compra *purchasing power.*
poder discrecional *discretion or discretionary power.*
poder reglamentario *regulatory power (of the executive).*

policía¹ (persona) n. *policeman, cop* (mod.). – Sin. guardián del orden.
oficial de policía *police officer.* – Sin. agente de policía.
policía de tránsito o tráfico *traffic police.*
policía vestido de civil *plain-clothes policeman.*
Rel: guardia, *guard;* vigilante, *guard.*

policía² (organización) n. *police.*
policíaco/policial adj. *pertaining to police.* – Sin. fuerza policíaca, *police force.* fuerza pública, *police force.*
estación de policía *police station.* – Sin. delegación de policía.
estación de policía *police station.*
fuerza policíaca *police force.* – Sin. fuerza pública.
patrulla o carro policíaco *police or squat car.*
policía de caminos *highway police.*
policía federal *federal police.*
policía judicial *judicial police.*
policía militar (PM) *military police.*
policía preventiva *preventive police.*
policía secreta *secret police.*
prefectura de policía *police headquarters.* – Sin. jefatura de la policía.
Rel: servicio secreto, *secret service.*

poligamia n. *polygamy.* **polígamo** n. *polygamous.*

polígrafo n. *polygraph.* – Sin. detector de mentiras, *lie detector.*

política¹ (poder) n. *politics.* **político** n. *politician.*

político adj. *political.* **políticamente** adv. *politically.*
  constitución política *constitution.*
  división política *political subdivision.*
  partido político *political party.*

política² (plan) n. *policy.*
  política arancelaria *tariff policy.*
  política exterior *foreign policy.*
  política económica *economic policy.*
  política fiscal *tax policy.*
  política monetaria *monetary policy.*

póliza de fletamiento *freight policy.*

póliza de seguro *insurance policy.* **tomador** n. *policy holder.* **beneficiario** n. *beneficiary.*

poner por escrito *reduce to writing.*

por lo expuesto y fundado *for the above mentioned reasons and statements.*

por propio derecho DER.PROC *on his or her own behalf.* – Sin. por derecho propio. por su propio derecho.

pormenores *particulars, details.*

pornografía n. *pornography.* **pornógrafo** n. *pornographer.* **pornográfico** adj. *pornographic.*
  • El cometer actos —expresados sobre todo en forma de publicaciones— que causan escándalo público por ser obscenos e ir contra la moral y buenas costumbres de la época y el lugar en donde se lleven a cabo. – Sin. impudicia, *immodesty, indecency.* indecencia, *indecency.* obscenidad, *obscenity.*

portación de armas (delito) *carrying a concealed weapon.*
  Rel: tenencia ilícita de armas, *possession of illegal weapons.*

portador n. *bearer, holder.* **portar** v. *to bear, hold.*
  al portador *to bearer.*

porte¹ (transportación) *transportation.* **portear** v. *to transport.* **porteador** n. *carrier.*
  carta de porte *waybill, bill of lading.*
  carta de porte aérea *air waybill.*
  Rel: contrato de transporte, *transportation contract.*

porte² (peaje) *transportation charge.*

posesión *possession.* **poseer** v. *to possess, hold.* **poseedor** n. *possessor, holder.* **posesorio** adj. *possessory.*
  • Es un estado de hecho que da a una persona el poder o señorío sobre una cosa para aprovecharse de ella con ánimo de dueño.

Cf: **posesión • tenencia • detentación.**
Términos usados frecuentemente en forma sinónima. Posesión se usa en ocasiones ampliamente significando simplemente poder físico sobre una cosa. En sentido más restringido, se refiere al poder directo, de hecho, ejercido sobre una cosa con la pretensión de ser su dueño. La tenencia, por su parte, se refiere al poder directo que una persona tiene sobre la cosa sin tener el ánimo de dueño, esto es, sin que exista una voluntad intencional de convertirse en su propietario. Si la tenencia es ilegítima, por ejemplo si el bien se robó, se dice que se trata ya, no de tenencia, sino de detentación. La tenencia, por tanto, requiere de la legitimidad del poder sobre la cosa, no así la detentación.

poseedor de buena fe *bona fide holder, holder in good faith.*

posesión continua *uninterrupted possession.*

posesión de buena fe *bona fide possession, possession in good faith.*

posesión de derecho *legal possession.*

posesión de hecho *actual possession.*

posesión de mala fe *mala fide possession, possession in bad faith.*

posesión pacífica *peaceable or undisturbed possession.*

posesión prescriptiva *adverse possession.*

posesión pública *notorious possession.*
Rel: detentación, *detainer;* precario, *detainer, holding;* tenencia, *tenancy.*

Comentario: "La posesión en el derecho romano significó, en esencia, una relación de hecho con la cosa, que llevaba consigo su dominación real y efectiva, unida a la intención de tener la cosa como propia. Tiene por el contrario, un sentido de ampliación progresiva de la idea de posesión la concepción moderna de ella, fundada en las tradiciones del Derecho germánico y el canónico, que ha ensanchado el ámbito de la misma, al considerarla no sólo como tenencia de las cosas del mundo exterior (es decir, como ejercicio o visibilidad del derecho de dominio), sino también como ejercicio del contenido de los demás derechos, especialmente de los de naturaleza real. En éste sentido amplio ... se define modernamente la posesión 'como el ejercicio, de hecho, de un derecho, independientemente de la consideración de si el derecho pertenece o no a quien lo ejercita, como derecho suyo.'" (II Vol. I Castan Tobeñas, 640-641)

Ver: *possession.*
Ref: (Ar)CC a.2351; (Ch)CC a.700; (CR)CC a.277-286; (Ec)CC a.734; (Esp)CC a.430; (Mx)CC a.790 ss.; (Pe)CC a.896ss.; (PR)CC a.360ss., 31 LPRA sec. 1421ss.; (Ur)CC a.646ss.; (Ve)CC a.771ss.

post mortem (lat.) *post mortem, occurring after death.*

postura legal *legal tender.* **postor** n. *bidder.*
mejor postor *highest bidder.*
mejor postura *highest bid.*
potestad n. *authority, power.*
• "Dominio, poder, jurisdicción o facultad que se tiene, ejerce sobre una persona o cosa." (Dicc. ed. Comares, 409) – Sin. autoridad, *authority.* dominio, *dominium.* poder, *power.* facultad, *power, authority.*
potestad disciplinaria *disciplinary authority.*
potestad discrecional *discretionary power.*
prácticas desleales de comercio *unfair business practices.*
prácticas discriminatorias *discriminatory practices.*
prácticas restrictivas de la competencia (Esp) *unfair competition practices.*
precario adj. *detainer, holding* || [ef]*revocable bailment.* **precariedad** n. *detaining, retaining.*
precarista adj. *holder.*
• Casos en que se posee un bien sin derecho alguno. También el uso gratuito de una cosa pudiendo revocarlo a su arbitrio.
precedente judicial *precedent.*
precepto n. *precept.* **preceptuar** v. *to issue precepts or rules.*
• Norma o regla parte de un ordenamiento.
– Sin. mandato, *precept, order.* regla, *rule.*
precepto legal *statute, rule.*
Rel: provisión, *measure, step.*
precio n. *price.* – Sin. importe. valor, *value.*
precio alzado o global *lump sum.*
precio cierto *price certain, fixed price.*
precio corriente *current price.*
precio de garantía *guaranteed price* || *lowest possible price.*
precio de menudeo *retail price.*
precio de mayoreo *wholesale price.*
precio de mercado *market price.*
precio de reposición *replacement value.*
precio de venta *asking price.*
precio en efectivo *cash price.*
precio máximo *ceiling price.*
precio mínimo *floor price.*
precio oficial *official price.*
precio tope *ceiling price.*
preclusión n. [ed]*extinction of a procedural right,* [rtrgido]*preclusion.* – Sin. caducidad, lapse, extinction.
Cf: **preclusión • caducidad.** Términos usados en ocasiones en forma intercambiable; son generalmente distinguidos por la doctrina y la legislación. La preclusión extingue expectativas o facultades de actuar válidamente y obedece a la inactividad de una de las partes, cerrando una etapa o fase procesal permitiendo al proceso continuar adelante. La caducidad en contraste, se refiere normalmente a la inactividad de ambas partes y extingue el proceso dejando sin efectos las actuaciones hechas.
Rel: caducidad de instancia, *nonsuit, laches;* prescripción, *prescription.*
predio *piece of land, lot.* **predial** adj. *pertaining to real property.*
predio colindante *adjoining lot or tenement.*
predio dominante *dominant estate or tenement.*
predio rural o rústico *rural property, rural land.*
predio sirviente *servient estate or tenement.*
predio urbano *urban real estate, urban property.*
Rel: finca, *farm, real estate;* fundo, *rural property.*
pregunta n. *question.* **preguntar** v. *to question, ask.* – Sin. cuestión, *question.*
pregunta capciosa *tricky question.* – Sin. pregunta insidiosa.
pregunta hipotética *hypothetical question, speculative question.*
pregunta impertinente *irrelevant question.*
pregunta sugestiva *leading question.*
Rel: absolución de posiciones, *reply to interrogatories;* interrogatorio, *interrogatory.*
prejudicial adj. *pretrial.*
prejuicio n. *prejudice.* – Sin. parcialidad, *bias.* preferencia, *preference.*
prejuicio racial *racial prejudice.*
prejuicio religioso *religious prejudice.*
prelación de créditos *priority of creditor's claims.*
premeditación n. *premeditation, prepense.*
premeditar v. *to premeditate.* **premeditado** adj. *premeditated.* **premeditadamente** adv. *premeditatedly.*
• "Deliberación o reflexión en torno a un delito que se tiene el propósito de cometer." (De Pina, 414) – Sin. deliberación, *deliberation.* reflexión, *reflection.*
Ver: agravantes.
prenda *pledge.* **pignorar** v. *to pledge, pawn.*
acreedor pignoraticio *pledgee.* **deudor pignoraticio** *pledgor.*
• Es un derecho real que se constituye sobre un bien mueble enajenable o un crédito para

asegurar el cumplimiento de una obligación, concediendo el derecho de vender el bien y otorgando una preferencia en su pago en caso de incumplimiento de la obligación asegurada. Prenda significa además el contrato de garantía llamado contrato de prenda en el que se constituye la misma, así como con frecuencia la cosa dada en garantía. <darse por recibido de la prenda> – Sin. pignus (lat.).

contrato de prenda *pledge agreement.*
dar en prenda *to furnish in pledge, to pledge.*
prenda con desplazamiento *pledge.*
prenda de valores *pledge of securities.*
– Sin. prenda sobre valores.
prenda flotante *floating pledge.*
prenda mercantil *commercial pledge.*
prenda sin desplazamiento *pledge in which property remains in pledgor's possession,* [ef]*chattel mortgage.* – Sin. prenda con registro. prenda registrable.
Ver: hipoteca.
Ref: (Ar)CC a.3204; (Ch)CC a.2384; (Ec)CC a. 2310-2332; (Esp)CC a.1863ss.; (Mx)CC a.2856ss.; (Pe) CC a.1055-1090; (Ur)CC a.2292-2321; (Ve)CC a. 1837-1854.

prescripción n. *prescription, limitation.*
prescribir v. *to prescribe.* **prescriptibilidad** n. [ed]*ability to own a right by adverse possession or to extinguish an obligation by lapsing.*
prescriptible adj. [ed]*able to be owned by adverse possession or extinguished by lapsing, prescribable.*
• Prescripción es un medio de adquirir un derecho o de liberarse de una obligación por el transcurso del tiempo.
interrupción de la prescripción *interruption of the limitation period.*
prescripción de la acción *limitation of action.*
prescripción de la pena *limitation of criminal punishment.*
prescripción del delito *limitation of criminal liability.*
prescripción extintiva *extinctive prescription.* [prest.]*liberative prescription.* – Sin. prescripción negativa, *negative prescription.*
prescripción positiva *positive prescription (if personalty), adverse possession (if realty),* [prest.]*acquisitive prescription.* – Sin. prescripción adquisitiva. usucapión.
término prescriptivo *limitation period.*
Rel: caducidad, *lapse;* preclusión, *extinction of a procedural right.*
presentación extemporánea DER.PROCESAL *late filing.*
presidente n. *president.* **presidencia** n. *presidency.*

presidencial adj. *presidential.*
presidencialismo n. *presidential system of government.*
presidente de la asociación *president of the association.*
Presidente de la República *President of the Republic.*
presidente del consejo de administración *Chairman of the Board.*
presidente del tribunal *chief judge, presiding judge.*
presidente municipal *municipal president.*
presidio n. *prison.* **presidiario** n. *prisoner, inmate.*
presidiable adj. *imprisonable.*
Ver: prisión.
preso n. *prisoner, inmate.* – Sin. encarcelado, *jailed.* presidiario. prisionero. recluso. reo.
preso político *political prisoner.*
preso por delitos de orden común *in detention accused of committing a state crime (in federal systems)* || *in detention accused of committing a felony or misdemeanor (not considered a political crime).*
prestación de una obligación OBLIGACIONES *to do, not to do, or to turn over (property, use, etc).*
prestación de servicios *rendering of services.*
prestaciones del seguro social *benefits provided by social security, social security benefits.* – Sin. beneficios del seguro social. prestaciones sociales.
Tipos: invalidez, *disability;* incapacidad, *disability;* desempleo, *unemployment;* jubilación, *retirement;* maternidad, *maternity benefits;* muerte, *death;* orfandad, *orphan protection;* servicios de salud, *health services;* viudedad o viudez, *widow's benefits.*
préstamo (contrato) n. *loan.* **prestar** v. *to lend.*
prestador n. *lender.* **prestamista** n. *moneylender.* **prestatario** n. *borrower.*
• "Contrato en virtud el cual una persona — mediante intereses o sin ellos— transfiere a otra una suma de dinero o cosas fungibles, quedando ésta obligada a devolver otro tanto de la misma especie o calidad." (De Pina, 415)
– Sin. crédito, *credit.* mutuo, *mutuum, loan.*
Cf: **préstamo • mutuo • comodato.** Contratos similares que se refieren a la operación de préstamo de bienes. Préstamo y mutuo son sinónimos ya que expresan contratos que transfieren la propiedad de sumas de dinero o bienes fungibles, en contraste el comodato expresa un contrato que transfiere la propiedad de bienes no fungibles en forma gratuita. Al

contrato de mutuo se le conoce tradicional-mente como "préstamo de consumo", en tanto que al comodato se le conoce como "préstamo de uso".

garantizar un préstamo *to secure a loan.*
gestionar un préstamo *to arrange for a loan.*
préstamo a la gruesa DER.MARÍTIMO *bottomry,* [lat.]*respondentia.*
préstamo bancario *bank loan.*
préstamo con garantía hipotecaria *mortgage loan.*
préstamo con garantía prendaria *loan secured by property pledged.*
préstamo con interés *loan with interest.*
préstamo de habilitación o avío *loan to industrial enterprises secured with inventories.*
préstamo garantizado *secured loan, guaranteed loan.* – Sin. préstamo con garantía.
préstamo hipotecario *mortgage loan.*
préstamo leonino *shark loan.*
préstamo mercantil *commercial loan.*
préstamo no garantizado *unsecured loan, straight loan.* – Sin. préstamo quirografario.
préstamo prendario *pledge loan.*
préstamo puente *bridge-loan.*
préstamo refaccionario *bank loan secured with capital assets.*
préstamo sin intereses *interest-free loan.*
préstamo sindicado *syndicated loan.*
Rel: comodato, [prest.][lat.]*commodatum,* [ef] *gratuitous bailment;* empréstito, *government loan.*
Ver: crédito[1].

prestanombre n. *straw man.*
• Persona que actúa en nombre e interés de otro permitiendo la realización de actos u operaciones que no puede o quiere llevar a cabo aquél por quien se actúa. – Sin. testaferro. persona interpuesta, *front person.* tapadera, *cover.*

prestar juramento *to take an oath, to be sworn in.*

presunción DER.PROC n. *presumption.* **presuntivo** adj. *presumed.* **presuntamente** adv. *presumably.* **presuntivamente** adv. *conjecturally.*
• La presunción es la consecuencia que la propia ley o el juez infieren de un hecho conocido para comprobar la existencia de otro desconocido. – Sin. conjetura, *conjecture.* indicio. suposición, *supposition, assumption.*
Cf: **presunción • indicio.** Ambos términos se usan sinónimamente con frecuencia, sin embargo en estricto rigor indicio tiene un signi-

ficado más amplio, ya que se le entiende no solamente como presunción sino también simplemente como un rastro, vestigio o clave en la comisión de un delito.

presunción de derecho *legal presumption.*
presunción de hecho *presumption of fact.*
presunción de inocencia *presumption of innocence.*
presunción de legítima defensa *presumption of self-defense.*
presunción de legitimidad *presumption of legitimacy.*
presunción de muerte *presumption of death.*
presunción iuris et de iure *presumption juris et de jure, conclusive presumption.*
presunción iuris tantum *rebuttable presumption.* – Sin. presunción que admite prueba en contrario.
presunción legal *statutory presumption.*

presupuesto n. *budget.* **presupuestar** v. *to budget.* **presupuestal** adj. *budgetary.*
asignación presupuestal *budget appropriation.*
control presupuestal *budgetary control.*
déficit presupuestal *budgetary deficit.*

presupuestos procesales [ed]*procedural basic conditions.*

pretensión n. *claim.* – Sin. pretensión jurídica. Ver: acción. demanda.

preterintencionalidad DER.PENAL n. [ed]*criminal action which causes a greater harm than the one initially intended.* **preterintencional** adj. [ed]*pertaining to a criminal action causing a greater harm than the one initially intended.* **preterintención** n. [ed]*criminal intent to cause a less serious injury than the one caused.*
• La discordancia entre la intención del delincuente y el resultado de su acción delictiva cuando el resultando excede la intención de su intento.

prevaricación n. *breach of duties by public officials.* **prevaricar** v. *to breach public duties.* **prevaricador** n. *public official who breaches his or her public duties.*
• Denominación genérica dada a los diferentes actos de falta de probidad en que puede incurrir un funcionario en el desempeño de su encargo, especialmente aquellos que implican decisiones o resoluciones. – Sin. prevaricato.

previsión social *social welfare legislation.*

prima[1] **(margen)** n. *margin, mark up.*
– Sin. sobreprecio, *surcharge.* prima, *mark up.*

prima² (aumento) n. *bonus.* – Sin. aumento, *increase, raise.* gratificación. plus (Esp), *extra pay, bonus.* premio, *premium.* recompensa, *reward.*

prima de seguro *insurance premium.*

prima facie (lat.) *prima facie, at first sight.*

• A primera vista. A primera impresión sin ver el caso a fondo.

primera instancia *first instance.*

principio de legalidad *due process of law || rule of law.*

principios generales del derecho [prest.][el]*general principles of law.*

• Principios derivados de un código u ordenación jurídica o de la totalidad del orden jurídico (e incluso los principios del derecho natural) para resolver aquellos casos que no se encuentran comprendidos en las disposiciones vigentes.

⊶ No hay concepto equivalente en el derecho angloamericano. Los principios generales del derecho derivan del método jurídico basado en la sistematización y racionalización propias de las normas del derecho romano-germánico. El derecho angloamericano basa su desarrollo de principios en la interpretación de las decisiones individualizadas, destacando la precisión y la correspondencia con la realidad. Se pudiera decir que mientras los principios generales del derecho, como una manifestación esencial de la naturaleza sistemática del derecho romano-germano, lo describen como un proceso totalizador; los precedentes judiciales, como la exposición central de la naturaleza pragmática y detallista del derecho angloamericano, lo definen como un proceso esencialmente atomista. El concepto jurídico de *common law* más cercano al contenido de los principios generales del derecho es el histórico principio de *equity*, como un elemento atemperante de la rigidez legalista con un contenido impreciso de justicia. Se trata de un mismo objetivo jurídico, algunos dirían similar función, aunque el contexto y la aplicación sean totalmente diferentes.

Comentario: "No es posible hacer una enumeración exhaustiva de los principios generales del derecho, pues el conocimiento de ellos se va perfeccionando poco a poco y por lo mismo su número y contenido han ido variando, sin embargo, por vía de ejemplo se pueden mencionar algunos: la equidad, o sea la prudente aplicación de la ley al caso concreto; la buena fe o lealtad a la palabra empeñada; la obligación de cumplir los convenios; … etc." (Dicc. UNAM, 2543)

prisión¹ (reclusión) n. *imprisonment.* **preso** n. *prisoner, inmate.* **prisionero** n. *prisoner.*

• Poner en prisión; confinar. – Sin. arresto (Esp). aprisionamiento. encarcelamiento, *jailing.* reclusión, *confinement.*

poner en prisión *to put in prison, to put in jail.*

prisión administrativa *administrative hold or detention.*

prisión preventiva *preventive or temporary detention pending trial.*

salir de prisión, *get out of prison, be discharged.*

sentencia de prisión *prison term judgment.*

prisión² (inmueble) n. *prison.*

• Centro de reclusión en donde purgan condenas los reos que han sido encontrados culpables. – Sin. correccional, *correctional.* penal, *prison, penitentiary.* penitenciaría, *penitentiary.* presidio.

Cf: **prisión • cárcel.** Términos que se usan frecuentemente en forma sinónima e intercambiable, pero que en estricto rigor técnico se distinguen por el hecho de que prisión se considera el lugar de resguardo de aquellos que han sido sentenciados a término de prisión, esto es, los condenados en justicia; mientras que cárcel se refiere, en la mayoría de los casos, al lugar en donde se encuentran detenidos los procesados, encausados, e incluso los detenidos preventivamente.

prisión de máxima seguridad *maximum security prison.*

prisión de mínima seguridad *minimum security prison.*

prisión estatal *state prison.*

Rel: cárcel, *jail.*

privacía n. *privacy.*

derecho de privacía *privacy rights.*

– Sin. derecho de privacidad.

privación ilegal de la libertad (delito) *false imprisonment, unlawful imprisonment.*

• La detención de una persona sin derecho, frecuentemente por fuerzas policíacas o militares. – Sin. [rtrgido]detención arbitraria (Co). detención ilegal (Esp). restricción de la libertad (PR). Rel: secuestro, *kidnapping;* desaparecido, *missing.*

privilegio¹ (prerrogativa) n. *privilege.* **privilegiar** v. *to grant a privilege.* **privilegiado** n. *privileged person.* **privilegiado** adj. *privileged.*

• "[L]a prerrogativa o gracia que se concede a uno, liberándole de carga o gravamen o confi-

riéndole un derecho de que no gozan los demás."
(VI Cabanellas, 424-25) – Sin. fuero, *legal privilege*. prerrogativa, *prerogative*. ventaja, *advantage*.

privilegio convencional *contractual privilege*.
privilegio personal *personal privilege*.
Rel: inmunidad, *immunity*.

privilegio²(garantía) n. *lien*.
privilegios marítimos *maritime liens*.
privilegio de pobreza *in forma pauperis*.

pro indiviso *pro indiviso, as undivided*.
Ver: indivisión.

probatoria n. *discovery period*.

procedimiento¹ (amplio) *procedure*.
procedimental adj. *procedural*.
• Secuencia ordenada de actos a través de los cuales se desenvuelve todo un proceso.
– Sin. enjuiciamiento.
Cf: **procedimiento • proceso**. Ambos términos se emplean como sinónimos o son intercambiables con frecuencia. Sin embargo la doctrina ha establecido una clara distinción con aceptación hoy en día generalizada: el proceso se encuentra dirigido a la resolución jurisdiccional de un litigio, mientras que el procedimiento se reduce a ser una coordinación de actos en marcha relacionados entre sí por el efecto jurídico final; el enfoque del proceso es primordialmente teleológico o finalista, el del procedimiento es de índole formal. Se puede decir que todo proceso requiere para su ejecución de un procedimiento, pero no todo procedimiento es un proceso.

procedimiento contencioso administrativo
[ed]*judicial proceedings involving administrative matters*.

procedimiento laboral o de trabajo
[ed]*proceedings regarding employee claims or labor disputes*.
Rel: juicio, *trial*.
Ver: procedimiento civil. procedimiento penal.

procedimiento² (restringido) *proceeding*.
• Conjunto de actos cumplidos para lograr una solución judicial específica.

procedimiento abreviado *summary proceeding*.

procedimiento administrativo *administrative proceeding*.

procedimiento de apremio *enforcement proceeding, distress proceeding*.

procedimiento de deportación *deportation proceeding*.

procedimiento de ejecución *enforcement proceeding*.

procedimiento de liquidación *liquidation proceeding*.

procedimiento ejecutivo hipotecario
foreclosure proceedings.

procedimiento civil *civil procedure*.
– Sin. enjuiciamiento civil.

El procedimiento civil en países hispanos está organizado alrededor de un procedimiento típico o modelo, llamado "ordinario," al que se ajustan la mayoría de los casos y sobre el que se modelan o definen los demás procedimientos (denominados "especiales"), mediante la introducción de las variaciones requeridas por las peculiaridades de que se trate.

Aunque los países hispanos entre sí presentan diferencias considerables en detalle, el procedimiento ordinario, generalmente denominado "juicio ordinario" o "vía ordinaria," puede ser descrito como una actuación judicial dividida en cuatro etapas y un procedimiento especial de ejecución de sentencia.

La primera etapa es de carácter preliminar y se refiere a la realización de actos preparatorios o medidas cautelares, como el arraigo y el secuestro de bienes, y otros requisitos que en ocasiones la ley exige para poder iniciar la acción. La segunda etapa, denominada expositiva o de fijación de la litis, tiene por objeto que las partes expongan sus pretensiones así como los hechos y el derecho que las apoyan. Se desarrolla a través de la demanda, el emplazamiento del demandado, la contestación de la demanda y las demás actuaciones que contribuyan a formar la litis (o determinación de los puntos controvertidos) incluyendo frecuentemente una audiencia que se denomina audiencia preliminar. El procedimiento pasa inmediatamente después al período probatorio en el cual se ofrecen y desahogan las pruebas. Es frecuente la realización de una audiencia de pruebas, pero no es necesaria en todo caso. Concluido el período probatorio se presentan los alegatos o conclusiones de las partes, que son hechos generalmente en forma escrita y una vez presentados éstos se "cita para sentencia," es decir se señala que se procederá a estudiar el caso por el juez y a dictar la sentencia correspondiente.

☛ Cuando se le compara con el derecho angloamericano, el procedimiento civil de los países hispanos presenta varias diferencias importantes: no hay el elaborado procedimiento de *pretrial discovery*, que tiene como función el permitir a las partes la localización y obtención de pruebas; ni el elaborado uso de *motions*, que permite a las partes actuar con flexibilidad y activamente en defensa de su causa. Estas ausencias en el procedimiento romano-germánico ponen de relieve el carácter menos contencioso entre las partes y explica la actuación más activa y participativa del juez.

Asimismo, puede decirse que el *trial*, como lo entiende el derecho angloamericano, esto es un evento oral culminante y único, no existe en derecho romano-germánico, en el que se entiende por juicio la totalidad del procedimiento, esto es, una sucesión de actos, escritos, audiencias y diligencias dirigidas a dar al juez los elementos de conocimiento necesarios para dictar la sentencia y en los que la oralidad es muy limitada.

procedimiento legal debidamente establecido *due process of law.* – Sin. debido proceso legal. principio de legalidad.

procedimiento penal *criminal procedure.*
– Sin. enjuiciamiento criminal.

El procedimiento penal en países hispanos está dividido en dos grandes etapas conocidas, entre otros nombres, como la instrucción y el plenario.

La instrucción, también llamada sumario o juicio informativo, se encamina a la recolección de datos y, en su caso, la determinación de la existencia o inexistencia de un hecho delictuoso y la probable responsabilidad del acusado. A su vez el plenario, también llamado juicio penal, proceso principal o debate, está orientado a una presentación legal o jurídica, deducida de los hechos, de la pretensión de la parte acusadora y de lo que alegue en su defensa el acusado, concluyendo con la sentencia. Los autos, audiencias y diligencias que forman el proceso penal en su totalidad varían considerablemente de país a país, y aun dentro de un mismo país, como en el caso de los sistemas federales. En la mayoría de los procedimientos, sin embargo, se pueden encontrar ciertos elementos procesales comunes. Entre ellos destacan en el orden en que generalmente aparecen:

La averiguación previa o período de investigación administrativa preliminar. El procesamiento o sea la promoción y ejercicio de la acción penal por parte del órgano de acusación. El auto de radicación o aceptación por el juez del inicio del proceso y su exigencia del apersonamiento o presentación del acusado. La consi-

guiente declaración preparatoria o indagatoria del acusado al acudir al llamamiento. El llamado auto de procesamiento o auto de sujeción a proceso, y el auto de libertad o auto de no sujeción a proceso, según el juez decida por uno u otro. Si el acusado es sujeto a proceso, se abre el plenario o juicio penal con la presentación de la demanda y la contestación, llamadas también conclusiones, que plantean la posición jurídica de las partes. A éstas le siguen el período probatorio, la citación para la audiencia final y, dentro de ésta, los alegatos o argumentos finales de las partes. Por último se dicta el auto de citación para sentencia y la sentencia penal.

☞ A grandes rasgos el procedimiento penal basado en el derecho romano-germánico se distingue del basado en el derecho angloamericano, entre otros aspectos, por la importancia y extensión dada a la averiguación previa o preliminar que conduce en algunos países un juez y en otros un fiscal, por la amplitud que tiene el acusado para ofrecer cualquier prueba que considere pertinente y por la función altamente participativa del juez en las diligencias, audiencias y el procedimiento en general. Aunque el procedimiento penal en sistemas romano-germánicos tiene un mayor contenido oral que el correspondiente procedimiento civil, sigue siendo primordialmente un procedimiento escrito, basado en la formación de un expediente o los llamados autos. Asimismo, es un procedimiento consistente en una serie de actuaciones que a diferencia del *trial* angloamericano no termina en un evento oral culminante y único.

procesal adj. *procedural.* **procesalista** n. *lawyer specialized in procedural law.*

procesamiento de datos *data processing.*

procesar DER.PENAL v. *to prosecute.* **procesado** n. *indicted or arraigned defendant.*

proceso n. *process.*
proceso político *political process.*

proceso judicial n. [rtrgido]*proceeding.*

• "Es una serie de actos jurídicos que se suceden regularmente en el tiempo y se encuentran concatenados entre sí por el fin u objeto que se quiere realizar con ellos." (Pallares, 640)

☞ El proceso judicial es un concepto que no tiene equivalente en el derecho angloamericano. *Proceeding*, entendido como la sucesión de actos que conforman un juicio es un término cercano que se usa frecuentemente como equivalente, sin embargo proceso es un concepto más amplio y abstracto que pone énfasis en la conexión de los actos procesales en función del fin que se persigue.

proceso civil *civil proceeding.*
proceso penal *criminal proceeding.*
proceso sumario *summary proceeding.*
Rel: causa judicial, *cause;* juicio, *trial;* pleito, *lawsuit.*
Ver: procedimiento.

proceso legislativo *legislative process.*

• Las etapas que deben cumplirse para que una ley sea debidamente iniciada, deliberada, aprobada, sancionada y promulgada.
Rel: aprobación, *approval;* cámara de origen, *Chamber or assembly where a bill is first brought for consideration;* cámara revisora, *Chamber or assembly voting on a bill for final approval;* debate, *debate;* deliberación, *deliberation;* iniciativa de ley, *bill;* sanción, *signing a bill into law, enactment.*

procuración de justicia *law enforcement.*

procuraduría[1] **(abogar)** n. *legal representation.*
procurador n. *barrister, lawyer.* **procuración** n. *legal power or authorization.*

• Representante debidamente facultado mediante poder para actuar ante los tribunales.
Rel: patrocinio, *legal representation.*

procuraduría[2] **(acusar)** n. *prosecution.*
procurador n. *prosecuting attorney.*
• Entidad a cargo del ejercicio de la acción penal en contra del presunto autor de un delito.
– Sin. ministerio público.
Procurador federal *Attorney general.*

producto interno bruto (PIB) *gross domestic product.*

producto nacional bruto (PNB) *gross national product.*

productos n. *proceeds, gains.* – Sin. frutos, *proceeds, fruits.*
productos del capital *capital gains.*
productos del trabajo *earned income.*

proemio n. *preamble.*

profanación del cadáver *desecration of a corpse.*

prófugo n. *escapee, fugitive.* – Sin. evadido. fugitivo, *fugitive.* huido, *fleer.*

prohibición n. *prohibition.* **prohibir** v. *to prohibit.* **prohibitivo** adj. *prohibitive.*

promesa n. *promise.* **prometer** v. *to promise.*
promitente n. *promisor.*
• "Declaración unilateral de voluntad por la cual consiente uno en obligarse a dar o hacer una cosa en tiempo futuro." (VI Cabanellas, 455)
– Sin. ofrecimiento, *offer.* promisión.

promesa de contrato *promise to execute a contract at a later date.* – Sin. precontrato.
promesa de matrimonio *promise to marry.*
promesa de recompensa *promise to pay a reward.*

promoción[1] **(petición)** n. *request, motion, petition.* **promover** v. *to motion, request.*
promovente n. *claimant, petitioner, applicant.*
• Acción de promover. Indica el acto por el que se inicia una causa o se da impulso a una causa en marcha. – Sin. pedimento. petición.
Cf: **promoción • petición • pedimento.**
Términos sinónimos usados intercambiablemente con frecuencia. Promoción enfatiza la idea de iniciar o continuar el movimiento de un proceso, con frecuencia usándose como verbo; <promover el juicio de deshaucio> mientras petición es un término considerado más general que pone de relieve el contenido de la solicitud hecha. <petición de herencia> Por su parte, pedimento se entiende como una solicitud hecha ante un juez e incluso, en ocasiones, como todo escrito presentado ante un órgano jurisdiccional. <pedimento ex parte>
presentar una promoción *to file a motion.*
promover un juicio *to file a suit, to bring a suit.*
promover una excepción *to plead a defense.*
Ver: *motion.*

promoción[2] **(avance)** n. *promotion.* **promover** v. *to promote.*
• Mejoramiento o avance en un empleo, actividad, productividad, etc.
obtener una promoción *to get a promotion.*
ser promovido *to be promoted.*

promulgación de la ley *promulgation of a statute.*
• La autorización formal de una ley o reglamento por la autoridad facultada para ello, para que sea dada a conocer y cumplida por el público.
fecha de la promulgación *date of promulgation.*
Rel: proceso legislativo, *legislative process.*

pronunciamiento n. *rebellion, revolt.*
– Sin. rebelión, *rebellion.* sedición, *uprising.*

propiedad n. *property, ownership.* **propietario** n. *owner.*
• Es el poder jurídico que se ejerce sobre una cosa en forma directa e inmediata consistente en el derecho de gozar y disponer de una cosa

sin más límites que los establecidos en las leyes. – Sin. dominio, *dominium*.

Cf: **propiedad • plena propiedad • nudapropiedad.** Términos que tienen un significado similar pero que se usan normalmente con la intención de lograr una mayor precisión jurídica: propiedad es el término más amplio y neutro, plena propiedad es la forma de expresar el concepto propiedad sin que ésta esté desmembrada, mientras nudapropiedad se refiere al término propiedad cuando la propiedad ha sido desmembrada, esto es cuando se han creado usufructos, habitaciones, etc.

↪ Mientras el sistema de la *common law* desarrolló la doctrina de los *estates* como su sistema de propiedad real, el sistema de derecho civil "adoptó el dominio, que significa un derecho de propiedad casi absoluto. 'El propietario tiene un título absoluto, tiene un derecho absoluto de disposición de la cosa bajo su propiedad, y su derecho de uso y disfrute se encontraba restringido por tan pocas limitaciones de derecho público que, éste también, podría ser considerado casi absoluto. El tipo de cargas que podía tenerse se redujeron al mínimo y aquellas existentes se distinguieron cuidadosamente del dominio sobre la cosa, el que se consideró como reteniendo su naturaleza de derecho general y único sobre la cosa pudiendo recuperar su plenitud original al desaparecer las cargas.' Esto no significa que el Derecho romano no haya reconocido derechos reales de propiedad, además del de dominio." (Cribbet & Johnson, 22. Traducción del editor).

propiedad absoluta *absolute property.*
propiedad comunal *communal land.*
propiedad ejidal (Mx) [prest.]*ejido property.*
propiedad en común *joint ownership, common property.*
propiedad en condominio *condominium.* – Sin. propiedad horizontal.
propiedad en cooperativa *cooperative ownership.*
propiedad fiduciaria *trust property.*
propiedad industrial *industrial property.*
propiedad inmobiliaria *real estate.*
propiedad intelectual *intellectual property.*
propiedad literaria *literary property.*
propiedad originaria *original ownership.*
propiedad privada *private property.* – Sin. propiedad particular.
propiedad pública *public property.*
propiedad real *real property.*

propiedad social *collectively-held property.* – Sin. propiedad colectiva.
propiedad urbana *urban property.*
Rel: posesión, *possession;* uso, [ed]*entitlement or right to use another's property;* usufructo, [prest.]*usufruct,* [ef]*life tenancy.*
Ref: (Ar)CC a.2506; (Ch)CC a.582; (CR)CC a.264-276; (Ec)CC a.618; (Esp)CC a.348; (Mx)CC a. 830 ss.; (Pe)CC a.923ss.; (PR)CC a.290, 31 LPRA sec 1111; (RD)CC a.544; (Ur)CC a.486-492; (Ve)CC a. 545.
Ver: dominio. tenencia.

propuesta n. *proposal.* **proponer** v. *to make a proposal.* **proponente** n. *proponent, proposer.* – Sin. proposición, *proposition.*

prorrata n. *pro rata.* **prorratear** v. *to divide pro rata.* **prorrateo** n. *pro rata division.*
• Parte o porción que corresponde a cada uno de algo que se reparte en forma proporcional.

prórroga[1] **(continuación)** n. *extension.* **prorrogar** v. *to extend a term.* **prorrogado** adj. *extended.* **prorrogación** *extension.* **prorrogable** adj. *extendable.*
• La continuación de un plazo o un término. – Sin. prolongación. continuación, *continuance.*
prórroga de jurisdicción *expansion of jurisdiction.*
prórroga de plazo *extension of a deadline.*
prórroga del contrato de arrendamiento *extension of the lease agreement.*

prórroga[2] **(aplazamiento)** n. *deferment, deferral.* **prorrogar** v. *to defer.* **prorrogado** adj. *deferred.* **prorrogación** *postponement.* **prorrogable** adj. *deferrable.*
• Aplazamiento temporal, normalmente para el cumplimiento de un deber. – Sin. aplazamiento, *postponement.* moratoria, *moratorium.* posposición, *postponement.* diferimiento, *deferment.*

proscripción n. *proscription, expulsion or deportation.* **proscribir** v. *to proscribe.* **proscripto** n. *deportee.* **proscripto** adj. *proscribed, exiled.* **proscriptor** n. *proscriber.* **proscriptor** adj. *proscribing.* **proscrito** n. *proscribed, outlaw.* – Sin. expatriación, *expatriation.* expulsión, *expulsion, expelling.*

prostitución n. *prostitution.* **prostituir** v. *to prostitute (a man, woman or oneself)* **prostíbulo** n. *brothel, whorehouse.* – Sin. ramería, *prostitution, streetwalking, hooking.* vida airada (euph). vida alegre (euph). vida galante (euph).
Rel: burdel, *brothel;* lenocinio, *pandering, procuring.*

prostituta n. *prostitute, streetwalker, hooker.* - Sin. ninfa. pupila. meretriz. puta. zorra. buscona. ramera. mujer pública.

protectorado DER.INTL n. *protectorate.*

protesta[1] **(afirmación)** n. *solemn attestation or affirmation.*

• "Promesa con aseveración o atestación de ejecutar una cosa." (II Dicc. REA, 1682)

Cf: **protesta de decir verdad • juramento • promesa solemne.** Protesta de decir verdad se usa modernamente en substitución del juramento de decir verdad, con frecuencia como un acto preliminar a una declaración formal. Juramento, a diferencia de la protesta, tiene una connotación y origen religioso que ha ido perdiendo favor en materias civiles en las que se va reduciendo su uso. Por otro lado, una promesa solemne se refiere a los casos en los que una declaración formal debe expresarse con cierta solemnidad para que sea válida, como lo es el caso de la toma de posesión de altos funcionarios públicos.

bajo protesta *under solemn attestation or affirmation.*

protesta de decir verdad *affirmation to tell the truth.*

rendir protesta *to attest or affirm solemnly.*

Rel: juramento, *oath.*

protesta[2] **(inconformidad)** n. *protest.* **protestar** v. *to protest.* **protestante** n. *protester.* **protestante** adj. *protester, protesting.*

• Manifestación o declaración dirigida a preservar un derecho o evitar un daño.

protesta pública *public protest.*

protesto TÍTULOS DE CRÉDITO n. *protest.*

protocolo[1] **(registro)** n. *registry, record.* **protocolizar** v. *to record in the notarial registry.* **protocolización** n. *to make an entry in the notarial registry.*

• Registro de escrituras matrices expedidas por un notario en cumplimiento de sus funciones de fedatario.

protocolizar un acta *to make a written record part of a notarial registry.*

protocolizar un documento *to make a document part of a notarial registry.*

protocolo[2] **(diplomacia)** n. *protocol.*

proveer de conformidad *to take the appropriate measures.*

proveído n. *interlocutory order or decision.*

• Se dice de la resolución de mero trámite o interlocutoria.

se dicta el proveído correspondiente *the corresponding interlocutory order is issued.*

proveído adj. *provided.*

proveimiento n. *decision, act of providing.*

providencia *order, decision, measures.*

• Para algunos autores es cualquier resolución judicial, exceptuada la sentencia. Para otros es la "resolución judicial no fundada expresamente, que decide sobre cuestiones de trámite y en cuanto a peticiones secundarias y accidentales." (VI Cabanellas, 491) - Sin. medidas, *measures.* orden, *order.* provisión, *measure, step.*

"La providencia fija el curso del procedimiento o sea la manera como debe seguirse el juicio, no en términos generales, sino para cada trámite en particular." (Pallares, 660)

providencia de mero trámite *interlocutory order.*

providencias para mejor proveer [ed]*orders to facilitate the expedient resolution of the case or to clarify facts or evidence.*

providencias precautorias [ed]*orders or decisions issued to preserve the subject matter of the trial and to prevent harm to the parties,* [el] *protective measures.* - Sin. providencias o medidas cautelares.

providencias preparatorias a juicio [ed] *pretrial orders or decisions to ensure a fair and correct trial.*

provisión de fondos *provision of funds.*

provocación n. *provocation.* **provocar** v. *to provoke.* **provocador** n. *provocative.* **provocativo** adj. *provocative.* - Sin. desafío, *challenge.* reto, *challenge, dare.* incitación, *incitement.*

proxenetismo n. *pimping, procuring.* **proxeneta** n. *pimp.* **proxenético** adj. *pertaining to a procurer or panderer.*

• El favorecer, promover o facilitar la prostitución ajena con propósito de lucro. - Sin. alcahuetismo. lenocinio. rufianería.

proyecto de ley *draft of a bill.*

Rel: iniciativa de ley, *bill.*

prueba[1] **(exámen)** n. *test.* **probar** v. *to test.* - Sin. análisis, *analysis.* examen, *exam.*

prueba de la emisión de un vehículo *emission test.*

prueba del analizador de aliento *breathalyzer test.*

Rel: cromatografía en base gaseosa, *gas chromatography;* espectrofotometría por absorción atómica, *atomic absorption spectrophotometry;* espectrofotometría por ultravioleta, *ultraviolet*

prueba

spectrophotometry; análisis de espectroscopia infrarroja, *infrared spectroscopy.*

prueba[2] **(demostración)** n. *evidence, proof.* **probar** v. *to prove.* **probatorio** adj. *evidenciary, probative.*

• La demostración, mediante los medios y formas permitidos por la ley, de la veracidad de los hechos controvertidos. – Sin. comprobación, *proof.* demostración, *demonstration.* evidencia, *evidence.*

↪ **prueba** • **evidencia.** Ambos términos son sinónimos y se usan con tal calidad con frecuencia. Prueba, sin embargo, es el término generalmente preferido para designar la demostración en un proceso judicial, en tanto que evidencia corresponde a una descripción de aplicación más general y frecuentemente menos técnica. Mientras en la mayoría de los países hispano parlantes se acepta esta distinción, en Puerto Rico, con motivo de la influencia del derecho y el vocabulario ingleses, la situación contraria prevalece: evidencia es el término preferido y prueba es normalmente una denominación no técnica y de uso general.

carga de la prueba *burden of proof.* – Sin. peso de la prueba.

desahogo de la prueba (Mx) *presentation of evidence.*

descubrimiento de prueba (PR) *discovery.*

evaluación de la prueba *weighing of the evidence.* – Sin. apreciación de la prueba.

exhibición de pruebas *tendering of evidence.*

prueba contaminada *tainted evidence.*

prueba documental *documentary evidence.* – Sin. prueba instrumental.

prueba inadmisible *inadmissible evidence.*

prueba legal *legally weighed evidence.* – Sin. prueba tasada.

prueba pericial *expert evidence.*

prueba plena *incontrovertible proof, conclusive evidence.* – Sin. prueba concluyente o conclusiva.

prueba presuncional *presumptive evidence.*

prueba testimonial *testimony, testimonial evidence.*

pruebas admisibles *admissible evidence.*

pruebas circunstanciales *circumstantial evidence.* – Sin. prueba indiciaria.

pruebas confirmatorias *corroborating evidence.*

pruebas contradictorias *conflicting or contradictory evidence.*

pruebas materiales *physical evidence.*

pruebas periciales médicas *medical evidence.*

pruebas preconstituidas *evidence produced or prepared before the filing of the lawsuit,* [amplio]*pretrial discovery.*

pruebas sobrevinientes *post-trial evidence.*

recabar una prueba *to obtain evidence.*

valor probatorio *probative value, weight given to specific evidence.*

Rel: medios de prueba, *evidence.*

Ver.: *evidence.*

pruebas (de campo) para determinar la sobriedad o ebriedad *(field) sobriety tests.* Rel: caminar sobre la línea, *walking the line test;* prueba de equilibrio, *balance test;* punta del pié al talón, *heel to toe;* tocar la punta de la nariz con la punta del dedo, *finger to nose test.* Ver: alcohol.

psicoanálisis n. *psychoanalysis.* **psicoanalista** n. *psychoanalyst.* **psicoanalítico** adj. *psychoanalytic, psychoanalytical.* – También: sicoanálisis.

psicología n. *psychology.* **psicólogo** *psychologist.* **psicológico** adj. *psychological.* – También: sicología.

psicopatología n. *psychopathology.*

psicosis n. *psychosis.* **psicópata** n. *psychopath.* – También: sicosis.

• "Nombre genérico de las enfermedades mentales mayores, que afectan profundamente la yoidad" y que incluyen a la esquizofrenia, paranoia, psicosis maniaco-depresiva y estados afines (Dicc. ed. Comares, 438).

psicotrópicos n. *psychotropic drugs.*

psiquiatría n. *psychiatry.* **psiquiatra** n. *psychiatrist.* – También: siquiatría.

pubertad n. *puberty.* **púber** n. *pubescent.* **pubescente** adj. *pubescent.*

publicación n. *publication.* **publicar** v. *to publish.* – Sin. divulgación. proclamación, *proclamation.* **notificación por publicación** *service by publication.* **publicación de la ley** *publication of statutes or regulations.*

publicidad n. *publicity, advertising.* **publicista** n. *publicist.* – Sin. anuncio, *ad, advertisement.* **publicidad engañosa** *deceiving advertising.*

puerto n. *port, harbor.* **portuario** adj. *port, related to ports.* – Sin. fondeadero, *anchorage place.* desembarcadero, *wharf, quay.* **puerto de destino** *port of destination.* **puerto de matrícula** *port of registration.*

puerto de origen *port of origin.*

puerto libre *free port.*

punibilidad DER.PROC. n. [ed]*punishability,* [el]*punitiveness.* **punir** v. *to punish.* **punitivo** adj. *punitive.* **punición** n. *punishment.* **punible** adj. *punishable.*

• "Por punibilidad entendemos la amenaza de pena que el estado asocia a la violación de los deberes consignados en las normas jurídicas, dictadas para garantizar la permanencia del orden social." (Pavón Vasconcelos. Derecho Penal, 486)

Rel: culpabilidad, *culpability;* excusa absolutoria, [ed]*excuse resulting in absolution of the accused.*

Ver: delito.

puntos resolutorios (sentencia) *holding (of a sentence).* – Sin. fallo. – También: puntos resolutivos.

pupilo n. *ward* || *minor.* **pupilaje** n. *pupilage.* **pupilar** adj. *pertaining to a minor orphan.* – Sin. huérfano, *orphan.*

putativo adj. *putative.*

QQQQ

quebramiento de condena *violations of terms of criminal sentence.* – Sin. quebramiento de sanción (Mx).

queja¹ (acusación) n. *criminal accusation.* **quejoso** n. *complainant.* – Sin. querella, *complaint.*

queja²(recurso) n. [ed]*motion in the form of appeal against court decisions which are not appealable.* **quejoso** n. *aggrieved party.*

• Acto procesal contra un juez o tribunal para anular o rectificar una resolución que no es objeto de apelación.

recurso de queja *motion in the form of appeal.*

Rel: recursos, *remedies.*

queja³ (reclamación) n. *complaint, grievance.*

querella DER.PROC.PENAL n. *complaint made by complaining witness pressing charges.* **querellarse** v. *to file a complaint.* **querellante** n. *complaining witness (in crimes prosecuted only if complaining witness is pressing charges).*

• Declaración del ofendido dirigida al órgano de autoridad competente haciendo de su conocimiento la comisión de un delito y dando su consentimiento para que éste se persiga, o ejerciendo la acción penal directamente, o como coadyuvante, cuando lo permita la ley.

– Sin. [rtrgido]acusador particular (Ar,Esp). [rtrgido] acusador privado (Ar,Esp), *private prosecutor.*

Cf: **querella** • **acusador particular** • **acusador privado.** Querella es el término genérico que indica la formalidad que una persona asume para iniciar una acción penal o legitimar al fiscal para que la inicie a su petición. El acusador particular es la persona que ejercita la acción penal directamente en los sistemas en que se permite la acción popular (esto es la acción pública directa del ofendido en un número limitado de casos). Por su parte, el acusador privado actúa ejercitando la acción directamente si se trata de un delito específicamente señalado como privado (esto es un delito en el que existe una relación entre el acusado y la víctima que se desea proteger).

Rel: delito perseguible a instancia de parte, *crime to be prosecuted only if complainant is pressing charges;* delito perseguible de oficio, *crime to be prosecuted regardless of whether a complaining witness is pressing charges or not;* denuncia, *criminal complaint;* ofendido, *injured party.*

Ref: (Ar)CPP a.176; (Ch)CPP a.18, NCPPCh a.261; (Ec)CPP a.57; (Esp)LECr a.270-281; (Mx)CFPP a. 113.

Ver: acusación. denuncia.

quid pro quo (lat.) *quid pro quo, something for something.*

• Se refiere al intercambio de una cosa por otra de igual o similar valor.

quiebra n. *bankruptcy.* **quebrado** n. *bankrupt.*

• La quiebra es un procedimiento que se aplica a todos los bienes de un comerciante, cuando le es imposible atender el pago de sus obligaciones por encontrarse en estado de insolvencia, con el propósito de distribuirlos entre sus acreedores en la proporción y con las prioridades establecidas en la ley. – Sin. bancarrota, *bankruptcy.*

Cf: **quiebra** • **bancarrota** • **concurso.** La quiebra y la bancarrota son términos sinónimos que se usan indistintamente. El concurso, por su parte, es el concepto equivalente al de quiebra aplicado a una persona que no es comerciante. Generalmente se usa la expresión "concurso de acreedores" o "concurso civil" para referirse a esta figura. Inicialmente concurso se usó como la descripción de un método de solución de insolvencias de comerciantes, siendo un antecedente e incluso un sinónimo de quiebra, pero esa acepción obsoleta ahora ha desaparecido casi totalmente.

administración de la quiebra *bankruptcy receivership.*

declaración de quiebra determination *of bankruptcy.* – Sin. auto de quiebra.

demanda de la declaración de quiebra *petition in bankruptcy.*

extinción de la quiebra *termination of bankruptcy proceedings, completion of bankruptcy proceedings.*

ley de quiebras *bankruptcy law.*

masa de la quiebra *bankruptcy estate.*

quiebra culpable *negligent bankruptcy.* – Sin. quiebra culposa.

quiebra fortuita *unintentional bankruptcy.*

quiebra fraudulenta *fraudulent bankruptcy.* – Sin. alzamiento de bienes.

Rel: concurso, [ed]*bankruptcy under civil code regulations;* insolvencia, *insolvency;* junta de acreedores, *meeting of creditors;* síndico, *trustee;* suspensión de pagos, *automatic stay.* Ref: (Ar)CCo a.1435,1379ss.; (Ch)Ley de Quiebras a.1-3.; (Mx)Ley de Quiebras a.380-393; (ES)CCo. a. 498ss.; (Esp)CCo a.874ss. LEC a.1318-1396; (Ve) CCo. a.914ss.

quita OBLIGACIONES n. *partial discharge of a debt.*
• Remisión o renuncia parcial de una deuda hecha al deudor. – Sin. liberación, *release.* remisión, *remission, release of debt.*

quita y espera *composition or extension of payments, deed of arrangement.*

quórum n. *quorum.*

RRRR

radicación[1] **(admisión)** n. [ed]*court admission of a civil complaint or criminal accusation.*
• Arraigar judicialmente, especialmente un juicio o demanda.

auto de radicación [ed]*court order admitting a criminal cause,* [ef]*court order establishing jurisdiction (over a cause of action).*

radicación de una apelación *admission of an appeal (by the appellate court), court order admitting an appeal.*

radicación de una demanda *admission of a complaint (by the court), court order admitting a complaint.*

Rel: presentación, *filing (of a complaint, appeal, etc.).*

radicación[2] **(residencia)** n. *residence.* **radicar** v. *to be domiciled, to be located.*

radicado en el extranjero *resident abroad.*

rapto n. *abduction.* **raptar** v. *to abduct.* **raptor** n. *abductor.*

• Restricción a la libertad individual, generalmente con la intención de atentar contra la libertad sexual de la persona.

matrimonio por rapto *forced marriage by prior abduction.*

rapto o secuestro de un menor *child abduction.* – Sin. rapto de niños.

ratero n. *petty thief, shoplifter.* **ratería** n. *pilfering, filching.* **ratero** adj. *thieving.*

ratificación n. *ratification.* **ratificar** v. *to ratify.* **ratificatorio** adj. *ratifying.*
• Manifestación de voluntad por la que una persona legitimada para ello aprueba o adopta un acto o contrato celebrado por otro, o por la persona misma pero en otro tiempo o lugar. – Sin. reafirmación, *reaffirmation.*
Rel: acknowledgment, *reconocimiento;* confirmación, *confirmation;* corroboración, *corroboration;* reafirmación, *reaffirmation.*

razón social *corporate name.*

reaseguro n. *reinsurance.*

rebeldía n. *default, nonappearance.* **rebelde** adj. *in default, defaulter.*
• Situación jurídica del demandado que debidamente emplazado no comparece ante el juez que preside el proceso, o que habiendo comparecido abandona el tribunal después.

acusar rebeldía *to give notice of default or non-appearance.* – Sin. acusar la rebeldía.

declaración de rebeldía *finding of default or non-appearance.*

juicio en rebeldía *proceeding in default.*
Rel: juicio en ausencia, [ext.lexico.]*proceedings in absentia.*

rebelión (delito) n. *rebellion.* **rebelarse** v. *to rebel.* **rebelde** n. *rebel.*
• Delito consistente en el levantamiento armado contra el gobierno constituido con la finalidad de derrocarlo, abolir las leyes, tomar el poder e instituir un nuevo régimen.
Cf: **rebelión • sedición • motín • asonada.**
Términos que se refieren a delitos o actividades contra el estado o las autoridades. Rebelión y sedición son definidos en los códigos como delitos, apareciendo claramente diferenciados: el primero constituyendo el atentado más grave que un grupo puede realizar contra el estado, en tanto que el segundo se considera un alzamiento en circunstancias menos graves y que, aún infringiendo la seguridad del estado, no llama por el cambio de régimen o por la abolición del sistema legal imperante. Motín y asonada son términos en cuyas definiciones

hay menos consenso. Motín es en ocasiones considerado un delito, pero mayormente se le considera una conducta de grupo consistente en la creación de un disturbio, normalmente de civiles (pero no exclusivamente), dirigido a quebrantar el orden público; mientras que asonada, es una palabra usada primordialmente en el habla común para significar una manifestación tumultuaria, que alterando el orden público, persigue finalidades de carácter social, económico o político. Es frecuente que asonada se refiera a un movimiento de militares, aunque no exclusivamente. De la misma manera es común considerar a la asonada como uno de los elementos constitutivos de la rebelión y la sedición.

rebelión militar *military rebellion, military insurrection.*

Rel: alzamiento, *uprising;* asonada, *tumultuary demonstration, mutinous demonstration*; insurrección, *insurrection;* levantamiento, *uprising;* motín, *riot, mutiny;* pronunciamiento, *insurrection;* sublevación, *revolt, insurrection.*
Ver: sedición.

rebus sic stantibus (lat.)(max.) *rebus sic stantibus. things standing thus.*

• El principio implícito de que todos los acuerdos son obligatorios conforme se pacten a menos que haya un cambio en las circunstancias.

recargo n. *surcharge.* – Sin. sobreprecio, *extra charge.*
  recargo fiscal *surtax.*

recaudación n. *collection, collecting.*

receso n. *recess.*

recibimiento a prueba (proc.civil) *probative period, period for producing evidence.*
  recibir a prueba *to admit as evidence* || *to open the probative period.*

recibo n. *receipt.* – Sin. comprobante, *voucher, proof.*
  recibo de almacén *warehouse receipt.*
  recibo de pago *proof of payment, receipt.*
  recibo de salarios *payroll stub.*

reciprocidad DER.INTL.PRIVADO n. *reciprocity.*

reclamación n. *claim, demand* || *grievance.* **reclamar** v. *to claim, complain.* **reclamo** n. *claim, complaint.* **reclamante** n. *claimant, complainer.* **reclamante** adj. *claiming.*

• Una expresión de insatisfacción o una oposición expresada oralmente o por escrito. También, la petición o exigencia de una cosa por una persona que tiene el derecho para hacerla. – Sin. exigencia, *demand.* reclamo.

reclamación de seguros *insurance claim.*
reclamación previa (Esp.) *grievance.*
reclamar en juicio *to sue, to bring a lawsuit.*

reclusión n. *confinement, reclusion.* **recluir** v. *to confine.* **recluso** n. *inmate, confined person.* **reclusorio** n. *prison.* – Sin. internamiento, *internment.* encerramiento, *locking up.*
enclaustramiento, *to put in seclusion, to hide away.*
  reclusión de un menor *confinement of a minor.*
  reclusorio preventivo *provisional confinement center, jail.*

recomendación n. *recommendation.*
  recomendar v. *to recommend.* **recomendante** adj. *recommending.* **recomendatorio** adj. *recommendatory.* – Sin. encomienda, *commendation.*

recompensa n. *reward.* **recompensar** v. *to reward.* **recompensable** adj. *rewardable.* – Sin. premio, *prize.* gratificación, *reward, gratuity.* prima, *bonus.*

reconciliación n. *reconciliation.* **reconciliar** v. *to reconcile.* **reconciliador** adj. *reconciling.* – Sin. hacer las paces (pop.), *to make up.*
  reconciliación conyugal *marital reconciliation.*

reconducción n. *renewal.*
  tácita reconducción *constructive renewal (of a lease),* [ef]*tenancy at sufferance.*

reconocimiento[1] **(aceptación)** n. *recognition.*
  reconocer v. *to recognize.*

• Admitir o aceptar que algo es cierto, que ha ocurrido, o que significa un nuevo estado de cosas. – Sin. aceptación, *acceptance.*
  reconocimiento de beligerancia *recognition of belligerence.*
  reconocimiento de estado *recognition of state.*
  reconocimiento de insurgencia *recognition of insurgency.*
  reconocimiento de gobierno *recognition of government.*
  reconocimiento de hijo *acknowledgment of children born out of wedlock.*
  reconocimiento de persona *identification of a person.*

reconocimiento[2] **(admisión)** n. *admission.* **reconocer** v. *to admit.*

• Confesar o hacer suya una deuda o una obligación. – Sin. admisión, *admission.*
  reconocimiento de deuda *admission of indebtedness.*

reconocimiento de documentos privados *admission of authenticity of private documents.*

reconocimiento[3] **(escrutinio)** n. *scrutiny.* **reconocer** v. *to scrutinize.*
• Examinar o registrar personas, documentos o cosas. – Sin. escrutinio, *scrutiny.* inspección, *inspection.*

reconocimiento aduanal *customs inspection.*
reconocimiento en fila *line-up identification.* – Sin. rueda de reconocimiento.
reconocimiento judicial *judicial examination.*

reconsideración administrativa *administrative review.*

reconstrucción de hechos *reconstruction of the facts.*

reconvención DER.PROC.CIVIL n. *counterclaim, cross-claim.* **reconvenir** v. *to counterclaim.* – Sin. contrademanda, *counterclaim.*

recopilación n. *compilation of statutes in force (in a given subject)* || *code.* Ver: código.

rectificación n. *rectification, correction.* **rectificar** v. *to rectify, correct.* **rectificable** adj. *rectifiable.* **rectificador** adj. *rectifying.* **rectificativo** adj. *rectifying.* – Sin. corrección, *correction.* enmienda, *amendment.*
rectificación de error *amendment of error.*
rectificación de sentencia *modification of judgment.*

recuperación de nacionalidad *recovery of nationality.*

recurso DER.PROCESAL n. [el]*legal recourse,* [ef] *appeal.* **recurrir** v. *to appeal, to file a legal recourse.* **recurrente** n. *petitioner, appellant.* **recurrido** n. *appellee.* **recurrible** adj. *appealable.*
• "Es el medio de impugnación que se interpone contra una resolución judicial pronunciada en un proceso ya iniciado, generalmente ante un juez o tribunal de mayor jerarquía y de manera excepcional ante el mismo juzgador, con el objeto de que dicha resolución sea revisada, modificada o anulada." (Dicc. UNAM, 2702-703)
Cf: **recurso • impugnación • apelación.** Estos tres términos, significando el atacar una resolución judicial, son usados frecuentemente en forma sinónima e intercambiable cuando se les considera genéricamente; sin embargo, estos mismos términos son considerados como distinguibles y definitivamente no intercambiables entre sí cuando se les considera especí-

ficamente. Impugnación es tradicionalmente considerado el género, refiriéndose al ataque que se da a los actos o instrumentos que adoleciendo de deficiencias, errores o injusticia deben corregirse o modificarse. El recurso es el medio de impugnación concreto que ataca a una decisión judicial promoviendo, ante el juez superior jerárquico del que la dictó, las razones que la ley establece como procedentes. Por su parte la apelación, en su acepción específica, es uno de los varios recursos que pueden promoverse y que consiste en la petición de un nuevo examen y fallo de una sentencia en segunda instancia.
escrito de interposición de recurso *notice of appeal or legal recourse.*
recurso contencioso-administrativo *judicial complaint against an administrative decision.*
recurso de aclaración *motion for clarification of sentence.*
recurso de amparo [exp.léxica]*writ of amparo,* [exp.léxica]*suit of amparo.* – Sin. amparo.
recurso de apelación o de alzada *appeal.*
recurso de casación [prest.]*cassation,* [ed]*direct appeal to the cassation court.*
recurso de hábeas corpus *writ of habeas corpus.*
recurso de queja [ed]*motion in the form of appeal against court decisions which are not appealable.*
recurso de revisión *motion to reopen a case, motion for a new trial.*
recurso de revocación o revocatoria *motion to recall an interlocutory order (in a civil suit).* – Sin. recurso de reposición.
recurso de súplica *interlocutory appeal (in cases before appeal courts).*
Rel: apelación, *appeal;* impugnación, [ed] *challenging a court decision;* remedio, *relief, remedy.*
Comentario: El concepto genérico de impugnación incluye tradicionalmente a aquellas peticiones hechas ante el mismo juez que las dictó, frecuentemente designados como remedios procesales, así como a aquellas presentadas ante el juez superior, que generalmente se denominan recursos. En ocasiones también incluye procedimientos autónomos, generalmente aplicables en el ámbito administrativo. Los remedios incluyen en la mayoría de los casos a la súplica, la reposición, y la reforma; por su parte, los recursos incluyen generalmente a la apelación, la queja, la reclamación, la casación, y la revisión.

recusación n. [prest.]*recusation.* **recusar** v. *to recuse.* **recusante** n. *person challenging for recusation.* **recusado** n. *recused person.*

• Petición que hacen las partes en un proceso civil o penal para apartar al juez, magistrado o secretario del conocimiento de la causa por razones establecidas en la ley y que invalidan su imparcialidad. - Sin. exclusión, *exclusion.*

recusación de un juez *motion to recuse a judge, recusal of a judge.*

Rel: descalificación, *disqualification.*

Ver: *recusal.*

redacción de un contrato *drafting of a contract, drawing up of a contract.*

redención n. *redemption, recuperación, rescate.*

rédito n. *income, yield.* **redituar** v. *to yield, produce.* **redituable** adj. *income-producing.* - Sin. beneficio, *benefit.* ganancia, *profit.* interés, *interest.* rendimiento, *yield.* renta.

reenvío CONFLICTO DE LEYES n. *renvoi.*

• En un caso de conflicto de leyes se da el reenvío cuando la ley extranjera que resultare aplicable señale como ley definitivamente aplicable, ya a la parte de derecho material de la ley que originalmente conoció del caso, ya a la ley de un tercero.

Ver: conflicto de leyes.

referéndum n. *referendum.*

Ver: plebiscito.

reforma constitucional *constitutional amendment.*

Cf: **reforma • enmienda.** Términos sinónimos pero no necesariamente intercambiables. Reforma es el término tradicionalmente usado en derecho constitucional para designar las modificaciones a la Constitución. Enmienda, por su parte, es la palabra usada para designar las reformas constitucionales en países de derecho anglo-americano, especialmente las de los Estados Unidos de América. Es común el uso de enmienda en éste sentido por parte de hispanoparlantes.

reformatorio n. *reformatory.* - Sin. correccional, *correctional.*

refrendo n. *legalization or authentication of a document by countersigning || renewal (of documentary rights by legalization or authentication).* **refrendar** v. *to renew, countersign.* **refrendario** n. *person who legalizes or authenticates.*

• Legalización de un despacho o documento por la firma de la persona designada para firmar inmediatamente después del titular o superior. También se aplica a la renovación de la validez de un documento por la firma de la persona legalmente autorizada para ello. - Sin. autorización, *authorization.* confirmación, *confirmation.*

refrendar un pasaporte *to renew a passport.*

refrendar una orden ministerial *to countersign a minister's order (to legalize it).*

refugiado n. *refugee.* **refugiar** v. *to give refuge or asylum.* **refugio** n. *refuge, asylum.* - Sin. asilado, *asylee.*

regalías n. *royalties.* - Sin. canon (Esp).

régimen económico del matrimonio *marital property system.*

Las legislaciones de los países hispanoparlantes permiten en el matrimonio tanto la comunidad de bienes como su separación; sin embargo, existe una marcada tendencia a otorgar a los regímenes de comunidad de bienes la calidad de supletorios y preferentes. Se pueden enumerar cuatro formas relevantes de regímenes de comunidad de bienes, a saber: la comunidad universal de bienes, en la que participan todos los bienes de los esposos sin exclusiones o limitaciones; la comunidad de gananciales o ganancias, en la que la masa común de bienes se forma con las ganancias o rentas de cualquier tipo provenientes de los bienes de ambos cónyuges; la comunidad en participación, en la que cada cónyuge retiene posesión y dominio de sus bienes, pero al extinguirse el régimen, cada uno tiene frente al otro un derecho de participación ya en los bienes, ya en las ganancias; y finalmente la comunidad de bienes muebles y gananciales, en la que la masa común está compuesta por todos los bienes muebles propiedad de los esposos más las ganancias de los inmuebles que cada uno posea.

Rel: comunidad de bienes, *community property system;* gananciales, [ed]*community of property earned by husband and wife during marriage;* separación de bienes, *separate property* system.

registro[1] (inspección) n. *search.* **registrar** v. *to search, examine.* **registrado** n. *person searched.* - Sin. cacheo, *pat down.* examen, *examination.*

entrada y registro (Esp) *entry and search.*

registro superficial *cursory search.*

Ver: cateo.

registro[2] (archivo) n. *registry, registrar's office.* **registrador** n. *registrar, recorder.* - Sin. matrícula.

registro civil *civil registry.*

registro de comercio *registry of commerce.*

registro de la propiedad industrial *industrial property registry.*

registro de la propiedad *real estate registry.*

registro de minas *mining claims office.*

registro de patentes y marcas *patent office registry.*

registro de vehículos *registry of vehicles.*

registro mercantil *commercial registry.*

registro[3] **(inscripción)** n. *registration.* **registrar** v. *to register, record.* **registrador** n. *registrar, recorder.* **registrado** adj. *registered.* **regístrese** *be it registered.*

registro de aeronaves *registration of aircraft.*

registro de buques *registration of ships.*
– Sin. matrícula de buques.

registro de cooperativas *cooperative registration.*

registro de partidos políticos *political parties registration.*

registro[4] **(partida)** n. *entry.* – Sin. asiento, *entry.*

regla de derecho *legal rule* || *juridical norm.*

reglas del procedimiento *rules of procedure.*

reglamentación n. *regulation.* **reglamentar** v. *to regulate.* **reglamentario** adj. *regulatory.*
– Sin. regulación, *regulation.*

reglamento[1] DER.ADMVO n. *administrative regulations or rule, regulations.*

• Es una disposición de carácter complementario o supletorio, expedida por el titular del Poder ejecutivo, con la finalidad de lograr la aplicación de una ley expedida con anterioridad.

facultad reglamentaria (del ejecutivo) *regulating authority (of the Executive branch), delegated rulemaking authority (of the Executive branch).*

reglamento ejecutivo *executive order or decree.*
Ref: (Ar)C a.99-2; (Bo)C a.96-1; (Ch)C a.32-3; (Co) C a.189-11; (CR)C a.140-3; (Ec)C a.171-5; (ES)C a.168-14; (Esp)C a.90; (Gu)C 183-5; (Ho)C a. 245. 11; (Mx)C a.89-I; (Ni)C 150-4; (Pa)C a.179-14; (Pe) C 118-7; (Ur)C 236-10; (Ve)C a.236-8.

reglamento[2] **(reglas de gobierno)** *regulations, rules.*

• Las directrices o instrucciones escritas que para su control y administración se da una empresa u organización.

reglamento de policía *police regulations.*

reglamento[3] DER.MILITAR n. *military rules and regulations.*

• "[I]nstrucciones o normas técnicas para las distintas Armas y para describir y emplear su peculiar armamento." (VII Cabanellas, 104)

reglamento de trabajo *work rules.*
– Sin. reglamento de empresa. reglamento de fábrica. reglamento de taller. reglamento de trabajo. reglamento de servicio. reglamento interior o interno de trabajo.

regulación n. *regulation.* **regular** v. *to regulate.* **regulador** adj. *regulating.* **regulatorio** adj. *regulatory.* **regulado** adj. *regulated.*
– Sin. reglado.

regularización de calidad migratoria *adjustment of immigration status.*

rehabilitación n. *rehabilitation.* **rehabilitar** v. *rehabilitate.* **rehabilitado** n. *person rehabilitated.*

rehabilitación del comerciante *discharge of an insolvent businessman.*

rehabilitación del quebrado *discharge of a bankrupt.* – Sin. rehabilitación del fallido.

rehabilitación física *physical rehabilitation.*

rehabilitación vocacional *vocational rehabilitation.*

rehén n. *hostage.*

reincidencia n. *recidivism.* **reincidir** v. *to be a recidivist.* **reincidente** n. *recidivist, repeat offender.* – Sin. recaída, *relapse.*

delincuente reincidente *repeat offender, recidivist.* – Sin. multirreincidente.

reinstalación del trabajador *rehiring of fired workers, reinstatement of dismissed workers.*

reivindicación n. *replevin (chattels), ejectment (land).* **reivindicar** v. *to replevy, eject.* **reivindicatorio** adj. *replevying, ejecting.* **reivindicable** adj. *able to be replevied or ejected.*

• Acción que se ejerce judicialmente para demandar la propiedad de una cosa o derecho contra su poseedor.

➥ A diferencia del derecho romano-germánico, el *common law* inglés no desarrolló una acción reivindicatoria de bienes muebles; en su lugar, se otorga al propietario despojado la acción de *detinue*, basada en la comisión de un ilícito penal, el delito de *conversion*. Mientras *detinue* aún subsiste, en forma limitada en los Estados Unidos, se encuentra ya abolida en Inglaterra. Por su parte *replevin* se refiere a una acción para recuperar la posesión de un bien mueble cuando el demandante tenga derecho a la posesión inmediata de la cosa, en tanto que *ejectment* es la acción que ejerce el propietario de un bien inmueble para recuperar la posesión de la que ha sido ilegalmente privado.

Reivindicación es una acción que procede tanto en el caso de bienes muebles, como de inmuebles, y requiere que el demandante se produzca como el propietario.
acción reivindicatoria *replevin (chattels), ejectment (land).* – Sin. acción de reivindicación.
relación fiduciaria *fiduciary relationship.*
relación jurídica *juridical relationship.*
relación laboral *master and servant, employee-employer relationship.* – Sin. relación de trabajo. Ver: contrato de trabajo.
relaciones consulares *consular relations.*
relaciones diplomáticas *diplomatic relations.*
relaciones familiares *domestic relations.*
relaciones sexuales *sexual relations.*
remate judicial *judicial auction.*
remedio *relief, remedy.* Ver: recurso.
remisión de deuda *remission, forgiveness or cancellation of a debt, release from a debt.* – Sin. perdón de deuda.
remisión convencional *conventional remission.*
remisión tácita *tacit remission.* Rel: quita, *partial discharge of a debt;* renuncia, *waiver.*
remisión de la pena *conditional sentence.* – Sin. condena condicional. redención de pena.
remisión automática *work-release program.*
remisión condicional *conditional discharge.* – Sin. remisión condicionada. Rel: libertad condicional, *parole.* Ver: perdón.
remoción n. *removal.* **remover** v. *to remove.*
• Remoción de cargo o empleo.
– Sin. separación, *separation.* destitución, *destitution.*
remoción de albacea *removal of executor.*
remoción de un juez *removal of judge.*
remoción de tutor o curador *removal of guardian or curator of a minor.*
remuneración n. *remuneration.* **remunerar** v. *to remunerate, pay.* **remunerado** adj. *remunerated, paid.* **remunerador** adj. *remunerating.* **remunerador** n. *remunerator.* **remunerativo** adj. *remunerative.* – Sin. retribución, *repayment.* compensación, *compensation.* pago, *pay.*
trabajo remunerado *paying job.*
rendición de cuentas *rendering of accounts.*
rendimiento n. *return, yield.* – Sin. ganancia, *profit, gain.* rédito, *income.* renta, *yield,*

interest. utilidad, *profit, earnings.*
rendimiento de capital *return on capital.*
rendimiento financiero *financial yield.*
rendimiento tributario (Esp) *taxable income.* – Sin. ingreso fiscal.
renta[1] **(ingreso)** n. *revenue, income.*
• Incremento total producido o presumido por la ley en el patrimonio del sujeto pasivo durante un período dado. – Sin. ingreso.
impuesto sobre la renta *income tax.* – Sin. contribución sobre la renta (Esp).
renta fija *fixed income.*
renta gravable *taxable income.* – Sin. ingreso gravable.
renta nacional *national product or revenue.*
renta[2] **(rédito)** n. *yield, interest.* **rentista** n. *person who lives off revenues from investments.* **rentable** adj. *rentable.* **rentabilidad** n. *rentability, profitability.*
• "Utilidad o beneficio que rinde anualmente una cosa, o lo que de ella se cobra." (II Dicc. REA, 1770) – Sin. interés, *interest.* rédito, *yield, interest.*
renta del capital *interest.*
renta fija *fixed yield.*
renta variable *variable yield.*
renta vitalicia *life annuity.*
rentabilidad de una inversión *profitability of an investment.*
renta[3] **(arrendamiento)** n. *rent, rental.* **rentar** v. *to rent.* **rentado** adj. *rented, leased.*
• La cantidad que paga periódicamente un arrendatario. – Sin. alquiler, *rent.*
congelación de rentas *rent freeze.*
renta de un inmueble *rent obtained from leasing real estate.*
renta urbana *urban rent.*
rentas atrasadas *unpaid rent, behind in the rent.*
renuncia n. *waiver, renunciation.* **renunciante** n. *person who waives.* **renunciar** v. *to waive.* **renunciable** adj. *renounceable.* **renunciación** n. *renunciation, waiver.*
• "Acción y efecto de abandonar o dejar voluntariamente una cosa o derecho que se tienen, resignando la facultad de poseerlos o ejercerlos." (Couture, 517) – Sin. desistimiento, *abandonment, voluntary dismissal.*
presentar una renuncia *to hand in a resignation, to resign.*
renuncia al trabajo *resignation, quitting.*
renuncia de jurisdicción *waiver of venue.*
renuncia de la nacionalidad *renunciation of citizenship.*

renuncia de un derecho *waiver of a right.*
renuncia expresa *express resignation or waiver.*
renuncia tácita *implied resignation or waiver.*
renuncia voluntaria *voluntary resignation or waiver.*
Rel: abandono, *abandonment;* dimisión, *resignation.*

reo n. *convict,* [brder]*inmate.*

• Es la persona condenada a una pena, como resultado de haber sido encontrada culpable de un ilícito penal, en un proceso llevado a cabo con motivo de la comisión de un delito.
– Sin. condenado, *condemned, convict.*
convicto, *convict.* penado, *person subject to punishment, convict.*

reparación del daño DER.PROC.PENAL [ef]*restitution,* [el]*indemnification for damage caused (in the commission of a crime).*

• Pena pecuniaria que compensa la pérdida sufrida por la víctima de un delito, en la medida necesaria para reestablecer la situación anterior a su comisión, y resarcir los perjuicios provocados. – Sin. resarcimiento, *compensation.* restitución, *restitution.*
reparación extrajudicial *out of court restitution.*
Ref: (Ar)CP a.29-33; (Bo)CP a.65,87; (Co)CP a.265; (Esp)CP a.112; (Mx)CP a.29; (Pe)CP a.92-101; (RD) CP a.10; (Ur)CP 104-106.

reparto de utilidades *profit sharing.*

réplica DER.PROC.CIVIL n. *reply.*

• Segundo escrito en el que el actor impugna las defensas y excepciones presentadas por el demandado en su contestación.

reporte n. *report.* – Sin. dictamen. informe. parte. relación escrita.
reporte de un accidente *accident report.*
reporte de un perito *expert witness report.*

reporto (contrato) n. *repurchase agreement (of securities).* – Sin. contrato de doble (Esp). operación de pase (Ar).

reposesión n. *repossession* || [rtrgido]*reentry.*

reposición n. *replacement, reinstatement.*

repregunta n. *questioning of a prior reply, cross-examination.* **repreguntar** v. *to cross-examine.*

represalia n. *reprisal.* – Sin. desquite, *revenge.* venganza, *revenge.* vindicación, *vindication.*
represalias internacionales *international reprisals.*

Rel: retorsión, *retaliation.*

representación¹ (legal) n. *representation.*
representar v. *to represent.* **representante** n. *representative.* **representado** adj. *person or entity represented.* **representativo** adj. *representative.*
• Mediante la representación una persona, (representado), es substituido por otro, (representante) que actúa en su nombre e interés.
– Sin. delegación, *delegation, authorization of agency.*
acreditar su representación *to prove that one has authority, to establish one's authority.*
legítimo representante *legal representative.*
representación judicial *court-ordered representation.*
representación legal *legal representation arising by operation of law.*
representación procesal *representation in court proceedings or litigation.*
Rel: mandato, *agency agreement;* poder, *power of attorney.*

representación² (política) n. *representation.*
representar v. *to represent.* **representante** n. *representative.* **representativo** adj. *representative.*
representación indirecta *indirect representation.*
representación política *political representation.*
representación popular *popular representation.*
representación proporcional *proportional representation.*
representante a la Cámara *House representative* (EEUU,Au), *member of Parliament* (RU, Ca,NZ), *parliamentary representative.* – Sin. representante en la Cámara.

repudio de la deuda pública *repudiation of public debt.* – Sin. desconocimiento de la deuda pública.

repudio de la herencia *renunciation of inheritance.* – Sin. repudiación de la herencia.

reputación n. *reputation.*
Rel: celebridad, *celebrity;* fama, *fame;* prestigio, *prestige;* renombre, *renown.*

requerimiento n. *request, demand.* **requerir** v. *to require, demand.* **requirente** n. *requester.*
• Acto, generalmente hecho con cierta formalidad o en forma judicial, por el cual se ordena a una persona que entregue, haga o deje de hacer alguna cosa. – Sin. demanda, *demand.* exigencia, *demand, requirement.*

requerimiento de pago *demand for payment, request of payment.*

requerimiento judicial *court order, judicial order to do or refrain from doing something.*

requisa[1] **(embargo)** n. *requisition.* **requisar** v. *to requisition.* **requisable** adj. *able to be requisitioned.* – Sin. requisición, *requisition.*

requisa[2] **(inspección)** n. *inspection, review.* – Sin. revista. *inspection.*

requisición[1] **(embargo)** n. *requisition.*
• Demanda imperiosa hecha por el gobierno para que se ponga a su disposición a personas y cosas que se necesiten con urgencia para atender una necesidad pública. – Sin. requisa. Ver: expropiación.

requisición[2] **(orden)** n. *court order.*
• Acto judicial por el que se intima se haga algo.

requisito n. *requirement.* **requisitar** v. *to meet requirements, fulfilling requirements.* – Sin. condición, *condition.* formalidad, *formality.*

requisitos fiscales *fiscal requirements.*

requisitoria[1] **(orden)** *criminal summons.*

requisitoria[2] **(comunicación)** *request made to a judge by another to execute a sentence.* – Sin. despacho.
Rel: exhorto, *letter of request, requisitory letter;* suplicatorio, *communication issued to a higher court (by a lower court).*

res (lat.) *res, thing.* – Sin. corpus, *corpus.* cosa.
res derelicta (lat.) *res derelicta, abandoned property.*
res judicata (lat.) *res judicata, a thing adjudicated.*
res nullius (lat.) *res nullius, ownerless chattel.*
res publica (lat.) *res publica, public things.*
Ver: bienes.

res inter alios acta (lat.)(max.) *res inter alios acta, a thing done between others.*
• Los efectos jurídicos de un contrato sólo puede afectar a aquellos que lo celebraron.

resarcimiento *compensation, indemnification.*
resarcir v. *to compensate, indemnify.*
resarcible adj. *compensable.* – Sin. indemnización, *indemnification.* reparación, *redress.* compensación, *compensation.*
resarcimiento de daños *recovery of damages.*

rescisión n. *rescission.* **rescindir** *to rescind.*
rescisorio adj. *rescissory, rescinding.*
rescindible adj. *rescindable.*

• Destrucción de un acto o negocio jurídico válido mediante una declaración de voluntad que priva de efectos futuros al acto por conllevar ciertas consecuencias injustas, causando perjuicio económico a alguna de las partes o a sus acreedores. – Sin. anulación, *annulment.* invalidación, *invalidation.*
Cf: **rescisión • resolución.** Se les confunde en ocasiones, aunque tradicionalmente se ha distinguido a la rescisión como la terminación de un acto o contrato por declaración con motivo de factores externos que implican perjuicio, mientras que la resolución es considerada la terminación del acto o contrato causada por el incumplimiento de una de las partes o por la realización de la condición resolutoria a la que se sujetó.

rescisión contractual *rescission of a contract, contractual rescission.*
Ver: ineficacia.

reserva a un tratado *reservation of a treaty.*

reserva de derechos *without prejudice to legal rights.*

reserva de dominio *reservation of right of ownership.*

reserva legal DER.BANCARIO *legal reserve.*

reserva militar *military reserve, national guard.*

residencia n. *residence.* **residir** v. *to reside.*
residente n. *resident.* **residencial** adj. *residential.*
• El lugar en el que una persona mora habitualmente. – Sin. domicilio, *domicile.*
residencia extranjera *foreign residence.*
residencia habitual *habitual residence, usual residence, usual place of abode.* – Sin. morada habitual. vivienda habitual.
residencia legal *legal residence.*
residencia permanente *permanent residence.*
Rel: morada, *dwelling, abode.*

resistencia armada *armed resistance.*

resistencia a la autoridad *resistance to authority.*

resolución[1] **(resolver)** n. *resolution, decision, solving a problem or issue.* **resolver** v. *to decide, solve.* – Sin. resolver. solventar.
resolución administrativa *administrative adjudication.* – Sin. decisión administrativa.
resolución de un conflicto *resolution of a conflict.*
resolución final *final decision.*

resuélvase lo conducente *have this matter resolved accordingly.*

se resolvió que *it was held that, it was adopted that.*

resolución² (**terminación**) n. *termination.*
– Sin. terminación.

resolución de un contrato *termination of a contract.*

resolución de una obligación *termination of an obligation.*

resolución de una venta *dissolution of a sale.*
Ver: rescisión.

resolución judicial *court's disposition, decision.*
• Son los pronunciamientos de los jueces y tribunales a través de los cuales acuerdan determinaciones que sustancían el procedimiento, de conformidad con la ley y la instigación y derecho de las partes al promover sus intereses.
– Sin. decisión judicial, *judicial decision.* determinación judicial, *court's disposition.*
Las resoluciones judiciales generalmente comprenden los *decretos*, que son simples determinaciones de trámite; los *autos,* cuando deciden cualquier punto dentro del proceso; y las *sentencias* si resuelven el fondo del negocio.
Rel: auto, *court order or decree;* decreto o providencia, *order, measures;* sentencia, *judgment.*
Ref: (Esp)LOPJ a.248; (Mx)CPC a.79 CFPP a.94.

responsabilidad n. *liability, responsibility.*
responsabilizar v. *to make someone responsible or accountable.* **responsable** adj. *responsible, accountable.*
• Es la obligación o deber de reparar y satisfacer la pérdida causada, el mal inferido o el daño originado con motivo de una acción u omisión ilícitas.
La palabra responsabilidad tiene diferentes acepciones en su uso común: Se le puede entender como capacidad mental cuando se habla de que una persona ha sido responsable de ciertos actos; como causa de un acontecimiento cuando se dice que un cierto evento o conducta fueron responsables de los consecuentes sucesos; como el deber de un cargo cuando se señala que era responsabilidad del capitán la seguridad del barco. A diferencia de estas connotaciones de responsabilidad, la acepción jurídica generalmente aceptada es la que resulta en la posibilidad de una sanción en virtud del incumplimiento de una obligación o deber que el orden jurídico le impone a la persona. En este sentido se habla de responsabilidad penal cuando nos referimos a la resultante de la comisión de un delito, de responsabilidad civil cuando resulta como aplicación de normas o instituciones de naturaleza civil, ya directamente ya en forma supletoria. Por otro lado, la responsabilidad puede derivarse de la culpa en que haya incurrido el autor del daño y se dice entonces que se trata de la responsabilidad subjetiva o de culpa; o bien, puede derivarse de la relación de causalidad entre el acto del agente y el daño producido, independientemente de la intencionalidad o falta de diligencia o cuidado, y se dice entonces que se trata de la responsabilidad objetiva o teoría del riesgo causal. En la actualidad, la responsabilidad objetiva se aplica por excepción a ciertas materias, como accidentes de tráfico, navegación aérea y caza, por ejemplo, en las demás se aplica formalmente el principio de la responsabilidad subjetiva, basada en la culpa, y en su necesidad probatoria.

fincar responsabilidad *to determine accountability.*

presunta responsabilidad *alleged liability.*

responsabilidad civil *civil liability, tort.*

responsabilidad del producto (**R. del P.**) *product liability.*

responsabilidad mancomunada *joint liability.*

responsabilidad objetiva o absoluta *strict liability.*

responsabilidad oficial *official misconduct.*

responsabilidad penal *criminal responsibility.* – Sin. responsabilidad criminal.

responsabilidad por culpa *liability arising from fault.*

responsabilidad por decreto de la ley *statutory liability.*

responsabilidad por terceros *vicarious liability.*

responsabilidad profesional *professional liability.*

responsabilidad solidaria *joint and several liability.*

responsabilidad tributaria o fiscal *tax liability.*

responsable por daños y perjuicios *liable for damages.*
Rel: obligación, *obligation.*

restitución n. *restitution.* **restituir** v. *to restore, reinstate.* – Sin. reparación del daño. reposición. reintegración, *restoration.*

Rel: devolución, *return, refund.*

restricción domiciliaria *home confinement.*
– Sin. confinamiento domiciliario.

resultandos (sentencia) *the facts (of a sentence).*
• Son las consideraciones hechas en la senten-cia de los antecedentes del asunto expresadas en forma descriptiva.
Rel: considerandos, *points of law, applicable law (of a sentence);* puntos resolutorios, *holding.*

retención fiscal *tax withholding.*

retención del salario *withholding of salary.*

retiro n. *retirement.* **retirarse** v. *to retire.*
retirado adj. *retired.* – Sin. jubilación.

retracto n. *revocation, retraction.* **retractar** v. *to retract, to revoke.* **retractación** n. *retrac-tation.* **retractable** adj. *retractable.*
• "Acción de revocar un acto voluntariamente cumplido, con el fin de destruir sus efectos." (Couture, 526) – Sin. revocación, *revocation.*
retractación de una confesión *retraction of a confession, recantation.*
retracto convencional *right of revocation (of a sales contract), right of redemption.*
retracto legal *legal right of revocation.*

retraso n. *delay, late.* **retrasar** v. *to delay.*
retrasado adj. *in arrears.* – Sin. atraso. retardo. demora. dilación.
retraso en el pago *late payment.*

retraso mental *mental retardation.* **retrasado** n. *retarded.* – Sin. oligofrenia, *oligophrenia.*
Rel: debilidad mental, *mental deficiency, feeble-mindedness;* idiotez, *idiocy;* imbecili-dad, *imbecility.*

retrato hablado [fr.]*portrait parle, composite picture or sketch,* [ed]*suspect's sketch (made by a police artist).*
• Descripción oral de tipo fisonómico para reproducir la cara de una persona a través de sus rasgos faciales.
Glosario: barba saliente, *protruding chin;* barba, *beard;* barbilla puntiaguda, *pointed chin;* base de la nariz, *base of nose;* bien parecido, *good-looking;* calvo, *bold;* cejas arqueadas, *arched eyebrows;* cejas pobladas, *bushy eyebrows;* do-ble papada, *double chin;* labio superior saliente, *overhanging upper lip;* labios resaltados, *pro-truding lips;* marca de nacimiento, *birthmark;* mejilla, *cheek;* mentón, *chin;* nariz abultada, *bulbous nose;* nariz aquilina, *aquiline nose;* nariz bilobulada, *bilobed nose;* nariz cóncava, *concave nose;* nariz convexa, *convex nose;* pómulo, *cheek bone;* puente de la nariz, *bridge of nose;* tabique de la nariz, *septum of nose;* tener entradas, *receding hairline.*

retroactividad n. *retroactivity.* **retrotraer** v. *to have retroactive effect.* **retroactivo** adj. *retroactive.*
• "Por autoridad de Derecho o hecho, exten-derse una ley a hechos anteriores a su promulgación." (VII Cabanellas, 220) – Ant. irre-troactividad, *non-retroactivity.*
retroactividad de una ley *retroactivity of an statute.*

retroventa n. [ed]*right of repurchase,* [rtrgido] *right of redemption.*
• Derecho que tiene una persona para recupe-rar la cosa vendida pagando su precio.
pacto de retroventa *repurchase clause, repurchase agreement.*

revalidación n. *revalidation, republication.*
revalidar v. *to revalidate.*
Rel: ratificación, *ratification.*

revelación de secretos *revealing or divulging secrets, disclosure of secrets.*

reventa n. *resale, scalping.* **revender** v. *to resell.* **revendedor** n. *reseller, scalper.*

reversión (expropiación) n. *reversion.* **revertir** v. *to revert.* **reversible** adj. *reversible.*

revisión[1] **(verificación)** *revision, review.* **revisar** v. *to revise, review.* **revisor** n. *reviewer.*
– Sin. examen, *examination.* comprobación, *verification.*
lugar o caseta de revisión *checkpoint.*
revisión contable *audit.* – Sin. revisión de cuentas.
revisión de la causa *rehearing.*
revisión fiscal *tax inspection.*
revisión judicial *judicial review.* – Sin. interven-ción judicial.
revisión salarial *salary negotiations* || *salary review.*

revisión[2] **(recurso)** [ed]*review of a case by a higher court (on grounds of an error of fact).*
• "Recurso extraordinario que tiene por objeto la revisión de una sentencia dictada por error de hecho, para hacer posible la resolución justa, en un nuevo juicio, de la cuestión a que el fallo anulado se refiere." (De Pina, 445) Se daría por ejemplo, en el caso de la constatación de estar viva la víctima de un homicidio.
recurso de revisión [ed]*legal recourse of review of a case by a higher court (on grounds of an error of fact).*

revisión de oficio [ed]*review of a case made by the decision and initiative of a higher court judge.*
Ver: recurso.

revocación[1] **(extinción)** n. *revocation.* **revocar** v. *to revoke.* **revocador** n. *revoker.* **revocador** adj. *revoking.*

• Es un acto por el que se da por terminado otro acto jurídico válido por razones de conveniencia y por voluntad del autor. La revocación se da primordialmente en el campo civil y administrativo.

"Sólo puede hablarse de revocación [civil] en negocios jurídicos unilaterales (testamentos) y aquellos que tengan causa gratuita (donaciones). En ambos casos, la ineficacia se produce por una declaración unilateral, siempre que se cumplan los presupuestos previstos legalmente para que el acto de revocar sea válido." (IV Enciclopedia ed. Cívitas, 6011)

Cf: **revocación – nulidad.** La revocación se distingue de la nulidad por su unilateralidad, por ser causada por razones de conveniencia y por no requerir de una declaración judicial. En contraste, la nulidad debe ser declarada por un juez y tiene como causa la existencia de un defecto o vicio de origen del acto de que se trate.

revocación de un testamento *revocation of a will.*

revocación de una donación *reversion of a gift.* – Sin. reversión de donaciones.
Rel: cancelación, *cancellation;* nulidad, *void;* terminación, *termination, extinguishment.*
Ver: abrogación.

revocación[2] **(recurso)** *recall, set aside.*

• Recurso que procede generalmente contra autos y decretos no apelables, tramitándose ante el mismo juez de la causa.
– Sin. revocatoria.

revocar un auto *recall a court order, set aside a court order.*

revolución n. *revolution.* **revolucionario** n.adj. *revolutionary.*
Rel: golpe de estado, *coup d'état.* rebelión, *rebellion.*

riesgo n. *risk.* **riesgoso** adj. *risky, dangerous.*
• El riesgo es el peligro o la contingencia de que ocurra un daño.
Cf: **riesgo – peligro.** Términos usados a veces sinónimamente pero que son generalmente diferenciados. Se considera que la diferencia entre riesgo y peligro es que el riesgo es even-tual, puede existir, en cambio el peligro es actual y positivo, existe.

riesgo cambiario *foreign exchange risk.*

riesgo creado [ed]*liability born out of inherently dangerous things or animals.*

riesgo profesional *occupational hazard.*
– Sin. riesgo de trabajo.
Rel: asunción de riesgo (PR), *assumption of risk;* peligro, *danger.*

riña n. *quarrel, fight.* – Sin. pelea, *fight.*

robo (delito) n. *robbery.* **robar** v. *to rob or steal with violence or intimidation.*

• Delito que consiste en el apoderamiento ilegítimo "de una cosa mueble, total o parcialmente ajena, con fuerza en las cosas o violencia física en las personas."(Ar-CP, a.164)
– Sin. atraco (pop.), *stick up, hold up.* rapiña (Ur), robo con violencia.

Cf: **robo – hurto.** Hurto y robo se refieren a la apropiación de un bien mueble ajeno sin derecho y sin permiso del dueño; en el hurto se trata de un apoderamiento sin fuerza en las cosas o violencia en las personas, mientras que en el robo el apoderamiento se da precisamente mediante el uso de dicha fuerza o violencia.

robo a mano armada *armed robbery.*

robo de fluido *theft of electrical service.*
Rel: arrebatar, *to snatch;* despojo, *dispossession, robbing;* hurto, *larceny, theft;* ratería, *pilfering.*
Comentario: A diferencia de la mayoría de los países de habla hispana, México no hace la distinción tradicional entre hurto y robo. Para la legislación mexicana el robo simple es la modalidad de hurto y el robo con calificativos es la forma de robo en sí. El término hurto en México es una palabra de uso popular que significa un hurto de pequeña cuantía o una ratería.
Ref: (Bo)CP a.331-332; (Ch)CP a.433; (Ec)CP a. 550-553; (Esp)CP a.237ss.; (Gu)CP a.251; (Mx)CP a.372; (Pe)CP a.188; (PR)CP a.173, 33 LPRA sec. 4279; (RD)CP a.382; (Ur)CP a.344ss.; (Ve)CP a.457-58.

rogatorio adj. *rogatory.*

rúbrica n. *signature.* **rubricar** v. *to sign.*

rubro n. *caption, label.*

rueda de presos *lineup.* – Sin. galería de sospechosos. línea de presos. rueda de detenidos. rueda de sospechosos.

SSSS

sabotaje (delito) n. *sabotage.* **sabotear** v. *to sabotage.* **saboteador** n. *saboteur.*

salario DER.LABORAL n. *salary.* **salariado** adj. *salaried.* **asalariado** n. *salaried worker.*

• Es la compensación o retribución dada al trabajador por el patrono por el trabajo realizado bajo su dirección y supervisión. – Sin. emolumento, *emolument.* estipendio, *stipend.* jornal, *day's wages.* paga, *pay.* raya (pop.)(Mx), *pay.* sueldo, *wage.*

Normalmente comprende toda retribución, tanto en efectivo como en especie, que se da como contraprestación por los servicios del trabajador o se considera como tal por la legislación laboral (como en el caso de vacaciones y días de asueto pagados).

Cf: **salario ● sueldo ● estipendio ● jornal ● gratificación ● remuneración.** Todos estos términos se usan sinónima y frecuentemente en forma intercambiable. Salario y sueldo son los términos más generales refiriéndose a cualquier pago hecho por el patrón como compensación por el trabajo realizado por el trabajador. En general ambos se usan indistintamente aunque en ocasiones son distinguidos: salario se usa a veces para indicar un nivel de trabajo profesional o especializado, mientras sueldo se refiere a pagos hechos a trabajadores menos calificados o pagados a diario o semanalmente. Tanto salario como sueldo indican, sin embargo, un modo de pago periódico que cubre un período ya semanal, ya quincenal, ya de mayor plazo. Un estipendio se refiere a la paga que ha sido convenida con anticipación. Un jornal indica que los pagos se hacen diariamente. Una gratificación es un pago dado a título extraordinario con motivo de una causa específica que lo justifica. Finalmente, se habla de remuneración cuando se quiere expresar la idea opuesta a la de una actividad gratuita.

deducciones del salario *payroll deductions.*
impuesto sobre salarios *payroll tax.* – Sin. impuesto sobre nóminas.
nómina de salarios *payroll.*
salario a comisión *salary on commission.*
salario a destajo *pay by the piece or by the job.*
salario base *base salary.* – Sin. salario básico.
salario de subsistencia *subsistence wage.*
salario devengado *accrued wages.*
salario efectivo *take-home pay.*
salario en especie *salary paid in kind.*
salario en metálico *salary paid in cash.* – Sin. salario en dinero.
salario mínimo *minimum wage.*

salario neto *take-home pay, net salary.*
salario nominal *nominal salary.*
salario por hora *hourly wage.*
salario por unidad de obra *salary paid on a completion or piece basis.*
salario por unidad de tiempo *salary paid on a time basis.*
salarios caídos *back pay.*
Rel: aguinaldo, *year-end bonus;* gratificación, *bonus;* honorarios, *fees;* propina, *tip;* remuneración, *remuneration.*

saldo n. *balance.*
saldo acreedor *credit balance.*
saldo deudor *debit balance.*
saldo final *closing balance.*
saldo inicial *opening balance.*
saldo insoluto *unpaid balance.*

salvo buen cobro *due collection provided.*
salvo pacto en contrario *unless otherwise agreed.*
salvoconducto n. *safe conduct, pass.* – Sin. pase, *pass.* salvaguardia.

sanción[1] **(aprobación)** *sanction.* **sancionar** v. *to sanction.*

• Aprobación o autorización dada a un acto, en particular la dada a una ley. – Sin. aprobación, *approval.* autorización, *authorization.*
sanción de una ley *official approval of a statute.*

sanción[2] **(castigo)** *punishment, sanction.* **sancionar** v. *to punish.* **sancionable** adj. *punishable.*

• Pena o castigo señalado para aquél que infringe una disposición de la que se desprende alguna responsabilidad. – Sin. castigo, *punishment.* pena, *penalty, punishment.* punición, *punishment.*
sanción administrativa *administrative sanction.*
sanciones disciplinarias *disciplinary measures.*
sanciones internacionales *international sanctions.*
sanciones penales *criminal punishment.*
sanciones DER.INTL n. *sanctions.*

saneamiento n. [ed]*duty of seller to guarantee against hidden defects and the buyer's quiet enjoyment,* [ed]*warranty against hidden defects and the buyer's quiet enjoyment.*
sanear v. *to cure errors or defects.*

• Obligación que tiene un vendedor de responder de la posesión pacífica y útil de la cosa vendida.

saneamiento de un título *warranty against defects in title.*

saneamiento para el caso de evicción [ed] *duty of seller to guarantee buyer's quiet enjoyment (in the event of disturbance or conversion of property sold),* [ef]*warranty against dispossession or conversion.*

saneamiento por vicios ocultos [ed]*duty of seller of curing latent defects of property sold,* [ef]*warranty against hidden defects.*

saqueo n. *looting.* **saquear** v. *to loot.*

secesión n. *secession.* **secesionismo** n. *secessionism.* **secesionista** n. *secessionist.* – Sin. separatismo, *separatism.*

Secretaría DER ADMVO n. *Ministry || department.* Ver: Ministerio.

secretario del juzgado [el]*court clerk,* [ed] *court's assisting attorney.* – Sin. secretario judicial.

• Funcionario de un juzgado que prepara los acuerdos que recaen a las promociones o peticiones hechas por las partes, que interviene como fedatario de las actuaciones judiciales celebradas ante él, y que lleva a cabo otras funciones administrativas varias.

secretario de acuerdos [ed]*court's assisting attorney in charge of drafting court orders and other court dispositions.*

secretario proyectista [ed]*court's assisting attorney in charge of drafting sentence proposals.*

secretario administrativo [ed]*court clerk in charge of administrative matters.*

Comentario: El secretario del juzgado en los sistemas judiciales hispanos tiene un papel mayor y más relevante que su contraparte en los sistemas de origen anglosajón. Los secretarios generalmente son abogados titulados y dictan los acuerdos judiciales, incluyendo con frecuencia los proyectos de sentencia de los casos sujetos a su control, con la debida aprobación del juez. También son responsables de la guarda de valores, del manejo de los expedientes y frecuentemente de deberes administrativos.

Ver: actuario.

secreto bancario *bank secrecy.*

secreto profesional *professional confidentiality, confidential communication.*

secuestro¹ (de personas)(delito) n. *kidnapping, hijacking.* **secuestrar** v. *to kidnap.*

secuestrador n. *kidnapper, hijacker.*

• Apoderamiento y detención de una persona con el objeto de pedir rescate por su retorno. – Sin. plagio (obs.). secuestro extorsivo.

Cf: **secuestro ● privación ilegal de la libertad.** Ambos términos se usan sinónimamente con frecuencia, pero son generalmente considerados como dos delitos individualmente identificables: secuestro es una detención ilegal con el propósito de obtener un beneficio económico, mientras que privación ilegal de la libertad es una detención ilegal sin que se pida rescate. En estricto sentido privación ilegal aparece en varias legislaciones como el género al que pertenecen como variantes los diferentes tipos de secuestros y en ocasiones el rapto.

secuestro de automóvil *carjacking.*

secuestro de avión *aircraft hijacking, skyjacking.* – Sin. apoderamiento y desvío de aeronave.

secuestro extorsivo *kidnapping for ransom.*

secuestro exprés (Mx) [ed]*short term kidnapping (to forcefully demand withdrawal of funds from bank cash machines).* Ref: (Bo)CP a.334; (Ch)CP a.141; (Co)CP a.168-71; (Esp)CP a.163ss.; (Gu)CP a.201; (Mx)CP a.366; (Pe) CP a.152; (PR)CP a.137-138 33 LPRA sec. 4178-179; (Ur)CP a.346; (Ve)CP a.462.

secuestro² (judicial) n. *sequestration, seizure.*

• Secuestro "consiste en una medida de carácter procesal, civil o penal, que implica la custodia temporal de cosa ajena, por la administración judicial o administrativa, sin prejuzgamiento acerca de la propiedad de la cosa secuestrada." (Fernández Vázquez, 697) – Sin. depósito judicial.

secuestro de bienes *sequestration of personal property, seizure of personal property.* Ver: embargo.

sedición (delito) n. *uprising, revolt.* **sedicioso** adj. *insurgent.* **sediciosamente** adv. *insurgently.*

• Es un levantamiento multitudinario en contra de la autoridad, el orden público o la disciplina militar si efectuada por militares. – Sin. alzamiento. levantamiento.

Cf: **sedición ● rebelión.** Ambos son clasificados como delitos contra la seguridad del estado y claramente distinguibles, ya que la sedición es generalmente considerado como un delito menos grave y menos intenso que la rebelión; tradicionalmente se le define como un levantamiento colectivo, no armado y que no incide en la seguridad nacional, con finalidades que pueden o no ser políticas. La rebelión es normalmente considerada como un alzamiento general, en tanto que la sedición lo es como un alzamiento local.

sedición militar *military uprising.*

Rel: rebelión, *rebellion;* revolución, *revolution.*

segregación racial *racial segregation.*

segunda instancia [ef]*appeal,* [ed]*first appeal.*
elevar a segunda instancia *to appeal, to send a case to an appeals court.*

seguridad n. *safety, security.* – Sin. protección, *protection.*
cuerpo de seguridad *security.*
seguridad internacional *international security.* – Sin. seguridad colectiva.
seguridad nacional *national security.*
seguridad pública *public safety,*
seguridad social *social security.* – Sin. seguro social.
seguridad jurídica *the rule of law* || *legal certainty.*

seguro n. *insurance.* **asegurar** v. *to insure.* **asegurado** n. *insured.*
• En virtud del contrato de seguro se asumen los riesgos de pérdidas o daños a que está expuesto el patrimonio del asegurado a cambio del pago de una cantidad, denominada prima.
agente de seguros *insurance agent.*
ajustador de seguros *insurance adjuster.*
compañía de seguros *insurance company, insurer, insurance carrier.* – Sin. compañía aseguradora.
demanda o reclamación de seguros *insurance claim.*
ley de seguros *insurance law.*
póliza de seguro *insurance policy.*
prima de seguro *insurance premium.*
reclamación de seguros *insurance claim.*
seguro a plazo fijo *term insurance.*
seguro automovilístico *automobile insurance.*
seguro colectivo *group insurance.* – Sin. seguro de grupo.
seguro contra robo *theft insurance.*
seguro de accidentes *accident insurance.*
seguro de cobertura amplia *comprehensive insurance, all-risk insurance.*
seguro de colisión *collision insurance.*
seguro de crédito *credit insurance.*
seguro de desempleo *unemployment insurance.*
seguro de incendio *fire insurance.*
seguro de pérdida marina *marine loss insurance.*
seguro de propiedad *property insurance.*
seguro de responsabilidad civil *liability insurance.*
seguro de salud *health insurance.* – Sin. seguro de enfermedad.

seguro de vida colectivo *group life insurance.* – Sin. seguro colectivo de vida.
seguro de vida *life insurance.*
seguro médico *health insurance.*
Rel: actuario, *actuary;* beneficiario, *beneficiary;* coseguro, *coinsurance;* cobertura, *coverage;* deducible, *deductible;* exclusiones, *exclusions;* riesgo, *risk;* siniestro, *casualty;* pérdida, *loss.*
seguro social *social security.* – Sin. seguridad social.
Rel: cotización, *payment;* prestaciones del seguro social, *social security benefits.*

sello n. *seal, stamp.* **sellar** v. *to stamp, seal.*
violación de sellos *breaking of seals.*
los sellos se encontraron íntegros *the seals were found intact.*
llevar el sello *under seal.* – Sin. estar sellados.

sentencia[1] **(decision)** n. *judgment,* [amplio]*decision.* **sentenciar** v. *to render a judgment or verdict.* **sentenciador** n. *judge, person issuing a decision.* **sentenciador** adj. *sentencing.* **sentenciado** adj. *condemned, sentenced.*
• Es la decisión judicial que pronuncia el juez o tribunal para resolver el fondo del litigio, conflicto o controversia dando por terminado el proceso. – Sin. decisión, *decision.* fallo, *ruling.* resolución judicial.
"La sentencia, como declaración de voluntad del órgano jurisdiccional, está sometida a un riguroso formalismo escrito en papel sellado que tiene carácter de documento público. Se inicia con el encabezamiento en el que se exponen los datos de los sujetos procesales, antecedentes del fallo y circunstancias del lugar y tiempo de la sentencia. A continuación, y mediante párrafos separados y numerados, se expondrán los motivos de hecho que hayan sido alegados; éstos párrafos se denominan resultandos. Tras éstos, en párrafos asimismo separados y numerados, se expondrán las consideraciones de derecho; son los denominados considerandos. Por último, el fallo, que contiene la parte dispositiva de la sentencia." (Ribó Durán, 289)
aclaración de sentencia *clarification of judgment.*
fundamento o fundamentación de la sentencia *legal grounds of a sentence.*
motivos de la sentencia *reasoning supporting a judgment.*
sentencia absolutoria *not-guilty judgment, not-guilty verdict, judgment for defendant (in a civil case).* – Sin. sentencia desestimatoria.

sentencia arbitral *arbitration award.*

sentencia condenatoria *conviction, guilty verdict (in a criminal case), judgment for plaintiff or petitioner (in a civil case).*

sentencia convenida *consented judgment.*

sentencia de divorcio *decree of divorce.*

sentencia de muerte *death sentence.*

sentencia de primera instancia *judgment issued in the first instance, trial court judgment.*

sentencia de prisión *prison term.*

sentencia de remate *order of judicial sale.*

sentencia de segunda instancia *appellate court decision, judgment on appeal.*

sentencia de separación *separation decree.*

sentencia declarativa *declaratory judgment.*

sentencia definitiva *final judgment.*

sentencia ejecutoriada *executed judgment.*

sentencia firme *final unappealable judgment or sentence.*

sentencia interlocutoria *interlocutory sentence.*

Rel: considerandos, *points of law;* dictamen, *opinion;* encabezamiento, *caption, heading;* laudo, *award;* resultandos, *the facts;* veredicto, *verdict.*

Ref: (Ar)CPCC a.163; (Bo)CPC a.190; (Ch) NCPP Ch a.341ss.; (Ec)CPC a.273; (Esp)LEC a.434 y 447; (Mx)CPC a.79-V y 1323; (Ve)CPC a.242-254.

sentencia²(pena) *sentence.* **sentenciar** v. *to sentencing.*

cumplir una sentencia *to complete a sentence.*

recibir una sentencia de x años *to receive a sentence of x years.*

Ver: *sentence².*

separación¹ DER.CIVIL n. *separation.* **separar** v. *to separate.* **separado** adj. *separated.*

• La cesación de la vida en común de los cónyuges sin que resulte en la ruptura o terminación del matrimonio. – Sin. separación de cuerpos.

orden judicial de separación *court order of separation.*

separación conyugal *marital separation.*

separación de común acuerdo *separation by mutual agreement.*

separación del hogar conyugal *desertion of spouse.*

separación legal *legal separation.*

Rel: divorcio, *divorce.*

separación² DER.ADMVO n. *separation.*

separación de la iglesia y del estado *separation of church and state.*

separación de poderes *separation of powers.*

separación de bienes *separate ownership of property during marriage, separate property system.*

servicio civil *civil service.*

Rel: puesto de carrera, *career civil servant position.*

servicio militar *military service.*

servicio social *social service.*

servicios públicos *public services.*

servidumbre n. *easement.*

• "[Derecho] real que se constituye gravando una cosa con la prestación de servicios determinados en provecho exclusivo de persona que no es dueño, o de finca que corresponde a otro propietario." (Dicc. ed. Comares, 492) – Sin. carga, *servitude, charge or burden in another's land.* gravamen, *encumbrance, lien.*

Cf: **servidumbre ● carga.** Servidumbre y carga son términos sinónimos e intercambiables. Servidumbre es el término preferido en la literatura jurídica, mientras que carga tiene una acepción más amplia ya que se le usa también como sinónimo de gravamen real.

servidumbre de acueducto *easement to run an aqueduct through another's land.*

servidumbre de desagüe de edificios *sewer drainage easement.* – Sin. servidumbre de desagüe.

servidumbre de luces y vistas [ed]*easement prohibiting window openings, balconies or other intrusions next to or over the adjoining land.* [ed]*easement prohibiting openings over adjoining land.*

servidumbre de medianería *easement related to a dividing wall.*

servidumbre de paso de energía eléctrica *easement to run electrical transmission equipment.*

servidumbre de paso *right of way.*

servidumbre personal *easement in gross.*

servidumbre real *easement appurtenant.*

Rel: predio dominante, *dominant land or tenement;* predio sirviente, *servient land or tenement.*

Ref: (Ar)CC a.2970ss.; (Ch)CC a.820ss.; (CR)CC a.370ss.; (Ec)CC a.876-952; (Esp)CC a.530 y 531; (Mx)CC a.1057ss.; (Pe)CC a.1035; (PR)CC a.461, 31 LPRA sec. 1631; (RD)CC a.637; (Ur)CC a.550 ss.; (Ve)CC a.709ss.

sesión n. *session.* **sesionar** v. *to be in session.*

abrir la sesión *to call a meeting to order.*

levantar la sesión *to adjourn the session.*

sesión a puerta cerrada *closed session.*

sesión del Congreso *congressional session, parliamentary session.*
sesión plenaria *plenary session.*
Rel: asamblea, *assembly;* reunión, *meeting.*
sevicia n. *extreme cruelty.* – Sin. ensañamiento, *aggravated brutality.*
sexo n. *sex.* **sexual** adj. *sexual.* **sexualidad** n. *sexuality.*
abuso sexual *sexual abuse.*
delitos sexuales *sexual crimes.*
enfermedades sexuales *sexual diseases.*
Rel: prostitución, *prostitution.*
sicario n. *hired killer.* – Sin.: asesino a sueldo.
signatario n.adj. *signatory.*
signatario de un tratado *signatory of a treaty.*
simulación n. *simulation.* **simular** v. *to simulate.*
simulado adj. *simulated.*
sin dejar testamento [lat.]*ab intestato, without leaving a will.*
sin que conste en autos *off the record.*
sinalagmático adj. *mutually obligatory (bargained for).*
• Un acto o contrato bilateral del que nacen obligaciones para ambas partes.
sindicación de acciones *pooling agreement, voting agreement.* – Abr. s de a. – Sin. sindicato accionario.
sindicato DER.LABORAL n. *union, labor union.*
sindicar v. *to unionize.* **sindical** adj. *pertaining to unions.* **sindicalista** n. *unionist.*
sindicalismo n. *labor unionism.*
• "Es la asociación de trabajadores o patrones, constituida para el estudio, mejoramiento y defensa de sus respectivos intereses." (Mx-LFT, a.356).
En Argentina las organizaciones de trabajadores y de empleadores se denominan asociaciones profesionales. Las asociaciones de trabajadores pueden usar la denominación sindicato o unión, pero no pueden contratar colectivamente. Aquellas asociaciones que lo pueden hacer se denominan asociaciones profesionales con personería gremial y se encuentran limitadas en número.
cuota sindical *union fees.*
sindicato de empresa *union including workers of one single company.*
sindicato de industria *industrial union.*
– Sin. sindicato industrial.
sindicato gremial *craft union, trade union.*
– Sin. sindicato de oficio. sindicato horizontal.

sindicato obrero *labor union.*
sindicato patronal *employer's association.*
Rel: colegio, *college, association;* contrato colectivo de trabajo, *collective bargaining agreement;* gremio, *guild;* huelga, *strike.*
síndico[1] **(administrador)** n. *receiver or trustee.*
sindicatura n. *receivership.*
• Administrador que representa o substituye al quebrado y a los acreedores y se encarga de la administración y liquidación de la masa, así como de las gestiones y actuaciones requeridas por su cometido. – Sin. administrador, *administrator.*
síndico definitivo o liquidador *receiver, trustee.*
síndico en bancarrota *receiver or trustee in bankruptcy.* – Sin. síndico de la quiebra.
síndico en concurso de acreedores *receiver or trustee in insolvency proceedings.*
síndico[2] **(fiscalizador)** n. [ed]*stockholder's auditor.*
– Sin. comisario.
sine qua non (lat.) *sine qua non, essential condition.*
causa sine qua non *causa sine qua non, a necessary cause.*
siniestro (seguros) n. *casualty, loss.*
• Realización del riesgo asegurado.
sistema electoral *electoral system.*
soberanía n. *sovereignty.* **soberano** adj. *sovereign.*
• Potestad o poder que tiene una entidad para ejercitarlo sin que exista otra potestad o poder superior. – Sin. dominio, *dominium.* imperio, *imperium.*
soberanía nacional *national sovereignty.*
soberanía popular *popular sovereignty.*
soberanía sobre el espacio aéreo *sovereignty over air space.*
soberanía territorial *territorial sovereignty.*
soborno (delito) n. *bribery.* **sobornar** v. *to bribe.*
sobornado adj. *bribed.* **sobornador** n. *briber.*
Cf: **soborno ● cohecho.** Ambos términos suelen usarse sinónimamente, sin embargo puede señalarse que el delito de cohecho se refiere por lo general a la aceptación de una dádiva indebida por parte de un funcionario público, mientras que se habla de soborno cuando la dádiva es entregada o prometida a una persona sin tal calidad, aunque frecuentemente actuando en la administración de la justicia, como lo es el caso de testigos o jurados por ejemplo.
sobornar al jurado *embracery.*

sobregiro

Rel: cohecho, *bribery (of a public official);* corrupción, *corruption.*

sobregiro n. *overdraft.* **sobregirar** v. to *overdraft.*
sobregirar una cuenta, *to overdraw an
account.*

sobreseer[1] **(suspender)** v. *to dismiss, to stay.*
sobreseer[2] **(reemplazar)** v. *to supersede.*
sobreseimiento n. *dismissal, nonsuit.* **sobreseer**
v. *to dismiss, stay.*
• "Es la resolución judicial por la cual se declara que existe un obstáculo jurídico o de hecho
que impide la decisión sobre el fondo de la
controversia." (Dicc. UNAM, 2937)
sobreseimiento de la instancia *dismissal with
prejudice, stay of petition.*
sobreseimiento provisional *dismissal without
prejudice.* – Sin. absolución de la instancia.
sobreseimiento total DER.PENAL *dismissal in full.*
Rel: caducidad, *lapse;* improcedencia, *inadmissibility, denial.*

sociedad n. [fr.]*société,* [rtrgido]*partnership,
company.* **socio** n. *partner, shareholder.*
• "Organización voluntaria civil o comercial,
en la cual dos o más personas, físicas o jurídicas, denominadas socios, ponen en común sus
capitales, su trabajo o ambos a la vez, con el
propósito de dividir sus eventuales utilidades."
(Couture, 546).
La sociedad como concepto jurídico incluye a
la sociedad civil y a la sociedad mercantil. La
distinción entre sociedad civil y mercantil ha
sido recogida por todas las legislaciones que,
sobre la base del modelo francés, consagraron
una legislación diferenciada promulgando códigos separados para las disciplinas civiles y
mercantiles.
Cf: **sociedad • asociación.** Ambos conceptos se
refieren a la empresa en la que participan los
socios para la consecución de una finalidad
común. La distinción fundamental consiste en
que mientras la finalidad es primordialmente
no económica en la asociación (pudiendo ser
de beneficencia, cultural, educativa, etc.), es
por lo contrario primordialmente económica
en la sociedad, en la que hay la intención de
generar y repartir ganancias.
↳ El concepto sociedad es un término genérico
que no tiene un equivalente exacto en inglés.
Los sistemas jurídicos romano-germánico y
anglo-americano al regular las organizaciones
y empresas desarrollaron dos esquemas
diferentes, que no tienen una correspondencia
fácil. La sociedad definida como un esfuerzo
común de los socios logrando una utilidad co-

rresponde a la descripción de un *partnership,*
pero también puede incluir a una *corporation;*
algunos arguyen incluso, que ciertas *associations* podrían caer dentro del concepto de
sociedad. Si el término sociedad considerado
en forma genérica presenta dificultad en su
equivalencia, afortunadamente las categorías
específicas de sociedades tienen una mayor
correspondencia con la dualidad *partnership-
corporation* del derecho angloamericano.
sociedad accidental o momentánea *joint
venture, participation association.* – Sin. asociación en participación.
sociedad civil *civil society* || [ed]*partnerships
or legal entities regulated by the civil code,*
[ef]*non-business partnerships or associations.*
sociedad comercial *business entity, business
company.*
sociedad controladora *holding company.*
sociedad cooperativa *cooperative, co-op.*
sociedad de inversión *mutual fund.*
sociedad filial *subsidiary.* – Sin. subsidiaria.
sociedad irregular *de facto corporation.*
– Sin. sociedad de hecho.
sociedad matriz *parent company.*
sociedad mercantil [ed]*commercial or
mercantile partnership or corporation.*
sociedad mutualista *mutual benefit company.*
sociedad oculta [ed]*non-disclosed business
partnership or association.*
sociedad unimembre *sole proprietorship.*
Rel: asociación, *association;* compañía, *company;* consorcio, *consortium;* cooperativa, *cooperative;* empresa, *firm, business.*
Ver: sociedades mercantiles.

sociedad anónima [ed]*incorporated joint stock
company,* [ef][amplio]*corporation.*
[prest.]*sociedad anónima,* [fr.]*société anonyme.*
• La sociedad anónima es una sociedad mercantil formada por la aportación de capital,
dividido en acciones, hecha por socios cuya
responsabilidad se limita a tal aportación.
– Sin. compañía anónima.
fundación de sociedad anónima *incorporation of a joint stock company, formation of a
joint stock company.* – Sin. constitución de la
sociedad anónima.
Rel: administrador, *member of the Board;*
asamblea, *shareholder's meeting;* comisario,
shareholder's auditor; escritura constitutiva,
corporate charter.
Ref: (Ch)LSA a.1; (Co)CCo. a.233ss.; (Ec)LC, a.
143- 144; (ES)CCo a.191ss.; (Esp)TRLSA a.1;
(Mx)LGSM a.87; (Pa)LSA a.1; (Ve)CCo. a.242ss.
Ver: *corporation.*

sociedad conyugal *community property, marital property.* – Sin. comunidad de bienes (maritales).

sociedades mercantiles [el]*mercantile companies, business entities.*

• Son sociedades mercantiles aquellas cuyo objeto es la obtención de utilidades realizando operaciones mercantiles. – Sin. compañía mercantil (PR). Tradicionalmente son consideradas sociedades mercantiles: la sociedad anónima, la sociedad colectiva o en nombre colectivo, la sociedad comanditaria o en comandita, y la sociedad de responsabilidad limitada.

sociedad anónima [ed]*incorporated joint stock company,* [ef][amplio]*corporation.*

sociedad colectiva *general commercial partnership, general partnership.* – Sin. sociedad en nombre colectivo.

sociedad comanditaria por acciones *partnership limited by shares.* – Sin. sociedad en comandita por acciones.

sociedad comanditaria simple *limited partnership.* – Sin. sociedad en comandita simple.

sociedad cooperativa *cooperative corporation, cooperative.*

sociedad de responsabilidad limitada *limited liability company.*

socio n. *partner, shareholder.* – Sin. accionista, shareholder. asociado, *associate.*

⌐ El término socio se refiere tanto a la calidad de *partner* como a la de *shareholder* o *stockholder.* Generalmente se usa *partner* cuando se trata de una sociedad en la que cuando menos algunos de los socios son ilimitadamente responsables y las aportaciones no están representadas por acciones. Se usa, por otro lado, *shareholder* o *stockholder* cuando la responsabilidad de los participantes es limitada y el capital está representado accionariamente.

socio accionista *shareholder, stockholder.*

socio capitalista *capital partner, partner investing capital and/or goods.*

socio de trabajo *partner investing labor.*

socio fundador *founding partner.*

socio industrial *partner investing labor and/or services.* – Sin. socio de industria.

sodomía n. *sodomy.*

solemnidad n. *solemnity.* **solemnizar** v. *to solemnize.* **solemne** adj. *solemn.* **solemnemente** adv. *solemnly.*

• Los rituales necesarios para cumplimentar las formalidades exigidas para la validez de un acto o contrato. – Sin. ceremonial, *ceremonial.* ritual, *ritual.*

solemnidades *formalities.*

solicitud n. *application, petition.* – Sin. petición, *petition.*

llenar una solicitud *to fill out an application.* **presentar una solicitud** *to file an application.* **requerir una solicitud** *to request an application* || *an application is needed.*

solidaridad[1] **(unión)** n. *solidarity.* **solidarizar** v. *to join together.* **solidario** adj. *solidary.*

solidaridad[2] **(responsabilidad)** n. *joint liability.* **solidarizar** v. *to make joint and severally responsible.* **solidario** adj. *joint and several.*

• Caso de pluralidad de deudores o acreedores en el que a cada uno de ellos se le puede exigir (en el caso de deudores) o se le puede pagar (en el caso de acreedores) la totalidad de la obligación.

obligación solidaria *joint and several obligation.*

solventar una deuda *discharge a debt.*

sordera n. *deafness.* **sordo** n. *deaf.* **sordomudez** n. *deaf-muteness.* **sordomudo** n. *deaf-mute.*

sororicidio n. *sororicide.* **sororicida** n. *sororicide.*

sospechoso n. *suspect.* – Sin. autor. indiciado. presunto.

status quo (lat.) *status quo, the situation that currently exists.*

strictu sensu (lat.) *strictu sensu, in strict sense.*

subarriendo o subarrendamiento n. *sublease, sublet.* **subarrendar** v. *to sublease.*

subarrendador n. *sublessor.*

subarrendatario n. *subtenant, sublessee.*

subasta n. *auction.* **subastar** v. *to auction.*

subastador n. *auctioneer.* – Sin. remate, *auction.*

subasta judicial *judicial auction.*

subasta pública *public auction.* – Sin. almoneda.

subcontratista n. *subcontractor.* **subcontratar** v. *to subcontract.* **subcontrato** n. *subcontract.*

subrogación OBLIGACIONES n. *subrogation.* **subrogado** n. *subrogee.*

• Es la substitución admitida por la ley de una persona por otra, permaneciendo idéntica e invariable la relación obligatoria en la que se ha efectuado tal substitución. – Sin. substitución, *substitution.*

subrogación convencional *conventional subrogation.*

subsidio

subrogación legal *legal subrogation.*
subrogación personal *substitution of subrogor.*
subrogación real *substitution of subrogee.*
subsidio n. *subsidy.* **subsidiar** v. *to subsidize.*
• Apoyo económico que la administración pública otorga a particulares con el objeto de fomentar las actividades productivas en forma temporal. En España la palabra subsidio se usa frecuentemente como sinónimo de prestación social. <subsidio de desempleo> – Sin. subvención, *subvention.*
Cf. **subsidio • subvención • incentivo.** Subsidio y subvención son sinónimos y frecuentemente se les usa indistintamente. Subvención es el término genérico que se refiere al apoyo económico que otorga el estado para auspiciar el desarrollo de actividades económicas. El subsidio, se dice, es una especie de subvención sin que esté claramente diferenciado por la doctrina. Por lo que se refiere a los incentivos, este apoyo económico por lo general se da exencionando a los particulares de impuestos o derechos a pagar. A los incentivos también se les refiere como estímulos, y aún más específicamente como estímulos fiscales o tributarios. Rel: apoyo, *assistance;* beneficio económico, *economic benefit;* estímulo, *incentive;* incentivo, *incentive.*

sustanciación n. [ed]*the act of carrying on the due procedural steps in the suit or case, trying a case.* **sustanciar** v. *to litigate, carry on a case.*
sustancias tóxicas *toxic substances.*
Rel: arsénico, *arsenic;* cianuro, *cyanide;* estricnina, *strychnine;* insecticida, *insecticide;* monóxido de carbono, *carbon monoxide.*
substitución n. *substitution.* **substituir** v. *to substitute.* **substituto** n. *substitute.* **substituible** adj. *replaceable.* **substitutivo** adj. *substitutive.* – Sin. reemplazo, *replacement.* suplencia. También: sustitución.
substitución de las penas *substitution of penalty or criminal punishment.*
substitución fiduciaria [ed]*designation in a will of the beneficiaries who will inherit at the death of the first designated heir,* [el]*fiduciary substitution (of a designated heir).*
substitución patronal *substitution of employer.*
substitución procesal *substitution of parties in a trial.*
substitución vulgar [ed]*appointment in a will of a substitute contingent heir.*

subsuelo n. *subsoil.*
subvención n. *subvention.* **subvencionar** v. *to grant a subvention.*
Ver: subsidio.
subversión n. *subversion.* **subvertir** v. *to subvert.* **subversivo** adj. *subversive.* – Sin. desorden, *disorder, disturbance.* trastorno, *upheaval, disturbance.*
elementos subversivos *subverting elements.*
sucesión n. *succession.* **sucesor** n. *successor.*
• Es la transmisión de los bienes, derechos y obligaciones de una persona a los herederos que él haya designado en testamento o que sean señalados por la ley. – Sin. herencia, *inheritance.*
↪ A diferencia del sistema anglosajón, la sucesión en países de tradición romano-germánica transmite la titularidad de los bienes del decujus ipso jure (esto es en forma inmediata y automáticamente), evitando en consecuencia el procedimiento de *probate,* típico del sistema anglosajón. Otra distinción importante es la existencia de la sucesión legítima en los países hispanos, la que limita la transmisión de bienes por sucesión, especificando una porción obligatoria a ciertas personas.
colación de la sucesión *hotchpot, hodgepodge, collation* (EEUU-La).
línea de sucesión *line of succession.*
partición de la herencia *partition of the estate.*
sucesión hereditaria *hereditary succession.*
sucesión intestada o legítima *intestate succession.* – Sin. sucesión legal.
sucesión por cabezas *per capita succession.* – Sin. sucesión in capita.
sucesión por estirpe *per stirpes succession.* – Sin. sucesión por representación.
sucesión por líneas *lineal descendibility, lineal ascendancy, in line of succession (ascendancy or descendancy).* – Sin. sucesión in líneas.
sucesión testamentaria *testamentary succession.*
sucesión universal [prest.]*universal succession,* [ed]*succession to an entire estate of another.*
Rel: intestado, *intestate;* legado, *legacy;* masa hereditaria, *decedent's estate, corpus of the estate;* testamento, *will.*
Ref: (Ar)CC a.3279ss.; (Ch)CC a.951ss.; (Ec)CC a. 1015; (Esp)CC a.657-58; (Mx)CC a.1281ss.; (Pe) CC a.660; (Ur)CC. a.776-778; (Ve)CC a.807.
sucursal *branch, subsidiary.*

sueldo n. *salary, wage.*
retención de sueldo *wage withholding.*
sueldo anual complementario *year-end bonus.* – Sin. aguinaldo. mes 13.
sueldo base *base salary.*
Ver: salario.

suelo n. *soil, ground.* – Sin. solar, plot. terreno, land, terrain. tierra, land, soil.
regulación del uso del suelo *zoning.*

sufragio[1] (derecho) n. *suffrage.*
sufragio restringido *restricted suffrage.*
sufragio universal *universal suffrage.*

sufragio[2] (votar) n. *vote, voting.*

sufragio[3] (ayuda) n. *aid, help.* – Sin. auxilio. ayuda.

suicidio n. *suicide.* **suicidarse** v. *to commit suicide.* **suicida** n. *suicide.* **suicida** adj. *suicidal.* – Sin. quitarse o arrebatarse la vida, *to take own's life.*
auxilio e inducción al suicidio *aiding and abetting a suicide.* – Sin. instigación al suicidio, cooperación al suicidio.

sujeto activo del delito *participant in the crime, party to the crime.*

sujeto de derecho *legal entity or being,* [ed] *being capable of rights and duties,* [ef]*legal person.* – Sin. persona.

sujeto pasivo del delito *victim of the crime.*

sumario[1] (expedito) *summary proceeding.*
sumariamente adv. *summarily.* – Sin. abreviado, shortened, accelerated.
enjuiciar sumariamente *being summarily tried.*
juicio sumario *summary proceeding.*
juicio sumarísimo DER.MILITAR *accelerated summary proceeding.*

sumario[2] DER.PROC.PENAL n. [ed]*preliminary stage (of criminal proceedings).* [ef]*probable cause phase (of a criminal cause).* – Sin. instrucción.
El sumario es la etapa inicial que se sigue en un juicio penal con motivo de la comisión de un delito. En ella se hace una investigación por el juzgador para determinar la existencia de los delitos y la responsabilidad o falta de responsabilidad del acusado.
instruir un sumario [ed]*to conduct the preliminary stage (of criminal proceedings),* [ef] *to proceed with the probable cause phase (of a criminal cause).*
Rel: auto de cabeza de proceso, *judicial admission of a cause (by the court);* auto de no sujeción a proceso, *court order dismissing charges (for lack of evidence);* auto de procesa-

miento, *indictment and order to stand trial;* averiguación previa, *preliminary investigation;* indagatoria, *first statement made by defendant before a judge (regarding the facts of the case);* orden de personación del inculpado, *order compelling appearance of defendant.*
Ver: procedimiento penal.

suministro n. *supply.* **suministrar** v. *to supply.*
suministrador n. *supplier.* – Sin. abastecimiento. provisión. suministración. aprovisionamiento.
contrato de suministro *supply contract, provisions contract, contract to supply goods continuously (to purchaser).*

superávit n. *surplus.*

supérstite adj. *surviving (another person).* – Sin. sobreviviente. superviviente.
cónyuge supérstite *surviving spouse.*

suplencia de la queja [ed]*court's discretion to amend and correct claim and motions from disadvantaged litigants,* [ed]*sua sponte court's amendment of motions and complaints.*
☛ Suplencia de la queja, siendo la actuación directa de juez en reposición de las omisiones de una de las partes, no tiene un equivalente exacto en inglés. Se basa en la naturaleza directiva y participativa que tiene el juez en el proceso dentro de la tradición romano-germánica, que no se da en el sistema de la *common law,* en donde los jueces presiden un proceso esencialmente contencioso o *adversarial,* y en el que las partes se responsabilizan en todo momento de sus propias actuaciones. El juez en el sistema de la *common law* no está facultado para participar en suplencia de alguna de las partes, ya que desvirtuaría la naturaleza de su participación y posición en el proceso.

supletoriedad n. [ed]*suppletive,* [ed]*replacing.*
supletorio adj. *suppletive, replacing.*
• La supletoriedad es el principio desarrollado por el derecho privado de señalar a ciertas normas, generalmente parte de un ordenamiento, como aquellas a las que se referirá el aplicador cuando no hay normas directamente aplicables que permitan resolver la situación planteada.
☛ La supletoriedad es un concepto desconocido en el derecho angloamericano. Las normas en el derecho romano-germánico, entre otras clasificaciones, pueden ser imperativas o supletorias: son imperativas aquellas que obligan en todo caso a los particulares, con independencia de su voluntad; son supletorias aquellas que se aplican sólo en ausencia de una regula-

ción que normalmente le corresponde establecer a los contratantes.

ley supletoria [prest.]*suppletive statute.* [ed] *statute to be applied in the absence of other applicable statute or code* – Sin. norma supletiva.
Rel: norma imperativa o taxativa, *mandatory norm.*

suplicatorio[1] (desafuero) n. [ed]*request (made by the court) for authorization to charge a member of the legislature with a crime.*
• Solicitud hecha a la legislatura para que se autorice el proceder contra un diputado o senador por la comisión de un delito.
Rel: desafuero, *deprivation of legal privilege;* fuero parlamentario, *parliamentary privilege.*

suplicatorio[2] (comunicación) n. *communication or request from a lower to a higher court.*
• Es una súplica, esto es una simple petición, hecha por un juez inferior a uno superior, de informes o datos relacionados a algún asunto en particular.
Ver: comunicaciones procesales.

Suprema Corte de Justicia *Supreme Court.* – Sin. Corte Suprema de Justicia. Tribunal Supremo. Tribunal Supremo de Justicia.
Rel: Tribunal Superior de Justicia, *Superior Court, High Court.*
Ver: *Supreme Court.*

surtir efecto *to take effect, to acquire legal force.*

susodicho n. *aforesaid, above-mentioned.* – Sin. antedicho, *above-mentioned.* sobredicho, *aforesaid.*

suspensión[1] (detención) n. *suspension, adjournment.* **suspender** v. *to suspend, adjourn.* **suspensivo** adj. *suspensive, adjourning.* **suspendido** n.adj. *suspended.*
Cf: **suspensión • receso.** Una sesión se suspende cuando se da por terminada y se resumirá en otra ocasión o lugar; un receso, en cambio, es una suspensión breve durante el transcurso de la misma sesión.

suspensión de la asamblea de accionistas *adjournment of the shareholder's meeting.*

suspensión de operaciones *discontinuance or suspension of operations.*

suspensión[2] (posponer) n. *suspension, stay.* **suspender** v. *to suspend, stay.* **suspendido** n.adj. *suspended.* **suspensivo** adj. *suspensive, staying.*

suspensión de la condena *suspended sentence.* – Sin. [rtrgido]suspensión de la pena.

suspensión de pagos *suspension of payments.*

suspensión del procedimiento *stay of proceedings.*

suspensión del procedimiento administrativo de ejecución *stay of administrative execution proceedings.*

suspensión del proceso *suspension of the suit or case.*

suspensión[3] (castigo) n. *suspension, sanction.*

suspensión de derechos *suspension of constitutional guarantees.* – Sin. suspensión de garantías.

sustracción de menores (Esp) *child abduction.*

TTTT

tácito adj. *implied, tacit.* **tácitamente** adv. *implicitly, tacitly.* – Sin. implícito, *implied.*

tácita reconducción *constructive renewal.*

tácita reconducción de un arrendamiento [ef]*tenancy at sufferance, constructive renewal of a lease.*

tacha de falsedad *challenge of testimony.*

tacha de testigos *impeachment of witnesses.*

tanatología *thanatology.*
• Parte de la medicina legal que estudia todo lo relativo a la muerte y al cadáver.
Rel: exhumación, *exhumation, disinterment;* inhumación, *inhumation, burial.*

tanteo n. *right of first refusal, first option to buy.*
• Derecho de preferencia para adquirir ciertos bienes concretamente especificados, dado a ciertas personas por la ley o por acuerdo entre las partes. – Sin. derecho de preferencia por el tanto. derecho de tanteo. derecho del tanto.

tanteo convencional *right of first refusal (by agreement).*

tanteo legal *statutory right of first refusal.*

tarjeta de débito *debit card.*

tarjeta de crédito *credit card.*

tasa[1] (tributo) *tax, charge.* **tasar** v. *to tax.* **tasado** adj. *taxed.*
• Es un tributo como contraprestación a un servicio publico, la utilización del dominio público o la realización de una actividad pública que beneficie a un particular. – Sin. derecho (Mx).

tasas estatales *state charges.*

tasas municipales *municipal charges.* – Sin. tasas locales.

tasa[2] (proporción) *rate.*

tasa de cambio *rate of exchange.*

tasa de descuento *discount rate.*

tasa de desempleo *unemployment rate.*
tasa de interés *interest rate.*
tasa fiscal *tax rate.*
tasa[3] **(valuación)** n. *valuation, appraisal.* **tasación** n. *appraisal, assessment.* **tasar** v. *to apprise, to assess.* **tasador** n. *appraiser, adjuster.* **tasado** adj. *appraised, assessed.* – Sin. valuación. estimación, *estimate.*
tasación de costas o costos *assessment of costs.*
tasación de las costas *assessment of court costs.*
tecnología n. *technology.*
tecnología de punta o de vanguardia *state-of-the-art technology.*
tecnología libremente disponible *freely available technology.*
tecnología obsoleta *obsolete technology.*
Rel: conocimiento técnico, *technical know-how;* técnica, *technique.*
temor fundado *reasonable fear.*
teneduría de libros *bookkeeping.*
tenencia n. *tenancy, holding.* **tenedor** n. *tenant, holder.*
• Se refiere a tener el control de una cosa en forma legítima sin que se tenga la posesión, dominio o propiedad de la misma.
Cf: **propiedad ● tenencia.** La propiedad es un poder jurídico que una persona ejerce en forma directa e inmediata sobre una cosa para su goce y disposición, siendo oponible a los demás. La tenencia es el ejercicio de un poder físico sobre la cosa en forma legal sin tener el ánimo de dueño, esto es, detentando la cosa por otro.
↵ Tenencia y *tenancy* son términos equivalentes al referirse al poder de control ejercido sobre un bien en forma justificada legalmente. Se apartan el uno del otro en el énfasis que el derecho angloamericano da a *tenancy* como un concepto fundamental del derecho inmobiliario, <life tenancy> en tanto que el derecho romano-germánico presenta una mayor inclinación a favor de tenencia como un concepto aplicable a diferentes materias jurídicas, <tenencia de vehículo> sin otorgarle un relieve sobresaliente en alguna de ellas.
tenedor de acciones *stockholder.*
tenencia de armas *possession of weapons.*
tenencia de la tierra *land tenancy.*
Rel: detentación, *detainer;* posesión, *possession.*
Ver: posesión.
tentativa n. *attempt.*

• Hay tentativa cuando el sujeto inicia la ejecución del delito, practicando todos o parte de los actos necesarios para su consecución, sin que se produzca éste por causas independientes a la voluntad del autor. – Sin. intento.
Cf: **tentativa ● intento.** Términos sinónimos e intercambiables entre sí. Tentativa es el término legal preferido, mientras que intento es el término usado en el habla popular preferentemente, pero que ha adquirido status legal en ciertas expresiones. <intento de suicidio>.
tentativa de homicidio *attempted murder.*
terapia n. *therapy.* **terapeuta** n. *therapist.*
terapéutico adj. *therapeutic.* – Sin. terapéutica. tratamiento, *treatment.*
bioterapia *biotherapy.*
quemoterapia *chemotherapy.*
terapia de grupo *group therapy.*
terapia electroconvulsiva *electroconvulsive therapy.*
terapia ocupacional *occupational therapy.*
tercería DER.PROC.CIVIL n. *intervention.*
tercero/tercerista n. *third party, intervener.*
• Tercería es la participación de un tercero en un proceso con el objeto de hacer valer derechos propios que pudieran resultar afectados con motivo del litigio.
tercería coadyuvante *co-litigation.*
tercería excluyente [ed]*intervener alleges having opposing interest (to that advanced by the other parties).*
tercería forzosa *impleader, to bring a third party into a lawsuit.* – Sin. tercería necesaria.
tercería voluntaria *voluntary intervention.*
terceros en el proceso *third parties interveners.*
tercero DER.CIVIL n. *third party.*
• En derecho civil el tercero es aquél que no es parte en el contrato o negocio jurídico.
tercero contractual *contractual third party.*
oponible a terceros *enforceable against third parties, binding on third parties.*
terminación n. *termination.* – Sin. cesación, *cessation.* conclusión, *conclusion.* extinción, *extinguishing, extinguishment.* término, *limit, end.*
terminación anticipada *early termination.*
terminación de un contrato *termination of contract.* – Sin. resiliación de un contrato.
Rel: cancelación, *cancellation;* nulidad, *void, voidable;* rescisión, *rescission;* revocación, *revocation.*
término n. *term, period (of time).*

término convencional *agreed or stipulated term or deadline.*
término fatal *fatal deadline.*
término improrrogable *final deadline.*
término legal *legal term or period, legal deadline.*
término perentorio *procedural term which expires automatically.*
término probatorio [ed]*period open (to the parties) for discovery and to offer evidence.*
– Sin. período probatorio.
término probatorio *evidentiary period.*
término procesal *term or period set by procedural rules.*
término prorrogable *extendable term or deadline.*
Ver: plazo.

terrateniente n. [ext.lexico.]*terre-tenant, land-tenant.*
terreno n. *land.* **tierra** n. *land, ground.*
– Sin. tierra, *land, ground.*
terreno baldío *empty lot, uncultivated land.*
terreno contiguo *adjacent land, adjacent lot.*
terreno rural *rural property.*
terreno urbano *urban property.*
terrenos nacionales *national lands, public lands.*
Rel: parcela, *plot, lot;* predio, *lot.*

territorialidad n. *territoriality.* **territorial** adj. *territorial.*
• Ámbito de jurisdicción geográfico de un Estado para aplicar con validez sus leyes.
principio de territorialidad *territorialism.*
Rel: extraterritorialidad, *extraterritoriality.*

territorio DER.INTL n. *territory.* **territorial** adj. *territorial.* – Sin. espacio geográfico.
territorio bajo administración fiduciaria o tutela *trust territory.*
territorio no autónomo *non-self-governing territory.*

terrorismo n. *terrorism.* **terrorista** n. *terrorist.*
• "Se entiende por terrorismo toda actividad violenta, que no constituya rebelión, cualquiera que sean los medios empleados, que pretenda obtener, mediante el grave temor provocado en la comunidad, o en un sector de ella, la alteración de la paz social interior, la desestabilización del gobierno, o el logro de éste, de ciertas ventajas de índole político o social." (Pavón Vasconcelos Dicc., 966)
atentado terrorista *terrorist attack.*
terrorismo de estado *state terrorism.*
terrorismo internacional *international terrorism.*
Rel: atentado, *criminal assault or attack;* secuestro, *kidnapping.*

tesoro n. *treasure-trove.*
• Depósito oculto o ignorado de dinero, alhajas u otros objetos preciosos cuya legítima pertenencia se ignore.

testaferro n. *straw man.*
Ver: prestanombre.

testamento SUCESIONES n. *will, testament.* **testador** n. *testator, testatrix.* **testado** adj. *testate.* **testamentario** adj. *testamentary.*
• El acto por el cual una persona dispone, en forma libre y revocable, para después de su muerte de todos sus bienes o derechos o sólo parte de ellos. También se refiere al documento que contiene ésta disposición de última voluntad. – Sin. última disposición, *last will and testament.*
impugnar un testamento *to contest a will.*
redactar un testamento *to draft a will, to draw up a will.*
revocación de un testamento *revocation of a will.*
testamento abierto [ed]*will drafted and certified by a public notary.*
testamento cerrado *sealed will.*
testamento en lengua extranjera *will written in a foreign language.*
testamento marítimo *mariner's will, seaman's will.*
testamento militar *soldier's will.*
testamento ológrafo *holographic will.*
testamento privado *nuncupative will.*
Rel: legado, *legacy;* sucesión, *succession;* testamentaria, *testamentary execution.*
Ref: (Ar)CC a.3607; (Ch)CC a.999; (CR)CC a.577 ss.; (Ec)CC a.1063ss.; (Esp)CC a.667; (Mx) CC a.1297ss.; (Pe)CC a.686ss.; (Ur)CC a.779; (Ve)CC a.833ss.

testar¹ (cancelar) v. *to delete, cross out.* **testado** v. *stricken, deleted.*
testar² (will) v. *to make a will.*
testigo n. *witness.* **testificar** v. *to testify, to take the stand.* **testificación** n. *giving testimony.*
testificante adj. *testifying.* – Sin. declarante, *declarant, deponent.*
testigo de cargo *witness for the prosecution.*
testigo de coartada *alibi witness.*
testigo de conocimiento *identifying witness.*
testigo de descargo *witness for the defense.*
testigo de oídas o referencia *hearsay witness.*
testigo desfavorable *adverse witness.*
testigo idóneo *qualified witness.*

testigo instrumental *documentary witness.*
testigo no confiable *unreliable witness.*
testigo parcial *zealous witness.*
testigo presencial *eyewitness.* – Sin. testigo de vista. testigo ocular.
testigo renuente *reluctant witness, hostile witness.*
testigo único *sole witness.*
testigo veraz *credible witness.*
testimonio[1] **(declaración)** n. *testimony.* **testimoniar** v. *to testify.* **testimonial** adj. *testimonial.*
• Declaración que hace un testigo en juicio. – Sin. atestiguación. prueba testimonial. testificación, *testification.*
en testimonio de lo cual *in witness whereof.*
rebatir un testimonio *to rebut a witness's testimony, to impech a witness.*
testimonio acerca de lo dicho por un tercero *hearsay testimony.*
testimonio de una persona no competente *incompetent testimony.*
testimonio extrajudicial *deposition.*
testimonio falso *false testimony.*
testimonio inverosímil *incredible testimony.*
testimonio[2] **(documento)** *notarial document.*
• Documento expedido bajo la fe de notario en el que se transcribe una escritura o acta así como los documentos anexos a las mismas. – Sin. testimonio notarial.
Cf: **acta de declaración jurada** • **acta de declaración notarizada** • **testimonio notarial.**
Una acta de declaración jurada es aquella que expresa una declaración hecha mediante juramento que le da validez. Por su parte, tanto un acta de declaración notariada o notarizada, como un testimonio notarial son hechos mediante la fe del notario público, que similarmente los valida.
tiempo compartido *timeshare.*
timbre n. *stamp.* **timbrado** adj. *stamped.* – Sin. sello, *seal.* estampilla, *stamp.*
impuesto del timbre *stamp tax.*
timo n. *swindle.* **timador** n. *swindler.* – Sin. estafa. engaño, *deceit, trick.*
tipicidad DER.PENAL n. [ed]*fit between the facts and the statutory description of a crime.*
• Coincidencia de la conducta del acusado con la descripción de los elementos del delito (tipo) descritos por la ley penal.
Rel: tipo, [ed]*statutory description of a crime.*
tipo de cambio *rate of exchange.*
título[1] **(relación jurídica)** n. *title, reason.*

a título de dominio *by right of ownership.*
a título gratuito *without valuable consideration, as a gift.*
a título oneroso *for valuable consideration.*
a título particular *by a special right.*
a título sucesorio *under succession rights.*
a título universal *by a general right, inclusive of an entire estate.*
justo título *legitimate title.*
título de propiedad *title deed.*
título libre de gravámenes *clear title.*
título perfecto *perfect title.*
título profesional *professional certification.*
título translativo de dominio *deed or instrument transferring ownership.* – Sin. título traslaticio de dominio.
título[2] **(documento)** n. *document, certificate.*
titular adj. *title-holder.*
título de acciones *stock certificate.*
título ejecutivo [ed]*document providing executory process.* – Sin. título sumario.
título nominativo *registered instrument.*
título[3] **(distinción)** n. *title.*
título de director de departamento *title of director of department.*
título nobiliario *title of nobility.* – Sin. título de nobleza.
títulos de crédito [ef]*negotiable instruments.*
• Título de crédito es el documento necesario para ejercitar el derecho literal y autónomo que en él se incorpora. – Sin. título valor. papel comercial, *commercial paper.*
cancelación de un título de crédito *cancellation of a negotiable instrument.*
emisión de un título de crédito *issuance of a negotiable instrument.*
reposición de un título de crédito *replacement of a negotiable instrument.*
Rel: acción cambiaria, *right of recourse, collection action based on a negotiable instrument;* aceptación, *acceptance;* aval, *accommodation endorsement;* cheque, *check;* endoso, *indorsement;* giro, *draft;* letra de cambio, *bill of exchange, draft;* pagaré, *promissory note.*
tomar posesión *to assume (office).*
tortura n. *torture.* **torturar** v. *to torture.*
torturador n. *torturer.*
• La aplicación de violencia física o moral a una persona, generalmente para obligarla a decir o hacer algo. – Sin. martirio. tormento, *torment.* suplicio, *torture, torment.*
Rel: azotes, *flogging, lashing;* cepo, *pillory;* garrucha, *pulley, block;* lavado de cerebro,

brain washing; molino, *treadmill;* patíbulo, *gallows, gibbet;* picana, *goading;* rueda, *wheel;* tablillas, *splint.*

tóxico adj. *toxic.* **intoxicar** v. *to intoxicate, poison.* **toxicomanía** n. *drug addiction.*
toxicómano n. *drug addict.* **toxicidad** adj. *toxicity.* – Sin. toxicante. venenoso, *poisonous.*
toxicología n. *toxicology.*
traba de la litis *pleadings.*
Ver: fijación de la litis.
trabajador n. *worker.* **trabajar** v. *to work.*
trabajador adj. *working.* – Sin. empleado, *employee.* obrero, *worker.*
cuadrilla de trabajadores *workers' crew.*
trabajador a domicilio *worker who works at home.*
trabajador a prueba *worker under a trial period.*
trabajador a tiempo parcial *part-time worker.*
trabajador agrícola *agricultural worker.*
trabajador de confianza *management or supervisory personnel.*
trabajador dependiente *employee.*
trabajador doméstico *domestic worker.*
trabajador eventual *casual worker.*
– Sin. trabajador accidental.
trabajador indocumentado *undocumented worker.*
trabajador interino *substitute worker.*
trabajador no sindicalizado *non-unionized worker.*
trabajador por cuenta ajena *hired worker, employed person.*
trabajador por cuenta propia *self-employed person, independent contractor.*
– Sin. trabajador autónomo.
trabajador social *social worker.*
trabajador temporal *temporary worker.*
trabajo[1] **(faena)** n. *work, labor.* **trabajar** v. *to work.* – Sin. chamba (mod.), *work.* labor, *labor.* tarea, *task.*
trabajo a destajo *piecework.*
trabajo a domicilio *work performed at home.*
trabajo de menores *work performed by minors, child labor.*
trabajo diurno *day work.*
trabajo forzado *forced labor.*
trabajo nocturno *night work.*
trabajo ocasional *temporary emergency work.*
– Sin. trabajo accidental. trabajo transitorio.
trabajo peligroso *hazardous work.*
trabajo penitenciario *prison work.*

Rel: instrumentos de trabajo, *work tools or implements.*
trabajo[2] **(ocupación)** n. *job, employment.*
– Sin. empleo. ocupación, *occupation.*
conseguir trabajo *to find work.*
faltar al trabajo *to miss work, to be absent.*
trabajos públicos *public works.*
trabar ejecución *attachment and execution of a judgment.*
trabar embargo *to levy an attachment of assets, to seize in attachment.*
tracto sucesivo CONTRATOS *periodic performance (contract).*
tradición n. *delivery.* **tradente** n. *deliverer, person surrendering something to another.*
adquirente/ adquiriente n. *acquirer, transferee.*
• Entrega real o simbólica de la cosa. – Sin. entrega.
tradición por ministerio de la ley *delivery by operation of law.* – Sin. tradición jurídica.
tradición real o material *actual delivery.*
tradición simbólica *constructive delivery.*
tradición virtual *symbolic delivery.*
– Sin. tradición fingida.
traducción n. *translation.* **traducir** v. *to translate.* **traductor** n. *translator.* – Sin. traslación.
traducción consecutiva *consecutive translation.*
traducción legal *legal translation.*
traducción literal *literal translation.*
traducción literaria *literary translation.*
traducción oficial *official translation.*
traducción simultánea *simultaneous translation.*
traducción técnica *technical translation.*
traductor certificado *certified translator.*
Rel: interpretación, *interpretation;* transposición, *transposition.*
tráfico de drogas *drug traffic.*
• Constituye tráfico ilícito todas las operaciones de cultivo, adquisición, enajenación, importación, exportación, depósito, almacenamiento, transporte, distribución y tránsito de sustancias estupefacientes. – Sin. narcotráfico. tráfico de estupefacientes. tráfico ilegal de drogas, *illegal drug traffic.*
Generalmente se usa la denominación estupefaciente para incluir a todo estupefaciente, psico trópico y demás sustancias susceptibles de constituir adicción e incluidas en los listados

de sustancias ilegales de las autoridades de salud correspondientes.

traficante de drogas *drug dealer.*
Rel: estupefacientes, *narcotics and similar substances;* fabricación de drogas, *drug production;* posesión de drogas, *drug possession.*

tráfico de influencias (delito) *influence peddling.*
• Delito que cometen los funcionarios públicos al procurar, por sí mismos u otras personas, la solución favorable de determinados asuntos y proteger así ilícitamente intereses propios o ajenos.
Rel: influyentismo o compadrazgo (Mx), *old boys network;* favoritismo, *favoritism;* nepotismo, *nepotism;* tener palanca (pop.), *to be connected;* enchufe (PR), *connections.*

tráfico ilegal de mano de obra (Esp) *trafficking of illegal workers.*

traición *treason.* **traicionar** v. *to commit treason.* **traidor** n. *traitor.* **traicionero** n. *traitor.* **traicionero** adj. *traitorous, treacherous.*
• "Toda persona que debiendo obediencia a la Nación por razón de su empleo o función pública, tomare las armas contra ésta, se uniere a sus enemigos o les prestare cualquier ayuda o socorro." (Valletta, 662)
Se trata de un delito que atenta contra la seguridad exterior del estado, y que tradicionalmente se basa en la violación del vínculo de lealtad que deben guardar los nacionales de un país para con el mismo, o el peligro a que expone a una nación aquél que entrega secretos, divulga información sensitiva o toma acciones similares.

alta traición *high treason.*
traición a la patria *treason,* [obs.]*high treason.*
traición militar *military treason.*

trámites n. *steps, formalities.* **tramitar** v. *to carry through formalities.* **tramitación** n. *formalities and procedures.* – Sin. pasos, *steps.* formalidades, *formalities.*
de mero trámite *routine matters, a mere formality.*
estar en trámite *being processed already.*
realizar un trámite *to fulfill a formality, to process a transaction, to file a document.*
sin más trámite *without further formalities.*
trámites administrativos *administrative formalities and procedures.*
Rel: papeleo, *red tape.*

transacción¹ ((finiquito) n. *accord and satisfaction.* **transigir** v. *to settle.* **transaccional** adj.

settlement, pertaining to a settlement.
• "Contrato en virtud del cual las partes, mediante recíprocas concesiones, ponen término a una controversia presente o previenen una futura." (Mx-CC, a.2944)
Cf: **transacción ▪ convenio transaccional.**
Términos muy similares, ambos refiriéndose a un acuerdo que pone fin a una controversia. Convenio transaccional se refiere con mayor énfasis al hecho del cumplimiento de una obligación o la ejecución del convenio, en cambio transacción implica mayormente la resolución de un conflicto o desacuerdo entre las partes.
Ver: autocomposición.

transacción²(trato) n. *transaction, deal.*

transferencia n. *transfer.* **transferir** v. *to transfer.* **transferible** adj. *transferable.*
– Sin. cesión, *assignment.* transmisión. traspaso.

transferencia de tecnología *transfer of technology.*
Glosario: asistencia técnica, *technical assistance;* derechos y licencias, *rights and licensing;* conocimientos técnicos, *technical know-how;* maquiladoras, *in bond plants;* ingeniería básica y de detalle, *basic and detail engineering;* capacitación, *training;* precio de insumos, *price of inputs;* prohibición de exportar, *export prohibition;* regalías, *royalties;* secretos industriales, *industrial secrets;* técnicos extranjeros, *foreign technicians.*

transgresión n. *transgression.* **transgredir** v. *to transgress, break.* **transgresor** n. *lawbreaker.*
– Sin. infracción, *infraction.* quebranto, *breaking.* violación, *violation.*

transgresión de la ley *violation of the law, breaking the law.*

transmisión de acciones *stock transfer.*

transmisión de obligaciones *subrogation or assignment of obligations.* – Sin. transferencia.
Rel: cesión de derechos, *assignment of rights;* cesión de deudas, *assignment of credits or debts;* subrogación, *subrogation.*

transmisión de propiedad *transfer of ownership.*

transmisión de un derecho real *conveyance of a right in rem.*

transporte (contrato) n. *transportation, transport.* **transportar** v. *to transport.*
transportador/ transportista n. *carrier, transporter.*
• "Contrato en virtud del cual una de las partes se obliga respecto de la otra, a trasladar de un

lugar a otro, por tierra, por el agua o por el aire, personas, animales, mercancías o cualesquiera otros objetos mediante un precio." (De Pina, 484) – Sin. transportación, *transportation.*
comisionista de transporte *freight forwarder.* – Sin. transitario.
transporte aéreo *air transportation.*
transporte de línea *line transportation.*
transporte de mercancías *transportation of cargo.*
transporte de personas *transportation of passengers.*
transporte público *public transportation, common carrier.*
transporte privado *private carrier.*
transporte terrestre *ground transportation.*
Rel: embalaje, *packing, crating, bailing;* transbordo, *transshipment.*
transporte marítimo *maritime or ocean transportation.*
Rel: línea de conferencia, *conference line;* línea marítima regular, *regular maritime line;* manifiesto, *manifest.*
traslación de dominio *transfer of title.*
traslación del impuesto *tax transfer.*
– Sin. traslación tributaria. traslado de impuestos.
traslado de la demanda *to serve notice of complaint or petition (made to the opposing party in a lawsuit).*
correr traslado *to serve copies to the opposing party or parties.*
traspaso n. *transfer, conveyance.* **traspasar** v. *to transfer, alienate.* – Sin. cesión, *assignment.* transferencia, *transference, transfer.*
trasplante de órganos *organ transplant.*
Rel: donante, *donor;* receptor, *recipient.*
trata de blancas *white slave trade.*
trata de esclavos *slave trade.*
tratado DER.INTL n. *treaty.*
• Tratado es todo acuerdo concluido entre dos o más sujetos de derecho internacional y ratificado por sus órganos internos. – Sin. concordato, *concordat.* convención, *convention.*
ratificación de un tratado *ratification of a treaty.*
reserva de un tratado *reservation of a treaty.*
tratado de asistencia mutua *treaty of mutual assistance.*
tratado de comercio *commercial treaty.*
tratado de doble nacionalidad *double nationality treaty.*
tratado de extradición *extradition treaty.*

tratado de paz *peace treaty.*
tratado internacional *international treaty.*
Rel: firma, *signature;* negociación, *negotiation;* ratificación, *ratification.*
Tratado Norteamericano de Libre Comercio (TNLC) *North American Free Trade Agreement* (NAFTA).
tratos crueles inhumanos o degradantes *cruel, inhuman or degrading treatment.*
tribunal n. *tribunal, court.*
• "Organo de jurisdicción destinado a la aplicación del derecho por la vía del proceso." (De Pina, 485) – Sin. corte, *court.* juzgado, *court.* órgano jurisdiccional, *court.*
"A los órganos colegiados suele denominárseles con el nombre de tribunales, aunque esta denominación también se utiliza frecuentemente como comprensiva de todos los órganos jurisdiccionales e indistintamente para los unipersonales y colegiados." (IV Enciclopedia ed. Cívitas, 6689)
tribunal colegiado *collegiate court,* [ed]*tribunal made up of more than one judge.*
tribunal de circuito *circuit court.*
tribunal de lo contencioso administrativo *administrative court.*
tribunal de primera instancia *court of first instance, trial court.*
tribunal de segunda instancia *appellate court.* – Sin. tribunal de apelación.
tribunal de última instancia *court of last resort.*
tribunal electoral *board of elections.*
tribunal en pleno *court in full.* – Sin. tribunal plenario.
tribunal fiscal *tax court.*
tribunal militar *military court, military tribunal.*
tribunal para menores *juvenile court.*
Tribunal Supremo *Supreme Court.*
tribunal superior *superior court.*
Rel: sala (de un tribunal), *division of a court* || *courtroom.*
tributo n. *tax.* **tributar** v. *to pay taxes.* **tributación** n. *paying of taxes, tribute.* **tributante** n. *taxpayer.* **tributario** adj. *pertaining to taxes or duties.* **tributante** adj. *taxable.* **contribuyente** n. *taxpayer.*
• El tributo es una prestación obligatoria, comúnmente en dinero, debida coactivamente al Estado y que se genera al caer el causante en los supuestos que establece la ley. – Sin. carga tributaria. contribución. gabela. gravamen (obs.).

Cf: **tributo ● impuesto.** Ambos términos se usan sinónimamente con frecuencia, pero existe unanimidad entre los tratadistas en el sentido de considerar al tributo como el término genérico que incluye tanto al impuesto como a los otros cargos públicos (contribuciones, tasas, derechos, productos, etc.).

derecho tributario *tax law.* – Sin. derecho fiscal.

ley general tributaria (Esp) *tax law, tax act.* – Sin. código fiscal.

potestad tributaria *taxing power.*

reforma tributaria *tax reform.* – Sin. reforma fiscal.

Rel: alcabala (obs.), *sales tax;* contribuciones, *contribution, levy, tax;* derechos, *duties, fees;* impuesto, *tax;* peaje, *toll;* productos, *yield, rent, proceeds;* tasa, *duty, tax.*

Comentario: "A pesar de que el tributo es la institución central de un sector perfectamente diferenciado dentro del Derecho Financiero, sus contornos no son siempre precisos en la doctrina y en la jurisprudencia. Nuestra legislación [española] no define el tributo, aunque presupone la existencia del mismo, pues existe una Ley que dice, entre otras cosas, que los tributos se clasifican en tasas, contribuciones especiales e impuestos." (IV Enciclopedia ed. Cívitas, 6712) Ver: impuesto. *international taxation.*

trueque n. *barter.* **trocar** v. *to barter.* – Sin. trocamiento. trueco. cambio, *exchange.* permuta, *exchange.*

tutela FAMILIA n. *guardianship,* [prest.]*tutorship* (EEUU-La). **tutelar** v. *to protect, guard.* **tutor** n. *guardian.* **tutelado** adj. *subject to guardianship.* **pupilo** *minor ward.* **tutoría** n. *guardianship.*

• Autoridad que se otorga substituyendo a la patria potestad para la guarda de menores o incapacitados y la protección de sus bienes. – Sin. guarda, *ward.* tutoría, *guardianship.*

Cf: **tutela ● curatela.** Términos claramente distinguibles aunque frecuentemente se les confunde. La tutela es una institución por la que se otorga la guarda de personas y bienes de menores sin padres o mayores incapacitados. La curatela es un tipo especial de tutela que tiene la finalidad principal de proteger los bienes de ciertas personas (señaladas específicamente por la ley), ya directamente, ya mediante la supervisión del tutor.

tutela dativa *court-appointed guardianship.*

tutela legítima *statutory guardianship.*

tutela testamentaria *testamentary guardianship.*

Rel: curatela, *curatorship;* custodia, *custody.*

Ref: (Ar)CC a.377; (Ch)CC a.338; (Ec)CC a.385ss.; (Esp)CC a.215ss.; (Mx)CC a.450; (Pe)CC a.502-563; (PR)CC a.167, 31 LPRA 661; (Ur)CC a.313ss.; (Ve)CC 301ss.

tutela jurídica *relief, protection of the law.*

tutela jurisdiccional *judicial relief.*

UUUU

ubicación *location.* **ubicar** v. *to locate.* **ubicado** adj. *located.* – Sin. localización, *location.*

la mejor ubicación *prime location.*

ultimátum DER.INTL n. *ultimatum.*

ultraje a la moral pública *offending public morality.*

ultraje al pudor *criminal sexual contact.* – Sin. abuso deshonesto.

unilateral adj. *unilateral.*

unión aduanera *customs union.*

unión de crédito *credit union.*

unión de sociedades *combination.* Rel: cártel o consorcio, *cartel;* fusión, *merger.*

unión libre *common law marriage.* – Sin. amancebamiento. concubinato.

Unión Postal Universal (UPU) *Universal Post Union* (UPU).

urbano adj. *urban.* **urbanizador** n. *developer.*

uso¹ (práctica) n. *usage.*

• Norma de naturaleza y forma consuetudinaria que, una vez reconocida por el legislador, entra a formar parte del ordenamiento vigente. – Sin. usanza, *usage.*

uso inveterado *inveterate usage.*

uso jurídico *lawful usage.*

uso y costumbre *custom and usage.*

usos del comercio *business practices.*

usos mercantiles *trade usage.*

usos sociales *social conventions.* Rel: costumbre, *custom;* práctica, *practice.*

uso² (derecho real) n. [ed]*entitlement or right to use another's property.* [lat.]*usus.* **usuario** n. *tenant, user.*

• Derecho real que faculta al usuario para percibir los frutos de un bien ajeno con el objeto de satisfacer las necesidades propias y las de su familia. – Sin. derecho de uso.

usuario n. *customer, user.*

usuario final *end user.*

usucapión n. *acquisition of ownership by adverse possession,* [prest.]*usucaption.* – Sin. prescripción positiva.

usufructo [prest.]*usufruct*. [ef]*life tenancy,* [ef]*life estate*. **usufructuar** v. *to benefit from an usufruct*. **usufructuario** n. *usufructuary, holder of an usufruct*.

• "El usufructo es un derecho real, temporal, por naturaleza vitalicio, para usar y disfrutar de los bienes ajenos sin alterar su forma ni substancia." (II Rojina Villegas, 118)

↳ El término *life estate* o *life tenancy* se usa con frecuencia como equivalente de usufructo. En la mayoría de las veces esta equiparación es apropiada ya que usufructo es mayormente un derecho que se "desmiembra" del derecho de propiedad permitiendo que el propietario conserve el dominio y ceda el uso o disfrute, en forma generalmente vitalicia. Esta descripción es muy similar, en términos funcionales, al concepto de *life estate* o *life tenancy* que consiste no en un "desmembramiento" de la propiedad sino en la creación de un derecho similar nuevo y siempre vitalicio, a partir del derecho original del propietario. La similitud funcional se extiende al derecho que reciben el usufructuario y *reversioner* después de otorgado el usufructo o creado el *life estate*, pero debe tenerse en cuenta que mientras el usufructuario tiene un derecho real sobre una propiedad que le pertenece a otro, el *revisioner* es el titular, podría decirse, no de un derecho, sino de un *estate* consistente en un *future interest* sobre el bien inmueble.

usufructo múltiple *usufruct granted to several persons.*

usufructo múltiple simultáneo [ext.lexico.]*usufruct granted to several persons simultaneously.*

usufructo múltiple sucesivo [ext.lexico.]*usufruct granted to several persons successively.*

usufructo particular [ext.lexico.]*usufruct over specified things.*

usufructo testamentario [ext.lexico.]*usufruct granted by will*. – Sin. usufructo voluntario.

Rel: derecho de goce, *right to enjoy another's property;* derecho de uso, *right to use another's property;* nudapropiedad, *naked ownership.*

Ver: propiedad.

usura n. *usury*. **usurear** v. *to practice usury*. **usurero** n. *usurer*. **usurariamente** adv. *usuriously.*

• La práctica de hacer préstamos de dinero a tasas de interés excesivas o exorbitantes.

usurpación n. *usurpation, encroachment*. **usurpar** v. *to usurp*. **usurpador** n. *usurper*. **usurpador** adj. *usurping.*

• Desposesión de una propiedad inmueble en forma violenta e indebida.

usurpación de aguas *unlawful appropriation of waters.*

usurpación de tierras *usurpation of land, illegal taking of land.*

usurpación de estado civil *usurpation of another's legal status.*

usurpación de funciones *usurpation of authority.* – Sin. usurpación de cargo público, usurpación de funciones públicas.

usus fori (lat.) *usus fori, rule of court.*

• La práctica del foro o los tribunales.

utilidad pública *public benefit.*

utilidades (contab.) n. *profits, earnings.* – Sin. beneficios. ganancias, *earnings, gains.* provecho, *profit.*

pago de utilidades *profit distribution.*

reinversión de utilidades *reinvestment of earnings.*

tasa de utilidad *profit rate.*

utilidad bruta *gross profit.*

utilidad de operación *operating profit.*

utilidad fiscal *taxable profit.*

utilidad neta *net income.*

utilidad por acción (UPA) *earnings per share (EPS).*

utilidades antes de impuestos *profits before taxes.*

utilidades extraordinarias *extraordinary profit.*

utilidades no distribuidas *retained earnings.* – Sin. utilidades retenidas.

uxoricidio n. *uxoricide*. **uxoricida** n. *uxoricide*. **uxoricida** adj. *uxoricide.*

• Homicidio de un cónyuge cometido por el otro.

VVVV

vacaciones n. *vacation*. **vacacionar** v. *to vacation*, **vacacionista** n. *vacationer*. **vacaciones pagadas** *paid vacation.*

vagancia n. *vagrancy* || *loitering*. **vagar** v. *to wander, roam*. **vago** n. *vagrant*. **vagante** adj. *vagrant*. – Sin. vagabundeo.

vale[1] (recibo) n. *voucher.* **vale de caja** *cash voucher.*

vale[2] (pagaré) n. *promissory note.*

Ver: pagaré.

validez n. *validity.* **validar** v. *to validate, make valid.* **válido** adj. *valid.* **válidamente** adv. *validly.* – Sin. eficacia, *effectiveness, validity.* vigencia, *force and effect.*

elementos de validez de un contrato [el] *elements of validity of a contract, requirements needed for a contract to be valid.*

validez de un testamento *validity of a will.*

valor[1] **(cuantía)** n. *value.*

valor al menudeo *retail value.*

valor catastral *assessed value.*

valor de avalúo *appraised value.*

valor de costo *cost value.*

valor de deshecho *scrap value.* – Sin. valor de desperdicio.

valor de mercado *market value.*

valor de reposición *replacement value.*

valor de rescate *surrender value.*

valor en aduana *customs assessed value.*

valor en efectivo *cash value.*

valor en libros *book value.* – Sin. valor en libros.

valor fiscal *tax value.*

valor gravable *taxable value.*

valor nominal *face or nominal value.*

valor recibido *value received.*

valor[2] **(títulos)** *securities.* – Sin. valores mobiliarios.

valores al portador *bearer securities.*

valores bursátiles *stock-exchange listed securities.*

valores de inversión *investment securities.*

valores de renta fija *fixed-yield or fixed-income securities.*

valores de renta variable *variable-yield securities.*

valores en depósito *custody of securities.*

valores en garantía *pledged securities.*

valores listados *listed securities.*

valores negociables *marketable securities.*

valuación n. *appraisal.* **valuar** v. *to value, appraise.* **valuador** n. *appraiser, assessor.* – Sin. aprecio. tasación. valorización, *valuation, appraisal.*

vandalismo n. *vandalism.* **vándalo** n. *vandal.* **vandálico** adj. *pertaining to vandalism.*

• Actos de violencia o destrucción realizados en una manifestación pública contra otros o contra propiedades públicas o privadas. – Sin. barbarie, *barbarism.* depredación, *depredation.*

veda n. *prohibition, ban.*

vehículo *vehicle.* **vehicular** adj. *vehicular.*

Rel: automóvil, *automobile.*

velo corporativo *corporate veil.*

vencimiento n. *due, maturity.* **vencer** v. *to expire.* **vencido** adj. *due, matured.*

• El momento en que una obligación se convierte en exigible y en el que puede demandarse su pago o cumplimiento.

vencimiento a la vista *due on demand, due on sight, payable on sight.*

vencimiento a un plazo desde la fecha *due a certain length of time after the date of issue, payable x days from the date of issue.* – Sin. vencimiento a días fecha. vencimiento a cierto tiempo fecha.

vencimiento a un plazo desde la vista *due a certain length of time after presentment, payable x days from presentment.* – Sin. vencimiento a días vista. vencimiento a cierto tiempo vista.

vencimiento a una fecha *due on a specific date, payable on a fixed date.*

venganza n. *vengeance, revenge.* **vengar** v. *to avenge.* **vengador** n. *avenger.* **vengador** adj. *avenging.* – Sin. desquite. represalia, *reprisal, retaliation.* revancha, *revenge, retaliation.* vindicación, *vindication.* vindicta.

Rel: linchamiento, *lynching;* vigilantismo, *vigilantism.*

venia[1] **(permiso)** n. *permission, authorization.*

con la venia de la sala *may it please the court, by leave of the court.*

venia[2] **(perdón)** n. *pardon.*

venta n. *sale.* **vender** v. *to sell.* **vendedor** n. *seller, vendor.* **revendedor** *reseller.* **vendido** adj. *sold.* – Sin. compraventa, *sale.*

venta a crédito *sale on credit.*

venta a domicilio *door to door sale.*

venta a plazos *installment sale.* – Sin. venta en abonos.

venta a prueba [ed]*sale subject to buyer's acceptance (at the buyer's reasonable discretion).* – Sin. venta a calidad de prueba. venta a calidad de ensayo.

venta al contado *cash sale.*

venta al menudeo *retail sale.*

venta con pacto de retroventa *sale with repurchase clause, sale with right of redemption.* – Sin. venta con pacto de retracto.

venta de acciones *sale of stock or shares.*

venta de activo fijo *sale of fixed assets.*

venta de cosa ajena *sale of property of another.*

venta de liquidación *clearance, clearance*

sale, close out sale.

venta de mercancías *sale of goods.*
venta de primera mano *first sale.*
venta en almoneda *auction sale.*
venta en consignación *consignment sale.*
venta en subasta *auction sale.*
venta firme *executed sale.*
venta judicial *judicial sale.*
venta por suministro *procurement contract.*
– Sin. venta de suministro.
venta sobre muestras *sale by sample.*

verdugo n. *executioner.*

veredicto n. *verdict.*

veredicto de culpabilidad *guilty verdict.*
veredicto de inocencia *not-guilty verdict,*
acquittal.

verificación n. *verification.* **verificar** v. *to*
verify. **verificador** n. *verifier.* **verificador** adj.
verifying. **verificado** adj. *verified.* – Sin. comprobación. constatación.

Rel: cotejo, *comparison, collation.*

veto n. *veto.* **vetar** v. *to veto.*

vía administrativa *administrative proceeding.*

vía de apremio *enforcement proceedings.*
– Sin. procedimiento de apremio.

vía judicial *litigation, process of law, legal*
means.
recurrir a la vía judicial *to resort to*
litigation.

vía ordinaria *ordinary procedure, ordinary*
proceedings.
Ver: procedimiento civil.

vía sumaria *summary proceedings, summary*
procedure.

viáticos *travel expenses.*

vicio n. *defect, vice.* **viciar** v. *to make imperfect*
or faulty. **viciado** adj. *defectively.*
• Defecto en la celebración de un acto jurídico
o un contrato. – Sin. defecto. vicio de fondo
substantive defect.
vicio de forma *procedural defect.*
vicio jurídico *legal defects.*
vicios ocultos o redhibitorios *latent defects.*
vicios del consentimiento CONTRATOS [ed]*defects in*
the formation of contractual consent, [prest.]
vices of consent (EEUU-La). **viciar** v. *to form*
or create with a defect. **viciado** adj. *with a vice*
or defect.
• Vicios del consentimiento son la ausencia
o realización incompleta de elementos esenciales para que se manifieste debidamente
el consentimiento de las partes en la forma-

ción de un contrato, ocasionando la posible
nulidad o ineficacia del mismo. – Sin. vicios de
la voluntad.
Son vicios del consentimiento en los contratos
todo hecho o actitud que restrinja o anule la
libertad de la persona y el conocimiento con
que deba formularse una declaración, tales
como el dolo, el error, las amenazas o intimi-
daciones, la violencia, la mala fe, la lesión y
el fraude. La lista final varía en las diferentes
legislaciones según la doctrina que se adopte.
Rel: dolo, *dolus;* error, *error;* lesión, *lesion;*
mala fe, *bad faith;* violencia o fuerza, *violence.*

víctima n. *victim.*

vida n. *life.*
costarle la vida *to cost someone his or her life.*
de por vida *for life, life.*
nivel de vida *standard of living.*
sin vida *lifeless, devoid of life.*

vigencia n. *in effect, duration.* **vigente** adj. *in*
force and effect.
• Que tiene validez y por tanto se encuentra en
vigor. – Sin. eficacia, *effectiveness, validity.*
validez, *validity.*
Cf: **vigencia • duración.** Vigencia y duración
son usados como sinónimos constantemente,
sin embargo son dos conceptos a veces identificables separadamente. La vigencia se refiere a la validez de la norma, de la ley y por
extensión a la de cualquier disposición. Una
norma o ley abrogada o declarada inconstitucional no es una norma o ley válida, como tal
se dice que no está vigente. La duración por
su parte se refiere al plazo de tiempo que dura-
rá la norma o ley. Por lo general la duración
de una norma, ley o disposición depende de
su validez y por ello hay coincidencia y sinonimia. Estrictamente hablando sin embargo,
la vigencia expresa la validez, mientras la
duración pone de relieve el período de tiempo.
entrar en vigencia *to take effect.*
vigencia de la garantía *validity of the warran-*
ty, duration of the warranty.
vigencia de la ley *effective date of the statute,*
duration of the statute.
vigencia del contrato *term or duration of the*
contract.
Rel: duración, *duration.*

vigilancia n. *vigilance, watchfulness.* **vigilar** v.
to keep vigil. **vigilante** n. *guard, watchman.*
– Sin. guardia, *guard.* vigilia, *vigil, watch.*
compañía privada de vigilancia *security*
private company.
vigilante nocturno *night watchman.*

vínculo jurídico *legal relationship.*

violación[1] **(infracción)** n. *violation.* **violar** v. *to violate.* **violador** n. *violator.*

• Infringir o quebrantar una disposición o precepto. – Sin. infracción, *infraction.* quebrantamiento.

violación de correspondencia *mail tampering.* – Sin. intercepción de correspondencia. interceptación de correspondencia.

violación de derechos constitucionales *violation of constitutional rights.*

violación de derechos *violation of rights.*

violación de garantías *violation of constitutional protections or guarantees.*

violación de la ley *violation of the law.*

violación de neutralidad *violation of neutrality.*

violación de patente *infringement of a patent.*

violación de sepulturas *desecration of tombs or graves.*

violación de una disposición *infringement of regulations.*

violación del secreto profesional *violation of professional secrets, violation of professional confidentiality.*

violación[2] **(delito)** n. *rape,* [amplio]*sexual assault.* **violar** v. *to rape.* **violador** n. *rapist.* **violada** n. *raped woman.*

• Violación es el tener cópula con mujer mediante la fuerza o la intimidación, considerándose también conducta constitutiva de este delito cuando la mujer fuese menor de cierta edad (generalmente tratándose de una impúber), aun sin mediar la fuerza o intimidación. – Sin. agresión sexual (Esp). acceso carnal violento (Co).

violación mediante el uso de la fuerza *forcible rape.* – Sin. violación con violencia.

Rel: cópula, *copulation;* estupro, *statutory rape;* violencia física o moral, *physical violence or intimidation.*

Ref: (Ar)CP a.119; (Bo)CP a.308; (Ch)CP a.361; (Co)CP a.205-207; (Ec)CP a.512; (Gu)CP a.173; (Mx)CP a.265; (Pa)CP a.216; (Pe)CP a.170; (PR) CP a. 99, 33 LPRA sec. 4061; (RD)CP a.331; (Ur) CP a.272.

violación[3] DER.CANÓNICO n. *desecration of a holy place, profanation of a sacred place.*

violación de domicilio (delito)(Ar) *unauthorized entry in another's home, home invasion.* Ver: allanamiento de morada.

violencia n. *violence.* **violentar** v. *to do violence.* force. **violento** adj. *violent.* **violentamente** adv. *violently.* – Sin. fuerza, *force.*

desatarse la violencia *violence to break loose.*

violencia doméstica *domestic violence.* – Sin. violencia sobre familiares.

violencia física *physical violence.*

violencia moral *intimidation.*

visa n. *visa.* **visar** v. *to grant a visa.* **visado** n. *visa.*

Cf: **legalización** • **certificación** • **visa.** Estos tres términos se usan como sinónimos frecuentemente en el ámbito consular, aunque cada uno de ellos puede diferenciarse: la legalización se refiere a la autentificación de funcionarios o fedadores públicos extranjeros hecha por un agente consular; la certificación es la anotación hecha por un funcionario consular señalando que tuvo a la vista el documento respectivo; y la visa o visado es la autorización consular que le da efecto legal al documento en el que consta, normalmente se sujetan a visa los pasaportes y documentos como certificados de origen, certificados de sanidad animal y similares.

visa de estudiante *student visa.*

visa de hombre de negocios *businessman visa.*

visa de residente *resident's visa.*

visa de turista *tourist visa.*

visa diplomática *diplomatic visa.*

visa oficial *official visa.*

visa temporal *temporary visa.*

Rel: inmigración, *immigration;* pasaporte, *passport.*

Ver: legalización.

visita conyugal *conjugal visit.*

visita domiciliaria *home visit.*

visitante de intercambio DER.INTL *exchange visitor.*

vista[1] **(pedir una actuación)** n. [ed]*notify a party to act or motion accordingly (in a lawsuit).*

dése vista a la contraria [ed]*notify the opposing party (to act or motion accordingly).*

dése vista para sentencia [ed]*notify the parties (to act or motion accordingly) before judgment is issued.*

vista[2] **(audiencia)** n. *hearing, proceeding.*

• Actuación judicial o audiencia en la que se escucha a las partes con motivo de una causa o incidente para resolver mediante sentencia.

vista en primera instancia *hearing at trial court level, hearing in the first instance.*

vista preliminar *preliminary hearing.* – Sin. examen preliminar.

vista[3] **(inspector)** n. *inspector.*

vista aduanal *customs inspector.*

visto bueno

visto bueno *approval.* – Abr. Vo.Bo.
dar el visto bueno *to approve (something).*
vistos los autos *the record having been reviewed.*
viudedad (Esp) *widowhood* ǁ *widow's pension.*
viuda n. *widow.* **viudo** n. *widower.*
– Sin. viudez.
voluntad n. *will, intent.* **voluntario** adj. *voluntary, willful.* **voluntariamente** adv. *voluntarily.*
• La voluntad se refiere al poder o la facultad de la persona para obrar o abstenerse, a la posibilidad de elegir libremente el actuar, en otras palabras, se refiere a su libre albedrío.
Cf: **voluntad•intención.** Términos similares que se usan en ocasiones en forma intercambiable, <la voluntad del legislador> <la intención del legislador> pero que sin embargo han desarrollado varios usos ya firmemente establecidos en el campo jurídico. Voluntad entendida como un querer generalmente se asocia con la idea de libertad y "libre albedrío", <la voluntad de las partes> en tanto que intención se inclina más en poner de relieve la especificidad del propósito que pretende el querer de una persona. <la intención delictiva>.
por motivos ajenos a su voluntad *for reasons beyond one's control.*
voluntad de las partes *actual intent of the parties.*
voluntad del legislador *legislator's intent.*
voluntad del testador *intent of the testator.*
voluntad expresa *express intent.*
voluntad presunta *constructive intent.*
voluntad tácita *implicit intent.*
Rel: declaración unilateral de voluntad, *express promise.*
voto[1] (dictámen) n. *vote, ballot.* **votar** v. *to vote.*
votante n. *voter.*
con derecho a voto *with a right to vote.*

emitir un voto *to cast a vote.*
no tener ni voz ni voto *without a right to take part in neither discussions nor vote.*
voto de calidad *casting vote.*
voto de censura *vote of censure.*
voto de confianza *confidence vote.*
voto disidente *dissenting vote.* – Sin. voto en disidencia.
voto secreto *secret ballot.*
voto[2] (elección) n. *voting, election.* **votación** n. *voting.* – Sin. elección.
voto oral *voice vote.* – Sin. votación oral.
voto secreto *vote by secret ballot, secret vote.*
– Sin. votación secreta.
Rel: sufragio, *suffrage.*

XXXX
xenofobia n. *xenophobia.* **xenófobo** n. *xenophobe.* **xenófobo** adj. *xenophobic.*

YYYY
yacente *inheritance in abeyance.* – Sin. herencia yacente.

ZZZZ
zona contigua *contiguous zone.*
zona de guerra *war zone.*
zona de libre comercio *fee-trade zone.*
zona económica exclusiva *exclusive economic zone.*
zona fronteriza *border country, border area.*
zona libre o franca *free zone, duty-free zone.*

APPENDIXES – APÉNDICES

APPENDIX-APÉNDICE A
ABBREVIATIONS
(US LAW PRACTICE)

ABA American Bar Association *Barra de Abogados Americana.*

ABH actual bodily harm *lesión corporal.*

AFF'D affirmed *confirmado a ratificado.*

AKA also know as *también conocido como.*

ASA Assistant State's Attorney *Asistente o Agente del Fiscal, Fiscal.*

B/A by agreement *de común acuerdo.*

CC case closed *caso terminado o concluido.*

CDTP criminal damage to property *daño en propiedad ajena.*

CFT continued for trial *se continúa en juicio.*

CNFT continued not for trial *se continúa sin juicio.*

CLIN clinical evaluation *evaluación clínica.*

CT. court *corte, juzgado.*

CTTV criminal trespass to vehicle *entrar u ocupar un vehículo ilícitamente.*

DBA doing business as *operando mercantilmente como, en negocios bajo el nombre de, haciendo negocios como* (PR).

DOA dead on arrival *declarado muerto al llegar.*

DEL/DELQ delinquent *delincuente.*

DEN denial *se niega, negativa.*

DOC Department of Corrections *Departamento de Correcciones.*

DWOP dismissed without prejudice *sobreseimiento sin precluir el ejercicio de acciones procedentes.*

DWP dismissed with prejudice *sobreseimiento precluyendo el ejercicio de cualquier acción.*

DUI Driving under the influence *conducir en estado de ebriedad.*

ET UX. et uxor (and wife) *y esposa.*

EV. EVID. evidence *pruebas.*

FDG finding *decisión, fallo, declaración.*

GAL guardian at litem *tutor judicial temporal, tutor at litem.*

INS Immigration and Naturalization Service *Servicio de Inmigración y Naturalización.*

JAW Juvenile arrest warrant *orden de detención de un menor.*

LTD limited *limitado.*

L.S. locus sigilli. *sello.*

M/R motion of the respondent *petición o promoción del demandado.*

M/S motion of the State *petición o promoción del Fiscal.*

MTV motion to vacate *petición o promoción de revocación.*

NKA now known as *ahora conocido como.*

OD overdoses *sobredosis.*

O/C order of court *orden de la corte.*

P/C probable cause *causa probable.*

PD Public Defender *Defensor Público.*

PO probation *condena condicional,* [le]*probación.*

REM'G remanding *devuélvase (los autos).*

RVP return parole violator *recibido por violación de la libertad preparatoria.*

SOJ substitution of judge *substitución de juez.*

SOL stricken on leave to reinstate *sobreseimiento o desistimiento con reserva de reposición (de la acción).*

TCC trial commenced and concluded *juicio iniciado y concluido.*

TCS term considered served *pena de prisión considerada como cumplida.*

UUW unlawful use of weapons *uso ilegal de armas.*

VOP violation of probation *violación de las condiciones de la condena condicional.*

VOS violation of supervision *violación de las condiciones de supervisión.*

NOIC no officer in court *el oficial de policía no se encuentra en la corte.*

BFW bond forfeiture warrant *orden de detención por violación de las condiciones de la fianza.*

APPENDIX-APÉNDICE B
ACCOUNTING TERMS
TÉRMINOS CONTABLES

ENGLISH-SPANISH

acceptance *aceptación.*
account *cuenta.*
accountant *contador.*
accounts payable *cuentas por pagar, cuentas a pagar.*
accounts payable ledger *mayor documentos a pagar.*
accounts receivable *cuentas a cobrar.*
accounts receivable ledger *mayor de clientes, mayor de cuentas a cobrar.*
accrual *acumulación.*
accrued depreciation *depreciación acumulada.*
accrued depreciation *depreciación acumulada.*
accrued dividend *dividendo acumulado.*
accrued income *ingresos acumulados, ingresos devengados.*
accrued liabilities *pasivo acumulado o devengado.*
accrued payroll *nómina a pagar, nómina acumulada.*
accrued revenue *ingresos acumulados.*
acelerated depreciation *depreciación acelerada.*
actual cost *costo efectivo.*
amortization *amortización.*
assets *activos.*
audit *auditoría, intervención.*
average life *vida promedio.*
bad debts *cuentas malas, cuentas incobrables, créditos incobrables.*
balance *saldo, balance.*
balance sheet *Balance general, Estado de situación.*
bill *cuenta, factura, documento.*
billing *facturación.*
book value *valor en libros.*
bookkeeper *tenedor de libros.*
books of account *libros de contabilidad.*
budget *presupuesto.*
capital assets *activo fijo.* [Syn] fixed assets.
capital expenditure *desembolso capitalizable, inversión en activo fijo, gasto capitalizable* (Mx).
capital expenditures *desembolso capitalizable, inversión en activo fijo, gasto capitalizable* (Mx).
capital gains *ganancias en bienes de capital.*
capital reserves *reservas de capital.*

capital surplus *superávit de capital.*
cash *efectivo.*
cash account *cuenta de caja.*
cash discount *descuento por pronto pago.*
cash dividends *dividendos en efectivo.*
cash flow statement *estado de movimiento de efectivo.*
cash fund *fondo de caja.*
cash in bank *effectivo en banco.*
cash sale *venta al contado.*
ceiling price *precio tope.*
certified public accountant *Contador público titulado* (Mx), *Contador público nacional* (Arg), *Contador registrado* (Ch), *Contador público* (Pe,Uru).
charge *cargo, débito.*
chart of accounts *Clasificación de cuentas, Código de cuentas* (Ur), *Catálogo de cuentas* (Mx).
closing inventory *inventario final, inventario de cierre.*
contra accounts *cuentas cruzadas, cuentas de orden, cuentas compensadas, contracuentas* (Mx).
cost *costo, coste.*
cost of goods sold *costo de la mercancía vendida.*
credit *crédito, abono, haber, data.*
credit balance *saldo acreedor.*
credit entry *asiento de abono, asiento de crédito.*
credit sale *venta a crédito.*
creditor *acreedor.*
current assets *activo corriente, activo circulante.* [Syn] circulating assets.
current income *ingresos del período.*
current liabilities *pasivo corriente, pasivo a corto plazo, pasivo circulante, pasivo flotante, deuda flotante, pasivo exigible* (Ch).
current price *precio corriente.*
cut off date *fecha de corte de operaciones.*
debit *debe, cargo, dédito.*
debit entry *asiento de cargo o de débito.*
debtor *deudor.*
deferred income *ingresos diferidos.*
deficit *déficit.*
depletion *agotamiento.*
deposit slip *hoja, boleta o ficha de depósito.*

depreciation *depreciación.*
depreciation expense *gasto o provisión para depreciación.*
discount *descuento, bonificación.* [Syn] allowance.
dividend *dividendo.*
double taxation *doble imposición.*
draft *giro, letra de cambio, borrador.*
due date *fecha de vencimiento.*
earned income *ingresos devengados.*
earnings *ingreso, ganancia.*
entry *asiento, entrada.*
expenditure *desembolso.*
expense account *cuenta de gastos, informe de gastos.*
expenses *gastos.*
first-in-first-out (FIFO) *primeras entradas primeras salidas, valoración en el orden de entrada.*
fiscal year *año social, año económico, año fiscal, ejercicio* (Mx).
fixed assets *activo fijo, activo inmobilizado.*
fixed cost *costo fijo.*
fund *fondo.*
gains *ganancias, utilidades.*
general journal *diario general.*
goodwill *plusvalía mercantil.*
gross profit *utilidad bruta, ganancia bruta.*
gross sales *ventas brutas.*
in arrears *atrasado, vencido.*
income *ingreso, producto, renta, ganancias.*
income statement *estado de ingresos, estado de ingresos y gastos, estados de resultados.*
income tax *impuesto sobre la renta, impuesto sobre los ingresos, impuesto a los réditos* (Ar), *impuesto cedular* (Ch).
installment *plazo, pago parcial, abono.*
installment sales *ventas a plazos, ventas en abonos* (Mx).
interest *interés, rédito, participación.*
inventory *inventario, bienes de cambio* (Ar).
inventory turnover *rotación del inventario.*
invoice *factura.*
journal *diario, libro diario.*
last-in-first-out (LIFO) *valoración en el orden inverso de entrada.*
ledger *mayor, libro mayor.*
liabilities *pasivo, deudas, obligaciones.*
liabilities reserves *reservas de pasivo.*
loan *préstamo.*
long term debt *deuda a largo plazo, pasivo a largo plazo.*
long-term liabilities *pasivo a largo plazo, deuda a largo plazo.*

loss *pérdida.*
lump sum *cantidad global.*
marginal cost *costo marginal.*
markdown *reducción.*
minimo wages *salario mínimo, jornal mínimo.*
net price *precio neto.*
net proceeds *producto líquido.*
net profit *beneficio neto, utilidad neta, ganancia neta.*
net value *valor neto.*
net worth *capital líquido, capital neto, patrimonio neto* (Ar), *pasivo no exigible* (Ar), *activo líquido, capital contable* (Mx), *neto patrimonial* (Sp). [Syn] net assets.
notes payable *efectos a pagar, documentos por pagar.*
notes receivable *efectos a cobrar, pagarés por cobrar, letras por cobrar, letras a recibir, documentos a cobrar* (Mx).
opening inventory *inventario inicial, inventario de apertura.*
operating expenses *gastos de operación.*
overdraft *sobregiro, giro en descubierto* (Ar), *descubierto* (Ur).
overdue *atrasado vencido.*
overhead *gastos generales, gastos fijos.*
payroll *nómina, planilla de sueldos* (Ar,Ur).
payroll taxes *impuesto sobre la nómina.*
perpetual inventory *inventario perpetuo o constante.*
petty cash *caja chica, caja pequeña.*
physical inventory *inventario físico.*
prepaid expense *gastos pagados por adelantado.*
prepaid interest *interés pagado por adelantado.*
profit *utilidad, ganancia, beneficio.*
profit and loss statement *estado de pérdidas y ganancias.*
rate of interest *tipo de interés, tasa de interés.*
rebate *descuento en devolución.*
receipts and disbursements statement *estado de entradas y salidas.*
receivables *partidas a cobrar.*
reconciliation *reconciliación.*
record *registro.*
replacement cost *costo de reposición.*
reserve *reserva.*
reserve for bad debts *reserva de cuentas malas, reserva de cuentas incobrables.*
reserve for depreciation and amortization *reserva para depreciación y amortización.*
revenue *ingresos.* [Syn] receipts.
revenue accrued *ingresos acumulados.*

reversing entry *asiento de reversión.*
salary *salario, sueldo.*
sales allowance *bonificación sobre ventas.*
short-term liabilities *pasivo a corto plazo.*
social security taxes *impuesto del seguro social, cargas sociales* (Ar), *cuotas de seguros sociales* (Sp).
straight line depreciation *método directo de depreciación, cálculo de depreciación en línea recta.*
summary entry *asiento de resumen.*
surcharge *recargo.*
surplus *superávit, sobrante, reservas y resultados* (Ar).
surtax *impuesto adicional.*
tax examination *inspección de impuestos,*

exámen de impuestos, auditoría fiscal (Mx).
tax witheld *impuesto retenido.*
taxable income *ganancia gravable, ganancia imponible, utilidad gravable.*
to credit *abonar, acreditar.*
to debit *cargar, debitar, adeudar.*
to post *registrar (un asiento).*
trade-in value *valor de cambio.*
trust fund *fondo fiduciario.*
variable cost *costo variable.*
variance *variación.*
voucher *comprobante, justificante, póliza* (Mx).
voucher journal *comprobante de diario.*
wages *salario, jornal.*
write off *cancelación, castigo* (Mx).
year-end adjustments *ajuste de cierre de año.*

ESPAÑOL-INGLÉS

abonar *to credit, make partial payments.* [Sin]acreditar.
abono *credit.* [Sin]crédito, haber.
acciones comunes *ordinary shares, common stock.*
acciones preferentes *preferred shares, preferred stock.*
aceptación *acceptance.*
acreedor *creditor.*
activo *assets.*
activo circulante *current assets.* [Sin]activo corriente.
activo de realización inmediata *cash assets.*
activo diferido *deferred assets.*
activo disponible *cash on hand and with banks.*
activo fijo *fixed assets, capital assets.* [Sin]activo inmobilizado.
activo intangible *intangible assets.*
agotamiento *depletion.*
ajuste de cierre de año *year-end adjustments.*
amortización *amortization.*
anticipos *advance payments.*
anualidades *annuities.*
año social *fiscal year.* [Sin]año económico, año fiscal, ejercicio (Mx).
aportaciones de capital *paid-in capital.*
apreciación *appreciation.*
arqueo de caja *cash count.*
asiento *entry.* [Sin]entrada.
asiento compuesto *compound entry.*
asiento cruzado *cross entry.*
asiento de abono *credit entry.* [Sin]asiento de crédito.
asiento de ajuste *adjusting entry.*
asiento de cargo o de débito *debit entry.*

asiento de resumen *summary entry.*
asiento de reversión *reversing entry.*
atrazado *overdue.*
auditoría *audit.* [Sin]intervención.
balance general *balance sheet.* [Sin]Estado de situación.
bancos de depósito *commercial banks.*
beneficio neto *net profit.* [Sin]utilidad neta. ganancia neta.
boleta o ficha de depósito *deposit slip.*
bonificación sobre ventas *sales allowance.*
caja chica *petty cash.* [Sin]caja pequeña.
cantidad global *lump sum.*
capital autorizado *authorized capital.*
capital contable *net worth, net assets.*
capital de trabajo *working capital.*
capital inflado *watered capital.*
capital insoluto *unpaid capital.*
capital líquido *net worth.* [Sin]capital neto, patrimonio neto (Ar), pasivo no exigible (Ar), activo líquido, capital contable (Mx), neto patrimonial (Esp).
capital social *capital stock.*
cargar *to debit.* [Sin]debitar, adeudar.
cartera *notes and accounts receivable.*
cartera vencida *overdue notes receivable.*
catálogo de cuentas *chart of accounts.*
cerrar los libros *close the books.*
Clasificación de cuentas *chart of accounts.* [Sin]Código de cuentas (Ur), Catálogo de cuentas (Mx).
comprobante *voucher.* [Sin]justificante, póliza (Mx).
comprobante de diario *voucher journal.*
contador *accountant.*

contador público titulado (Mx) *certified public accountant.* [Sin]contador público nacional (Ar), contador registrado (Ch), contador público (Pe,Ur).

contracuenta *contra account.*

contralor *comptroller.*

costo *cost.* [Sin]coste.

costo de entrega *delivery cost.*

costo de la mercancía vendida *cost of goods sold.*

costo de manufactura *manufacturing cost.*

costo de mercado *market cost.*

costo de reemplazo *replacement cost.* [Sin] costo de reposición.

costo efectivo *actual cost.*

costo fijo *fixed cost.*

costo marginal *marginal cost.*

costo unitario *unit cost.*

costo variable *variable cost.*

costos directos *direct costs.*

costos indirectos *indirect costs.*

crédito *credit.*

cuantahabiente *depositor.*

cuenta *account.*

cuenta *bill.* [Sin]factura, documento.

cuenta corriente *current account.*

cuenta de caja *cash account.*

cuenta de gastos *expense account.* [Sin]informe de gastos.

cuentas a cobrar *accounts receivable*

cuentas compensadas *contra accounts.* [Sin]cuentas de orden. cuentas cruzadas. contracuentas (Mx).

cuentas malas *bad debts.* [Sin]cuentas incobrables, créditos incobrables.

cuentas por cobrar *account receivable.*

cuentas por pagar *accounts payable.* [Sin]cuentas a pagar.

dédito *debit.* [Sin]debe, cargo.

déficit *deficit.*

depreciación *depreciation.*

depreciación acelerada *accelerated depreciation.*

depreciación acumulada *accrued depreciation.*

depreciación cálculo por quebrados *declining or increasing balance method depreciation.*

depreciación en línea recta *straight-line depreciation.*

descuento *discount.* [Sin]bonificación.

descuento en devolución *rebate.*

descuento por pronto pago *cash discount.*

desembolso *expenditure.*

deuda a largo plazo *long term debt.* [Sin]pasivo a largo plazo.

deudor *debtor.*

diario general *general journal.*

diario *journal.* [Sin]libro diario.

dictámen de auditoría *audit report.*

dividendo *dividend.*

dividendos acumulados *accrued dividends.*

dividendos decretados *declared dividends.*

dividendos diferidos *deferred dividends.*

dividendos en efectivo *cash dividends.*

doble imposición *double taxation.*

documentos a cargo de clientes *customer's note receivable.*

documentos por cobrar *notes receivable.* [Sin]efectos a cobrar. pagarés por cobrar. letras por cobrar. letras a recibir.

documentos por pagar *notes payable.* [Sin]efectos a pagar.

efectivo *cash.*

effectivo en banco *cash in bank.*

egresos *disbursements.*

ejercicio fiscal *fiscal year.* [Sin]año fiscal. año social.

enseres *fixtures.*

estado de entradas y salidas *receipts and disbursements statement.*

estado de ingresos *income statement.* [Sin]estado de ingresos y gastos. estados de resultados.

estado de movimiento de efectivo *cash flow statement.*

estado de pérdidas y ganancias *statement of profit and loss.*

factura *invoice.*

facturación *billing.*

fecha de corte de operaciones *cut off date.*

fecha de vencimiento *due date.*

fondo *fund.*

fondo de amortización *sinking fund.*

fondo de caja *cash fund.*

fondo fiduciario *trust fund.*

ganancia gravable *taxable income.* [Sin]ganancia imponible. utilidad gravable.

ganancias brutas *gross earnings.*

ganancias en bienes de capital *capital gains.*

gasto capitalizable (Mx) *capital expenditures,* [Sin]inversión en activo fijo.

gasto o provisión para depreciación *depreciation expense.*

gastos *expenses.*

gastos de operación *operating expenses.*

gastos fijos *fixed expenses.*

gastos generales *overhead.*

gastos pagados por adelantado *prepaid expense.*

haber *credit.*

impuesto adicional *surtax.*

impuesto del seguro social *social security taxes.* [Sin]cargas sociales (Ar), cuotas de seguros sociales (Esp), cuotas del seguro social (Mx).

impuesto retenido tax witheld.

impuesto sobre la nómina *payroll taxes.*

impuesto sobre la renta *income tax.* [Sin]impuesto sobre los ingresos. impuesto a los réditos (Ar), impuesto cedular (Ch).

ingreso *income, revenue.* [Sin]producto. renta. ganancias.

ingresos acumulados *accrued revenue or income.*

ingresos del período *current income.*

ingresos devengados *earned income.*

ingresos diferidos *deferred income.*

inspección de impuestos *tax examination.* [Sin]exámen de impuestos. auditoría fiscal (Mx).

interés *interest.* [Sin]rédito. participación.

interés compuesto *compound interest.*

interés legal *legal interest.*

interés pagado por adelantado *prepaid interest.*

inventario *inventory.* [Sin]bienes de cambio (Ar).

inventario final *closing inventory.* [Sin]inventario de cierre.

inventario físico *physical inventory.*

inventario inicial *opening inventory.* [Sin]inventario de apertura.

inventario perpetuo o constante *perpetual inventory.*

inversión en activo fijo *capital expenditure.* [Sin]gasto capitalizable (Mx). desembolso capitalizable.

libro mayor, *ledger.* [Sin]mayor.

libros de contabilidad *books of account.*

mayor *ledger.* **mayor de cuentas a cobrar** *accounts receivable ledger.* [Sin]mayor de clientes.

mayor documentos a pagar *accounts payable ledger.*

método directo de depreciación *straight line depreciation.* [Sin]cálculo de depreciación en línea recta.

nómina *payroll.* [Sin]planilla de sueldos (Ar,Ur).

nómina a pagar *accrued payroll.* [Sin]nómina acumulada.

operaciones de diario *journal entries.*

origen de recursos *sources of funds.*

pago parcial *installment.* [Sin]abono.

papel comercial *commercial paper.*

partidas a cobrar *receivables.*

pasivo *liabilities.* [Sin]deudas. obligaciones.

pasivo a corto plazo short-term liabilities.

pasivo a largo plazo *long-term liabilities.* [Sin]deuda a largo plazo.

pasivo acumulado o devengado *accrued liabilities.*

pasivo circulante o exigible *current liabilities.*

pasivo contingente *contingent liabilities.*

pasivo corriente *current liabilities.* [Sin]pasivo a corto plazo. pasivo circulante. pasivo flotante. deuda flotante. pasivo exigible (Ar).

pasivo diferido *deferred liabilities.*

pasivo fijo *fixed liabilities.*

pasivo vencido *past due liabilities.*

pérdida *loss.*

pérdida bruta *gross loss.*

pérdida neta *net loss.*

plusvalía mercantil *goodwill.*

póliza de egreso *disbursement voucher.*

posición corta *short position.*

posición larga *long position.*

precio corriente *current price.*

precio neto *net price.*

precio tope *ceiling price.*

presupuesto *budget.*

primeras entradas primeras salidas *first-in-first-out* (FIFO). [Sin]valoración en el orden de entrada.

producto líquido *net proceeds.*

productos brutos *gross income.*

productos de inversiones *income from investments.*

punto de equilibrio *break-even point.*

razón de capital contable a pasivo total *net worth to liabilities ratio.*

recargo *surcharge.*

reconciliación *reconciliation.*

reducción *markdown.*

registrar (un asiento) *to post (an entry).*

registro *record.*

reserva *reserve.*

reserva legal *legal reserve.*

reserva para agotamiento *reserve for depletion.*

reserva para amortización *reserve for amortization.*

reserva para bonificaciones o descuentos *allowance reserve.*

reserva para cuentas incobrables *reserve for uncollectible accounts, reserve for bad debts.* [Sin]reserva para cuentas malas.

reserva para depreciación *reserve for depreciation.*

reserva secreta *secret account, hidden account.*

reservas de capital *capital reserves.*

reservas de pasivo *liabilities reserves.*

rotación del inventario *inventory turnover.*

salario wages. [Sin]jornal. sueldo.

salario mínimo *mínimo wages.* [Sin]jornal mínimo.

saldo *balance.* [Sin]balance.

saldo acreedor *credit balance.*

sobrante superavit, surplus.

sobregiro *overdraft.* [Sin]giro en descubierto (Ar), descubierto (Ur).

superávit *surplus.* [Sin]sobrante. reservas y resultados (Ar).

superávit de capital *capital surplus.*

tasa nominal *nominal rate.*

tenedor de libros *bookkeeper.*

tipo de interés *rate of interest.* [Sin]tasa de interés.

utilidad *profit.* [Sin]ganancia. beneficio.

utilidad bruta *gross profit.* [Sin]ganancia bruta.

utilidad de operación *operating profit.*

utilidades del ejercicio *fiscal year profits.*

utilidades distribuidas *distributed profits.*

utilidades en libros *book profits.*

utilidades no realizadas *paper profits, accrued profits.*

utilidades realizadas *realized profits.*

vale de caja *cash voucher.*

valor de cambio *trade-in value.*

valor de costo *cost value.*

valor de liquidación *liquidation value.*

valor de mercado *market value.*

valor de rescate *surrender value.*

valor en libros *book value.*

valor neto *net value.*

valor nominal *face value.*

valoración en el orden inverso de entrada *last-in-first-out* (LIFO).

valores mobiliarios *securities.*

vencido *in arrears.*

venta a crédito *credit sale.*

venta al contado *cash sale.*

ventas a plazos *installment sales.* [Sin]ventas en abonos (Mx).

ventas brutas *gross sales.*

APPENDIX-APÉNDICE C
LATIN TERMS
LATINISMOS

a contrario sensu *on the other hand, in the contrary sense.* en contrario.

a fortiori *much more so, by so much stronger reason.* con mayor razón.

a posteriori *from the effect to the cause.* del efecto a la causa.

a priori *from the cause to the effect.* lo que ocurrió antes.

ab initio *from the beginning.* desde el principio.

ab intestato *from an intestate.* sin dejar testamento.

actio in personam *a personal acton.* acción personal.

actio in rem *an action for the recovery of the very thing.* acción real.

ad hoc *for a particular or special purpose.* para propósito específico.

ad hominem *to the person.* a la persona.

ad infinitum *without limit. indefinitely.* al infinito.

ad interim *in the meantime.* interinamente.

ad litem *for the purpose of the suit.* para el pleito.

ad valorem *according to value.* según el valor.

amicus curiae *a friend of the court.* amigo del tribunal.

animus defamandi *the intention to defame.* intención de difamar.

animus donandi *with intention fo giving or making a gift.* ánimo donativo.

animus possidendi *the intention of possessing.* ánimo posesivo.

bona fide *in or with good faith.* de buena fé.

bonae fidei emptor *a purchaser in good faith.* comprador de buena fé.

capitis diminutio *reduction of status.* disminución de la capacidad.

casus belli *an occurrence giving rise or justifying war,* una causa de guerra.

causa mortis *in contemplation of impending death.* en causa de muerte.

causa proxima *the proximate or immediate cause.* la causa inmediata.

caveat emptor *let the buyer be aware.* que el comprador sepa.

contra bonos mores *that which is against good morals.* contra las buenas morales.

corpus delicti *body of the crime.* cuerpo del delito.

damnum *damage.* daño.

de cuius *from whom.* de quién.

de facto *in fact.* de hecho.

de jure *of right.* de derecho.

de novo *anew.* de nuevo.

dolus *fraud.* dolo.

dominium *absolute ownership.* dominium.

donatio mortis causa *gift in contemplation of death.* donación por causa de muerte inminente.

erga omnes *against all men.* respecto de todos.

error nominis *mistke in the name.* error en el nombre.

et al: *and others.* y otros.

et sequ.: *and the following.* y los siguientes.

ex contractu *out of a contract.* del contrato.

ex delicto *from a fault.* de una falta.

ex lege *by virtue of law.* como cuestión de ley.

ex parte *on one side only.* de una sola parte.

exceptio *an exception, plea.* excepción.

flagrante delicto *in the very act of committing the crime.* en flagrante delito.

forum *court.* tribunal.

fructus *fruits.* frutos.

furtum *theft.* robo.

ignorantia legis neminem excusat *ignorance of law excuses no one.* la ignorancia de la ley no excusa su cumplimiento.

imperium *power or dominion.* poder o imperio.

in articulo mortis *at the point of death.* al momento de la muerte.

in dubio pro reo *in doubt benefit the accused.* la duda beneficia al reo.

in fraganti *in the act.* en el acto.

in pari delicto *in equal fault.* en delito igual.

in personam *against a person.* procedimiento contra una persona.

in rem *against a thing.* procedimiento contra una cosa.

in terrorem *by way of threat.* con amenaza.

injuria *injury.* lesión.

inter alia *among other things.* entre otras cosas.

inter vivos *between the living.* entre vivos.

ipso facto *by the fact itself.* por el hecho mismo.

ipso jure *by the law itself.* por ministerio de la ley.

juris et de jure *of law and of right.* por ley y por derecho, presunción conclusiva.

juris tantum *of law only.* tan sólo de derecho, presunción que admite prueba en contrario.

jus cogens *compelling law.* derecho que obliga.

jus gentium *law of nations.* derecho de gentes, ley de las naciones.

jus naturale *natural law.* derecho natural.

jus sanguinis *right of blood.* derecho de la sangre.

jus soli *right of the soil.* derecho del lugar de nacimiento.

lex *law, statute.* ley.

lis pendens *a suit or action pending in court.* pendiente el caso.

litis *contested issue, litigation.* litigio.

mala fides *bad faith.* mala fé.

malum in se *evil in itself.* malo por si.

malum prohibitum *prohibited evil.* mal prohibido.

modus operandi *the manner of doing business.* forma de operación.

modus vivendi *means of living.* forma de vivir.

mortis causa *by reason of or in contemplation of death.* por causa de muerte.

negotiorum gestio *a manager of affairs.* gestión de negocios.

nolens volens *willing or unwilling.* con o sin consentimiento.

nolo contendere *I do not wish to contend.* no quiero litigar.

non bis in idem *not twice for the same thing.* no dos veces por lo mismo. *Also* ne bis in idem.

non sequitur *it does not follow.* no tiene secuencia.

nulla poena sine lege *there ought to be no punishment without legal authority.* no hay pena sin ley.

obiter *by the way.* de paso, incidentalmente.

obligatio *obligation.* obligación.

pacta sunt servanda *agreements must be kept.* los acuerdos deben cumplirse conforme se pactaron.

per capita *by the head.* por cabeza.

per se *by himself.* por sí.

pignus *pledge.* prenda.

post-mortem *after death.* después de la muerte.

prima facie *on the face of it.* a primera vista.

pro forma *as a matter of form.* por la forma.

pro indiviso *undivided.* sin división.

pro se *for himself.* por sí mismo.

quasi *analogous to.* casi.

ratio decidenci *the ground or reasons for a decision.* razón de decidir.

res derelicta *property abandoned by owner.* cosa derelicta.

res ipsa loquitur *the thing speaks by itself.* la cosa habla por sí misma.

res judicata *a matter adjudged or settled by judgment.* cosa juzgada.

res nullius *thing of no one.* cosa sin dueño.

scintilla *a spark of right.* el más mínimo indicio.

sine die *without assigned day.* sin un día determinado.

sine qua non *whitout which not.* sin el cual no.

situs *location.* lugar.

stare decisis *to stand by things decided.* acatar los precedentes judiciales.

statu quo *the state of things at a given time.* el estado de las cosas como están.

strictu sensu *in a restricted sense.* sentido estricto.

sua sponte *voluntarily, on its own motion.* voluntariamente, por sí.

subpoena *(to appear) under penalty.* citación, notificación.

sui generis *of its own kind.* de su propio género o especie.

traditio *delivery.* tradición.

ultra vires *beyond powers.* exceder los poderes.

APPENDIX-APÉNDICE D
STOCK EXCHANGE GLOSSARY
GLOSARIO DE LA BOLSA DE VALORES

ENGLISH-SPANISH

above par *sobre la par.*

accrued interest *intereses devengados o acumulados.*

all or none order *orden de venta "a todo o nada."*

American Depositary Receipt (ADR) *recibo americano de depósito (a cambio de acciones en compañías extranjeras).*

arbitrage *arbitraje.*

asked price *precio de oferta.*

at the close *al cierre.*

at the opening *a la apertura.*

automatic reinvestment of distributions *reinversión automática de utilidades.*

bear market *mercado a la baja general.*

bearer security *valor al portador.*

bid *oferta de compra inmediata.*

block trade *compraventa en bloque.*

bond *bono.*

bond premium *por encima de la par, sobre par.*

book value *valor en libros.*

brokerage commission *comisión bursátil, comisión de intermediación bursátil.*

bull market *mercado al alza general.*

buy stop order *orden de compra a cifra tope detemina.*

callable security *título sujeto a redención anticipada.*

capital gain or loss *ganancia o pérdida de capital.*

cash dividend *dividendos en efectivo.*

clearing house *cámara de compensación.*

closing quotation *cotización al cierre.*

commission *comisión.*

common stock *acción común, accion ordinaria.*

convertibles *acciones convertibles.*

corporate bond *bono corporativo.*

coupon *coupón.*

date of record *fecha de registro.*

dealer *agente de valores.*

discount *descuento.*

dividend *dividendo.*

earnings per share *utilidades por acción.*

face value *valor nominal.*

fair market value *precio de mercado justo, justo valor en el mercado.*

fill or kill order *order ejecutar o cancelar.*

firm order *order en firme.*

floor trader *operador de piso.*

futures market *mercado de futuros.* [Sin]commodities market.

in-the-money *dentro del precio.*

initial public offering (IPO) *nueva emisión de acciones.*

inside information *información intena o privilegiada.*

insider trading *uso indebido de información privilegiada.*

institutional investor *inversionista institucional.*

interest rate *tasa de interés.*

investment company *sociedad de inversión.*

leverage *apalancamiento.*

limit order *orden límite.*

London interbank offered rate (LIBOR) *tasa de interés ofrecida del mercado interbancario de Londres.*

long position *posición a largo.*

margin account *cuenta de margen.*

market order *orden de mercado.*

market value *precio actual de mercado.*

maturity *vencimiento.*

money market *mercado de capitales, mercado de valores de renta fija.*

mutual fund *fondo de inversiones bursátiles, fondo común de inversiones* (Ar), *fondo mutuo de inversión* (Co), *fondo mutual de inversiones* (Ve).

net asset value *valor del activo neto.*

nominal price *precio nominal.*

open order *order abierta.*

opening price *precio de apertura.*

option *opción.*

out-of-the-money *fuera del precio.*

at par *a la par.*

portfolio *portafolio.*

premium *sobreprecio, por encima de la par, sobre par.*

present value *valor presente, valor actual.*

price limit *precio límite.*

price-earnings ratio *relación precio-beneficio, relación precio-utilidad.*

price spread *precio diferencial.*

profit *utilidades.*

prospectus *prospecto, folleto bursátil* (Sp).

put *opción de venta.*
quote *cotización.*
rate of return *tasa de rendimiento.*
redemption price *precio de rescate, precio de redención.*
safekeeping *custodia.*
securities analyst *analista de valores.*
securities company *sociedad bursátil.*
sell stop order *orden de venta tope.*
settlement date *fecha de ejecución.*
short position *posición a corto.*
sinking fund *fondo de amortizaión.*

small investor *inversionista particular.*
split *cambio de valor nominal.*
spread in price *diferencial de precio.*
stop limit order *orden tope con límite.*
stop order *orden tope.*
technical analysis *análisis técnico.*
thin market *mercado inactivo.*
under par *bajo la par.*
unlisted securities *valores no registrados.*
yield *rendimiento.*
yield to maturity *rendimiento al vencimiento.*

ESPAÑOL-INGLÉS

a la apertura *at the opening.*
acciones comunes *common stock.*
acción *share.*
acciones convertibles *convertibles.*
agente de bolsa *stokbroker.*
agente de valores *dealer.*
al cierre *at the close.*
análisis técnico *technical analysis.*
analista de valores *securities analyst.*
apalancamiento *leverage.*
arbitraje *arbitrage.*
bajo par *under par.*
al portador *to bearer.*
bolsa de valores *stock exchange.*
bond *bono.*
bono corporativo *corporate bond.*
cámara de compensación *clearing house.*
cartera de valores *portfolio.*
casa de bolsa *securities firm.*
comisión bursátil *brokerage commission.*
cotización *quote.*
cotización al cierre *closing quotation.*
cotización de compra *bid.*
cotización de venta *offer.*
descuento *discount.*
diferencial de precio *spread in price.*
dividendo *dividend.*
dividendos en efectivo *cash dividend.*
fondo de amortizaión *sinking fund.*
información interna *inside information.*
    [Sin]información privilegiada.
intereses devengados *accrued interest.*
    [Sin]intereses acumulados.
inversionista institucional *institutional investor.*
margen *margin.*
mercado a la baja (generalizada) *bear market.*
mercado al alza (generalizada) *bull market.*

mercado de futuros *futures market, commodities market.*
oferta pública *public offer.*
opción *option.*
opción de venta *put.*
operador de piso *floor trader.*
orden abierta *open order.*
orden de mercado *market order.*
orden de venta tope *sell stop order.*
orden en firme *firm order.*
orden límite *limit order.*
orden tope con límite *stop limit order.*
orden tope *stop order.*
order abierta *open order.*
order ejecutar o cancelar *fill or kill order.*
order en firme *firm order.*
posición a corto *short position.*
posición a largo *long position.*
precio actual de mercado *market value.*
precio de apertura *opening price.*
precio de mercado justo *fair market value.*
    [Sin]justo valor en el mercado.
precio de oferta *asked price.*
precio de redención *redemption price.*
precio diferencial *price spread.*
precio límite *price limit.*
precio nominal *nominal price.*
prospecto *prospectus.* [Sin]folleto bursátil (Sp).
reinversión automática de utilidades *automatic reinvestment of distributions.*
rendimiento al vencimiento *yield to maturity.*
rendimiento *yield.*
salón de remates *tradig floor.*
sesiones de remate *trading session.*
sociedad bursátil *securities company.*
sociedad de inversión *investment company.*
fondo de inversiónes bursátiles (de renta variable) *mutual fund.* [Sin]fondo mutual de

inversiones (Ve), fondo común de inversiones (Ar). fondo mutuo de inversión (Co).

relación precio-beneficio *price-earnings ratio.* [Sin]relación precio-ganancias.

fecha de cierre *settlement date.*

tasa de interés *interest rate.*

tasa de rendimiento *rate of return.*

tasa prima *prime rate.*

utilidades *profit.*

utilidades por acción *earnings per share.*

valor del activo neto *net asset value.*

valor en libros *book value.*

valor nominal *face value.*

valor presente *present value.*

vencimiento *maturity.*

venta en corto *short sale.*

APPENDIX-APÉNDICE E
TAX LAW GLOSSARY
GLOSARIO DE DERECHO FISCAL

ENGLISH-SPANISH

abatment of tax *reducción o rebaja de impuestos.*

administrative appeal *apelación contencioso-administrativa.*

assessment of deficiency *determinación del saldo fiscal a deber o déficit fiscal.*

back taxes *impuestos atrasados.*

delinquent penalty *multa por mora, multa moratoria.*

demand for payment *intimación de pago, pedir pago.*

double taxation *doble imposición tributaria.*

estimated tax *impuesto estimado, contribución estimada* (PR).

false statement *declaración falsa.*

fraudulent return *declaración fraudulenta.*

frivolous return *declaración de impuestos improcedente o sin fundamento.*

individual income tax *impuesto sobre el ingreso personal.*

inheritance tax *impuesto hereditario, impuesto sucesorio o de sucesiones.*

Internal Revenue Service (US) *Hacienda pública, fisco, Servicio de Impuestos Internos, Servicio de Rentas Internas* (PR).

levy *imposición de un impuesto.*

notice of assessment *notificación de crédito fiscal a pagar.*

payroll tax *impuesto sobre la nómina* ‖ *impuesto deducido del ingreso neto de un trabajador o empleado.*

penalties *multas.*

real estate tax *impuesto sobre propiedad inmueble.*

self-employment tax *contribución al seguro social hecha por un trabajador que trabaja por cuenta propia.*

tax settlement *acuerdo o convenio fiscal.*

state taxes *impuestos estatales, contribuciones estatales* (PR).

tax audit *auditoría fiscal.*

tax auditor *auditor fiscal, inspector de impuestos* (PR).

tax avoidance *elusión impositiva.*

tax bracket *categoría impositiva, tramo de la escala del impuesto, tramo de la escala contributiva* (PR).

tax collection *cobro de impuestos.*

tax consultant *asesor fiscal.*

tax credit *deducción directa del impuesto a pagar.*

tax deductible *deducible de impuestos.*

tax deduction *deducción fiscal.*

tax evasion *evasión fiscal, evasión de impuestos.*

tax exempt *exento de impuestos.*

tax form *forma de impuestos, anexo, formulario de impuestos o fiscal.*

tax fraud *fraude o defraudación fiscal.*

tax holiday *suspensión temporal de pago de impuestos.*

tax home *domicilio fiscal, domicilio tributario.*

tax incentive *estímulo fiscal.*

tax investigation *investigación fiscal.*

tax liability *impuesto por pagar, crédito fiscal.*

tax lien *gravámen fiscal.*

tax loophole *laguna fiscal.*

tax loss *pérdida fiscal.*

tax procedure *procedimiento fiscal.*

tax rate schedule *tarifa del impuesto.*

tax rate *tasa fiscal, tasa de impuesto, tasa de contribución* (PR).

tax rebate *devolución de impuestos por reducción de impuestos.*

tax refund *devolución de impuestos por sobrepago.*

tax relief *desgravación impositiva.*

tax shelter *[le]abrigo tributario, [de]esquema tributario que elude o prorroga el pago de impuestos, beneficio contributivo* (PR).

tax table *tabla del impuesto, tabla de contribución* (PR).

tax withholding *retención fiscal.*

tax write-off *deducción fiscal por pérdidas.*

tax year *ejercicio fiscal, año tributario, año contributivo (PR).*

taxable income *ingreso base del impuesto, ingreso sujeto a contribución* (PR).

willful failure to file or pay *no declarar o pagar impuestos en forma dolosa o intencional.*

withholding taxes *impuestos retenidos.*

ESPAÑOL-INGLÉS

actividad gravable *taxable activity.*

acuerdo o convenio fiscal *tax settlement.*

asesor fiscal *tax consultant.*

auditor fiscal , *tax auditor.* [Sin]inspector de impuestos (PR).

auditoría fiscal *tax audit.*

base del impuesto *tax basis.*

categoría impositiva *tax bracket.* [Sin]tramo de la escala del impuesto, tramo de la escala contributiva (PR).

cobro de impuestos *tax collection.*

contribuyente *taxpayer.*

crédito fiscal *tax owed, tax liability.*

declaración de impuestos *tax return.*

declaración falsa *false tax return.*

declaración fraudulenta *fraudulent return.*

deducción fiscal *tax deduction.*

deducible de impuestos *tax deductible.*

depreciación *depreciation.*

desgravación impositiva *tax relief.*

determinación de un impuesto *assessment of tax.*

determinación del saldo fiscal a deber o déficit fiscal *assessment of deficiency.*

devolución de impuestos (por sobrepago) *tax refund.*

devolución de impuestos (por reeducción) *tax rebate.*

doble imposición tributaria *double taxation.*

domicilio fiscal *tax home.* [Sin]domicilio tributario.

ejercicio fiscal *tax year.* [Sin]año tributario, año contributivo (PR).

elusión impositiva *tax avoidance.*

estímulos fiscales *tax incentives.*

evasión fiscal *tax evasion.* [Sin]evasión de impuestos.

exención *exemption.*

exento de impuestos *tax exempt.*

fraude o defraudación fiscal *tax fraud.*

gastos de ejecución *execution costs.*

gastos deducibles *deductible expenses.*

gravámen fiscal *tax lien.*

impuesto estimado *estimated tax.* [Sin]contribución estimada (PR).

impuesto hereditario *inheritance tax.* [Sin]impuesto sucesorio o de sucesiones.

impuesto predial *property tax.*

impuesto sobre bienes inmuebles *real estate tax.*

impuesto sobre el ingreso personal *individual income tax.*

impuestos atrasados *back taxes.*

impuestos estatales *state taxes.* [Sin]contribuciones estatales (PR).

impuestos retenidos *taxes withheld.*

ingreso base del impuesto *taxable income.* [Sin]ingreso sujeto a contribución (PR).

investigación fiscal *tax investigation.*

multa por mora *delinquent penalty.* [Sin]multa moratoria.

multa *fine.*

no declarado *unreported.*

no llevar contabilidad *failure to keep accounting books.*

no presentar declaración *failure to file a tax return.*

notificación de crédito fiscal a pagar *tax assessment notice.*

oficina recaudadora *tax collector's office.*

pago espontáneo *voluntary payment.*

pago provisional *estimated payment.*

percepciones *income, receipts.*

pérdida fiscal *tax loss.*

política fiscal *tax policy.*

procedimiento fiscal *tax procedure.*

recargos *penalty.*

receptor de rentas *tax collector.*

reducción o rebaja de impuestos *abatment of tax.*

renta *income, revenue.*

retención de impuestos *tax withholding.* [Sin]retención fiscal.

sobretasa *surcharge.*

tarifa del impuesto *tax rate schedule.*

tasa fiscal *tax rate.* [Sin]tasa de impuesto, tasa de contribución (PR).

tribunal fiscal o tributario, *tax court.*

tributación *taxation.*

unidad económica *economic unit.*

utilidad bruta *gross profit.*

viáticos *travel expenses.*

vida útil estimada *estimated useful life.*

Organs. - *Organos.*

General Assembly, *Asamblea General.*

Security Council, *Consejo de Seguridad.*

Economic and Social Council (ECOSOC), *Consejo Económico y Social.*

Trusteeship Council, *Consejo de Administración Fiduciaria.*

International Court of Justice, *Corte Internacional de Justicia.*

Secretary-General, *Secretario General.*

Programs and Funds. - *Programas y Fondos.*

United Nations Conference on Trade and Development (UNCTAD). *Conferencia de la Naciones Unidas sobre Comercio y Desarrollo (UNCTAD).*

International Trade Centre (ITC), *Centro de Comercio Internacional (CCI).*

United Nations Drug Control Programme (UNDCP), *Programa de las Naciones Unidas para la Fiscalización Internacional de Drogas (PNUFID).*

United Nations Environment Programme (UNEP), *Programa de las Naciones Unidas para el Medio Ambiente (PNUMA).*

United Nations Human Settlements Programme (UNHSP, UN-HABITAT), *Programa de las Naciones Unidas para los Asentamientos Humanos (PNUAH).*

United Nations Development Programme (UNDP), *Programa de las Naciones Unidas para el Desarrollo (PNUD).*

United Nations Development Fund for Women (UNIFEM), *Fondo de Desarrollo de las Naciones Unidas para la mujer (UNIFEM).*

United Nations Volunteers (UNV), *Voluntarios de las Naciones Unidas (VNU).*

United Nations Population Fund (UNFPA), *Fondo de Población de las Naciones Unidas (FNUAP).*

Office of the United Nations High Commissioner for Reefugees (UNHCR). *Fondo del Alto Comisionado de las Naciones Unidas para los Refujiados (ACNUR).*

United Nations Children's Fund (UNICEF). *Fondo de las Naciones Unidas para la Infancia (UNICEF).*

World Food Programme (WFP), *Programa Mundial de Alimentos (PMA).*

Specialized Agencies. *Organismos Especializados.*

Food and Agriculture Organization (FAO), *Organización de las Naciones Unidas para la Agricultura y la Alimentación (FAO).*

International Maritime Organization (IMO), *Organización Marítima Internacional.*

International Bank for Reconstruction and Development (IBRD), *Banco Internacional de Reconstrucción y Fomento (BIRD).*

International Civil Aviation Organization (ICAO), *Organización Internacional de Aviación Civil.*

International Development Association (IDA), *Asociación Internacional de Desarrollo (AID).*

International Finance Corporation (IFC), *Corporación Financiera Internacional.*

International Labor Organization (ILO), *Organización Internacional del Trabajo (OIT).*

International Monetary Fund (IMF), *Fondo Monetario Internacional (FMI).*

International Telecommunications Union (ITU), *Unión Internacional de Comunicación (ITU).*

United Nations Educational, Scientific and Cultural Organization (UNESCO), *Organización de las Naciones Unidas para la Educación, la Ciencia y la Cultura (UNESCO).*

Universal Postal Union (UPU), *Unión Postal Universal (UPU).*

World Health Organization (WHO), *Organización Mundial de la Salud (OMS).*

World Meteorological Organization (WMO), *Organización Meteorológica Mundial (OMM).*

World Intellectual Property Organization (WIPO), *Organización Mundial de la Propiedad Industrial (OMPI).*

International Fund for Agricultural Development (IFAD), *Fondo Internacional de Desarrollo Agrícola.*

United Nations Industrial Development Organization (UNIDO), *Organización de las Naciones Unidas para el Desarrollo Industrial.*

REFERENCES-BIBLIOGRAFÍA

List of References mentioned – Lista de obras mencionadas

II. English Language sources – Títulos en idioma inglés.

A Concise Dictionary of Law (Oxford 2nd ed. 1990).
American Jurisprudence 1st.
American Jurisprudence 2d.
Baker Richard D. *Judicial Review in Mexico. A Study of the Amparo Suit.* (1971).
Ballentine James A. *Ballentine's Law Dictionary.* (3rd ed. 1969).
Ballentine's Law Dictionary. Legal Assistant Edition (Jack G. Handler ed. 1994).
Black's Law Dictionary (Bryan A. Garner ed. 8th ed. 2004).
Black's Law Dictionary (Abridged 5th ed. 1983).
Bledsoe R. L. &. B. A. Boczec. *The International Law Dictionary* (1987).
Bradley Craig M. *Criminal Procedure. A Worldwide study.* (1999).
Brown G. W. *Legal Terminology* (3rd ed. 1998).
Brown R. A. *The Law of Personl Property* (2nd ed. 1955).
Bruce J. B. *Real Estate Finance in a Nutshell* (2nd ed. 1985).
Burton William C. *Legal Thesaurus.* (1980).
Calamari J. D. & J.M. Perillo. *Contracts.* (2nd ed. 1987).
Chandler R. C.; R.A. Enslen & P.G. Renstrom. *The Constitutional Law Dictionary.* (1985).
Clark David S. *Comparative and Private International Law* (1990).
Collin Peter H. *Spanish Law Dictionary. Diccionario de Términos Jurídicos.* (1999).
Collin Peter. H. *Dictionary of Law.* (2nd ed. 1999).
Comparative Juridical Review.
Cribbet J.E. & Johnson C. W. *The Principles of the Law of Propety.* (3rd. ed. 1989).
Cunninham R. A.; W. B. Stoebuck & D. A. Whitman. *The Law of Property* (1993).
Dahl Henry Saint. *Dahl's Law Dictionary. Diccionario Jurídico Dahl.* (3rd. ed. 1999).
Danner Richard & Marie-Louise H. Bernal. *Introduction to Foreign Legal Systems.* (1994).
David Rene & John E. C. Brierley. *Major Legal Systems in the World today: An Introduction to the Comparative Study of Law* (3rd ed. 1985).
De Cruz Peter. *A Modern Approach to Comparative Law* (Netherlands 1993).
DeVries Henry P. *Civil Law and the Anglo-American lawyer* (1976).
Downes John & Jordan Elliot Goodman. *Dictionary of Finance and Investment Terms* (3rd ed. 1991).
Dukelow D A. & B. Nuse. *The Dictionary of Canadian Law* (2nd ed. 1995).
Eder Phanor J. *A Comparative survey of Anglo-American and Latin-American Law.* (1950).
Ehrmann Henry W. *Comparative Legal Cultures* (1976).
Environmental regulation: Law Science and Policy (1996) in Law and the Environment. (Compiled by R.B. Percival & D.C. Alevizatos 1997).
Fishman Clifford S. *Jones on Evidence Civil & Criminal.* (1992).
Garner Bryan A. *A Dictionary of Modern Legal Usage* (2nd ed. 1995).
Gifis Steven H. *Law Dictionary* (4th ed. 1996).

Glendon Mary Ann; Michael W. Gordon & Paolo G. Carozza. *Comparative Legal Traditions in a Nutshell* (2nd ed. 1999).

Glendon Mary & Michael W. Gordon. Christoper Osakwer. *Comparative Legal Traditions in a nutshell.* (1982).

Gutteridge H. C. *Comparative Law* (2nd ed. 1971).

Hamilton R. W. *The law of Corportations in a Nutshell* (4th ed. 1996).

Hill David S. *Landlord and Tenant Law in a Nutshell* (1986).

Hynes Dennis J. *Agency Partnership and the LLC. in a nutshell* (1997).

InterAmerican Law Review-Revista Jurídica Interamericana.

International Encyclopaedia of Laws. (Netherlands).

International Encyclopedia of Comparative Law. (Netherlands).

Jackson T. H. *The Logic and Limits of Bankruptcy Law* (1986).

Kaplan B. M. *A Guide to Modern Business and Commercial Law* (1985).

Keeton R. E. & A.I. Widiss. *Insurance Law* (1988).

Lawson Frederick H. *A common lawyer looks at the civil law.* (1955).

McClintock H. L. *Handbook of the Principles of Equity* (2nd ed. 1948).

Mellinkoff David. *Mellinkoff's Dictionary of American Legal Usage.* (1992).

Merriam Webster's Dictionary of Law. (1996).

Merryman John H. *The Civil Law Tradition. An Introduction to the Legal Systems of Western Europe and Latin America.* (2nd ed. 1985).

Merryman John H. *The Loneliness of the Comparative Lawyer.* (1999).

Merryman John H. David S. Clark & John D. Haley. *The Civil Law Tradition. Europe Latin America and East Asia.* (1994).

Osmanczyk Edmund Jan. *The Encyclopedia of the United Nations and International Relations.* (2nd ed. 1990).

Oxford Dictionary of Law (Oxford 4th ed. 1997).

Peter de Cruz. *Comparative Law in a changing world.* (2nd ed. 1999).

Plano J. C. & R. Olton. *The International Relations Dictionary.* (4th ed. 1988).

Prosser & Keeton on The Law of Torts (5th ed. 1984).

Rabin E. H. *Fundamentals of Modern Real Property Law* (2nd ed. 1982).

Radin Max. *Radin Law Dictionary.* (2nd ed. 1970).

Redden Kenneth R. & Enid L. Veron. *Modern Legal Glossary.* (1980).

Renstrom Peter G. *The American Law Dictionary* (1991).

Restatement (Second) of Contracts.

Restatement (Revised) of Foreign Relations Law.

Rodgers Jr. W. H. *Environmental Law* (1977).

Romañach Jr Julio. *Dictionary of Legal terms. Dictionario de Términos Jurídicos.* (1989).

Šarčević Susan. *New Approach to Legal Translation.* (1997).

Schaber G. D. & C.D. Rohwer. *Contracts in a Nutshell* (3rd ed. 1990).

Schauer Frederick. *Law and Language.* (1993).

Schlesinger R. B. *Comparative Law* (2nd 1959).

Schoenbaum T. J. *Admiralty and Maritime Law* (1987).

Schwartz Bernard. *The Code Napoleon and the Common-law World.* (1975).

Simes L.M. *Future interests* (2nd ed. 1966).

Simon and Schuster's International Dictionary (1973).

Smith P.F. & S.H. Bailey. *The Modern English Legal System* (1984).

Sodhi D. S. *The Canadian Law Dictionary* (1980).

Stein J. A. Damages and Recovery. *Personal Injury and Death actions* (1972).

Sterling J. A. L. *World Copyright Law* (1998).
Sykes E. & M. C. Pryles. *International and Interstate Conflic of Laws* (2nd ed.).
Stroud's Judicial Dictionary of Words and Phrases (John S. James ed. 4th ed. 1971).
The American Journal of Comparative Law.
The University of Miami Inter-American Law Review.
Uniform Comercial Code (U.S.).
Uniform Partnership Act (U.S.).
Walker David M. *The Oxford Companion to Law* (1980).
Watson Alan. *Legal Transplants.* An approach to Comparative Law (1974).
Webster Encyclopedic Unabridged Dictionary (1989).
West's Legal and Commercial Dictionary in five Languages (1985).
Wharton's Criminal Evidence (15th ed. 1997).
Wharton's Criminal Law (Charles E. Torcia ed. 1994).
Williston Samuel. *A Treatise on the Law of Contracts* (4th ed. 1990).
Words and Phrases (West. Permanent Edition).
Ynterna Hessel E. & Rodolfo Batiza. *The law of negotiable Instruments (Bills of exchange) in the Americas.* (1969).
Yogis John A. *Canadian Law Dictionary* (4th ed. 1998).
Zweigert Konrad & Hein Kotz. *Introduction to Comparative Law* (3rd ed. 1998).

II. Títulos en idioma español. Spanish Language sources.

Achával Alfredo. Práctica Forense. *Manual de Medicina Legal.* (Argentina 4ª ed. 1980).
Alcalá-Zamora y Castillo Niceto. *Clínica Procesal.* (México 1963).
Alessandri Rodriguez A. *De los Contratos.* (Chile 1992).
Alsina Hugo. *Tratado Teórico Práctico de Derecho Procesal Civil y Comercial.* (Argentina 2a. ed. 1957).
Alvarez Varó Enrique y Brian Hughes. *Diccionario de Términos Jurídicos.* (España 1993).
Arellano García Carlos. *Teoría General del Proceso.* (México 8ª ed. 1999).
Bonilla Carlos E. *Manual de Técnica Policial.* (Argentina 2ª. ed. 1995).
Burgoa O. Ignacio. *El juicio de amparo.* (México 33a. ed. 1997).
Bustos Ramírez Juan J. y Hernán Hormazábal Malarée. *Lecciones de Derecho Penal.* (España 1998).
Cabanellas Guillermo. *Diccionario Enciclopédico de Derecho Usual.* (Argentina 20ª ed. 1981).
Cabanellas Guillermo & Eleanor C. Hoague. *Diccionario Jurídico. Law Dictionary* (Argentina 1996).
Carrancá y Trujillo Raúl; y Carrancá y Rivas Raúl. *Derecho Penal Mexicano. Parte General.* (México 20ª ed. 1999).
Castan Tobeñas José. *Derecho Civil Español Común y Foral.* (España 14a ed. 1992).
Cavero-Lataillade Iñigo; y Tomás Zamora Rodriguez. *Introducción al Derecho Constitucional.* (Madrid 1995).
Colín Sanchez Guillermo. *Derecho Mexicano de Procedimientos Penales.* (México 17ª. ed. 1998).

REFERENCES-BIBLIOGRAFÍA

Corral Salvador Carlos; y José Arteaga Embil. *Diccionario de Derecho Canónico.* (España 1989).

Couture Eduardo J. *Vocabulario Jurídico.* (Argentina 5ª reimpr. 1993).

Cury Urzua Enrique. *Derecho Penal. Parte General* (Chile 2ª. ed. 1992).

David René. *Los Grandes Sistemas Jurídicos Contemporáneos.* Editorial Aguilar. (Traducción 2ª edición francesa por Pedro Bravo Gala 1968).

De la Cruz Agüero Leopoldo. *Procedimiento Penal Mexicano* (México 2a ed. 1966).

De la Cueva Mario. *El Nuevo Derecho Mexicano del Trabajo.* (México 16ª. ed. 1999).

De la Fuente Félix. *Diccionario Jurídico de la Unión Europea.* (España 1994).

De Pina Rafael y Rafael De Pina Vara. *Diccionario de Derecho.* (México 27ª ed. 1999).

Devis Echandía Hernando. *Teoría General del Proceso.* (Argentina 1984).

Diccionario Básico Jurídico. (España Ed. Comares 1997).

Diccionario de la Lengua Española. (España RAE 21a. 1992).

Diccionario Jurídico Mexicano. (México UNAM 2ª. ed. 1988).

Digesto de Puerto Rico. (E.U. A. Butterworth 1992).

Enciclopedia Jurídica Básica. (España Ed. Civitas 1995).

Enciclopedia Jurídica Omeba. (Argentina Ed. Bibliográfica Argentina 1991).

Escobar Raúl Tomás. *Diccionario del Hampa y del Delito.* (Argentina 1986).

Fernández Vasquez Emilio. *Diccionario de Derecho Público.* (Argentina 1981).

Flores Zavala Ernesto. *Finanzas Públicas Mexicanas.* (México 32a. ed. 1998).

Fontán Balestra Carlos. *Tratado de Derecho Penal.* (Argentina 1980).

García Maynez Eduardo. *Introducción al Estudio del Derecho.* (México 48a. ed. 1996).

García Trinidad. *Lecciones de Derecho Civil.* (México 30ª. ed. 1998).

Garrido de Palma Victor Manuel. Estudios sobre la Sociedad Anónima. (España 1991).

Garrone Jose Albeto. *Diccionario Jurídico Abeledo-Perrot.* (Argentina 1986).

Ghersi Carlos A. *Accidentes de Tránsito.* (Argentina 1995).

Giuliani Fonrouge Carlos M. *Derecho Financiero.* (Argentina 5a ed. 1993).

Gómez Lara Cipriano. *Teoria General del Proceso.* (México 9ª Ed. 1990).

Gonzalez Ramirez Jorge A. y Luis M. Fernandez. *Manual de Legislación Militar.* (Argentina 1986).

Gutierrez y Gonzalez Ernesto. *Derecho de las Obligaciones.* (México 2ª. ed. 1965).

Lopez Monroy José de Jesús. *El Sistema Jurídico del Common Law.* México 1997).

Machado Schiaffino Carlos. *Diccionario Jurídico Polilingüe.* (Argentina 1996).

Madrid-Malo Garizabal Mario. *Diccionario Jurídico Colombiano.* (Colombia 1988).

Mancera Hermanos. *Terminología del Contador.* (México 7ª. ed. 1966).

Martínez Marín J.; J. Martín Martín y C. Avila Martín. *Diccionario de Términos Jurídicos.* (España 1994).

Mascareñas Carlos E. *Nueva Enciclopedia Jurídica.* (España 1983).

Meilij de Romero Gabriela. *Vocabulario Legal y Empresario. Legal and Business Terms* (Argentina 1987).

Morrison Tirso R. M. *Gran Diccionario de Sinónimos Antónimos e ideas afines* (México 1987).

Pachón Muñoz Manuel. *Manual de Derechos de Autor.* (Colombia 1988).

Pallares Eduardo. *Diccionario de Derecho Procesal Civil.* (México 24ª ed. 1998).

Pavón Vasconcelos Francisco. *Derecho Penal Mexicano* (12ª Ed. 1995).

Pavón Vasconcelos Francisco. *Diccionario de Derecho Penal.* (México 2ª ed. 1999).

Plano Jack C. & Roy Olton. *Diccionario de Relaciones Internationales.* (Spanish Translation 1991).

Prieto-Castro y Ferrandis Leonardo. *Derecho Procesal Civil.* (España 5a. ed. 1989).

Rabasa Oscar. *El Derecho angloamericano.* (México 2a ed. 1982).

Ramírez Gronda Juan D. *Diccionario Jurídico* (Argentina 11a. ed. 1994).

Reyes Echandía Alfonso. *Culpabilidad.* (Colombia 3ª ed. 1997).

Ribó Durán Luis. *Diccionario de derecho* (España 1987).

Rojina Villegas Rafael. *Compendio de Derecho Civil.* (México 1962).

Rubinstein Santiago J. *Diccionario de Derecho del Trabajo y de la Seguridad Social.* (Argentina 1983).

Sanchez Medal Ramón. *De los Contratos Civil.* (México 16ª ed. 1988).

Seara Vasquez Modesto. *Derecho Internacional Público* (México 17a. ed. 1998).

Seara Vazquez Modesto. *Derecho Internacional Público.* (México 15ª ed. 1994).

Silva Silva Alberto. *Derecho Procesal Penal* (México 2ª ed. 1995).

Tratado Teórico Práctico de Derecho Procesal Civil y Comercial. (Argentina 1957).

Valdés Acosta Ramón. *Curso de Derecho Tributario.* (Colombia 2ª. ed. 1996).

Valletta M. Laura. *Diccionario Jurídico.* (Argentina 1999).

Miranda Rights

"You have the right to remain silent. Anything you say can and will be used against you in a court of law. You have the right to talk to a lawyer and have him present with you while you are being questioned. If you cannot afford to hire a lawyer one will be appointed to represent you before any questioning if you wish one." (Miranda v. Arizona 384 U.S. 436, 444-45)

"Usted tiene derecho a no decir nada. Cualquier cosa que usted diga podrá y será usada en su contra en una corte judicial. Usted tiene el derecho de hablar con un abogado y de que él esté presente con usted cuando se le esté interrogando. Si usted no puede pagar para contratar a un abogado uno le será nombrado, si usted desea tenerlo, para que lo represente antes de cualquier interrogatorio."

Merl Publications

MerlPublications.com

Order Form
Merl Publications

e-mail orders: Visit our Web site at www.merlpublications.com

Mail Orders: Mail this order form with payment by check or money order in U.S. currency to: Merl Publications 1658 Milwaukee Ave. # 242 Chicago, IL 60647

SHIPPING ADDRESS
Name: _____

Address: _____ Apt. _____

City: _____ State: _____ ZIP Code: _____

Telephone: _____ e-mail address: _____

DESCRIPTION	Quantity	Price each	Total
Merl Bilingual Law Dictionary			
Shipping and handling (See below)			
IL residents must add 9% sales tax			
Total			

Price: Merl Bilingual Law Dictionary, single copy $34.95

Shipping and handling: For U.S. destinations add $4.00 for first book, $6.00 for two copies, $8.00 for three copies, $10.00 for four copies. for quantities of more than four copies, increase the $10.00 four-book charge by $1.00 for each additional copy.
For international destinations charges may vary depending upon location and date of order. For up to date information or estimates please contact Merl's Publications web site, www.merlpublications.com.